Microsoft® POWERPOINT® 2013

COMPREHENSIVE ENHANCED EDITION

Microsoft® POWERPOINT® 2013

COMPREHENSIVE
ENHANCED EDITION

Susan L. Sebok

CENGAGE
Learning®

SHELLY
CASHMAN
SERIES.

Australia • Brazil • Japan • Korea • Mexico • Singapore • Spain • United Kingdom • United States

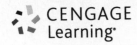

CENGAGE Learning·

Microsoft® PowerPoint® 2013: Comprehensive Enhanced Edition
Susan L. Sebok

Product Director: Kathleen McMahon

Senior Director of Development: Marah Bellegarde

Senior Product Team Manager: Lauren Murphy

Product Team Manager: Brian Hyland

Product Development Manager: Leigh Hefferon

Content Developer: Jon Farnham

Associate Content Developer: Crystal Parenteau

Product Assistant: Brianna Vorce

Development Editors: Deb Kaufmann

Director of Production: Patty Stephan

Senior Content Project Manager: Matthew Hutchinson

Marketing Director: Michele McTighe

Marketing Manager: Kristie Clark

Manufacturing Planner: Julio Esperas

QA Manuscript Reviewers: Jeffrey Schwartz, John Freitas, Serge Palladino, Susan Pedicini, Danielle Shaw, Susan Whalen

Composition: Lumina Datamatics, Inc.

Art Director: Marissa Falco

Text Design: Joel Sadagursky

Cover Design: Lisa Kuhn, Curio Press, LCC

Cover Photo: Tom Kates Photography

Proofreader: Lumina Datamatics, Inc.

For product information and technology assistance, contact us at
Cengage Learning Customer & Sales Support, 1-800-354-9706

For permission to use material from this text or product,
submit all requests online at **cengage.com/permissions**
Further permissions questions can be emailed to
permissionrequest@cengage.com

Library of Congress Control Number: 2015934771

ISBN-13: 978-1-305-50753-1
ISBN-10: 1-305-50753-3

Cengage Learning
20 Channel Center Street
Boston, MA 02210
USA

Cengage Learning is a leading provider of customized learning solutions with office locations around the globe, including Singapore, the United Kingdom, Australia, Mexico, Brazil, and Japan. Locate your local office at:
international.cengage.com/region

Cengage Learning products are represented in Canada by Nelson Education, Ltd.

To learn more about Cengage Learning, visit **www.cengage.com**

Purchase any of our products at your local college bookstore or at our preferred online store at **www.cengagebrain.com**

We dedicate this book to the memory of Thomas J. Cashman (4/29/32 – 1/7/15). As one of the founders of the Shelly Cashman Series, Tom partnered with Gary Shelly to write and publish their first computer education textbook in 1969, revolutionizing the introductory computing course and changing the path of computing course materials. From 1969 through his retirement in 2008, Tom served as educator, author, leader, and inspiration to his fellow authors and Shelly Cashman Series team members. His mark on the series and the introductory computing market is indelible and he will be both remembered and missed.

Printed in the United States of America
Print Number: 1   Print Year: 2015

Microsoft POWERPOINT 2013
COMPREHENSIVE ENHANCED EDITION

Contents

CHAPTER FIVE
Collaborating on and Delivering a Presentation

Preface

The Shelly Cashman Series® offers the finest textbooks in computer education. We are proud that since Microsoft® Office 4.3, our series of Microsoft Office textbooks have been the most widely used books in education. With each new edition of our Office books, we make significant improvements based on the software and comments made by instructors and students. For this Microsoft® PowerPoint® 2013 text, the Shelly Cashman Series development team carefully reviewed our pedagogy and analyzed its effectiveness in teaching today's Office student. Students today read less, but need to retain more. They need not only to be able to perform skills, but to retain those skills and know how to apply them to different settings. Today's students need to be continually engaged and challenged to retain what they're learning.

With this Microsoft PowerPoint 2013 text, we continue our commitment to focusing on the users and how they learn best.

Objectives of This Textbook

Microsoft PowerPoint 2013: Comprehensive is intended for a ten- to fifteen-week period in a course that teaches PowerPoint 2013 as the primary component. No experience with a computer is assumed, and no mathematics beyond the high school freshman level is required. The objectives of this book are:

- To offer a comprehensive presentation of Microsoft PowerPoint 2013
- To expose students to practical examples of the computer as a useful tool
- To acquaint students with the proper procedures to create presentations suitable for coursework, professional purposes, and personal use
- To help students discover the underlying functionality of PowerPoint 2013 so they can become more productive
- To develop an exercise-oriented approach that allows learning by doing

The Shelly Cashman Approach

A Proven Pedagogy with an Emphasis on Project Planning

Each chapter presents a practical problem to be solved within a project planning framework. The project orientation is strengthened by the use of the Roadmap, which provides a visual framework for the project. Step-by-step instructions with supporting screens guide students through the steps. Instructional steps are supported by the Q&A, Experimental Step, and BTW features.

A Visually Engaging Book that Maintains Student Interest

The step-by-step tasks, with supporting figures, provide a rich visual experience for the student. Call-outs on the screens that present both explanatory and navigational information provide students with information they need when they need to know it.

Supporting Reference Materials (Quick Reference)

With the Quick Reference, students can quickly look up information about a single task, such as keyboard shortcuts, and find page references to where in the book the task is illustrated.

Integration of the World Wide Web

The World Wide Web is integrated into the PowerPoint 2013 learning experience with (1) BTW annotations; (2) BTW, Q&A, and Quick Reference Summary Web pages; and (3) the Learn Online resources for each chapter.

End-of-Chapter Student Activities

Extensive end-of-chapter activities provide a variety of reinforcement opportunities for students to apply and expand their skills through individual and group work. To complete some of these assignments, you will be required to use the Data Files for Students. Visit www.cengage.com/ct/studentdownload for detailed access instructions or contact your instructor for information about accessing the required files.

New to this Edition

Enhanced Coverage of Critical Thinking Skills

A new Consider This element poses thought-provoking questions throughout each chapter, providing an increased emphasis on critical thinking and problem-solving skills. Also, every task in the project now includes a reason *why* the students are performing the task and *why* the task is necessary.

Enhanced Retention and Transference

A new Roadmap element provides a visual framework for each project, showing students where they are in the process of creating each project, and reinforcing the context of smaller tasks by showing how they fit into the larger project.

Integration of Office with Cloud and Web Technologies

A new Lab focuses entirely on integrating cloud and web technologies with PowerPoint 2013, using technologies like blogs and social networks.

More Personalization

Each chapter project includes an optional instruction for the student to personalize his or her solution, if required by an instructor, making each student's solution unique.

More Collaboration

A new Research and Collaboration project has been added to the Consider This: Your Turn assignment at the end of each chapter.

Instructor Resources

The Instructor Resources include both teaching and testing aids and can be accessed at www.cengage.com/login.

Instructor's Manual Includes lecture notes summarizing the chapter sections, figures and boxed elements found in every chapter, teacher tips, classroom activities, lab activities, and quick quizzes in Microsoft Word files.

Syllabus Easily customizable sample syllabi that cover policies, assignments, exams, and other course information.

Figure Files Illustrations for every figure in the textbook in electronic form.

PowerPoint Presentations A multimedia lecture presentation system that provides slides for each chapter. Presentations are based on chapter objectives.

Solutions to Exercises Includes solutions for all end-of-chapter and chapter reinforcement exercises.

Test Bank & Test Engine Test banks powered by Cognero include 112 questions for every chapter, featuring objective-based and critical thinking question types, and including page number references and figure references, when appropriate.

Data Files for Students Includes all the files that are required by students to complete the exercises.

Additional Activities for Students Consists of Chapter Reinforcement Exercises, which are true/false, multiple-choice, and short answer questions that help students gain confidence in the material learned.

Learn Online

CengageBrain.com is the premier destination for purchasing or renting Cengage Learning textbooks, eBooks, eChapters, and study tools at a significant discount (eBooks up to 50% off Print). In addition, CengageBrain.com provides direct access to all digital products, including eBooks, eChapters, and digital solutions, such as MindTap and SAM, regardless of where purchased. The following are some examples of what is available for this product on www.cengagebrain.com.

SAM: Skills Assessment Manager Get your students workplace-ready with SAM, the market-leading proficiency-based assessment and training solution for Microsoft Office! SAM's active, hands-on environment helps students master Microsoft Office skills and computer concepts that are essential to academic and career success, delivering the most comprehensive online learning solution for your course!

Through skill-based assessments, interactive trainings, business-centric projects, and comprehensive remediation, SAM engages students in mastering the latest Microsoft Office programs on their own, giving instructors more time to focus on teaching. Computer concepts labs supplement instruction of important technology-related topics and issues through engaging simulations and interactive, auto-graded assessments. With enhancements including streamlined course setup, more robust grading and reporting features, and the integration of fully interactive MindTap Readers containing Cengage Learning's premier textbook content, SAM provides the best teaching and learning solution for your course.

MindLinks MindLinks is a new Cengage Learning Service designed to provide the best possible user experience and facilitate the highest levels of learning retention and outcomes, enabled through a deep integration of Cengage Learning's digital suite into an instructor's Learning Management System (LMS). MindLinks works on any LMS that supports the IMS Basic LTI open standard. Advanced features, including gradebook exchange, are the result of active, enhanced LTI collaborations with industry-leading LMS partners to drive the evolving technology standards forward.

CourseNotes

Cengage Learning's CourseNotes are six-panel quick reference cards that reinforce the most important and widely used features of a software application in a visual and user-friendly format. CourseNotes serve as a great reference tool during and after the course. CourseNotes are available for software applications, such as Microsoft Office 2013. There are also topic-based CourseNotes available for Best Practices in Social Networking, Hot Topics in Technology, and Web 2.0. Visit www.cengagebrain.com to learn more!

Certification Prep Tool

This textbook was developed to instruct on the Microsoft® Office® 2013 certification objectives. Microsoft Corporation has developed a set of standardized, performance-based examinations that you can take to demonstrate your overall expertise with Microsoft Office 2013 programs. Microsoft Office 2013 certification provides a number of benefits for you:

- Differentiate yourself in the employment marketplace from those who are not Microsoft Office Specialist or Expert certified.
- Prove skills and expertise when using Microsoft Office 2013.
- Perform at a higher skill level in your job.
- Work at a higher professional level than those who are not certified.
- Broaden your employment opportunities and advance your career more rapidly.

For more information about Microsoft Office 2013 certification, including a complete list of certification objectives, visit the Microsoft web site, http://www.microsoft.com /learning. To see which Microsoft Office 2013 certification objectives are addressed by the contents of this text and where each is included in the text, visit the Certification resource on the Student Companion Site located on www.cengagebrain.com. For detailed instructions about accessing available resources, visit www.cengage.com /ct/studentdownload or contact your instructor for information about accessing the required files.

About Our Covers

The Shelly Cashman Series is continually updating our approach and content to reflect the way today's students learn and experience new technology. This focus on student success is reflected on our covers, which feature real students from the University of Rhode Island using the Shelly Cashman Series in their courses, and reflect the varied ages and backgrounds of the students learning with our books. When you use the Shelly Cashman Series, you can be assured that you are learning computer skills using the most effective courseware available.

Textbook Walk-Through

The Shelly Cashman Series Pedagogy: Project-Based — Step-by-Step — Variety of Assessments

Roadmaps provide a visual framework for each project, showing the students where they are in the process of creating each project.

Step-by-step instructions provide a context beyond the point-and-click. Each step provides information on why students are performing each task and what will occur as a result.

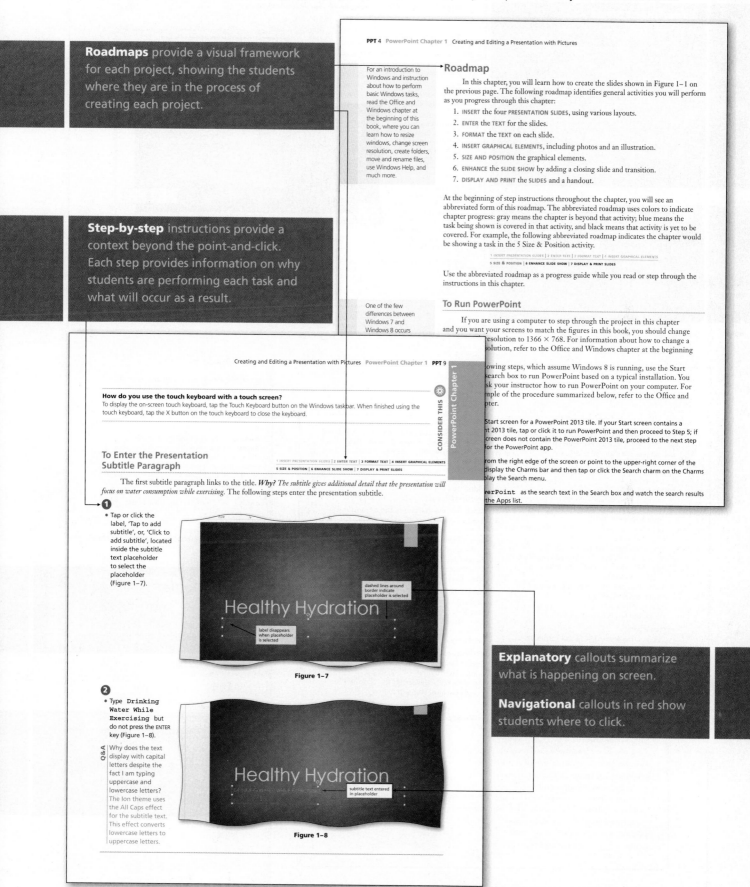

For an introduction to Windows and instruction about how to perform basic Windows tasks, read the Office and Windows chapter at the beginning of this book, where you can learn how to resize windows, change screen resolution, create folders, move and rename files, use Windows Help, and much more.

Roadmap

In this chapter, you will learn how to create the slides shown in Figure 1–1 on the previous page. The following roadmap identifies general activities you will perform as you progress through this chapter:

1. INSERT the four PRESENTATION SLIDES, using various layouts.
2. ENTER the TEXT for the slides.
3. FORMAT the TEXT on each slide.
4. INSERT GRAPHICAL ELEMENTS, including photos and an illustration.
5. SIZE AND POSITION the graphical elements.
6. ENHANCE the SLIDE SHOW by adding a closing slide and transition.
7. DISPLAY AND PRINT the SLIDES and a handout.

At the beginning of step instructions throughout the chapter, you will see an abbreviated form of this roadmap. The abbreviated roadmap uses colors to indicate chapter progress: gray means the chapter is beyond that activity; blue means the task being shown is covered in that activity, and black means that activity is yet to be covered. For example, the following abbreviated roadmap indicates the chapter would be showing a task in the 5 Size & Position activity.

1 INSERT PRESENTATION SLIDES | 2 ENTER TEXT | 3 FORMAT TEXT | 4 INSERT GRAPHICAL ELEMENTS
5 SIZE & POSITION | 6 ENHANCE SLIDE SHOW | 7 DISPLAY & PRINT SLIDES

Use the abbreviated roadmap as a progress guide while you read or step through the instructions in this chapter.

To Run PowerPoint

One of the few differences between Windows 7 and Windows 8 occurs

If you are using a computer to step through the project in this chapter and you want your screens to match the figures in this book, you should change resolution to 1366 × 768. For information about how to change a resolution, refer to the Office and Windows chapter at the beginning

owing steps, which assume Windows 8 is running, use the Start search box to run PowerPoint based on a typical installation. You sk your instructor how to run PowerPoint on your computer. For mple of the procedure summarized below, refer to the Office and pter.

Start screen for a PowerPoint 2013 tile. If your Start screen contains a nt 2013 tile, tap or click it to run PowerPoint and then proceed to Step 5; if creen does not contain the PowerPoint 2013 tile, proceed to the next step for the PowerPoint app.

rom the right edge of the screen or point to the upper-right corner of the display the Charms bar and then tap or click the Search charm on the Charms play the Search menu.

werPoint as the search text in the Search box and watch the search results the Apps list.

CONSIDER THIS

PowerPoint Chapter 1

How do you use the touch keyboard with a touch screen?
To display the on-screen touch keyboard, tap the Touch Keyboard button on the Windows taskbar. When finished using the touch keyboard, tap the X button on the touch keyboard to close the keyboard.

To Enter the Presentation Subtitle Paragraph

1 INSERT PRESENTATION SLIDES | 2 ENTER TEXT | 3 FORMAT TEXT | 4 INSERT GRAPHICAL ELEMENTS
5 SIZE & POSITION | 6 ENHANCE SLIDE SHOW | 7 DISPLAY & PRINT SLIDES

The first subtitle paragraph links to the title. *Why? The subtitle gives additional detail that the presentation will focus on water consumption while exercising.* The following steps enter the presentation subtitle.

1
• Tap or click the label, 'Tap to add subtitle', or, 'Click to add subtitle', located inside the subtitle text placeholder to select the placeholder (Figure 1–7).

dashed lines around border indicate placeholder is selected

Healthy Hydration

label disappears when placeholder is selected

Figure 1–7

2
• Type **Drinking Water While Exercising** but do not press the ENTER key (Figure 1–8).

Q&A Why does the text display with capital letters despite the fact I am typing uppercase and lowercase letters? The Ion theme uses the All Caps effect for the subtitle text. This effect converts lowercase letters to uppercase letters.

Healthy Hydration

subtitle text entered in placeholder

Figure 1–8

Explanatory callouts summarize what is happening on screen.

Navigational callouts in red show students where to click.

Textbook Walk-Through

Experiment Steps within the step-by-step instructions encourage students to explore, experiment, and take advantage of the features of the Office 2013 user interface. These steps are not necessary to complete the projects, but are designed to increase confidence with the software and build problem-solving skills.

Q&A boxes anticipate questions students may have when working through the steps and provide additional information about what they are doing right where they need it.

To Zoom a Slide

1 INSERT PRESENTATION SLIDES | 2 ENTER TEXT | 3 FORMAT TEXT | 4 INSERT GRAPHICAL ELEMENTS
5 SIZE & POSITION | 6 ENHANCE SLIDE SHOW | 7 DISPLAY & PRINT SLIDES

You will be modifying the text and other slide components as you create the presentation, so you can enlarge the slide on the screen. **Why?** *Zooming the slide can help you see slide elements more clearly so that you can position them precisely where desired.* The following step changes the zoom to 80 percent.

Experiment

- Repeatedly tap or click the Zoom In and Zoom Out buttons on the status bar and watch the size of the slide change in the Slide pane.

- Tap or click the Zoom In or Zoom Out button as many times as necessary until the Zoom button on the status bar displays 80% on its face (Figure 1–9).

Figure 1–9

Q&A If I change the zoom percentage, will the slide display differently when I run the presentation?
No. Changing the zoom helps you develop the slide content and does not affect the slide show.

Other Ways

1. Drag Zoom slider on status bar	2. Tap or click Zoom level button on status bar, select desired zoom percent or type (Zoom dialog box), tap or click OK button	3. Tap or click Zoom button (VIEW tab | Zoom group), select desired zoom percent or type (Zoom dialog box), tap or click OK button	4. For touch screens: Pinch two fingers together in Slide pane (zoom out) or stretch two fingers apart (zoom in)

Formatting Characters in a Presentation

...determines the color scheme, font set, and layout of ...ic document theme and then change the characters' ...after you type the text.

...e screen are a specific shape and size. Examples of ...e, or format, of these typed characters on the screen ...ont, **style**, size, and color. The **font**, or typeface, ...f the letters, numbers, punctuation marks, and ...aracters are formatted. PowerPoint's text font styles ...d italic. **Size** specifies the height of the characters ...tem that uses points. A **point** is 1/72 of an inch in ...t size of 36 is 36/72 (or 1/2) of an inch in height. ...ters.

Chapter Summary

In this chapter you have learned how to apply and change a document theme and variant, create a title slide and text slides with a bulleted list, insert photos and an illustration and then resize and move them on a slide, format and edit text, add a slide transition, view the presentation in Slide Show view, and print slides as handouts. The items listed below include all the new PowerPoint skills you have learned in this chapter, with the tasks grouped by activity.

Enter and Edit Text
Enter the Presentation Title (PPT 7)
Enter the Presentation Subtitle Paragraph (PPT 9)
Zoom a Slide (PPT 10)
Add a New Text Slide with a Bulleted List (PPT 15)
Enter a Slide Title (PPT 17)
Type a Multilevel Bulleted List (PPT 18)
Add a Slide with the Title Only Layout (PPT 23)
Add a New Slide and Enter a Slide Title and Headings (PPT 24)
Move to Another Slide in Normal View (PPT 29)
Duplicate a Slide (PPT 41)
Arrange a Slide (PPT 42)
Delete Text in a Placeholder (PPT 43)

Format a Slide
Choose a Document Theme and Variant (PPT 5)
Change the Theme (PPT 26)
Change the Variant (PPT 27)

Format Text
Italicize Text (PPT 11)
Increase Font Size (PPT 12, 22)

Change the Text Color (PPT 13)
Bold Text (PPT 21)

Enhance Slides with Pictures and a Transition
Insert a Picture from Office.com into the Title Slide (PPT 31)
Insert a Picture from Office.com into a Content Placeholder (PPT 34)
Proportionally Resize Pictures (PPT 36)
Move Pictures (PPT 39)
Add a Transition between Slides (PPT 45)

Run and Print a Slide Show
Change Document Properties (PPT 48)
Start Slide Show View (PPT 49)
Move Manually through Slides in a Slide Show (PPT 50)
Print a Presentation (PPT 52)

Select Text and Slide Elements
Select a Paragraph (PPT 11)
Select a Word (PPT 12)
Select a Text Placeholder (PPT 18)
Select a Group of Words (PPT 20)

CONSIDER THIS

What decisions will you need to make when creating your next presentation?
Use these guidelines as you complete the assignments in this chapter and create your own slide show decks outside of this class.

1. Determine the content you want to include on your slides.

2. Determine which theme and variant are appropriate.

3. Identify the slide layouts that best communicate your message.

4. Format various text elements to emphasize important points.

   a) Select appropriate font sizes.
   b) Emphasize important words with bold or italic type and color.

5. Locate graphical elements, such as photos and illustrations, that reinforce your message.

   a) Size and position them aesthetically on slides.

6. Determine a storage location for the presentation.

7. Determine the best method for distributing the presentation.

Chapter Summary A listing of the tasks completed within the chapter, grouped into major task categories in an outline format.

Consider This: Plan Ahead box presents a single master planning guide that students can use as they create documents on their own.

Consider This boxes pose thought-provoking questions with answers throughout each chapter, promoting critical thought along with immediate feedback.

Apply Your Knowledge This exercise usually requires students to open and manipulate a file that parallels the activities learned in the chapter.

How should you submit solutions to questions in the assignments identified with a ✹ symbol?

Every assignment in this book contains one or more questions identified with a ✹ symbol. These questions require you to think beyond the assigned presentation. Present your solutions to the questions in the format required by your instructor. Possible formats may include one or more of these options: write the answer; create a document that contains the answer; present your answer to the class; discuss your answer in a group; record the answer as audio or video using a webcam, smartphone, or portable media player; or post answers on a blog, wiki, or website.

CONSIDER THIS

Apply Your Knowledge

Reinforce the skills and apply the concepts you learned in this chapter.

Modifying Character Formats and Paragraph Levels and Moving an Illustration
Note: To complete this assignment, you will be required to use the Data Files for Students. Visit www.cengage.com/ct/studentdownload for detailed instructions or contact your instructor for information about accessing the required files.

Instructions: Run PowerPoint. Open the presentation, Apply 1-1 Effective Writing, from the Data Files for Students.

The two slides in the presentation discuss steps to follow when writing a persuasive essay. The document you open is an unformatted presentation. You are to modify the document theme, indent the paragraphs, resize and move the photo, and format the text so the slides look like Figure 1–80 on this page and the next page.

Perform the following tasks:

1. Change the document theme to Ion.
2. On the title slide, use your name in place of Student Name and bold and italicize your name.
3. If requested by your instructor, change your first name to your grandmother's first name on the title slide.
4. Increase the size of using a font size of 9-point Size and position the photo using the Smart Guides title placeholder, as shown in Figure 1–80a.

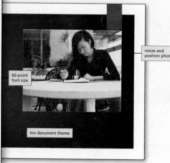

resize and position photo

60-point font size

Ion document theme

(a) Slide with a Picture)
Figure 1–80

Continued >

Apply Your Knowledge *continued*

5. On Slide 2, increase the indent of the third and fourth paragraphs to second-level paragraphs. Then combine paragraphs six and seven (To change readers' minds? and To confirm opinions?) to read, To change readers' minds or confirm opinions?, as shown in Figure 1–80b. Increase the indent of this paragraph to second level.
6. Save the presentation using the file name, Apply 1-1 Effective Writing Strategies.
7. Submit the revised document in the format specified by your instructor.
8. ✹ In Step 5 you combined two paragraphs. How did this action improve the slide content?

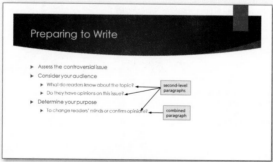

Preparing to Write

▸ Assess the controversial issue
▸ Consider your audience
  ▸ What do readers know about the topic? ← second-level paragraphs
  ▸ Do they have opinions on this issue?
▸ Determine your purpose
  ▸ To change readers' minds or confirm opinions? ← combined paragraph

(b) Slide 2 (Multilevel Bulleted List)
Figure 1–80 (Continued)

Extend Your Knowledge

Extend the skills you learned in this chapter and experiment with new skills. You may need to use Help to complete the assignment.

Changing Slide Theme, Layout, and Text
Note: To complete this assignment, you will be required to use the Data Files for Students. Visit www.cengage.com/ct/studentdownload for detailed instructions or contact your instructor for information about accessing the required files.

Instructions: Run PowerPoint. Open the presentation that you are going to prepare for your brother's horseback riding business, Extend 1-1 Horseback Riding, from the Data Files for Students. You will choose a theme, format slides, and create a closing slide.

Perform the following tasks:

1. Apply an appropriate document theme.
2. On Slide 1 (Figure 1–81), use your name in place of Student Name. Format the text on this slide using techniques you learned in this chapter, such as changing the font size and color and bolding and italicizing words.
3. Delete the bullets in the subtitle text.
4. Resize the photo and move it to an appropriate area on the slide.
5. On Slide 2, add bullets to the paragraphs in the Beginners and Advanced boxes, and then change the look of the default bullets.

Extend Your Knowledge projects at the end of each chapter allow students to extend and expand on the skills learned within the chapter. Students use critical thinking to experiment with new skills to complete each project.

Textbook Walk-Through

(d) Slide 4
Figure 2–85 (Continued)

Analyze, Correct, Improve projects call on the students to analyze a file, discover errors in it, fix the errors, and then improve upon the file using the skills they learned in the chapter.

then bold the text. Use the Format Painter to format the text in the two arrows with the same features as the first arrow. Move the arrows so that each one points to the correct ring, as shown in Figure 2–85d. Delete the bulleted text in the text placeholder.

12. Apply an appropriate transition to all slides.
13. Save the presentation using the file name, Extend 2-1 Field Archery Scoring.
14. Submit the revised document in the format specified by your instructor.
15. ⚙ In this assignment, you changed the transparency of the inserted background photo on the title slide to 50%. How did this transparency change enhance your title slide?

Analyze, Correct, Improve

Analyze a presentation, correct all errors, and improve it.

Correcting Formatting, Adding Slide Numbers, and Correcting Spelling
Note: To complete this assignment, you will be required to use the Data Files for Students. Visit www.cengage.com/ct/studentdownload for detailed instructions or contact your instructor for information about accessing the required files.

Instructions: Run PowerPoint. Open the presentation, Analyze 2-1 Avoid the Flu, from the Data Files for Students. This presentation contains four slides and explains why doctors recommend you should get an annual flu shot. Figure 2–86 on the next page shows the uncorrected title slide. Modify the slides by making the indicated corrections and improvements.

1. Correct
   a. Change the variant to blue (the second variant in the gallery).
   b. Decrease the font size of the Slide 1 title text and change the font color. Also, capitalize the letter F in the word, flu.
   c. Use your name in place of Student Name on Slide 1.

In the Lab Three in-depth assignments in each chapter that require students to apply the chapter concepts and techniques to solve problems. One Lab is devoted entirely to Cloud and Web 2.0 integration.

Continued >

In the Labs

Design and/or create a presentation using the guidelines, concepts, and skills presented in this chapter. Labs 1 and 2, which increase in difficulty, require you to create solutions based on what you learned in the chapter; Lab 3 requires you to create a solution, which uses cloud and web technologies, by learning and investigating on your own from general guidance.

Lab 1: Creating a Presentation with Bulleted Lists, a Closing Slide, and Pictures

Problem: You are majoring in accounting and work part-time at a tax-filing service. Your clients have asked you numerous times what documents they should keep at home to support their tax returns. You decide to put together a presentation that would offer some basic guidelines about how to organize personal documents. You develop the outline shown in Figure 1–83 and then prepare the PowerPoint presentation shown in Figures 1–84a through 1–84e on pages PPT 62–64.

Files or Piles
    Document Storage and Retention at Home

Store and Retain
    In Home Office Safe
        Tax records for six years
        Pay stubs until W2 arrives
        Credit card statements
        Canceled checks
        Utility bills
    In Bank Safe Deposit Box
        Wills, deeds, and titles
        Birth and death certificates
        Passports
        Military records

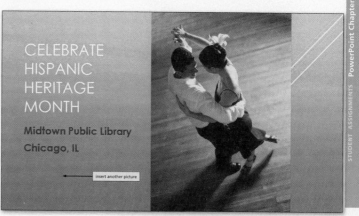

Figure 1–87   Slide 1 (Title Slide)

✴ Consider This: Your Turn

Apply your creative thinking and problem-solving skills to design and implement a solution.

1. Design and Create a Presentation about Mars Exploration
Personal

Part 1:   Your astronomy class is studying the solar system, and you have been assigned the topic of the Mars Curiosity rover and its exploration of that planet. You have learned that the rover was launched from Cape Canaveral, Florida, on November 26, 2011, and landed in the Gale Crater on Mars on August 6, 2012. The mission was scheduled to last two years and had the major goal of assessing whether Mars was or is capable of supporting life. The Curiosity rover is the size of a car and has a MastCam equipped with two camera systems to take photos of the landscape as it maneuvers around the rocky surface. The rover also can scoop up samples of the Martian soil, fire a laser at rocks as far away as nine feet (2.7 meters), and make weather station readings. Use the concepts and techniques you learned in the chapter to create a PowerPoint presentation with a suitable theme, a title slide, and three text slides with bulleted lists. Add pictures from Office.com and apply a transition. Submit your assignment in the format specified by your instructor.

Part 2:   ✴ You made several decisions while creating the presentation in this assignment: what theme to use, where to place text, how to format the text (font, font size, paragraph alignment, bulleted paragraphs, italics, bold, color). You also decided which graphical images to use, where to position the graphical images, if a closing slide would be useful, and which transition would be most effective. What was the rationale behind each of these decisions? When you proofed the document, what further revisions did you make and why? Where would you recommend showing this slide show?

Continued >

Consider This: Your Turn
exercises call on students to apply creative thinking and problem solving skills to design and implement a solution.

Student Success Guide

On the Path to Success

In this Student Success Guide, you explore tools, techniques, and skills essential to your success as a student. In particular, you focus on planning, time management, study tools, critical thinking, and problem solving. As you explore effective practices in these areas, you will also be introduced to Microsoft OneNote 2013, a free-form note-taking application in the Microsoft Office suite that lets you gather, organize, and share digital notes.

Microsoft product screenshots used with permission from Microsoft Corporation.

Objectives

You will have mastered the material in this chapter when you can:

- Use Microsoft OneNote to track tasks and organize ideas
- Set and achieve short-term and long-term goals
- Take notes during PowerPoint presentations
- Share OneNote content with others
- Apply critical-thinking strategies to evaluate information
- Follow a four-step process to solve problems

Planning Sets You Free

Benjamin Franklin once said, "If you fail to plan, you are planning to fail." When you set goals and manage time, your life does not just happen by chance. Instead, you design your life. Planning sets you free.

Without planning, you simply dig in and start writing or generating material you might use — but might not. You can actually be less productive and busier at the same time. Planning replaces this haphazard behavior with clearly defined outcomes and action steps.

Planning is a creative venture that continues for a lifetime. Following are planning suggestions that flow directly from this point of view and apply to any type of project or activity, from daily tasks to a multiyear career:

- **Schedule for flexibility and fun.** Be realistic. Expect the unexpected. Set aside time for essential tasks and errands, but don't forget to make room for fun.

- **Back up to view a bigger picture.** Consider your longer-range goals — what you want to accomplish in the next six months, the next year, the next five years, and beyond. Ask whether the activities you're about to schedule actually contribute to those goals.

- **Look boldly for things to change.** Don't accept the idea that you have to put up with substandard results in a certain area of your life. Staying open-minded about what is possible to achieve can lead to a future you never dreamed was possible.

- **Look for what's missing — and what to maintain.** Goals are often fueled by problems you need to resolve, projects you need to complete, relationships you want to develop, and careers you want to pursue. However, consider other goals that maintain your achievements and the activities you already perform effectively.

- **Think even further into the future.** To have fun and unleash your creativity while planning, set goals as far into the future as you can.

- **Return to the present.** Once you've stated your longest-range goals, work backward until you can define a next step to take now. Write down the shorter-term goals along the way. Leave some space in your schedule for unplanned events. Give yourself time to deal with obstacles before they derail you from realizing your dreams.

- **Schedule fixed blocks of time first.** When planning your week, start with class time and work time. Next, schedule essential daily activities such as sleeping and eating. In addition, schedule some time each week for actions that lead directly to one of your written goals.

- **Set clear starting and stopping times.** Set a timer and stick to it. Set aside a specific number of minutes or hours to spend on a certain task. Feeling rushed or sacrificing quality is not the goal here. The point is to push yourself and discover your actual time requirements.

- **Plan for changes in your workload.** To manage your workload over the length of a term or project, plan for a change of pace. Stay on top of your assignments right from the start. Whenever possible, work ahead.

- **Involve others when appropriate.** When you schedule a task that depends on another person's involvement, let that person know — the sooner, the better.

- **Start the day with your Most Important Task.** Review your to-do list and calendar first thing each morning. For an extra level of clarity, condense your to-do list to only one top-priority item — your Most Important Task. Do it as early in the day as possible, impeccably, and with total attention.

- **Plan in a way that works for you.** You can perform the kind of planning that sets you free with any set of tools. What matters above all is clear thinking and specific intentions. You can take any path that leads to your goal.

As you continue through this chapter, you will learn how to use Microsoft OneNote to plan, organize, and maintain the important information and ideas in your life. You will also explore methods for setting and achieving goals, improving study practices, and thinking critically to solve problems.

Quick Tour of Microsoft OneNote

Microsoft OneNote is part of the Microsoft Office suite and provides a single location for storing everything that is important to you, accessible from any device or on the web. Using OneNote, you store information in a **notebook**, a collection of electronic pages with text, graphics, and other content, including sound and video recordings. You organize the pages into tabbed sections as you would a tabbed ring binder. In your school notebook, for example, create a section for each of your courses, and then take notes during class on the pages within each section.

Exploring the OneNote Interface

As part of the Microsoft Office suite, the Microsoft OneNote 2013 desktop application contains a ribbon at the top of the window with seven default tabs: FILE, HOME, INSERT, DRAW, HISTORY, REVIEW, and VIEW. See Figure 1.

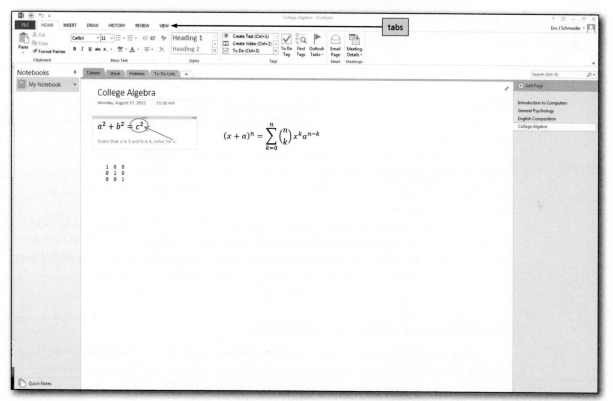

Figure 1 Microsoft OneNote 2013 ribbon

Each tab contains the following types of commands and features:

- **HOME tab**: This tab contains the most commonly used commands and features of Microsoft OneNote, which are divided into six groups: Clipboard, Basic Text, Styles, Tags, Email, and Meetings.
- **INSERT tab**: This tab includes commands for inserting tables, files, images, links, audio and video recordings, date/time stamps, page templates, and symbols.
- **DRAW tab**: This tab includes commands and tools for writing notes on pages, inserting shapes, arranging content, and converting handwritten notes to text or mathematical symbols.
- **HISTORY tab**: This tab includes tools for reviewing unread notes, managing multiple authors in a notebook, and reviewing pages and content in previous versions or pages and content that have been placed in the Notebook Recycle Bin.
- **REVIEW tab**: This tab provides research tools, including a spelling checker and thesaurus, language and translation tools, password-protection options, and links to other notebook sections and pages.
- **VIEW tab**: This tab contains page setup options, zoom tools, and application views, including docking options and the Send to OneNote tool.

Using Page Templates

To get started with OneNote and fill a blank page more quickly and easily, OneNote provides a collection of page templates. A **page template** is a design you apply to new pages in your notebook to provide an appealing background or to create a consistent layout. The OneNote page templates are organized into five categories: Academic, Blank, Business, Decorative, and Planners.

Additional templates are available on Office.com. After you define a standard way of organizing information, you can also create your own templates.

Time Management

When you say you don't have enough time, the problem might be that you are not spending the time you do have in the way you want. This section surveys ways to solve that time-management problem.

Time is an equal-opportunity resource. Everyone, regardless of gender, race, creed, or national origin, has exactly the same number of hours in a week. No matter how famous you are, no matter how rich or poor, you have 168 hours to spend each week — no more, no less.

As you explore time management in this section, you will learn how to set and achieve goals, how to apply the ABC method to writing a daily to-do list, and how to use technology for effective time management, with a special focus on using Microsoft OneNote to brainstorm ideas, set and achieve goals, and create to-do lists.

Setting and Achieving Goals

You can employ many useful methods for setting goals. One method is based on writing goals that relate to several periods and areas of your life. Writing down your goals greatly increases your chances of meeting them. Writing exposes incomplete information, undefined terms, unrealistic deadlines, and other symptoms of fuzzy thinking.

WRITE SPECIFIC GOALS

State your written goals as observable actions or measurable results. Think in detail about what will be different when you attain your goals. List the changes in what you'll see, feel, touch, taste, hear, be, do, or have. Specific goals make clear what actions you need to take or what results you can expect. Figure 2 compares vague and specific goals.

Vague Goal	Specific Goal
Get a good education.	Graduate with BS degree in engineering, with honors, by 2017.
Get good grades.	Earn a 3.5 grade point average next semester.
Enhance my spiritual life.	Meditate for 15 minutes daily.
Improve my appearance.	Lose 6 pounds during the next 6 months.
Gain control of my money.	Transfer $100 to my savings account each month.

© 2016 Cengage Learning

Figure 2 Vague and specific goals

WRITE GOALS FOR SEVERAL TIME FRAMES

To develop a comprehensive vision of your future, write down the following types of goals:

- **Long-term goals**: Long-term goals represent major targets in your life. They can include goals in education, careers, personal relationships, travel, financial security, and more — whatever is important to you.

- **Midterm goals**: Midterm goals are objectives you can accomplish in one to five years. They include goals such as completing a course of education, paying off a car loan, or achieving a specific career level. These goals usually support your long-term goals.

- **Short-term goals**: Short-term goals are the ones you can accomplish in a year or less. These goals are specific achievements that require action now or in the near future.

WRITE GOALS IN SEVERAL AREAS OF LIFE

People who set goals in only one area of life may find that their personal growth becomes one-sided. They might experience success at work while neglecting their health or relationships with family members and friends.

To avoid this outcome, set goals in a variety of categories, such as education, career, financial life, family life or relationships, social life, contribution (volunteer activities, community services), spiritual life, and level of health. Add goals in other areas as they occur to you.

REFLECT ON YOUR GOALS

Each week, take a few minutes to think about your goals. You can perform the following spot checks:

- **Check in with your feelings.** Think about how it feels to set your goals. Consider the satisfaction you'll gain in attaining your objectives. If you don't feel a significant emotional connection with a written goal, consider letting it go or filing it away to review later.

- **Check for alignment.** Look for connections among your short-term to midterm goals and your midterm to long-term goals. Look for a fit between all of your goals and your purpose for taking part in higher education as well as your overall purpose in life.
- **Check for obstacles.** Complications can come between you and your goals, such as constraints on time and money. Anticipate obstacles and look for solutions.
- **Check for next steps.** Decide on a series of small, achievable steps you can take to accomplish your short-term goals. Write down these small steps on a daily to-do list. Note your progress and celebrate your successes.

TAKE ACTION IMMEDIATELY

To increase your odds of success, take immediate action. Decrease the gap between stating a goal and starting to achieve it. If you slip and forget about the goal, you can get back on track at any time by *doing* something about it.

Using OneNote to Set Goals

The versatility of Microsoft OneNote allows you to write ideas anywhere on the page, identify notes with a variety of tags, and organize notes into pages and sections, making it a great tool for writing down your goals, organizing your thoughts and ideas, and building connections among them all.

BRAINSTORM WITH QUICK NOTES

Ideas often present themselves without order, structure, or clear fit in the organization of your existing content. Microsoft OneNote provides a feature called Quick Notes for such ideas. A **Quick Note** is a small window you can move anywhere on-screen and use to write reminders and other short notes. Getting the ideas on paper (or in your OneNote notebook) can be the first step in using them to define larger ideas and related goals. Quick Notes are initially unfiled within your notebook, but you can easily move or copy them to other sections. Think of an electronic Quick Note as you would a sticky note on your desk.

ORGANIZE LARGER IDEAS WITH SECTIONS AND PAGES

For larger or more defined ideas, establish an organization system in your OneNote notebook so you can easily locate related information. OneNote provides multiple levels of organization within a notebook.

Most OneNote users store content on pages within sections. As your use of OneNote increases, you can organize related sections into groups or increase the detail of pages by creating subpages for better organization. See Figure 3.

Figure 3 OneNote section tabs and Pages pane

Use Tags to Organize Content in OneNote

OneNote lets you mark notes and other content with tags — keywords that help you find important information — to set reminders, classify information, or set priorities, for example. OneNote provides the following tags by default: To Do, Important, Question, Remember for later, Definition, Highlight, Contact, Address, Phone number, website to visit, Idea, Password, Critical, Project A, Project B, Movie to see, Book to read, Music to listen to, Source for article, Remember for blog, Discuss with <Person A>, Discuss with <Person B>, Discuss with manager, Send in email, Schedule meeting, Call back, To Do priority 1, To Do priority 2, and Client request.

You assign a tag to page content by moving the insertion point to the text you want to tag and then selecting an item from the Tags gallery on the HOME tab of the ribbon. You can create custom tags to meet personal needs for organizing OneNote content in your notebooks.

Creating an ABC Daily To-Do List

One advantage to keeping a daily to-do list is that you don't have to remember what to do next. It's on the list. A typical day in the life of a student is full of separate, often unrelated tasks — reading, attending lectures, reviewing notes, working at a job, writing papers, researching special projects, and running errands. It's easy to forget an important task on a busy day. When that task is written down, you don't have to rely on your memory.

The following steps present the ABC method for creating and using to-do lists. This method involves ranking each item on your list according to three levels of importance: A, B, or C.

Step 1: Brainstorm Tasks

To get started, list all of the tasks you want to complete in a day. Each task will become an item on a to-do list. Don't worry about putting the entries in order or scheduling them yet. Just list everything you want to accomplish.

Step 2: Estimate Time

For each task you wrote down in Step 1, estimate how long it will take to complete the task. Estimating can be tricky. If you allow too little time, you end up feeling rushed. If you allow too much time, you become less productive. For now, use your best guess. If you are unsure, overestimate rather than underestimate how long you need for each task.

Add up the time you estimated to complete all your to-do items. Also add up the number of unscheduled hours in your day. Then compare the two totals. If you have more time assigned to tasks than unscheduled hours in the day, that's a potential problem. To solve it, proceed to Step 3.

Step 3: Rate Each Task by Priority

To prevent overscheduling, decide which to-do items are the most important given the time you have available. One suggestion for making this decision comes from the book *How to Get Control of Your Time and Your Life*, by Alan Lakein — simply label each task A, B, or C:

- The A tasks on your list are the most critical. They include assignments that are coming due or jobs that need to be done immediately.

- The B tasks on your list are important, but less so than the A tasks. They can be postponed, if necessary, for another day.

- The C tasks do not require immediate attention. C tasks are often small, easy jobs with no set deadline. They too can be postponed.

After labeling the items on your to-do list, schedule time for all of the A tasks.

Step 4: Cross off Tasks

Keep your to-do list with you at all times. Cross off, check, or otherwise mark activities when you finish them, and add new tasks when you think of them.

When using the ABC method, you might experience an ailment common to students: C fever. Symptoms include the uncontrollable urge to drop an A task and begin crossing off C items on your to-do list. The reason C fever is so common is that A tasks are usually more difficult or time consuming to achieve and have a higher risk of failure.

Use your to-do list to keep yourself on track, working on your A tasks. Don't panic or berate yourself when you realize that in the last six hours, you have completed nine Cs and not a single A. Just calmly return to the A tasks.

Step 5: Evaluate

At the end of the day, evaluate your performance. Look for A priorities you didn't complete. Look for items that repeatedly turn up as Bs or Cs on your list and never seem to get done. Consider changing them to A tasks or dropping them altogether. Similarly, you might consider lowering the priority of an A task you didn't complete to a B or C task.

When you're finished evaluating, start on tomorrow's to-do list. That way, you can wake up and start working on tasks productively without panicking about what to do.

Creating To-Do Lists in OneNote

The To Do tag in OneNote makes it easy to change any notebook item into a task. When you select an item and then assign the To Do tag to it, a check box appears next to the item. Insert a check mark in the box when you complete the task. You can also use the Planners subcategory of Page Templates in OneNote to generate Simple To Do Lists, Prioritized To Do Lists, and Project To Do Lists quickly and easily — leaving you to merely provide the action items. Figure 4 shows a to-do list based on the Simple To-Do List page template.

Figure 4 List based on the Simple To-Do List page template

Finding Time

Good news: You have enough time to accomplish the tasks you want to do. All it takes is thinking about the possibilities and making conscious choices.

Everything written about time management can be reduced to three main ideas:

1. Know exactly *what* you want. State your wants as clear, specific goals. Put them in writing.

2. Know *how* to get what you want. Take action to meet your goals. Determine what you'll do *today* to get what you want in the future. Put those actions in writing as well.

3. Strive for balance. When your life lacks balance, you spend most of your time responding to interruptions, last-minute projects, and emergencies. Life feels like a scramble just to survive. You're so busy achieving someone else's goals that you forget about getting what *you* want.

According to Stephen R. Covey, author of *The Seven Habits of Highly Effective People*, the purpose of planning is to carve out space in your life for tasks that are not urgent but are truly important. Examples are exercising regularly, reading, praying or meditating, spending quality time alone or with family members and friends, traveling, and cooking nutritious meals. Each of these tasks contributes directly to your personal goals for the future and to the overall quality of your life in the present.

Think of time management as time *investment*. Spend your most valuable resource in the way you choose.

Study Tools

In this section, you will learn ways to effectively use technology to promote positive study habits and successful results. Specifically, you explore ways to integrate Microsoft OneNote with PowerPoint presentations, web content, and **screen clippings**, also called screenshots, which are images of your screen that you capture using a OneNote tool. You will also learn techniques for interacting with e-books and for collaborating with others through the sharing features of OneNote and Office Online.

Turning PowerPoint Presentations into Powerful Notes

Some students stop taking notes during a PowerPoint presentation. This choice can be hazardous to your academic health for three major reasons:

- **PowerPoint presentations don't include everything.** Instructors and other speakers use PowerPoint to organize their presentations. Topics covered in the slides make up an outline of what your instructor considers important. Speakers create slides to flag the main points and signal transitions between topics. However, speakers usually enhance a presentation with examples and explanations that don't appear on the slides. In addition, slides will not contain any material from class discussion, including any answers that the instructor gives in response to questions.

- **You stop learning.** Taking notes forces you to capture ideas and information in your own words. The act of writing also helps you remember the material. If you stop writing and let your attention drift, you can quickly lose track of the presentation or topic.

- **You end up with major gaps in your notes.** When it's time to review your notes, you'll find that material from PowerPoint presentations is missing. This can be a major problem at exam time.

To create value from PowerPoint presentations, take notes directly on the slides. Continue to observe, record, and review. Use the presentation as a way to *guide* rather than to *replace* your own note taking.

PREPARE BEFORE THE PRESENTATION

Sometimes instructors make PowerPoint slides available before a lecture. Scan the slides, just as you would preview a reading assignment. Consider printing the slides and bringing them along to class. You can take notes directly on the printed pages.

If you use a laptop for taking notes during class, then you might not want to bother with printing. Open the PowerPoint presentation file and type your notes in the Notes pane, which appears below each slide.

CREATE ONENOTE PAGE CONTENT FROM POWERPOINT SLIDES

Use the File Printout button on the OneNote INSERT tab in the Files group to print PowerPoint slides directly to OneNote. You can store the slides where you keep your other notes and then take notes on the same page of your notebook as the slide content.

TAKE NOTES DURING THE PRESENTATION

As you take notes during a presentation, be selective in what you write down. Determine what kind of material appears on each slide. Stay alert for new topics, main points, and important details. Taking too many notes makes it hard to keep up with a speaker and separate main points from minor details.

In any case, go *beyond* the slides. Record valuable questions and answers that come up during a discussion, even if they are not a planned part of the presentation.

USE DRAWING OBJECTS, AUDIO, AND VIDEO IN YOUR NOTES

On touch interface devices, OneNote makes it easy to handwrite your notes or draw symbols and shapes on the notebook pages. For mouse users, the OneNote DRAW tab contains predefined shapes and pen options for creating notes that are more than just text.

On devices that include microphones or webcams, you can use OneNote to capture audio and video recordings in your notebook pages, ensuring that every moment of an important lecture is captured for later review and study.

REVIEW AFTER THE PRESENTATION

If you printed out slides before class and took notes on those pages, then find a way to integrate them with the rest of your notes. For example, add references in your notebook to specific slides. Create summary notes that include the major topics and points from readings, class meetings, and PowerPoint presentations.

If you have a copy of the presentation, consider editing it. Cut slides that don't include information you want to remember. Rearrange slides so that the order makes more sense to you. Remember that you can open the original file later to see exactly what your instructor presented.

ADD LINKS TO OTHER NOTEBOOK CONTENT

When creating summary note pages in your OneNote notebook, it is good practice to link text or content on the summary page to the detailed notes elsewhere in your notebook. To do so, select the content you want to use as the link, click the Link button in the Links group on the INSERT tab to open the Link dialog box (shown in Figure 5), and then select the location in the OneNote notebook with the detailed content.

text to display at link location

page location containing linked content

Figure 5 Link dialog box in OneNote 2013

SEARCH NOTES AND PRINTOUTS

You can quickly locate content in your OneNote notebooks using the built-in search features of OneNote 2013. For basic text searches, you can limit the results to content on the current page, current section, current section group, current notebook, or all open notebooks.

After you apply tags to content within the notebook, use the Find Tags button in the Tags group on the HOME tab to locate and filter results based on tags.

Extending Reading to Webpages and E-Books

While reading, skilled readers focus on finding answers to their questions and flagging them in the text. E-books offer features that help with the following steps:

- **Access the table of contents.** For a bigger picture of the text, look for a table of contents that lists chapter headings and subheadings. Click a heading to expand the text for that part of the book.

- **Use navigation tools.** To flip electronic pages, look for Previous and Next buttons or arrows on the right and left borders of each page. Many e-books also offer a Go to Page feature that allows you to enter a specific page number to access the page.

- **Search the text.** Look for a search box that allows you to enter key words and find all the places in the text where those words are mentioned.

- **Follow links to definitions and related information.** Many e-books supply a definition to any word in the text. All you need to do is highlight a word and then click it.

- **Highlight and annotate.** E-books allow you to select words, sentences, or entire paragraphs and highlight them in a bright color. You can also annotate a book by entering your own notes on the pages.

COLLECT WEB CONTENT IN ONENOTE

OneNote makes it easy to collect content with notations and links to the original source. When copying content from an electronic source, OneNote adds a reference to the original location below the pasted content. For web-based resources, OneNote inserts a hyperlink so you can access the source again later.

INSERT SCREEN CLIPPINGS

In addition to copying content directly from websites, you can use the Screen Clipping tool to collect an image from any open application. To insert a screen clipping into a notebook, display the item you want to capture in another application, switch to OneNote, and then click the Screen Clipping button in the Images group on the INSERT tab. OneNote is minimized and the most recently used application is displayed with a transparent overlay. Draw a box around the area you want to capture to insert the screen clipping into the OneNote page as an image with details of when you collected the screen clipping. You can include additional notes and annotations using other text and drawing tools in OneNote.

Setting Limits on Screen Time

To get an accurate picture of your involvement in social networking and other online activity, monitor how much time you spend on them for one week. Make conscious choices about how much time you want to spend online and on the phone. Don't let social networking distract you from meeting personal and academic goals.

Using Technology to Collaborate

When planning group projects, look for tools that allow you to create, edit, and share documents, spreadsheets, drawings, presentations, and other files. You can find a growing list of applications for these purposes, including Office Online, which includes an online version of OneNote.

When using collaborative technology, your people skills are as important as your technology skills. Set up a process to make sure that everyone's voice is heard during a virtual meeting. People who are silenced will probably tune out.

Function as a professional whenever you're online. Team members might get to know you mainly through emails and instant messages. Consider the impression you're making with your online presence. Avoid slang, idioms, sarcastic humor, and other expressions that can create misunderstanding. A small dose of civility can make a big difference in the quality of your virtual team experience.

USE OFFICE ONLINE

Office Online is the free, online version of Microsoft Word, Microsoft Excel, Microsoft PowerPoint, and Microsoft OneNote available through Office 365, SharePoint Online, and OneDrive accounts. These tools provide basic functionality from the desktop applications directly in a web browser, giving you the ability to view and edit documents, workbooks, presentations, and notebooks from virtually any device with an Internet connection.

Supported by the cloud storage options associated with Office 365, SharePoint Online, and OneDrive, Office Online makes it easy to do real-time collaborative editing of shared files with classmates, friends, family, and colleagues.

SHARE CONTENT FROM ONENOTE

If you store OneNote notebooks on OneDrive or SharePoint, you can share pages, sections, or entire notebooks with others by using the commands in the Share group on the OneNote FILE tab. You can even share paragraphs of text on pages by right-clicking selected content and then clicking the Copy Link to Paragraph option on the shortcut menu. Export pages, sections, or entire notebooks from OneNote in various formats, including PDF and XPS, for sharing with users who don't have Microsoft OneNote.

Critical Thinking and Problem Solving

It has been said that human beings are rational creatures. Yet no one is born as an effective thinker. Critical thinking — the objective analysis and evaluation of an issue in order to form a judgment — is a learned skill. This is one reason that you study so many subjects in higher education. A broad base of courses helps you develop as a thinker, giving you a foundation for dealing with complex challenges in your career, your relationships, and your community.

Following a Process for Critical Thinking

Learning to think well matters. The rewards are many, and the stakes are high. Major decisions in life — from choosing a major to choosing a spouse — depend on your thinking skills.

Following are strategies that you can use to move freely through six levels of thinking: remembering, understanding, applying, analyzing, evaluating, and creating. The strategies fall into three major categories: check your attitudes, check for logic, and check for evidence.

CHECK YOUR ATTITUDES

The following suggestions help you understand and analyze information free from bias and other filters that cloud clear thinking:

- **Be willing to find various points of view on any issue.** People can have dozens of viewpoints on every important issue. In fact, few problems have any single, permanent solution. Begin seeking alternative views with an open mind. When talking to another person, be willing to walk away with a new point of view — even if it's similar to your original idea, supported with new evidence.

- **Practice tolerance.** One path to critical thinking is tolerance for a wide range of opinions. Taking a position on important issues is natural. Problems emerge, however, when people become so attached to their current viewpoints that they refuse to consider alternatives.

- **Understand before criticizing.** The six levels of thinking build on each other. Before you agree or disagree with an idea, make sure that you *remember* it accurately and truly *understand* it. Polished debaters make a habit of doing this. Often they can sum up their opponent's viewpoint better than anyone else can. This puts them in a much stronger position to *apply, analyze, evaluate,* and *create* ideas.

- **Watch for hot spots.** Many people have mental "hot spots" — topics that provoke strong opinions and feelings. To become more skilled at examining various points of view, notice your own particular hot spots. In addition, be sensitive to other people's hot spots. Demonstrate tolerance and respect before discussing personal issues.

- **Be willing to be uncertain.** Some of the most profound thinkers have practiced the art of thinking by using a magic sentence: "I'm not sure yet." It is courageous and unusual to take the time to pause, look, examine, be thoughtful, consider many points of view — and be unsure. Uncertainty calls for patience. Give yourself permission to experiment, practice, and learn from mistakes.

CHECK FOR LOGIC

Learning to think logically offers many benefits: When you think logically, you take your reading, writing, speaking, and listening skills to a higher level. You avoid costly mistakes in decision making. You can join discussions and debates with more confidence, cast your votes with a clear head, and become a better-informed citizen.

The following suggestions will help you work with the building blocks of logical thinking — terms, assertions, arguments, and assumptions:

- **Define key terms.** A *term* is a word or phrase that refers to a clearly defined concept. Terms with several different meanings are ambiguous — fuzzy, vague, and unclear. One common goal of critical thinking is to remove ambiguous terms or define them clearly.

- **Look for assertions.** An *assertion* is a complete sentence that contains one or more key terms. The purpose of an assertion is to define a term or to state relationships between terms. These relationships are the essence of what we mean by the term *knowledge*.

- **Look for arguments.** For specialists in logic, an *argument* is a series of related assertions. There are two major types of reasoning used in building arguments — deductive and inductive. *Deductive reasoning* builds arguments by starting with a general assertion and leading to a more specific one. With *inductive reasoning*, the chain of logic proceeds in the opposite direction — from specific to general.

- **Remember the power of assumptions.** Assumptions are beliefs that guide our thinking and behavior. Assumptions can be simple and ordinary. In other cases, assumptions are more complex and have larger effects. Despite the power to influence our speaking and actions, assumptions are often unstated. People can remain unaware of their most basic and far-reaching assumptions — the very ideas that shape their lives. Heated conflict and hard feelings often result when people argue on the level of opinions and forget that the real conflict lies at the level of their assumptions.

- **Look for stated assumptions.** Stated assumptions are literally a thinker's starting points. Critical thinkers produce logical arguments and evidence to support most of their assertions. However, they are also willing to take other assertions as "self-evident" — so obvious or fundamental that they do not need to be proved.

- **Look for unstated assumptions.** In many cases, speakers and writers do not state their assumptions or offer evidence for them. In addition, people often hold many assumptions at the same time, with some of those assumptions contradicting each other. This makes uncovering assumptions a feat worthy of the greatest detective. You can follow a two-step method for testing the validity of any argument. First, state the assumptions. Second, see whether you can find any exceptions to the assumptions. Uncovering assumptions and looking for exceptions can help you detect many errors in logic.

CHECK FOR EVIDENCE

In addition to testing arguments with the tools of logic, look carefully at the evidence used to support those arguments. Evidence comes in several forms, including facts, comments from recognized experts in a field, and examples.

Thinking Critically About Information on the Internet

Sources of information on the Internet range from the reputable (such as the Library of Congress) to the flamboyant (such as the *National Enquirer*). People are free to post *anything* on the Internet, including outdated facts as well as intentional misinformation.

Taking a few simple precautions when you surf the Internet can keep you from crashing onto the rocky shore of misinformation.

DISTINGUISH BETWEEN IDEAS AND INFORMATION

To think more powerfully about what you find on the Internet, remember the difference between information and ideas. *Information* refers to facts that can be verified by independent observers. *Ideas* are interpretations or opinions based on facts. Several people with the same information might adopt different ideas based on that information.

Don't assume that an idea is more current, reasonable, or accurate just because you find it on the Internet. Apply your critical thinking skills to all published material — print and online.

LOOK FOR OVERALL QUALITY

Examine the features of a website in general. Notice the effectiveness of the text and visuals as a whole. Also note how well the site is organized and whether you can navigate the site's features with ease. Look for the date that crucial information was posted, and determine how often the site is updated.

Next, get an overview of the site's content. Examine several of the site's pages, and look for consistency of facts, quality of information, and competency with grammar and spelling. Evaluate the site's links to related webpages. Look for links to pages of reputable organizations.

LOOK AT THE SOURCE

Find a clear description of the person or organization responsible for the website. If a site asks you to subscribe or become a member, then find out what it does with the personal information that you provide. Look for a way to contact the site's publisher with questions and comments.

LOOK FOR DOCUMENTATION

When you encounter an assertion on a webpage or another Internet resource, note the types and quality of the evidence offered. Look for credible examples, quotations from authorities in the field, documented statistics, or summaries of scientific studies.

SET AN EXAMPLE

In the midst of the Internet's chaotic growth, you can light a path of rationality. Whether you're sending a short email message or building a massive website, bring your own critical thinking skills into play. Every word and image that you send down the wires to the web can display the hallmarks of critical thinking: sound logic, credible evidence, and respect for your audience.

Using OneNote to Enhance Critical Thinking

Using Microsoft OneNote as a tool for collecting your thoughts and ideas into organized sections of information puts your broad base of knowledge in a single searchable location for retrieval, analysis, and connection. During the critical thinking process, you can create a new section or a new page in OneNote and use the techniques discussed earlier in this chapter to link information from multiple areas of your notebook and synthesize those concepts into a final product.

Completing Four Steps to Solve Problems

Think of problem solving as a process with four Ps: Define the *problem*, generate *possibilities*, create a *plan*, and *perform* your plan.

DEFINE THE PROBLEM

To define a problem effectively, understand what a problem is: a mismatch between what you want and what you have. Problem solving is all about reducing the gap between these two factors. One simple and powerful strategy for defining problems is simply to put them in writing. When you do this, you might find that potential solutions appear as well.

GENERATE POSSIBILITIES

Now put on your creative thinking hat. Open up. Brainstorm as many possible solutions to the problem as you can. As you generate possibilities, gather relevant facts.

CREATE A PLAN

After rereading your problem definition and list of possible solutions, choose the solution that seems most workable. Think about specific actions that will reduce the gap between what you have and what you want. Visualize the steps you will take to make this solution a reality, and arrange them in chronological order. To make your plan even more powerful, put it in writing.

PERFORM YOUR PLAN

Ultimately, your skill in solving problems lies in how well you perform your plan. Through the quality of your actions, you become the architect of your own success.

Office 2013 and Windows 8: Essential Concepts and Skills

Microsoft product screen shots used with permission from Microsoft Corporation.

Objectives

You will have mastered the material in this chapter when you can:

- Use a touch screen
- Perform basic mouse operations
- Start Windows and sign in to an account
- Identify the objects in the Windows 8 desktop
- Identify the apps in and versions of Microsoft Office 2013
- Run an app
- Identify the components of the Microsoft Office ribbon

- Create folders
- Save files
- Change screen resolution
- Perform basic tasks in Microsoft Office apps
- Manage files
- Use Microsoft Office Help and Windows Help

Office 2013 and Windows 8: Essential Concepts and Skills

This introductory chapter uses PowerPoint 2013 to cover features and functions common to Office 2013 apps, as well as the basics of Windows 8.

Roadmap

In this chapter, you will learn how to perform basic tasks in Windows and PowerPoint. The following roadmap identifies general activities you will perform as you progress through this chapter:

1. SIGN IN to an account
2. USE WINDOWS
3. USE Features in PowerPoint that are Common across Office APPS
4. FILE and Folder MANAGEMENT
5. SWITCH between APPS
6. SAVE and Manage FILES
7. CHANGE SCREEN RESOLUTION
8. EXIT APPS
9. USE ADDITIONAL Office APP FEATURES
10. USE Office and Windows HELP

At the beginning of the step instructions throughout the chapter, you will see an abbreviated form of this roadmap. The abbreviated roadmap uses colors to indicate chapter progress: gray means the chapter is beyond that activity, blue means the task being shown is covered in that activity, and black means that activity is yet to be covered. For example, the following abbreviated roadmap indicates the chapter would be showing a task in the 3 USE APPS activity.

1 SIGN IN | 2 USE WINDOWS | 3 USE APPS | 4 FILE MANAGEMENT | 5 SWITCH APPS | 6 SAVE FILES
7 CHANGE SCREEN RESOLUTION | 8 EXIT APPS | 9 USE ADDITIONAL APP FEATURES | 10 USE HELP

Use the abbreviated roadmap as a progress guide while you read or step through the instructions in this chapter.

Introduction to the Windows 8 Operating System

Windows 8 is the newest version of Microsoft Windows, which is a popular and widely used operating system. An **operating system** is a computer program (set of computer instructions) that coordinates all the activities of computer hardware, such as memory, storage devices, and printers, and provides the capability for you to communicate with the computer.

The Windows operating system simplifies the process of working with documents and apps by organizing the manner in which you interact with the computer. Windows is used to run apps. An **app** (short for application) consists of programs designed to make users more productive and/or assist them with personal tasks, such as creating presentations or browsing the web.

The Windows 8 interface begins with the **Start screen**, which shows tiles (Figure 1). A **tile** is a shortcut to an app or other content. The tiles on the Start screen include installed apps that you use regularly. From the Start screen, you can choose which apps to run using a touch screen, mouse, or other input device.

Figure 1

Using a Touch Screen and a Mouse

Windows users who have computers or devices with touch screen capability can interact with the screen using gestures. A **gesture** is a motion you make on a touch screen with the tip of one or more fingers or your hand. Touch screens are convenient because they do not require a separate device for input. Table 1 on the next page presents common ways to interact with a touch screen.

If you are using your finger on a touch screen and are having difficulty completing the steps in this chapter, consider using a stylus. Many people find it easier to be precise with a stylus than with a finger. In addition, with a stylus you see the pointer. If you still are having trouble completing the steps with a stylus, try using a mouse.

Table 1 Touch Screen Gestures

Motion	Description	Common Uses
Tap	Quickly touch and release one finger one time.	Activate a link (built-in connection) Press a button Run a program or an app
Double-tap	Quickly touch and release one finger two times.	Run a program or an app Zoom in (show a smaller area on the screen, so that contents appear larger) at the location of the double-tap
Press and hold	Press and hold one finger to cause an action to occur, or until an action occurs.	Display a shortcut menu (immediate access to allowable actions) Activate a mode enabling you to move an item with one finger to a new location
Drag, or slide	Press and hold one finger on an object and then move the finger to the new location.	Move an item around the screen Scroll
Swipe	Press and hold one finger and then move the finger horizontally or vertically on the screen.	Select an object Swipe from edge to display a bar such as the Charms bar, Apps bar, and Navigation bar (all discussed later)
Stretch	Move two fingers apart.	Zoom in (show a smaller area on the screen, so that contents appear larger)
Pinch	Move two fingers together.	Zoom out (show a larger area on the screen, so that contents appear smaller)

© 2014 Cengage Learning

BTW

BTWs

For a complete list of the BTWs found in the margins of this book, visit the BTW resource on the Student Companion Site located on www.cengagebrain.com. For detailed instructions about accessing available resources, visit www.cengage.com/ct/studentdownload or contact your instructor for information about accessing the required files.

BTW

Touch Screen Differences

The Office and Windows interfaces may vary if you are using a touch screen. For this reason, you might notice that the function or appearance of your touch screen differs slightly from this chapter's presentation.

CONSIDER THIS

Will your screen look different if you are using a touch screen?

The Windows and Microsoft Office interface varies slightly if you are using a touch screen. For this reason, you might notice that your Windows or PowerPoint screens look slightly different from the screens in this book.

Windows users who do not have touch screen capabilities typically work with a mouse that has at least two buttons. For a right-handed user, the left button usually is the primary mouse button, and the right mouse button is the secondary mouse button. Left-handed people, however, can reverse the function of these buttons.

Table 2 explains how to perform a variety of mouse operations. Some apps also use keys in combination with the mouse to perform certain actions. For example, when you hold down the CTRL key while rolling the mouse wheel, text on the screen may become larger or smaller based on the direction you roll the wheel. The function of the mouse buttons and the wheel varies depending on the app.

Table 2 Mouse Operations

Operation	Mouse Action	Example*
Point	Move the mouse until the pointer on the desktop is positioned on the item of choice.	Position the pointer on the screen.
Click	Press and release the primary mouse button, which usually is the left mouse button.	Select or deselect items on the screen or run an app or app feature.
Right-click	Press and release the secondary mouse button, which usually is the right mouse button.	Display a shortcut menu.
Double-click	Quickly press and release the primary mouse button twice without moving the mouse.	Run an app or app feature.
Triple-click	Quickly press and release the primary mouse button three times without moving the mouse.	Select a paragraph.
Drag	Point to an item, hold down the primary mouse button, move the item to the desired location on the screen, and then release the mouse button.	Move an object from one location to another or draw pictures.
Right-drag	Point to an item, hold down the right mouse button, move the item to the desired location on the screen, and then release the right mouse button.	Display a shortcut menu after moving an object from one location to another.
Rotate wheel	Roll the wheel forward or backward.	Scroll vertically (up and down).
Free-spin wheel	Whirl the wheel forward or backward so that it spins freely on its own.	Scroll through many pages in seconds.
Press wheel	Press the wheel button while moving the mouse.	Scroll continuously.
Tilt wheel	Press the wheel toward the right or left.	Scroll horizontally (left and right).
Press thumb button	Press the button on the side of the mouse with your thumb.	Move forward or backward through webpages and/or control media, games, etc.

© 2014 Cengage Learning

*Note: The examples presented in this column are discussed as they are demonstrated in this chapter.

Scrolling

A **scroll bar** is a horizontal or vertical bar that appears when the contents of an area may not be visible completely on the screen (Figure 2). A scroll bar contains **scroll arrows** and a **scroll box** that enable you to view areas that currently cannot be seen on the screen. Tapping or clicking the up and down scroll arrows moves the screen content up or down one line. You also can tap or click above or below the scroll box to move up or down a section, or drag the scroll box up or down to move to a specific location.

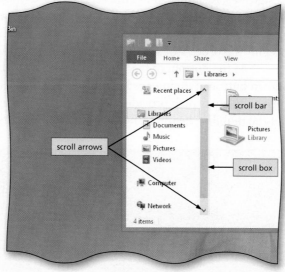

Figure 2

What should you do if you are running Windows 7 instead of Windows 8?
Although Windows 8 includes several user interface and feature enhancements, many of the steps in this book work in both Windows 7 and Windows 8. If you have any questions about differences between the two operating systems or how to perform tasks in an earlier version of Windows, contact your instructor.

CONSIDER THIS

Keyboard Shortcuts

In many cases, you can use the keyboard instead of the mouse to accomplish a task. To perform tasks using the keyboard, you press one or more keyboard keys, sometimes identified as a **keyboard shortcut**. Some keyboard shortcuts consist of a single key, such as the F1 key. For example, to obtain help in many apps, you can press the F1 key. Other keyboard shortcuts consist of multiple keys, in which case a plus sign separates the key names, such as CTRL+ESC. This notation means to press and hold down the first key listed, press one or more additional keys, and then release all keys. For example, to display the Start screen, press CTRL+ESC, that is, hold down the CTRL key, press the ESC key, and then release both keys.

Starting Windows

It is not unusual for multiple people to use the same computer in a work, educational, recreational, or home setting. Windows enables each user to establish a **user account**, which identifies to Windows the resources, such as apps and storage locations, a user can access when working with the computer.

Each user account has a user name and may have a password and an icon, as well. A **user name** is a unique combination of letters or numbers that identifies a specific user to Windows. A **password** is a private combination of letters, numbers, and special characters associated with the user name that allows access to a user's account resources. An icon is a small image that represents an object, thus a **user icon** is a picture associated with a user name.

When you turn on a computer, Windows starts and displays a **lock screen** consisting of the time and date (Figure 3a). To unlock the screen, swipe up or click the lock screen. Depending on your computer's settings, Windows may or may not display a sign-in screen that shows the user names and user icons for users who have accounts on the computer (Figure 3b). This **sign-in screen** enables you to sign in to your user account and makes the computer available for use. Tapping or clicking the user icon begins the process of signing in, also called logging on, to your user account.

At the bottom of the sign-in screen is the 'Ease of access' button and a Shut down button. Tapping or clicking the 'Ease of access' button displays the Ease of access menu, which provides tools to optimize a computer to accommodate the needs of the mobility, hearing, and vision impaired users. Tapping or clicking the Shut down

Figure 3a

SC Series user icon

Note: To help you locate screen elements that are referenced in the step instructions, such as buttons and commands, this book uses red boxes to point to these screen elements.

Figure 3b

button displays a menu containing commands related to restarting the computer, putting it in a low-power state, and shutting it down. The commands available on your computer may differ.

- The Sleep command saves your work, turns off the computer fans and hard disk, and places the computer in a lower-power state. To wake the computer from sleep mode, press the power button or lift a laptop's cover, and sign in to your account.
- The Shut down command exits running apps, shuts down Windows, and then turns off the computer.
- The Restart command exits running apps, shuts down Windows, and then restarts Windows.

BTW

Q&As

For a complete list of the Q&As found in many of the step-by-step sequences in this book, visit the Q&A resource on the Student Companion Site located on www.cengagebrain.com. For detailed instructions about accessing available resources, visit www.cengage.com/ct/studentdownload or contact your instructor for information about accessing the required files.

1 SIGN IN | 2 USE WINDOWS | 3 USE APPS | 4 FILE MANAGEMENT | 5 SWITCH APPS | 6 SAVE FILES
7 CHANGE SCREEN RESOLUTION | 8 EXIT APPS | 9 USE ADDITIONAL APP FEATURES | 10 USE HELP

To Sign In to an Account

The following steps, which use SC Series as the user name, sign in to an account based on a typical Windows installation. *Why? After starting Windows, you might be required to sign in to an account to access the computer's resources.* You may need to ask your instructor how to sign in to your account. If you are using Windows 7, skip these steps and instead perform the steps in the yellow box that immediately follows these Windows 8 steps.

1

- Swipe up or click the lock screen (shown in Figure 3a) to display a sign-in screen (shown in Figure 3b).

- Tap or click the user icon (for SC Series, in this case) on the sign-in screen, which depending on settings, either will display a second sign-in screen that contains a Password text box (Figure 4) or will display the Windows Start screen (shown in Figure 5 on the next page).

Q&A

Why do I not see a user icon?
Your computer may require you to type a user name instead of tapping or clicking an icon.

What is a text box?
A text box is a rectangular box in which you type text.

Why does my screen not show a Password text box?
Your account does not require a password.

password text box

SC Series

Password

Submit button

'Ease of access' button

Shut down button

Figure 4

- If Windows displays a sign-in screen with a Password text box, type your password in the text box.

2

- Tap or click the Submit button (shown in Figure 4 on the previous page) to sign in to your account and display the Windows Start screen (Figure 5).

Q&A Why does my Start screen look different from the one in Figure 5?
The Windows Start screen is customizable, and your school or employer may have modified the screen to meet its needs. Also, your screen resolution, which affects the size of the elements on the screen, may differ from the screen resolution used in this book. Later in this chapter, you learn how to change screen resolution.

How do I type if my tablet has no keyboard?
You can use your fingers to press keys on a keyboard that appears on the screen, called an on-screen keyboard, or you can purchase a separate physical keyboard that attaches to or wirelessly communicates with the tablet.

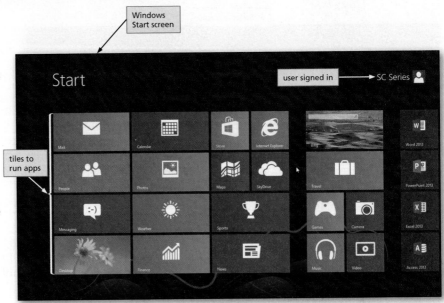

Figure 5

To Sign In to an Account Using Windows 7

If you are using Windows 7, perform these steps to sign in to an account instead of the previous steps that use Windows 8.

1. Click the user icon on the Welcome screen; depending on settings, this either will display a password text box or will sign in to the account and display the Windows 7 desktop.

2. If Windows 7 displays a password text box, type your password in the text box and then click the arrow button to sign in to the account and display the Windows 7 desktop.

The Windows Start Screen

BTW
Modern UI
The new Windows 8 user interface also is referred to as the Modern UI (user interface).

The Windows Start screen provides a scrollable space for you to access apps that have been pinned to the Start screen (shown in Figure 5). Pinned apps appear as tiles on the Start screen. In addition to running apps, you can perform tasks such as pinning apps (placing tiles) on the Start screen, moving the tiles around the Start screen, and unpinning apps (removing tiles) from the Start screen.

If you swipe up from the bottom of or right-click an open space on the Start screen, the App bar will appear. The **App bar** includes a button that enables you to display all of your apps. When working with tiles, the App bar also provides options for manipulating the tiles, such as resizing them.

How do you pin apps, move tiles, and unpin apps?

- To pin an app, swipe up from the bottom of the Start screen or right-click an open space on the Start screen to display the App bar, tap or click the All apps button on the App bar to display the Apps list, swipe down on or right-click the app you want to pin, and then tap or click the 'Pin to Start' button on the App bar. One way to return to the Start screen is to swipe up from the bottom or right-click an open space in the Apps list and then tap or click the All apps button again.

- To move a tile, drag the tile to the desired location.

- To unpin an app, swipe down on or right-click the app to display the App bar and then tap or click the 'Unpin from Start' button on the App bar.

Introduction to Microsoft Office 2013

Microsoft Office 2013 is the newest version of Microsoft Office, offering features that provide users with better functionality and easier ways to work with the various files they create. These features include enhanced design tools, such as improved picture formatting tools and new themes, shared notebooks for working in groups, mobile versions of Office apps, broadcast presentations for the web, and a digital notebook for managing and sharing multimedia information.

Microsoft Office 2013 Apps

Microsoft Office 2013 includes a wide variety of apps such as Word, PowerPoint, Excel, Access, Outlook, Publisher, OneNote, InfoPath, SharePoint Workspace, and Lync:

- **Microsoft Word 2013**, or Word, is a full-featured word processing app that allows you to create professional-looking documents and revise them easily.

- **Microsoft PowerPoint 2013**, or PowerPoint, is a complete presentation app that enables you to produce professional-looking presentations and then deliver them to an audience.

- **Microsoft Excel 2013**, or Excel, is a powerful spreadsheet app that allows you to organize data, complete calculations, make decisions, graph data, develop professional-looking reports, publish organized data to the web, and access real-time data from websites.

- **Microsoft Access 2013**, or Access, is a database management system that enables you to create a database; add, change, and delete data in the database; ask questions concerning the data in the database; and create forms and reports using the data in the database.

- **Microsoft Outlook 2013**, or Outlook, is a communications and scheduling app that allows you to manage email accounts, calendars, contacts, and access to other Internet content.

- **Microsoft Publisher 2013**, or Publisher, is a desktop publishing app that helps you create professional-quality publications and marketing materials that can be shared easily.

- **Microsoft OneNote 2013**, or OneNote, is a note taking app that allows you to store and share information in notebooks with other people.

- **Microsoft InfoPath Designer 2013**, or InfoPath, is a form development app that helps you create forms for use on the web and gather data from these forms.

- **Microsoft SharePoint Workspace 2013**, or SharePoint, is a collaboration app that allows you to access and revise files stored on your computer from other locations.

- **Microsoft Lync 2013** is a communications app that allows you to use various modes of communications such as instant messaging, videoconferencing, and sharing files and apps.

Microsoft Office 2013 Suites

A **suite** is a collection of individual apps available together as a unit. Microsoft offers a variety of Office suites, including a stand-alone desktop app (boxed software), Microsoft Office 365, and Microsoft Office Web Apps. **Microsoft Office 365**, or Office 365, provides plans that allow organizations to use Office in a mobile setting while also being able to communicate and share files, depending upon the type of plan selected by the organization. **Microsoft Office Web Apps**, or Web Apps, are apps that allow you to edit and share files on the web using the familiar Office interface. Table 3 on the next page outlines the differences among these Office suites.

Table 3 Office Suites					
Apps/ Licenses	Office 365 Home Premium	Office 365 Small Business Premium	Office Home & Student	Office Home & Business	Office Professional
Word	✓	✓	✓	✓	✓
PowerPoint	✓	✓	✓	✓	✓
Excel	✓	✓	✓	✓	✓
Access	✓	✓			✓
Outlook	✓	✓		✓	✓
Publisher	✓	✓			✓
Lync		✓			
OneNote			✓	✓	✓
InfoPath		✓			
Licenses	5	5	1	1	1

© 2014 Cengage Learning

During the Office 365 installation, you select a plan, and depending on your plan, you receive different apps and services. Office Web Apps do not require a local installation and are accessed through SkyDrive and your browser. **SkyDrive** is a cloud storage service that provides storage and other services, such as Office Web Apps, to computer users.

CONSIDER THIS

How do you sign up for a SkyDrive account?

• Use your browser to navigate to skydrive.live.com.

• Create a Microsoft account by tapping or clicking the 'Sign up now' link (or a similar link) and then entering your information to create the account.

• Sign in to SkyDrive using your new account or use it in PowerPoint to save your files on SkyDrive.

Apps in a suite, such as Microsoft Office, typically use a similar interface and share features. Once you are comfortable working with the elements and the interface and performing tasks in one app, the similarity can help you apply the knowledge and skills you have learned to another app(s) in the suite. For example, the process for saving a file in Word is the same in PowerPoint, Excel, and the other Office apps. While briefly showing how to use PowerPoint, this chapter illustrates some of the common functions across the Office apps and identifies the characteristics unique to PowerPoint.

Running and Using an App

To use an app, such as PowerPoint, you must instruct the operating system to run the app. Windows provides many different ways to run an app, one of which is presented in this section (other ways to run an app are presented throughout this chapter). After an app is running, you can use it to perform a variety of tasks. The following pages use PowerPoint to discuss some elements of the Office interface and to perform tasks that are common to other Office apps.

PowerPoint

PowerPoint is a full-featured presentation app that allows you to produce compelling presentations to deliver and share with an audience. A PowerPoint **presentation** also is called a **slide show**. PowerPoint contains many features to design, develop, and organize slides, including formatting text, adding and editing video and audio clips, creating tables and charts, applying artistic effects to pictures, animating graphics, and collaborating with friends and colleagues. You then can turn your presentation into a video, broadcast your slide show on the web, or create a photo album.

To Run an App from the Start Screen

1 SIGN IN | 2 USE WINDOWS | 3 USE APPS | 4 FILE MANAGEMENT | 5 SWITCH APPS | 6 SAVE FILES
7 CHANGE SCREEN RESOLUTION | 8 EXIT APPS | 9 USE ADDITIONAL APP FEATURES | 10 USE HELP

The Start screen contains tiles that allow you to run apps, some of which may be stored on your computer. **Why?** *When you install an app, for example, tiles are added to the Start screen for the various Office apps included in the suite.*

The following steps, which assume Windows is running, use the Start screen to run PowerPoint based on a typical installation. You may need to ask your instructor how to run PowerPoint on your computer. Although the steps illustrate running the PowerPoint app, the steps to run any Office app are similar. If you are using Windows 7, skip these steps and instead perform the steps in the yellow box that immediately follows these Windows 8 steps.

1

- If necessary, scroll to display the PowerPoint tile on the Start screen (Figure 6).

Q&A

Why does my Start screen look different?
It may look different because of your computer's configuration. The Start screen may be customized for several reasons, such as usage requirements or security restrictions.

What if the app I want to run is not on the Start screen?
You can display all installed apps by swiping up from the bottom of the Start screen or right-clicking an open space on the Start screen and then tapping or clicking the All apps button on the App bar.

How do I scroll on a touch screen?
Use the slide gesture; that is, press and hold your finger on the screen and then move your finger in the direction you wish to scroll.

Figure 6

2

- Tap or click the PowerPoint 2013 tile to run the PowerPoint app and display the PowerPoint start screen (Figure 7).

Figure 7

3

- Tap or click the Blank Presentation thumbnail on the PowerPoint start screen to create a blank PowerPoint document in the PowerPoint window (Figure 8).

Q&A What happens when you run an app?

Some apps provide a means for you to create a blank document, as shown in Figure 7 on the previous page; others immediately display a blank document in an app window, such as the PowerPoint window shown in Figure 8. A **window** is a rectangular area that displays data and information. The top of a window has a **title bar**, which is a horizontal space that contains the window's name.

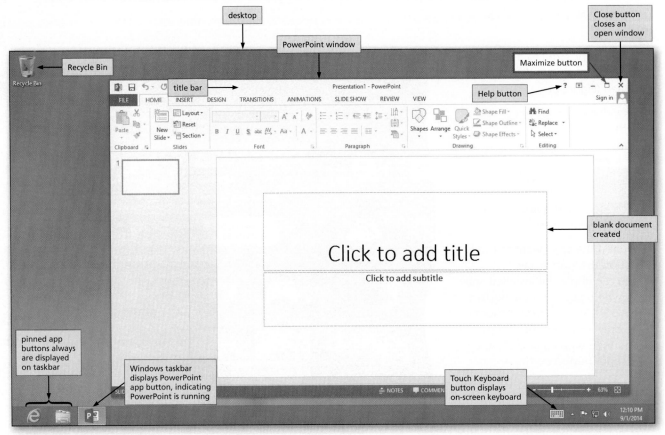

Figure 8

Other Ways

1. Tap or click Search charm on Charms bar, type app name in search box, tap or click app name in results list

2. Double-tap or double-click file created in app you want to run

---

BTW

Touch Keyboard

To display the on-screen touch keyboard, tap the Touch Keyboard button on the Windows taskbar. When finished using the touch keyboard, tap the X button on the touch keyboard to close the keyboard.

To Run an App Using the Start Menu Using Windows 7

If you are using Windows 7, perform these steps to run PowerPoint using the Start menu instead of the previous steps that use Windows 8.

1. Click the Start button on the Windows 7 taskbar to display the Start menu.

2. Click All Programs at the bottom of the left pane on the Start menu to display the All Programs list.

3. If the PowerPoint app is located in a folder, click, or scroll to and then click, the folder in the All Programs list to display a list of the folder's contents.

4. Click, or scroll to and then click, the app name (PowerPoint, in this case) in the list to run the selected app.

Windows Desktop

When you run an app in Windows, it may appear in an on-screen work area app, called the **desktop** (shown in Figure 8). You can perform tasks such as placing objects in the desktop, moving the objects around the desktop, and removing items from the desktop.

Some icons also may be displayed in the desktop. For instance, the icon for the **Recycle Bin**, the location of files that have been deleted, appears in the desktop by default. A **file** is a named unit of storage. Files can contain text, images, audio, and video. You can customize your desktop so that icons representing apps and files you use often appear in the desktop.

To Switch between an App and the Start Screen

1 SIGN IN | 2 USE WINDOWS | 3 USE APPS | 4 FILE MANAGEMENT | 5 SWITCH APPS | 6 SAVE FILES
7 CHANGE SCREEN RESOLUTION | 8 EXIT APPS | 9 USE ADDITIONAL APP FEATURES | 10 USE HELP

While working with an app, such as PowerPoint, or in the desktop, you easily can return to the Start screen. The following steps switch from the PowerPoint app to the Start screen. *Why? Returning to the Start screen allows you to run any of your other apps.* If you are using Windows 7, read these steps without performing them because Windows 7 does not have a Start screen.

- Swipe in from the left edge of the screen, and then back to the left, or point to the lower-left corner of the PowerPoint app to display a thumbnail of the Start screen (Figure 9).

Figure 9

- Tap or click the thumbnail of the Start screen to display the Start screen (Figure 10).

- Tap or click the Desktop tile to redisplay the PowerPoint app in the desktop (shown in Figure 8).

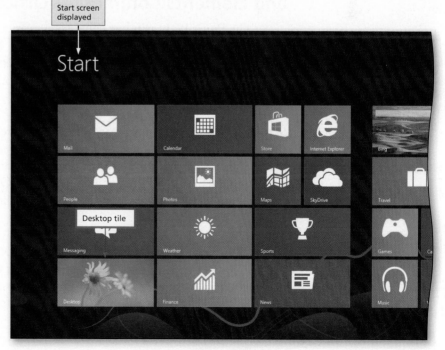

Figure 10

Other Ways

1. Press WINDOWS key to display Start screen

OFF 14   **Office 2013 and Windows 8 Chapter**   Essential Concepts and Skills

1 SIGN IN | 2 USE WINDOWS | 3 USE APPS | 4 FILE MANAGEMENT | 5 SWITCH APPS | 6 SAVE FILES
7 CHANGE SCREEN RESOLUTION | 8 EXIT APPS | 9 USE ADDITIONAL APP FEATURES | 10 USE HELP

To Maximize a Window

Sometimes content is not visible completely in a window. One method of displaying the entire contents of a window is to **maximize** it, or enlarge the window so that it fills the entire screen. The following step maximizes the PowerPoint window; however, any Office app's window can be maximized using this step. *Why?* *A maximized window provides the most space available for using the app.*

- If the PowerPoint window is not maximized already, tap or click the Maximize button (shown in Figure 8 on page OFF 12) next to the Close button on the window's title bar to maximize the window (Figure 11).

Figure 11

Q&A

What happened to the Maximize button?
It changed to a Restore Down button, which you can use to return a window to its size and location before you maximized it.

How do I know whether a window is maximized?
A window is maximized if it fills the entire display area and the Restore Down button is displayed on the title bar.

Other Ways

1. Double-tap or double-click title bar   2. Drag title bar to top of screen

PowerPoint Document Window, Ribbon, and Elements Common to Office Apps

The PowerPoint window consists of a variety of components to make your work more efficient and documents more professional. These include the document window, ribbon, mini toolbar, shortcut menus, Quick Access Toolbar, and Microsoft Account area. Most of these components are common to other Microsoft Office apps; others are unique to PowerPoint.

Scroll Bars   You use a scroll bar to display different portions of a presentation in the document window. At the right edge of the document window is a vertical scroll bar. If a slide is too wide to fit in the document window, a horizontal scroll bar also appears at the bottom of the document window. On a scroll bar, the position of the scroll box reflects the location of the portion of the presentation that is displayed in the document window.

Status Bar   The **status bar**, located at the bottom of the document window above the Windows taskbar, presents information about the presentation, the progress of current tasks, and the status of certain commands and keys; it also provides controls for viewing the presentation. As you type text or perform certain tasks, various indicators and buttons may appear on the status bar.

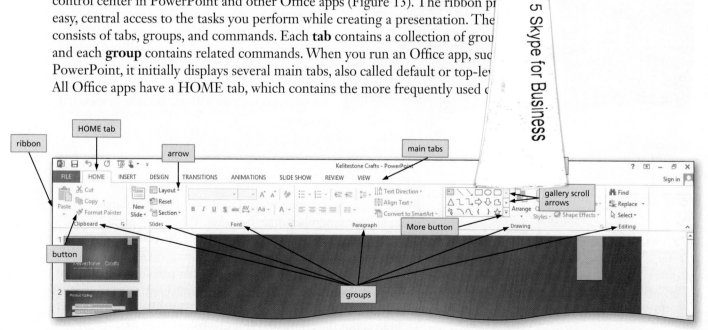

Figure 12

The left side of the status bar in Figure 12 shows the current slide followed by the total number of slides in the presentation and an icon to check spelling. The side of the status bar includes buttons and controls you can use to change the v presentation and adjust the size of the displayed slide.

Ribbon The ribbon, located near the top of the window below the title bar, is control center in PowerPoint and other Office apps (Figure 13). The ribbon pr easy, central access to the tasks you perform while creating a presentation. The consists of tabs, groups, and commands. Each **tab** contains a collection of grou and each **group** contains related commands. When you run an Office app, suc PowerPoint, it initially displays several main tabs, also called default or top-le All Office apps have a HOME tab, which contains the more frequently used o

Figure 13

In addition to the main tabs, the Office apps display **tool tabs**, also called contextual tabs (Figure 14), when you perform certain tasks or work with objects such as pictures or tables. If you insert a picture in a PowerPoint slide, for example, the PICTURE TOOLS tab and its related subordinate FORMAT tab appear, collectively referred to as the PICTURE TOOLS FORMAT tab. When you are finished working with the picture, the PICTURE TOOLS FORMAT tab disappears from the ribbon. PowerPoint and other Office apps determine when tool tabs should appear and disappear based on tasks you perform. Some tool tabs, such as the TABLE TOOLS tab, have more than one related subordinate tab.

Figure 14

Figure 15

Items on the ribbon include buttons, boxes, and galleries (shown in Figure 13 on the previous page). A **gallery** is a set of choices, often graphical, arranged in a grid or in a list. You can scroll through choices in an in-ribbon gallery by tapping or clicking the gallery's scroll arrows. Or, you can tap or click a gallery's More button to view more gallery options on the screen at a time.

Some buttons and boxes have arrows that, when tapped or clicked, also display a gallery; others always cause a gallery to be displayed when tapped or clicked. Most galleries support **live preview**, which is a feature that allows you to point to a gallery choice and see its effect in the document — without actually selecting the choice (Figure 15). Live preview works only if you are using a mouse; if you are using a touch screen, you will not be able to view live previews.

Figure 16

Some commands on the ribbon display an image to help you remember their function. When you point to a command on the ribbon, all or part of the command glows in a shade of blue, and a ScreenTip appears on the screen. A **ScreenTip** is an on-screen note that provides the name of the command, available keyboard shortcut(s), a description of the command, and sometimes instructions for how to obtain help about the command (Figure 16).

Some groups on the ribbon have a small arrow in the lower-right corner, called a **Dialog Box Launcher**, that when tapped or clicked, displays a dialog box or a task pane with additional options for the group (Figure 17). When presented with a dialog box, you make selections and must close the dialog box before returning to the document. A **task pane**, in contrast to a dialog box, is a window that can remain open and visible while you work in the document.

BTW
Touch Mode
The Office and Windows interfaces may vary if you are using Touch mode. For this reason, you might notice that the function or appearance of your touch screen in PowerPoint differs slightly from this book's presentation.

Figure 17

Mini Toolbar   The **mini toolbar**, which appears automatically based on tasks you perform, contains commands related to changing the appearance of text in a document (Figure 18). If you do not use the mini toolbar, it disappears from the screen. The buttons, arrows, and boxes on the mini toolbar vary, depending on whether you are using Touch mode versus Mouse mode. If you press and hold or right-click an item in the document window, PowerPoint displays both the mini toolbar and a shortcut menu, which is discussed in a later section in this chapter.

All commands on the mini toolbar also exist on the ribbon. The purpose of the mini toolbar is to minimize hand or mouse movement.

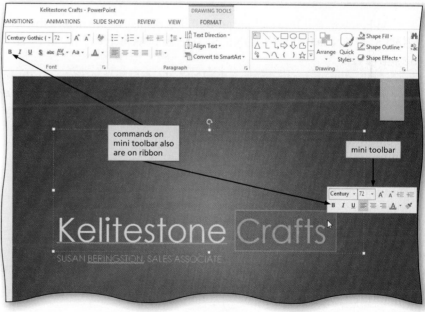

Figure 18

Quick Access Toolbar   The **Quick Access Toolbar**, located initially (by default) above the ribbon at the left edge of the title bar, provides convenient, one-tap or one-click access to frequently used commands (shown in Figure 16). The commands on the Quick Access Toolbar always are available, regardless of the task you are performing. The Touch/Mouse Mode button on the Quick Access Toolbar allows you to switch between Touch mode and Mouse mode. If you primarily are using touch gestures, Touch mode will add more

BTW
Turning Off the Mini Toolbar
If you do not want the mini toolbar to appear, tap or click FILE on the ribbon to open the Backstage view, tap or click Options in the Backstage view, tap or click General (Options dialog box), remove the check mark from the 'Show Mini Toolbar on selection' check box, and then tap or click the OK button.

space between commands on menus and on the ribbon so that they are easier to tap. While touch gestures are convenient ways to interact with Office apps, not all features are supported when you are using Touch mode. If you are using a mouse, Mouse mode will not add the extra space between buttons and commands. The Quick Access Toolbar is discussed in more depth later in the chapter.

KeyTips   If you prefer using the keyboard instead of the mouse, you can press the ALT key on the keyboard to display **KeyTips**, or keyboard code icons, for certain commands (Figure 19). To select a command using the keyboard, press the letter or number displayed in the KeyTip, which may cause additional KeyTips related to the selected command to appear. To remove KeyTips from the screen, press the ALT key or the ESC key until all KeyTips disappear, or tap or click anywhere in the app window.

Microsoft Account Area   In this area, you can use the Sign in link to sign in to your Microsoft account. Once signed in, you will see your account information as well as a picture if you have included one in your Microsoft account.

Figure 19

1 SIGN IN | 2 USE WINDOWS | 3 USE APPS | 4 FILE MANAGEMENT | 5 SWITCH APPS | 6 SAVE FILES
7 CHANGE SCREEN RESOLUTION | 8 EXIT APPS | 9 USE ADDITIONAL APP FEATURES | 10 USE HELP

To Display a Different Tab on the Ribbon

When you run PowerPoint, the ribbon displays nine main tabs: FILE, HOME, INSERT, DESIGN, TRANSITIONS, ANIMATIONS, SLIDE SHOW, REVIEW, and VIEW. The tab currently displayed is called the **active tab**.

The following step displays the INSERT tab, that is, makes it the active tab. *Why? When working with an Office app, you may need to switch tabs to access other options for working with a document.*

1

- Tap or click INSERT on the ribbon to display the INSERT tab (Figure 20).

 Experiment

- Tap or click the other tabs on the ribbon to view their contents. When you are finished, tap or click INSERT on the ribbon to redisplay the INSERT tab.

Q&A | If I am working in a different Office app, such as Word or Access, how do I display a different tab on the ribbon?
Follow this same procedure; that is, tap or click the desired tab on the ribbon.

Figure 20

To Collapse and Expand the Ribbon and Use Full Screen Mode

To display more of a document or other item in the window of an Office app, some users prefer to collapse the ribbon, which hides the groups on the ribbon and displays only the main tabs, or to use **Full Screen mode**, which hides all the commands and just displays the document. Each time you run an Office app, such as PowerPoint, the ribbon appears the same way it did the last time you used that Office app. The chapters in this book, however, begin with the ribbon appearing as it did at the initial installation of Office or PowerPoint.

The following steps collapse, expand, and restore the ribbon in PowerPoint and then switch to Full Screen mode. **Why?** *If you need more space on the screen to work with your document, you may consider collapsing the ribbon or switching to Full Screen mode to gain additional workspace.*

1

- Tap or click the 'Collapse the Ribbon' button on the ribbon (shown in Figure 20) to collapse the ribbon (Figure 21).

Q&A What happened to the groups on the ribbon?
When you collapse the ribbon, the groups disappear so that the ribbon does not take up as much space on the screen.

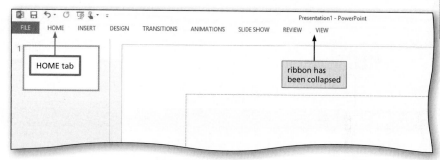

Figure 21

What happened to the 'Collapse the Ribbon' button?
The 'Pin the ribbon' button replaces the 'Collapse the Ribbon' button when the ribbon is collapsed. You will see the 'Pin the ribbon' button only when you expand a ribbon by tapping or clicking a tab.

2

- Tap or click HOME on the ribbon to expand the HOME tab (Figure 22).

Q&A Why would I click the HOME tab?
If you want to use a command on a collapsed ribbon, tap or click the main tab to display the groups for that tab. After you select a command on the ribbon, the groups will be collapsed once

Figure 22

again. If you decide not to use a command on the ribbon, you can collapse the groups by tapping or clicking the same main tab or tapping or clicking in the app window.

 Experiment

- Tap or click HOME on the ribbon to collapse the groups again. Tap or click HOME on the ribbon to expand the HOME tab.

3

- Tap or click the 'Pin the ribbon' button on the expanded HOME tab to restore the ribbon.

- Tap or click the 'Ribbon Display Options' button to display the Ribbon Display Options menu (Figure 23).

Figure 23

• Tap or click Auto-hide Ribbon to use Full Screen mode, which hides all the commands from the screen (Figure 24).

• Tap or click the ellipsis to display the ribbon temporarily.

• Tap or click the 'Ribbon Display Options' button to display the Ribbon Display Options menu (shown in Figure 23).

• Tap or click 'Show Tabs and Commands' to exit Full Screen mode.

Figure 24

Other Ways

1. Double-tap or double-click a main tab on the ribbon   2. Press CTRL+F1

To Use a Shortcut Menu to Relocate the Quick Access Toolbar

1 SIGN IN | 2 USE WINDOWS | 3 USE APPS | 4 FILE MANAGEMENT | 5 SWITCH APPS | 6 SAVE FILES
7 CHANGE SCREEN RESOLUTION | 8 EXIT APPS | 9 USE ADDITIONAL APP FEATURES | 10 USE HELP

When you press and hold or right-click certain areas of the PowerPoint and other Office app windows, a shortcut menu will appear. A **shortcut menu** is a list of frequently used commands that relate to an object. *Why? You can use shortcut menus to access common commands quickly.* When you press and hold or right-click the status bar, for example, a shortcut menu appears with commands related to the status bar. When you press and hold or right-click the Quick Access Toolbar, a shortcut menu appears with commands related to the Quick Access Toolbar. The following steps use a shortcut menu to move the Quick Access Toolbar, which by default is located on the title bar.

• Press and hold or right-click the Quick Access Toolbar to display a shortcut menu that presents a list of commands related to the Quick Access Toolbar (Figure 25).

Q&A

What if I cannot make the shortcut menu appear using the touch instruction?

When you use the press and hold technique, be sure to release your finger when the circle appears on the screen to display the shortcut menu. If the technique still does not work, you might need to add more space around objects on the screen, making it easier for you to press or tap them. Click the 'Customize Quick Access Toolbar' button and then click Touch/Mouse Mode on the menu. Another option is to use the stylus.

Figure 25

2

- Tap or click 'Show Quick Access Toolbar Below the Ribbon' on the shortcut menu to display the Quick Access Toolbar below the ribbon (Figure 26).

Figure 26

3

- Press and hold or right-click the Quick Access Toolbar to display a shortcut menu (Figure 27).

4

- Tap or click 'Show Quick Access Toolbar Above the Ribbon' on the shortcut menu to return the Quick Access Toolbar to its original position (shown in Figure 25).

Figure 27

Other Ways

1. Tap or click 'Customize Quick Access Toolbar' button on Quick Access Toolbar, tap or click 'Show Below the Ribbon' or 'Show Above the Ribbon'

To Customize the Quick Access Toolbar

1 SIGN IN | 2 USE WINDOWS | 3 USE APPS | 4 FILE MANAGEMENT | 5 SWITCH APPS | 6 SAVE FILES
7 CHANGE SCREEN RESOLUTION | 8 EXIT APPS | 9 USE ADDITIONAL APP FEATURES | 10 USE HELP

The Quick Access Toolbar provides easy access to some of the more frequently used commands in the Office apps. By default, the Quick Access Toolbar contains buttons for the Save, Undo, and Redo commands. You can customize the Quick Access Toolbar by changing its location in the window, as shown in the previous steps, and by adding more buttons to reflect commands you would like to access easily. The following steps add the Quick Print button to the Quick Access Toolbar in the PowerPoint window. *Why? Adding the Quick Print button to the Quick Access Toolbar speeds up the process of printing.*

1

- Tap or click the 'Customize Quick Access Toolbar' button to display the Customize Quick Access Toolbar menu (Figure 28).

Q&A

Which commands are listed on the Customize Quick Access Toolbar menu?

It lists commands that commonly are added to the Quick Access Toolbar.

What do the check marks next to some commands signify?

Check marks appear next to commands that already are on the Quick Access Toolbar. When you add a button to the Quick Access Toolbar, a check mark will be displayed next to its command name.

Figure 28

Figure 29

- Tap or click Quick Print on the Customize Quick Access Toolbar menu to add the Quick Print button to the Quick Access Toolbar (Figure 29).

Q&A How would I remove a button from the Quick Access Toolbar?
You would press and hold or right-click the button you wish to remove and then tap or click 'Remove from Quick Access Toolbar' on the shortcut menu or tap or click the 'Customize Quick Access Toolbar' button on the Quick Access Toolbar and then click the button name in the Customize Quick Access Toolbar menu to remove the check mark.

To Enter Content in a Title Slide

1 SIGN IN | 2 USE WINDOWS | 3 USE APPS | 4 FILE MANAGEMENT | 5 SWITCH APPS | 6 SAVE FILES
7 CHANGE SCREEN RESOLUTION | 8 EXIT APPS | 9 USE ADDITIONAL APP FEATURES | **10 USE HELP**

With the exception of a blank slide, PowerPoint assumes every new slide has a title. Many of PowerPoint's layouts have both a title text placeholder and at least one content placeholder. To make creating a presentation easier, any text you type after a new slide appears becomes title text in the title text placeholder. As you begin typing text in the title text placeholder, the title text also is displayed in the Slide 1 thumbnail in the Thumbnail pane. The title for this presentation is Kelitestone Crafts. The steps on the next page enter a presentation title on the title slide. *Why? In general, every presentation should have a title to describe what the presentation will be covering.*

- Tap or click the 'Click to add title' label located inside the title text placeholder to select the placeholder (Figure 30).

Q&A What are the white squares that appear around the title text placeholder as I type the presentation title?
The white squares are sizing handles, which you can drag to change the size of the title text placeholder. Sizing handles also can be found around other placeholders and objects within an Office app.

Figure 30

- Type **Kelitestone Crafts** in the title text placeholder. Do not press the ENTER key because you do not want to create a new line of text (Figure 31).

Figure 31

Office 2013 and Windows 8 Chapter

Saving and Organizing Files

While you are creating a document, the computer stores it in memory. When you save a document, the computer places it on a storage medium such as a hard disk, solid state drive (SSD), USB flash drive, or optical disc. The storage medium can be permanent in your computer, may be portable where you remove it from your computer, or may be on a web server you access through a network or the Internet.

A saved document is referred to as a file. A **file name** is the name assigned to a file when it is saved. When saving files, you should organize them so that you easily can find them later. Windows provides tools to help you organize files.

CONSIDER THIS

How often should you save a document?

It is important to save a document frequently for the following reasons:

- The document in memory might be lost if the computer is turned off or you lose electrical power while an app is running.

- If you run out of time before completing a project, you may finish it at a future time without starting over.

Organizing Files and Folders

A file contains data. This data can range from a research paper to an accounting spreadsheet to an electronic math quiz. You should organize and store files in folders to avoid misplacing a file and to help you find a file quickly.

If you are taking an introductory computer class (CIS 101, for example), you may want to design a series of folders for the different subjects covered in the class. To accomplish this, you can arrange the folders in a hierarchy for the class, as shown in Figure 32.

The hierarchy contains three levels. The first level contains the storage medium, such as a hard disk. The second level contains the class folder (CIS 101, in this case), and the third level contains seven folders, one each for a different Office app that will be covered in the class (Word, PowerPoint, Excel, Access, Outlook, Publisher, and OneNote).

When the hierarchy in Figure 32 is created, the storage medium is said to contain the CIS 101 folder, and the CIS 101 folder is said to contain the separate Office folders (i.e., Word, PowerPoint, Excel, etc.). In addition, this hierarchy easily can be expanded to include folders from other classes taken during additional semesters.

The vertical and horizontal lines in Figure 32 form a pathway that allows you to navigate to a drive or folder on a computer or network. A **path** consists of a drive letter (preceded by a drive name when necessary) and colon, to identify the storage device, and one or more folder names. A hard disk typically has a drive letter of C. Each drive or folder in the hierarchy has a corresponding path.

By default, Windows saves documents in the Documents library, music in the Music library, pictures in the Pictures library, and videos in the Videos library. A **library** helps you manage multiple folders stored in various locations on a computer and devices. It does not store the folder contents; rather, it keeps track of their locations so that you can access the folders and their contents quickly. For example, you can save pictures from a digital camera in any folder on any storage location on a computer. Normally, this would make organizing the different folders difficult. If you add the folders to a library, however, you can access all the pictures from one location regardless of where they are stored.

BTW

File Type

Depending on your Windows settings, the file type .pptx may be displayed immediately to the right of the file name after you save the file. The file type .pptx is a PowerPoint 2013 document.

Figure 32

The following pages illustrate the steps to organize the folders for this class and save a file in a folder:

1. Create the folder identifying your class.
2. Create the PowerPoint folder in the folder identifying your class.
3. Save a file in the PowerPoint folder.
4. Verify the location of the saved file.

To Create a Folder

When you create a folder, such as the CIS 101 folder shown in Figure 32 on the previous page, you must name the folder. A folder name should describe the folder and its contents. A folder name can contain spaces and any uppercase or lowercase characters, except a backslash (\), slash (/), colon (:), asterisk (*), question mark (?), quotation marks ("), less than symbol (<), greater than symbol (>), or vertical bar (|). Folder names cannot be CON, AUX, COM1, COM2, COM3, COM4, LPT1, LPT2, LPT3, PRN, or NUL. The same rules for naming folders also apply to naming files.

The following steps create a class folder (CIS 101, in this case) in the Documents library. *Why? When storing files, you should organize the files so that it will be easier to find them later.* If you are using Windows 7, skip these steps and instead perform the steps in the yellow box that immediately follows these Windows 8 steps.

• Tap or click the File Explorer app button on the taskbar to run the File Explorer app (Figure 33).

Q&A | Why does the title bar say Libraries?
File Explorer, by default, displays the name of the selected library or folder on the title bar.

Figure 33

- Tap or click the Documents library in the navigation pane to display the contents of the Documents library in the file list (Figure 34).

Q&A
What if my screen does not show the Documents, Music, Pictures, and Videos libraries?
Double-tap or double-click Libraries in the navigation pane to expand the list.

Figure 34

- Tap or click the New folder button on the Quick Access Toolbar to create a new folder with the name, New folder, selected in a text box (Figure 35).

Q&A
Why is the folder icon displayed differently on my computer?
Windows might be configured to display contents differently on your computer.

Figure 35

- Type CIS 101 (or your class code) in the text box as the new folder name.

- If requested by your instructor, add your last name to the end of the folder name.

- Press the ENTER key to change the folder name from New folder to a folder name identifying your class (Figure 36).

Q&A
What happens when I press the ENTER key?
The class folder (CIS 101, in this case) is displayed in the file list, which contains the folder name, date modified, type, and size.

Figure 36

Other Ways

1. Press CTRL+SHIFT+N   2. Tap or click the New folder button (Home tab | New group)

To Create a Folder Using Windows 7

If you are using Windows 7, perform these steps to create a folder instead of the previous steps that use Windows 8.

1. Click the Windows Explorer button on the taskbar to run Windows Explorer.
2. Click the Documents library in the navigation pane to display the contents of the Documents library in the file list.
3. Click the New folder button on the toolbar to display a new folder icon with the name, New folder, selected in a text box.
4. Type `CIS 101` (or your class code) in the text box to name the folder.
5. Press the ENTER key to create the folder.

Folder Windows

The Documents window (shown in Figure 36 on the previous page) is called a folder window. Recall that a folder is a specific named location on a storage medium that contains related files. Most users rely on **folder windows** for finding, viewing, and managing information on their computers. Folder windows have common design elements, including the following (shown in Figure 36).

- The **address bar** provides quick navigation options. The arrows on the address bar allow you to visit different locations on the computer.
- The buttons to the left of the address bar allow you to navigate the contents of the navigation pane and view recent pages.
- The **Previous Locations arrow** displays the locations you have visited.
- The **Refresh button** on the right side of the address bar refreshes the contents of the folder list.
- The **search box** contains the dimmed words, Search Documents. You can type a term in the search box for a list of files, folders, shortcuts, and elements containing that term within the location you are searching. A **shortcut** is an icon on the desktop that provides a user with immediate access to an app or file.
- The **ribbon** contains five tabs used to accomplish various tasks on the computer related to organizing and managing the contents of the open window. This ribbon works similarly to the ribbon in the Office apps.
- The **navigation pane** on the left contains the Favorites area, Libraries area, Homegroup area, Computer area, and Network area.
- The **Favorites area** shows your favorite locations. By default, this list contains only links to your Desktop, Downloads, and Recent places.
- The **Libraries area** shows folders included in a library.

1 SIGN IN | 2 USE WINDOWS | 3 USE APPS | 4 FILE MANAGEMENT | 5 SWITCH APPS | 6 SAVE FILES
7 CHANGE SCREEN RESOLUTION | 8 EXIT APPS | 9 USE ADDITIONAL APP FEATURES | 10 USE HELP

To Create a Folder within a Folder

With the class folder created, you can create folders that will store the files you create using PowerPoint. The following steps create a PowerPoint folder in the CIS 101 folder (or the folder identifying your class). *Why? To be able to organize your files, you should create a folder structure.* If you are using Windows 7, skip these steps and instead perform the steps in the yellow box that immediately follows these Windows 8 steps.

- Double-tap or double-click the icon or folder name for the CIS 101 folder (or the folder identifying your class) in the file list to open the folder (Figure 37).

Figure 37

- Tap or click the New folder button on the Quick Access Toolbar to create a new folder with the name, New folder, selected in a text box folder.

- Type **PowerPoint** in the text box as the new folder name.

- Press the ENTER key to rename the folder (Figure 38).

Figure 38

Other Ways

1. Press CTRL+SHIFT+N   2. Tap or click the New folder button (Home tab | New group)

TO CREATE A FOLDER WITHIN A FOLDER USING WINDOWS 7

If you are using Windows 7, perform these steps to create a folder within a folder instead of the previous steps that use Windows 8.

1. Double-click the icon or folder name for the CIS 101 folder (or the folder identifying your class) in the file list to open the folder.

2. Click the New folder button on the toolbar to display a new folder icon and text box for the folder.

3. Type **PowerPoint** in the text box to name the folder.

4. Press the ENTER key to create the folder.

To Expand a Folder, Scroll through Folder Contents, and Collapse a Folder

1 SIGN IN | 2 USE WINDOWS | 3 USE APPS | 4 FILE MANAGEMENT | 5 SWITCH APPS | 6 SAVE FILES
7 CHANGE SCREEN RESOLUTION | 8 EXIT APPS | 9 USE ADDITIONAL APP FEATURES | 10 USE HELP

Folder windows display the hierarchy of items and the contents of drives and folders in the file list. You might want to expand a library or folder in the navigation pane to view its contents, slide or scroll through its contents, and collapse it when you are finished viewing its contents. *Why? When a folder is expanded, you can see all the folders it contains. By contrast, a collapsed folder hides the folders it contains.* The following steps expand, slide or scroll through, and then collapse the folder identifying your class (CIS 101, in this case).

- Double-tap or double-click the Documents library in the navigation pane, which expands the library to display its contents and displays a black arrow to the left of the Documents library icon (Figure 39).

Figure 39

- Double-tap or double-click the My Documents folder, which expands the folder to display its contents and displays a black arrow to the left of the My Documents folder icon.

 What is the My Documents folder?
When you save files on your hard disk, the My Documents folder is the default save location.

- Double-tap or double-click the CIS 101 folder, which expands the folder to display its contents and displays a black arrow to the left of the folder icon (Figure 40).

Figure 40

 Experiment

- Slide the scroll bar down or click the down scroll arrow on the vertical scroll bar to display additional folders at the bottom of the navigation pane. Slide the scroll bar up or click the scroll bar above the scroll box to move the scroll box to the top of the navigation pane. Drag the scroll box down the scroll bar until the scroll box is halfway down the scroll bar.

- Double-tap or double-click the folder identifying your class (CIS 101, in this case) to collapse the folder (Figure 41).

 Why are some folders indented below others?
A folder contains the indented folders below it.

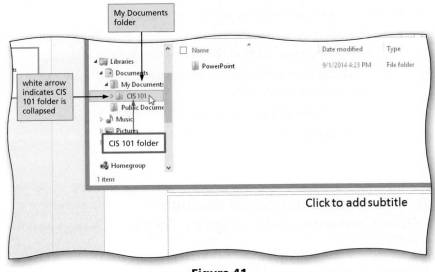

Figure 41

Other Ways

1. Point to display arrows in navigation pane, tap or click white arrow to expand or tap or click black arrow to collapse

2. Select folder to expand or collapse using arrow keys, press RIGHT ARROW to expand; press LEFT ARROW to collapse.

---

1 SIGN IN | 2 USE WINDOWS | 3 USE APPS | 4 FILE MANAGEMENT | 5 SWITCH APPS | 6 SAVE FILES

To Switch from One App to Another

7 CHANGE SCREEN RESOLUTION | 8 EXIT APPS | 9 USE ADDITIONAL APP FEATURES | 10 USE HELP

The next step is to save the PowerPoint file containing the title text you typed earlier. PowerPoint, however, currently is not the active window. You can use the app button on the taskbar and live preview to switch to PowerPoint and then save the document in the PowerPoint document window.

Why? *By clicking the appropriate app button on the taskbar, you can switch to the open app you want to use.* The following steps switch to the PowerPoint window; however, the steps are the same for any active Office app currently displayed as an app button on the taskbar.

1

- If you are using a mouse, point to the PowerPoint app button on the taskbar to see a live preview of the open document(s) or the window title(s) of the open document(s), depending on your computer's configuration (Figure 42).

Figure 42

2

- Tap or click the PowerPoint app button or the live preview to make the app associated with the app button the active window (Figure 43).

Q&A What if multiple documents are open in an app?
Tap or click the desired live preview to switch to the window you want to use.

Figure 43

To Save a File in a Folder

1 SIGN IN | 2 USE WINDOWS | 3 USE APPS | 4 FILE MANAGEMENT | 5 SWITCH APPS | 6 **SAVE FILES**
7 CHANGE SCREEN RESOLUTION | 8 EXIT APPS | 9 USE ADDITIONAL APP FEATURES | 10 USE HELP

With the PowerPoint folder created, you can save the PowerPoint document shown in the document window in the PowerPoint folder. *Why? Without saving a file, you may lose all the work you have completed and will be unable to reuse or share it with others later.* The following steps save a file in the PowerPoint folder contained in your class folder (CIS 101, in this case) using the file name, Craft Store.

- Tap or click the Save button (shown in Figure 43) on the Quick Access Toolbar, which depending on settings, will display either the Save As gallery in the Backstage view (Figure 44) or the Save As dialog box (Figure 45 on the next page).

Q&A What is the Backstage view?
The **Backstage view** contains a set of commands that enable you to manage documents and data about the documents.

Figure 44

What if the Save As gallery is not displayed in the Backstage view?
Tap or click the Save As tab to display the Save As gallery.

How do I close the Backstage view?
Tap or click the Back button in the upper-left corner of the Backstage view to return to the PowerPoint window.

2

• If your screen displays the Backstage view, tap or click Computer, if necessary, to display options in the right pane related to saving on your computer; if your screen already displays the Save As dialog box, proceed to Step 3.

Q&A What if I wanted to save on SkyDrive instead?
You would tap or click SkyDrive. Saving on SkyDrive is discussed in a later section in this chapter.

• Tap or click the Browse button in the right pane to display the Save As dialog box (Figure 45).

Q&A Why does a file name already appear in the File name box?
PowerPoint automatically suggests a file name the first time you save a document. The file name normally consists of the first few words contained in the title text. Because the suggested file name is selected, you do not need to delete it; as soon as you begin typing, the new file name replaces the selected text.

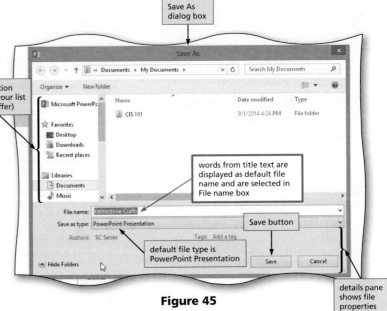

Figure 45

3

• Type **Craft Store** in the File name box (Save As dialog box) to change the file name. Do not press the ENTER key after typing the file name because you do not want to close the dialog box at this time (Figure 46).

Q&A What characters can I use in a file name?
The only invalid characters are the backslash (\\), slash (/), colon (:), asterisk (*), question mark (?), quotation mark ("), less than symbol (<), greater than symbol (>), and vertical bar (|).

Figure 46

4

• Navigate to the desired save location (in this case, the PowerPoint folder in the CIS 101 folder [or your class folder] in the My Documents folder in the Documents library) by performing the tasks in Steps 4a and 4b.

4a

• If the Documents library is not displayed in the navigation pane, slide to scroll or drag the scroll bar in the navigation pane until Documents appears.

• If the Documents library is not expanded in the navigation pane, double-tap or double-click Documents to display its folders in the navigation pane.

Figure 47

• If the My Documents folder is not expanded in the navigation pane, double-tap or double-click My Documents to display its folders in the navigation pane.

• If your class folder (CIS 101, in this case) is not expanded, double-tap or double-click the CIS 101 folder to select the folder and display its contents in the navigation pane (Figure 47).

Q&A What if I do not want to save in a folder?
Although storing files in folders is an effective technique for organizing files, some users prefer not to store files in folders. If you prefer not to save this file in a folder, select the storage device on which you wish to save the file and then proceed to Step 5.

4b

- Tap or click the PowerPoint folder in the navigation pane to select it as the new save location and display its contents in the file list (Figure 48).

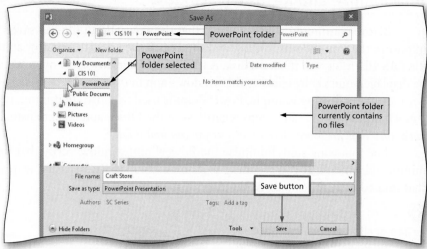

Figure 48

5

- Tap or click the Save button (Save As dialog box) to save the document in the selected folder in the selected location with the entered file name (Figure 49).

Q&A

How do I know that the file is saved?
While an Office app such as PowerPoint is saving a file, it briefly displays a message on the status bar indicating the amount of the file saved. In addition, the file name appears on the title bar.

Figure 49

Other Ways

1. Tap or click FILE on ribbon, tap or click Save As in Backstage view, tap or click Computer, tap or click Browse button, type file name (Save As dialog box), navigate to desired save location, tap or click Save button

2. Press F12, type file name (Save As dialog box), navigate to desired save location, tap or click Save button

Navigating in Dialog Boxes

Navigating is the process of finding a location on a storage device. While saving the Craft Store file, for example, Steps 4a and 4b in the previous set of steps navigated to the PowerPoint folder located in the CIS 101 folder in the My Documents folder in the Documents library. When performing certain functions in Windows apps, such as saving a file, opening a file, or inserting a picture in an existing document, you most likely will have to navigate to the location where you want to save the file or to the folder containing the file you want to open or insert. Most dialog boxes in Windows apps requiring navigation follow a similar procedure; that is, the way you navigate to a folder in one dialog box, such as the Save As dialog box, is similar to how you might navigate in another dialog box, such as the Open dialog box. If you chose to navigate to a specific location in a dialog box, you would follow the instructions in Steps 4a and 4b.

To Minimize and Restore a Window

Before continuing, you can verify that the PowerPoint file was saved properly. To do this, you will minimize the PowerPoint window and then open the CIS 101 window so that you can verify the file is stored in the CIS 101 folder on the hard disk. A **minimized window** is an open window that is hidden from view but can be displayed quickly by clicking the window's app button on the taskbar.

In the following example, PowerPoint is used to illustrate minimizing and restoring windows; however, you would follow the same steps regardless of the Office app you are using. *Why? Before closing an app, you should make sure your file saved correctly so that you can find it later.*

The following steps minimize the PowerPoint window, verify that the file is saved, and then restore the minimized window. If you are using Windows 7, skip these steps and instead perform the steps in the yellow box that immediately follows these Windows 8 steps.

- Tap or click the Minimize button on the PowerPoint window title bar (shown in Figure 49 on the previous page) to minimize the window (Figure 50).

Q&A Is the minimized window still available?
The minimized window, PowerPoint in this case, remains available but no longer is the active window. It is minimized as an app button on the taskbar.

- If the File Explorer window is not open on the screen, tap or click the File Explorer app button on the taskbar to make the File folder window the active window.

Figure 50

- Double-tap or double-click the PowerPoint folder in the file list to select the folder and display its contents (Figure 51).

Q&A Why does the File Explorer app button on the taskbar change?
A selected app button indicates that the app is active on the screen. When the button is not selected, the app is running but not active.

- After viewing the contents of the selected folder, tap or click the PowerPoint app button on the taskbar to restore the minimized window (as shown in Figure 49 on the previous page).

Figure 51

Other Ways

1. Press and hold or right-click title bar, tap or click Minimize on shortcut menu, tap or click taskbar button in taskbar button area

2. Press WINDOWS+M, press WINDOWS+SHIFT+M

TO MINIMIZE AND RESTORE A WINDOW USING WINDOWS 7

If you are using Windows 7, perform these steps to minimize and restore a window instead of the previous steps that use Windows 8.

1. Click the Minimize button on the app's title bar to minimize the window.

2. If the Windows Explorer window is not open on the screen, click the Windows Explorer button on the taskbar to make the Windows Explorer window the active window.

3. Double-click the PowerPoint folder in the file list to select the folder and display its contents.

4. After viewing the contents of the selected folder, click the PowerPoint button on the taskbar to restore the minimized window.

To Save a File on SkyDrive

1 SIGN IN | 2 USE WINDOWS | 3 USE APPS | 4 FILE MANAGEMENT | 5 SWITCH APPS | 6 SAVE FILES
7 CHANGE SCREEN RESOLUTION | 8 EXIT APPS | 9 USE ADDITIONAL APP FEATURES | 10 USE HELP

One of the features of Office is the capability to save files on SkyDrive so that you can use the files on multiple computers without having to use external storage devices such as a USB flash drive. Storing files on SkyDrive also enables you to share files more efficiently with others, such as when using Office Web Apps and Office 365.

In the following example, PowerPoint is used to save a file to SkyDrive. *Why? Storing files on SkyDrive provides more portability options than are available from storing files in the Documents library.*

You can save files directly to SkyDrive from within Word, PowerPoint, and Excel. The following steps save the current PowerPoint file to the SkyDrive. These steps require you have a Microsoft account and an Internet connection.

• Tap or click FILE on the ribbon to open the Backstage view (Figure 52).

Q&A What is the purpose of the FILE tab?
The FILE tab opens the Backstage view for each Office app, including PowerPoint.

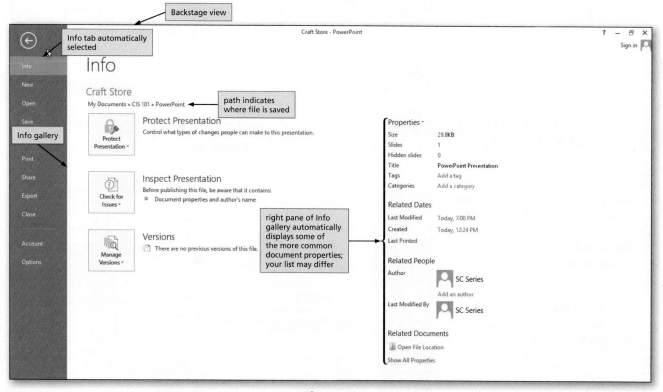

Figure 52

2

- Tap or click the Save As tab in the Backstage view to display the Save As gallery.

- Tap or click SkyDrive to display SkyDrive saving options or a Sign In button, if you are not signed in already to your Microsoft account (Figure 53).

Q&A What if my Save As gallery does not display SkyDrive as a save location?

Tap or click 'Add a Place' and proceed to Step 3.

Figure 53

3

- If your screen displays a Sign In button, tap or click it to display the Sign in dialog box (Figure 54).

Q&A What if the Sign In button does not appear?

If you already are signed into your Microsoft account, the Sign In button will not be displayed. In this case, proceed to Step 5.

Figure 54

4

- Type your Microsoft account user name and password in the text boxes and then tap or click the Sign in button (Sign in dialog box) to sign in to SkyDrive.

5

- Tap or click your SkyDrive to select your SkyDrive as the storage location (Figure 55).

Figure 55

- Tap or click the Browse button to contact the SkyDrive server (which may take some time, depending on the speed of your Internet connection) and then display the Save As dialog box (Figure 56).

Q&A Why does the path in the address bar contain various letters and numbers?
The letters and numbers in the address bar uniquely identify the location of your SkyDrive files and folders.

- Tap or click the Save button (Save As dialog box) to save the file on SkyDrive.

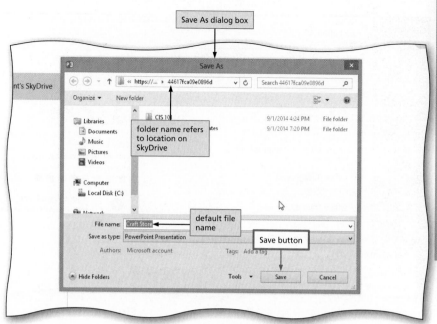

Figure 56

To Sign Out of a Microsoft Account

If you are using a public computer or otherwise wish to sign out of your Microsoft account, you should sign out of the account from the Accounts gallery in the Backstage view. Signing out of the account is the safest way to make sure that nobody else can access online files or settings stored in your Microsoft account. **Why?** *For security reasons, you should sign out of your Microsoft account when you are finished using a public or shared computer. Staying signed in to your Microsoft account might enable others to access your files.*

The following steps sign out of a Microsoft account from PowerPoint. You would use the same steps in any Office app. If you do not wish to sign out of your Microsoft account, read these steps without performing them.

1 Tap or click FILE on the ribbon to open the Backstage view.

2 Tap or click the Account tab to display the Account gallery (Figure 57 on the next page).

3 Tap or click the Sign out link, which displays the Remove Account dialog box. If a Can't remove Windows accounts dialog box appears instead of the Remove Account dialog box, click the OK button and skip the remaining steps.

Q&A Why does a Can't remove Windows accounts dialog box appear?
If you signed in to Windows using your Microsoft account, then you also must sign out from Windows, rather than signing out from within PowerPoint. When you are finished using Windows, be sure to sign out at that time.

4 Tap or click the Yes button (Remove Account dialog box) to sign out of your Microsoft account on this computer.

Q&A Should I sign out of Windows after removing my Microsoft account?
When you are finished using the computer, you should sign out of Windows for maximum security.

5 Tap or click the Back button in the upper-left corner of the Backstage view to return to the document.

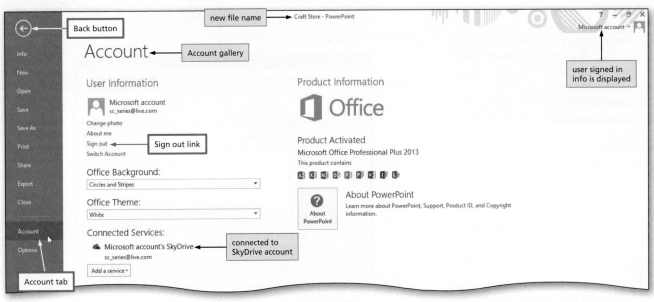

Figure 57

Screen Resolution

Screen resolution indicates the number of pixels (dots) that the computer uses to display the letters, numbers, graphics, and background you see on the screen. When you increase the screen resolution, Windows displays more information on the screen, but the information decreases in size. The reverse also is true: as you decrease the screen resolution, Windows displays less information on the screen, but the information increases in size.

Screen resolution usually is stated as the product of two numbers, such as 1366×768 (pronounced "thirteen sixty-six by seven sixty-eight"). A 1366×768 screen resolution results in a display of 1366 distinct pixels on each of 768 lines, or about 1,050,624 pixels. Changing the screen resolution affects how the ribbon appears in Office apps and some Windows dialog boxes. Figure 58, for example, shows the PowerPoint ribbon at screen resolutions of 1366×768 and 1024×768. All of the same commands are available regardless of screen resolution. The app (PowerPoint, in this case), however, makes changes to the groups and the buttons within the groups to accommodate the various screen resolutions. The result is that certain commands may need to be accessed differently depending on the resolution chosen. A command that is visible on the ribbon and available by tapping or clicking a button at one resolution may not be visible and may need to be accessed using its Dialog Box Launcher at a different resolution.

Comparing the two ribbons in Figure 58, notice the changes in content and layout of the groups and galleries. In some cases, the content of a group is the same in each resolution, but the layout of the group differs. For example, the same gallery and buttons appear in the Styles groups in the two resolutions, but the layouts differ. In other cases, the content and layout are the same across the resolution, but the level of detail differs with the resolution.

(a) Ribbon at 1366 × 768 Resolution

Figure 58

(b) Ribbon at 1024 x 768 Resolution

Figure 58 (Continued)

To Change the Screen Resolution

1 SIGN IN | 2 USE WINDOWS | 3 USE APPS | 4 FILE MANAGEMENT | 5 SWITCH APPS | 6 SAVE FILES

7 CHANGE SCREEN RESOLUTION | 8 EXIT APPS | 9 USE ADDITIONAL APP FEATURES | 10 USE HELP

If you are using a computer to step through the chapters in this book and you want your screen to match the figures, you may need to change your screen's resolution. *Why? The figures in this book use a screen resolution of 1366 × 768.* The following steps change the screen resolution to 1366 × 768. Your computer already may be set to 1366 × 768. Keep in mind that many computer labs prevent users from changing the screen resolution; in that case, read the following steps for illustration purposes.

- Tap or click the Show desktop button, which is located at the far-right edge of the taskbar, to display the Windows desktop.

Q&A I cannot see the Show desktop button. Why not?
When you point to the far-right edge of the taskbar, a small outline appears to mark the Show desktop button.

Figure 59

- Press and hold or right-click an empty area on the Windows desktop to display a shortcut menu that contains a list of commands related to the desktop (Figure 59).

Q&A Why does my shortcut menu display different commands?
Depending on your computer's hardware and configuration, different commands might appear on the shortcut menu.

- Tap or click Screen resolution on the shortcut menu to open the Screen Resolution window (Figure 60).

- Tap or click the Resolution button in the Screen Resolution window to display the resolution slider.

Figure 60

4

- If necessary, drag the resolution slider until the desired screen resolution (in this case, 1366 × 768) is selected (Figure 61).

Q&A What if my computer does not support the 1366 × 768 resolution?

Some computers do not support the 1366 ×768 resolution. In this case, select a resolution that is close to the 1366 × 768 resolution.

What is a slider?

A **slider** is an object that allows users to choose from multiple predetermined options. In most cases, these options represent some type of numeric value. In most cases, one end of the slider (usually the left or bottom) represents the lowest of available values, and the opposite end (usually the right or top) represents the highest available value.

Figure 61

5

- Tap or click an empty area of the Screen Resolution window to close the resolution slider.

- Tap or click the OK button to change the screen resolution and display the Display Settings dialog box (Figure 62).

- Tap or click the Keep changes button (Display Settings dialog box) to accept the new screen resolution.

Q&A Why does a message display stating that the image quality can be improved?

Some computer monitors or screens are designed to display contents better at a certain screen resolution, sometimes referred to as an optimal resolution.

Figure 62

To Exit an App with One Document Open

1 SIGN IN | 2 USE WINDOWS | 3 USE APPS | 4 FILE MANAGEMENT | 5 SWITCH APPS | 6 SAVE FILES
7 CHANGE SCREEN RESOLUTION | 8 EXIT APPS | 9 USE ADDITIONAL APP FEATURES | 10 USE HELP

When you exit an Office app, such as PowerPoint, if you have made changes to a file since the last time the file was saved, the app displays a dialog box asking if you want to save the changes you made to the file before it closes the app window. *Why? The dialog box contains three buttons with these resulting actions: the Save button saves the changes and then exits the Office app, the Don't Save button exits the Office app without saving changes, and the Cancel button closes the dialog box and redisplays the file without saving the changes.*

If no changes have been made to an open document since the last time the file was saved, the Office app will close the window without displaying a dialog box.

The following steps exit PowerPoint. You would follow similar steps in other Office apps.

1

- If necessary, tap or click the PowerPoint app button on the taskbar (shown in Figure 62) to display the PowerPoint window on the desktop.

- If you are using a mouse, point to the Close button on the right side of the PowerPoint window title bar (Figure 63).

Figure 63

- Tap or click the Close button to close the document and exit PowerPoint.

Q&A What if I have more than one document open in PowerPoint?
You could click the Close button for each open document. When you click the last open document's Close button, you also exit PowerPoint. As an alternative that is more efficient, you could press and hold or right-click the PowerPoint app button on the taskbar and then tap or click 'Close all windows' on the shortcut menu to close all open documents and exit PowerPoint.

❸

- If a Microsoft PowerPoint dialog box appears, tap or click the Save button to save any changes made to the document since the last save.

Other Ways

1. Press and hold or right-click the PowerPoint app button on Windows taskbar, click 'Close all windows' on shortcut menu   2. Press ALT + F4

To Copy a Folder to a USB Flash Drive

1 SIGN IN | 2 USE WINDOWS | 3 USE APPS | 4 FILE MANAGEMENT | 5 SWITCH APPS | 6 SAVE FILES
7 CHANGE SCREEN RESOLUTION | 8 EXIT APPS | 9 USE ADDITIONAL APP FEATURES | 10 USE HELP

To store files and folders on a USB flash drive, you must connect the USB flash drive to an available USB port on a computer. The following steps copy your CIS 101 folder to a USB flash drive. *Why? It often is good practice to have a backup of your files. Besides SkyDrive, you can save files to a portable storage device, such as a USB flash drive.* If you are using Windows 7, skip these steps and instead perform the steps in the yellow box that immediately follows these Windows 8 steps.

❶

- Insert a USB flash drive in an available USB port on the computer to connect the USB flash drive.

Q&A How can I ensure the USB flash drive is connected?
In File Explorer, you can use the navigation bar to find the USB flash drive. If it is not showing, then it is not connected properly.

❷

- Tap or click the File Explorer app button on the taskbar to make the folder window the active window.

- If necessary, navigate to the CIS 101 folder in the File Explorer window (see Step 4a on page OFF 30 for instructions about navigating to a folder location).

- Press and hold or right-click the CIS 101 folder to display a shortcut menu (Figure 64).

Figure 64

❸

- Tap or point to Send to, which causes a submenu to appear (Figure 65).

Figure 65

4

- Tap or click the USB flash drive to copy the folder to the USB flash drive (Figure 66).

Q&A

Why does the drive letter of my USB flash drive differ?
Windows assigns the next available drive letter to your USB flash drive when you connect it. The next available drive letter may vary by computer, depending on the number of storage devices that currently are connected.

Figure 66

To Copy a Folder to a USB Flash Drive Using Windows 7

If you are using Windows 7, perform these steps to copy a folder to a USB flash drive instead of the previous steps that use Windows 8.

1. Insert a USB flash drive in an available USB port on the computer to open the AutoPlay window.
2. Click the 'Open folder to view files' link in the AutoPlay window to open the Windows Explorer window.
3. Navigate to the Documents library.
4. Right-click the CIS 101 folder to display a shortcut menu.
5. Point to Send to, which causes a submenu to appear.
6. Click the USB flash drive to copy the folder to the USB flash drive.

Break Point: If you wish to take a break, this is a good place to do so. To resume at a later time, continue to follow the steps from this location forward.

Additional Common Features of Office Apps

The previous section used PowerPoint to illustrate common features of Office and some basic elements unique to PowerPoint. The following sections continue to use PowerPoint to present additional common features of Office.

In the following pages, you will learn how to do the following:

1. Run PowerPoint using the search box.
2. Open a document in PowerPoint.
3. Close the document.
4. Reopen the document just closed.
5. Create a blank PowerPoint document from Windows Explorer and then open the file.
6. Save a document with a new file name.

1 SIGN IN | 2 USE WINDOWS | 3 USE APPS | 4 FILE MANAGEMENT | 5 SWITCH APPS | 6 SAVE FILES
7 CHANGE SCREEN RESOLUTION | 8 EXIT APPS | 9 USE ADDITIONAL APP FEATURES | 10 USE HELP

To Run an App Using the Search Box

The following steps, which assume Windows is running, use the search box to run the PowerPoint app based on a typical installation; however, you would follow similar steps to run any app. *Why? Sometimes an app does not appear on the Start screen, so you can find it quickly by searching.* You may need to ask your instructor how to run apps for your computer. If you are using Windows 7, skip these steps and instead perform the steps in the yellow box that immediately follows these Windows 8 steps.

1

- Swipe in from the right edge of the screen or point to the upper-right corner of the screen to display the Charms bar (Figure 67).

Figure 67

2

- Tap or click the Search charm on the Charms bar to display the Search menu (Figure 68).

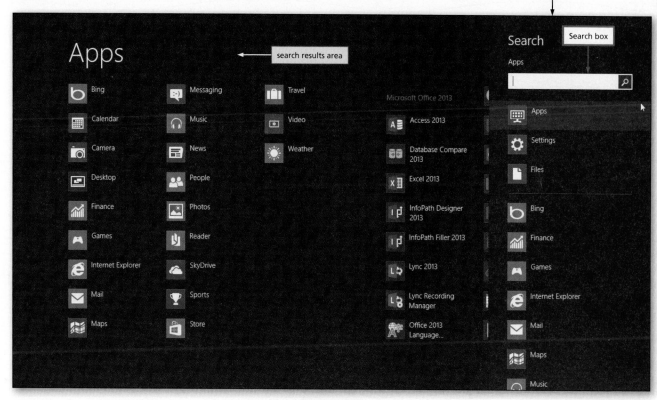

Figure 68

3

- Type `PowerPoint 2013` as the search text in the Search box and watch the search results appear in the Apps list (Figure 69).

Q&A | Do I need to type the complete app name or use correct capitalization?
No, you need to type just enough characters of the app name for it to appear in the Apps list. For example, you may be able to type PowerPoint or powerpoint, instead of PowerPoint 2013.

Figure 69

4

- Tap or click PowerPoint 2013 in the search results to run PowerPoint.

- Tap or click the Blank Presentation thumbnail to create a blank presentation and display it in the PowerPoint window.

- If the PowerPoint window is not maximized, tap or click the Maximize button on its title bar to maximize the window (Figure 70).

Figure 70

TO RUN AN APP USING THE SEARCH BOX USING WINDOWS 7

If you are using Windows 7, perform these steps to run an app using the search box instead of the previous steps that use Windows 8.

1. Click the Start button on the Windows 7 taskbar to display the Start menu.

2. Type `PowerPoint 2013` as the search text in the 'Search programs and files' text box and watch the search results appear on the Start menu.

3. Click PowerPoint 2013 in the search results on the Start menu to run PowerPoint.

4. Click the Blank Presentation thumbnail to create a blank presentation and display it in the PowerPoint window.

5. If the PowerPoint window is not maximized, click the Maximize button on its title bar to maximize the window.

---

1 SIGN IN | 2 USE WINDOWS | 3 USE APPS | 4 FILE MANAGEMENT | 5 SWITCH APPS | 6 SAVE FILES
7 CHANGE SCREEN RESOLUTION | 8 EXIT APPS | 9 USE ADDITIONAL APP FEATURES | 10 USE HELP

To Open an Existing File

As discussed earlier, the Backstage view contains a set of commands that enable you to manage documents and data about the documents. *Why? From the Backstage view in PowerPoint, for example, you can create, open, print, and save documents. You also can share documents, manage versions, set permissions, and modify document properties. In other Office 2013 apps, the Backstage view may contain features specific to those apps.* The following steps open a saved file, specifically the Craft Store file, that recently was saved.

- Tap or click FILE on the ribbon to open the Backstage view and then tap or click Open in the Backstage view to display the Open gallery in the Backstage view.

- Tap or click Computer to display recent folders accessed on your computer.

- Tap or click the Browse button to display the Open dialog box.

- If necessary, navigate to the location of the file to open as described in Steps 4a and 4b on pages OFF 30 and OFF 31.

- Tap or click the file to open, Craft Store in this case, to select the file (Figure 71).

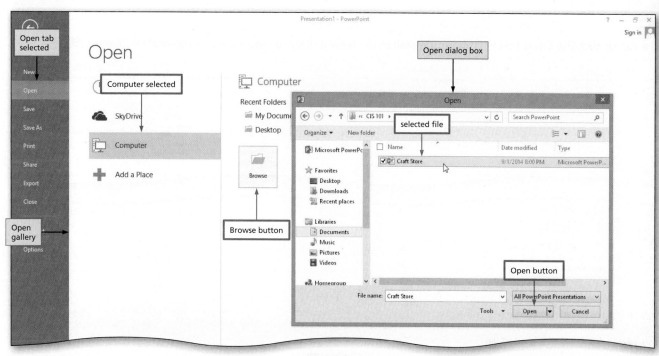

Figure 71

2

- Tap or click the Open button (Open dialog box) to open the file (shown in Figure 49 on page OFF 31).

Other Ways
1. Press CTRL+O   2. Navigate to file in File Explorer window, double-tap or double-click file

To Create a New Document from the Backstage View

1 SIGN IN | 2 USE WINDOWS | 3 USE APPS | 4 FILE MANAGEMENT | 5 SWITCH APPS | 6 SAVE FILES
7 CHANGE SCREEN RESOLUTION | 8 EXIT APPS | 9 USE ADDITIONAL APP FEATURES | 10 USE HELP

You can open multiple documents in an Office program, such as PowerPoint, so that you can work on the documents at the same time. The following steps create a file, a blank presentation in this case, from the Backstage view. **Why?** *You want to create a new document while keeping the current document open.*

1

- Tap or click FILE on the ribbon to open the Backstage view.

- Tap or click the New tab in the Backstage view to display the New gallery (Figure 72).

Q&A Can I create documents through the Backstage view in other Office apps?
Yes. If the Office app has a New tab in the Backstage view, the New gallery displays various options for creating a new file.

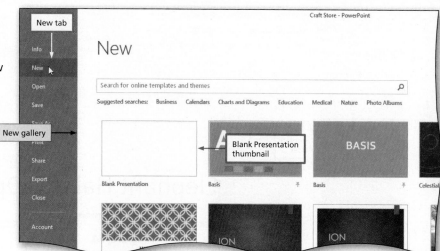

Figure 72

2
- Tap or click the Blank Presentation thumbnail in the New gallery to create a new presentation (Figure 73).

Figure 73

Other Ways

1. Press CTRL+N

To Enter Content in a Title Slide of a Second PowerPoint Presentation

The presentation title for this presentation is Elephant Habitat Opening. The following steps enter a presentation title on the title slide.

1 Tap or click the title text placeholder to select it.

2 Type **Elephant Habitat Opening** in the title text placeholder. Do not press the ENTER key (Figure 74).

Figure 74

To Save a File in a Folder

The following steps save the second presentation in the PowerPoint folder in the class folder (CIS 101, in this case) in the My Documents folder in the Documents library using the file name, Elephant Habitat Opening.

1 Tap or click the Save button on the Quick Access Toolbar (shown in Figure 74), which depending on settings will display either the Save As gallery in the Backstage view or the Save As dialog box.

2 If your screen displays the Backstage view, tap or click Computer, if necessary, to display options in the right pane related to saving on your computer; if your screen already displays the Save As dialog box, proceed to Step 4.

3 Tap or click the Browse button in the right pane to display the Save As dialog box.

4 If necessary, type **Elephant Habitat Opening** in the File name box (Save As dialog box) to change the file name. Do not press the ENTER key after typing the file name because you do not want to close the dialog box at this time.

5 If necessary, navigate to the desired save location (in this case, the PowerPoint folder in the CIS 101 folder [or your class folder] in the My Documents folder in the Documents library). For specific instructions, perform the tasks in Steps 4a and 4b on pages OFF 30 and OFF 31.

6 Tap or click the Save button (Save As dialog box) to save the presentation in the selected folder on the selected drive with the entered file name.

BTW

Customizing the Ribbon
In addition to customizing the Quick Access Toolbar, you can add items to and remove items from the ribbon. To customize the ribbon, click FILE on the ribbon to open the Backstage view, click Options in the Backstage view, and then click Customize Ribbon in the left pane of the Options dialog box. More information about customizing the ribbon is presented in a later chapter.

To Close a File Using the Backstage View

1 SIGN IN | 2 USE WINDOWS | 3 USE APPS | 4 FILE MANAGEMENT | 5 SWITCH APPS | 6 SAVE FILES
7 CHANGE SCREEN RESOLUTION | 8 EXIT APPS | 9 USE ADDITIONAL APP FEATURES | 10 USE HELP

Sometimes, you may want to close an Office file, such as a PowerPoint presentation, entirely and start over with a new file. *Why else would I close a file? You also may want to close a file when you are finished working with it so that you can begin a new file.* The following steps close the current active PowerPoint file, that is, the Elephant Habitat Opening presentation, without exiting the active app (PowerPoint, in this case).

1

- Tap or click FILE on the ribbon (shown in Figure 74) to open the Backstage view (Figure 75).

2

- Tap or click Close in the Backstage view to close the open file (Elephant Habitat Opening, in this case) without exiting the active app.

Q&A

What if PowerPoint displays a dialog box about saving?
Tap or click the Save button if you want to save the changes, tap or click the Don't Save button if you want to ignore the changes since the last time you saved, and tap or click the Cancel button if you do not want to close the document.

Can I use the Backstage view to close an open file in other Office apps, such as Word and Excel?
Yes.

Figure 75

Other Ways

1. Press CTRL+F4

To Open a Recent File Using the Backstage View

You sometimes need to open a file that you recently modified. *Why? You may have more changes to make, such as adding more content or correcting errors.* The Backstage view allows you to access recent files easily. The following steps reopen the Elephant Habitat Opening file just closed.

- Tap or click FILE on the ribbon to open the Backstage view.
- Tap or click the Open tab in the Backstage view to display the Open gallery (Figure 76).

- Tap or click the desired file name in the Recent Presentations list, Elephant Habitat Opening in this case, to open the file (shown in Figure 74 on page OFF 44).

Figure 76

Q&A Can I use the Backstage view to open a recent file in other Office apps, such as Word and Excel?
Yes, as long as the file name appears in the list of recent files.

Other Ways

1. Tap or click FILE on ribbon, tap or click Open in Backstage view, tap or click Computer, tap or click Browse, navigate to file (Open dialog box), tap or click Open button

To Create a New Blank Document from File Explorer

File Explorer provides a means to create a blank Office document without running an Office app. The following steps use File Explorer to create a blank PowerPoint document. *Why? Sometimes you might need to create a blank document and then return to it later for editing.* If you are using Windows 7, skip these steps and instead perform the steps in the yellow box that immediately follows these Windows 8 steps.

- Double-tap or double-click the File Explorer app button on the taskbar to make the folder window the active window.
- If necessary, double-tap or double-click the Documents library in the navigation pane to expand the Documents library.
- If necessary, double-tap or double-click the My Documents folder in the navigation pane to expand the My Documents folder.
- If necessary, double-tap or double-click your class folder (CIS 101, in this case) in the navigation pane to expand the folder.
- Tap or click the PowerPoint folder in the navigation pane to display its contents in the file list.
- With the PowerPoint folder selected, press and hold or right-click an open area in the file list to display a shortcut menu.
- Tap or point to New on the shortcut menu to display the New submenu (Figure 77).

Figure 77

- Tap or click 'Microsoft PowerPoint Presentation' on the New submenu to display an icon and text box for a new file in the current folder window with the file name, New Microsoft PowerPoint Presentation, selected (Figure 78).

Figure 78

3

- Type **Elephant Habitat Volunteers** in the text box and then press the ENTER key to assign a new name to the new file in the current folder (Figure 79).

Figure 79

TO CREATE A NEW BLANK DOCUMENT FROM WINDOWS EXPLORER USING WINDOWS 7

If you are using Windows 7, perform these steps to create a new blank Office document from Windows Explorer instead of the previous steps that use Windows 8.

1. If necessary, click the Windows Explorer button on the taskbar to make the folder window the active window.

2. If necessary, double-click the Documents library in the navigation pane to expand the Documents library.

3. If necessary, double-click the My Documents folder in the navigation pane to expand the My Documents folder.

4. If necessary, double-click your class folder (CIS 101, in this case) in the navigation pane to expand the folder.

5. Click the PowerPoint folder in the navigation pane to display its contents in the file list.

6. With the PowerPoint folder selected, right-click an open area in the file list to display a shortcut menu.

7. Point to New on the shortcut menu to display the New submenu.

8. Click 'Microsoft PowerPoint Presentation' on the New submenu to display an icon and text box for a new file in the current folder window with the name, New Microsoft PowerPoint Presentation, selected.

9. Type **Elephant Habitat Volunteers** in the text box and then press the ENTER key to assign a new name to the new file in the current folder.

To Run an App from File Explorer and Open a File

1 SIGN IN | 2 USE WINDOWS | 3 USE APPS | 4 FILE MANAGEMENT | 5 SWITCH APPS | 6 SAVE FILES
7 CHANGE SCREEN RESOLUTION | 8 EXIT APPS | 9 USE ADDITIONAL APP FEATURES | 10 USE HELP

Previously, you learned how to run PowerPoint using the Start screen and the Search charm. The steps on the next page, which assume Windows is running, use File Explorer to run PowerPoint based on a typical installation. *Why? Another way to run an Office app is to open an existing file from File Explorer, which causes the app in which the file was created to run and then open the selected file.* You may need to ask your instructor how to run PowerPoint for your computer. If you are using Windows 7, follow the steps in the yellow box that immediately follows these Windows 8 steps.

- If necessary, display the file to open in the folder window in File Explorer (shown in Figure 79 on the previous page).

- Press and hold or right-click the file icon or file name (Elephant Habitat Volunteers, in this case) to display a shortcut menu (Figure 80).

Figure 80

- Tap or click Open on the shortcut menu to open the selected file in the app used to create the file, PowerPoint in this case (Figure 81).

- If the PowerPoint window is not maximized, tap or click the Maximize button on the title bar to maximize the window.

- Click the slide to display Slide 1 with the Title Slide layout applied.

Figure 81

To Run an App from Windows Explorer and Open a File Using Windows 7

If you are using Windows 7, perform these steps to run an app from Windows Explorer and open a file instead of the previous steps that use Windows 8.

1. Display the file to open in the folder window in Windows Explorer.

2. Right-click the file icon or file name (Elephant Habitat Volunteers, in this case) to display a shortcut menu.

3. Click Open on the shortcut menu to open the selected file in the app used to create the file, PowerPoint in this case.

4. If the PowerPoint window is not maximized, click the Maximize button on the title bar to maximize the window.

To Enter Text in a Document

The next step is to enter text in this blank PowerPoint document. The following step enters a line of text.

 Type **Elephant Habitat Volunteers** in the title text placeholder (shown in Figure 82).

To Save an Existing File with the Same File Name

1 SIGN IN | 2 USE WINDOWS | 3 USE APPS | 4 FILE MANAGEMENT | 5 SWITCH APPS | 6 SAVE FILES
7 CHANGE SCREEN RESOLUTION | 8 EXIT APPS | 9 USE ADDITIONAL APP FEATURES | 10 USE HELP

Saving frequently cannot be overemphasized. *Why? You have made modifications to the file (presentation) since you created it. Thus, you should save again. Similarly, you should continue saving files frequently so that you do not lose the changes you have made since the time you last saved the file.* You can use the same file name, such as Elephant Habitat Volunteers, to save the changes made to the document. The following step saves a file again with the same file name.

1

• Tap or click the Save button on the Quick Access Toolbar to overwrite the previously saved file (Elephant Habitat Volunteers, in this case) in the PowerPoint folder (Figure 82).

Figure 82

Other Ways

1. Press CTRL+S or press SHIFT+F12

To Save a File with a New File Name

You might want to save a file with a different name or to a different location. For example, you might start a homework assignment with a data file and then save it with a final file name for submission to your instructor, saving it to a location designated by your instructor. The following steps save a file with a different file name.

1 Tap or click the FILE tab to open the Backstage view.

2 Tap or click the Save As tab to display the Save As gallery.

3 If necessary, tap or click Computer to display options in the right pane related to saving on your computer.

4 Tap or click the Browse button in the right pane to display the Save As dialog box.

5 Type **Elephant Habitat Staff and Volunteers** in the File name box (Save As dialog box) to change the file name. Do not press the ENTER key after typing the file name because you do not want to close the dialog box at this time.

6 If necessary, navigate to the desired save location (in this case, the PowerPoint folder in the CIS 101 folder [or your class folder] in the My Documents folder in the Documents library). For specific instructions, perform the tasks in Steps 4a and 4b on pages OFF 30 and OFF 31.

7 Tap or click the Save button (Save As dialog box) to save the presentation in the selected folder on the selected drive with the entered file name.

To Exit an Office App

You are finished using PowerPoint. The following steps exit PowerPoint. You would use similar steps to exit other Office apps.

1 Because you have multiple PowerPoint documents open, press and hold or right-click the app button on the taskbar and then tap or click 'Close all windows' on the shortcut menu to close all open documents and exit PowerPoint.

2 If a dialog box appears, tap or click the Save button to save any changes made to the file since the last save.

Renaming, Moving, and Deleting Files

Earlier in this chapter, you learned how to organize files in folders, which is part of a process known as **file management**. The following sections cover additional file management topics including renaming, moving, and deleting files.

To Rename a File

1 SIGN IN | 2 USE WINDOWS | 3 USE APPS | **4 FILE MANAGEMENT** | 5 SWITCH APPS | 6 SAVE FILES
7 CHANGE SCREEN RESOLUTION | 8 EXIT APPS | 9 USE ADDITIONAL APP FEATURES | **10 USE HELP**

In some circumstances, you may want to change the name of, or rename, a file or a folder. *Why? You may want to distinguish a file in one folder or drive from a copy of a similar file, or you may decide to rename a file to better identify its contents.* The PowerPoint folder shown in Figure 66 on page OFF 40 contains the PowerPoint document, Craft Store. The following steps change the name of the Craft Store file in the PowerPoint folder to Craft Store Presentation. If you are using Windows 7, skip these steps and instead perform the steps in the yellow box that immediately follows these Windows 8 steps.

- If necessary, tap or click the File Explorer app button on the taskbar to make the folder window the active window.

- If necessary, navigate to the location of the file to be renamed (in this case, the PowerPoint folder in the CIS 101 [or your class folder] folder in the My Documents folder in the Documents library) to display the file(s) it contains in the file list.

- Press and hold or right-click the Craft Store icon or file name in the file list to select the Craft Store file and display a shortcut menu that presents a list of commands related to files (Figure 83).

Figure 83

- Tap or click Rename on the shortcut menu to place the current file name in a text box.

- Type `Craft Store Presentation` in the text box and then press the ENTER key (Figure 84).

Q&A
Are any risks involved in renaming files that are located on a hard disk?
If you inadvertently rename a file that is associated with certain apps, the apps may not be able to find the file and, therefore, may not run properly. Always use caution when renaming files.

Can I rename a file when it is open?
No, a file must be closed to change the file name.

Figure 84

Other Ways

1. Select file, press F2, type new file name, press ENTER   2. Select file, tap or click Rename (Home tab | Organize group), type new file name, press ENTER

TO RENAME A FILE USING WINDOWS 7

If you are using Windows 7, perform these steps to rename a file instead of the previous steps that use Windows 8.

1. If necessary, click the Windows Explorer app button on the taskbar to make the folder window the active window.

2. Navigate to the location of the file to be renamed (in this case, the PowerPoint folder in the CIS 101 [or your class folder] folder in the My Documents folder in the Documents library) to display the file(s) it contains in the file list.

3. Right-click the Craft Store icon or file name in the file list to select the Craft Store file and display a shortcut menu that presents a list of commands related to files.

4. Click Rename on the shortcut menu to place the current file name in a text box.

5. Type **Craft Store Presentation** in the text box and then press the ENTER key.

To Move a File

1 SIGN IN | 2 USE WINDOWS | 3 USE APPS | **4 FILE MANAGEMENT** | 5 SWITCH APPS | 6 SAVE FILES
7 CHANGE SCREEN RESOLUTION | 8 EXIT APPS | 9 USE ADDITIONAL APP FEATURES | **10 USE HELP**

Why? *At some time, you may want to move a file from one folder, called the source folder, to another, called the destination folder.* When you move a file, it no longer appears in the original folder. If the destination and the source folders are on the same media, you can move a file by dragging it. If the folders are on different media, then you will need to press and hold and then drag, or right-drag the file, and then click Move here on the shortcut menu. The following step moves the Elephant Habitat Volunteers file from the PowerPoint folder to the CIS 101 folder. If you are using Windows 7, skip these steps and instead perform the steps in the yellow box that immediately follows these Windows 8 steps.

1

- In File Explorer, if necessary, navigate to the location of the file to be moved (in this case, the PowerPoint folder in the CIS 101 folder [or your class folder] in the Documents library).

- If necessary, tap or click the PowerPoint folder in the navigation pane to display the files it contains in the right pane.

- Drag the Elephant Habitat Volunteers file in the right pane to the CIS 101 folder in the navigation pane and notice the ScreenTip as you drag the mouse (Figure 85).

Figure 85

 Experiment

- Tap or click the CIS 101 folder in the navigation pane to verify that the file was moved.

Other Ways

1. Press and hold or right-click file to move, tap or click Cut on shortcut menu, press and hold or right-click destination folder, tap or click Paste on shortcut menu

2. Select file to move, press CTRL+X, select destination folder, press CTRL+V

TO MOVE A FILE USING WINDOWS 7

If you are using Windows 7, perform these steps to move a file instead of the previous steps that use Windows 8.

1. In Windows Explorer, navigate to the location of the file to be moved (in this case, the PowerPoint folder in the CIS 101 folder [or your class folder] in the Documents library).

2. Click the PowerPoint folder in the navigation pane to display the files it contains in the right pane.

3. Drag the Elephant Habitat Volunteers file in the right pane to the CIS 101 folder in the navigation pane.

1 SIGN IN | 2 USE WINDOWS | 3 USE APPS | 4 FILE MANAGEMENT | 5 SWITCH APPS | 6 SAVE FILES
7 CHANGE SCREEN RESOLUTION | 8 EXIT APPS | 9 USE ADDITIONAL APP FEATURES | 10 USE HELP

To Delete a File

A final task you may want to perform is to delete a file. Exercise extreme caution when deleting a file or files. When you delete a file from a hard disk, the deleted file is stored in the Recycle Bin where you can recover it until you empty the Recycle Bin. If you delete a file from removable media, such as a USB flash drive, the file is deleted permanently. The next steps delete the Elephant Habitat Volunteers file from the CIS 101 folder. *Why? When a file no longer is needed, you can delete it to conserve space in your storage location.* If you are using Windows 7, skip these steps and instead perform the steps in the yellow box that immediately follows these Windows 8 steps.

- In File Explorer, navigate to the location of the file to be deleted (in this case, the CIS 101 folder [or your class folder] in the Documents library).

- Press and hold or right-click the Elephant Habitat Volunteers icon or file name in the right pane to select the file and display a shortcut menu (Figure 86).

- Tap or click Delete on the shortcut menu to delete the file.

- If a dialog box appears, tap or click the Yes button to delete the file.

Q&A Can I use this same technique to delete a folder?
Yes. Right-click the folder and then click Delete on the shortcut menu. When you delete a folder, all of the files and folders contained in the folder you are deleting, together with any files and folders on lower hierarchical levels, are deleted as well.

Figure 86

Other Ways

1. Select icon, press DELETE

TO DELETE A FILE USING WINDOWS 7

If you are using Windows 7, perform these steps to delete a file instead of the previous steps that use Windows 8.

1. In Windows Explorer, navigate to the location of the file to be deleted (in this case, the CIS 101 folder [or your class folder] in the Documents library).

2. Right-click the Elephant Habitat Volunteers icon or file name in the right pane to select the file and display a shortcut menu.

3. Click Delete on the shortcut menu to delete the file.

4. If a dialog box appears, click the Yes button to delete the file.

Microsoft Office and Windows Help

At any time while you are using one of the Office apps, such as PowerPoint, you can use Office Help to display information about all topics associated with the app. This section illustrates the use of PowerPoint Help. Help in other Office apps operates in a similar fashion.

In Office, Help is presented in a window that has browser-style navigation buttons. Each Office app has its own Help home page, which is the starting Help page that is displayed in the Help window. If your computer is connected to the Internet, the contents of the Help page reflect both the local help files installed on the computer and material from Microsoft's website.

To Open the Help Window in an Office App

1 SIGN IN | 2 USE WINDOWS | 3 USE APPS | 4 FILE MANAGEMENT | 5 SWITCH APPS | 6 SAVE FILES
7 CHANGE SCREEN RESOLUTION | 8 EXIT APPS | 9 USE ADDITIONAL APP FEATURES | 10 USE HELP

The following step opens the PowerPoint Help window. *Why? You might not understand how certain commands or operations work in PowerPoint, so you can obtain the necessary information using help. The step to open a Help window in other Office programs is similar.*

- Run PowerPoint.

- Tap or click the Microsoft PowerPoint Help button near the upper-right corner of the app window to open the PowerPoint Help window (Figure 87).

Figure 87

Other Ways
1. Press F1

Moving and Resizing Windows

At times, it is useful, or even necessary, to have more than one window open and visible on the screen at the same time. You can resize and move these open windows so that you can view different areas of and elements in the window. In the case of the Help window, for example, it could be covering document text in the PowerPoint window that you need to see.

To Move a Window by Dragging

1 SIGN IN | **2 USE WINDOWS** | 3 USE APPS | 4 FILE MANAGEMENT | 5 SWITCH APPS | 6 SAVE FILES
7 CHANGE SCREEN RESOLUTION | 8 EXIT APPS | 9 USE ADDITIONAL APP FEATURES | 10 USE HELP

You can move any open window that is not maximized to another location on the desktop by dragging the title bar of the window. *Why? You might want to have a better view of what is behind the window or just want to move the window so that you can see it better.* The step on the next page drags the PowerPoint Help window to the upper-left corner of the desktop.

- Drag the window title bar (the PowerPoint Help window title bar, in this case) so that the window moves to the upper-left corner of the desktop, as shown in Figure 88.

Figure 88

To Resize a Window by Dragging

1 SIGN IN | **2 USE WINDOWS** | 3 USE APPS | 4 FILE MANAGEMENT | 5 SWITCH APPS | 6 SAVE FILES
7 CHANGE SCREEN RESOLUTION | 8 EXIT APPS | 9 USE ADDITIONAL APP FEATURES | 10 USE HELP

A method used to change the size of the window is to drag the window borders. The following step changes the size of the PowerPoint Help window by dragging its borders. *Why? Sometimes, information is not visible completely in a window, and you want to increase the size of the window.*

- If you are using a mouse, point to the lower-right corner of the window (the PowerPoint Help window, in this case) until the pointer changes to a two-headed arrow.

- Drag the bottom border downward to display more of the active window (Figure 89).

Q&A

Can I drag other borders on the window to enlarge or shrink the window?
Yes, you can drag the left, right, and top borders and any window corner to resize a window.

Will Windows remember the new size of the window after I close it?
Yes. When you reopen the window, Windows will display it at the same size it was when you closed it.

Figure 89

Using Office Help

Once an Office app's Help window is open, several methods exist for navigating Help. You can search for help by using any of the three following methods from the Help window:

1. Enter search text in the 'Search online help' text box.

2. Click the links in the Help window.

3. Use the Table of Contents.

To Obtain Help Using the 'Search online help' Text Box

1 SIGN IN | 2 USE WINDOWS | 3 USE APPS | 4 FILE MANAGEMENT | 5 SWITCH APPS | 6 SAVE FILES
7 CHANGE SCREEN RESOLUTION | 8 EXIT APPS | 9 USE ADDITIONAL APP FEATURES | **10 USE HELP**

Assume for the following example that you want to know more about fonts. The following steps use the 'Search online help' text box to obtain useful information about fonts by entering the word, fonts, as search text. *Why?* *You may not know the exact help topic you are looking to find, so using keywords can help narrow your search.*

1

- Type **fonts** in the 'Search online help' text box at the top of the PowerPoint Help window to enter the search text.

- Tap or click the 'Search online help' button to display the search results (Figure 90).

Q&A

Why do my search results differ?
If you do not have an Internet connection, your results will reflect only the content of the Help files on your computer. When searching for help online, results also can change as material is added, deleted, and updated on the online Help webpages maintained by Microsoft.

Why were my search results not very helpful?
When initiating a search, be sure to check the spelling of the search text; also, keep your search specific to return the most accurate results.

Figure 90

2

- Tap or click the 'Change the fonts' link to display the Help information associated with the selected topic (Figure 91).

Figure 91

- Tap or click the Home button in the Help window to clear the search results and redisplay the Help home page (Figure 92).

Figure 92

To Obtain Help Using Help Links

1 SIGN IN | 2 USE WINDOWS | 3 USE APPS | 4 FILE MANAGEMENT | 5 SWITCH APPS | 6 SAVE FILES
7 CHANGE SCREEN RESOLUTION | 8 EXIT APPS | 9 USE ADDITIONAL APP FEATURES | 10 USE HELP

If your topic of interest is listed in the Help window, you can click the link to begin browsing the Help categories instead of entering search text. ***Why?*** *You browse Help just as you would browse a website. If you know which category contains your Help information, you may wish to use these links.* The following step finds the Portrait information using the Portrait link from the PowerPoint Help home page.

- Tap or click the Portrait link on the Help home page (shown in Figure 92) to display the Portrait help links (Figure 93).

- After reviewing the page, tap or click the Close button to close the Help window.

- Tap or click PowerPoint's Close button to exit PowerPoint.

Q&A
Why does my Help window display different links?
The content of your Help window may differ because Microsoft continually updates its Help information.

Figure 93

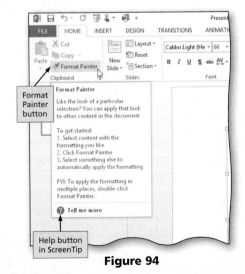

Figure 94

Obtaining Help while Working in an Office App

Help in the Office apps, such as PowerPoint, provides you with the ability to obtain help directly, without opening the Help window and initiating a search. For example, you may be unsure about how a particular command works, or you may be presented with a dialog box that you are not sure how to use.

Figure 94 shows one option for obtaining help while working in an Office app. If you want to learn more about a command, point to its button and wait for the ScreenTip to appear. If the Help icon appears in the ScreenTip, press the F1 key while pointing to the button to open the Help window associated with that command.

Figure 95 shows a dialog box that contains a Help button. Pressing the F1 key while the dialog box is displayed opens a Help window. The Help window contains help about that dialog box, if available. If no help file is available for that particular dialog box, then the main Help window opens.

Using Windows Help and Support

One of the more powerful Windows features is Windows Help and Support. **Windows Help and Support** is available when using Windows or when using any Microsoft app running in Windows. The same methods used for searching Microsoft Office Help can be used in Windows Help and Support. The difference is that Windows Help and Support displays help for Windows, instead of for Microsoft Office.

Figure 95

To Use Windows Help and Support

1 SIGN IN | 2 USE WINDOWS | 3 USE APPS | 4 FILE MANAGEMENT | 5 SWITCH APPS | 6 SAVE FILES
7 CHANGE SCREEN RESOLUTION | 8 EXIT APPS | 9 USE ADDITIONAL APP FEATURES | 10 USE HELP

The following steps use Windows Help and Support and open the Windows Help and Support window, which contains links to more information about Windows. *Why? This feature is designed to assist you in using Windows or the various apps.* If you are using Windows 7, skip these steps and instead perform the steps in the yellow box that immediately follows these Windows 8 steps.

- Swipe in from the right edge of the screen or point to the upper-right corner of the screen to display the Charms bar (Figure 96).

Figure 96

2

- Tap or click the Settings charm on the Charms bar to display the Settings menu (Figure 97).

Figure 97

3

- Tap or click Help to open the Windows Help and Support window (Figure 98).

4

- After reviewing the Windows Help and Support window, tap or click the Close button to close the Windows Help and Support window.

Figure 98

Other Ways

1. Press WINDOWS + F1

TO USE WINDOWS HELP AND SUPPORT WITH WINDOWS 7

If you are using Windows 7, perform these steps to start Windows Help and Support instead of the previous steps that use Windows 8.

1. Click the Start button on the taskbar to display the Start menu.

2. Click Help and Support on the Start menu to open the Windows Help and Support window.

3. After reviewing the Windows Help and Support window, click the Close button to exit Windows Help and Support.

Chapter Summary

In this chapter, you learned how to use the Windows interface, several touch screen and mouse operations, and file and folder management. You also learned some basic features of PowerPoint and discovered the common elements that exist among Microsoft Office apps. The items listed below include all of the new Windows and PowerPoint skills you have learned in this chapter, with the tasks grouped by activity.

CONSIDER THIS: PLAN AHEAD

What guidelines should you follow to plan your projects?

The process of communicating specific information is a learned, rational skill. Computers and software, especially Microsoft Office 2013, can help you develop ideas and present detailed information to a particular audience and minimize much of the laborious work of drafting and revising projects. No matter what method you use to plan a project, it is beneficial to follow some specific guidelines from the onset to arrive at a final product that is informative, relevant, and effective. Use some aspects of these guidelines every time you undertake a project, and others as needed in specific instances.

1. Determine the project's purpose.
    a) Clearly define why you are undertaking this assignment.
    b) Begin to draft ideas of how best to communicate information by handwriting ideas on paper; composing directly on a laptop, tablet, or mobile device; or developing a strategy that fits your particular thinking and writing style.

2. Analyze your audience.
    a) Learn about the people who will read, analyze, or view your work.
    b) Determine their interests and needs so that you can present the information they need to know and omit the information they already possess.
    c) Form a mental picture of these people or find photos of people who fit this profile so that you can develop a project with the audience in mind.

3. Gather possible content.
    a) Locate existing information that may reside in spreadsheets, databases, or other files.
    b) Conduct a web search to find relevant websites.
    c) Read pamphlets, magazine and newspaper articles, and books to gain insights of how others have approached your topic.
    d) Conduct personal interviews to obtain perspectives not available by any other means.
    e) Consider video and audio clips as potential sources for material that might complement or support the factual data you uncover.

4. Determine what content to present to your audience.
  a) Write three or four major ideas you want an audience member to remember after reading or viewing your project.
  b) Envision your project's endpoint, the key fact you wish to emphasize, so that all project elements lead to this final element.
  c) Determine relevant time factors, such as the length of time to develop the project, how long readers will spend reviewing your project, or the amount of time allocated for your speaking engagement.
  d) Decide whether a graph, photo, or artistic element can express or enhance a particular concept.
  e) Be mindful of the order in which you plan to present the content, and place the most important material at the top or bottom of the page, because readers and audience members generally remember the first and last pieces of information they see and hear.

CONSIDER THIS

How should you submit solutions to questions in the assignments identified with a symbol?
Every assignment in this book contains one or more questions identified with a symbol. These questions require you to think beyond the assigned file. Present your solutions to the questions in the format required by your instructor. Possible formats may include one or more of these options: write the answer; create a document that contains the answer; present your answer to the class; discuss your answer in a group; record the answer as audio or video using a webcam, smartphone, or portable media player; or post answers on a blog, wiki, or website.

Apply Your Knowledge

Reinforce the skills and apply the concepts you learned in this chapter.

Creating a Folder and a Presentation
Instructions: You will create a PowerPoint folder and then create a PowerPoint presentation and save it in the folder.

Perform the following tasks:

1. Open the File Explorer window and then double-tap or double-click to open the Documents library.

2. Tap or click the New folder button on the Quick Access Toolbar to display a new folder icon and text box for the folder name.

3. Type **PowerPoint** in the text box to name the folder. Press the ENTER key to create the folder in the Documents library.

4. Run PowerPoint.

5. Enter the text shown in Figure 99 in a new blank title slide.

6. If requested by your instructor, enter your name in the PowerPoint presentation.

Figure 99

7. Tap or click the Save button on the Quick Access Toolbar. Navigate to the PowerPoint folder in the Documents library and then save the document using the file name, Apply 1 Speech.

8. If your Quick Access Toolbar does not show the Quick Print button, add the Quick Print button to the Quick Access Toolbar. Print the document using the Quick Print button on the Quick Access Toolbar. When you are finished printing, remove the Quick Print button from the Quick Access Toolbar.

9. Submit the printout to your instructor.

10. Exit PowerPoint.

11. What other commands might you find useful to include on the Quick Access Toolbar?

Extend Your Knowledge

Extend the skills you learned in this chapter and experiment with new skills. You will use Help to complete the assignment.

Using Help

Instructions: Use PowerPoint Help to perform the following tasks.

Perform the following tasks:

1. Run PowerPoint.

2. Tap or click the Microsoft PowerPoint Help button to open the PowerPoint Help window (Figure 100).

3. Search PowerPoint Help to answer the following questions.

   a. What are three features new to PowerPoint 2013?
   b. What type of training courses are available through Help?
   c. What are the steps to add a new group to the ribbon?
   d. How do you add speaker notes to slides?
   e. How do you insert clip art?
   f. Where do you find templates that have complete formatting?
   g. How do Smart Guides help align slide content?
   h. What is a SmartArt graphic?
   i. What is cropping?
   j. How do you add sound to a presentation?

Figure 100

4. Type the answers from your searches in a new blank PowerPoint presentation. Save the document with a new file name and then submit it in the format specified by your instructor.

5. If requested by your instructor, enter your name in the PowerPoint document.

6. Exit PowerPoint.

7. ✸ What search text did you use to perform the searches above? Did it take multiple attempts to search and locate the exact information for which you were searching?

Analyze, Correct, Improve

Analyze a file structure, correct all errors, and improve the design.

Organizing Vacation Photos

Note: To complete this assignment, you will be required to use the Data Files for Students. Visit www.cengage.com/ct/student-download for detailed instructions or contact your instructor for information about accessing the required files.

Instructions: Traditionally, you have stored photos from past vacations together in one folder. The photos are becoming difficult to manage, and you now want to store them in appropriate folders. You will create the folder structure shown in Figure 101. You then will move the photos to the folders so that they will be organized properly.

Figure 101

© 2014 Cengage Learning

1. Correct Create the folder structure in Figure 101 so that you are able to store the photos in an organized manner. If requested by your instructor, add another folder using your last name as the folder name.

2. Improve View each photo and drag it to the appropriate folder to improve the organization. Submit the assignment in the format specified by your instructor.

3. ✸ In which folder did you place each photo? Think about the files you have stored on your computer. What folder hierarchy would be best to manage your files?

In the Labs

Use the guidelines, concepts, and skills presented in this chapter to increase your knowledge of Windows 8 and PowerPoint 2013. Labs 1 and 2, which increase in difficulty, require you to create solutions based on what you learned in the chapter; Lab 3 requires you to create a solution, which uses cloud and web technologies, by learning and investigating on your own from general guidance.

Lab 1: Creating Folders for a Video Store

Problem: Your friend works for Ebaird Video. He would like to organize his files in relation to the types of videos available in the store. He has six main categories: drama, action, romance, foreign, biographical, and comedy. You are to create a folder structure similar to Figure 102.

Instructions: Perform the following tasks:

1. Insert a USB flash drive in an available USB port and then open the USB flash drive window.

2. Create the main folder for Ebaird Video.

3. Navigate to the Ebaird Video folder.

4. Within the Ebaird Video folder, create a folder for each of the following: Drama, Action, Romance, Foreign, Biographical, and Comedy.

5. Within the Action folder, create two additional folders, one for Science Fiction and the second for Western.

Figure 102

6. If requested by your instructor, add another folder using your last name as the folder name.

7. Submit the assignment in the format specified by your instructor.

8. ✹ Think about how you use your computer for various tasks (consider personal, professional, and academic reasons). What folders do you think will be required on your computer to store the files you save?

Lab 2: Saving Files in Folders

Problem: You are taking a class that requires you to complete three PowerPoint chapters. You will save the work completed in each chapter in a different folder (Figure 103).

Instructions: Create the folders shown in Figure 103. Then, using PowerPoint, create three small files to save in each folder.

1. Create a PowerPoint document containing the text, First PowerPoint Chapter.

2. In the Backstage view, tap or click Save As and then tap or click Computer.

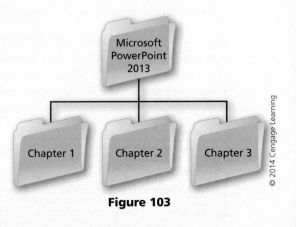

Figure 103

3. Tap or click the Browse button to display the Save As dialog box.

4. Tap or click Documents to open the Documents library. Next, create the folder structure shown in Figure 103 using the New folder button.

5. Navigate to the Chapter 1 folder and then save the file in the Chapter 1 folder using the file name, PowerPoint Chapter 1 Document.

6. Create another PowerPoint document containing the text, Second PowerPoint Chapter, and then save it in the Chapter 2 folder using the file name, PowerPoint Chapter 2 Document.

7. Create a third PowerPoint document containing the text, Third PowerPoint Chapter, and then save it in the Chapter 3 folder using the file name, PowerPoint Chapter 3 Document.

8. If requested by your instructor, add your name to each of the three PowerPoint files.

9. Submit the assignment in the format specified by your instructor.

10. ✸ Based on your current knowledge of Windows and PowerPoint how will you organize folders for assignments in this class? Why?

Lab 3: Expand Your World: Cloud and Web Technologies
Creating Folders on SkyDrive and Using the PowerPoint Web App

Problem: You are taking a class that requires you to create folders on SkyDrive, use the PowerPoint Web App to create a document, and then save the document in a folder on SkyDrive (Figure 104).

Instructions: Perform the following tasks:

1. Sign in to SkyDrive in your browser.

2. Use the Create button to create the folder structure shown in Figure 104.

3. In the Notes folder, use the Create button to create a PowerPoint document with the file name, Notes, and containing the text, Important Test on Tuesday, on Slide 1.

4. If requested by your instructor, add your name to the PowerPoint document.

5. Save the document in the Notes folder and then exit the app.

6. Submit the assignment in the format specified by your instructor.

7. ✸ Based on your current knowledge of SkyDrive, do you think you will use it? What about the PowerPoint Web App?

Figure 104

© 2014 Cengage Learning

✸ Consider This: Your Turn

Apply your creative thinking and problem solving skills to design and implement a solution.

1: Creating Beginning Files for Classes

Personal

Part 1: You are taking the following classes: Introduction to Sociology, Chemistry, Calculus, and Marketing. Create folders for each of the classes. Create a folder structure that will store the documents for each of these classes. Use PowerPoint to create a separate PowerPoint presentation for each class. Each document should contain the name of each class and the class meeting locations and times: Introduction to Sociology meets on Mondays and Wednesdays from 8:00 a.m. to 10:00 a.m.; Chemistry meets on Tuesdays and Thursdays from 11:00 a.m. to 1:00 p.m.; Calculus

Continued >

Consider This: Your Turn *continued*

meets on Mondays, Wednesdays, and Fridays from 1:30 p.m. to 3:00 p.m.; and Marketing meets on Tuesdays from 5:00 to 8:00 p.m. If requested by your instructor, add your name to each of the PowerPoint documents. Use the concepts and techniques presented in this chapter to create the folders and files, and store the files in their respective locations. Submit your assignment in the format specified by your instructor.

Part 2: ✷ You made several decisions while determining the folder structure in this assignment. What was the rationale behind these decisions? Are there any other decisions that also might have worked?

2: Creating Folders

Professional

Part 1: Your boss at the media store where you work part-time has asked for help with organizing his files. After looking through the files, you decided upon a file structure for her to use, including the following folders: CDs, DVDs, and general merchandise. Use PowerPoint to create separate PowerPoint presentations that list examples in each category. For example, CDs include music [blues, rock, country, new age, pop, and soundtracks], blank discs, books, and games; DVDs include movies [action, documentary, music videos, mystery, and drama], television series, and blank discs; and general merchandise includes clothing, portable media players, cases, earbuds, chargers, and cables. If requested by your instructor, add your name to each of the PowerPoint documents. Use the concepts and techniques presented in this chapter to create the folders. Submit your assignment in the format specified by your instructor.

Part 2: ✷ You made several decisions while determining the folder structure in this assignment. What was the rationale behind these decisions? Justify why you feel this folder structure will help your boss organize her files.

3: Using Help

Research and Collaboration

Part 1: You have just installed a new computer with the Windows operating system and want to be sure that it is protected from the threat of viruses. You ask two of your friends to help research computer viruses, virus prevention, and virus removal. In a team of three people, each person should choose a topic (computer viruses, virus prevention, and virus removal) to research. Use the concepts and techniques presented in this chapter to use Help to find information regarding these topics. Create a PowerPoint document that contains steps to properly safeguard a computer from viruses, ways to prevent viruses, as well as the different ways to remove a virus should your computer become infected. Submit your assignment in the format specified by your instructor.

Part 2: ✷ You made several decisions while searching Windows Help and Support for this assignment. What decisions did you make? What was the rationale behind these decisions? How did you locate the required information about viruses in help?

Learn Online

Reinforce what you learned in this chapter with games, exercises, training, and many other online activities and resources.

Student Companion Site Reinforcement activities and resources are available at no additional cost on www.cengagebrain.com. Visit www.cengage.com/ct/studentdownload for detailed instructions about accessing the resources available at the Student Companion Site.

SAM Put your skills into practice with SAM Projects! If you have a SAM account, go to www.cengage.com/sam2013 to access SAM assignments for this chapter.

Office 365 Essentials

Microsoft product screen shots used with permission from Microsoft Corporation.

Objectives

You will have mastered the material in this chapter when you can:

- Describe the components of Office 365
- Compare Office 2013 to Office 365 subscription plans
- Understand the productivity tools of Office 365
- Sync multiple devices using Office 365
- Describe how business teams collaborate using SharePoint
- Describe how to use a SharePoint template to design a public website
- Describe how to conduct an online meeting with Lync

Explore Office 365

Introduction to Office 365

Microsoft Office 365 uses the cloud to deliver a subscription-based service offering the newest Office suite and much more. The Microsoft cloud provides Office software and information stored on remote servers all over the world. Your documents are located online or on the cloud, which provides you access to your information anywhere using a PC, Mac, tablet, mobile phone, or other device with an Internet connection. For businesses and students alike, Office 365 offers significant cost savings compared to the traditional cost of purchasing Microsoft Office 2013. In addition to the core desktop Office suite, Office 365 provides access to email, calendars, conferencing, file sharing, and website design, which sync across multiple devices.

Cloud Computing

Cloud computing refers to a collection of computer servers that house resources users access through the Internet (Figure 1). These resources include email messages, schedules, music, photos, videos, games, websites, programs, apps, servers, storage, and more. Instead of accessing these resources on your computer or mobile device, you access them on the cloud.

Figure 1

Cloud computing can help businesses be more efficient and save them money by shifting usage and the consumption of resources, such as servers and programs, from a local environment to the Internet. For example, an employee working during the day in California could use computing resources located in an office in London that is closed for the evening. When the company in California uses the computing resources, it pays a fee that is based on the amount of computing time and other resources it consumes, much in the same way that consumers pay utility companies for the amount of electricity they use.

Cloud computing is changing how users access and pay for software applications. Fading fast are the days when software packages were sold in boxes at a physical store location with a one-time purchase software license fee. Instead, the new pricing structure is a subscription-based model, where users pay a monthly or annual fee for the software that you can use on multiple devices. The cloud-based Office 365 offers the Office suite with added features that allow you to communicate and collaborate with others in real time.

When you create a free Microsoft account, do you get free cloud storage space?
Yes, when you create a free Microsoft account at Outlook.com, you have access to 15 GB of cloud storage for any types of files.

CONSIDER THIS

What Is Office 365?

Office 365 is a collection of programs and services, which includes the Microsoft Office suite, file storage, online collaboration, and file synchronization, as shown in Figure 2 on the next page. You can access these services using your computer, tablet (Windows, iPad, or Android), any browser, or supported mobile device. For example, a business has two options for providing Office to their employees. A business could purchase Office 2013 and install the software on company computers and servers; however, this traditional Office 2013 package with perpetual licensing does not include the communication and collaboration tools. Employees could not access the Office software if they were not using their work computers. In contrast, if the business purchases a monthly subscription to Office 365, each employee has access to the Office suite on up to five different computers, whether at home or work; company-wide email; web conferencing; website creation capabilities; unlimited cloud storage; and shared files. An employee can begin a departmental budget on Excel on their office PC, finish the budget on their iPad at home, and review the final budget on their smartphone using Office 365. For a lower price, Office 365 provides many more features. In addition, a business may prefer a subscription plan with predictable monthly costs and no up-front infrastructure costs.

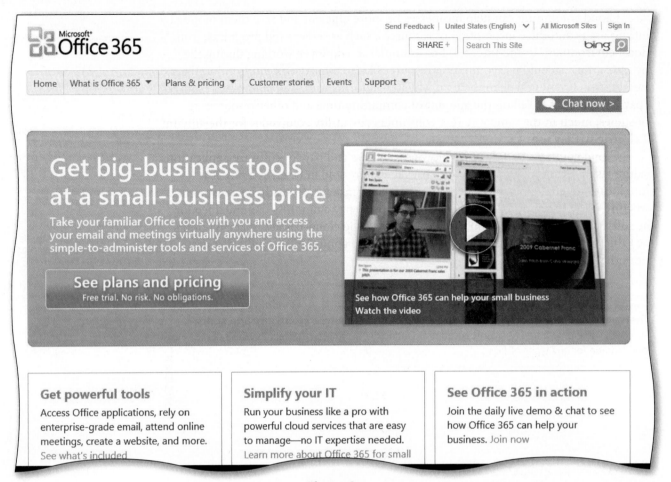

Figure 2

Office 2013 and Office 365 Features Comparison

Office 2013 is the name of the perpetual software package that includes individual applications that can be installed on a single computer. An Office 365 subscription comes with a license to install the software on multiple PCs, Macs, iPad tablets, or smartphones at the same time, giving you more flexibility to use your Office products in your home, school, or workplace, whether on a computer, tablet, or a mobile device. Office 365 provides updated Office 2013 programs as part of a subscription service that includes online storage, sharing, and syncing via Microsoft cloud services as shown in Table 1. A limited version of Office 365 including Word, Excel, PowerPoint, and OneNote can be downloaded from the appropriate app store on mobile devices, such as an iPad or smartphone. Office documents can be created, viewed, and edited using an iPhone, Android, or Windows smartphone. Office applications differ across different platforms and are tailored to work best on each device. The Office applications are available for Mac users and the version numbers may be different from those available for PC users.

Office 365 is available in business, consumer, education, and government editions. Office 365 combines the full version of the Microsoft Office desktop suite with cloud-based versions of Microsoft's communications and collaboration services. The subscription package includes:

- Microsoft Exchange online for shared email and calendars
- Microsoft SharePoint Online for shared file access and public website creation
- Microsoft Office Online for browser viewing
- Microsoft Lync Online for communication services

Table 1 Office 2013 and Office 365 Feature Comparison for PCs and Macs	
Office 2013 Professional (Installed on a single device)	**Office 365 Subscription (Installed on 2 to 5 devices)**
Microsoft Word	Microsoft Word
Microsoft Excel	Microsoft Excel
Microsoft PowerPoint	Microsoft PowerPoint
Microsoft Access (Mac version not available)	Microsoft Access (Mac version not available)
Microsoft Outlook	Microsoft Outlook
Microsoft Publisher	Microsoft Publisher
Microsoft OneNote	Microsoft OneNote
	email and calendars (Exchange Online)
	file sharing (SharePoint Online and Yammer)
	public website design and publishing (SharePoint Online)
	browser-based Office Online
	instant messaging (Lync Online and Yammer)
	audio and video web conferencing (Lync Online)
	screen sharing with shared control (Lync Online)
	technical support

© 2014 Cengage Learning

Subscription-Based Office 365 Plans

Microsoft provides various subscription plans for Office 365 with different benefits for each individual or organization. Subscription plans include Office 365 Home Premium for home users, Office 365 ProPlus programs for students and teachers, Office 365 Small Business, Office 365 Small Business Premium, Office 365 Midsize Business, and Office 365 Enterprise and Government. During the Office 365 sign-up process, you create a Microsoft email address and password to use on your multiple devices. A single subscription to an Office 365 Home Premium account can cover an entire household. The Office 365 Home Premium subscription allows up to five concurrent installations by using the same email address and password combination. This means that your mother could be on the main family computer while you use your tablet and smartphone at the same time. You each can sign in with your individual Microsoft accounts using your settings and accessing your own documents using a single Office 365 subscription.

The educational Office 365 ProPlus subscription plan is designed for K12 and higher-education full-time and part-time students, faculty, and staff. By submitting the proper credentials, such as a school email address, students, faculty, and school staff can download Office 365, including full online copies of Word, PowerPoint, Excel, Access, Outlook, Publisher, and OneNote for free if their school has an Office 2013 or 365 site wide license agreement (office.com/getoffice365). In addition, Office 365 ProPlus provides users with unlimited OneDrive cloud storage rather than the free 15 GB provided by a Microsoft account, and 60 Skype world minutes per month for videoconferencing. The Office 365 ProPlus program is limited to five home computers, tablets, or smartphones.

The Microsoft Office 365 Business Plans can provide full support for employees to work from any location, whether they are in their traditional business office, commuting to and from work across the country, or working from a home office. Office 365 Business accommodates up to 300 users. Office 365 Enterprise Plan fits organizations ranging in size from a single employee to 50,000-plus users. Each employee can install Microsoft Office 365 on five different computers.

First Look at Office 365

Microsoft Office 365 subscription plans offer all the same applications that are available in the Microsoft Office Professional 2013 suite in addition to multiple communication and collaboration tools. With Office 365 you can retrieve, edit, and save Office documents on the Office 365 cloud, coauthor documents in real time with others, and quickly initiate computer-based calls, instant messages, and web conferences with others. Microsoft continues to update Office 365 to include new features, so over time expect greater differences between Office 2013 and Office 365.

Productivity Tools

Whether you are inserting audio and video into a Word document to create a high-impact business plan proposal or utilizing the visualization tools in Excel to chart the return on investment of a new mobile marketing program, Office 365 uses a quick-start installation technology, called **Click-to-Run**, that downloads and installs the basics within minutes, so that users are able to start working almost immediately. In effect, the Office 365 subscription provides access to the full Office applications wherever you are working. When you access your Office 365 account management panel, three choices are listed: 32- and 64-bit versions of Office 2013, and Office for Mac. Selecting the third option will initiate a download of an installer that must be run in the standard OS X fashion. When you install Office 365 on a Mac, the most current Mac version of Office is installed.

CONSIDER THIS

Unlike Google, which offers online documents, spreadsheets, and presentations called Google Docs, Microsoft Office 365 installs locally on your computer in addition to being available online.

Email and Calendars

In business, sharing information is essential to meeting the needs of your customers and staff. Office 365 offers shared access to business email, calendars, and contacts using **Exchange Online** from a computer, tablet, phone, and browser. The cloud-based Exchange Online enables business people to access Outlook information from anywhere at any time, while eliminating the cost of purchasing and maintaining servers to store data. If you need to meet with a colleague about a new project, you can compare calendars to view availability, confirm conference room availability, share project contacts, search email messages related to the project, and send email invitations to the project meeting. Exchange Online also allows you to search and access your company's address list.

Online Meetings

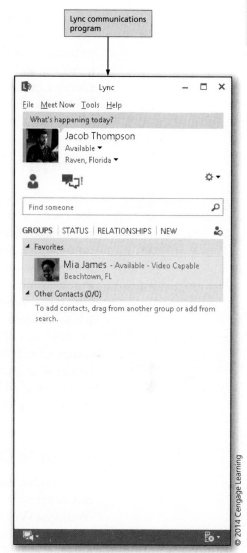

Lync communications program

When you are working with a team on a project that requires interaction, email and text communications can slow the communications process. Microsoft Lync connects you with others by facilitating real-time, interactive presentations and meetings over the Internet using both video and audio calling. As shown in Figure 3, you can conduct an online meeting with a team member or customer that includes an instant messaging conversation, audio, high-definition video, virtual whiteboards, and screen sharing. If the customer does not have an Office 365 subscription, they still can join the meeting through the invitation link, which runs the Lync Web App.

Skype is another tool in the Office 365 subscription, which enables users to place video calls to computers and smartphones and voice calls to landlines. Skype also supports instant message and file sharing to computers and mobile devices. While Skype may be adequate for simple communication, Lync provides for more robust, comprehensive communications. These robust features include high-definition (HD) videoconferencing capabilities, a whiteboard, and a larger audience. Using Lync, meeting attendees simultaneously can view up to five participants' videos, identify the active speaker, and associate names with faces. Lync supports up to 250 attendees per meeting. Unlike Skype, Lync meetings can be recorded for replaying at a later time. This enables businesses and schools to schedule meetings or organize online classes using Lync capabilities.

In addition to Lync, Microsoft Office 365 Business includes a business social networking tool named Yammer. With Yammer, employees create an online team workspace to discuss projects, deadlines, and share files. By sharing your profile and expertise, coworkers can easily find each other and post messages to keep all team members in the loop.

Figure 3

File Sharing

Office 365 includes a team site, which is a password-protected portal that supports sharing of large, difficult-to-email files and provides a single location for the latest versions of documents. In business, for example, colleagues working on common projects can save valuable time by being able to access instantly the latest master copy of each document. Security can be managed through different levels of user access so that users see only what they are supposed to see. Office 365 provides access to shared files using the cloud, making writing, editing, and sharing documents easier. If a construction company creates a commercial bid for a building project, the customers can be invited to view an Excel spreadsheet bid, construction timetable with a shared calendar, and an Access database of all the materials needed using the file sharing feature online.

Website Creation

Office 365 business plan subscriptions include a built-in hosted public website, where customers and clients can find an online storefront of a company. This public website, called the Website, can be customized to market a company by using various templates within the Office 365 cloud. The website creation tools include those for adding a theme, graphics, fonts, maps, directions, blogs, stock tickers, slide shows, PayPal, weather, and videos to interact with the website's visitors.

Synchronization

Office 365 subscription plans provide a central place to store and access your documents and business information. A feature of Office 365 ensures the original and backup computer files in two or more locations are identical through a process called **Active Directory Synchronization**. For example, if you open a PowerPoint presentation on your smartphone while you are riding a city bus and then add a new slide as you head to school, the PowerPoint presentation automatically is synced with Office 365. When you arrive on campus and open the PowerPoint presentation on a school computer, your new slide already is part of the finished slide show. By storing your files in Office 365, you can access your files on another computer if your home computer fails, with no loss of time or important information. When using your mobile phone's data plan, you do not need to search for a Wi-Fi hot spot to connect to the Office 365 cloud. Computer labs in schools can be configured to synchronize automatically all student files to Office 365 online.

Multiple Device Access to Office 365

With a single sign-in process, Office 365 provides access to multiple computers and mobile devices, including Android smartphones and tablets, Apple iPhones and iPads, and Windows phones. After you configure your devices' email settings, you can view your Microsoft account calendar, contacts, and email. Your personalized settings, preferences, and documents can be synchronized among all the different devices included in your Office 365 premium subscription. With the mobility of Office 365, students and employees can work anywhere, accessing information and responding to email requests immediately. If you lose your phone, Office 365 includes a feature that allows you to remotely wipe your phone clean of any data. By wiping your phone's data, you can prevent any unauthorized access to sensitive information, such as your banking information, passwords, and contacts, as well as discourage identity theft. Because your phone contacts and other information are stored on the Microsoft cloud, damaged or lost equipment is never a problem.

CONSIDER THIS

A thief can be quite resourceful if he or she steals your phone. Before you can alert your parents or spouse to the theft, they might receive a text from "you" asking for your ATM or credit card PIN number. Your parents or spouse might then reply with the PIN number. Your bank account could be emptied in minutes.

Teams Using Office 365 in Business

In the business world, rarely does an employee work in isolation. Companies need their employees to collaborate, whether they work in the same office or in locations around the world. Telecommuters working from home can communicate as if they were on-site by using a common team website and conferencing software. SharePoint Online and Lync Online provide seamless communication.

Small business subscription plans as low as $8.25 per user per month allow employees to create and store Word documents, Excel spreadsheets, and PowerPoint presentations online and communicate with one another via email, instant messaging, or video chat as they work on projects together. As shown in Figure 4, a team portal page is shown when you subscribe at https://portal.microsoftonline.com. Larger companies and those requiring more features can take advantage of the Office 365 business premium package, which, in addition to the features listed above, provides access to the Office 365 portal website and eliminates the effort and cost of the users maintaining their own costly computer servers.

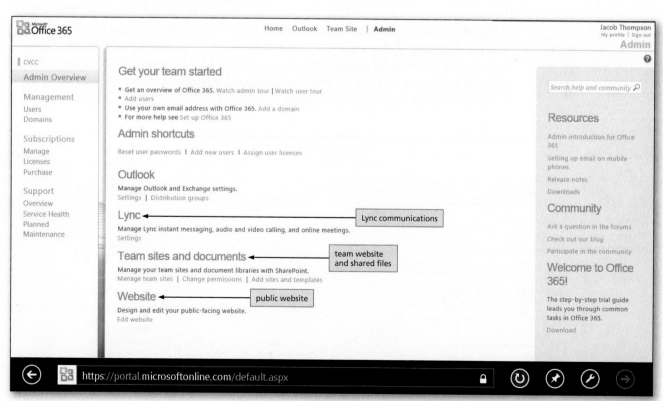

Figure 4

Email Communication Using Exchange

Office 365 includes Exchange Online, an email-based collaborative communications server for business. Exchange enables employees to be more productive by effectively managing email across multiple devices and facilitating teamwork.

Collaboration Using SharePoint

SharePoint Online, a part of Office 365 subscription plans, allows employees to collaborate with one another, share documents, post announcements, and track tasks, as shown in Table 2.

Table 2 Office 365 SharePoint Features	
Team Site Feature	**Description**
Calendar	Track important dates
Shared Document Library	Store related documents according to topic; picture, report, and slide libraries often are included
Task List	Track team tasks according to who is responsible for completion
Team Discussion Board	Discuss the topics at hand in an open forum
Contacts List	Share contact lists of employees, customers, contractors, and suppliers

© 2014 Cengage Learning

Office 365 provides the tools to plan meetings. Users can share calendars side by side, view availability, and suggest meeting times from shared calendars. Typically, a SharePoint team administrator or website owner establishes a folder structure to share and manage documents. The team website is fully searchable online, making locating and sharing data more efficient than using a local server. With a team website, everyone on the team has a central location to store and find all the information for a project, client, or department, as shown in Figure 5.

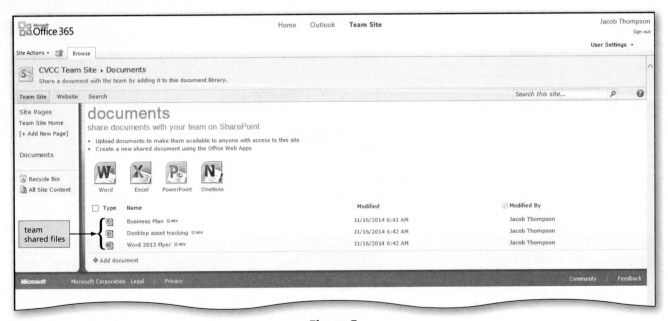

Figure 5

Website Design Using SharePoint

SharePoint provides templates to create a professional looking, public website for an online presence to market your business. As shown in Figure 6, a local pet sitting business is setting up a business website by customizing a SharePoint template. SharePoint Public Website includes features within the Design Manager that you use to customize and design your website by adding your own images, forms, style sheets, maps, themes, and social networking tools. When you finish customizing your business site, you can apply your own domain name to the site. A **domain** is a unique web address that identifies where your website can be found. Office 365 SharePoint hosts your website as part of your subscription. Your customers easily can find your business online and learn about your services.

BTW

Creating SharePoint Intranet Sites
A SharePoint website also can be customized to serve as an internal company website for private communications within the company.

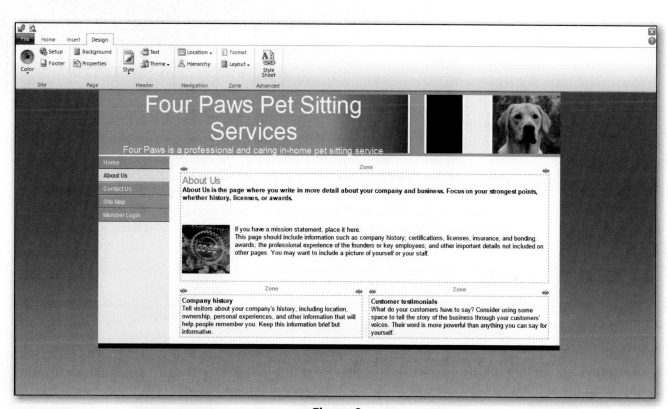

Figure 6

Real-Time Communications Using Lync

Lync Online is Microsoft's server platform for online team communications and comes bundled with Office 365 business subscriptions. As shown in Figure 7, Lync connects in real time to allow instant messaging, videoconferencing, and voice communications; it also integrates with email and Microsoft Office applications.

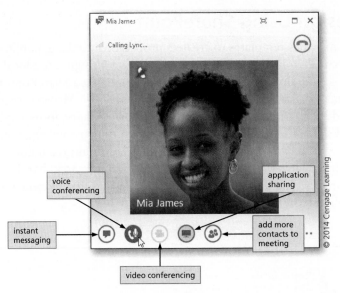

Figure 7

Lync allows you to connect with staff at remote locations using instant messaging capabilities, desktop sharing, videoconferencing, and shared agendas or documents. Lync is integrated into Office 365, which allows staff to start communicating from within the applications in which they currently are working. For example, while an employee is creating a PowerPoint presentation for a new product line, as shown in Figure 8, Lync enables him or her to collaborate with the entire team about the details of the product presentation. The team can view the presenter's screen displaying the PowerPoint presentation. The presenter can share control with any member of the team and can share his or her screen at any time during the Lync meeting.

Figure 8

Users can send a Lync meeting request to schedule a team meeting, or an impromptu conversation can be started immediately using the Meet Now feature. Participants receive a Lync meeting request link via an email message, and when they click the meeting request link, Lync automatically connects them to the online conference. If the participant does not have Lync installed, the Lync Web App automatically connects to the Lync meeting through the user's PC or Mac OS X browser. If a participant is away from his or her computer, he or she still can participate using the Lync Mobile apps for Windows Phone, iOS, and Android. As shown in Figure 9, Lync utilizes **instant messaging** (IM), allowing two or more people to share text messages. They can communicate in real time, similar to a voice conversation. In addition to a simple instant message, Lync provides a feature called **persistent chat**, which allows end-users to participate in a working session of instant messages that is persistent or sustained over a specified amount of time in a moderated chat room. Consider having an instant messaging session with a group of colleagues in different parts of your organization, regardless of geographic region, where you all are working on the same project. Over the course of the project, different people post questions and concerns, and others are able to respond to all those who have subscribed to your topic or been admitted to the chat room. Instead of a long trail of email messages, a team can keep information in a controlled environment with a full history of the discussion in one location.

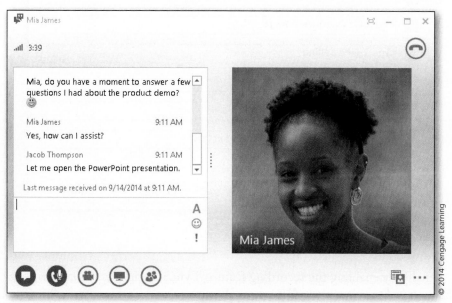

Figure 9

Lync also delivers support for full high-definition (HD) videoconferencing, so that a team can have a clear view of the participants, products, and demos. Before you join the video feed, you can preview your video feed to make sure your video camera is at the correct angle, your image is centered within the video frame, and that your room lighting provides for a clear image. The Lync preview option is important in creating a positive first impression over video. Your audio devices can be tested for clarity to make sure your headset, microphone, and speakers are functioning properly.

Lync provides a polling feature that presenters can use to ask the participants' opinions during a meeting (Figure 10). The poll question can consist of up to seven possible choices. The presenter has the option to view the results privately or share the results with the entire group.

Create a Poll

Poll name:

Office 365 Features

Question:

Which business feature is most useful feature in Office 365?

Choices:

Lync Online screen sharing

SharePoint Online sites

Microsoft OneDrive storage

Lync Online polling

Lync Online whiteboard

Lync Online video conferencing

Microsoft Exchange email unlimited access

Create   Cancel

Figure 10

Finally, by enabling the recording feature, Lync meetings and conversations can be captured for viewing at a later time. For instance, you can capture the audio, video, instant messaging (IM), screen sharing, Microsoft PowerPoint presentations, whiteboard, and polling portions of the Lync session and then play them back just as they transpired during the live Lync event. The meeting recordings can be made available to others so that they can view all or part of the Lync event. Instructors can record Lync online class sessions for students who were unable to attend the original presentation. The recording starts in Microsoft Lync; recordings then can be viewed within the Recording Manager feature.

Chapter Summary

In this chapter, you have learned how to subscribe to Office 365, which provides local and online access to Office applications, email, document sharing, web conferencing, and business websites. You also learned how a business can utilize Office 365 features on the cloud to facilitate teamwork. Finally, you learned about the features of SharePoint, Yammer, and Lync, which provide collaboration and communications for business teams using Office 365.

✸ Consider This: Your Turn

Apply your creative thinking and problem solving skills to design and implement a solution.

1: Comparing Office 365 Personal Plans

Personal

Part 1:   After graduation, you are considering if it would be a better value to subscribe to Office 365 Personal or Office 365 Home Premium. Write a one-page document comparing the pros and cons of the two subscription plans. Research the different subscriptions in detail at Office365.com. Submit your assignment in the format specified by your instructor.

Part 2: ✸ Which type of computer and/or devices would you use with your Office 365 subscription? If you are at a friend's home that does not have Office 365, how could you access your Office files if you do not have your computer or mobile device with you?

2: Upgrading a Local Business to Office 365

Professional

Part 1:   You are an employee at Impact Digital Marketing, a small marketing firm with 12 employees. The firm is setting up an Office 365 Business subscription next week, and you need to compose an email message with multiple paragraphs to explain the features of this new subscription plan to the members of your firm. Research the Office 365 Business subscription plan in detail at Office365.com, and compile your findings in an email message. Submit your assignment in the format specified by your instructor.

Part 2: ✸ Give three examples of how a marketing firm could use Lync. How could a marketing firm use the SharePoint Websites feature?

3: Conducting a Lync Meeting

Research and Collaboration

* Students need an Office 365 subscription to complete the following assignment.

Part 1:   Using your Office 365 subscription, conduct a meeting using Lync. Working with a partner, use your Office 365 subscription to research how to use Lync. Then, conduct a 15-minute Lync meeting, including instant messaging, to discuss the features of Lync. Use the concepts and techniques presented in this chapter to create the Lync meeting. Submit your assignment in the format specified by your instructor.

Part 2: ✸ When using Lync in an online class, when would the screen recording feature best be utilized?

1 Creating and Editing a Presentation with Pictures

Microsoft product screenshots used with permission from Microsoft Corporation.

Objectives

You will have mastered the material in this chapter when you can:

- Select and change a document theme and variant

- Create a title slide and a text slide with a multilevel bulleted list

- Add new slides and change slide layouts

- Insert photos and illustrations into slides with and without content placeholders

- Move and resize photos and illustrations

- Change font size and color

- Bold and italicize text

- Duplicate a slide

- Arrange slides

- Select slide transitions

- View a presentation in Slide Show view

- Print a presentation

1 | Creating and Editing a Presentation with Pictures

Introduction

A PowerPoint **presentation,** also called a **slide show,** can help you deliver a dynamic, professional-looking message to an audience. PowerPoint allows you to produce slides to use in an academic, business, or other environment. The collection of slides in a presentation is called a **deck,** resembling a deck of cards that are stacked on top of each other. A common use of slide decks is to enhance an oral presentation. A speaker might desire to convey information, such as urging students to volunteer at a fund-raising event, explaining changes in employee compensation packages, or describing a new laboratory procedure. The PowerPoint slides should reinforce the speaker's message and help the audience retain the information presented. Custom slides can fit your specific needs and contain diagrams, charts, tables, pictures, shapes, video, sound, and animation effects to make your presentation more effective. An accompanying handout gives audience members reference notes and review material for your presentation.

Project — Presentation with a Bulleted List, Photos, and an Illustration

In this chapter's project, you will follow proper design guidelines and learn to use PowerPoint to create, save, and print the slides shown in Figures 1–1a through 1–1e. The objective is to produce a presentation, titled Keeping Hydrated, to help athletes understand the need to drink water before, during, and after a workout. This slide show has a variety of pictures and visual elements to add interest and give facts about proper hydration. Some of the text has formatting and color enhancements. Transitions help one slide flow gracefully into the next during a slide show. In addition, you will print a handout of your slides to distribute to audience members.

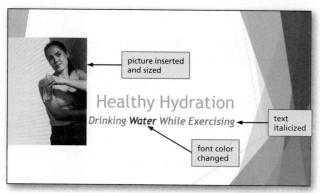

(a) Slide 1 (Title Slide with Photo)

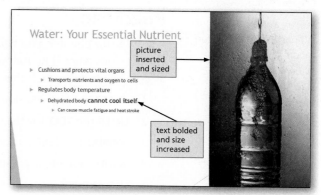

(b) Slide 2 (Multilevel Bulleted List with Photo)

(c) Slide 3 (Title and Illustration)

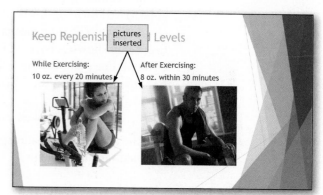

(d) Slide 4 (Comparison Layout and Photos)

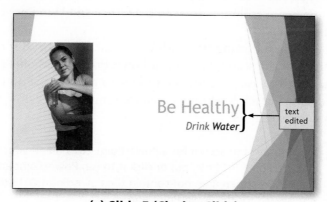

(e) Slide 5 (Closing Slide)

Figure 1–1

For an introduction to Windows and instruction about how to perform basic Windows tasks, read the Office and Windows chapter at the beginning of this book, where you can learn how to resize windows, change screen resolution, create folders, move and rename files, use Windows Help, and much more.

Roadmap

In this chapter, you will learn how to create the slides shown in Figure 1–1 on the previous page. The following roadmap identifies general activities you will perform as you progress through this chapter:

1. INSERT the four PRESENTATION SLIDES, using various layouts.
2. ENTER the TEXT for the slides.
3. FORMAT the TEXT on each slide.
4. INSERT GRAPHICAL ELEMENTS, including photos and an illustration.
5. SIZE AND POSITION the graphical elements.
6. ENHANCE the SLIDE SHOW by adding a closing slide and transition.
7. DISPLAY AND PRINT the SLIDES and a handout.

At the beginning of step instructions throughout the chapter, you will see an abbreviated form of this roadmap. The abbreviated roadmap uses colors to indicate chapter progress: gray means the chapter is beyond that activity; blue means the task being shown is covered in that activity, and black means that activity is yet to be covered. For example, the following abbreviated roadmap indicates the chapter would be showing a task in the 5 Size & Position activity.

1 INSERT PRESENTATION SLIDES | 2 ENTER TEXT | 3 FORMAT TEXT | 4 INSERT GRAPHICAL ELEMENTS
5 SIZE & POSITION | 6 ENHANCE SLIDE SHOW | 7 DISPLAY & PRINT SLIDES

Use the abbreviated roadmap as a progress guide while you read or step through the instructions in this chapter.

To Run PowerPoint

One of the few differences between Windows 7 and Windows 8 occurs in the steps to run PowerPoint. If you are using Windows 7, click the Start button, type **PowerPoint** in the 'Search programs and files' box, click PowerPoint 2013, and then, if necessary, maximize the PowerPoint window. For detailed steps to run PowerPoint in Windows 7, refer to the Office and Windows chapter at the beginning of this book. For a summary of the steps, refer to the Quick Reference located at the back of this book.

If you are using a computer to step through the project in this chapter and you want your screens to match the figures in this book, you should change your screen's resolution to 1366×768. For information about how to change a computer's resolution, refer to the Office and Windows chapter at the beginning of this book.

The following steps, which assume Windows 8 is running, use the Start screen or the search box to run PowerPoint based on a typical installation. You may need to ask your instructor how to run PowerPoint on your computer. For a detailed example of the procedure summarized below, refer to the Office and Windows chapter.

1 Scroll the Start screen for a PowerPoint 2013 tile. If your Start screen contains a PowerPoint 2013 tile, tap or click it to run PowerPoint and then proceed to Step 5; if the Start screen does not contain the PowerPoint 2013 tile, proceed to the next step to search for the PowerPoint app.

2 Swipe in from the right edge of the screen or point to the upper-right corner of the screen to display the Charms bar and then tap or click the Search charm on the Charms bar to display the Search menu.

3 Type **PowerPoint** as the search text in the Search box and watch the search results appear in the Apps list.

4 Tap or click PowerPoint 2013 in the search results to run PowerPoint.

5 If the PowerPoint window is not maximized, tap or click the Maximize button on its title bar to maximize the window.

Choosing a Document Theme and Variant

You easily can give the slides in a presentation a professional and integrated appearance by using a theme. A document **theme** is a specific design with coordinating colors, fonts, and special effects such as shadows and reflections. Several themes are available when you run PowerPoint, each with a specific name. Using one of the formatted themes makes creating a professional-looking presentation easier and quicker than using the Blank Presentation template, where you would need to make all design decisions.

Each theme has a set of four alternate designs, called **variants.** Each variant has the same overall composition, but the colors, fonts, and design elements differ. Once you select a theme, you then can select a variation that best fits your overall design needs. If you later decide that another theme or variant would better fit the presentation's general theme, you can change these elements while you are developing slides.

To Choose a Document Theme and Variant

1 INSERT PRESENTATION SLIDES | 2 ENTER TEXT | 3 FORMAT TEXT | 4 INSERT GRAPHICAL ELEMENTS
5 SIZE & POSITION | 6 ENHANCE SLIDE SHOW | 7 DISPLAY & PRINT SLIDES

When you begin creating a new PowerPoint presentation, you need to select a theme. You either can start with no design elements by using the Blank Presentation, or you select one of the available professionally designed themes. The following steps apply the Ion theme and then change the variant. *Why? The title slide will have text and a photo, so you want to select a theme, like Ion, with an uncluttered background. The presentation discusses the importance of drinking water while exercising, and blue is the color commonly associated with water in lakes and oceans. The default Ion theme is predominantly green and white, but one of its variants is blue and is an appropriate choice to relate to the water concept.*

- Press and hold or point to the Ion theme on the New screen (Figure 1–2).

Q&A | Why are my theme images, called thumbnails, displaying in a different order?
PowerPoint places the themes you have used recently in the first rows. You may need to scroll down to locate the Ion theme.

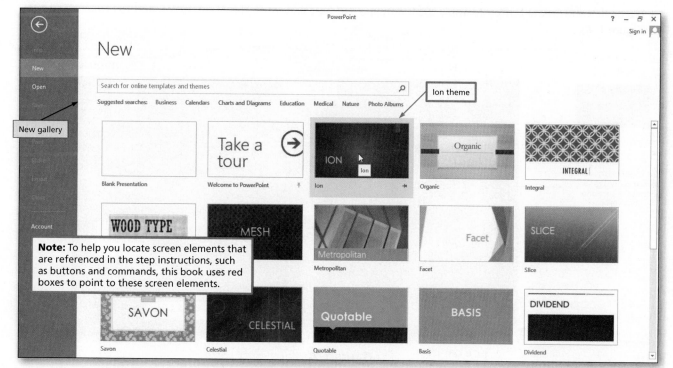

Figure 1–2

2

- Tap or click the Ion theme to display a theme preview dialog box with a thumbnail view of the theme and its variants (Figure 1–3).

Q&A Can I see previews of other themes?
Yes. Tap or click the right or left arrows on the sides of the theme preview dialog box.

Figure 1–3

3

- Tap or click the upper-right (blue) variant to view previews of that style applied to the thumbnail.

Q&A Can I see previews of the Ion theme and blue variant applied to layouts other than the title slide?
Yes. Tap or click the right or left arrows beside the words, More Images, below the thumbnail. Three other layouts will be displayed: Title and Content, Two Content, and Photo.

- Tap or click the Create button to apply the Ion theme and blue variant to the presentation and to display Slide 1 (Figure 1–4).

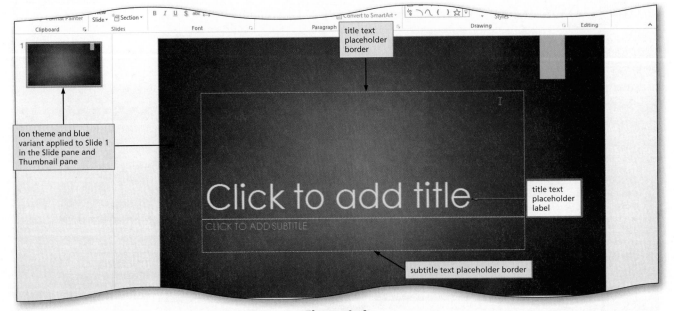

Figure 1–4

Creating a Title Slide

When you open a new presentation, the default **Title Slide** layout appears. The purpose of this layout is to introduce the presentation to the audience. PowerPoint includes other standard layouts for each of the themes. The slide layouts are set up in **landscape orientation**, where the slide width is greater than its height. In landscape orientation, the slide size is preset to 10 inches wide and 7.5 inches high when printed on a standard sheet of paper measuring 11 inches wide and 8.5 inches high.

    Placeholders are boxes with dotted or hatch-marked borders that are displayed when you create a new slide. Most layouts have both a title text placeholder and at least one content placeholder. Depending on the particular slide layout selected, title and subtitle placeholders are displayed for the slide title and subtitle; a content text placeholder is displayed for text, art, or a table, chart, picture, graphic, or movie. The title slide has two text placeholders where you can type the main heading, or title, of a new slide and the subtitle.

    With the exception of the Blank slide layout, PowerPoint assumes every new slide has a title. To make creating a presentation easier, any text you type after a new slide appears becomes title text in the title text placeholder. The following steps create the title slide for this presentation.

Choose the words for the slide.

All presentations should follow the 7 × 7 rule, which states that each slide should have a maximum of seven lines, and each line should have a maximum of seven words. PowerPoint designers must choose their words carefully and, in turn, help viewers read the slides easily.

Avoid line wraps. Your audience's eyes want to stop at the end of a line. Thus, you must plan your words carefully or adjust the font size so that each point displays on only one line.

To Enter the Presentation Title

1 INSERT PRESENTATION SLIDES | 2 ENTER TEXT | 3 FORMAT TEXT | 4 INSERT GRAPHICAL ELEMENTS
5 SIZE & POSITION | 6 ENHANCE SLIDE SHOW | 7 DISPLAY & PRINT SLIDES

    The presentation title for Project 1 is Healthy Hydration. *Why? The presentation discusses the importance of drinking water while exercising, and blue is the color associated with water.* The following step creates the slide show's title.

1
- Tap or click the label, 'Tap to add title', or, 'Click to add title', located inside the title text placeholder to select the placeholder (Figure 1–5).

Figure 1–5

● Type **Healthy Hydration** in the title text placeholder. Do not press the ENTER key (Figure 1–6).

Figure 1–6

Correcting a Mistake When Typing

If you type the wrong letter, press the BACKSPACE key to erase all the characters back to and including the one that is incorrect. If you mistakenly press the ENTER key after typing the title and the insertion point is on the new line, simply press the BACKSPACE key to return the insertion point to the right of the letter in the word, Water.

When you install PowerPoint, the default setting allows you to reverse up to the last 20 changes by tapping or clicking the Undo button on the Quick Access Toolbar. The ScreenTip that appears when you point to the Undo button changes to indicate the type of change just made. For example, if you type text in the title text placeholder and then point to the Undo button, the ScreenTip that appears is Undo Typing. For clarity, when referencing the Undo button in this project, the name displaying in the ScreenTip is referenced. You can reapply a change that you reversed with the Undo button by tapping or clicking the Redo button on the Quick Access Toolbar. Tapping or clicking the Redo button reverses the last undo action. The ScreenTip name reflects the type of reversal last performed.

Paragraphs

Text in the subtitle text placeholder supports the title text. It can appear on one or more lines in the placeholder. To create more than one subtitle line, you press the ENTER key after typing some words. PowerPoint creates a new line, which is the second paragraph in the placeholder. A **paragraph** is a segment of text with the same format that begins when you press the ENTER key and ends when you press the ENTER key again. This new paragraph is the same level as the previous paragraph. A **level** is a position within a structure, such as an outline, that indicates the magnitude of importance. PowerPoint allows for five paragraph levels.

How do you use the touch keyboard with a touch screen?

To display the on-screen touch keyboard, tap the Touch Keyboard button on the Windows taskbar. When finished using the touch keyboard, tap the X button on the touch keyboard to close the keyboard.

To Enter the Presentation Subtitle Paragraph

1 INSERT PRESENTATION SLIDES | 2 ENTER TEXT | 3 FORMAT TEXT | 4 INSERT GRAPHICAL ELEMENTS
5 SIZE & POSITION | 6 ENHANCE SLIDE SHOW | 7 DISPLAY & PRINT SLIDES

The first subtitle paragraph links to the title. *Why? The subtitle gives additional detail that the presentation will focus on water consumption while exercising.* The following steps enter the presentation subtitle.

- Tap or click the label, 'Tap to add subtitle', or, 'Click to add subtitle', located inside the subtitle text placeholder to select the placeholder (Figure 1–7).

Figure 1–7

- Type `Drinking Water While Exercising` but do not press the ENTER key (Figure 1–8).

Q&A
Why does the text display with capital letters despite the fact I am typing uppercase and lowercase letters? The Ion theme uses the All Caps effect for the subtitle text. This effect converts lowercase letters to uppercase letters.

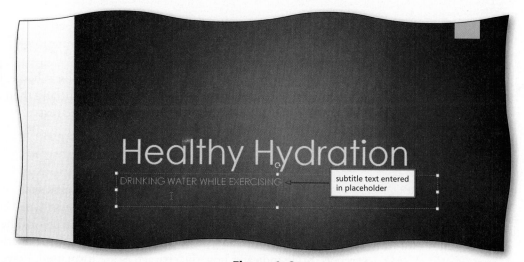

Figure 1–8

To Zoom a Slide

You will be modifying the text and other slide components as you create the presentation, so you can enlarge the slide on the screen. *Why? Zooming the slide can help you see slide elements more clearly so that you can position them precisely where desired.* The following step changes the zoom to 80 percent.

1

 Experiment

- Repeatedly tap or click the Zoom In and Zoom Out buttons on the status bar and watch the size of the slide change in the Slide pane.

- Tap or click the Zoom In or Zoom Out button as many times as necessary until the Zoom button on the status bar displays 80% on its face (Figure 1–9).

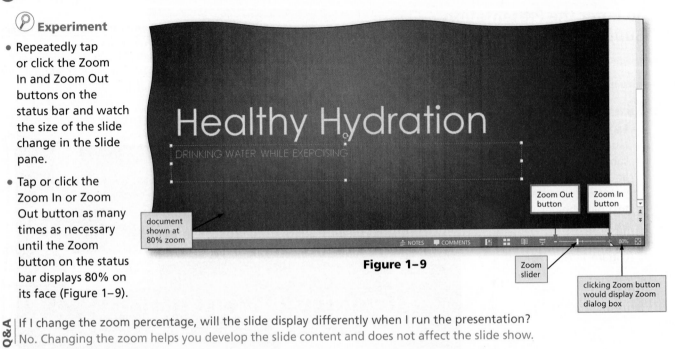

Figure 1–9

Q&A | If I change the zoom percentage, will the slide display differently when I run the presentation?
No. Changing the zoom helps you develop the slide content and does not affect the slide show.

Other Ways

1. Drag Zoom slider on status bar	2. Tap or click Zoom level button on status bar, select desired zoom percent or type (Zoom dialog box), tap or click OK button	3. Tap or click Zoom button (VIEW tab | Zoom group), select desired zoom percent or type (Zoom dialog box), tap or click OK button	4. For touch screens: Pinch two fingers together in Slide pane (zoom out) or stretch two fingers apart (zoom in)

Formatting Characters in a Presentation

BTW

BTWs
For a complete list of the BTWs found in the margins of this book, visit the BTW resource on the Student Companion Site located on www.cengagebrain.com. For detailed instructions about accessing available resources, visit www.cengage.com/ct/studentdownload or see the inside back cover of this book.

Recall that each document theme determines the color scheme, font set, and layout of a presentation. You can use a specific document theme and then change the characters' formats any time before, during, or after you type the text.

Fonts and Font Styles

Characters that appear on the screen are a specific shape and size. Examples of how you can modify the appearance, or **format**, of these typed characters on the screen and in print include changing the font, style, size, and color. The **font**, or typeface, defines the appearance and shape of the letters, numbers, punctuation marks, and symbols. **Style** indicates how the characters are formatted. PowerPoint's text font styles include regular, italic, bold, and bold italic. **Size** specifies the height of the characters and is gauged by a measurement system that uses points. A **point** is 1/72 of an inch in height. Thus, a character with a font size of 36 is 36/72 (or 1/2) of an inch in height. **Color** defines the hue of the characters.

This presentation uses the Ion document theme, which has particular font styles and font sizes. The Ion document theme default title text font is named Century Gothic. It has no special effects, and its size is 54 point. The Ion default subtitle text font also is Century Gothic with a font size of 18 point.

To Select a Paragraph

You can use many techniques to format characters. When you want to apply the same formats to multiple words or paragraphs, it is helpful to select these words. *Why? It is efficient to select the desired text and then make the desired changes to all the characters simultaneously.* The first formatting change you will make will apply to the title slide subtitle. The following step selects this paragraph.

- If you are using a touch screen, tap to position the insertion point in the text to select, and then drag the selection handles as necessary to select the entire paragraph; if you are using a mouse, triple-click the paragraph, Drinking Water While Exercising, in the subtitle text placeholder to select the paragraph (Figure 1–10).

Figure 1–10

Q&A | What is the selection handle?
When working on a touch screen, a **selection handle** (small circle) appears below the insertion point. Using a fingertip, you drag the selection handle to select text.

Other Ways

1. Position pointer to left of first paragraph and drag to end of line

To Italicize Text

Different font styles often are used on slides. *Why? These style changes make the words more appealing to the reader and emphasize particular text.* **Italicized** text has a slanted appearance. Used sparingly, it draws the readers' eyes to these characters. The following step adds emphasis to the line of the subtitle text by changing regular text to italic text.

- With the subtitle text still selected, tap or click the Italic button on the mini toolbar to italicize that text on the slide (Figure 1–11).

Q&A | If I change my mind and decide not to italicize the text, how can I remove this style?
Tap or click the Italic button a second time, immediately tap or click the Undo button on the Quick Access Toolbar, or press CTRL+Z.

Figure 1–11

Other Ways

1. Tap 'Show Context Menu' button on mini toolbar or right-click selected text, tap or click Font on shortcut menu, tap or click Font tab (Font dialog box), tap or click Italic in Font style list, tap or click OK button
2. Select text, tap or click Italic button (HOME tab | Font group)
3. Tap or click Font dialog box launcher (HOME tab | Font group), tap or click Font tab (Font dialog box), tap or click Italic in Font style list, tap or click OK button
4. Select text, press CTRL+I

To Increase Font Size

Why? *To add emphasis, you increase the font size for the subtitle text.* The Increase Font Size button on the mini toolbar increases the font size in preset increments. The following step uses this button to increase the font size.

- Tap or click the 'Increase Font Size' button on the mini toolbar three times to increase the font size of the selected text from 20 to 32 point (Figure 1–12).

Figure 1–12

Other Ways

1. Tap or click Font Size arrow on mini toolbar, tap or click desired font size in Font Size gallery

2. Tap or click Increase Font Size button (HOME tab | Font group)

3. Tap or click Font Size arrow (HOME tab | Font group), tap or click desired font size in Font size gallery

4. Press CTRL+SHIFT+>

To Select a Word

PowerPoint designers use many techniques to emphasize words and characters on a slide. To accentuate the word, Water, on your slide, you want to increase the font size and change the font color to dark blue for the word, WATER, in the subtitle text. To make these changes, you should begin by selecting the word, WATER. *Why? You could perform these actions separately, but it is more efficient to select the word and then change the font attributes.* The following steps select a word.

- Position the pointer somewhere in the word to be selected (in this case, in the word, WATER) (Figure 1–13).

Figure 1–13

- Double-tap or double-click the word to select it (Figure 1–14).

entire word is selected

Figure 1–14

Other Ways

1. Position pointer before first character, press CTRL+SHIFT+RIGHT ARROW

To Change the Text Color

1 INSERT PRESENTATION SLIDES │ 2 ENTER TEXT │ 3 FORMAT TEXT │ 4 INSERT GRAPHICAL ELEMENTS
5 SIZE & POSITION │ 6 ENHANCE SLIDE SHOW │ 7 DISPLAY & PRINT SLIDES

PowerPoint allows you to use one or more text colors in a presentation. You decide to change the color of the word you selected, WATER. *Why? The color, blue, is associated with water, and you want to add more emphasis, subtly, to that word in your subtitle slide text.* The following steps add emphasis to this word by changing the font color from green to blue.

- With the word, WATER, selected, tap or click the Font Color arrow on the mini toolbar to display the Font Color gallery, which includes Theme Colors and Standard Colors (Figure 1–15).

Q&A
If the mini toolbar disappears from the screen, how can I display it once again?
Press and hold or right-click the text, and the mini toolbar should appear.

Experiment

- If you are using a mouse, point to various colors in the gallery and watch the word's font color change.

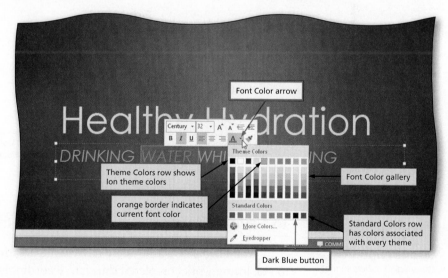

Font Color arrow

Theme Colors row shows Ion theme colors

orange border indicates current font color

Font Color gallery

Standard Colors row has colors associated with every theme

Dark Blue button

Figure 1–15

2

• Tap or click Dark Blue in the Standard Colors row on the mini toolbar (second color from right) to change the font color to Dark Blue (Figure 1–16).

◀ Q&A

Why did I select the color Dark Blue?
Dark Blue is one of the 10 standard colors associated with every document theme, and it is a universal color representing the natural resource of water. The color will emphasize the fact that the presentation focuses on water.

What is the difference between the colors shown in the Theme Colors area and the Standard Colors?
The 10 colors in the top row of the Theme Colors area are two text, two background, and six accent colors in the Ion theme; the five colors in each column under the top row display different transparencies. The Standard Colors are available in every document theme.

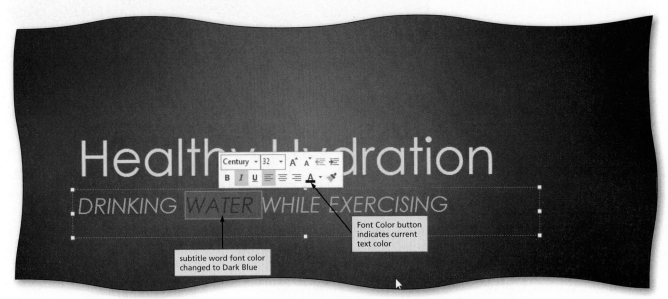

Figure 1–16

3

• Tap or click outside the selected area to deselect the word.

Other Ways	
1. Tap 'Show Context Menu' button on mini toolbar or right-click selected text, tap or click Font on shortcut menu, tap or click Font Color button, tap or click Dark Blue in Standard Colors row	2. Tap or click Font Color arrow (HOME tab | Font group), tap or click Dark Blue in Standard Colors row

BTW
Organizing Files and Folders
You should organize and store files in folders so that you easily can find the files later. For example, if you are taking an introductory computer class called CIS 101, a good practice would be to save all PowerPoint files in a PowerPoint folder in a CIS 101 folder. For a discussion of folders and detailed examples of creating folders, refer to the Office and Windows chapter at the beginning of this book.

To Save a Presentation with a New File Name

You have performed many tasks while creating this presentation and do not want to risk losing work completed thus far. Accordingly, you should save the presentation on your hard disk, SkyDrive, or a location that is most appropriate to your situation.

The following steps assume you already have created folders for storing your files, for example, a CIS 101 folder (for your class) that contains a PowerPoint folder (for your assignments). Thus, these steps save the presentation in the PowerPoint folder in the CIS 101 folder on your desired save location. For a detailed example of the procedure for saving a file in a folder or saving a file on SkyDrive, refer to the Office and Windows chapter at the beginning of this book.

1 Tap or click the Save button on the Quick Access Toolbar, which depending on settings, will display either the Save As gallery in the Backstage view or the Save As dialog box.

2 To save on a hard disk or other storage media on your computer, proceed to Step 2a. To save on SkyDrive, proceed to Step 2b.

2a If your screen opens the Backstage view and you want to save on storage media on your computer, tap or click Computer in the left pane, if necessary, to display options in the right pane related to saving on your computer. If your screen already displays the Save As dialog box, proceed to Step 3.

2b If your screen opens the Backstage view and you want to save on SkyDrive, tap or click SkyDrive in the left pane to display SkyDrive saving options or a Sign In button. If your screen displays a Sign In button, tap or click it and then sign in to SkyDrive.

3 Tap or click the Browse button in the right pane to display the Save As dialog box associated with the selected save location (i.e., Computer or SkyDrive).

4 Type **Keeping Hydrated** in the File name box to change the file name. Do not press the ENTER key after typing the file name because you do not want to close the dialog box at this time.

5 Navigate to the desired save location (in this case, the PowerPoint folder in the CIS 101 folder [or your class folder] on your computer or SkyDrive).

6 Tap or click the Save button (Save As dialog box) to save the presentation in the selected folder on the selected save location with the entered file name.

BTW

The Ribbon and Screen Resolution
PowerPoint may change how the groups and buttons within the groups appear on the ribbon, depending on the computer's screen resolution. Thus, your ribbon may look different from the ones in this book if you are using a screen resolution other than 1366 × 768.

Adding a New Slide to a Presentation

With the text for the title slide for the presentation created, the next step is to add the first text slide immediately after the title slide. Usually, when you create a presentation, you add slides with text, pictures, graphics, or charts. Some placeholders allow you to double-tap or double-click the placeholder and then access other objects, such as videos, charts, diagrams, and organization charts. You can change the layout for a slide at any time during the creation of a presentation.

To Add a New Text Slide with a Bulleted List

1 INSERT PRESENTATION SLIDES | 2 ENTER TEXT | 3 FORMAT TEXT | 4 INSERT GRAPHICAL ELEMENTS
5 SIZE & POSITION | 6 ENHANCE SLIDE SHOW | 7 DISPLAY & PRINT SLIDES

When you add a new slide, PowerPoint uses the Title and Content slide layout. This layout provides a title placeholder and a content area for text, art, charts, and other graphics. A vertical scroll bar appears in the Slide pane when you add the second slide. *Why? The scroll bar allows you to move from slide to slide easily.* A small image of this slide also appears in the Thumbnail pane. The step on the next page adds a new slide with the Title and Content slide layout.

1

- Tap or click the New Slide button (HOME tab | Slides group) to insert a new slide with the Title and Content layout (Figure 1–17).

Q&A Why does the bullet character display a green triangle?
The Ion document theme determines the bullet characters. Each paragraph level has an associated bullet character.

I clicked the New Slide arrow instead of the New Slide button. What should I do?
Tap or click the Title and Content slide thumbnail in the Ion layout gallery.

How do I know which slide number I am viewing?
The left edge of the status bar shows the current slide number followed by the total number of slides in the document. In addition, the slide number is displayed to the left of the slide thumbnail.

What are those six icons grouped in the middle of the Slide pane?
You can tap or click one of the icons to insert a specific type of content: table, chart, SmartArt graphic, pictures, online pictures, or video.

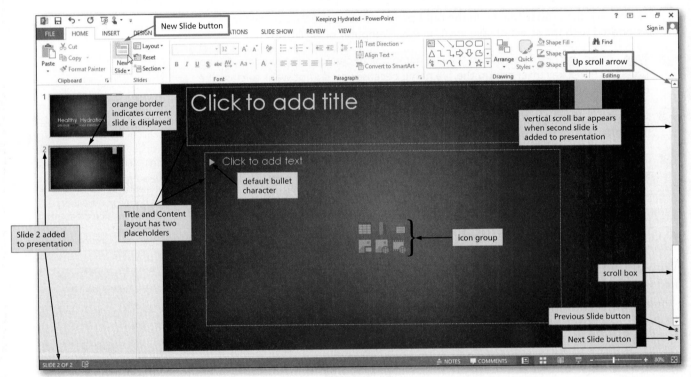

Figure 1–17

Other Ways

1. Press CTRL+M

Creating a Text Slide with a Multilevel Bulleted List

The information in the Slide 2 text placeholder is presented in a bulleted list with three levels. A **bulleted list** is a list of paragraphs, each of which may be preceded by a bullet character, such as a dot, arrow, or checkmark. Some themes, such as the Ion theme, do not display a bullet character at the start of a paragraph by default. A slide that consists of more than one level of bulleted text is called a **multilevel bulleted list slide**. In a multilevel bulleted list, a lower-level paragraph is a subset of a higher-level paragraph. It usually contains information that supports the topic in the paragraph immediately above it.

As you can see in Figure 1–1b on page PPT 3, two of the Slide 2 paragraphs appear at the same level, called the first level: Cushions and protects vital organs, and Regulates body temperature. Beginning with the second level, each paragraph indents to the right of the preceding level and is pushed down to a lower level. For example, if you increase the indent of a first-level paragraph, it becomes a second-level paragraph. The second, fourth, and fifth paragraphs on Slide 2 are second-level paragraphs. The last paragraph, Can cause muscle fatigue and heat stroke, is a third-level paragraph.

Creating a text slide with a multilevel bulleted list requires several steps. Initially, you enter a slide title in the title text placeholder. Next, you select the content text placeholder. Then, you type the text for the multilevel bulleted list, increasing and decreasing the indents as needed. The next several sections add a slide with a multilevel bulleted list.

BTW

Touch Screen Differences
The Office and Windows interfaces may vary if you are using a touch screen. For this reason, you might notice that the function or appearance of your touch screen differs slightly from this chapter's presentation.

To Enter a Slide Title

1 INSERT PRESENTATION SLIDES | **2 ENTER TEXT** | 3 FORMAT TEXT | **4 INSERT GRAPHICAL ELEMENTS**
5 SIZE & POSITION | 6 ENHANCE SLIDE SHOW | 7 DISPLAY & PRINT SLIDES

PowerPoint assumes every new slide has a title. *Why? The audience members read the title and then can begin to focus their attention on the information being presented on that slide.* The title for Slide 2 is Water: Your Essential Nutrient. The following step enters this title.

1
• Tap or click the label, 'Tap to add title', or, 'Click to add title', to select it and then type `Water: Your Essential Nutrient` in the title text placeholder. Do not press the ENTER key (Figure 1–18).

Figure 1–18

To Select a Text Placeholder

1 INSERT PRESENTATION SLIDES | 2 ENTER TEXT | 3 FORMAT TEXT | 4 INSERT GRAPHICAL ELEMENTS
5 SIZE & POSITION | 6 ENHANCE SLIDE SHOW | 7 DISPLAY & PRINT SLIDES

Why? Before you can type text into a content placeholder, you first must select it. The following step selects the text placeholder on Slide 2.

• Tap or click the label, 'Tap to add text', or 'Click to add text', to select the content placeholder (Figure 1–19).

Q&A Why does my pointer have a different shape?
If you move the pointer away from the bullet, it will change shape.

Figure 1–19

Other Ways

1. Press CTRL+ENTER

To Type a Multilevel Bulleted List

1 INSERT PRESENTATION SLIDES | 2 ENTER TEXT | 3 FORMAT TEXT | 4 INSERT GRAPHICAL ELEMENTS
5 SIZE & POSITION | 6 ENHANCE SLIDE SHOW | 7 DISPLAY & PRINT SLIDES

The content placeholder provides an area for the text characters. When you tap or click inside a placeholder, you then can type or paste text. As discussed previously, a bulleted list is a list of paragraphs, each of which is preceded by a bullet. A paragraph is a segment of text ended by pressing the ENTER key. The theme determines the bullets for each level. *Why? The bullet variations are determined by the specific paragraph levels, and they generally vary in size, shape, and color.*

The content text placeholder is selected, so the next step is to type the multilevel bulleted list that consists of six paragraphs, as shown in Figure 1–1b on page PPT 3. Creating a lower-level paragraph is called **demoting** text; creating a higher-level paragraph is called **promoting** text. The following steps create a multilevel bulleted list consisting of three levels.

• Type Cushions and protects vital organs and then press the ENTER key (Figure 1–20).

Figure 1–20

2

- Tap or click the 'Increase List Level' button (HOME tab | Paragraph group) to indent the second paragraph below the first and create a second-level paragraph (Figure 1–21).

Q&A Why does the bullet for this paragraph have a different size? A different bullet is assigned to each paragraph level.

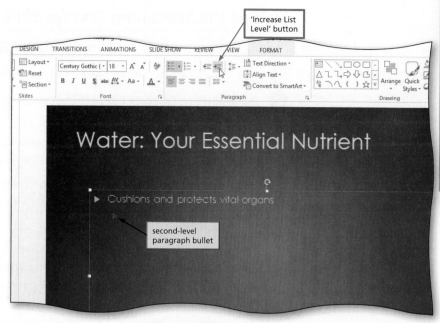

Figure 1–21

3

- Type **Transports nutrients and oxygen to cells** and then press the ENTER key (Figure 1–22).

Figure 1–22

4

- Tap or click the 'Decrease List Level' button (HOME tab | Paragraph group) so that the second-level paragraph becomes a first-level paragraph (Figure 1–23).

Q&A Can I delete bullets on a slide? Yes. If you do not want bullets to display in a particular paragraph, tap or click the Bullets button (HOME tab | Paragraph group) or press and hold or right-click the paragraph and then tap or click the Bullets button on the shortcut menu.

Figure 1–23

Other Ways

1. Press TAB to promote paragraph; press SHIFT+TAB to demote paragraph

To Type the Remaining Text for Slide 2

The following steps complete the text for Slide 2.

1 Type `Regulates body temperature` and then press the ENTER key.

2 Tap or click the 'Increase List Level' button (HOME tab | Paragraph group) to demote the paragraph to the second level.

3 Type `Dehydrated body cannot cool itself` and then press the ENTER key to add a new paragraph at the same level as the previous paragraph.

4 Tap or click the 'Increase List Level' button (HOME tab | Paragraph group) to demote the paragraph to the third level.

5 Type `Can cause muscle fatigue and heat stroke` but do not press the ENTER key (Figure 1–24).

Q&A I pressed the ENTER key in error, and now a new bullet appears after the last entry on this slide. How can I remove this extra bullet?

Press the BACKSPACE key twice.

remaining text for slide

Figure 1–24

To Select a Group of Words

1 INSERT PRESENTATION SLIDES | 2 ENTER TEXT | 3 FORMAT TEXT | 4 INSERT GRAPHICAL ELEMENTS
5 SIZE & POSITION | 6 ENHANCE SLIDE SHOW | 7 DISPLAY & PRINT SLIDES

PowerPoint designers use many techniques to emphasize words and characters on a slide. To highlight your slide show's concept of the dangers of not drinking water while exercising, you want to bold and increase the font size of the words, cannot cool itself, in the body text. The following steps select three words. *Why? You could perform these actions separately, but it is more efficient to select the words and then change the font attributes.*

1

- Position the pointer immediately to the left of the first character of the text to be selected (in this case, the c in the word, cannot) (Figure 1–25).

pointer

words to select

Figure 1–25

- Drag the pointer through the last character of the text to be selected (in this case, the f in the word, itself) (Figure 1–26).

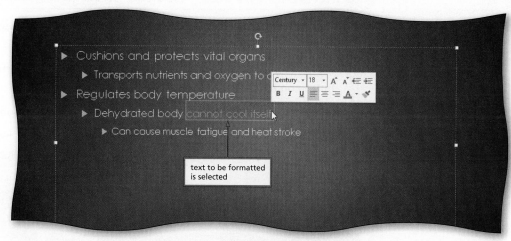

Figure 1–26

Other Ways

1. Press CTRL+SHIFT+RIGHT ARROW repeatedly until desired words are selected

To Bold Text

1 INSERT PRESENTATION SLIDES | 2 ENTER TEXT | 3 FORMAT TEXT | 4 INSERT GRAPHICAL ELEMENTS

5 SIZE & POSITION | 6 ENHANCE SLIDE SHOW | 7 DISPLAY & PRINT SLIDES

Why? *Bold characters display somewhat thicker and darker than those that display in a regular font style.* Tapping or clicking the Bold button on the mini toolbar is an efficient method of bolding text. To add more emphasis to the fact that the body needs water for cooling purposes, you want to bold the words, cannot cool itself. The following step bolds this text.

- With the words, cannot cool itself, selected, tap or click the Bold button on the mini toolbar to bold the three words (Figure 1–27).

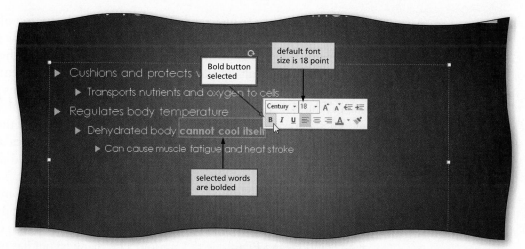

Figure 1–27

Other Ways

1. Tap 'Show Context Menu' button on mini toolbar or right-click selected text, tap or click Font on shortcut menu, tap or click Font tab (Font dialog box), tap or click Bold in Font style list, tap or click OK button

2. Select text, tap or click Bold button (HOME tab | Font group)

3. Tap or click Font dialog box launcher (HOME tab | Font group), tap or click Font tab (Font dialog box), tap or click Bold in Font style list, tap or click OK button

4. Select text, press CTRL+B

To Increase Font Size

Why? To add emphasis, you increase the font size for the words, cannot cool itself. The following steps increase the font size from 18 to 20 point.

1 With the words, cannot cool itself, still selected, tap or click the 'Increase Font Size' button on the mini toolbar once (Figure 1–28).

2 Tap or click outside the selected area to deselect the three words.

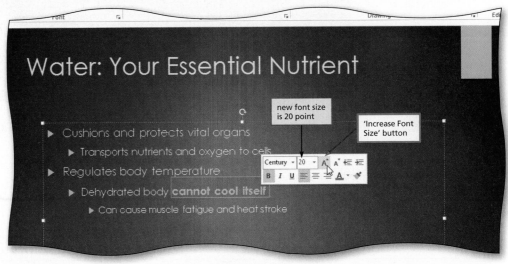

Figure 1–28

Adding New Slides, Changing Slide Layouts, and Changing the Theme

Slide 3 in Figure 1–1c on page PPT 3 contains an illustration of a character drinking water and does not contain a bulleted list. When you add a new slide, PowerPoint applies the Title and Content layout. This layout, along with the Title Slide layout for Slide 1, are the default styles. A **layout** specifies the arrangement of placeholders on a slide. These placeholders are arranged in various configurations and can contain text, such as the slide title or a bulleted list, or they can contain content, such as SmartArt graphics, photos, charts, tables, and shapes. The placement of the text, in relationship to content, depends on the slide layout. You can specify a particular slide layout when you add a new slide to a presentation or after you have created the slide.

Using the **layout gallery**, you can choose a slide layout. The nine layouts in this gallery have a variety of placeholders to define text and content positioning and formatting. Three layouts are for text: Title Slide, Section Header, and Title Only. Five are for text and content: Title and Content, Two Content, Comparison, Content with Caption, and Picture with Caption. The Blank layout has no placeholders. If none of these standard layouts meets your design needs, you can create a **custom layout**. A custom layout specifies the number, size, and location of placeholders, background content, and optional slide and placeholder-level properties.

When you change the layout of a slide, PowerPoint retains the text and objects and repositions them into the appropriate placeholders. Using slide layouts eliminates the need to resize objects and the font size because PowerPoint automatically sizes the objects and text to fit the placeholders. At any time when creating the slide content, you can change the theme and variant to give the presentation a different look and feel.

To Add a Slide with the Title Only Layout

1 INSERT PRESENTATION SLIDES | 2 ENTER TEXT | 3 FORMAT TEXT | 4 INSERT GRAPHICAL ELEMENTS
5 SIZE & POSITION | 6 ENHANCE SLIDE SHOW | 7 DISPLAY & PRINT SLIDES

The following steps add Slide 3 to the presentation with the Title Only slide layout style. *Why? The only text on the slide is the title, and the majority of the slide content is the illustration.*

1
- If necessary, tap or click HOME on the ribbon to display the HOME tab.

- Tap or click the New Slide arrow (HOME tab | Slides group) to display the Ion layout gallery (Figure 1–29).

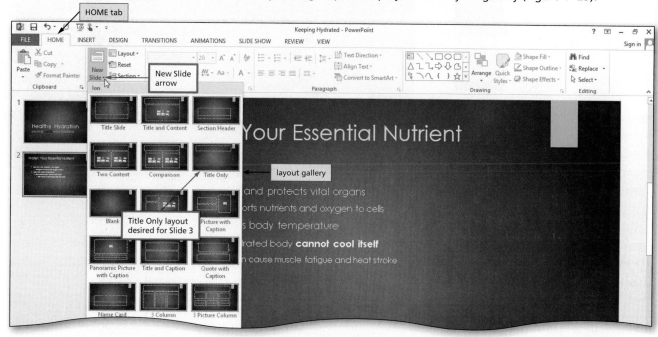

Figure 1–29

2
- Tap or click Title Only to add a new slide and apply that layout to Slide 3.

- If necessary, swipe up or click the Up scroll arrow several times until the title text placeholder is visible (Figure 1–30).

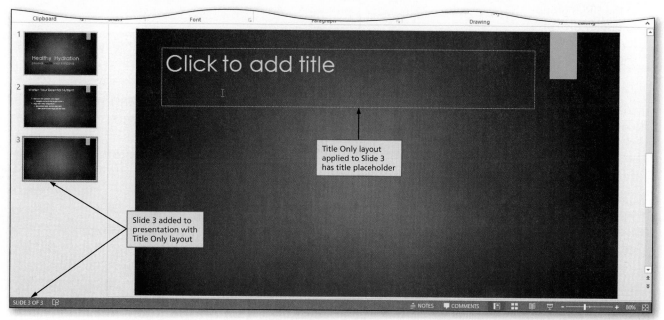

Figure 1–30

To Enter a Slide Title

The only text on Slide 3 is the title. The following step enters the title text for this slide.

1 Type `Begin Workout with Plenty of Water` as the title text but do not press the ENTER key (Figure 1–31).

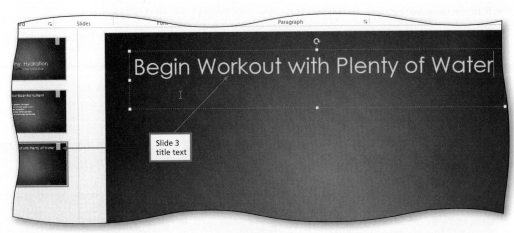

Figure 1–31

To Add a New Slide and Enter a Slide Title and Headings

1 INSERT PRESENTATION SLIDES | 2 ENTER TEXT | 3 FORMAT TEXT | 4 INSERT GRAPHICAL ELEMENTS
5 SIZE & POSITION | 6 ENHANCE SLIDE SHOW | 7 DISPLAY & PRINT SLIDES

The text on Slide 4 in Figure 1–1d on page PPT 3 consists of a title and two headings. The appropriate layout for this slide is named Comparison. **Why?** *The Comparison layout has two headings and two text placeholders adjacent to each other, so an audience member easily can compare and contrast the items shown side by side.* The following steps add Slide 4 to the presentation with the Comparison layout and then enter the title and heading text for this slide.

- Tap or click the New Slide arrow in the Slides group to display the Ion layout gallery (Figure 1–32).

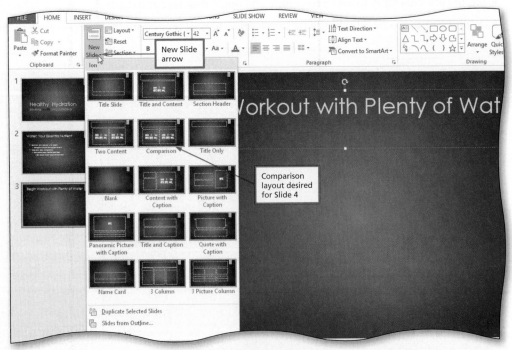

Figure 1–32

2

- Tap or click Comparison to add Slide 4 and apply that layout (Figure 1–33).

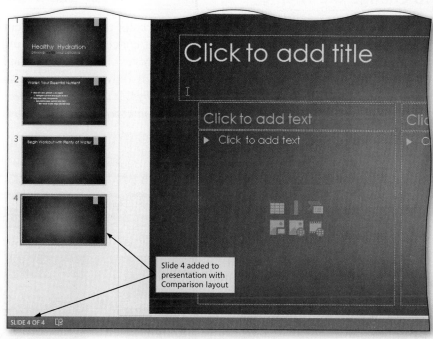

Figure 1–33

3

- Type **Keep Replenishing Fluid Levels** in the title text placeholder.

- Tap or click the left heading placeholder with the label, 'Tap to add text', or 'Click to add text', to select this placeholder (Figure 1–34).

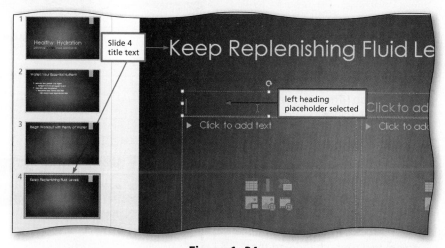

Figure 1–34

4

- Type **While Exercising:** and then press the ENTER key.

- Type **10 oz. every 20 minutes** but do not press the ENTER key.

- Select the right heading placeholder and then type **After Exercising:** and press the ENTER key.

- Type **8 oz. within 30 minutes** but do not press the ENTER key (Figure 1–35).

Figure 1–35

Q&A What is the white box with the arrow between the placeholders?

The text is too large to fit in the placeholder using the default font and paragraph attributes, so PowerPoint adjusts the text so it displays properly. That icon informs you that the font was altered.

To Change the Theme

A theme provides consistency in design and color throughout the entire presentation by setting the color scheme, font set, and layout of a presentation. This collection of formatting choices includes a set of colors (the Theme Colors group), a set of heading and content text fonts (the Theme Fonts group), and a set of lines and fill effects (the Theme Effects group). These groups allow you to choose and change the appearance of all the slides or individual slides in your presentation. *Why? At any time while creating the slide deck, you may decide to switch the theme so that the slides have a totally different appearance.* The following steps change the theme for this presentation from Ion to Facet.

● Tap or click DESIGN on the ribbon to display the DESIGN tab (Figure 1–36).

Figure 1–36

● Tap or click the More button (DESIGN tab | Themes group) to expand the gallery, which shows more theme gallery options (Figure 1–37).

 Experiment

● If you are using a mouse, point to various document themes in the Themes gallery and watch the colors and fonts change on the title slide.

Figure 1–37

Are the themes displayed in a specific order?
They are listed in alphabetical order in two groups: Facet to Wisp beginning in the first row and Banded to Wood Type beginning in the second row. If you are using a mouse and point to a theme, a ScreenTip with the theme's name appears on the screen.

● Tap or click the Facet theme to apply this theme to all four slides (Figure 1–38).

The Facet theme is visible in the first row of the gallery, so why did I click the More button to expand the gallery? While it is not necessary to view all the thumbnails, it sometimes is helpful to see all possible themes when deciding which one best fits the presentation.

If I decide at some future time that this design does not fit the theme of my presentation, can I apply a different design? Yes. You can repeat these steps at any time while creating your presentation.

Figure 1–38

To Change the Variant

1 INSERT PRESENTATION SLIDES | 2 ENTER TEXT | 3 FORMAT TEXT | 4 INSERT GRAPHICAL ELEMENTS
5 SIZE & POSITION | 6 ENHANCE SLIDE SHOW | 7 DISPLAY & PRINT SLIDES

When you began creating this presentation, you selected the Ion theme and then chose a blue variant. You can change the color variation at any time for any theme. ***Why?*** *The new Facet theme has a default green color, but you want to emphasize the blue color associated with water, just like you initially did when you chose the blue variant for the Ion theme.* The following steps change the variant from green to blue.

❶

- If you are using a mouse, point to the blue variation (DESIGN tab | Variants group) to see a preview of the blue variation on Slide 4 (Figure 1–39).

 Experiment

- If you are using a mouse, point to the pink and black variants and watch the colors change on the slide.

Figure 1–39

2
- Tap or click the blue variant to apply this color to all four slides (Figure 1–40).

Q&A If I decide at some future time that this color variation does not fit the theme of my presentation, can I apply a different variant?
Yes. You can repeat these steps at any time while creating your presentation.

Figure 1–40

To Save an Existing Presentation with the Same File Name

You have made several modifications to the presentation since you last saved it. Thus, you should save it again. The following step saves the presentation again. For an example of the step listed below, refer to the Office and Windows chapter at the beginning of this book.

1 Tap or click the Save button on the Quick Access Toolbar to overwrite the previously saved file.

Break Point: If you wish to take a break, this is a good place to do so. You can exit PowerPoint now (refer to page PPT 55 for instructions). To resume at a later time, run PowerPoint (refer to page PPT 4 for instructions), open the file called Keeping Hydrated, and continue following the steps from this location forward.

BTW
Welcome Back!
If you are designing a slide in your deck other than Slide 1 and then save and close the document, PowerPoint's new Welcome back! feature allows you to continue where you left off at the last save when you open the document. You may need to adjust the zoom if you are working at a different level than the default setting.

PowerPoint Views

The PowerPoint window display varies depending on the view. A **view** is the mode in which the presentation appears on the screen. You will use some views when you are developing slides and others when you are delivering your presentation. When creating a presentation, you most likely will use Normal, Slide Sorter, Notes Page, and Outline views. When presenting your slides to an audience, you most likely will use Slide Sorter, Presenter, and Reading views.

The default view is **Normal view**, which is composed of three areas that allow you to work on various aspects of a presentation simultaneously. The large area in the middle, called the **Slide pane**, displays the slide you currently are developing and allows you to enter text, tables, charts, graphics, pictures, video, and other elements. As you create the slides, miniature views of the individual slides, called thumbnails, are displayed in the **Thumbnail pane**. You can rearrange the thumbnails in this pane. The **Notes pane**, by default, is hidden at the bottom of the window. If you want to type notes to yourself or remarks to share with your audience, you can click the Notes button in the status bar to open the Notes pane. After you have created at least two slides, a scroll bar containing **scroll arrows** and **scroll boxes** will appear on the right edge of the window.

To Move to Another Slide in Normal View

1 INSERT PRESENTATION SLIDES | 2 ENTER TEXT | 3 FORMAT TEXT | 4 INSERT GRAPHICAL ELEMENTS
5 SIZE & POSITION | 6 ENHANCE SLIDE SHOW | 7 DISPLAY & PRINT SLIDES

Why? *When creating or editing a presentation in Normal view (the view you are currently using), you often want to display a slide other than the current one.* Before continuing with developing this project, you want to display the title slide. If you are using a touch screen, you can tap the desired slide in the Thumbnail pane; if you are using a mouse, you can click the desired slide in the Thumbnail pane or drag the scroll box on the vertical scroll bar. When you drag the scroll box, the **slide indicator** shows the number and title of the slide you are about to display. Releasing shows the slide. The following steps move from Slide 4 to Slide 1 using the scroll box in the Slide pane.

- Position the pointer on the scroll box.

- Press and hold down the mouse button so that Slide: 4 of 4 Keep Replenishing Fluid Levels appears in the slide indicator (Figure 1–41).

Figure 1–41

2

- Drag the scroll box up the vertical scroll bar until Slide: 1 of 4 Healthy Hydration appears in the slide indicator (Figure 1–42).

Figure 1–42

- Release so that Slide 1 appears in the Slide pane and the Slide 1 thumbnail has an orange border in the Thumbnail pane (Figure 1–43).

Figure 1–43

Other Ways

1. Click Next Slide button or Previous Slide button to move forward or back one slide

2. Tap or click slide in Thumbnail pane

3. Press PAGE DOWN or PAGE UP to move forward or back one slide

Inserting Photos and Illustrations into Slides

BTW
Microsoft Clip Organizer
Previous versions of Microsoft Office stored photos, illustrations, animations, videos, and other media in the Clip Organizer. Office 2013, however, has replaced this feature with the Insert Media dialog box, which allows you to search for and insert files from the Office.com Clip Art collection, Bing, Flickr, SkyDrive, Facebook, and other online sources.

A **clip** is a single media file, such as a photo, illustration, sound, or video. Adding a clip can help increase the visual and audio appeal of many slides and can offer a quick way to add professional-looking graphics and multimedia to a presentation without creating these files yourself. This material is contained in the **Office.com Clip Art** collection of drawings, photos, sounds, and other media files shared among Microsoft Office applications.

You also can add your own clips to slides. These images may include scanned photos, illustrations, and artwork from storage media, such as USB flash drives, hard disks, and memory cards. If you have a Microsoft account, you can add photos from other websites, including Flickr and SkyDrive.

You can add images from Office.com to your presentation in two ways. One way is by selecting one of the slide layouts that includes a content placeholder with an Online Pictures button. A second method is by tapping or clicking the Online Pictures button in the Images area on the INSERT tab. Tapping or clicking the Online Pictures button opens the Insert Pictures dialog box. The **Insert Pictures dialog box** allows you to search for clip art by using descriptive keywords. Clips have one or more keywords associated with various entities, activities, labels, and emotions.

If you have an active connection to the Internet, clips from the Microsoft Office.com website will display automatically as the result of your search. Microsoft constantly revises the content of Office.com, so you may not be able to locate the pictures used in this chapter. Contact your instructor if you need the photos and illustration used in the following steps.

How can you design a title slide that holds your audience's attention?

Develop a slide that reflects the content of your presentation but does so in a thought-provoking way. A title, at the very least, should prepare your audience for the material they are about to see and hear. Look for ways to focus attention on your theme and the method in which you plan to present this theme. A unique photograph or graphic can help generate interest. You may decide to introduce your topic with a startling fact, a rhetorical question, or a quotation. The device you choose depends upon your audience, the occasion, and the presentation's purpose.

To Insert a Picture from Office.com into the Title Slide

1 INSERT PRESENTATION SLIDES | 2 ENTER TEXT | 3 FORMAT TEXT | 4 INSERT GRAPHICAL ELEMENTS
5 SIZE & POSITION | 6 ENHANCE SLIDE SHOW | 7 DISPLAY & PRINT SLIDES

Slide 1 uses the Title Slide layout, which has two placeholders for text but none for graphical content. You desire to place a graphic on Slide 1. *Why? It is likely that your viewers will see an image on this slide before they read any text, so you want to include a photo to create interest in the presentation and introduce your audience to the topic. For this presentation, you will locate a photo of a person holding a water bottle and then insert this photo in this slide. Later in this chapter, you will resize and position the photo in an appropriate location.* The following steps add a photo to Slide 1.

1

- Tap or click INSERT on the ribbon to display the INSERT tab.

- Tap or click the Online Pictures button (INSERT tab | Images group) to display the Insert Pictures dialog box.

- With the insertion point in the Office.com Clip Art area, type **water bottle** in the search box (Figure 1–44).

Figure 1–44

2

- Tap or click the Search button (the magnifying glass) or press the ENTER key so that Office.com will search for and display all clips having the keywords, water bottle.

Q&A Why does the x button display when I begin typing the search terms?

Clicking the x button deletes all letters in the box.

3

- If necessary, slide or scroll down the list to display the photo shown in Figure 1–45.

- Tap or click the photo to select it (Figure 1–45).

Q&A What if the water bottle image displayed in Figure1–45 is not shown in my Office.com Clip Art dialog box?

Select a similar photo. Microsoft updates the files in the Office.com Clip art collection, so the images change constantly.

What are the words and numbers in the lower-left corner of the dialog box?

The words are the keywords associated with this photo, and the figures are the number of pixels associated with the width and height of the clip.

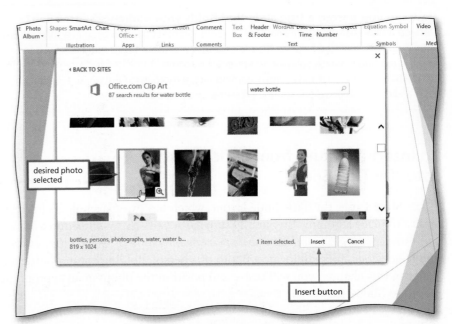

Figure 1–45

4

- Tap or click the Insert button to download the photo and insert it into the slide (Figure 1–46).

Q&A Can I double-tap or double-click the photo instead of selecting it and then tap or click the Insert button?

Yes. Either method downloads and inserts the photo.

Why is this photo displayed in this location on the slide?

The slide layout does not have a content placeholder, so PowerPoint inserts the file in the center of the slide.

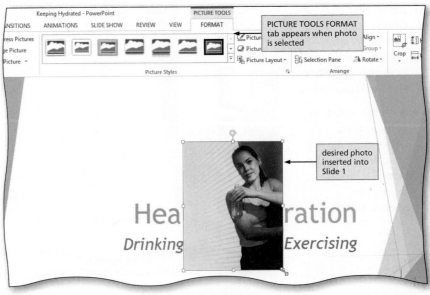

Figure 1–46

To Insert a Picture from Office.com into a Slide without a Content Placeholder

The next step is to add a water bottle photo to Slide 2. This slide has a bulleted list in the text placeholder, so the icon group does not display in the center of the placeholder. Later in this chapter, you will resize the inserted photo. The following steps add one photo to Slide 2.

1 Tap or click the Slide 2 thumbnail in the Thumbnail pane to display Slide 2.

2 Tap or click INSERT on the ribbon to display the INSERT tab and then tap or click the Online Pictures button (INSERT tab | Images group) to display the Insert Pictures dialog box.

3 Type `water bottle` in the Office.com Clip Art search box and then tap or click the Search button.

4 If necessary, slide or scroll down the list to display the water bottle photo shown in Figure 1–47, tap or click the photo to select it, and then tap or click the Insert button to download and insert the photo into Slide 2 (Figure 1–47).

Q&A Why is my photo a different size from the one shown in Figure1–1b on page PPT 3? The clip was inserted into the slide and not into a content placeholder. You will resize the photo later in this chapter.

Figure 1–47

To Insert an Illustration from Office.com into a Slide without a Content Placeholder

Next, you will add an illustration to Slide 3. You will not insert this file into a content placeholder, so it will display in the center of the slide. Later in this chapter, you will resize this illustration. You locate and download illustrations in the same manner you used to locate and download photos. The following steps add an illustration to Slide 3.

1 Tap or click the Slide 3 thumbnail in the Thumbnail pane.

2 Display the INSERT tab, tap or click the Online Pictures button, type `drinking water` as the search text, and then tap or click the Search button.

If necessary, slide or scroll down the list to display the picture of a character drinking water shown in Figure 1–48 and then insert it into Slide 3 (Figure 1–48).

Figure 1–48

To Insert a Picture from Office.com into a Content Placeholder

1 INSERT PRESENTATION SLIDES | 2 ENTER TEXT | 3 FORMAT TEXT | **4 INSERT GRAPHICAL ELEMENTS**
5 SIZE & POSITION | 6 ENHANCE SLIDE SHOW | 7 DISPLAY & PRINT SLIDES

Slide 4 uses the Comparison layout, which has a content placeholder below each of the two headings. You desire to insert photos into both content placeholders. ***Why?*** *You want to reinforce the concept that people should drink water during and after workouts.* The following steps insert photos of a female into the left content placeholder and a male into the right content placeholder on Slide 4.

1

• Tap or click the Slide 4 thumbnail in the Thumbnail pane to display Slide 4 (Figure 1–49).

Figure 1–49

- Tap or click the Online Pictures icon in the left content placeholder to select that placeholder and to open the Insert Pictures dialog box.

- Tap or click the search box, type **women bottled water** as the search text, and then press the ENTER key.

- If necessary, slide or scroll down the list to display the photo shown in Figure 1–50.

- Select the photo and then double-tap or double-click to download and insert it into the left content placeholder (Figure 1–50).

Figure 1–50

- Tap or click the Online Pictures icon in the right content placeholder to select that placeholder and to open the Insert Pictures dialog box.

- Tap or click the search box, type **men exercises hydration** as the search text, and press or tap the ENTER key.

- If necessary, slide or scroll down the list to display the photo shown in Figure 1–51.

- Insert the photo into the right content placeholder (Figure 1–51).

Figure 1–51

Break Point: If you wish to take a break, this is a good place to do so. You can save your presentation and then exit PowerPoint now. To resume at a later time, run PowerPoint, open the file called Keeping Hydrated, and continue following the steps from this location forward.

Resizing Photos and Illustrations

Sometimes it is necessary to change the size of photos and illustrations. **Resizing** includes enlarging or reducing the size of a graphic. You can resize these images using a variety of techniques. One method involves changing the size of a picture by specifying exact dimensions in a dialog box. Another method involves sliding or dragging one of the graphic's sizing handles to the desired location. A selected graphic appears surrounded by a **selection rectangle**, which has small squares and circles, called **sizing handles** or move handles, at each corner and middle location.

BTW
PowerPoint Help
At any time while using PowerPoint, you can find answers to questions and display information about various topics through PowerPoint Help. Used properly, this form of assistance can increase your productivity and reduce your frustrations by minimizing the time you spend learning how to use PowerPoint. For instruction about PowerPoint Help and exercises that will help you gain confidence in using it, read the Office and Windows chapter at the beginning of this book.

To Proportionally Resize Pictures

Why? On Slides 1, 2, and 3, the photo and illustration sizes are either too small or too large to display aesthetically on the slides. The photo and illustration on Slides 1 and 3 are too small, and the photo on Slide 2 is too large. The photo on Slide 1 is of a person, so it generally is important to maintain the proportions. To change the size of a photo and keep the width and height in proportion to each other, drag the corner sizing handles to view how the image will look on the slide. Using these corner handles maintains the graphic's original proportions. If, however, the proportions do not need to be maintained, as with the water bottle on Slide 2, drag the square sizing handles to alter the proportions so that the graphic's height and width become larger or smaller. The following steps proportionally increase the size of the Slide 1 photo using a corner sizing handle.

1

- Click the Slide 1 thumbnail in the Thumbnail pane to display Slide 1.

- Tap or click the photo to select it and display the selection rectangle.

- Point to the upper-right corner sizing handle on the illustration so that the pointer changes to a two-headed arrow (Figure 1–52).

Q&A I am using a touch screen and do not see a two-headed arrow when I press and hold the upper-right sizing handle. Why?
Touch screens may not display pointers; you can just press and slide sizing handles to resize.

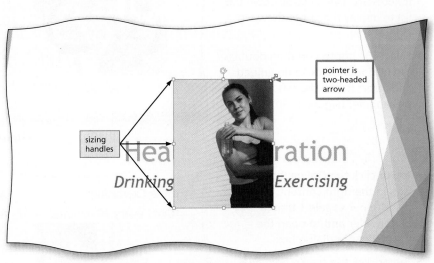

Figure 1–52

2

- Drag the sizing handle diagonally toward the upper-right corner of the slide until the upper-right sizing handle or the crosshair is positioned approximately as shown in Figure 1–53.

Q&A What if the illustration is not the same size as the one shown in Figure 1–53?
Repeat Steps 1 and 2.

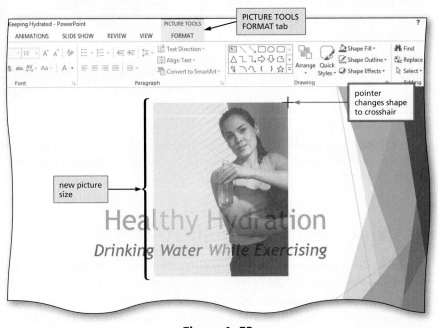

Figure 1–53

3

- Release to resize the illustration.

- Tap or click outside the illustration to deselect it (Figure 1–54).

Q&A What happened to the PICTURE TOOLS FORMAT tab?

When you tap or click outside the illustration, PowerPoint deselects the illustration and removes the PICTURE TOOLS FORMAT tab from the screen.

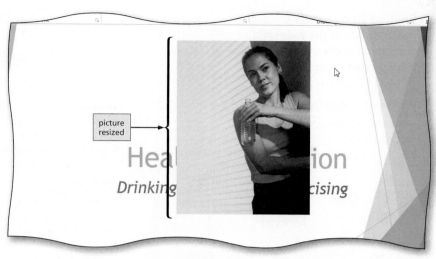

picture resized

Figure 1–54

To Nonproportionally Resize the Photograph on Slide 2

1 INSERT PRESENTATION SLIDES | 2 ENTER TEXT | 3 FORMAT TEXT | 4 INSERT GRAPHICAL ELEMENTS
5 SIZE & POSITION | 6 ENHANCE SLIDE SHOW | 7 DISPLAY & PRINT SLIDES

Why? *The height of the water bottle photo in Slide 2 extends from the top to the bottom of the slide. The width, however, will cover some of the text when the photo is positioned on the right side of the slide.* The width of this photo can be decreased slightly without negatively distorting the original image. You can decrease the width of a photo by sliding or dragging one of the square sizing handles on the sides of the image. The following steps resize the width of the water bottle photo using a sizing handle along the side of the image.

1

- Display Slide 2 and then tap or click the water bottle photo to select it and display the selection rectangle.

- Tap or click the Zoom Out button as many times as necessary until the Zoom level is 60%.

- Press or point to the sizing handle on the left side of the photo so that the pointer changes to a two-headed arrow (Figure 1–55).

pointer changes to a two-headed arrow

Zoom Out button

Zoom level is 70%

Figure 1–55

2

- Drag the sizing handle toward the right side of the slide until the sizing handle or crosshair is positioned approximately as shown in Figure 1–56.

Q&A What if the illustration is not the same size as the one shown in Figure 1–56?
Repeat Steps 1 and 2.

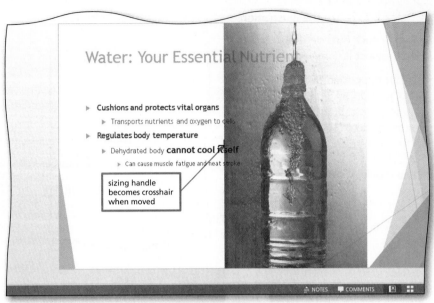

Figure 1–56

3

- Release to resize the photo.
- Tap or click outside the photo to deselect it (Figure 1–57).

Q&A What if I want to return the photo to its original size and start again?
With the photo selected, tap or click the Reset Picture arrow (PICTURE TOOLS FORMAT tab | Adjust group) and then click Reset Picture & Size in the Reset Picture gallery.

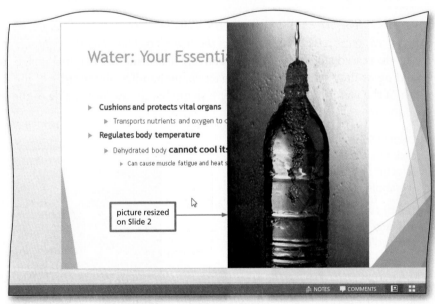

Figure 1–57

To Resize the Illustration on Slide 3

The illustration on Slide 3 can be reduced slightly to fit entirely on the slide. You resize an illustration in the same manner that you resize a photo. You want to maintain the proportions of the character and water in this illustration, so you will drag one of the corner sizing handles. The following steps resize this illustration using a corner sizing handle.

1 Display Slide 3 and then tap or click the character drinking water illustration to select it.

2 Drag the lower-left corner sizing handle on the illustration diagonally outward until the illustration is resized approximately as shown in Figure 1–58.

Figure 1–58

To Move Pictures

1 INSERT PRESENTATION SLIDES | 2 ENTER TEXT | 3 FORMAT TEXT | 4 INSERT GRAPHICAL ELEMENTS

5 SIZE & POSITION | 6 ENHANCE SLIDE SHOW | 7 DISPLAY & PRINT SLIDES

Why? After you insert a photo or an illustration on a slide, you might want to reposition it. The female athlete photo on Slide 1 could be moved to the left side of the slide, the water bottle on Slide 2 could be moved to the right side of the slide, and the illustration on Slide 3 could be positioned in the center of the slide. PowerPoint displays **Smart Guides** automatically when a photo, illustration, shape, or other object is close to lining up with another slide element. For example, a Smart Guide will display to help you align the right or left edge of a picture in relation to a text placeholder or to another picture. The following steps move the photos on Slides 1 and 2 and center the illustration on Slide 3.

1

- If necessary, tap or click the character illustration on Slide 3 to select it.

- Drag the illustration upward until the horizontal Smart Guide is displayed under the title text placeholder and the vertical Smart Guide is displayed through the center of the slide, as shown in Figure 1–59, and then release.

- If necessary, select the photo and then use the ARROW keys to position it precisely as shown in Figure 1–59.

Q&A The illustration still is not located exactly where I want it to display. What can I do to align the image?
Press the CTRL key while you press the ARROW keys. This key combination moves the illustration in smaller increments than when you press only an ARROW key.

Figure 1–59

● Display Slide 2 and then tap or click the water bottle photo to select it.

● Drag the photo to align with the right edge of the slide (Figure 1–60).

Q&A My water bottle photo is covering some of the title text on the slide. What should I do?

Either resize the photo to make it narrower or move the photo to the right so that it is hanging slightly off the side of the slide.

Figure 1–60

● Display Slide 1 and then tap or click the athlete photo to select it.

● Drag the photo to the left and either upward or downward until the horizontal center Smart Guide is displayed, as shown in Figure 1–61, and then release.

● Tap or click outside the photo to deselect it.

Figure 1–61

Q&A The athlete photo is too wide and is covering some of the text on the slide. What should I do?

Changing the width of a photo showing a person generally is not advisable because the altered proportions make the person appear tall and thin or short and overweight. In this case, move the photo to the left so that it is hanging slightly off the side of the slide, as shown in Figure1–61.

Ending a Slide Show with a Closing Slide

All the text for the slides in the Healthy Hydration slide show has been entered. This presentation thus far consists of a title slide, one text slide with a multilevel bulleted list, a third slide for a photo, and a fourth slide with a Comparison layout. A closing slide that resembles the title slide is the final slide to create.

CONSIDER THIS

What factors should you consider when developing a closing slide for the presentation?

After the last slide appears during a slide show, the default PowerPoint setting is to end the presentation with a **black slide**. This black slide appears only when the slide show is running and concludes the slide show, so your audience never sees the PowerPoint window. It is a good idea, however, to end your presentation with a final closing slide to display at the end of the presentation. This slide ends the presentation gracefully and should be an exact copy, or a very similar copy, of your title slide. The audience will recognize that the presentation is drawing to a close when this slide appears. It can remain on the screen when the audience asks questions, approaches the speaker for further information, or exits the room.

To Duplicate a Slide

Why? *When two slides contain similar information and have the same format, duplicating one slide and then making minor modifications to the new slide saves time and increases consistency.*

Slide 5 will have the same layout and design as Slide 1. The most expedient method of creating this slide is to copy Slide 1 and then make minor modifications to the new slide. The following steps duplicate the title slide.

1

- With Slide 1 selected, tap or click the New Slide arrow (HOME tab | Slides group) to display the Facet layout gallery (Figure 1–62).

Figure 1–62

2

- Tap or click 'Duplicate Selected Slides' in the Facet layout gallery to create a new Slide 2, which is a duplicate of Slide 1 (Figure 1–63).

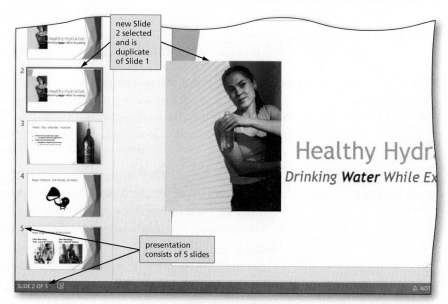

Figure 1–63

Break Point: If you wish to take a break, this is a good place to do so. Be sure to save the Keeping Hydrated file again and then you can exit PowerPoint. To resume at a later time, run PowerPoint, open the file called Keeping Hydrated, and continue following the steps from this location forward.

To Arrange a Slide

The new Slide 2 was inserted directly below Slide 1 because Slide 1 was the selected slide. This duplicate slide needs to display at the end of the presentation directly after the final title and content slide. *Why? It is a closing slide that reinforces the concept presented in Slide 1 and indicates to your audiences that your presentation is ending.*

Changing slide order is an easy process and is best performed in the Thumbnail pane. When you tap or click the thumbnail and begin to drag it to a new location, the remaining thumbnails realign to show the new sequence. When you release, the slide drops into the desired location. Hence, this process of sliding or dragging and then dropping the thumbnail in a new location is called **drag and drop**. You can use the drag-and-drop method to move any selected item, including text and graphics. The following step moves the new Slide 2 to the end of the presentation so that it becomes a closing slide.

- With Slide 2 selected, drag the Slide 2 slide thumbnail below the last slide in the Thumbnail pane (Figure 1–64).

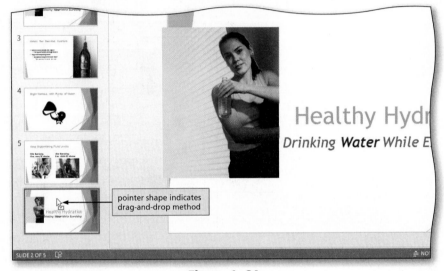

pointer shape indicates drag-and-drop method

Figure 1–64

Other Ways

1. Tap or click Slide Sorter button on status bar, drag thumbnail to new location

2. Tap or click Slide Sorter button (VIEW tab | Presentation Views group), tap or click slide thumbnail, drag thumbnail to new location

Making Changes to Slide Text Content

After creating slides in a presentation, you may find that you want to make changes to the text. Changes may be required because a slide contains an error, the scope of the presentation shifts, or the style is inconsistent. This section explains the types of changes that commonly occur when creating a presentation.

You generally make three types of changes to text in a presentation: additions, replacements, and deletions.

- Additions are necessary when you omit text from a slide and need to add it later. You may need to insert text in the form of a sentence, word, or single character. For example, you may want to add the presenter's middle name on the title slide.

- Replacements are needed when you want to revise the text in a presentation. For example, you may want to substitute the word, *their*, for the word, *there*.

- Deletions are required when text on a slide is incorrect or no longer is relevant to the presentation. For example, a slide may look cluttered. Therefore, you may want to remove one of the bulleted paragraphs to add more space.

Editing text in PowerPoint basically is the same as editing text in a word processing program. The following sections illustrate the most common changes made to text in a presentation.

Replacing Text in an Existing Slide

When you need to correct a word or phrase, you can replace the text by selecting the text to be replaced and then typing the new text. As soon as you press any key on the keyboard, the selected text is deleted and the new text is displayed.

PowerPoint inserts text to the left of the insertion point. The text to the right of the insertion point moves to the right (and shifts downward if necessary) to accommodate the added text.

Deleting Text

You can delete text using one of many methods. One is to use the BACKSPACE key to remove text just typed. The second is to position the insertion point to the left of the text you want to delete and then press the DELETE key. The third method is to drag through the text you want to delete and then tap or click the Cut button on the mini toolbar, press DELETE or BACKSPACE key, or press CTRL + X. Use the third method when deleting large sections of text.

To Delete Text in a Placeholder

Why? *To keep the ending slide clean and simple, you want to delete a few words in the slide title and subtitle text.* The following steps change Healthy Hydration to Be Healthy and then change Drinking Water While Exercising to Drink Water.

- With Slide 5 selected, position the pointer immediately to the right of the last character of the text to be selected in the title text placeholder (in this case, the n in the word, Hydration).

- Drag the pointer through the first character of the text to be selected (in this case, the space after the word, Healthy) (Figure 1–65).

Q&A

I am having difficulty selecting the required text. Can I drag from left to right or right to left?
Yes. You may need several attempts to select the correct characters.

Could I also have selected the word, Hydration, by double-tapping or double-clicking it?
Yes. Either method works to select a word.

Figure 1–65

● Tap or click the Cut button (HOME tab | Clipboard group) to delete the selected text and space.

● Position the pointer to the left of the word, Healthy, and then type **Be** and press the SPACEBAR as the first word in the title text placeholder (Figure 1–66).

● If requested by your instructor, add your mother's first name after the word, Healthy, in the title text placeholder.

Figure 1–66

● Position the pointer immediately to the right of the last character of the text to be selected in the subtitle text placeholder (in this case, the g in the word, Exercising).

● Drag the pointer to the left through the last character of the text to be selected (in this case, the space after the word, Water) (Figure 1–67).

Figure 1–67

4
- Tap or click the Cut button.
- Select the letters, ing, in the word, Drinking.
- Tap or click the Cut button (Figure 1–68).

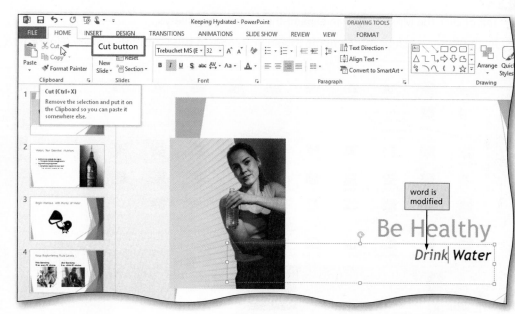

Figure 1–68

Other Ways

1. Tap 'Show Context Menu' button on mini toolbar or right-click selected text, tap or click Cut on shortcut menu

2. Select text, press DELETE or BACKSPACE key

3. Select text, press CTRL+X

Adding a Transition

PowerPoint includes a wide variety of visual and sound effects that can be applied to text or content. A **slide transition** is a special effect used to progress from one slide to the next in a slide show. You can control the speed of the transition effect and add a sound.

To Add a Transition between Slides

1 INSERT PRESENTATION SLIDES | 2 ENTER TEXT | 3 FORMAT TEXT | 4 INSERT GRAPHICAL ELEMENTS

5 SIZE & POSITION | 6 ENHANCE SLIDE SHOW | 7 DISPLAY & PRINT SLIDES

Why? *Transitions add interest when you advance the slides in a presentation and make a slide show presentation look professional.* In this presentation, you apply the Switch transition in the Exciting category to all slides and change the transition speed from 1.25 seconds to 2 seconds. The following steps apply this transition to the presentation.

1
- Tap or click the TRANSITIONS tab on the ribbon and then point to the More button (TRANSITIONS tab | Transition to This Slide group) in the Transition to This Slide gallery (Figure 1–69).

Figure 1–69

Is a transition applied now?

No. None, the first slide icon in the Transition to This Slide group, is selected, which indicates no transition has been applied.

2

• Tap or click the More button to expand the Transitions gallery.

• Point to the Switch transition in the Exciting category in the Transitions gallery (Figure 1–70).

Figure 1–70

3

• Tap or click Switch in the Exciting category in the Transitions gallery to apply this transition to the closing slide.

Q&A Why does a star appear next to Slide 5 in the Thumbnail pane?
The star indicates that a transition animation effect is applied to that slide.

• Tap or click the Duration up arrow (TRANSITIONS tab | Timing group) seven times to change the transition speed from 01.25 seconds to 03.00 seconds (Figure 1–71).

Q&A Why did the time change from the default 2.00 to 1.25?
Each transition has a default duration time. The default Switch transition time is 01.25 seconds.

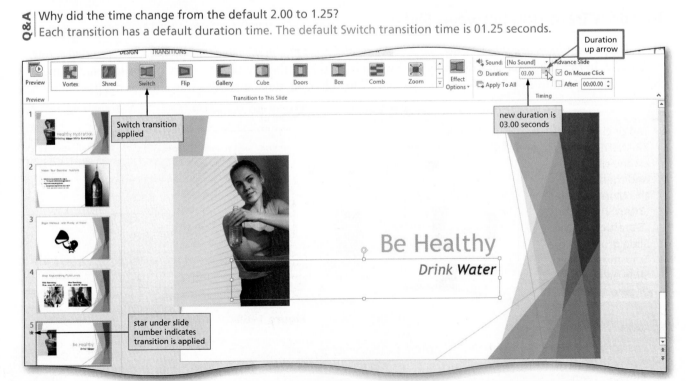

Figure 1–71

4

- Tap or click the Preview Transitions button (TRANSITIONS tab | Preview area) to view the transition and the new transition time (Figure 1–72).

Q&A Can I adjust the duration time I just set?

Yes. Tap or click the Duration up or down arrows or type a speed in the Duration box and preview the transition until you find the time that best fits your presentation.

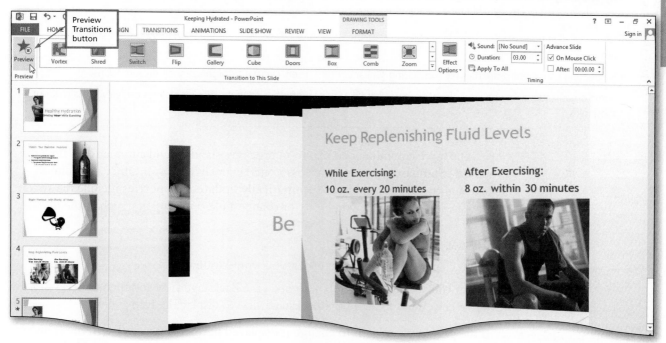

Figure 1–72

5

- Tap or click the 'Apply To All' button (TRANSITIONS tab | Timing group) to apply the Switch transition and the increased transition time to Slides 1 through 4 in the presentation (Figure 1–73).

Q&A What if I want to apply a different transition and duration to each slide in the presentation?

Repeat Steps 2 and 3 for each slide individually.

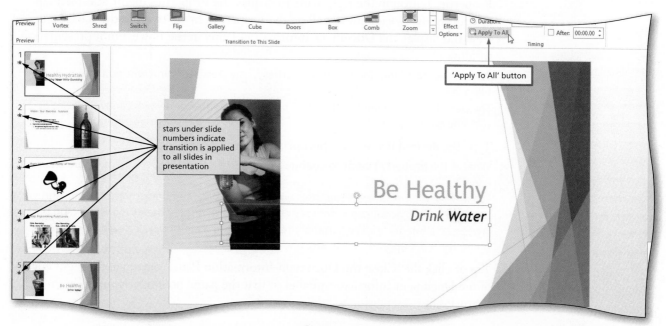

Figure 1–73

Document Properties

PowerPoint helps you organize and identify your files by using **document properties**, which are the details about a file such as the project author, title, and subject. For example, a class name or presentation topic can describe the file's purpose or content.

Why would you want to assign document properties to a presentation?

Document properties are valuable for a variety of reasons:

- Users can save time locating a particular file because they can view a file's document properties without opening the presentation.

- By creating consistent properties for files having similar content, users can better organize their presentations.

- Some organizations require PowerPoint users to add document properties so that other employees can view details about these files.

The more common document properties are standard and automatically updated properties. **Standard properties** are associated with all Microsoft Office files and include author, title, and subject. **Automatically updated properties** include file system properties, such as the date you create or change a file, and statistics, such as the file size.

To Change Document Properties

BTW
Printing Document Properties
PowerPoint 2013 does not allow you to print document properties. This feature, however, is available in other Office 2013 apps, including Word and Excel.

To change document properties, you would follow these steps.

1. Tap or click FILE on the ribbon to open the Backstage view and then, if necessary, tap or click the Info tab in the Backstage view to display the Info gallery.

2. If the property you wish to change is displayed in the Properties list in the right pane of the Info gallery, try to tap or click to the right of the property. If a box appears to the right of the property, type the text for the property in the box, and then tap or click the Back button in the upper-left corner of the Backstage view to return to the PowerPoint window. Skip the remaining steps.

3. If the property you wish to change is not displayed in the Properties list in the right pane of the Info gallery or you cannot change it in the Info gallery, tap or click the Properties button in the right pane to display the Properties menu, and then tap or click 'Show Document Panel' on the Properties menu to close the Backstage view and display the Document Information Panel in the PowerPoint presentation window.

Q&A Why are some of the document properties in my Document Information Panel already filled in?
The person who installed Office 2013 on your computer or network may have set or customized the properties.

4. Type the desired text in the appropriate property boxes.

Q&A What if the property I want to change is not displayed in the Document Information Panel?
Tap or click the Document Properties button in the Document Information Panel and then tap or click Advanced Properties on the menu to display the Properties dialog box. If necessary, tap or click the Summary tab (Properties dialog box) to display the Summary sheet, fill in the appropriate boxes, and then tap or click the OK button.

5. Tap or click the 'Close the Document Information Panel' button at the right edge of the Document Information Panel so that the panel no longer appears in the PowerPoint presentation window.

Viewing the Presentation in Slide Show View

The Start From Beginning button, located in the Quick Access Toolbar, allows you to show a presentation using a computer. As the name implies, the first slide to be displayed always will be Slide 1. You also can run a presentation starting with the slide currently displaying when you tap or click the Slide Show button on the status bar. In either case, PowerPoint displays the slides on the full screen without any of the PowerPoint window objects, such as the ribbon. The full-screen slide hides the toolbars, menus, and other PowerPoint window elements.

To Start Slide Show View

1 INSERT PRESENTATION SLIDES | 2 ENTER TEXT | 3 FORMAT TEXT | 4 INSERT GRAPHICAL ELEMENTS
5 SIZE & POSITION | 6 ENHANCE SLIDE SHOW | **7 DISPLAY & PRINT SLIDES**

Why? *You run a presentation in for your audience so they can see the slides in their entirety and view any transitions or other effects added to the slides.* When making a presentation, you use **Slide Show view**. You can start Slide Show view from Normal view or Slide Sorter view. Slide Show view begins when you tap or click the Start From Beginning button or the Slide Show button. The following steps start Slide Show view starting with Slide 1.

1

- If you are using a touch screen, proceed to Step 2. If you are using a mouse, point to the Start From Beginning button (Figure 1–74).

Q&A What would have displayed if I had tapped or clicked the Slide Show button instead of the Start From Beginning button?
When you tap or click the Slide Show button to start the presentation, PowerPoint begins the show with the currently displayed slide, which in this case is Slide 5. Only Slide 5 would display during the slide show.

Figure 1–74

● Tap or click the Start From Beginning button to display the title slide (Figure 1–75).

Q&A
Where is the PowerPoint window?
When you run a slide show, the PowerPoint window is hidden. It will reappear once you end your slide show.

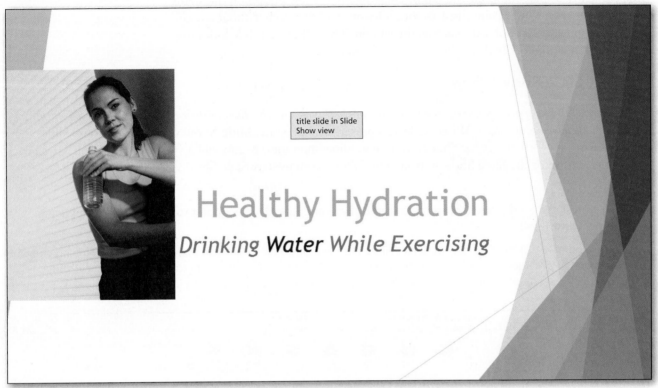

title slide in Slide Show view

Figure 1–75

Other Ways
1. Display Slide 1, tap or click Slide Show button on status bar	2. Tap or click Start From Beginning button (SLIDE SHOW tab | Start Slide Show group)	3. Press F5

To Move Manually through Slides in a Slide Show

1 INSERT PRESENTATION SLIDES | 2 ENTER TEXT | 3 FORMAT TEXT | 4 INSERT GRAPHICAL ELEMENTS
5 SIZE & POSITION | 6 ENHANCE SLIDE SHOW | **7 DISPLAY & PRINT SLIDES**

After you begin Slide Show view, you can move forward or backward through the slides. PowerPoint allows you to advance through the slides manually or automatically. During a slide show, each slide in the presentation shows on the screen, one slide at a time. Each time you tap or click, the next slide appears. The following steps move manually through the slides. *Why? You can control the length of time each slide is displayed and change the preset order if you need to review a slide already shown or jump ahead to another slide designed to display later in the presentation.*

- Swipe forward on or click each slide until Slide 5 (Be Healthy) is displayed (Figure 1–76).

Figure 1–76

- Swipe forward on or click Slide 5 so that the black slide appears with a message announcing the end of the slide show (Figure 1–77).

Q&A I see a small toolbar in the lower-left corner of my slide. What is this toolbar?
The Slide Show toolbar appears when you begin running a slide show and then tap a slide or move the pointer. The buttons on this toolbar allow you to navigate to the next slide, the previous slide, to mark up the current slide, or to change the current display.

Figure 1–77

- Swipe forward on or click the black slide to return to Normal view in the PowerPoint window.

Other Ways

1. Press PAGE DOWN to advance one slide at a time, or press PAGE UP to go back one slide at a time

2. Press RIGHT ARROW or DOWN ARROW to advance one slide at a time, or press LEFT ARROW or UP ARROW to go back one slide at a time

3. If Slide Show toolbar is displayed, tap or click Next Slide or Previous Slide button on toolbar

Printing a Presentation

After creating a presentation, you may want to print it. Printing a presentation enables you to distribute it to others in a form that can be read or viewed but typically not edited. It is a good practice to save a presentation before printing it, in the event you experience difficulties printing.

CONSIDER THIS

What is the best method for distributing a presentation?

The traditional method of distributing a presentation uses a printer to produce a hard copy. A **hard copy** or **printout** is information that exists on a physical medium such as paper. Hard copies can be useful for the following reasons:

- Some people prefer proofreading a hard copy of a presentation rather than viewing it on the screen to check for errors and readability.

- Hard copies can serve as a backup reference if your storage medium is lost or becomes corrupted and you need to recreate the presentation.

Instead of distributing a hard copy of a presentation, users can distribute the presentation as an electronic image that mirrors the original presentation's appearance. The electronic image of the presentation can be sent as an email attachment, posted on a website, or copied to a portable storage medium such as a USB flash drive. Two popular electronic image formats, sometimes called fixed formats, are PDF by Adobe Systems and XPS by Microsoft. In PowerPoint, you can create electronic image files through the Save As dialog box and the Export, Share, and Print tabs in the Backstage view. Electronic images of presentations, such as PDF and XPS, can be useful for the following reasons:

- Users can view electronic images of presentations without the software that created the original presentation (e.g., PowerPoint). Specifically, to view a PDF file, you use a program called Adobe Reader, which can be downloaded free from Adobe's website. Similarly, to view an XPS file, you use a program called XPS Viewer, which is included in the latest versions of Windows and Internet Explorer.

- Sending electronic presentations saves paper and printer supplies. Society encourages users to contribute to **green computing**, which involves reducing the electricity consumed and environmental waste generated when using computers, mobile devices, and related technologies.

To Print a Presentation

1 INSERT PRESENTATION SLIDES | 2 ENTER TEXT | 3 FORMAT TEXT | 4 INSERT GRAPHICAL ELEMENTS | 5 SIZE & POSITION | 6 ENHANCE SLIDE SHOW | **7 DISPLAY & PRINT SLIDES**

With the completed presentation saved, you may want to print it. ***Why?*** *You could distribute a handout of the slides to your audience members, or you might want to keep a printed copy as a backup in the event you experience technical difficulties before or during your speech. You, therefore, will print a hard copy on a printer.* The following steps print a hard copy of the contents of the saved Keeping Hydrated presentation.

1

- Tap or click FILE on the ribbon to open the Backstage view.
- Tap or click the Print tab in the Backstage view to display the Print gallery (Figure 1–78).

Q&A How do I preview Slides 2 through 5?
Tap or click the Next Page button in the Print gallery to scroll forward through pages in the document; similarly, tap or click the Previous Page button to scroll backward through pages.

How can I print multiple copies of my presentation?
Increase the number in the Copies box in the Print gallery.

What if I decide not to print the presentation at this time?
Tap or click the Back button in the upper-left corner of the Backstage view to return to the presentation window.

2

- Verify that the printer listed on the Printer Status button will print a hard copy of the presentation. If necessary, click the Printer Status button to display a list of available printer options and then click the desired printer to change the currently selected printer.

Q&A The selected printer is a black-and-white laser printer, so the preview is grayscale and shows varying shades of gray. If I change the currently selected printer to a color printer, will the preview display in color?
Yes, the preview will match the printer output.

BTW

Conserving Ink and Toner

If you want to conserve ink or toner, you can instruct PowerPoint to print draft quality documents by tapping or clicking FILE on the ribbon to open the Backstage view, tapping or clicking Options in the Backstage view to display the PowerPoint Options dialog box, tapping or clicking Advanced in the left pane (PowerPoint Options dialog box), sliding or scrolling to the Print area in the right pane, not placing a check mark in the High quality check box, and then tapping or clicking the OK button. Then, use the Backstage view to print the document as usual.

Figure 1–78

- Tap or click the Print button in the Print gallery to print the presentation on the currently selected printer.

- When the printer stops, retrieve the hard copy (Figure 1–79).

Q&A

Do I have to wait until my presentation is complete to print it?
No, you can follow these steps to print a presentation at any time while you are creating it.

What if I want to print an electronic image of a presentation instead of a hard copy?
You would click the Printer Status button in the Print gallery and then select the desired electronic image option, such as Microsoft XPS Document Writer, which would create an XPS file.

(a) Slide 1

(b) Slide 2

(c) Slide 3

(d) Slide 4

(e) Slide 5

Figure 1–79   (Handouts printed using a black-and-white printer)

Other Ways

1. Press CTRL+P, press ENTER

To Sign Out of a Microsoft Account

If you are signed in to a Microsoft account and are using a public computer or otherwise wish to sign out of your Microsoft account, you should sign out of the account from the Accounts gallery in the Backstage view before exiting PowerPoint. Signing out of the account is the safest way to make sure that nobody else can access SkyDrive files or settings stored in your Microsoft account. The following steps sign out of a Microsoft account from PowerPoint. For a detailed example of the procedure summarized below, refer to the Office and Windows chapter at the beginning of this book.

1 If you wish to sign out of your Microsoft account, tap or click FILE on the ribbon to open the Backstage view and then tap or click the Account tab to display the Account gallery.

2 Tap or click the Sign out link, which displays the Remove Account dialog box. If a Can't remove Windows accounts dialog box appears instead of the Remove Account dialog box, click the OK button and skip the remaining steps.

Q&A Why does a Can't remove Windows accounts dialog box appear?
If you signed in to Windows using your Microsoft account, then you also must sign out from Windows, rather than signing out from within PowerPoint. When you are finished using Windows, be sure to sign out at that time.

3 Tap or click the Yes button (Remove Account dialog box) to sign out of your Microsoft account on this computer.

Q&A Should I sign out of Windows after signing out of my Microsoft account?
When you are finished using the computer, you should sign out of your account for maximum security.

4 Tap or click the Back button in the upper-left corner of the Backstage view to return to the presentation.

BTW
Certification
The Microsoft Office Specialist (MOS) program provides an opportunity for you to obtain a valuable industry credential — proof that you have the PowerPoint 2013 skills required by employers. For more information, visit the Certification resource on the Student Companion Site located on www.cengagebrain.com. For detailed instructions about accessing available resources, visit www.cengage.com/ct/studentdownload or see the inside back cover of this book.

To Exit PowerPoint

This project now is complete. The following steps exit PowerPoint. For a detailed example of the procedure summarized below, refer to the Office and Windows chapter at the beginning of this book.

1a If you have one PowerPoint presentation open, tap or click the Close button on the right side of the title bar to close the open document and exit PowerPoint.

1b If you have multiple PowerPoint presentations open, press and hold or right-click the PowerPoint app button on the taskbar and then tap or click 'Close all windows' on the shortcut menu, or press ALT+F4 to close all open presentations and exit PowerPoint.

Q&A Could I press and hold or repeatedly click the Close button to close all open documents and exit PowerPoint?
Yes.

2 If a Microsoft PowerPoint dialog box appears, tap or click the Save button to save any changes made to the presentation since the last save.

BTW
Quick Reference
For a table that lists how to complete the tasks covered in this book using touch gestures, the mouse, ribbon, shortcut menu, and keyboard, see the Quick Reference Summary at the back of this book, or visit the Quick Reference resource on the Student Companion Site located on www.cengagebrain.com. For detailed instructions about accessing available resources, visit www.cengage.com/ct/studentdownload or see the inside back cover of this book.

Chapter Summary

In this chapter you have learned how to apply and change a document theme and variant, create a title slide and text slides with a bulleted list, insert photos and an illustration and then resize and move them on a slide, format and edit text, add a slide transition, view the presentation in Slide Show view, and print slides as handouts. The items listed below include all the new PowerPoint skills you have learned in this chapter, with the tasks grouped by activity.

Enter and Edit Text
Enter the Presentation Title (PPT 7)
Enter the Presentation Subtitle Paragraph (PPT 9)
Zoom a Slide (PPT 10)
Add a New Text Slide with a Bulleted List (PPT 15)
Enter a Slide Title (PPT 17)
Type a Multilevel Bulleted List (PPT 18)
Add a Slide with the Title Only Layout (PPT 23)
Add a New Slide and Enter a Slide Title and
    Headings (PPT 24)
Move to Another Slide in Normal View (PPT 29)
Duplicate a Slide (PPT 41)
Arrange a Slide (PPT 42)
Delete Text in a Placeholder (PPT 43)

Format a Slide
Choose a Document Theme and Variant (PPT 5)
Change the Theme (PPT 26)
Change the Variant (PPT 27)

Format Text
Italicize Text (PPT 11)
Increase Font Size (PPT 12, 22)

Change the Text Color (PPT 13)
Bold Text (PPT 21)

Enhance Slides with Pictures and a Transition
Insert a Picture from Office.com into the Title Slide
    (PPT 31)
Insert a Picture from Office.com into a Content
    Placeholder (PPT 34)
Proportionally Resize Pictures (PPT 36)
Move Pictures (PPT 39)
Add a Transition between Slides (PPT 45)

Run and Print a Slide Show
Change Document Properties (PPT 48)
Start Slide Show View (PPT 49)
Move Manually through Slides in a Slide
    Show (PPT 50)
Print a Presentation (PPT 52)

Select Text and Slide Elements
Select a Paragraph (PPT 11)
Select a Word (PPT 12)
Select a Text Placeholder (PPT 18)
Select a Group of Words (PPT 20)

CONSIDER THIS

What decisions will you need to make when creating your next presentation?
Use these guidelines as you complete the assignments in this chapter and create your own slide show decks outside of this class.

1. Determine the content you want to include on your slides.

2. Determine which theme and variant are appropriate.

3. Identify the slide layouts that best communicate your message.

4. Format various text elements to emphasize important points.

    a) Select appropriate font sizes.

    b) Emphasize important words with bold or italic type and color.

5. Locate graphical elements, such as photos and illustrations, that reinforce your message.

    a) Size and position them aesthetically on slides.

6. Determine a storage location for the presentation.

7. Determine the best method for distributing the presentation.

How should you submit solutions to questions in the assignments identified with a ✳ symbol?

Every assignment in this book contains one or more questions identified with a ✳ symbol. These questions require you to think beyond the assigned presentation. Present your solutions to the questions in the format required by your instructor. Possible formats may include one or more of these options: write the answer; create a document that contains the answer; present your answer to the class; discuss your answer in a group; record the answer as audio or video using a webcam, smartphone, or portable media player; or post answers on a blog, wiki, or website.

Apply Your Knowledge

Reinforce the skills and apply the concepts you learned in this chapter.

Modifying Character Formats and Paragraph Levels and Moving an Illustration

Note: To complete this assignment, you will be required to use the Data Files for Students. Visit www.cengage.com/ct/studentdownload for detailed instructions or contact your instructor for information about accessing the required files.

Instructions: Run PowerPoint. Open the presentation, Apply 1-1 Effective Writing, from the Data Files for Students.

The two slides in the presentation discuss steps to follow when writing a persuasive essay. The document you open is an unformatted presentation. You are to modify the document theme, indent the paragraphs, resize and move the photo, and format the text so the slides look like Figure 1–80 on this page and the next page.

Perform the following tasks:

1. Change the document theme to Ion.

2. On the title slide, use your name in place of Student Name and bold and italicize your name.

3. If requested by your instructor, change your first name to your grandmother's first name on the title slide.

4. Increase the title text font size to 60 point. Size and position the photo using the Smart Guides to align the image with the bottom of the title placeholder, as shown in Figure 1–80a.

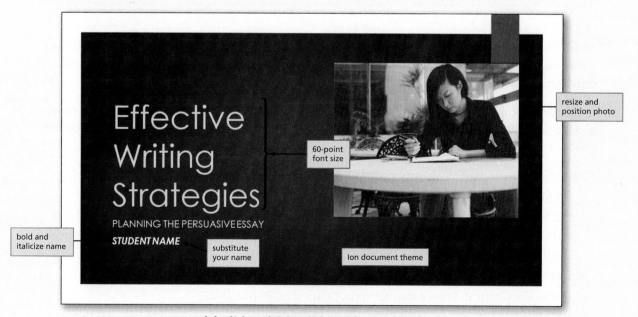

(a) Slide 1 (Title Slide with a Picture)
Figure 1–80

Continued >

Apply Your Knowledge *continued*

5. On Slide 2, increase the indent of the third and fourth paragraphs to second-level paragraphs. Then combine paragraphs six and seven (To change readers' minds? and To confirm opinions?) to read, To change readers' minds or confirm opinions?, as shown in Figure 1–80b. Increase the indent of this paragraph to second level.

6. Save the presentation using the file name, Apply 1-1 Effective Writing Strategies.

7. Submit the revised document in the format specified by your instructor.

8. ✳ In Step 5 you combined two paragraphs. How did this action improve the slide content?

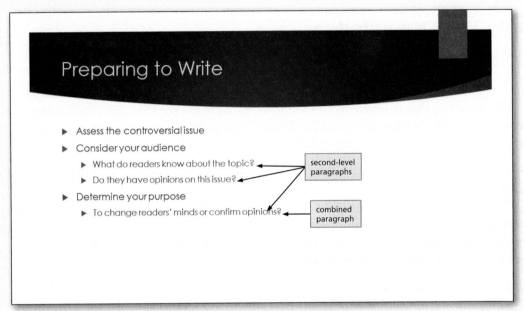

(b) Slide 2 (Multilevel Bulleted List)
Figure 1–80 (Continued)

Extend Your Knowledge

Extend the skills you learned in this chapter and experiment with new skills. You may need to use Help to complete the assignment.

Changing Slide Theme, Layout, and Text

Note: To complete this assignment, you will be required to use the Data Files for Students. Visit www.cengage.com/ct/studentdownload for detailed instructions or contact your instructor for information about accessing the required files.

Instructions: Run PowerPoint. Open the presentation that you are going to prepare for your brother's horseback riding business, Extend 1-1 Horseback Riding, from the Data Files for Students. You will choose a theme, format slides, and create a closing slide.

Perform the following tasks:

1. Apply an appropriate document theme.

2. On Slide 1 (Figure 1–81), use your name in place of Student Name. Format the text on this slide using techniques you learned in this chapter, such as changing the font size and color and bolding and italicizing words.

3. Delete the bullets in the subtitle text.

4. Resize the photo and move it to an appropriate area on the slide.

5. On Slide 2, add bullets to the paragraphs in the Beginners and Advanced boxes, and then change the look of the default bullets.

6. On Slide 3, create paragraphs and adjust the paragraph levels to create a bulleted list. Edit the text so that the slide meets the 7×7 rule, which states that each line should have a maximum of seven words, and each slide should have a maximum of seven lines.

7. Create an appropriate closing slide using the title slide as a guide. Change the title text to, See you at the Trails!

8. The slides contain a variety of pictures downloaded from Office.com. Size and move them when necessary.

9. Apply an appropriate transition to all slides.

10. Save the presentation using the file name, Extend 1-1 Horseback Riding Lessons.

11. Submit the revised document in the format specified by your instructor.

12. If requested by your instructor, replace the word, you, with your mother's first name on the closing slide.

13. ✳ In this assignment, you changed the bullet style on Slide 2. Which bullet style did you select and why?

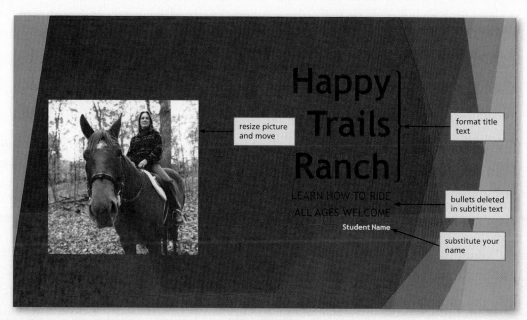

Figure 1–81

Analyze, Correct, Improve

Analyze a presentation, correct all errors, and improve it.

Correcting Formatting and List Levels

Note: To complete this assignment, you will be required to use the Data Files for Students. Visit www.cengage.com/ct/studentdownload for detailed instructions or contact your instructor for information about accessing the required files.

Instructions: Run PowerPoint. Open the presentation, Analyze 1-1 Math Tutor, from the Data Files for Students. As a part-time job while attending college, you decide to tutor students who are struggling with math. You decide to create a presentation promoting your service and begin with this document. Modify the slides by making the indicated corrections and improvements.

Continued >

Analyze, Correct, Improve *continued*

1. Correct

    a. Change the document theme from Office Theme Dark, shown in Figure 1–82, to Organic with the rightmost color variant.

    b. If requested by your instructor, change the Southtown Library Room number, 201, to your birth year on Slide 2.

    c. Correct the spelling errors on Slides 2 and 3.

    d. Use your name in place of Student Name on Slide 1.

2. Improve

    a. Adjust the size of the picture on Slide 1 and move it to the left of the subtitle text.

    b. Move Slide 2 to the end of the presentation so that it becomes the new Slide 3.

    c. On Slide 2, increase the font size of the Slide 2 title text, A Math Tutor Is Your Answer, to 54 point. Increase the size of the picture and move it to fill the white space on the right of the bulleted list. Align the picture using the right and bottom Smart Guides.

    d. On Slide 3, increase the font size of the title text, Schedule, to 60 point. Decrease the indent level for both bulleted lists to first level. Adjust the size of the picture and move it to the upper-right corner of the slide so that the upper edge of the image is aligned with the top edge of the title text placeholder.

    e. Apply the same transition and duration to all slides.

    f. Save the presentation using the file name, Analyze 1-1 – Math Tutor Info.

    g. Submit the revised document in the format specified by your instructor.

3. ✺ Which errors existed in the starting file? How did decreasing the indent level of the bulleted lists on Slide 3 and increasing the title text on Slides 2 and 3 enhance the presentation? When you adjusted the pictures, how did you determine their final sizes?

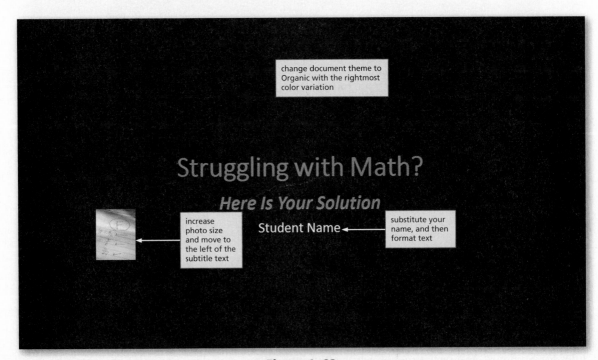

Figure 1–82

In the Labs

Design and/or create a presentation using the guidelines, concepts, and skills presented in this chapter. Labs 1 and 2, which increase in difficulty, require you to create solutions based on what you learned in the chapter; Lab 3 requires you to create a solution, which uses cloud and web technologies, by learning and investigating on your own from general guidance.

Lab 1: **Creating a Presentation with Bulleted Lists, a Closing Slide, and Pictures**

Problem: You are majoring in accounting and work part-time at a tax-filing service. Your clients have asked you numerous times what documents they should keep at home to support their tax returns. You decide to put together a presentation that would offer some basic guidelines about how to organize personal documents. You develop the outline shown in Figure 1–83 and then prepare the PowerPoint presentation shown in Figures 1–84a through 1–84e on pages PPT 62–64.

Files or Piles
    Document Storage and Retention at Home

Store and Retain
    In Home Office Safe
        Tax records for six years
        Pay stubs until W2 arrives
        Credit card statements
        Canceled checks
        Utility bills
    In Bank Safe Deposit Box
        Wills, deeds, and titles
        Birth and death certificates
        Passports
        Military records

Keep Indefinitely
    Personal health records
    Medical history
    Retirement benefit statements

General Rules
    Shred documents showing personal information
    Organize and store chronologically
    Keep list of important documents
        State their location
        Share with relative or friend

Figure 1–83

Continued >

In the Labs *continued*

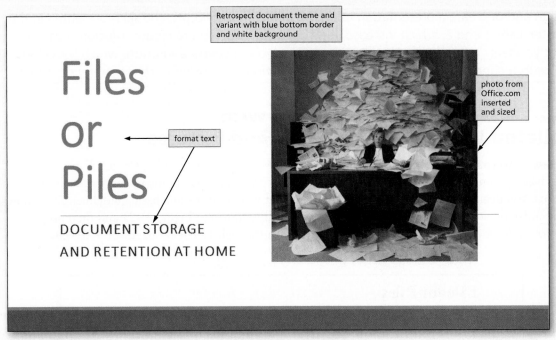

(a) Slide 1 (Title Slide)

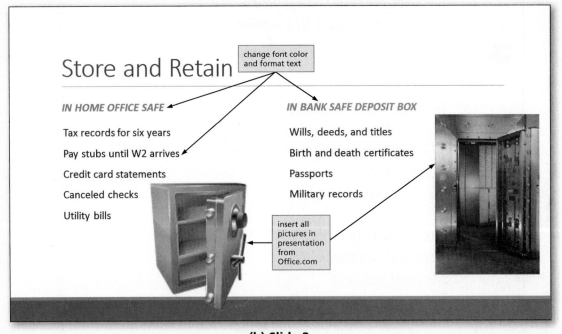

(b) Slide 2

Figure 1–84

(c) Slide 3

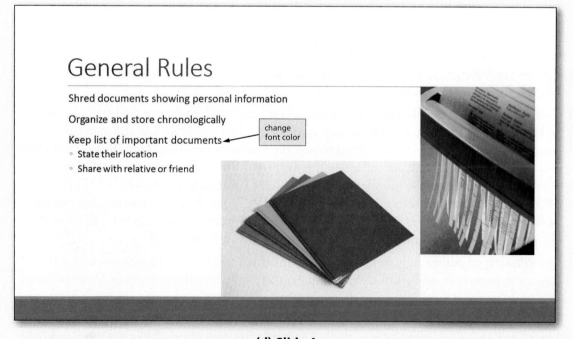

(d) Slide 4

Figure 1–84 (Continued)

Continued >

In the Labs *continued*

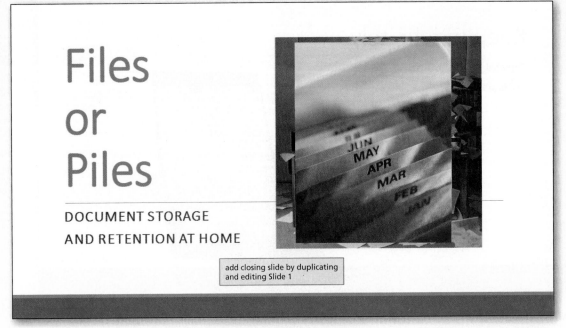

add closing slide by duplicating and editing Slide 1

(e) Slide 5 (Closing Slide)
Figure 1–84 (Continued)

Instructions: Perform the following tasks:

1. Create a new presentation using the Retrospect document theme and select the variant with the blue bottom border and white background.

2. Using the typed outline illustrated in Figure 1–83 on page PPT 61, create the title slide shown in Figure 1–84a. Press the ENTER key to place each word on a separate line and divide the title into three lines, as shown in the figure. Increase the font size of the title text to 88 point and bold this text. Change the font color to Green (the sixth color from left in the Standard Colors row). Increase the font size of the subtitle text, DOCUMENT STORAGE AND RETENTION AT HOME, to 28 point and bold this text. Press the ENTER key to divide the subtitle into two lines, as shown in the figure. Find and insert the picture from the Office.com Clip Art collection. Size the picture and use the Smart Guides to position it as shown in the figure.

3. Using the typed outline in Figure 1–83, create the three text slides with lists and find and insert the pictures from the Office.com Clip Art collection. Size the pictures and use the Smart Guides to position these images, as shown in Figures 1–84b, 1–84c, and 1–84d. You may want to zoom the slides to help you align these graphic elements.

4. On Slide 2, change the font color in the left and right heading placeholders to Green and bold and italicize this text.

5. On Slides 2, 3 and 4, change the font color of the lists to Dark Blue (second color from right in the Standard Colors row).

6. Create a closing slide by duplicating Slide 1 and adding the photo using the Smart Guides to center it on top of the existing photo.

7. If requested by your instructor, use your father's first name in place of the word, Piles, and replace the word, or, with the word, for, on Slide 5.

8. Apply the Shred transition in the Exciting category to all slides. Change the duration to 4.5 seconds.

9. Tap or click the Start From Beginning button to start the show from the first slide. Then swipe or click to display each slide.

10. Save the presentation using the file name, Lab 1-1 Document Storage at Home.

11. Submit the document in the format specified by your instructor.

12. ✳ What is the significance of placing the neat file folders photo on top of the messy desk photo on the closing slide? Why did you change the font color on Slides 2, 3, and 4 to Dark Blue?

Lab 2: Creating a Presentation with Bulleted Lists and Pictures

Problem: The number of reported West Nile Virus (WNV) cases across the continental United States has been growing steadily. After a discussion in your biology class, your instructor assigned everyone in the class to research WNV and to outline the facts that were discussed. You use your class notes to create the outline shown in Figure 1–85 and then create the presentation shown in Figures 1–86a through 1–86d on pages PPT 66–68.

West Nile Virus (WNV)
Facts, Signs, and Prevention
Student Name

What Is WNV?
    Transmitted by mosquitoes that bit infected birds
    First identified in eastern Africa in 1937
        Now worldwide in tropical and temperate climates
    Appeared in United States in 1999
        Now reported in 48 states
    At risk: People with weak immune systems

What Are the Symptoms?
    Most commonly resemble the flu
        High fever
        Headache
        Body aches
        Nausea / vomiting
        Vision problems

How Can I Avoid WNV?
    Protect against mosquito bites
        Wear repellent with EPA-recommended ingredients
        Avoid being outdoors at dawn and dusk
        Wear clothes that cover skin
    Remove standing water from yard vessels
    Repair damaged window and door screens

Figure 1–85

Continued >

In the Labs *continued*

Instructions: Perform the following tasks:

1. Create a new presentation using the Facet document theme.

2. Using the outline illustrated in Figure 1–85 on the previous page, create the title slide shown in Figure 1–86a, using your name in place of Student Name.

3. If requested by your instructor, substitute the name of your hometown in place of your last name.

4. On Slide 1, bold the text, West Nile Virus (WNV). Decrease the font size of the text, Facts, Signs, and Prevention, to 44 point. Change the font color of all the title text to Red, Accent 5 (second color from right in the Theme Colors row).

5. Using the outline in Figure 1–85, create the three text slides with bulleted lists shown in Figures 1–86b, 1–86c, and 1–86d. Change the color of the title text on these three text slides to Red, Accent 5.

6. Add the pictures shown in Figures 1–86a through 1–86d from Office.com. Zoom the slide and then resize the pictures when necessary.

7. Apply the Page Curl transition in the Exciting category to all slides. Change the duration to 2.25 seconds.

8. Tap or click the Start From Beginning button to start the slide show and then display each slide.

9. Save the presentation using the file name, Lab 1–2 West Nile Virus.

10. Submit the revised document in the format specified by your instructor.

11. ✹ How does changing the font color to red help reinforce the West Nile Virus prevention concept? What is the significance of adding a mosquito illustration to every slide?

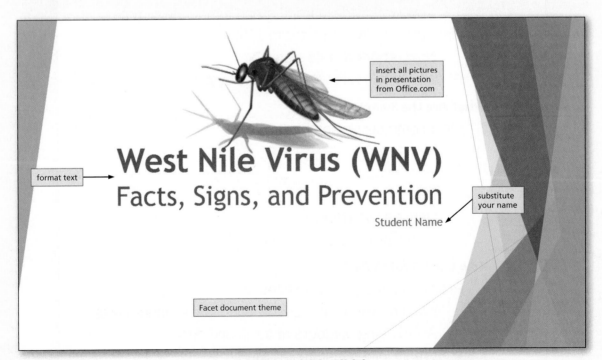

(a) Slide 1 (Title Slide)

Figure 1–86

(b) Slide 2

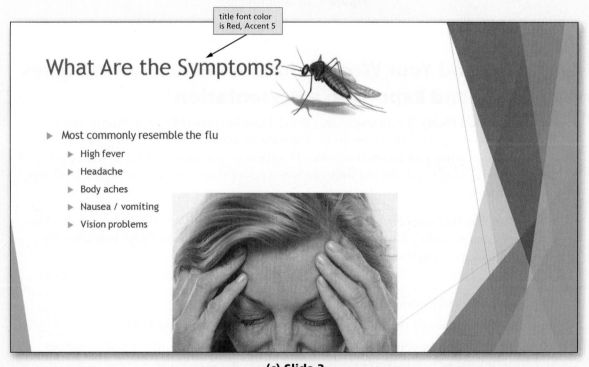

(c) Slide 3

Figure 1–86 (Continued)

Continued >

In the Labs *continued*

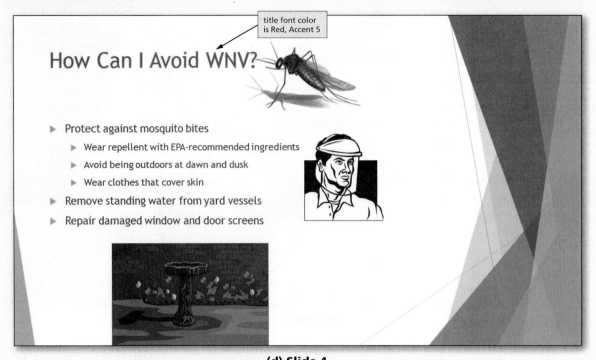

(d) Slide 4

Figure 1–86 (Continued)

Lab 3: Expand Your World: Cloud and Web Technologies
Modifying and Exporting a Presentation

Problem: Your local library is planning events to celebrate Hispanic Heritage Month, and you are part of a committee to publicize the event. You want to share the title slide of your preliminary PowerPoint presentation with fellow committee members, so you have decided to store the file on SkyDrive. You are going to modify the slide you have created thus far shown in Figure 1–87 and save it to SkyDrive.

Note: To complete this assignment, you will be required to use the Data Files for Students. Visit www.cengage.com/ct/studentdownload for detailed instructions or contact your instructor for information about accessing the required files.

Instructions:

1. Open the Lab 1–3 Hispanic Heritage file.

2. Insert another picture on the title slide in the area indicated in Figure 1–87.

3. If requested to do so by your instructor, change the city to the town where you were born.

4. Save the presentation using the file name, Lab 1–3 Heritage Month.

5. Export the file to your SkyDrive in the Chapter 01 folder in the PowerPoint folder.

6. Submit the assignment in the format specified by your instructor.

7. ✳ When would you save one of your files for school or your job to SkyDrive? Do you think using SkyDrive enhances collaboration efforts? Why?

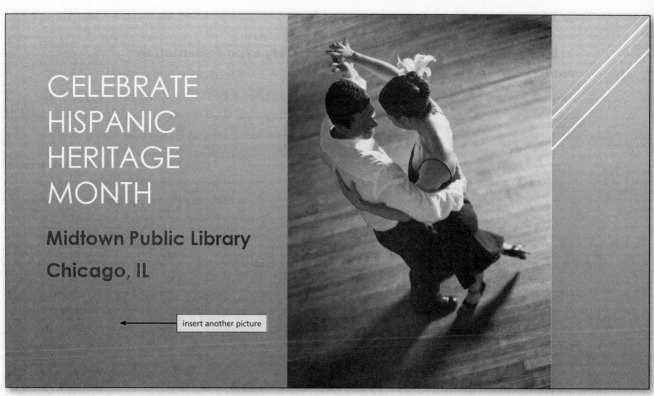

Figure 1–87 Slide 1 (Title Slide)

✸ Consider This: Your Turn

Apply your creative thinking and problem-solving skills to design and implement a solution.

1. Design and Create a Presentation about Mars Exploration

Personal

Part 1: Your astronomy class is studying the solar system, and you have been assigned the topic of the Mars Curiosity rover and its exploration of that planet. You have learned that the rover was launched from Cape Canaveral, Florida, on November 26, 2011, and landed in the Gale Crater on Mars on August 6, 2012. The mission was scheduled to last two years and had the major goal of assessing whether Mars was or is capable of supporting life. The Curiosity rover is the size of a car and has a MastCam equipped with two camera systems to take photos of the landscape as it maneuvers around the rocky surface. The rover also can scoop up samples of the Martian soil, fire a laser at rocks as far away as nine feet (2.7 meters), and make weather station readings. Use the concepts and techniques you learned in the chapter to create a PowerPoint presentation with a suitable theme, a title slide, and three text slides with bulleted lists. Add pictures from Office.com and apply a transition. Submit your assignment in the format specified by your instructor.

Part 2: ✸ You made several decisions while creating the presentation in this assignment: what theme to use, where to place text, how to format the text (font, font size, paragraph alignment, bulleted paragraphs, italics, bold, color). You also decided which graphical images to use, where to position the graphical images, if a closing slide would be useful, and which transition would be most effective. What was the rationale behind each of these decisions? When you proofed the document, what further revisions did you make and why? Where would you recommend showing this slide show?

Continued >

Consider This: Your Turn *continued*

2. Design and Create a Fire Department Safety Expo Presentation
Professional

Part 1: Your local fire department is sponsoring a Safety Expo one month from today at the local hardware store. The chief has asked you to prepare a slide show promoting the event, which will be held from noon to 5 p.m. A wide variety of demonstrations and informational booths will be present. They include: firefighters from your community's fire department, who will discuss home emergency planning, proper car seat installation, and fire extinguisher use; a local insurance agent, who will distribute tote bags filled with materials regarding adequate home and rental insurance coverage and also a nine-volt battery for a smoke alarm; and a children's workshop, where participants under 10 years of age can build a picture frame. Use the concepts and techniques presented in this chapter to develop and format this slide show with at least four slides with bulleted lists. Add pictures from Office.com and apply a transition. Submit your assignment in the format specified by your instructor.

Part 2: ✳ You made several decisions while creating the presentation in this assignment: what theme to use, where to place text, how to format the text (font, font size, paragraph alignment, bulleted paragraphs, italics, bold, color). You also decided which graphical images to use, where to position the graphical images, if a closing slide would be useful, and which transition would be most effective. What was the rationale behind each of these decisions? When you proofed the document, what further revisions did you make and why? Where would you recommend showing this slide show?

3. Design and Create a Presentation about Commemorative Postage Stamps
Research and Collaboration

Part 1: Stamp collecting is one of the world's more popular indoor hobbies. Collectors often seek postage stamps pertaining to a particular interest, such as birds, flowers, famous people, or ships. Have each member of your team gather information on these topics: stamp collecting equipment, popular commemorative stamps issued, current commemorative stamps for sale at your local post office, and rare stamps. After coordinating these facts, use the concepts and techniques presented in this chapter to prepare a presentation with a minimum of four slides that explore the subject of stamp collection. Select a suitable theme and include a title slide, bulleted lists, and a closing slide. Add pictures from Office.com and apply a transition. Submit your assignment in the format specified by your instructor.

Part 2: ✳ You made several decisions while creating the presentation in this assignment: what theme to use, where to place text, how to format the text (font, font size, paragraph alignment, bulleted paragraphs, italics, bold, color). You also decided which graphical images to use, where to position the graphical images, if a closing slide would be useful, and which transition would be most effective. What was the rationale behind each of these decisions? When you proofed the document, what further revisions did you make and why? Where would you recommend showing this slide show?

Learn Online

Reinforce what you learned in this chapter with games, exercises, training, and many other online activities and resources.

Student Companion Site   Reinforcement activities and resources are available at no additional cost on www.cengagebrain.com. Visit www.cengage.com/ct/studentdownload for detailed instructions about accessing the resources available at the Student Companion Site.

SAM   Put your skills into practice with SAM! If you have a SAM account, go to www.cengage.com/sam2013 to access SAM assignments for this chapter.

2 | Enhancing a Presentation with Pictures, Shapes, and WordArt

Microsoft product screenshots used with permission from Microsoft Corporation.

Objectives

You will have mastered the material in this chapter when you can:

- Search for and download an online theme
- Insert and format pictures
- Insert and size a shape
- Apply effects to a shape
- Add text to a shape
- Change the text font

- Insert and format WordArt
- Insert a picture to create a background
- Format slide backgrounds
- Find and replace text and check spelling
- Add and print speaker notes

2 | Enhancing a Presentation with Pictures, Shapes, and WordArt

Introduction

In our visually oriented culture, audience members enjoy viewing effective graphics. Whether reading a document or viewing a PowerPoint presentation, people increasingly want to see photographs, artwork, graphics, and a variety of typefaces. Researchers have known for decades that documents with visual elements are more effective than those that consist of only text because the illustrations motivate audiences to study the material. People remember at least one-third more information when the document they are seeing or reading contains visual elements. These graphics help clarify and emphasize details, so they appeal to audience members with differing backgrounds, reading levels, attention spans, and motivations.

Project — Presentation with Pictures, Shapes, and WordArt

The project in this chapter focuses on helping families plan for emergencies. Children need to prepare for the unexpected by collecting supplies to make an emergency supply kit, developing a communication plan, and realizing the need to be ready for any unexpected situation that may arise. The presentation shown in Figure 2–1 follows graphical guidelines and has a variety of illustrations and visual elements that are colorful and appealing to children. For example, the pictures have particular shapes and effects. The enhanced type has a style that blends well with the formatted background and illustrations. Pictures and type are formatted using picture styles and WordArt, which give the presentation a professional look. You plan to present the material during community safety open houses at fire stations and local hardware stores, so you want to add notes explaining concepts you will be discussing during the meeting.

BTW

BTWs
For a complete list of the BTWs found in the margins of this book, visit the BTW resource on the Student Companion Site located on www.cengagebrain.com. For detailed instructions about accessing available resources, visit www.cengage.com/ct/studentdownload or see the inside back cover of this book.

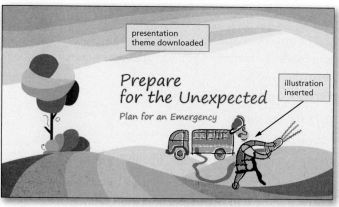

(a) Slide 1 (Title Slide)

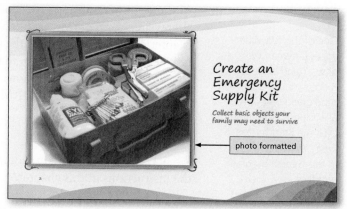

(b) Slide 2 (Formatted Picture)

(c) Slide 3 (Shapes Inserted and Formatted)

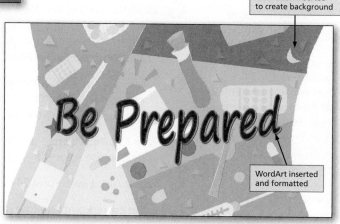

(d) Slide 4 (Picture Background)

Figure 2–1

For an introduction to Windows and instruction about how to perform basic Windows tasks, read the Office and Windows chapter at the beginning of this book, where you can learn how to resize windows, change screen resolution, create folders, move and re-name files, use Windows Help, and much more.

Roadmap

In this chapter, you will learn how to create the slides shown in Figure 2–1 on the previous page. The following roadmap identifies general activities you will perform as you progress through this chapter:

1. DOWNLOAD a theme and SELECT SLIDES for the presentation.
2. INSERT and FORMAT PICTURES for the slides.
3. INSERT and FORMAT SHAPES on one slide.
4. INSERT and FORMAT WORDART by changing the shape, fill, and outline.
5. FORMAT SLIDE BACKGROUNDS with a gradient, texture, and picture fill.
6. REVIEW and REVISE SLIDES by finding a synonym and checking spelling.

At the beginning of step instructions throughout the chapter, you will see an abbreviated form of this roadmap. The abbreviated roadmap uses colors to indicate chapter progress: gray means the chapter is beyond that activity; blue means the task being shown is covered in that activity, and black means that activity is yet to be covered. For example, the following abbreviated roadmap indicates the chapter would be showing a task in the 5 FORMAT SLIDE BACKGROUNDS activity.

One of the few differences between Windows 7 and Windows 8 occurs in the steps to run PowerPoint. If you are using Windows 7, click the Start button, type **PowerPoint** in the 'Search programs and files' box, click PowerPoint 2013, and then, if necessary, maximize the PowerPoint window. For detailed steps to run PowerPoint in Windows 7, refer to the Office and Windows chapter at the beginning of this book. For a summary of the steps, refer to the Quick Reference located at the back of this book.

1 DOWNLOAD & SELECT SLIDES	2 INSERT & FORMAT PICTURES	3 INSERT & FORMAT SHAPES
4 INSERT & FORMAT WORDART	**5 FORMAT SLIDE BACKGROUNDS**	6 REVIEW & REVISE SLIDES

Use the abbreviated roadmap as a progress guide while you read or step through the instructions in this chapter.

To Run PowerPoint

If you are using a computer to step through the project in this chapter and you want your screens to match the figures in this book, you should change your screen's resolution to 1366 × 768. For information about how to change a computer's resolution, refer to the Office and Windows chapter at the beginning of this book.

The following steps, which assume Windows 8 is running, use the Start screen or the search box to run PowerPoint based on a typical installation. You may need to ask your instructor how to run PowerPoint on your computer. For a detailed example of the procedure summarized below, refer to the Office and Windows chapter.

For an introduction to Office and instruction about how to perform basic tasks in Office apps, read the Office and Windows chapter at the beginning of this book, where you can learn how to run an application, use the ribbon, save a file, open a file, exit an application, use Help, and much more.

1 Scroll the Start screen for a PowerPoint 2013 tile. If your Start screen contains a PowerPoint 2013 tile, tap or click it to run PowerPoint and then proceed to Step 5; if the Start screen does not contain the PowerPoint 2013 tile, proceed to the next step to search for the PowerPoint app.

2 Swipe in from the right edge of the screen or point to the upper-right corner of the screen to display the Charms bar and then tap or click the Search charm on the Charms bar to display the Search menu.

3 Type **PowerPoint** as the search text in the Search box and watch the search results appear in the Apps list.

4 Tap or click PowerPoint 2013 in the search results to run PowerPoint.

5 If the PowerPoint window is not maximized, tap or click the Maximize button on its title bar to maximize the window.

Downloading a Theme and Editing Slides

In Chapter 1, you selected a theme and then typed the content for the title and text slides. In this chapter, you will type the slide content for the title and text slides, select a background, insert and format pictures and shapes, and then insert and format WordArt. To begin creating the four slides in this presentation, you will download a theme, delete unneeded slides in this downloaded presentation, and then enter text in three of the four slides.

To Search for and Download an Online Theme

1 DOWNLOAD & SELECT SLIDES | 2 INSERT & FORMAT PICTURES | 3 INSERT & FORMAT SHAPES
4 INSERT & FORMAT WORDART | 5 FORMAT SLIDE BACKGROUNDS | 6 REVIEW & REVISE SLIDES

PowerPoint displays many themes that are varied and appealing and give you an excellent start at designing a presentation. At times, however, you may have a specific topic and design concept and could use some assistance in starting to develop the presentation. Microsoft offers hundreds of predesigned themes and templates that could provide you with an excellent starting point. ***Why?*** *You can search for one of these ready-made presentations, or you can browse one of the predefined categories, such as business, medical, education, and nature. The themes and templates can save you time and help you develop content.* The following steps search for a theme that has an educational concept and is oriented toward children.

- Press and hold or point to Education in the Suggested searches list (Figure 2–2).

Q&A | Why does a Recent Presentation list display on the left side of my screen?
You can specify the number of recent presentations to display in the Advanced tab of the PowerPoint Options dialog box.

Figure 2–2

2

- Tap or click Education to search for themes with an academic subject.

Q&A Can I also use keywords to search for themes?
Yes. Tap or click the 'Search for online templates and themes' search box, type terms that relate to the topic of your presentation, and then click the Start searching button (the magnifying glass) or press the ENTER key so that Office.com will search for and display all themes with your keywords.

3

- Slide or scroll down about halfway through the theme thumbnails until the 'Colorful nature presentation, illustrated landscape design (widescreen)' theme, shown in Figure 2–3, is displayed.

Q&A Why are my theme thumbnails displaying in a different order?
Microsoft adds and modifies the themes, so the order may change.

4

- Tap or click the 'Colorful nature presentation, illustrated landscape design (widescreen)' theme to display a theme preview dialog box with a thumbnail view of the theme (Figure 2–3).

Q&A Can I see previews of the slides in this theme?
Yes. Click the right or left arrows beside the words, More Images, below the thumbnail. On some devices, a preview of all slides starts automatically after you tap the theme.

Figure 2–3

5

- Tap or click the Create button to download the theme and open a presentation with that theme in PowerPoint.

BTW
Additional Theme Information
You may see additional information regarding the theme in the theme preview dialog box if you are downloading the file for the first time. This information includes the provider (in this case, Microsoft Corporation), a description of the theme content and the intended audience, the file size (in this case, 2190 KB), and a rating.

To Delete a Slide

The downloaded theme has 13 slides with a variety of layouts. You will use four different layouts in your Be Prepared presentation, so you can delete the slides you downloaded that you will not need. *Why? Deleting the extra slides now helps reduce clutter and helps you focus on the layouts you will use.* The following steps delete the extra slides.

- If necessary, tap or click the Slide 1 thumbnail in the Thumbnail pane to select this slide.

- Swipe horizontally across each of the Slide 2, 3, and 4 thumbnails, or press and hold the SHIFT key and then click the thumbnail for Slide 4 to select slides 1 through 4 (Figure 2–4).

Q&A Why would I select Slide 1, the Title Slide layout, for deletion if I need a title slide for my presentation?
Slide 9 also will work well to format as the title slide (Slide 1) in this presentation.

Figure 2–4

- Press and hold or right-click any selected slide to display the shortcut menu (Figure 2–5).

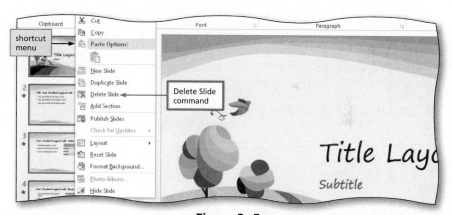

Figure 2–5

- Tap Delete or click Delete Slide to delete the selected slides from the presentation (Figure 2–6).

Q&A How would I delete several slides simultaneously if they are not sequential?
Repeat this procedure except make a short swipe across each slide thumbnail you want to delete to select it, or press and hold the CTRL key while you tap or click each slide you want to delete.

Figure 2–6

4

- Select the new Slides 2, 3, and 4, display the shortcut menu, and then delete these slides (Figure 2–7).

Q&A
Why am I selecting and then deleting these slides?
You want to use the current slides 1 and 5 in your presentation, so you need to delete the slides between these two slides.

Figure 2–7

5

- Tap or click the Slide 3 thumbnail to select this slide.

- Scroll down and then swipe the Slide 6 thumbnail or press and hold the CTRL key and then click the thumbnail for Slide 6 to select both slides 3 and 6 (Figure 2–8).

Q&A
Why did I press and hold down the CTRL key instead of the SHIFT key?
Holding down the CTRL key selects only the slides you tap or click, whereas holding the SHIFT key selects consecutive slides between the first and last selected slides.

Why am I selecting and then deleting these slides?
You want to use the current slides 4 and 5 in your presentation, so you need to delete slides 3 and 6.

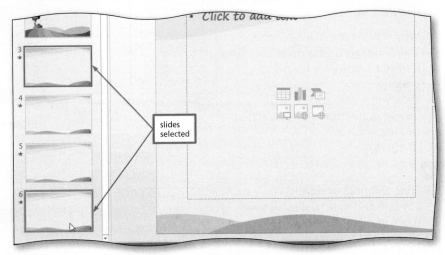

Figure 2–8

6

- Display the shortcut menu and then delete slides 3 and 6 (Figure 2–9).

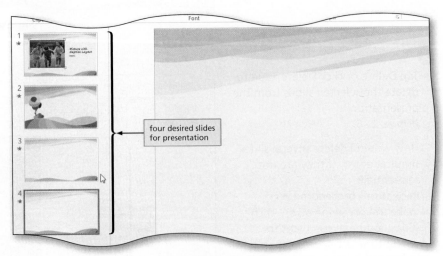

Figure 2–9

Other Ways

1. Select slide(s), press DELETE

To Create a Title Slide

Recall from Chapter 1 that the title slide introduces the presentation to the audience. In addition to introducing the presentation, this project uses the title slide to capture the audience's attention by using title text and an illustration. *Why? The presentation focuses on families and their need to work together to develop an emergency plan. The illustration of a fire truck and firefighter help introduce the concept.* The following steps rearrange Slide 1 and Slide 2 and then create the slide show's title slide.

1 Move Slide 2 in the Thumbnail pane above Slide 1 so that it becomes the first slide in the deck.

2 Type `Prepare` as the first text paragraph in the title text placeholder.

3 Press the ENTER key and then type `for the Unexpected` as the second paragraph in the title text placeholder.

4 Tap or click the subtitle text placeholder and then type `Plan for a Disaster` as the subtitle text (Figure 2–10).

Figure 2–10

To Create the First Text Slide

The first text slide you create in Chapter 2 emphasizes the need to make an emergency supply kit that contains supplies and other necessities for survival. The following steps create the Slide 2 text slide using the Picture with Caption layout.

1 Display Slide 2, select the text in the title text placeholder, and then type `Create a Disaster Supply Kit` in the placeholder.

2 Tap or click the caption placeholder and then type `Collect basic objects your family may need to stay alive` in this placeholder (Figure 2–11).

BTW

Q&As

For a complete list of the Q&As found in many of the step-by-step sequences in this book, visit the Q&A resource on the Student Companion Site located on www.cengagebrain.com. For detailed instructions about accessing available resources, visit www.cengage.com/ct/studentdownload or see the inside back cover of this book.

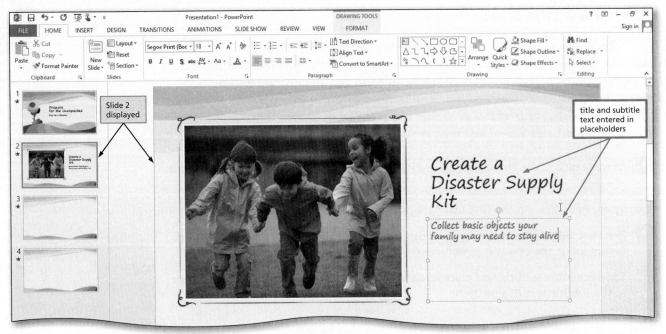

Figure 2–11

To Create the Second Text Slide

The second text slide you create shows two components of the family communication plan: carrying a contact list and arranging meeting places. The following step adds a title to Slide 3, which uses the Title Only layout.

Note: In the following step, the word, Communication, has been misspelled intentionally as Comunication to illustrate the use of PowerPoint's spell check feature. Your slides may contain different misspelled words, depending upon the accuracy of your typing.

1 Display Slide 3 and then type **Develop a Family Comunication Plan** in the title text placeholder. The word, Comunication, is intentionally misspelled; the red wavy line indicates the misspelling (Figure 2–12).

Figure 2–12

BTW

The Ribbon and Screen Resolution
PowerPoint may change how the groups and buttons within the groups appear on the ribbon, depending on the computer's screen resolution. Thus, your ribbon may look different from the ones in this book if you are using a screen resolution other than 1366 × 768.

To Save a Presentation

You have performed many tasks while creating this presentation and do not want to risk losing work completed thus far. Accordingly, you should save the presentation on your hard disk, SkyDrive, or a location that is most appropriate to your situation.

The following steps assume you already have created folders for storing your files, for example, a CIS 101 folder (for your class) that contains a PowerPoint folder (for your assignments). Thus, these steps save the presentation in the PowerPoint folder in the CIS 101 folder on your desired save location. For a detailed example of the procedure for saving a file in a folder or saving a file on SkyDrive, refer to the Office and Windows chapter at the beginning of this book.

1 Tap or click the Save button on the Quick Access Toolbar, which depending on settings, will display either the Save As gallery in the Backstage view or the Save As dialog box.

2 To save on a hard disk or other storage media on your computer, proceed to Step 2a. To save on SkyDrive, proceed to Step 2b.

2a If your screen opens the Backstage view and you want to save on storage media on your computer, tap or click Computer in the left pane, if necessary, to display options in the right pane related to saving on your computer. If your screen already displays the Save As dialog box, proceed to Step 3.

2b If your screen opens the Backstage view and you want to save on SkyDrive, tap or click SkyDrive in the left pane to display SkyDrive saving options or a Sign In button. If your screen displays a Sign In button, tap or click it and then sign in to SkyDrive.

3 Tap or click the Browse button in the right pane to display the Save As dialog box associated with the selected save location (i.e., Computer or SkyDrive).

4 Type `Emergency Plan` in the File name box to change the file name. Do not press the ENTER key after typing the file name because you do not want to close the dialog box at this time.

5 Navigate to the desired save location (in this case, the PowerPoint folder in the CIS 101 folder [or your class folder] on your computer or SkyDrive).

6 Tap or click the Save button (Save As dialog box) to save the presentation in the selected folder on the selected save location with the entered file name.

Inserting and Formatting Pictures in a Presentation

With the text entered in three of the four slides, the next step is to insert pictures into Slides 1 and 2 and then format the pictures. These graphical images draw the viewers' eyes to the slides and help them retain the information presented.

In the following pages, you will perform these tasks:

1. Insert the illustration into Slide 1.
2. Resize the illustration.
3. Change the Slide 2 photo.
4. Change the photo's brightness and contrast.
5. Change the photo's style and effect.
6. Add and modify the photo's border.

To Insert a Picture into a Slide without a Content Placeholder

1 DOWNLOAD & SELECT SLIDES | 2 INSERT & FORMAT PICTURES | 3 INSERT & FORMAT SHAPES
4 INSERT & FORMAT WORDART | 5 FORMAT SLIDE BACKGROUNDS | 6 REVIEW & REVISE SLIDES

In Chapter 1, you inserted photos and an illustration into slides without a content placeholder. *Why?* *Some slide layouts do not have a content placeholder, so you must insert and move the pictures to appropriate locations on the slide.* The illustration for Slide 1 is available on the Data Files for Students. Visit www.cengage.com/ct/studentdownload for detailed instructions or contact your instructor for information about accessing the

BTW

Organizing Files and Folders
You should organize and store files in folders so that you easily can find the files later. For example, if you are taking an introductory computer class called CIS 101, a good practice would be to save all PowerPoint files in a PowerPoint folder in a CIS 101 folder. For a discussion of folders and detailed examples of creating folders, refer to the Office and Windows chapter at the beginning of this book.

required files. The instructions in this chapter show the required files in the PowerPoint Chapter 2 folder in the CIS 101 folder on your computer. The following steps insert an illustration into the title slide.

1
- Display Slide 1 and then tap or click INSERT on the ribbon to display the INSERT tab.
- Tap or click the Pictures button (INSERT tab | Images group) to display the Insert Picture dialog box.

2
- If Computer is not displayed in the navigation pane, press and drag or drag the navigation pane scroll bar (Insert Picture dialog box) until Computer appears.
- Tap or click Computer in the navigation pane to display a list of available storage locations in the Insert Picture dialog box. If necessary, scroll through the dialog box until your class folder appears in the list.
- Double-tap or double-click your folder in the list of available storage locations to display a list of files and folders. Double-tap or double-click the Data Files for Students folder, double-tap or double-click the PowerPoint folder, and then double-tap or double-click the Chapter 02 folder to display a list of files in that folder.

- Slide or scroll down and then tap or click Fire Truck to select the file name (Figure 2–13).

Q&A
What if the picture is not in the folder?
Use the same process, but select the location containing the Chapter 2 data file pictures or search for the picture on Office.com.

Why do I see thumbnails of the pictures along with the file names in my folder?
Your view is different from the view shown in Figure 2–13.

Figure 2–13

3
- Tap or click the Insert button (Insert Picture dialog box) to insert the illustration into Slide 1.
- Drag the upper-right sizing handle diagonally toward the upper-right corner of the slide until the crosshair is positioned approximately as shown in Figure 2–14.

Figure 2–14

4
- Release to resize the illustration.

- Drag the illustration downward until the horizontal Smart Guide is displayed under the title text placeholder and the vertical Smart Guide is displayed near the right side of the slide, as shown in Figure 2–15, and then release.

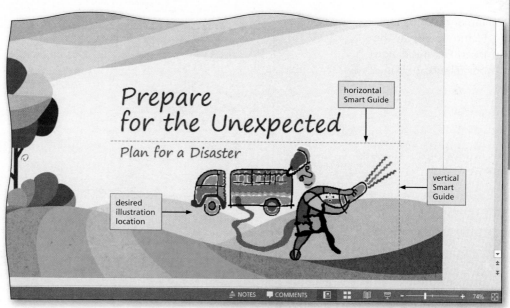

Figure 2–15

To Change a Picture

1 DOWNLOAD & SELECT SLIDES | 2 INSERT & FORMAT PICTURES | 3 INSERT & FORMAT SHAPES
4 INSERT & FORMAT WORDART | 5 FORMAT SLIDE BACKGROUNDS | 6 REVIEW & REVISE SLIDES

Why? *The downloaded theme included the photo of three children on Slide 2. You need to change the photo to reflect the emergency kit concept presented on this slide.* The next task in the presentation is to change the default picture on Slide 2 with one of the emergency pictures on the Data Files for Students. The following steps change the Slide 2 photo to the Emergency Kit photo, which, in this example, is located in the PowerPoint Chapter 02 folder that contains the saved presentation.

1
- Display Slide 2 and then press and hold or right-click the picture to display the shortcut menu (Figure 2–16).

Q&A Why are the Style and Crop buttons displayed above the shortcut menu on my screen?
These two buttons display either above or below the shortcut menu depending upon where you press and hold or right-click on the screen.

Figure 2–16

2

- Tap or click Change Picture to display the Insert Pictures dialog box (Figure 2–17).

Figure 2–17

3

- Tap or click the Browse button in the From a file area to display the Insert Pictures dialog box.

- If necessary, navigate to the PowerPoint Chapter 02 folder, slide or scroll down, and then click First Aid Kit to select the file name (Figure 2–18).

Figure 2–18

4

- Tap or click the Insert button (Insert Picture dialog box) to insert the photo into the Slide 2 picture placeholder (Figure 2–19).

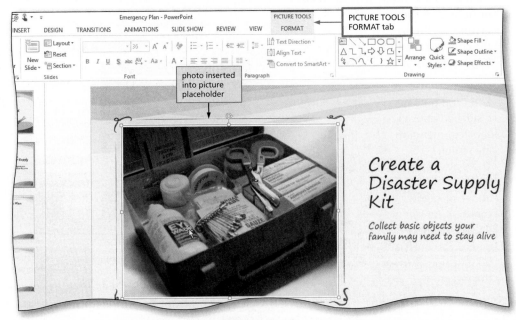

Figure 2–19

Other Ways

1. Tap or click Change Picture button (PICTURE TOOLS FORMAT tab | Adjust group)

To Correct a Picture

A photo's color intensity can be modified by changing the brightness and contrast. **Brightness** determines the overall lightness or darkness of the entire image, whereas **contrast** is the difference between the darkest and lightest areas of the image. The brightness and contrast are changed in predefined percentage increments. The following step increases the brightness and decreases the contrast. *Why? Altering the photo's brightness will coordinate with the vibrant colors in the slide design while decreasing the contrast will soften the image. It is important for the audience to recognize the first aid kit but not focus on each individual supply in the kit.*

1

- With the First Aid Kit photo on Slide 2 still selected, tap or click FORMAT on the ribbon to display the PICTURE TOOLS FORMAT tab.

- Tap or click the Corrections button (PICTURE TOOLS FORMAT tab | Adjust group) to display the Corrections gallery.

- If you are using a mouse, point to Brightness: +20% Contrast: −40% (the fourth picture in the first Brightness/Contrast row) to display a live preview of these corrections on the picture (Figure 2–20).

Q&A Can I use live preview on a touch screen?
Live preview is not available on a touch screen.

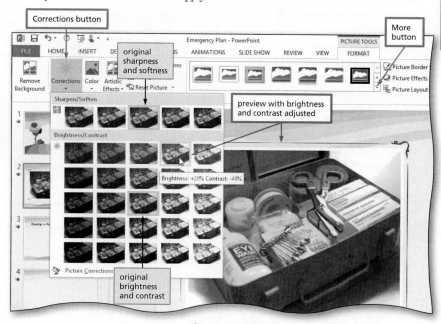

Figure 2–20

Why is a pink border surrounding the pictures in the center of the Sharpen/Soften and Brightness/Contrast areas of the gallery?
The image on Slide 2 currently has normal sharpness, brightness, and contrast (0%), which is represented by these center images in the gallery.

Experiment

- If you are using a mouse, point to various pictures in the Brightness and Contrast area and watch the brightness and contrast change on the picture in Slide 2.

- Tap or click Brightness: +20% Contrast: −40% to apply this correction to the First Aid Kit photo.

Q&A How can I remove all effects from the picture?
Tap or click the Reset Picture button (PICTURE TOOLS FORMAT tab | Adjust group).

Other Ways

1. Tap or click Picture Corrections Options (Corrections gallery), move Brightness or Contrast sliders or enter number in box next to slider (Format Picture task pane)

To Apply a Picture Style

A **style** is a named group of formatting characteristics. The picture on Slide 2 emphasizes the concept of assembling a supply kit, and you can increase its visual appeal by applying a style. *Why? PowerPoint provides more than 25 picture styles that enable you easily to change a picture's look to a more visually appealing style, including a variety of shapes, angles, borders, and reflections.* You want to use a style that applies a shadow to the First Aid Kit photo. The following steps apply a picture style to the Slide 2 photo.

1

- With the Slide 2 picture selected, if necessary tap or click the PICTURE TOOLS FORMAT tab and then tap or click the More button in the Picture Styles gallery (PICTURE TOOLS FORMAT tab | Picture Styles group) (shown in Figure 2–20) to expand the gallery.

- If you are using a mouse, point to Center Shadow Rectangle in the Picture Styles gallery (the sixth style in the second row) to display a live preview of that style applied to the picture in the document (Figure 2–21).

Figure 2–21

Experiment

- If you are using a mouse, point to various picture styles in the Picture Styles gallery and watch the style of the picture change in the document window.

2

- Tap or click Center Shadow Rectangle in the Picture Styles gallery to apply the style to the selected picture (Figure 2–22).

BTW

Touch Screen Differences

The Office and Windows interfaces may vary if you are using a touch screen. For this reason, you might notice that the function or appearance of your touch screen differs slightly from this chapter's presentation.

Figure 2–22

To Add a Picture Border

1 DOWNLOAD & SELECT SLIDES | 2 INSERT & FORMAT PICTURES | 3 INSERT & FORMAT SHAPES
4 INSERT & FORMAT WORDART | 5 FORMAT SLIDE BACKGROUNDS | 6 REVIEW & REVISE SLIDES

The next step is to add a border to the Slide 2 picture. *Why? Some picture styles do not have a border; others, such as the Center Shadow Rectangle style you applied to this picture, do have this edging. This border is small, and you want a larger edge around the photo to draw attention to the graphic.* The following steps add a border to the First Aid Kit picture.

❶
- With the Slide 2 picture still selected, tap or click the Picture Border arrow (PICTURE TOOLS FORMAT tab | Picture Styles group) to display the Picture Border gallery.

Q&A What if the PICTURE TOOLS FORMAT tab no longer is displayed on my ribbon?
Tap or click the picture to display the PICTURE TOOLS FORMAT tab.

❷
- Point to Weight on the Picture Border gallery to display the Weight gallery (Figure 2–23).

❸
- If you are using a mouse, point to 3 pt to display a live preview of this line weight on the picture.

Figure 2–23

Q&A Can I make the line width more than 6 pt?
Yes. Tap or click More Lines, tap or click Solid line in the LINE section of the Format Picture task pane, and then increase the amount in the Width box.

🔎 **Experiment**
- If you are using a mouse, point to various line weights in the Weight gallery and watch the line thickness change.

- Tap or click 3 pt to add this line weight to the picture.

To Change a Picture Border Color

1 DOWNLOAD & SELECT SLIDES | 2 INSERT & FORMAT PICTURES | 3 INSERT & FORMAT SHAPES
4 INSERT & FORMAT WORDART | 5 FORMAT SLIDE BACKGROUNDS | 6 REVIEW & REVISE SLIDES

The default color for the border you added to the Slide 2 picture is brown, but you will change the border color to light blue. *Why? The light blue color coordinates with other elements on the slide, especially the blue sky.* The following steps change the Slide 2 picture border color.

❶
- With the Slide 2 photo still selected, tap or click the Picture Border arrow (PICTURE TOOLS FORMAT tab | Picture Styles group) to display the Picture Border gallery.

❷
- If you are using a mouse, point to Light Blue, Background 2 (the third color in the first row) in the Picture Border gallery to display a live preview of that border color on the picture (Figure 2–24).

Figure 2–24

Experiment

- If you are using a mouse, point to various colors in the Picture Border gallery and watch the border on the picture change in the slide.

3

- Tap or click Light Blue, Background 2 in the Picture Border gallery to change the picture border color.

To Apply Picture Effects

1 DOWNLOAD & SELECT SLIDES | 2 INSERT & FORMAT PICTURES | 3 INSERT & FORMAT SHAPES
4 INSERT & FORMAT WORDART | 5 FORMAT SLIDE BACKGROUNDS | 6 REVIEW & REVISE SLIDES

Why? *The picture effect allows you to further customize a picture.* PowerPoint provides a variety of picture effects, including shadows, reflections, glow, soft edges, bevel, and 3-D rotation. The difference between the effects and the styles is that each effect has several options, providing you with more control over the exact look of the image.

In this presentation, the photo on Slide 2 has a blue glow effect and a bevel applied to its edges. The following steps apply picture effects to the selected picture.

1

- With the Slide 2 picture selected, tap or click the Picture Effects button (PICTURE TOOLS FORMAT tab | Picture Styles group) to display the Picture Effects menu.

Q&A
What if the PICTURE TOOLS FORMAT tab no longer is displayed on my ribbon?
Tap or double-click the picture to display the PICTURE TOOLS FORMAT tab.

- Point to Glow on the Picture Effects menu to display the Glow gallery.

Figure 2–25

- If you are using a mouse, point to Light Blue, 18 pt glow, Accent color 2 in the Glow Variations area (the second glow in the last row) to display a live preview of the selected glow effect applied to the picture in the document window (Figure 2–25).

Experiment

- If you are using a mouse, point to various glow effects in the Glow gallery and watch the picture change in the document window.

2

- Tap or click Light Blue, 18 pt glow, Accent color 2 in the Glow gallery to apply the selected picture effect.

3

- Tap or click the Picture Effects button (PICTURE TOOLS FORMAT tab | Picture Styles group) to display the Picture Effects menu again.

- Point to Bevel on the Picture Effects menu to display the Bevel gallery.

- If you are using a mouse, point to Relaxed Inset (the second bevel in the first row) to display a live preview of the selected bevel effect applied to the Slide 2 picture (Figure 2–26).

 Experiment

- If you are using a mouse, point to various bevel effects in the Bevel gallery and watch the picture change in the slide.

Figure 2–26

4

- Tap or click Relaxed Inset in the Bevel gallery to apply the selected picture effect.

Other Ways

1. Press and hold or right-click picture, click Format Picture on shortcut menu, select desired options (Format Picture task pane), tap or click Close button

2. Tap or click Format Shape task pane launcher (PICTURE TOOLS FORMAT tab | Picture Styles group), select desired options (Format Picture task pane), tap or click Close button

---

Break Point: If you wish to take a break, this is a good place to do so. Be sure to save the Emergency Plan file again and then you can exit PowerPoint. To resume at a later time, run PowerPoint, open the file called Emergency Plan, and continue following the steps from this location forward.

Inserting and Formatting a Shape

One method of getting the audience's attention and reinforcing the major concepts being presented is to have graphical elements on the title slide. PowerPoint provides a wide variety of predefined shapes that can add visual interest to a slide. Shape elements include lines, basic geometrical shapes, arrows, equation shapes, flowchart symbols, stars, banners, and callouts. After adding a shape to a slide, you can change its default characteristics by adding text, bullets, numbers, and styles. You also can combine multiple shapes to create a more complex graphic.

Slide 3 in this presentation is enhanced in a variety of ways. First, a scroll and a plus shape are inserted on Slide 4. Then, a rectangle is added and copied, and text is added to each rectangle and then formatted.

To Add a Shape

Many of the shapes included in the Shapes gallery can direct the viewer to important aspects of the presentation. The following steps add a scroll shape to Slide 3. *Why? A scroll shape helps emphasize the presentation's theme of drafting and finalizing a plan for dealing with emergencies in the household.*

1

- Display Slide 3 and then display the HOME tab (Figure 2–27).

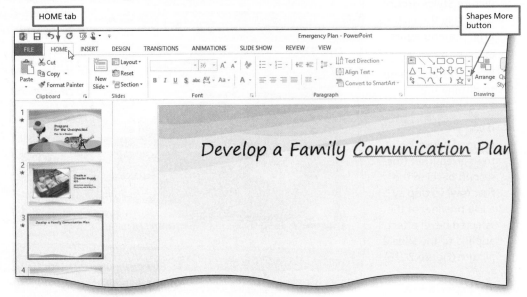

Figure 2–27

2

- Tap or click the Shapes More button (HOME tab | Drawing group) shown in Figure 2–27 to display the Shapes gallery (Figure 2–28).

Q&A
I do not see a Shapes More button and the three rows of the shapes shown in Figure 2–28. Instead, I have a Shapes button. Why? Monitor dimensions and resolution affect how buttons display on the ribbon. Tap or click the Shapes button to display the entire Shapes gallery.

Figure 2–28

- Tap or click the Vertical Scroll shape in the Stars and Banners area of the Shapes gallery.

Q&A Why did my pointer change shape?
The pointer changed to a plus shape to indicate the Vertical Scroll shape has been added to the Clipboard.

- Position the pointer (a crosshair) below the word, Develop, as shown in Figure 2–29.

Figure 2–29

④

- Tap or click Slide 3 to insert the Vertical Scroll shape.

Other Ways

1. Tap or click Shapes button (INSERT tab | Illustrations group)

To Resize a Shape

1 DOWNLOAD & SELECT SLIDES | 2 INSERT & FORMAT PICTURES | 3 INSERT & FORMAT SHAPES
4 INSERT & FORMAT WORDART | 5 FORMAT SLIDE BACKGROUNDS | 6 REVIEW & REVISE SLIDES

The next step is to resize the Vertical Scroll shape. *Why? The shape should be enlarged so that it fills the middle area of the left side of the slide.* The following steps resize the selected Vertical Scroll shape.

- Press and hold down the SHIFT key and then drag the lower-right corner sizing handle until the Vertical Scroll shape is resized approximately as shown in Figure 2–30.

Q&A Why did I need to press the SHIFT key while enlarging the shape?
Holding down the SHIFT key while dragging keeps the proportions of the original shape.

What if my shape is not selected?
To select a shape, click it.

If I am using a touch screen, how can I maintain the shape's original proportion?
If you drag one of the corner sizing handles, the object should stay in proportion.

Figure 2–30

2

- Release to resize the shape.

- Drag the scroll shape until the vertical Smart Guide is displayed along the left side of the slide, as shown in Figure 2–31, and then release.

What if I want to move the shape to a precise location on the slide? With the shape selected, press the ARROW keys or the CTRL+ARROW keys to move the shape to the desired location.

Figure 2–31

Other Ways

1. Enter shape height and width in Height and Width boxes (DRAWING TOOLS FORMAT tab | Size group)

2. Tap or click Size and Position task pane launcher (DRAWING TOOLS FORMAT tab | Size group), tap or click Size tab, enter desired height and width values in boxes, tap or click Close button

To Add Other Shapes

1 DOWNLOAD & SELECT SLIDES | 2 INSERT & FORMAT PICTURES | 3 INSERT & FORMAT SHAPES
4 INSERT & FORMAT WORDART | 5 FORMAT SLIDE BACKGROUNDS | 6 REVIEW & REVISE SLIDES

Circles, squares, arrows, stars, and equation shapes are among the items included in the Shapes gallery. These shapes can be combined to show relationships among the elements, and they can help illustrate the basic concepts presented in your slide show. The following steps add the Plus and Rectangle shapes to Slide 3.

1

- Tap or click the Shapes More button (HOME tab | Drawing group) to display the Shapes gallery (Figure 2–32).

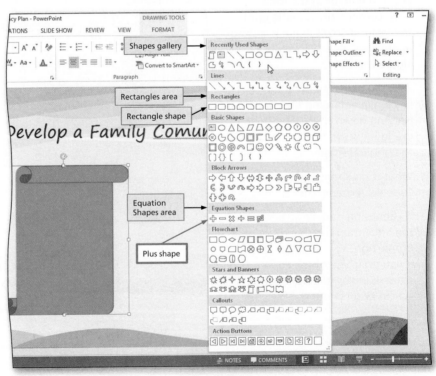

Figure 2–32

2

- Tap or click the Plus shape in the Equation Shapes area of the Shapes gallery.
- Position the pointer in the center of Slide 3 and then tap or click to insert the Plus shape.

3

- Press and hold down the SHIFT key and then drag a corner sizing handle until the Plus shape is the size shown in Figure 2–33.

 Q&A If I am using a touch screen, how can I maintain the Plus shape's original proportion?
The object should stay in proportion when you drag one of the corner sizing handles.

Figure 2–33

- Drag the Plus shape until the horizontal Smart Guide is displayed in the middle of the two shapes and the vertical Smart Guide is displayed between the two shapes, as shown in Figure 2–33, and then release.

4

- Display the Shapes gallery and then tap or click the Rectangle shape in the Rectangles area of the gallery.
- Position the pointer toward the upper-right side of the Plus shape and then tap or click to insert the Rectangle shape.

5

- Resize the Rectangle shape so that it is the size shown in Figure 2–34.
- Drag the Rectangle shape until the horizontal Smart Guide is displayed below the title text and the vertical Smart Guide is displayed between the Plus and the Rectangle shapes, as shown in Figure 2–34, and then release.

Figure 2–34

To Apply a Shape Style

1 DOWNLOAD & SELECT SLIDES | 2 INSERT & FORMAT PICTURES | 3 INSERT & FORMAT SHAPES
4 INSERT & FORMAT WORDART | 5 FORMAT SLIDE BACKGROUNDS | 6 REVIEW & REVISE SLIDES

Formatting text in a shape follows the same techniques as formatting text in a placeholder. You can change font, font color and size, and alignment. You later will add contact information to the scroll, but now you want to apply a shape style to the scroll. *Why? The style will give depth to the object so that it appears three-dimensional.* The Quick Styles gallery has a variety of styles that change depending upon the theme applied to the presentation. The following steps apply a style to the Vertical Scroll shape.

- Tap or click the
Vertical Scroll shape
to select it and then
tap or click the Quick
Styles button (HOME
tab | Drawing group)
(Figure 2–35).

Figure 2–35

- If you are using
a mouse, point
to Subtle Effect –
Lavender, Accent 6
in the Quick Styles
gallery (the last shape
in the fourth row) to
display a live preview
of that style applied
to the Vertical Scroll
shape in the slide
(Figure 2–36).

 Experiment

- If you are using a
mouse, point to
various styles in the
Quick Styles gallery
and watch the style
of the shape change.

Figure 2–36

- Tap or click Subtle Effect – Lavender, Accent 6 in the Quick Styles gallery to apply
the selected style to the Vertical Scroll shape.

Other Ways

1. Tap or click Shape Styles More button (DRAWING TOOLS FORMAT tab | Shape Styles group), select style

2. Press and hold or right-click shape, tap or click Format Shape on shortcut menu, select desired style (Format Shape task pane), tap or click Close button

To Apply Another Style

You later will add meeting place information to the rectangle, but now you want to format this shape. ***Why?*** *The formatting will add interest. In addition, the Plus shape helps join the scroll and the rectangle, both of which will contain components of the family communication plan. You can apply a coordinating shape style to the Plus sign.* The following steps apply styles to the Rectangle and Plus shapes.

1 Tap or click the Rectangle shape on Slide 3 to select it.

2 Tap or click the Quick Styles button (HOME tab | Drawing group) to display the Quick Styles gallery and then apply the Subtle Effect – Lavender, Accent 6 style to the Rectangle shape.

3 Tap or click the Plus shape on Slide 3 to select it and then tap or click the Quick Styles button.

4 Tap or click Colored Outline – Lavender, Accent 6 (the last style in the first row) to apply that style to the Plus shape (Figure 2–37).

Figure 2–37

To Add Text to a Shape

1 DOWNLOAD & SELECT SLIDES | 2 INSERT & FORMAT PICTURES | **3 INSERT & FORMAT SHAPES**
4 INSERT & FORMAT WORDART | 5 FORMAT SLIDE BACKGROUNDS | 6 REVIEW & REVISE SLIDES

The scroll and rectangle shapes on Slide 3 help call attention to the key aspects of your presentation. ***Why?*** *Your goal is to urge families to develop a communication plan by gathering contact information and determining meeting locations.* The next step is to add this information to Slide 3. The following steps add text to the two shapes.

1

- Tap or click the Vertical Scroll shape to select it and then type `Contact names & phone numbers` in the shape.

2

- Tap or click the Rectangle shape to select it and then type `Meeting place near house` in the shape (Figure 2–38).

Figure 2–38

To Change the Font

1 DOWNLOAD & SELECT SLIDES | 2 INSERT & FORMAT PICTURES | **3 INSERT & FORMAT SHAPES**
4 INSERT & FORMAT WORDART | 5 FORMAT SLIDE BACKGROUNDS | 6 REVIEW & REVISE SLIDES

The default theme font is Segoe Print. To draw more attention to text in the shapes and to help differentiate these slide elements from the title text, you want to change the font to Courier New. ***Why?*** *This font resembles the letters that typewriters produced.* To change the font, you must select the letters you want to format. In Chapter 1, you selected a paragraph and then formatted the characters, and you follow the same procedure to change the font. The following steps change the text font in the shape.

1

- Be certain the Rectangle shape is selected. If you are using a touch screen, tap to position the insertion point in the text to select and then drag the selection handles as necessary until all the characters are selected and the mini toolbar is displayed; if you are using a mouse, triple-click the text to select all the characters and display the mini toolbar (Figure 2–39).

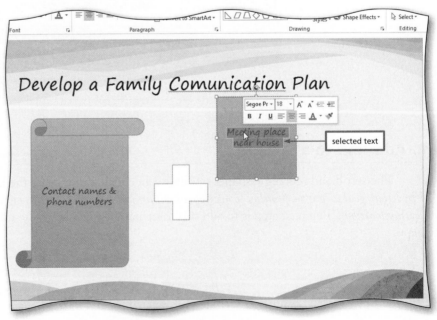

Figure 2–39

2

- Tap or click the Font arrow to display the Font gallery (Figure 2–40).

Q&A Will the fonts in my Font gallery be the same as those shown in Figure 2–40?
Your list of available fonts may differ, depending on what fonts you have installed and the type of printer you are using.

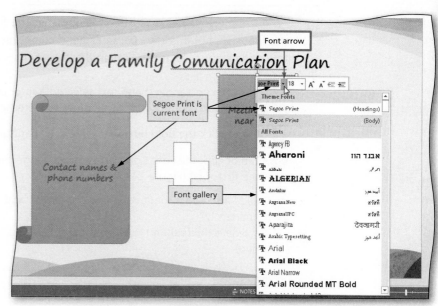

Figure 2–40

3

- If you are using a mouse, drag or scroll through the Font gallery and then point to Courier New (or a similar font) to display a live preview of the title text in the Courier New font (Figure 2–41).

Experiment

- If you are using a mouse, point to various fonts in the Font gallery and watch the subtitle text font change in the slide.

- Tap or click Courier New (or a similar font) to change the font of the selected text to Courier New.

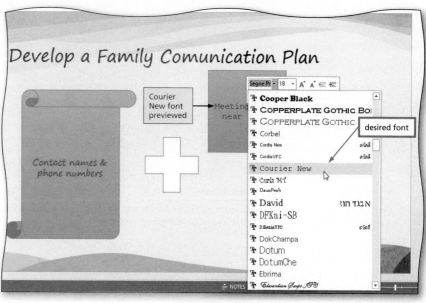

Figure 2–41

Other Ways

1. Tap or click Font arrow (HOME tab | Font group), tap or click desired font in Font gallery

2. Press and hold or right-click selected text, click Font on shortcut menu (Font dialog box), tap or click Font tab, select desired font in Font list, tap or click OK button

3. Tap or click Font dialog box launcher (HOME tab | Font group), tap or click Font tab (Font dialog box), select desired font in Font list, tap or click OK button

4. Press CTRL+SHIFT+F, click Font tab (Font dialog box), select desired font in the Font list, tap or click OK button

To Format the Text

To increase readability, you can format the Rectangle shape text by increasing the font size, bolding the characters, and changing the font color to black. The following steps format the Rectangle shape text.

1 With the Rectangle shape text selected, tap or click the Increase Font Size button (HOME tab | Font group) three times to increase the font size to 28 pt.

2 Tap or click the Bold button (HOME tab | Font group) to bold the text.

3 Tap or click the Font Color arrow and change the color to Black (the fourth color in the first row) (Figure 2–42).

Q&A Could I also add a shadow behind the text to add depth and help the letters display prominently?
Yes. Select the text and then tap or click the Text Shadow button (HOME tab | Font group).

Figure 2–42

Other Ways

1. Select text, tap 'Show Context Menu' button on mini toolbar or right-click selected text, tap or click desired text format button on mini toolbar

Format Painter

To save time and avoid formatting errors, you can use the Format Painter to apply custom formatting to other places in your presentation quickly and easily. You can use this feature in three ways:

- To copy only character attributes, such as font and font effects, select text that has these qualities.

- To copy both character attributes and paragraph attributes, such as alignment and indentation, select the entire paragraph.

- To apply the same formatting to multiple words, phrases, or paragraphs, double-tap or double-click the Format Painter button and then select each item you want to format. You then can press the ESC key or click the Format Painter button to turn off this feature.

To Format Text Using the Format Painter

Why? *To save time and duplicated effort, you quickly can use the Format Painter to copy formatting attributes from the Rectangle shape text and apply them to Vertical Scroll text.* The following steps use the Format Painter to copy formatting features.

- With the Rectangle shape text still selected, double-tap or double-click the Format Painter button (HOME tab | Clipboard group).

- Move the pointer off the ribbon (Figure 2–43).

Q&A Why did my pointer change shape?
The pointer changed shape by adding a paintbrush to indicate that the Format Painter function is active.

Figure 2–43

- Tap and drag the selection handles as necessary or triple-click the Vertical Scroll text to apply the format to all characters (Figure 2–44).

- Tap the Format Painter button or press the ESC key to turn off the Format Painter feature.

Figure 2–44

Other Ways

1. Select text, tap or click Format Painter button on mini toolbar

To Copy and Paste a Shape

When developing a communication plan, family members need to determine two meeting places: one near the house and a second outside the neighborhood. You already have created the shape stating the first meeting location. You now need to create a second shape with the instruction to decide where to meet away from the house. The following steps copy the Rectangle shape and then move the copy. *Why?* *You could repeat all the steps you performed to create the first rectangle, but it is much more efficient to duplicate the shape and then edit the text.*

- Select the Rectangle shape and then tap or click the Copy button (HOME tab | Clipboard group) (Figure 2–45).

Figure 2–45

2

- Tap or click the Paste button (HOME tab | Clipboard group) to insert a duplicate Rectangle shape on Slide 3.

- Drag the Rectangle shape below the first Rectangle shape (Figure 2–46).

Figure 2–46

3

- In the second Rectangle shape, select the text, near house, and then type **away from vicinity** as the replacement text (Figure 2–47).

Figure 2–47

Other Ways

1. Press and hold or right-click selected shape, tap or click Copy on shortcut menu, press and hold or right-click, tap or click Paste on shortcut menu

2. Select shape, press CTRL+C, press CTRL+V

Break Point: If you wish to take a break, this is a good place to do so. Be sure to save the Emergency Plan file again and then you can exit PowerPoint. To resume at a later time, run PowerPoint, open the file called Emergency Plan, and continue following the steps from this location forward.

Inserting and Formatting WordArt

One method of adding appealing visual elements to a presentation is by using **WordArt** styles. This feature is found in other Microsoft Office applications, including Word and Excel. This gallery of decorative effects allows you to type new text or convert existing text to WordArt. You then can add elements such as fills, outlines, and effects.

WordArt **fill** in the interior of a letter can consist of a solid color, texture, picture, or gradient. The WordArt **outline** is the exterior border surrounding each letter or symbol. PowerPoint allows you to change the outline color, weight, and style. You also can add an **effect**, which helps add emphasis or depth to the characters. Some effects are shadows, reflections, glows, bevels, and 3-D rotations.

BTW
Undo Text Formatting Changes
To remove a formatting change you have made to text, such as an underline or bolding, select the text and then tap or click the button that originally applied the format. For example, to undo bolding, select the text and then click the Bold button. If you apply a format and then immediately decide to remove this effect, click the Undo button on the Quick Access Toolbar.

To Insert WordArt

1 DOWNLOAD & SELECT SLIDES | 2 INSERT & FORMAT PICTURES | 3 INSERT & FORMAT SHAPES
4 INSERT & FORMAT WORDART | 5 FORMAT SLIDE BACKGROUNDS | 6 REVIEW & REVISE SLIDES

Having a communication plan is of utmost importance to prepare for the unexpected. You want to emphasize this concept, and the last slide in the presentation is an excellent location to urge your audience to take action. *Why? Audience members remember the first and last things they see and hear.* You quickly can add a visual element to the slide by selecting a WordArt style from the WordArt Styles gallery and then applying it to some text. The following steps insert WordArt.

- Display Slide 4 and then display the INSERT tab.

- Tap or click the WordArt button (INSERT tab | Text group) to display the WordArt gallery (Figure 2–48).

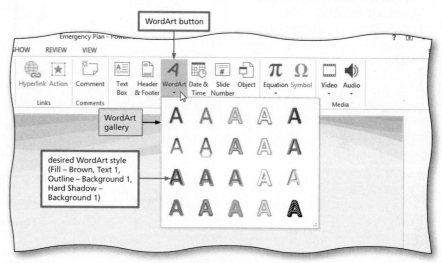

Figure 2–48

2

- Tap or click Fill – Brown, Text 1, Outline – Background 1, Hard Shadow – Background 1 (the first style in the third row) to insert the WordArt object (Figure 2–49).

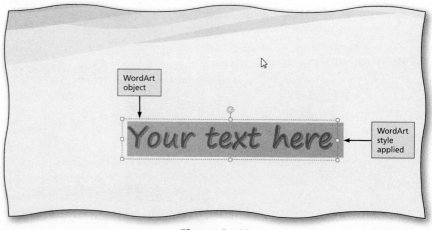

Figure 2–49

3

- Type **Be Prepared** in the object as the WordArt text (Figure 2–50).

Why did the DRAWING TOOLS FORMAT tab appear automatically in the ribbon?
It appears when you select text to which you could add a WordArt style or other effect.

Figure 2–50

To Change the WordArt Shape

1 DOWNLOAD & SELECT SLIDES | 2 INSERT & FORMAT PICTURES | 3 INSERT & FORMAT SHAPES
4 INSERT & FORMAT WORDART | 5 FORMAT SLIDE BACKGROUNDS | 6 REVIEW & REVISE SLIDES

Why? *The WordArt text is useful to emphasize the need to prepare for emergencies. You further can emphasize this text by changing its shape.* PowerPoint provides a variety of graphical shapes that add interest to WordArt text. The following steps change the WordArt shape to Inflate Bottom.

1

- With the WordArt object still selected, click the Text Effects button (DRAWING TOOLS FORMAT tab | WordArt Styles group) to display the Text Effects menu (Figure 2–51).

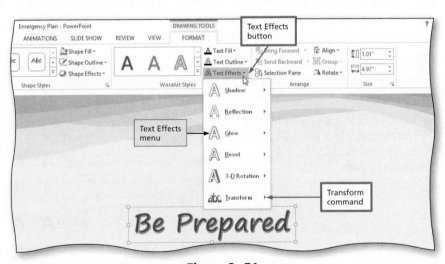

Figure 2–51

2

- Point to Transform in the Text Effects menu to display the WordArt Transform gallery (Figure 2–52).

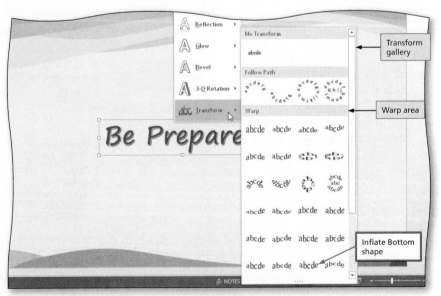

Figure 2–52

3

- If you are using a mouse, point to the Inflate Bottom shape in the Warp area (the third shape in the last row) to display a live preview of that text effect applied to the WordArt object (Figure 2–53).

 Experiment

- If you are using a mouse, point to various effects in the Transform gallery and watch the format of the text and borders change.

Q&A How can I see the preview of a Transform effect if the gallery is overlaying the WordArt letters? Move the WordArt box to the left or right side of the slide and then repeat Steps 1 and 2.

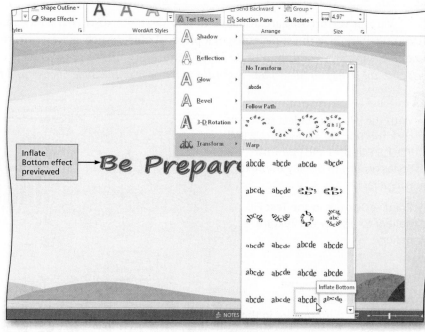

Figure 2–53

4

- Tap or click the Inflate Bottom shape to apply this text effect to the WordArt object.

Q&A Can I change the shape I applied to the WordArt? Yes. Position the insertion point in the box and then repeat Steps 1 and 2.

5

- Drag the upper-left sizing handle diagonally toward the upper-left corner of the slide until the crosshair is positioned approximately as shown in Figure 2–54.

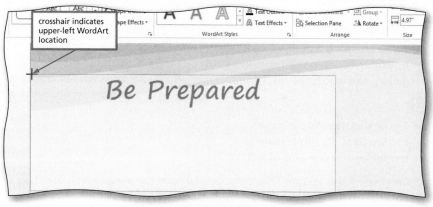

Figure 2–54

6

- Release to resize the WordArt object.

- Drag the WordArt object toward the center of the slide until it is positioned approximately as shown in Figure 2–55.

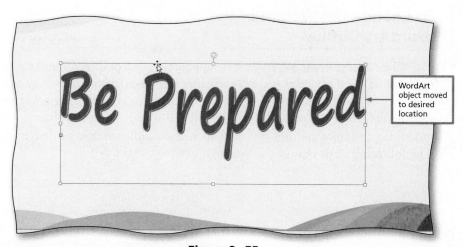

Figure 2–55

To Apply a WordArt Text Fill

Various texture fills are available to give your WordArt characters a unique look. The 24 pictures in the Texture gallery give the appearance of a physical object, such as water drops, sand, tissue paper, and a paper bag. The following steps add the Purple Mesh texture as a fill for the WordArt characters. **Why?** *Purple coordinates well with the shapes on Slide 3 and is similar to the color in the Slide1 flower and firefighter's hose.*

1

- With the WordArt object selected, click the Text Fill arrow (DRAWING TOOLS FORMAT tab | WordArt Styles group) to display the Text Fill gallery.

- Point to Texture in the Text Fill gallery to display the Texture gallery.

2

- If you are using a mouse, point to the Purple mesh texture (the third texture in the fifth row) to display a live preview of that texture applied to the WordArt object (Figure 2–56).

 Experiment

- If you are using a mouse, point to various styles in the Texture gallery and watch the fill change.

3

- Tap or click the Purple mesh texture to apply this texture as the fill for the WordArt object.

Figure 2–56

Q&A
Can I apply this texture simultaneously to text that appears in more than one place on my slide?
Yes. If you are not using a touch screen, you can select one area of text, press and then hold the CTRL key while you select the other text, and then apply the texture.

To Change the Weight of the WordArt Outline

The letters in the WordArt style applied have an outline around the edges. You can increase the width of the lines. **Why?** *The thicker line will emphasize this characteristic and add another visual element.* As with fonts, lines also are measured in point size, and PowerPoint gives you the option to change the line **weight**, or thickness, starting with ¼ point (pt) and increasing in one-fourth-point increments. Other outline options include modifying the color and the line style, such as changing to dots or dashes or a combination of dots and dashes. The following steps change the WordArt outline weight to 3 pt.

- With the WordArt object still selected, click the Text Outline arrow (DRAWING TOOLS FORMAT tab | WordArt Styles group) to display the Text Outline gallery.

- Point to Weight in the gallery to display the Weight list.

- If you are using a mouse, point to 3 pt to display a live preview of this line weight on the WordArt text outline (Figure 2–57).

Q&A Can I make the line width more than 6 pt?
Yes. Tap or click More Lines and increase the amount in the Width box.

Experiment

- If you are using a mouse, point to various line weights in the Weight list and watch the line thickness change.

Figure 2–57

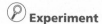

- Tap or click 3 pt to apply this line weight to the WordArt text outline.

Q&A Must my text have an outline?
No. To delete the outline, click No Outline in the Text Outline gallery.

To Change the Color of the WordArt Outline

1 DOWNLOAD & SELECT SLIDES | 2 INSERT & FORMAT PICTURES | 3 INSERT & FORMAT SHAPES
4 INSERT & FORMAT WORDART | 5 FORMAT SLIDE BACKGROUNDS | 6 REVIEW & REVISE SLIDES

Why? *The WordArt outline color and the slide background color are similar, so you can add contrast by changing one of these slide elements.* The following steps change the WordArt outline color.

1

- With the WordArt object still selected, display the Text Outline gallery.

- If you are using a mouse, point to Red (the second color in the Standard Colors row) to display a live preview of this outline color.

Experiment

- If you are using a mouse, point to various colors in the gallery and watch the outline colors change.

2

- Tap or click Red to apply this color to the WordArt outline.

- Tap or click outside of the WordArt box to deselect this slide element (Figure 2–58).

Figure 2–58

BTW
PowerPoint Help
At any time while using
PowerPoint, you can find
answers to questions and
display information about
various topics through
PowerPoint Help. Used
properly, this form of
assistance can increase your
productivity and reduce your
frustrations by minimizing
the time you spend learning
how to use PowerPoint. For
instruction about PowerPoint
Help and exercises that will
help you gain confidence
in using it, read the Office
and Windows chapter at the
beginning of this book.

Formatting Slide Backgrounds

A slide's background is an integral part of a presentation because it can generate audience interest. Every slide can have the same background, or different backgrounds can be used in a presentation. This background is considered fill, which is the content that makes up the interior of a shape, line, or character. Four fills are available: solid, gradient, picture or texture, and pattern. **Solid fill** is one color used throughout the entire slide. **Gradient fill** is one color shade gradually progressing to another shade of the same color or one color progressing to another color. **Picture** or **texture fill** uses a specific file or an image that simulates a material, such as cork, granite, marble, or canvas. **Pattern fill** adds designs, such as dots or diamonds, that repeat in rows across the slide.

Once you add a fill, you can adjust its appearance. For example, you can adjust its **transparency**, which allows you to see through the background, so that any text on the slide is visible. You also can select a color that is part of the theme or a custom color. You can use **offsets**, another background feature, to move the background away from the slide borders in varying distances by percentage. **Tiling options** repeat the background image many times vertically and horizontally on the slide; the smaller the tiling percentage, the greater the number of times the image is repeated.

To Insert a Picture to Create a Background

1 DOWNLOAD & SELECT SLIDES | 2 INSERT & FORMAT PICTURES | 3 INSERT & FORMAT SHAPES
4 INSERT & FORMAT WORDART | 5 FORMAT SLIDE BACKGROUNDS | 6 REVIEW & REVISE SLIDES

Why? *For variety and interest, you want to use an illustration as the Slide 4 background.* This picture is stored on the Data Files for Students. PowerPoint will stretch the height and width of this picture to fill the slide area. The following steps insert the picture, Emergency Collage, on Slide 4 only.

1

- With Slide 4 displaying, display the DESIGN tab and then click the Format Background button (DESIGN tab | Customize group).

- With the FILL section displaying (Format Background task pane) and 'Picture or texture fill' selected, tap or click the File button to display the Insert Picture dialog box (Figure 2–59).

- If necessary, navigate to the PowerPoint Chapter 02 folder or the location where your Data Files for Students folder is located.

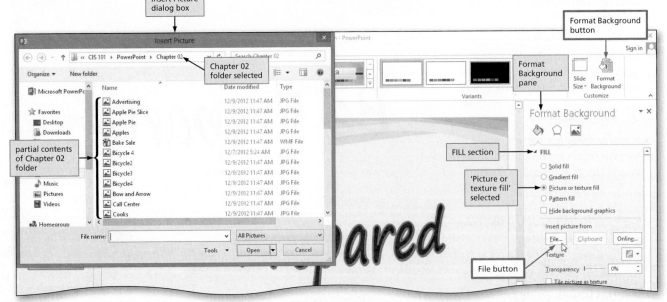

Figure 2–59

2

- If necessary, slide or scroll down and then click Emergency Collage to select the file name (Figure 2–60).

Figure 2–60

3

- Tap or click the Insert button (Insert Picture dialog box) to insert the Emergency Collage illustration as the Slide 4 background (Figure 2–61).

Q&A | What if I do not want to use this picture?
Tap or click the Undo button on the Quick Access Toolbar or tap or click the Reset Background button at the bottom of the Format Background task pane.

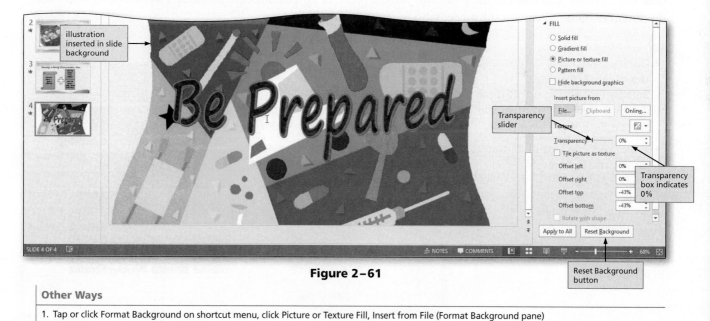

Figure 2–61

Other Ways

1. Tap or click Format Background on shortcut menu, click Picture or Texture Fill, Insert from File (Format Background pane)

To Format the Background Picture Fill Transparency

1 DOWNLOAD & SELECT SLIDES | 2 INSERT & FORMAT PICTURES | 3 INSERT & FORMAT SHAPES
4 INSERT & FORMAT WORDART | 5 FORMAT SLIDE BACKGROUNDS | 6 REVIEW & REVISE SLIDES

The Emergency Collage illustration on Slide 4 has vibrant colors and conflicts with the WordArt. One method of reducing this richness is to change the transparency. The **Transparency slider** indicates the amount of opaqueness. The default setting is 0, which is fully opaque. The opposite extreme is 100%, which is fully transparent. To change the transparency, you can move the Transparency slider or enter a number in the box next to the slider. The following step adjusts the transparency of the background picture to 60%.

1

- Tap or click the Transparency slider and drag it to the right until 60% is displayed in the Transparency box (Figure 2–62).

Q&A

Can I move the slider in small increments so that I can get a precise percentage easily?

Yes. Tap or click the up or down arrows in the Transparency box to move the slider in one-percent increments.

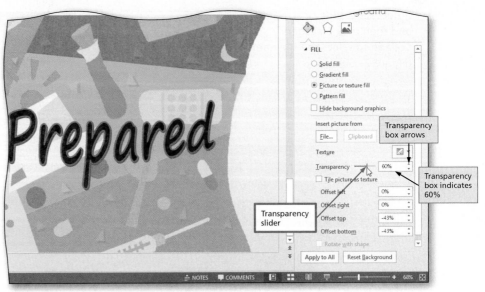

Figure 2–62

To Insert a Texture Fill

You used a texture fill to add interest to the WordArt characters. These same fills are available to add as a slide background. You also can use your own texture pictures for custom backgrounds. The following steps insert the Bouquet fill on Slide 3 in the presentation.

1

- Display Slide 3 and, if necessary, tap or click the Format Background button (DESIGN tab | Customize group) to display the Format Background task pane.

- Tap or click the Texture button to display the Texture gallery (Figure 2–63).

Figure 2–63

2

- Tap or click the Bouquet texture (the last texture in the fourth row) to insert this texture fill as the background on Slide 3 (Figure 2–64).

Q&A

Is a live preview available to see the various textures on this slide?

No. Live preview is not an option with the background textures and fills.

Could I insert this background on all four slides simultaneously?

Yes. You would click the 'Apply to All' button to insert the Bouquet background on all slides.

Figure 2–64

Other Ways

1. Press and hold or right-click background, click Format Background on shortcut menu, select desired options (Format Background pane)

To Format the Background Texture Fill Transparency

1 DOWNLOAD & SELECT SLIDES | 2 INSERT & FORMAT PICTURES | 3 INSERT & FORMAT SHAPES
4 INSERT & FORMAT WORDART | **5 FORMAT SLIDE BACKGROUNDS** | 6 REVIEW & REVISE SLIDES

The Bouquet texture on Slide 3 may detract from the three shapes because it does not offer sufficient contrast with the symbols and text. You can adjust the transparency of a slide texture in the same manner that you change a picture transparency. The following step adjusts the texture transparency to 35%.

- Click the Transparency slider and drag it to the right until 35% is displayed in the Transparency box (Figure 2–65).

Figure 2–65

To Insert a Gradient Fill

1 DOWNLOAD & SELECT SLIDES | 2 INSERT & FORMAT PICTURES | 3 INSERT & FORMAT SHAPES
4 INSERT & FORMAT WORDART | **5 FORMAT SLIDE BACKGROUNDS** | 6 REVIEW & REVISE SLIDES

Although you selected Bouquet texture fill on Slide 3 and changed the transparency, you decide that another type of background may be more suitable for your presentation. *Why? The Bouquet texture is very colorful and may detract from the messages presented in the symbols.* For each theme, PowerPoint provides 30 preset **gradient fills** with five designs for each of the six major theme colors. Each fill has one dark color shade that gradually lightens to either another shade of the same color or another color. The following steps replace the texture fill on Slide 3 to a preset gradient fill.

1

- Tap or click Gradient fill in the Format Background pane and then click the Preset gradients button to display the Preset gradients gallery (Figure 2–66).

Q&A Are the backgrounds displayed in a specific order?
Yes. The first row has light colors at the top of the background; the middle rows have darker fills at the bottom; the bottom row has overall dark fills on all edges.

Is a live preview available to see the various gradients on this slide?
No. Live preview is not an option with the background textures and fills.

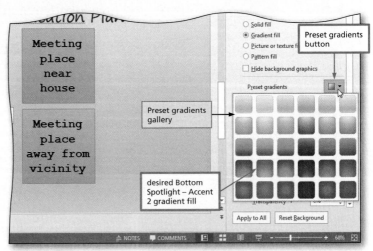

Figure 2–66

2

- Tap or click Bottom Spotlight – Accent 2 (the second fill in the fourth row) to apply that style to Slide 3 (Figure 2–67).

Q&A If I decide later that this background gradient does not fit the theme of my presentation, can I apply a different background?
Yes. You can repeat these steps at any time while creating your presentation.

What if I want to apply this background gradient to all slides in the presentation?
Tap or click the desired style or click the 'Apply to All' button at the bottom of the pane.

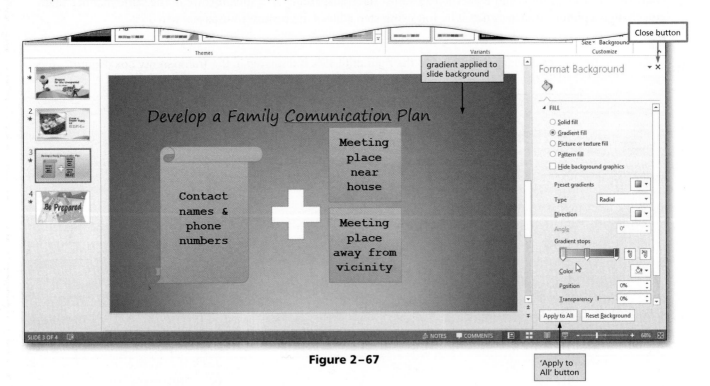

Figure 2–67

3

- Tap or click the Close button (Format Background pane) to close the pane and return to Slide 3.

Other Ways

1. Tap or click DESIGN tab on ribbon, tap or click Format Background button (Customize group), select desired options (Format Background pane)

2. Press and hold or right-click background, click Format Background on shortcut menu, select desired options (Format Background pane)

Reviewing and Revising Individual Slides

The text, pictures, and shapes for all slides in the Emergency Plan presentation have been entered. Once you complete a slide show, you might decide to change elements. PowerPoint provides several tools to assist you with making changes. They include finding and replacing text, inserting a synonym, and checking spelling. The following pages discuss these tools.

Replace Dialog Box

At times, you might want to change all occurrences of a word or phrase to another word or phrase. For example, an instructor may have one slide show to accompany a lecture for several introductory classes, and he wants to update slides with the particular class name and section that appear on several slides. He manually could change the characters, but PowerPoint includes an efficient method of replacing one word with another. The Find and Replace feature automatically locates specific text and then replaces it with desired text.

In some cases, you may want to replace only certain occurrences of a word or phrase, not all of them. To instruct PowerPoint to confirm each change, click the Find Next button in the Replace dialog box instead of the Replace All button. When PowerPoint locates an occurrence of the text, it pauses and waits for you to click either the Replace button or the Find Next button. Clicking the Replace button changes the text; clicking the Find Next button instructs PowerPoint to disregard that particular instance and look for the next occurrence of the Find what text.

To Find and Replace Text

1 DOWNLOAD & SELECT SLIDES | 2 INSERT & FORMAT PICTURES | 3 INSERT & FORMAT SHAPES
4 INSERT & FORMAT WORDART | 5 FORMAT SLIDE BACKGROUNDS | **6 REVIEW & REVISE SLIDES**

While reviewing your slides, you realize that the word, Emergency, would be a better choice than the word, Disaster. To change these words throughout a presentation, you could view each slide, look for the word, Disaster, delete the word, and then type the replacement word, Emergency. A more efficient and effective method of performing this action is to use PowerPoint's Find and Replace feature, which automatically locates each occurrence of a word or phrase and then replaces it with specified text. The word, Disaster, displays twice in the presentation. The following steps use Find and Replace to replace all occurrences of the words, a Disaster, with the words, an Emergency.

1

- Display the HOME tab and then tap or click the Replace button (HOME tab | Editing group) to display the Replace dialog box.

- Type **a Disaster** in the Find what box (Replace dialog box).

- Tap or click the Replace with box and then type **an Emergency** in the box (Figure 2–68).

Figure 2–68

2

- Tap or click the Replace All button (Replace dialog box) to instruct PowerPoint to replace all occurrences of the Find what words, a Disaster, with the Replace with words, an Emergency (Figure 2–69).

Q&A If I accidentally replaced the wrong text, can I undo this replacement?
Yes. Tap or click the Undo button on the Quick Access Toolbar to undo all replacements. If you had tapped or clicked the

Replace button instead of the Replace All button, PowerPoint would undo only the most recent replacement.

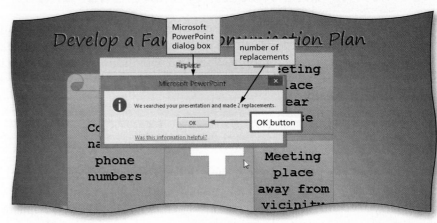

Figure 2–69

3

- Tap or click the OK button (Microsoft PowerPoint dialog box).
- Tap or click the Close btton (Replace dialog box).

BTW
Finding and Replacing Text
When finding and replacing text, you do not need to display the slide that contains the word for which you are searching. You can perform this action when any slide is displayed. To see the results of the search and replace action, however, you need to display the slide where the change occurred.

Other Ways

1. Press CTRL+H

To Find and Insert a Synonym

1 DOWNLOAD & SELECT SLIDES | 2 INSERT & FORMAT PICTURES | 3 INSERT & FORMAT SHAPES
4 INSERT & FORMAT WORDART | 5 FORMAT SLIDE BACKGROUNDS | **6 REVIEW & REVISE SLIDES**

When reviewing your slide show, you may decide that a particular word does not express the exact usage you intended or that you used the same word on multiple slides. In these cases, you could find a **synonym**, or word similar in meaning, to replace the inappropriate or duplicate word. PowerPoint provides a **thesaurus**, which is a list of synonyms and antonyms, to help you find a replacement word.

In this project, you want to find a synonym to replace the words, stay alive, on Slide 2. The following steps locate an appropriate synonym and replace the word.

1

- Display Slide 2 and then select the words, stay alive.

- If you are using a mouse, right-click to display a shortcut menu related to the words you right-clicked. Then, point to Synonyms on the shortcut menu to display a list of synonyms for these words (Figure 2–70).

Q&A If I want to locate a synonym for only one word, do I need to select it?
No. You simply need to place the insertion point in the word and then press and hold or right-click to display the shortcut menu.

- If you are using a touch screen, tap the Thesaurus button (REVIEW

Figure 2–70

tab | Proofing group) to display the Thesaurus task pane for the selected words. Then, in the task pane, tap the arrow next to the word survive if necessary to display a shortcut menu.

2

- Tap Insert or click the synonym you want (survive) on the Synonyms submenu to replace the words, stay alive, in the presentation with the word, survive (Figure 2–71).

Q&A What if a suitable word does not display in the Synonyms submenu?

You can display the Thesaurus task pane by tapping or clicking Thesaurus on the Synonyms submenu. A complete thesaurus with synonyms displays in the task pane along with an antonym, which is a word with an opposite meaning.

Figure 2–71

Other Ways	
1. Tap or click Thesaurus (REVIEW tab | Proofing group)	2. Press SHIFT+F7

To Add Notes

1 DOWNLOAD & SELECT SLIDES \| 2 INSERT & FORMAT PICTURES \| 3 INSERT & FORMAT SHAPES
4 INSERT & FORMAT WORDART \| 5 FORMAT SLIDE BACKGROUNDS \| **6 REVIEW & REVISE SLIDES**

As you create slides, you may find material you want to state verbally and do not want to include on the slide. You can type and format notes in the **Notes pane** as you work in Normal view and then print this information as **notes pages**. The Notes pane is hidden until you tap or click the Notes button on the status bar to open the pane. If you want to close the Notes pane, tap or click the Notes button again. After adding comments, you can print a set of speaker notes. These notes will print below a small image of the slide. Charts, tables, and pictures added to the Notes pane also print on these pages. The following steps add text to the Notes pane on Slides 2, 3, and 4.

Note: In the following step, the word, whistle, has been misspelled intentionally as wistle to illustrate the use of PowerPoint's spell check feature. Your slides may contain different misspelled words, depending upon the accuracy of your typing.

1

- Display Slide 2 and then if necessary tap or click the Notes button on the status bar to display the Notes pane.

Q&A Why might I need to tap or click the Notes pane?

By default, the Notes pane is closed when you begin a new presentation. Once you display the Notes pane for any slide, the Notes pane will remain open unless you tap or click the Notes button to close it.

- Tap or click the Notes pane and then type `The kit should include a flashlight, wistle, water, radio, batteries, three-day supply of food, three gallons of water for each family member, change of clothing, tools, and first aid kit.` (Figure 2–72).

Q&A What if I cannot see all the lines I typed?

You can drag the splitter bar up to enlarge the Notes pane. Clicking the Notes pane scroll arrows or swiping up or down on the Notes pane allows you to view the entire text.

Figure 2–72

- Display Slide 3, tap or click the Notes pane, and then type `One meeting place should be near the home, and the second should be outside the neighborhood. One out-of-state relative should be included in the contacts list.` (Figure 2–73).

Figure 2–73

- Display Slide 4 and then type `The Federal Emergency Management Agency (FEMA) has additional information about helping people prepare for emergency situations. Visit www.ready.gov.` in the Notes pane (Figure 2–74).

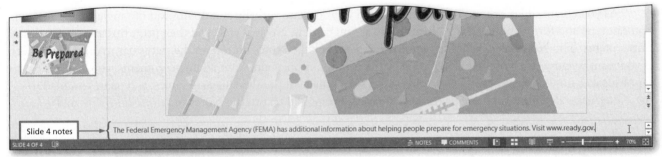

Figure 2–74

BTW
Formatting Notes Pane Text
You can format text in the Notes pane in the same manner you format text on a slide. For example, you can bold key words or change the font size and color to add emphasis.

BTW
Detecting Spelling Errors
The x in the Spell Check icon indicates PowerPoint detected a possible spelling error. A check mark in the icon indicates the entered text contains no spelling errors.

Checking Spelling

After you create a presentation, you should check it visually for spelling errors and style consistency. In addition, you use PowerPoint's Spelling tool to identify possible misspellings on the slides and in the notes. Do not rely on the spelling checker to catch all your mistakes. Although PowerPoint's spelling checker is a valuable tool, it is not infallible. You should proofread your presentation carefully by pointing to each word and saying it aloud as you point to it. Be mindful of commonly misused words such as its and it's, through and though, and to and too.

PowerPoint checks the entire presentation for spelling mistakes using a standard dictionary contained in the Microsoft Office group. This dictionary is shared with the other Microsoft Office applications such as Word and Excel. A custom dictionary is available if you want to add special words such as proper names, cities, and acronyms. When checking a presentation for spelling errors, PowerPoint opens the standard dictionary and the custom dictionary file, if one exists. When a word appears in the Spelling pane, you can perform one of several actions, as described in Table 2–1.

The standard dictionary contains commonly used English words. It does not, however, contain many proper names, abbreviations, technical terms, poetic contractions, or antiquated terms. PowerPoint treats words not found in the dictionaries as misspellings.

Table 2–1 Spelling Pane Buttons and Actions

Button Name/Action	When to Use	Action
Ignore	Word is spelled correctly but not found in dictionaries	PowerPoint continues checking rest of the presentation but will flag that word again if it appears later in document.
Ignore All	Word is spelled correctly but not found in dictionaries	PowerPoint ignores all occurrences of the word and continues checking rest of presentation.
Add	Add word to custom dictionary	PowerPoint opens custom dictionary, adds word, and continues checking rest of presentation.
Change	Word is misspelled	Click proper spelling of the word in Suggestions list. PowerPoint corrects word, continues checking rest of presentation, but will flag that word again if it appears later in document.
Change All	Word is misspelled	Click proper spelling of word in Suggestions list. PowerPoint changes all occurrences of misspelled word and continues checking rest of presentation.
Listen to the pronunciation	To hear the pronunciation of a word	Tap or click the audio speaker icon next to the properly spelled word near the bottom of the Spelling pane.
View synonyms	See some synonyms for the correctly spelled word	View the bullet list of synonyms below the correctly spelled word near the bottom of the Spelling pane.
Close	Stop spelling checker	PowerPoint closes spelling checker and returns to PowerPoint window.

To Check Spelling

1 DOWNLOAD & SELECT SLIDES | 2 INSERT & FORMAT PICTURES | 3 INSERT & FORMAT SHAPES
4 INSERT & FORMAT WORDART | 5 FORMAT SLIDE BACKGROUNDS | **6 REVIEW & REVISE SLIDES**

The following steps check the spelling on all slides in the Emergency Plan presentation.

1
- Tap or click REVIEW on the Ribbon to display the REVIEW tab.
- Tap or click the Spelling button (REVIEW Tab | Proofing group) to start the spelling checker and display the Spelling pane (Figure 2–75).

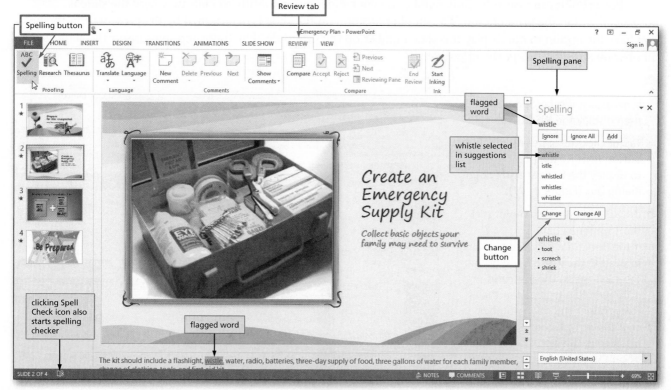

Figure 2–75

2

- With the word, wistle, selected in the list, tap or click the Change button (Spelling pane) to replace the misspelled flagged word, wistle, with the selected correctly spelled word, whistle, and then continue the spelling check (Figure 2–76).

Q&A Could I have tapped or clicked the Change All button instead of the Change button?
Yes. When you tap or click the Change All button, you change the current and future occurrences of the misspelled word. The misspelled word, wistle, appears only once in the presentation, so tapping or clicking the Change or the Change All button in this instance produces identical results.

Occasionally a correctly spelled word is flagged as a possible misspelled word. Why?
Your custom dictionary does not contain the word, so it is seen as spelled incorrectly. You can add this word to a custom dictionary to prevent the spelling checker from flagging it as a mistake.

Figure 2–76

3

- Replace the misspelled word, Comunication, with the word, Communication.

- Continue checking all flagged words in the presentation. When the Microsoft PowerPoint dialog box appears, tap or click the OK button (Microsoft PowerPoint dialog box) to close the spelling checker and return to the slide where a possible misspelled word appeared.

Other Ways

1. Tap or click Spell Check icon on status bar   2. Press and hold or right-click flagged word, tap or click correct word   3. Press F7

To Insert a Slide Number

1 DOWNLOAD & SELECT SLIDES | 2 INSERT & FORMAT PICTURES | 3 INSERT & FORMAT SHAPES
4 INSERT & FORMAT WORDART | 5 FORMAT SLIDE BACKGROUNDS | 6 REVIEW & REVISE SLIDES

PowerPoint can insert the slide number on your slides automatically to indicate where the slide is positioned within the presentation. The number location on the slide is determined by the presentation theme. You have the option to not display this slide number on the title slide. The following steps insert the slide number on all slides except the title slide.

1

- If necessary, display Slide 3 and then display the INSERT tab.

- Tap or click the Slide Number button (INSERT tab | Text group) to display the Header and Footer dialog box (Figure 2–77).

Q&A Why might I need to tap or click the Thumbnail pane?
If the final flagged word had been located in the Notes pane during the spell check, the insertion point would have been in the Notes pane. The page number, consequently, would have been inserted in the Notes pane instead of on the slide.

Figure 2–77

2

- Tap or click the Slide number check box (Header and Footer dialog box) to place a check mark in it.

- Tap or click the 'Don't show on title slide' check box (Header and Footer dialog box) to place a check mark in it (Figure 2–78).

Q&A Where does the slide number display on the slide?
Each theme determines where the slide number is displayed in the footer. In this theme, the slide number location is the left side of the footer, as indicated by the black box at the bottom of the Preview area.

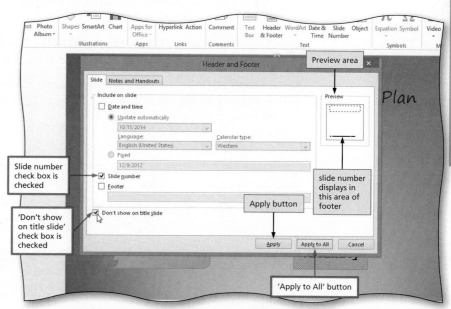

Figure 2–78

3

- Tap or click the Apply to All button (Header and Footer dialog box) to close the dialog box and insert the slide number on all slides except Slide 1 (Figure 2–79).

Q&A How does tapping or clicking the Apply to All button differ from tapping or clicking the Apply button?
The Apply button inserts the slide number only on the currently displayed slide whereas the Apply to All button inserts the slide number on every slide.

Figure 2–79

Other Ways

1. Tap or click Header & Footer button (INSERT tab | Text group), tap or click Slide Number box (Header and Footer dialog box), tap or click 'Slide number' and 'Don't show on title slide' boxes, tap or click Apply to All button

To Add a Transition between Slides

A final enhancement you will make in this presentation is to apply the Fracture transition in the Exciting category to all slides and increase the transition duration. The following steps apply this transition to the presentation.

1 Tap or click TRANSITIONS on the ribbon. Tap or click the More button (TRANSITIONS tab | Transition to This Slide group) to expand the Transitions gallery.

2 Tap or click the Fracture transition in the Exciting category to apply this transition.

3 Tap or click the Duration up arrow in the Timing group four times to change the transition speed from 02.00 to 03.00.

BTW
Certification
The Microsoft Office Specialist (MOS) program provides an opportunity for you to obtain a valuable industry credential — proof that you have the PowerPoint 2013 skills required by employers. For more information, visit the Certification resource on the Student Companion Site located on www.cengagebrain. com. For detailed instructions about accessing available resources, visit www.cengage.com/ct/ studentdownload or see the inside back cover of this book.

④ Tap or click the Preview Transitions button (TRANSITIONS tab | Preview area) to view the new transition time.

⑤ Tap or click the Apply To All button (TRANSITIONS tab | Timing group) to apply this transition and speed to all four slides in the presentation (Figure 2–80).

Q&A | Can I apply a particular transition or duration to one slide and then change the transition or timing for a different slide in the presentation?
| Yes. Select a slide and then select a transition and duration. Do not tap or click the Apply To All button. Repeat this process to apply the transition and duration to individual slides.

Figure 2–80

CONSIDER THIS

How can I use handouts to organize my speech?

As you develop a lengthy presentation with many visuals, handouts may help you organize your material. Print handouts with the maximum number of slides per page. Use scissors to cut each thumbnail and then place these miniature slide images adjacent to each other on a flat surface. Any type on the thumbnails will be too small to read, so the images will need to work with only the support of the verbal message you provide. You can rearrange these thumbnails as you organize your speech. When you return to your computer, you can rearrange the slides on your screen to match the order of your thumbnail printouts. Begin speaking the actual words you want to incorporate in the body of the talk. This process of glancing at the thumbnails and hearing yourself say the key ideas of the speech is one of the best methods of organizing and preparing for the actual presentation. Ultimately, when you deliver your speech in front of an audience, the images on the slides or on your note cards should be sufficient to remind you of the accompanying verbal message.

To Print Speaker Notes

Comments added to slides in the Notes pane give the speaker information that supplements the text on the slide. They will print with a small image of the slide at the top and the comments below the slide. The following steps print the speaker notes.

- Display Slide 1, tap or click FILE on the ribbon to open the Backstage view, and then tap or click the Print tab in the Backstage view to display Slide 1 in the Print gallery.

- Tap or click 'Full Page Slides' in the Settings area to display the Print gallery (Figure 2–81).

Q&A Why does the preview of my slide appear in color?
Your printer determines how the preview appears. If your printer is not capable of printing color images, the preview will not appear in color.

Figure 2–81

BTW

Distributing a Document
Instead of printing and distributing a hard copy of a document, you can distribute the document electronically. Options include sending the document via email; posting it on cloud storage (such as SkyDrive) and sharing the file with others; posting it on a social networking site, blog, or other website; and sharing a link associated with an online location of the document. You also can create and share a PDF or XPS image of the document, so that users can view the file in Acrobat Reader or XPS Viewer instead of in PowerPoint.

2

- Tap or click Notes Pages in the Print Layout area to select this option and then tap or click the Next Page button three times to display a preview of Slide 4 (Figure 2–82).

Q&A Can I preview Slides 1, 2, or 3 now?
Yes. Click the Previous Page button to preview the other slides.

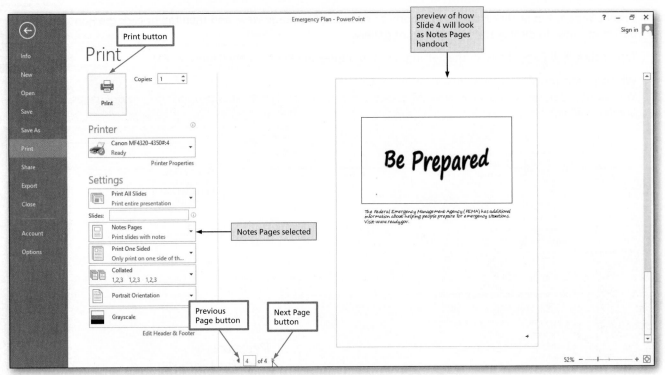

Figure 2–82

3

- Verify that the printer listed on the Printer Status button will print a hard copy of the presentation. If necessary, click the Printer Status button to display a list of available printer options and then click the desired printer to change the currently selected printer.

- Tap or click the Print button in the Print gallery to print the notes pages on the currently selected printer.

- When the printer stops, retrieve the hard copy (Figure 2–83).

Q&A Why does the background display on my printout but not in the figure?
Graphics are displayed depending upon the settings in the Print gallery. For example, the background will print if Color is specified whereas it will not with a Grayscale or Pure Black and White setting.

BTW
Printing Document Properties
To print document properties, tap or click FILE on the ribbon to open the Backstage view, tap or click the Print tab in the Backstage view to display the Print gallery, tap or click the first button in the Settings area to display a list of options specifying what you can print, tap or click Document Info in the list to specify you want to print the document properties instead of the actual document, and then tap or click the Print button in the Print gallery to print the document properties on the currently selected printer.

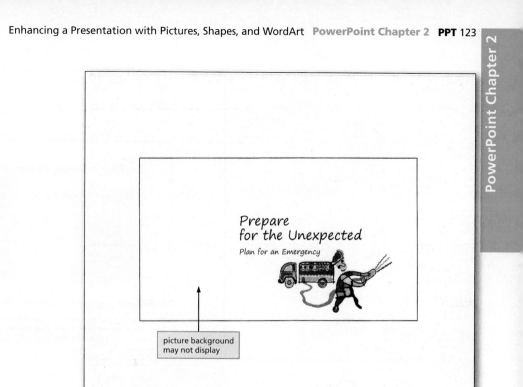

(a) Slide 1 – Speaker Notes

(b) Slide 2 – Speaker Notes

Figure 2–83 (Continued)

(c) Slide 3 – Speaker Notes

(d) Slide 4 – Speaker Notes
Figure 2–83 (Handouts printed using a black-and-white printer) (Continued)

Other Ways

1. Press CTRL+P, press ENTER

To Save the Presentation, Sign Out of a Microsoft Account, and Exit PowerPoint

You have made several changes to the presentation since you last saved it. Thus, you should save it again. The following steps save the presentation, sign out of your Microsoft account, and exit PowerPoint.

1 Tap or click the Save button on the Quick Access Toolbar.

2 If you wish to sign out of your Microsoft account, open the Backstage view, tap or click the Account tab to display the Account gallery, and then tap or click the Sign out link, which displays the Remove Account dialog box. If a Can't remove Windows accounts dialog box appears instead of the Remove Account dialog box, click the OK button and skip the remaining steps.

3 Tap or click the Yes button (Remove Account dialog box) to sign out of your Microsoft account on this computer.

4 Tap or click the Back button in the upper-left corner of the Backstage view to return to the presentation.

5a If you have one PowerPoint presentation open, tap or click the Close button on the right side of the title bar to close the open document and exit PowerPoint.

5b If you have multiple PowerPoint presentations open, press and hold or right-click the PowerPoint app button on the taskbar and then tap or click 'Close all windows' on the shortcut menu, or press ALT+F4 to close all open presentations and exit PowerPoint.

BTW
Quick Reference
For a table that lists how to complete the tasks covered in this book using touch gestures, the mouse, ribbon, shortcut menu, and keyboard, see the Quick Reference Summary at the back of this book, or visit the Quick Reference resource on the Student Companion Site located on www.cengagebrain.com. For detailed instructions about accessing available resources, visit www.cengage.com/ct/studentdownload or see the inside back cover of this book.

Chapter Summary

In this chapter you have learned how to insert and format pictures, add and format shapes, insert and format WordArt, add slide backgrounds, find and replace text, check spelling, add notes, and print speaker notes. The items listed below include all the new PowerPoint skills you have learned in this chapter, with the tasks grouped by activity.

Download and Modify Themes
Search for and Download an Online Theme (PPT 77)
Delete a Slide (PPT 79)

Format Fonts
Change the Font (PPT 98)
Format Text Using the Format Painter (PPT 101)

Format Slide Backgrounds
Insert a Picture to Create a Background (PPT 108)
Format the Background Picture Fill Transparency (PPT 109)
Insert a Texture Fill (PPT 110)
Format the Background Texture Fill Transparency (PPT 111)
Insert a Gradient Fill (PPT 111)

Insert and Format Pictures
Insert a Picture into a Slide without a Content Placeholder (PPT 83)
Change a Picture (PPT 85)
Correct a Picture (PPT 87)
Apply a Picture Style (PPT 87)
Add a Picture Border (PPT 88)
Change a Picture Border Color (PPT 89)
Apply Picture Effects (PPT 90)

Insert and Format Shapes
Add a Shape (PPT 92)
Resize a Shape (PPT 93)
Add Other Shapes (PPT 94)
Apply a Shape Style (PPT 95)
Add Text to a Shape (PPT 97)
Copy and Paste a Shape (PPT 101)

Insert and Format WordArt

Insert WordArt (PPT 103)

Change the WordArt Shape (PPT 104)

Apply a WordArt Text Fill (PPT 106)

Change the Weight of the WordArt Outline
(PPT 106)

Change the Color of the WordArt Outline
(PPT 107)

Review and Enhance Slides and Printouts

Find and Replace Text (PPT 113)

Find and Insert a Synonym (PPT 114)

Add Notes (PPT 115)

Check Spelling (PPT 117)

Insert a Slide Number (PPT 118)

Print Speaker Notes (PPT 121)

CONSIDER THIS

What decisions will you need to make when creating your next presentation?

Use these guidelines as you complete the assignments in this chapter and create your own slide show decks outside of this class.

1. Determine if an online theme can help you design and develop the presentation efficiently and effectively.

2. Identify personal pictures that would create interest and promote the message being presented.

3. Consider modifying pictures.

   a) Add corrections.

   b) Add styles.

   c) Add effects.

   d) Add and format borders.

4. Locate shapes that supplement the verbal and written message.

   a) Size and position them aesthetically on slides.

   b) Add styles.

5. Develop WordArt that emphasizes major presentation messages.

   a) Modify the shape.

   b) Change the weight and color to coordinate with slide elements.

6. Format individual slide backgrounds.

   a) Add and modify fills.

   b) Insert a picture.

7. Change fonts to emphasize particular slide components.

8. Search for synonyms that help express your thoughts.

9. Create speaker notes.

10. Check spelling.

How should you submit solutions to questions in the assignments identified with a ✹ symbol?

Every assignment in this book contains one or more questions identified with a ✹ symbol. These questions require you to think beyond the assigned presentation. Present your solutions to the questions in the format required by your instructor. Possible formats may include one or more of these options: write the answer; create a document that contains the answer; present your answer to the class; discuss your answer in a group; record the answer as audio or video using a webcam, smartphone, or portable media player; or post answers on a blog, wiki, or website.

Apply Your Knowledge

Reinforce the skills and apply the concepts you learned in this chapter.

Changing the Background and Adding Photos and WordArt

Note: To complete this assignment, you will be required to use the Data Files for Students. Visit www.cengage.com/ct/studentdownload for detailed instructions or contact your instructor for information about accessing the required files.

Instructions: Run PowerPoint. Open the presentation, Apply 2-1 Bicycle, from the Data Files for Students.

The five slides in the presentation discuss bicycle safety. The document you open is an unformatted presentation. You are to add photos, apply picture styles, add WordArt, change slide layouts, apply a transition, and use the Format Painter so the slides look like Figures 2–84a through 2–84e on pages PPT 127 through 130.

Perform the following tasks:

1. On the title slide, use your name in place of Student Name and bold and italicize your name.

2. If requested by your instructor, change your first name to your mother's first name on the title slide.

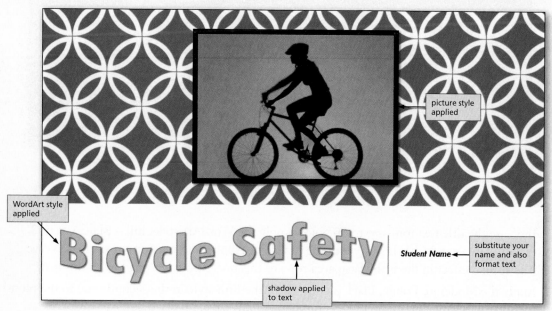

(a) Slide 1

Figure 2–84 (Continued)

Continued >

Apply Your Knowledge *continued*

(b) Slide 2

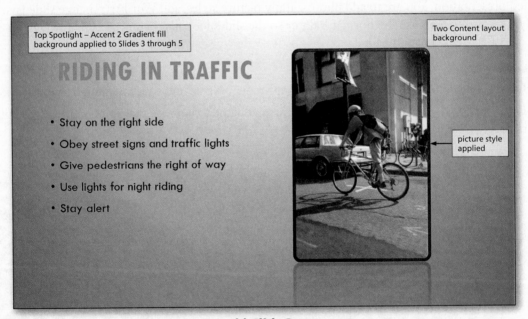

(c) Slide 3

Figure 2–84

3. Increase the title text font size to 60 point. Apply the WordArt style, Fill – Blue, Accent 2, Outline – Accent 2 (the third style in the first row). Apply the Transform text effect, Wave 2 (the second effect in the fifth Warp area row) to this text. Also add a shadow to this text.

4. Apply the Moderate Frame, Black picture style (the fifth style in the second row) to the photo on Slide 1, as shown in Figure 2–84a on the previous page.

5. On Slide 2, change the layout to Title and Content. Increase the title text font to 54 point, change the font color to Green (the sixth color in the Standard Colors row), and then bold this text. Increase the bulleted list font to 24 point, as shown in Figure 2–84b.

6. Create a background on Slide 2 by inserting the photo called Cyclist, which is available on the Data Files for Students.

7. On Slide 2, type **The average cost for a routine bike inspection is $20.** in the Notes pane.

8. On Slides 3 through 5, change the layout to Two Content. Insert the photos, as shown in Figures 2–84c through 2–84e on the next page. The photos to be inserted are called Bicycle2, Bicycle3, and Bicycle4 and are available on the Data Files for Students. Also, change the background to Top Spotlight – Accent 2 gradient fill (the second gradient in the second row) in the Preset gradients gallery on Slides 3 through 5.

9. On Slide 3, adjust the size of the photo and apply the Reflected Bevel, Black picture style (the fourth style in the fourth row) and change the photo brightness to +20% (the fourth picture in the third row in the Brightness and Contrast area).

10. On Slide 3, type **Laws for bicycles on the road vary in every state and country.** in the Notes pane.

11. On Slide 4, adjust the size of the photo, apply the Metal Oval picture style (the seventh style in the fourth row), and then change the photo border to Black, Text 1 (the second color in the first Theme Colors row), as shown in Figure 2–84d.

12. Use the thesaurus to change the word, suitable, to appropriate.

13. Type **Hydration is critical. Make sure your bike is equipped with a bottle holder.** in the Notes pane.

14. On Slide 5, adjust the size of the photo and apply the Bevel Perspective picture style (the first style in the fourth row) to the photo, as shown in Figure 2–84e on the next page.

15. Use the Format Painter to format the title text and the bulleted lists on Slides 3 through 5 with the same features as the title text and bulleted list on Slide 2.

16. Apply the Wind transition in the Exciting category to all slides. Change the duration to 2.50 seconds.

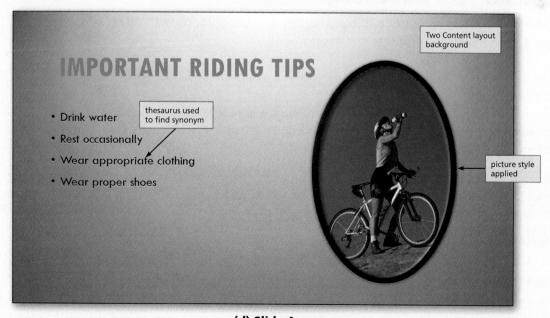

(d) Slide 4

Figure 2–84 (Continued)

Continued >

Apply Your Knowledge *continued*

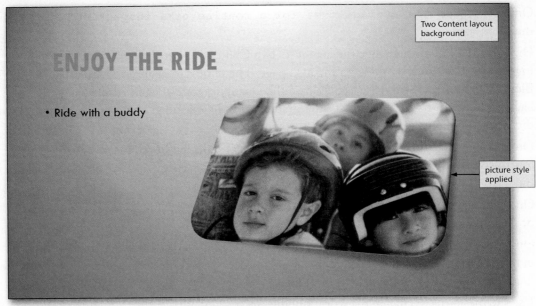

(e) Slide 5

Figure 2–84 (Continued)

17. Save the presentation using the file name, Apply 2-1 Bicycle Safety.

18. Submit the revised document in the format specified by your instructor.

19. ☀ In Step 4 you applied the Moderate Frame, Black picture style. How did this style improve the slide?

Extend Your Knowledge

Extend the skills you learned in this chapter and experiment with new skills. You may need to use Help to complete the assignment.

Changing Slide Backgrounds, Inserting Shapes and WordArt, and Finding and Replacing Text

Note: To complete this assignment, you will be required to use the Data Files for Students. Visit www.cengage.com/ct/studentdownload for detailed instructions or contact your instructor for information about accessing the required files.

Instructions: Run PowerPoint. Open the presentation, Extend 2-1 Field Archery, from the Data Files for Students. You will create backgrounds including inserting a photo to create a background, apply a WordArt Style and Effect, and add shapes to create the presentation shown in Figure 2–85.

Perform the following tasks:
1. Change the theme to Wisp and choose the second variant.

2. Find and replace the words, Bow and Arrow, with the word, Archery, on all slides.

3. On Slides 2 through 4, change the background style to Top Spotlight – Accent 5 (the fifth style in the second Preset gradients row). Also, change the title text to bold and change the font color to Orange, Accent 1 (the fifth color in the first Theme Colors row) on Slides 2 through 4.

4. On the title slide (Figure 2–85a), create a background by inserting the photo called Bow and Arrow, which is available on the Data Files for Students. Change the transparency to 50%.

5. Apply the WordArt style, Fill - Orange, Accent 1, Shadow (the second style in the first row), to the title text, center the text, and increase the font size to 72 point. Apply the WordArt Transform text effect, Arch Up (the first effect in the first Follow Path row), and then bold this text. Also, move the title text above the archer in the photo on the title slide.

6. If requested by your instructor, add your current or previous pet's name as the Slide 1 subtitle text.

7. On Slides 2 through 4, increase the font size of the first-level bulleted text to 22 point and the second-level bulleted text to 20 point.

8. On Slide 2, enlarge the illustration to the size shown in Figure 2–85b on the next page, apply the Reflected Bevel, Black picture style (the fourth style in the fourth row), and then move it to the location shown in the figure.

9. On Slide 3, apply the Soft Edge Oval picture style (the sixth style in the third row) to the photo and move the photo to the upper-right area of the slide. Also, apply the Orange, 18 pt glow, Accent color 1 glow variation (the first variation in the fourth Glow Variations row) to this photo, as shown in Figure 2–85c on the next page.

10. On Slide 4, select the Oval shape and while holding down the Shift key, draw a circle 6" × 6", as shown in Figure 2–85d on page PPT 133. Fill this shape with Black, Text 1, Lighter 15% and then change the shape outline to No Outline. Then copy and paste this shape two times. Change the shape size of the first pasted circle to 4" × 4". Hint: Use the Size and Position group on the PICTURE TOOLS FORMAT tab to enter the exact measurement of the shape. Change the Shape Fill to White and then center this shape over the original black circle using the Smart Guides. Select the second pasted circle and change the shape size to 2" × 2", the Shape Fill to Black, Text 1, Lighter 15% and then center this shape over the white circle shape using the Smart Guides.

photo inserted as background and transparency changed

bold and shadow the WordArt text and move up to new location

color variant changed

Wisp document theme

(a) Slide 1

Figure 2–85 (Continued)

Continued >

Extend Your Knowledge *continued*

(b) Slide 2

(c) Slide 3

Figure 2–85

11. Insert an arrow on Slide 4 by using the Right Arrow shape under Block Arrows. Size the arrow to 1.5" × 6" and then copy and paste this arrow shape two times. Copy and paste the three paragraphs from the bulleted list into the three arrow shapes. Select the text on one of these shapes, change the font size to 28 point, change the font color to black, center the text, and

(d) Slide 4
Figure 2–85 (Continued)

then bold the text. Use the Format Painter to format the text in the two arrows with the same features as the first arrow. Move the arrows so that each one points to the correct ring, as shown in Figure 2–85d. Delete the bulleted text in the text placeholder.

12. Apply an appropriate transition to all slides.

13. Save the presentation using the file name, Extend 2-1 Field Archery Scoring.

14. Submit the revised document in the format specified by your instructor.

15. ✳ In this assignment, you changed the transparency of the inserted background photo on the title slide to 50%. How did this transparency change enhance your title slide?

Analyze, Correct, Improve

Analyze a presentation, correct all errors, and improve it.

Correcting Formatting, Adding Slide Numbers, and Correcting Spelling

Note: To complete this assignment, you will be required to use the Data Files for Students. Visit www.cengage.com/ct/studentdownload for detailed instructions or contact your instructor for information about accessing the required files.

Instructions: Run PowerPoint. Open the presentation, Analyze 2-1 Avoid the Flu, from the Data Files for Students. This presentation contains four slides and explains why doctors recommend you should get an annual flu shot. Figure 2–86 on the next page shows the uncorrected title slide. Modify the slides by making the indicated corrections and improvements.

1. Correct

a. Change the variant to blue (the second variant in the gallery).

b. Decrease the font size of the Slide 1 title text and change the font color. Also, capitalize the letter F in the word, flu.

c. Use your name in place of Student Name on Slide 1.

Continued >

Analyze, Correct, Improve *continued*

d. If requested by your instructor, change your first name on Slide 1 to your mother's first name.

e. On Slides 2 through 4, adjust the photo sizes and move them so they do not overlap text and are the appropriate dimensions for the slide content.

f. On all slides, adjust font sizes and font color so they are the appropriate size and enhance the presentation.

g. Correct the spelling errors on all slides.

2. Improve

a. Increase the size of the medical symbol on the title slide and move the symbol to the right side of the slide.

b. On Slides 2 through 4, change the color of the title text and bold all the titles.

c. Change the photo border colors on all slides to make them more visually attractive.

d. Add the slide number to all slides except the title slide.

e. Apply the same transition and duration to all slides.

f. Save the presentation using the file name, Analyze 2-1 – Get Your Flu Shot.

g. Submit the revised document in the format specified by your instructor.

3. ✳ Which errors existed in the starting file? How did changing the variant color help? When you adjusted the photo sizes, how did you determine their final sizes?

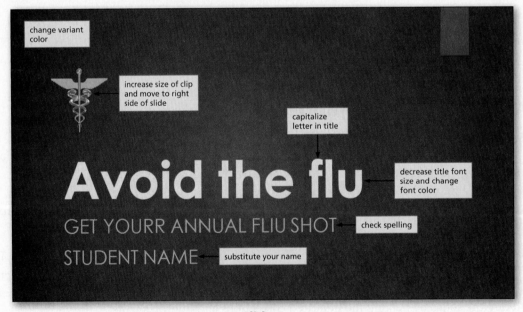

Slide 1

Figure 2–86

In the Labs

Design and/or create a presentation using the guidelines, concepts, and skills presented in this chapter. Labs 1 and 2, which increase in difficulty, require you to create solutions based on what you learned in the chapter; Lab 3 requires you to create a solution, which uses cloud and web technologies, by learning and investigating on your own from general guidance.

Lab 1: Creating a Presentation Inserting Photos, Applying Picture Styles, and Inserting Shapes

Problem: Your creative cooking class has volunteered to manage a bake sale to raise funds for victims of a tornado in a neighboring town. To encourage more students to participate in the bake sale, you decide to put together a presentation that would run in the cafeteria. You want to show your audience how easy it is to make an apple pie. Create the slides shown in Figure 2–87.

Instructions: Perform the following tasks:

1. Create a new presentation using the Retrospect theme. Do not change the brown variant.

2. On Slide 1, create a background by inserting the photo called Apple Pie from the Data Files for Students, as shown in Figure 2–87a. Change the transparency to 53%.

3. Type **Homemade Apple Pie** as the Slide 1 title text. Press the ENTER key after the word, Homemade, so the text is on two lines, and then center the text. Apply the WordArt style Fill – Orange, Accent 2, Outline – Accent 2 (the third style in the first row). Change the text fill to Dark Red (the first color in the Standard Colors row), and then change the text outline color to Green (the sixth color in the Standard Colors row) and the text outline weight to 3 pt. Also, apply the Transform text Effect, Chevron Up (the first effect in the second Warp row), to this text. Position this WordArt, as shown in Figure 2–87a. Type **BAKE SALE – SATURDAY JANUARY 20** in the subtitle placeholder. Change the font to MV Boli, increase the font size to 30 point, bold this text, and then center the text, as shown in the figure.

4. Create Slides 2 through 4 with the Two Content layout, Slide 5 with the Content with Caption layout, and Slide 6 with the Picture with Caption layout.

(a) Slide 1

Figure 2–87 (Continued)

Continued >

In the Labs *continued*

5. Type the title and content and insert all photos on Slides 2 through 5, as shown in Figures 2–87b through 2–87e. The photos to be inserted are called Apples, Ingredients, Cooks, and Apple Pie Slice, and are available on the Data Files for Students. Size the photos and then use the Smart Guides to position these images. You may want to zoom the slides to help you align these graphic elements.

6. On Slide 2, increase the title text size to 54 point, change the font color to Dark Red, and then bold this text. Use the Format Painter to apply these formatting changes to the title text on Slides 3 and 4. On Slide 2, change the list font size to 24 point. Apply the Bevel Perspective picture style (the first style in the fourth row) to the photo, change the border color to Light Green (the fifth color in the Standard Colors row), and then change the border weight to 6 pt, as shown in Figure 2–87b.

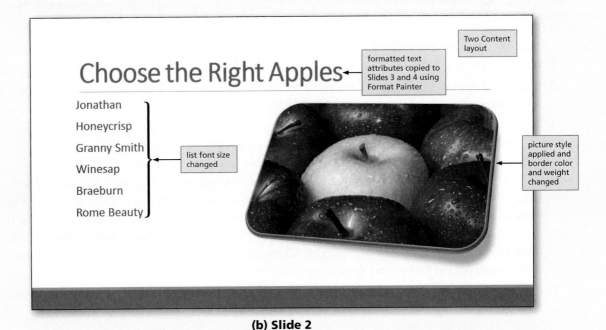

(b) Slide 2

(c) Slide 3

Figure 2–87

7. On Slide 3, change the list font size to 24 point. Insert the Pie shape located in the Basic Shapes area to the lower-left corner of the slide. Apply the Colored Fill – Brown, Accent 4 (the eighth color in the first row) to the shape. Size the shape as shown in the figure. Type the text, `Use Fresh Ingredients` in the shape. Bold this text, and change the font size to 24 point, as shown in Figure 2–87c.

8. On Slide 4, change the list font size to 20 point. Apply the Snip Diagonal Corner, White picture style (the first style in the third row) to the photo, change the border color to Dark Red (the first color in the Standard Colors row), and then apply the Reflection picture effect, Tight Reflection, touching (the first effect in the first Reflection Variations row). Copy the pie shape from Slide 3 and paste it in the bottom center of the slide. Type the text, `Bake 40 to 50 Minutes`, as shown in Figure 2–87d.

(d) Slide 4

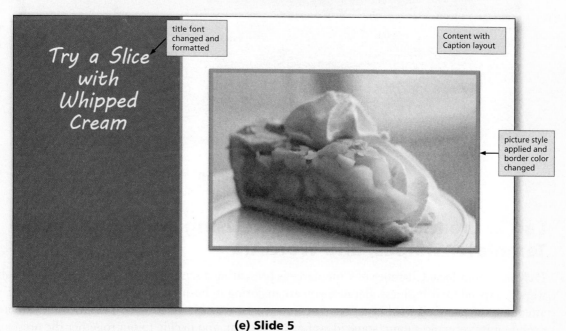

(e) Slide 5

Figure 2–87 (Continued)

Continued >

In the Labs *continued*

9. On Slide 5, change the title text font to MV Boli, change the font size to 40 point, and then center this text. Apply the Simple Frame, White picture style (the first style in the first row) to the slice of pie photo and then change the border color to Orange, Accent 1 (the fifth color in the Theme Colors row), as shown in Figure 2–87e on the previous page.

10. On Slide 6, change the caption title font to MV Boli, change the font size to 32 point, and then bold this text. Select the photo, click the Change Picture button (PICTURE TOOLS FORMAT tab | Adjust group), and then insert the Bake Sale illustration from the Data Files for Students, as shown in Figure 2–87f.

11. If requested by your instructor, type the name of the city or county in which you were born into the subtitle text placeholder on Slide 6.

12. Apply the Peel Off transition in the Exciting category to all slides. Change the duration to 2.5 seconds.

13. Check the spelling and correct any errors. Save the presentation using the file name, Lab 2-1 Homemade Apple Pie.

14. Submit the document in the format specified by your instructor.

15. ✸ What is the significance of changing the transparency of the photo on the title slide? Why did you put a red border on the photo on Slide 4? Explain why you did not follow the 7 × 7 rule on Slides 3 and 4.

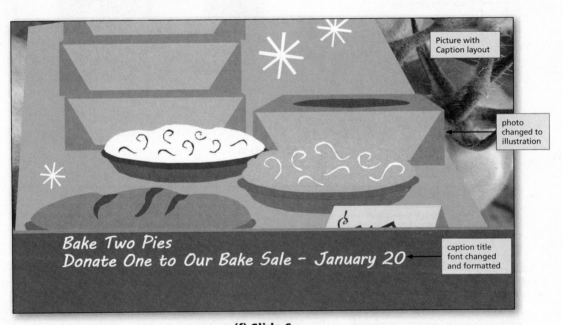

(f) Slide 6

Figure 2–87 (Continued)

Lab 2: Creating a Presentation Using an Online Theme Template, Shapes, and WordArt

Problem: Your local Chamber of Commerce is presenting a seminar to local business owners about ways to expand their business. Because you are majoring in business, your teacher thought that attending this meeting would be a good experience for you. He asked the Chamber of Commerce president if you could submit some ideas for the seminar. You decide to put together the presentation shown in Figure 2–88.

Instructions: Perform the following tasks:

1. Create a new presentation using the Business project plan presentation (widescreen) in the Business category under Suggested searches.

2. Delete Slides 7 through 14.

3. Apply the Two Content layout to Slide 2, the Alternate Content with Caption layout to Slide 3, the Content with Caption layout to Slide 4, the Title only layout to Slide 5, and the Section Header layout to Slide 6. Delete all titles and text content from Slides 2 through 6. Type the new title and text content for Slides 2, 3, and 4, as shown in Figures 2–88b through 2–88d on the next page.

4. Insert the photos and illustration shown in Figures 2–88b through 2–88e from the Data Files for Students. The photos and illustration are called Advertising, Delivery, Customer, and Call Center. Apply the Canvas texture fill (the second texture in the first row) to Slides 2 through 5 and change the transparency to 35%.

5. On the title slide, type the new title and subtitle content, increase the font size of the subtitle text to 28 point, and then change the font color to Orange (the third color in the Standard Colors row), as shown in Figure 2–88a.

6. If requested by your instructor, add the name of your hometown after the word, Business, in the subtitle placeholder. Type the word **in** before the name of your hometown.

7. On Slide 2, increase the font size of the title to 40 point, change the font color to Indigo, Text 2, Darker 25% (the fourth color in the fifth Theme Colors row), and then bold this text. Increase the font size of the bulleted list to 24 point. Apply the Perspective Shadow, White picture style (the fourth style in the third row) and resize the photo, as shown in Figure 2–88b.

8. On Slide 3, increase the font size of the title to 40 point and then bold this text. Increase the font size of the text to 24 point. Apply the Simple Frame picture style (the first style in the first row) to the photo, as shown in Figure 2–88c.

9. On Slide 4, increase the font size of the title text to 40 point, change the font color to Indigo, Text 2, Darker 25% (the fourth color in the fifth Theme Colors row), and then bold this text. Increase the font size of the bulleted list text to 24 point. Apply the Metal Frame picture style (the third style in the first row) to the photo, as shown in Figure 2–88d.

10. On Slide 5, increase the font size of the title to 40 point, change the font color to Indigo, Text 2, Darker 25% (the fourth color in the fifth Theme Colors row), and then bold this text. Move

(a) Slide 1

Figure 2–88 (Continued)

Continued >

In the Labs *continued*

(b) Slide 2

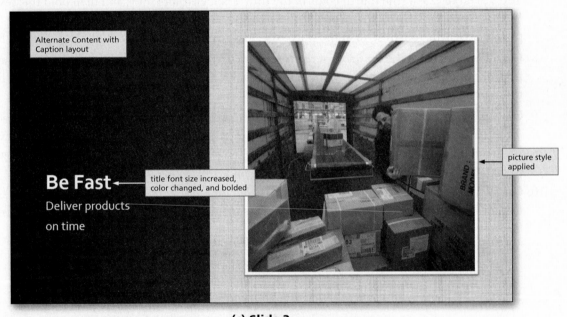

(c) Slide 3

Figure 2–88

the photo to the right side of the slide and then apply the Soft Edge Oval picture style (the sixth style in the third row) to the photo, as shown in Figure 2–88e.

11. Insert the Diamond shape located in the Basic Shapes area, resize the shape so that it is approximately 3.42" × 3.93", and then right-click the shape, click Style, and apply the Subtle Effect – Red, Accent 6 Shape Quick Style (the seventh style in the fourth row). Copy and paste the shape two times and move the shapes, as shown in Figure 2–88e. Type the text into the shape and then increase the text size to 24 point.

12. On Slide 6, type the new title and subtitle content, and create a background by inserting the Ladder photo from the Data Files for Students. Change the transparency to 40%. Decrease the title font size to 44 point, change the font color to Indigo, Text 2, Darker 25% (the fourth color in the fifth Theme Colors row), right-align the text, and then bold this text. Increase the font size of the subtitle text to 28 point, change the font color to Indigo, Text 2 (the fourth color in the first Theme

(d) Slide 4

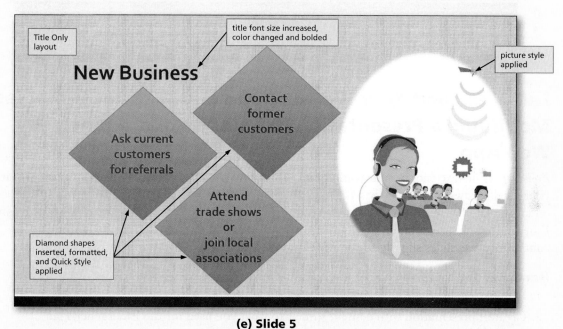

(e) Slide 5

Figure 2–88 (Continued)

Colors row), and then right-align this text, as shown in Figure 2–88f. Insert the Pentagon shape located in the Block Arrows area and then apply the Subtle Effect - Lime, Accent 1 Quick Style (the second style in the fourth row) to the shape. Type **Success** in the shape, change the font to Forte, change the font size to 60 point, and then change the font color to Gray – 80%, Text 1.

13. Change the transition to Doors in the Exciting category to all slides. Change the duration to 2.75 seconds.

14. Check spelling and correct all errors. Save the presentation using the file name, Lab 2-2 Small Business Seminar.

15. Submit the revised document in the format specified by your instructor.

16. ✳ You searched for an online theme under Business. Why? Do you think any of the other themes would have worked well for your presentation? How does changing the slide layouts help your presentation?

Continued >

In the Labs *continued*

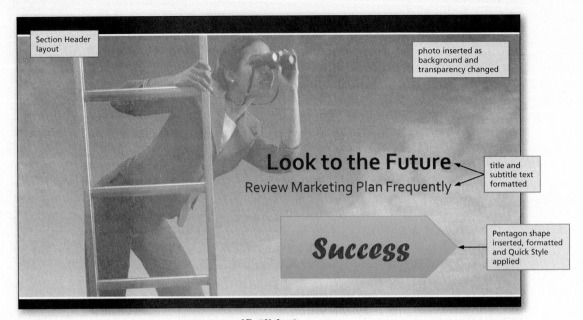

(f) Slide 6

Figure 2–88 (Continued)

Lab 3: Expand Your World: Cloud and Web Technologies
Modifying a Presentation Using the PowerPoint Web App

Problem: The fire chief in your community is planning a family security and safety workshop at your local hardware store. He has asked you to help him publicize the event, and he wants to focus on urging families to prepare for unexpected situations. You inform him that you have created an Emergency Plan presentation for your computer class, and he would like you to customize the content of these slides slightly to promote the workshop.

Instructions:

1. Sign in to your Microsoft account and run the PowerPoint web app.

2. Create a presentation with content similar to what you used for the Emergency Plan presentation.

3. On the title slide, add the name and address of the nearest hardware store. In addition, add the date that is exactly one month from today and a starting time of noon. Add the name of one of your elementary school teachers as the fire chief's name on this slide.

4. Save the presentation using the file name, Lab 2-3 Local Safety Workshop.

5. Submit the assignment in the format specified by your instructor.

6. ✸ Other than the content the chief asked you to include on the title slide, how does the presentation you created using the PowerPoint web app differ from the presentation you created in the Chapter 2 project? Which formatting features are not available in the web app? Do you think using the web app has sufficient functions to develop effective presentations? Why or why not?

✳ Consider This: Your Turn

Apply your creative thinking and problem-solving skills to design
and implement a solution.

1. Design and Create a Presentation about Skydiving from New Heights

Personal

Part 1:   Members of your skydiving club are discussing free-falling records of new heights reached by skydivers over the past years. They've been following the news reports about the man from Austria, 43-year-old Felix Baumgartner, who broke a record by completing the highest skydive and traveling faster than the speed of sound without being in an aircraft. At a recent meeting with your fellow sky-divers, many questions arose as to how this man was able to accomplish this, what risks were involved, and how long he trained for this venture. You researched facts about this record-breaking skydive and learned that the height he dove from (128,100 feet above Earth) was more than three times the cruising altitude of a passenger jet (hitting Mach 1.24 or 833.9 mph). It was the height at which wa-ter boils. If his pressurized spacesuit had malfunctioned, it would have been disastrous: a leak in his spacesuit would have caused his blood to boil instantly. Half of his nine-minute descent was a free fall of 119,846 feet. He trained for seven years. Use the concepts and techniques presented in this chapter to prepare a presentation with a minimum of four slides that explores this subject. Select a suitable theme, and include a title slide, bulleted lists, shapes, and WordArt. The presentation should contain photos and illustrations appropriately resized. Eight photos and illustrations are available on the Data Files for Students: Skydiving1, Skydiving2, Skydiving3, Skydiving4, Skydiving5, Skydiving6, Skydiv-ing7, and Skydiving8. You can add your own digital photos or photos from Office.com if they are ap-propriate for this topic. Apply picture styles and effects. Add a title slide and closing slide to complete your presentation. Format the title slide with a shape. Format the background with at least one photo and apply a background texture to at least one slide. Review and revise your presentation as needed. Submit your assignment in the format specified by your instructor.

Part 2:   ✳ You made several decisions while creating the presentation in this assignment: where to place text, how to format the text (such as font, font size, and where to use WordArt), which graphi-cal image(s) to use, what styles and effects to apply, where to position the graphical image, how to format the graphical images, and which shapes to use to add interest to the presentation. What was the rationale behind each of these decisions? When you reviewed the document, what further revi-sions did you make and why? Where would you recommend showing this slide show?

2. Design and Create a Presentation about Teaching Geometry to Elementary Students

Professional

Part 1:   You work part time for a tutoring agency. Because you are majoring in math, your boss asked if you would put together a teaching aid for teaching geometry to the elementary students. You decide to create a presentation with some basic shapes: squares, circles, and triangles. To make the slides appeal to your young students, you decide to use shapes and add photos and illustra-tions. Geometry for elementary students also can cover parallel lines, intersecting lines, and how intersecting lines form angles. You can show them shapes such as pentagons, heptagons, and octa-gons. They can look for shapes in their environment and draw them. You can teach them that even though a shape is turned upside down or rotated, it is still the same shape even if it looks different. Use the concepts and techniques presented in this chapter to create a presentation with at least four slides. Select a suitable theme, include a title slide, and add WordArt. Review and revise your pre-sentation as needed. Submit your assignment in the format specified by your instructor.

Part 2:   ✳ You made several decisions while creating the presentation in this assignment: where to place text, how to format the text (such as font, font size, and where to use WordArt), which graphical image(s) to use, what styles and effects to apply, where to position the graphical images,

Continued >

Consider This: Your Turn *continued*

and which shapes to use to add interest to the presentation. What was the rationale behind each of these decisions? When you reviewed the document, what further revisions did you make and why? Where would you recommend showing this slide show?

3. Design and Create a Presentation about Coyotes Roaming in Your Neighborhood
Research and Collaboration

Part 1: Many of your neighbors are concerned about the coyotes that have been spotted in your neighborhood. With the help of a friend who works part time at a local wildlife refuge, you suggest that each of you do some research about coyotes and discuss your findings and put together a presentation to share at the next town hall meeting. Your main concern is that the coyotes are finding outdoor food sources such as pet food, uncovered garbage cans, and areas near homes where rodents may be nesting. You want to make suggestions to your neighbors about how to deter the coyotes from staying in your neighborhood. You ask your friend who works at the wildlife refuge to research the habits of coyotes. You will gather information from the local newspaper where there have been articles written about the coyotes and your other neighbor will talk to other people in the neighbor about sightings of coyotes and possible photographs. After coordinating all the facts about the coyotes, use the concepts and techniques presented in this chapter to prepare a presentation with a minimum of four slides that explores the subject of coyotes. Summarize your research findings and type this information in the Notes pane of each slide. Select a suitable theme, include a title slide, bulleted lists, shapes, and WordArt. Seven photos and illustrations are available on the Data Files for Students: Coyote1, Coyote2, Coyote3, Coyote4, Coyote5, Coyote6, and Coyote7. Change the brightness and contrast for at least one photo. Insert shapes and WordArt to enhance your presentation. Apply a transition in the Subtle area to all slides and increase the duration. Review and revise your presentation as needed. Submit your assignment in the format specified by your instructor.

Part 2: ⚙ You made several decisions while creating the presentation in this assignment: where to place text, how to format the text (such as font, font size, and where to use WordArt), which graphical image(s) to use, what styles and effects to apply, where to position the graphical image, what shapes to use to add interest to the presentation. What was the rationale behind each of these decisions? When you reviewed the document, what further revisions did you make and why? Where would you recommend showing this slide show?

Learn Online
Reinforce what you learned in this chapter with games, exercises, training, and many other online activities and resources.

Student Companion Site Reinforcement activities and resources are available at no additional cost on www.cengagebrain.com. Visit www.cengage.com/ct/studentdownload for detailed instructions about accessing the resources available at the Student Companion Site.

SAM Put your skills into practice with SAM! If you have a SAM account, go to www.cengage.com/sam2013 to access SAM assignments for this chapter.

3 Reusing a Presentation and Adding Media and Animation

Microsoft product screenshots used with permission from Microsoft Corporation.

Objectives

You will have mastered the material in this chapter when you can:

- Color a photo
- Add an artistic effect to a photo
- Align paragraph text
- Change views
- Ungroup, change the color of, and regroup an illustration
- Copy a slide element from one slide to another

- Insert and edit a video clip
- Insert audio
- Control audio and video clips
- Insert entrance, emphasis, and exit effects
- Control animation timing
- Change theme colors
- Change a theme and variant on one slide
- Print handouts

3 | Reusing a Presentation and Adding Media and Animation

Introduction

BTW
Using Media in Presentations
PowerPoint makes it easy to insert media into a presentation. Well-produced video clips add value when they help explain a procedure or show movement that cannot be captured in a photo or illustration. A sound can emphasize an action. Before you insert these files on a slide, however, consider whether they really add any value to your overall slide show. If you are inserting them just because you can, you might want to reconsider your decision. Audiences quickly tire of extraneous movement and sounds on slides, and they will find these media clips annoying. Keep in mind that the audience's attention should focus primarily on the presenter; extraneous or inappropriate media files may divert their attention and, in turn, decrease the quality of the presentation.

At times, you will need to revise a PowerPoint presentation. Changes may include inserting and adding effects to photos, altering the colors of photos and illustrations, and updating visual elements displayed on a slide. Applying a different theme, changing fonts, and substituting graphical elements can give a slide show an entirely new look. Adding media, including sounds, video, and music, can enhance a presentation and help audience members retain the information being presented. Adding animation can reinforce important points and enliven a presentation.

Project — Presentation with Video, Audio, Animation, and Photos with Effects

The project in this chapter follows graphical guidelines and uses PowerPoint to create the presentation shown in Figure 3–1. The slides in this revised presentation, which discusses Watch for Motorcycles, have a variety of audio and visual elements. For example, the photos have artistic effects applied that soften the photos and help the audience focus on other elements on the slides. The car clip has colors that blend well with the background. The bullet list is animated with entrance, emphasis, and exit effects. The video has been edited to play only the portion with Watch for Motorcycles and has effects to add audience interest. Motorcycle sounds integrate with the visual elements. Overall, the slides have myriad media elements and effects that are exciting for your audience to watch and hear.

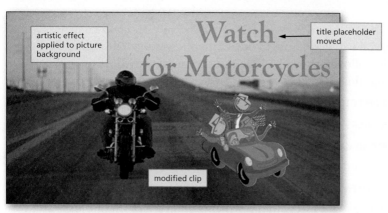

artistic effect applied to picture background

title placeholder moved

modified clip

(a) Slide 1 (Title Slide with Picture Background, Modified Clip, and Animated Clip)

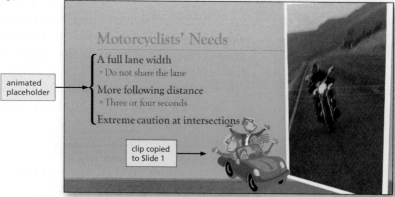

animated placeholder

clip copied to Slide 1

(b) Slide 2 (Bulleted List)

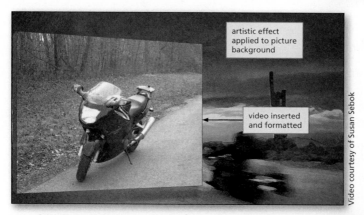

artistic effect applied to picture background

video inserted and formatted

Video courtesy of Susan Sebok

(c) Slide 3 (Picture Background and Video Clip)

video plays full screen

Video courtesy of Susan Sebok

(d) Slide 4 (Video Playing Full Screen)

Figure 3–1

For an introduction to Windows and instruction about how to perform basic Windows tasks, read the Office and Windows chapter at the beginning of this book, where you can learn how to resize windows, change screen resolution, create folders, move and rename files, use Windows Help, and much more.

One of the few differences between Windows 7 and Windows 8 occurs in the steps to run PowerPoint. If you are using Windows 7, click the Start button, type **PowerPoint** in the 'Search programs and files' box, click PowerPoint 2013, and then, if necessary, maximize the PowerPoint window. For detailed steps to run PowerPoint in Windows 7, refer to the Office and Windows chapter at the beginning of this book. For a summary of the steps, refer to the Quick Reference located at the back of this book.

Roadmap

In this chapter, you will learn how to create the slides shown in Figure 3–1 on the previous page. The following roadmap identifies general activities you will perform as you progress through this chapter:

1. INSERT and ADD EFFECTS to photos, including changing colors and styles.
2. MODIFY PLACEHOLDERS on the slides by moving and changing sizes.
3. MODIFY and COPY an ILLUSTRATION to customize its appearance.
4. ADD MEDIA files to slides.
5. ANIMATE SLIDE CONTENT with entrance, emphasis, and exit effects.
6. CUSTOMIZE SLIDE ELEMENTS by changing a theme and variant on one slide and changing the theme colors.

At the beginning of step instructions throughout the chapter, you will see an abbreviated form of this roadmap. The abbreviated roadmap uses colors to indicate chapter progress: gray means the chapter is beyond that activity; blue means the task being shown is covered in that activity, and black means that activity is yet to be covered. For example, the following abbreviated roadmap indicates the chapter would be showing a task in the 5 ANIMATE SLIDE CONTENT activity.

1 INSERT & ADD EFFECTS | 2 MODIFY PLACEHOLDERS | 3 MODIFY & COPY ILLUSTRATIONS
4 ADD MEDIA | **5 ANIMATE SLIDE CONTENT** | 6 CUSTOMIZE SLIDE ELEMENTS

Use the abbreviated roadmap as a progress guide while you read or step through the instructions in this chapter.

To Run PowerPoint

If you are using a computer to step through the project in this chapter and you want your screens to match the figures in this book, you should change your screen's resolution to 1366×768. For information about how to change a computer's resolution, refer to the Office and Windows chapter at the beginning of this book.

The following steps, which assume Windows 8 is running, use the Start screen or the search box to run PowerPoint based on a typical installation. You may need to ask your instructor how to run PowerPoint on your computer. For a detailed example of the procedure summarized below, refer to the Office and Windows chapter.

1 Scroll the Start screen for a PowerPoint 2013 tile. If your Start screen contains a PowerPoint 2013 tile, tap or click it to run PowerPoint and then proceed to Step 5; if the Start screen does not contain the PowerPoint 2013 tile, proceed to the next step to search for the PowerPoint app.

2 Swipe in from the right edge of the screen or point to the upper-right corner of the screen to display the Charms bar and then tap or click the Search charm on the Charms bar to display the Search menu.

3 Type **PowerPoint** as the search text in the Search text box and watch the search results appear in the Apps list.

4 Tap or click PowerPoint 2013 in the search results to run PowerPoint.

5 If the PowerPoint window is not maximized, tap or click the Maximize button on its title bar to maximize the window.

6 If necessary, navigate to the PowerPoint files location (in this case, the PowerPoint folder in the CIS 101 folder [or your class folder]). Visit www.cengage.com/ct/studentdownload for detailed instructions or contact your instructor for information about accessing the required files. Open the presentation, Motorcycle, from the Data Files for Students.

7 Save the presentation using the file name, Watch for Motorcycles.

Inserting Photos and Adding Effects

The Watch for Motorcycles presentation consists of three slides that have some text, a clip art image, a formatted background, and a transition applied to all slides. You will insert a photo into one slide and then modify it and another photo by adding artistic effects and recoloring. You also will copy the clip art from Slide 2 to Slide 1 and modify the objects in this clip. In Chapter 2, you inserted photos, made corrections, and added styles and effects; the new effects you apply in this chapter will add to your repertoire of photo enhancements that increase interest in your presentation.

In the following pages, you will perform these tasks:

1. Insert the first photo into Slide 1.
2. Recolor the Slide 1 photo.
3. Add an artistic effect to the Slide 3 photo.
4. Send the Slide 1 photo back behind all other slide objects.

To Insert and Resize a Photo into a Slide without Content Placeholders

The first step is to insert a photo into Slide 1. This photo is available on the Data Files for Students. Visit www.cengage.com/ct/studentdownload for detailed instructions or contact your instructor for information about accessing the required file.

The following steps insert a photo into Slide 1.

1 With Slide 1 displaying, tap or click INSERT on the ribbon to display the INSERT tab and then tap or click the Pictures button (INSERT tab | Images group) to display the Insert Picture dialog box.

2 If necessary, navigate to the photo location (in this case, the PowerPoint folder in the CIS 101 folder [or your class folder]).

3 Tap or click Highway Motorcycle to select the file.

4 Tap or click the Insert button (Insert Picture dialog box) to insert the photo into Slide 1.

5 Drag the sizing handles to resize the photo so that it covers the entire slide. You can tap or click the Height and Width arrows (PICTURE TOOLS FORMAT tab | Size group) to adjust the picture size (Figure 3–2 on the next page).

For an introduction to Office and instruction about how to perform basic tasks in Office apps, read the Office and Windows chapter at the beginning of this book, where you can learn how to run an application, use the ribbon, save a file, open a file, exit an application, use Help, and much more.

BTW
Organizing Files and Folders
You should organize and store files in folders so that you easily can find the files later. For example, if you are taking an introductory computer class called CIS 101, a good practice would be to save all PowerPoint files in a PowerPoint folder in a CIS 101 folder. For a discussion of folders and detailed examples of creating folders, refer to the Office and Windows chapter at the beginning of this book.

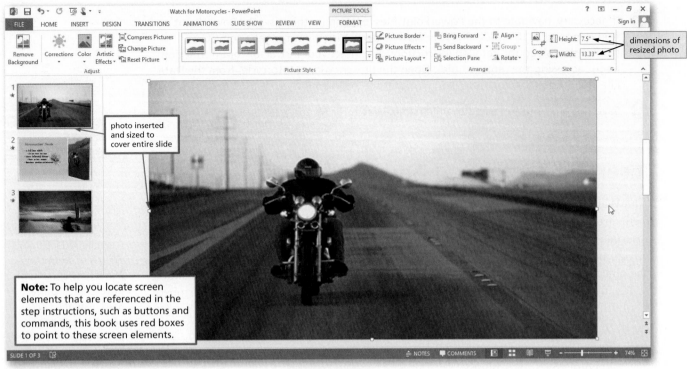

Figure 3–2

Adjusting Photo Colors

BTW
Touch Screen Differences
The Office and Windows interfaces may vary if you are using a touch screen. For this reason, you might notice that the function or appearance of your touch screen differs slightly from this chapter's presentation.

PowerPoint allows you to adjust colors to match or add contrast to slide elements by coloring photos. The Color gallery has a wide variety of preset formatting combinations. The thumbnails in the gallery display the more common color saturation, color tone, and recolor adjustments. **Color saturation** changes the intensity of colors. High saturation produces vivid colors; low saturation produces gray tones. **Color tone** affects the coolness, called blue, or the warmness, called orange, of photos. When a digital camera does not measure the tone correctly, a **color cast** occurs, and, as a result, one color dominates the photo. **Recolor** effects convert the photo into a wide variety of hues. The more common are **grayscale**, which changes the color photo into black, white, and shades of gray, and **sepia**, which changes the photo colors into brown, gold, and yellow, reminiscent of a faded photo. You also can fine-tune the color adjustments by tapping or clicking the Picture Color Options and More Variations commands in the Color gallery.

To Color a Photo

1 INSERT & ADD EFFECTS | 2 MODIFY PLACEHOLDERS | 3 MODIFY & COPY ILLUSTRATIONS
4 ADD MEDIA | 5 ANIMATE SLIDE CONTENT | 6 CUSTOMIZE SLIDE ELEMENTS

The Office theme and text on Slides 1 and 2 are simple and fulfill the need to communicate the presentation's safety message. The photos on Slides 1 and 3, in contrast, help set the tone of riding on an open road and enjoying the freedom that biking brings. You may want to add an effect to photos. *Why? An effect adds variety to the presentation and helps enhance ordinary photos.* The following steps recolor the Slide 1 photo to coordinate with the brown colors of a highway and barren desert landscape.

1

• With Slide 1 displaying and the Highway Motorcycle photo selected, tap or click the Color button (PICTURE TOOLS FORMAT tab | Adjust group) to display the Color gallery (Figure 3–3).

Q&A Why does the Adjust group look different on my screen?
Your monitor is set to a different resolution. See the Office and Windows chapter for an explanation of screen resolution and the appearance of the ribbon.

Why are pink borders surrounding the thumbnails in the Color Saturation, Color Tone, and Recolor areas in the gallery?
The image on Slide 1 currently has normal color saturation and a normal color tone.

Figure 3–3

2

• If you are using a mouse, point to Sepia (third photo in the first Recolor area row) to display a live preview of this adjustment on the photo.

 Experiment

• If you are using a mouse, point to various thumbnails in the Recolor area and watch the hues change on the photo in Slide 1.

• Tap or click Sepia to apply this recoloring to the Highway Motorcycle photo (Figure 3–4).

Q&A Could I have applied this recoloring to the photo if it had been a background instead of a file inserted into the slide?
No. Artistic effects and recoloring cannot be applied to backgrounds.

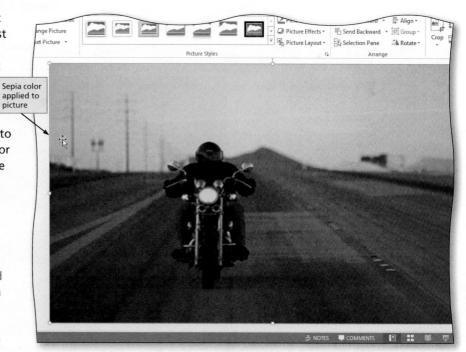

Figure 3–4

Other Ways

1. Tap or click Format Picture on shortcut menu, tap or click Picture icon, tap or click PICTURE COLOR, tap or click Recolor button (Format Picture pane)

To Add an Artistic Effect to a Photo

Artists use a variety of techniques to create effects in their paintings. They can vary the amount of paint on their brushstroke, use fine bristles to add details, mix colors to increase or decrease intensity, and smooth their paints together to blend the colors. You, likewise, can add similar effects to your photos using PowerPoint's built-in artistic effects. ***Why?*** *The completed Slide 3 will have both the photo and a video, so applying an artistic effect to the photo will provide a contrast between the two images.* The following steps add an artistic effect to the Slide 3 photo.

1

- Display Slide 3 and select the photo.

- Tap or click the Artistic Effects button (PICTURE TOOLS FORMAT tab | Adjust group) to display the Artistic Effects gallery (Figure 3–5).

Figure 3–5

2

- If you are using a mouse, point to Paint Brush (third photo in the second row) to display a live preview of this adjustment on the photo.

🔍 **Experiment**

- If you are using a mouse, point to various artistic effects and watch the hues change on the photo in Slide 3.

- Tap or click Paint Brush to apply this artistic effect to the photo (Figure 3–6).

Q&A Can I adjust a photo by recoloring and applying an artistic effect? Yes. You can apply both a color and an effect. You may prefer at times to mix these adjustments to create a unique image.

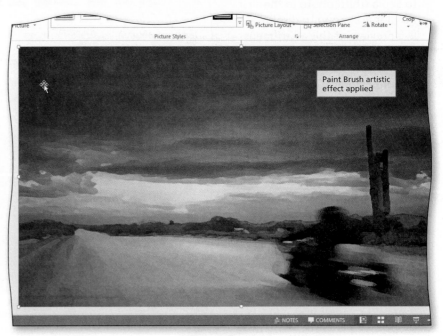

Figure 3–6

Other Ways

1. Tap or click Format Picture on shortcut menu, tap or click Effects icon, tap or click ARTISTIC EFFECTS

To Change the Stacking Order

The objects on a slide stack on top of each other, much like individual cards in a deck. To change the order of these objects, you use the Bring Forward and Send Backward commands. **Bring Forward** moves an object toward the top of the stack, and **Send Backward** moves an object underneath another object. When you tap or click the Bring Forward arrow, PowerPoint displays a menu with an additional command, **Bring to Front**, which moves a selected object to the top of the stack. Likewise, when you tap or click the Send Backward arrow, the **Send to Back** command moves the selected object underneath all objects on the slide. The following steps arrange the Slide 1 photo. *Why? On this slide, the photo is on top of the placeholders, so you no longer can see the text. If you send the photo to the bottom of the stack on the slide, the letters will become visible.*

- Display Slide 1 and then select the Highway Motorcycle photo.
- Tap or click the Send Backward arrow (PICTURE TOOLS FORMAT tab | Arrange group) to display the Send Backward menu (Figure 3–7).

Q&A
How can I see objects that are not on the top of the stack?
Press TAB or SHIFT+TAB to display each slide object.

Figure 3–7

- Tap or click Send to Back to move the photo underneath all slide objects (Figure 3–8).

Figure 3–8

Other Ways
1. Tap or click Send Backward arrow (PICTURE TOOLS FORMAT tab | Arrange group), press K   2. Press and hold or right-click photo, tap or click Send to Back on shortcut menu

Modifying Placeholders

You have become familiar with inserting text and graphical content in the three types of placeholders: title, subtitle, and content. These placeholders can be moved, resized, and deleted to meet desired design requirements. In addition, placeholders can be added to a slide when needed. After you have modified the placeholder locations, you can view thumbnails of all your slides simultaneously by changing views.

In the following pages, you will perform these tasks:

1. Resize the Slide 1 title placeholder.
2. Align the Slide 1 title text.
3. Move the Slide 1 title placeholder.
4. Delete the Slide 1 subtitle placeholder.
5. Change views.

BTW

Q&As

For a complete list of the Q&As found in many of the step-by-step sequences in this book, visit the Q&A resource on the Student Companion Site located on www.cengagebrain.com. For detailed instructions about accessing available resources, visit www.cengage.com/ct/studentdownload or see the inside back cover of this book.

To Resize a Placeholder

1 INSERT & ADD EFFECTS | 2 MODIFY PLACEHOLDERS | 3 MODIFY & COPY ILLUSTRATIONS
4 ADD MEDIA | 5 ANIMATE SLIDE CONTENT | 6 CUSTOMIZE SLIDE ELEMENTS

The AutoFit button displays on the left side of the Slide 1 title placeholder because the two lines of text exceed the placeholder's borders. PowerPoint attempts to reduce the font size when the text does not fit, and you can tap or click this button to resize the existing text in the placeholder so the spillover text will fit within the borders. The following step increases the Slide 1 title placeholder size. *Why? The two lines of text exceed the placeholder's borders, so you can resize the placeholder and fit the letters within the rectangle.*

1

- With Slide 1 displaying, tap or click somewhere in the title text paragraph to position the insertion point in the paragraph. Tap or click the border of the title placeholder to select it. Point to the top-middle sizing handle.

- Drag the top title placeholder border upward to enlarge the placeholder (Figure 3–9).

Q&A Can I drag other sizing handles to enlarge or shrink the placeholder? Yes, you also can drag the left, right, top, and corner sizing handles to resize a placeholder. When you drag a corner sizing handle, the box keeps the same proportion and simply enlarges the overall shape.

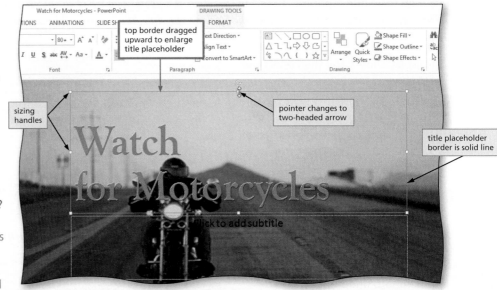

Figure 3–9

To Align Paragraph Text

1 INSERT & ADD EFFECTS | 2 MODIFY PLACEHOLDERS | 3 MODIFY & COPY ILLUSTRATIONS
4 ADD MEDIA | 5 ANIMATE SLIDE CONTENT | 6 CUSTOMIZE SLIDE ELEMENTS

The presentation theme determines the formatting characteristics of fonts and colors. It also establishes paragraph formatting, including the alignment of text. Some themes **center** the text paragraphs between the left and right placeholder borders, while others **left-align** the paragraph so that the first character of a text line is near the left border or **right-align** the paragraph so that the last character of a text line is near the right border. The paragraph also can be **justified** so that the text is aligned to both the left and right borders. When PowerPoint justifies text, it adds extras spaces between the words to fill the entire line.

The words, Watch for Motorcycles, are left-aligned in the Slide 1 title placeholder. Later, you will add an illustration below the words, for Motorcycles, so you desire to center the paragraph. *Why? Both the text and the picture will be centered, so the alignments complement each other.* The following steps change the alignment of the Slide 1 title placeholder.

1

- With the HOME tab displayed, tap or click somewhere in the title text paragraph of Slide 1 to position the insertion point in the paragraph to be formatted (Figure 3–10).

Figure 3–10

2

- Tap or click the Center button (HOME tab | Paragraph group) to center the paragraph (Figure 3–11).

Q&A What if I want to return the paragraph to left-alignment?
Tap or click the Align Left button (HOME tab | Paragraph group).

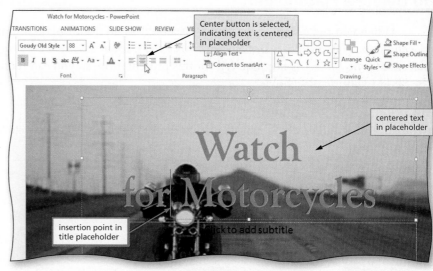

Figure 3–11

Other Ways			
1. Press and hold or right-click paragraph, tap or click Center button on mini toolbar	2. Press and hold or right-click paragraph, tap or click Paragraph on shortcut menu, tap or click Indents and Spacing tab (Paragraph dialog box), tap or click Alignment arrow, tap or click Centered, tap or click OK button	3. Tap or click Paragraph dialog box launcher (HOME tab | Paragraph group), tap or click Indents and Spacing tab (Paragraph dialog box), tap or click Alignment arrow, tap or click Centered, tap or click OK button	4. Press CTRL+E

To Move a Placeholder

1 INSERT & ADD EFFECTS | 2 MODIFY PLACEHOLDERS | 3 MODIFY & COPY ILLUSTRATIONS
4 ADD MEDIA | 5 ANIMATE SLIDE CONTENT | 6 CUSTOMIZE SLIDE ELEMENTS

Why? *If you desire to have a placeholder appear in a different area of the slide, you can move it to a new location.* The theme layouts determine where the text and content placeholders display on the slide. The Slide 1 title placeholder currently displays in the upper third of the slide, but the text in this placeholder would be more aesthetically pleasing if it were moved to the upper-right corner of the slide. The following step moves the Slide 1 title placeholder.

1

- Tap or click the border of the Slide 1 title placeholder to select it.

- With the title placeholder border displaying as a solid line or fine dots, point to an area of the left border between the middle and lower sizing handles so that the pointer changes to a four-headed arrow.

Q&A Can I tap or click any part of the border to select it?
Yes. You can tap or click any of the four border lines.

How do I know if the placeholder is selected?
The selection handles are displayed.

- Drag the placeholder upward and to the right so that the text is centered between the motorcyclist's helmet and the right edge of the slide (Figure 3–12).

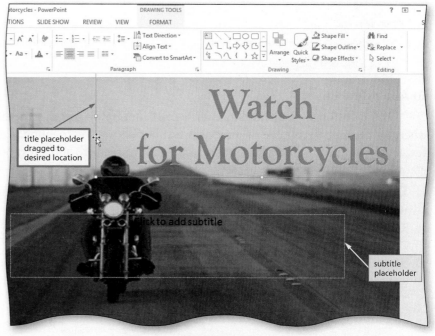

Figure 3–12

To Delete a Placeholder

When you run a slide show, empty placeholders do not display. You may desire to delete unused placeholders from a slide. ***Why?*** *So they are not a distraction when you are designing slide content.* The subtitle placeholder on Slide 1 is not required for this presentation, so you can remove it. The following steps remove the Slide 1 subtitle placeholder.

- Tap or click a border of the subtitle placeholder so that it displays as a solid line or fine dots (Figure 3–13).

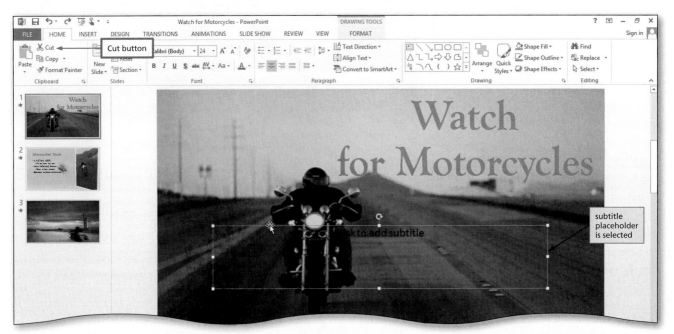

Figure 3–13

2

- Tap or click the Cut button (HOME tab | Clipboard group) to remove the placeholder.

Other Ways	
1. Select placeholder, press DELETE or BACKSPACE	2. Press and hold or right-click placeholder border, tap Cut on shortcut menu

To Add a Text Box

You occasionally may need to insert a small amount of text in an area of a slide where no content placeholder is located. A text box allows you to emphasize or set off text that you consider important for your audience to read. To add a text box to a slide, you would perform the following steps.

1. Tap or click the Text Box button (INSERT tab | Text group), click or tap the slide, and then drag the object to the desired location on the slide.

2. Click inside the text box to add or paste text.

3. If necessary, change the look and style of the text box characters by using formatting features (HOME tab | Font group).

Changing Views

You have been using Normal view to create and edit your slides. Once you completed your slides, you reviewed the final products by displaying each slide in Slide Show view, which occupies the full computer screen. You were able to view how the transitions, graphics, and effects will display in an actual presentation before an audience.

PowerPoint has other views to help review a presentation for content, organization, and overall appearance. Slide Sorter view allows you to look at several slides at one time. Reading view is similar to Slide Show view because each slide displays individually, but the slides do not fill the entire screen. Using this view, you easily can progress through the slides forward or backward with simple controls at the bottom of the window. Switching between Slide Sorter view, Reading view, and Normal view helps you review your presentation, assess whether the slides have an attractive design and adequate content, and make sure they are organized for the most impact. After reviewing the slides, you can change the view to Normal so that you may continue working on the presentation.

To Change Views

1 INSERT & ADD EFFECTS │ 2 MODIFY PLACEHOLDERS │ 3 MODIFY & COPY ILLUSTRATIONS
4 ADD MEDIA │ 5 ANIMATE SLIDE CONTENT │ 6 CUSTOMIZE SLIDE ELEMENTS

Why? You have made several modifications to the slides, so you should check for balance and consistency. The following steps change the view from Normal view to Slide Sorter view, then Reading view, and back to Normal view.

- Tap or click the Slide Sorter view button in the lower right of the PowerPoint window to display the presentation in Slide Sorter view (Figure 3–14).

Q&A Why is Slide 1 selected?
It is the current slide in the Thumbnails pane.

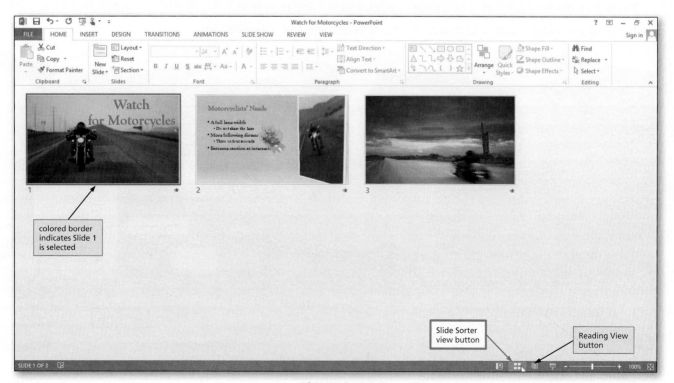

colored border indicates Slide 1 is selected

Slide Sorter view button

Reading View button

Figure 3–14

• Tap or click the Reading View button in the lower right of the PowerPoint window to display Slide 1 of the presentation in Reading view (Figure 3–15).

Figure 3–15

• Tap or click the Next button two times to advance through the presentation.

• Tap or click the Previous button two times to display Slide 2 and then Slide 1.

• Tap or click the Menu button to display commonly used commands (Figure 3–16).

Figure 3–16

• Tap or click End Show to return to Slide Sorter view, which is the view you were using before Reading view.

• Tap or click the Normal view button to display the presentation in Normal view.

Modifying and Copying an Illustration

Slides 1 and 2 (shown in Figures 3–1a and 3–1b on PPT 147) contain an illustration of a car that was downloaded from Office.com and then modified. You may want to modify an illustration for various reasons. Many times, you cannot find an illustration that precisely represents your topic. For example, you want a picture of a person wearing a red sweater, but the only available picture has a person with a blue sweater.

Occasionally, you may want to remove or change a portion of an illustration or you might want to combine two or more illustrations. For example, you can use one illustration for the background and another photo as the foreground. Other times, you may want to combine an illustration with another type of object. In this presentation, the tires on the car are orange, and you want to change the color to black. In addition, the car illustration has a highway below the tires and a colorful background, which are not required to display on the slide, so you will ungroup the illustration, change the color of the tires, and remove the highway and the background.

Modifying the clip on Slide 2 and then copying it to Slide 1 requires several steps. In the following pages, you will perform these tasks:

1. Zoom Slide 2 to examine the illustration.
2. Ungroup the illustration.
3. Change a color.
4. Delete objects.
5. Regroup the illustration.
6. Copy the illustration from Slide 2 to Slide 1.

BTW
BTWs
For a complete list of the BTWs found in the margins of this book, visit the BTW resource on the Student Companion Site located on www.cengagebrain.com. For detailed instructions about accessing available resources, visit www.cengage.com/ct/studentdownload or see the inside back cover of this book.

To Zoom a Slide

You will be modifying small areas of the illustration, so it will help you select the relevant pieces if the graphic is enlarged. The following step changes the zoom to 200 percent.

1 Display Slide 2 and then drag the Zoom slider or tap or click the Zoom level button or the Zoom In button to change the zoom level to 200% (Figure 3–17).

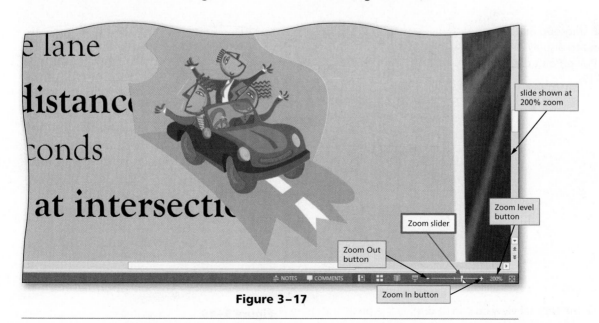

Figure 3–17

To Ungroup an Illustration

The next step is to ungroup the car illustration, also called a clip, on Slide 2. When you **ungroup** an illustration, PowerPoint breaks it into its component objects. A clip may be composed of a few individual objects or several complex groups of objects. These groups can be ungrouped repeatedly until they decompose into individual objects. *Why? Because an illustration is a collection of complex groups of objects, you may need to ungroup a complex object into less complex objects before being able to modify a specific object.* When you ungroup a clip and tap or click the Yes button in the Microsoft PowerPoint dialog box, PowerPoint converts the clip to a PowerPoint object. The following steps ungroup an illustration.

- Tap or click the car clip to select it and then tap or click FORMAT on the ribbon to display the PICTURE TOOLS FORMAT tab.

- Tap or click the Group button (PICTURE TOOLS FORMAT tab | Arrange group) to display the Group menu (Figure 3–18).

Q&A Why does the Group button look different on my screen?
Your monitor is set to a different resolution. See Chapter 1 for an explanation of screen resolution and the appearance of the ribbon.

Figure 3–18

2

- Tap or click Ungroup on the Group menu to display the Microsoft PowerPoint dialog box (Figure 3–19).

Figure 3–19

3

- Tap or click the Yes button (Microsoft PowerPoint dialog box) to convert the clip to a Microsoft Office drawing.

Q&A What happens if I tap or click the No button?
The clip will remain displayed on the slide as an illustration and will not ungroup.

- Tap or click FORMAT on the ribbon to display the DRAWING TOOLS FORMAT tab. Tap or click the Group button (DRAWING TOOLS FORMAT tab | Arrange group) and then tap or click Ungroup again to display the objects that constitute the car clip (Figure 3–20).

Q&A Why does the ribbon change from the PICTURE TOOLS DRAWING tab to the DRAWING TOOLS FORMAT tab and show different options this time?
The illustration has become a drawing object, so tools related to drawing now display.

Why do all those circles and squares display in the clip?
The circles and squares are sizing handles for each of the clip's objects, which resemble pieces of a jigsaw puzzle.

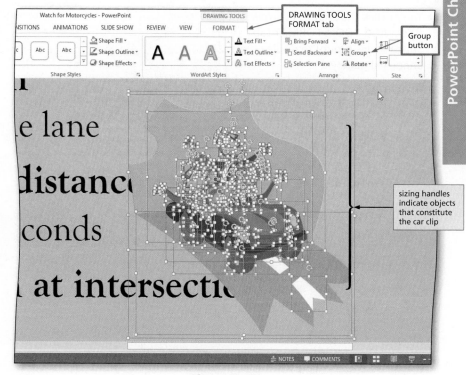

Figure 3–20

Other Ways

1. Press and hold or right-click clip, point to Group on shortcut menu, tap or click Ungroup   2. Press CTRL+SHIFT+G

To Change the Color of a Clip Object

1 INSERT & ADD EFFECTS | 2 MODIFY PLACEHOLDERS | 3 MODIFY & COPY ILLUSTRATIONS
4 ADD MEDIA | 5 ANIMATE SLIDE CONTENT | 6 CUSTOMIZE SLIDE ELEMENTS

Now that the car illustration is ungrouped, you can change the color of the objects. You must exercise care when selecting the correct object to modify. *Why? The clip is composed of hundreds of objects.* The following steps change the color of the car's tires from orange to black.

1

- Tap or click an area of the slide that is not part of the clip to deselect all the clip pieces.

- Tap or click the car's left front tire to display sizing handles around the orange colored area (Figure 3–21).

Q&A What if I selected a different area by mistake?
Tap or click outside the clip and retry.

Figure 3–21

2

- Tap or click the Shape Fill arrow (DRAWING TOOLS FORMAT tab | Shape Styles group) to display the Shape Fill gallery.

- If you are using a mouse, point to Black, Text 1 (second color in the first Theme Colors row) to display a live preview of the tire color (Figure 3–22).

Experiment

- If you are using a mouse, point to various colors and watch the car's tire color change.

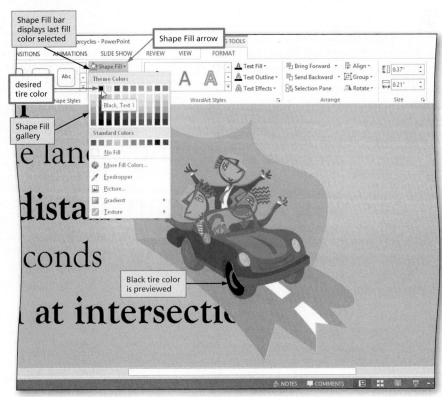

Figure 3–22

3

- Tap or click the color Black, Text 1 to change the car's tire color (Figure 3–23).

Q&A Why is the bar under the Shape Fill button now black?
The button displays the last fill color selected.

BTW

The Ribbon and Screen Resolution
PowerPoint may change how the groups and buttons within the groups appear on the ribbon, depending on the computer's screen resolution. Thus, your ribbon may look different from the ones in this book if you are using a screen resolution other than 1366 × 768.

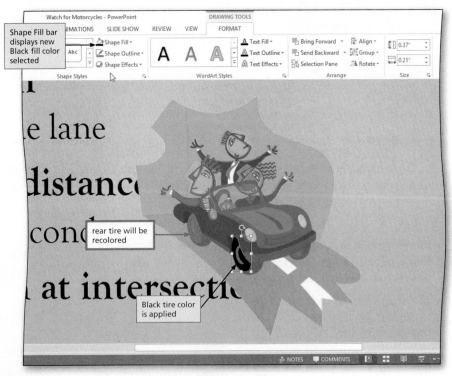

Figure 3–23

4

- Tap or click the left rear tire to select it.

- Tap or click the Shape Fill button to change the tire color to Black, Text 1 (Figure 3–24).

 Why did I not need to tap or click the Shape Fill arrow to select this color?
PowerPoint uses the last fill color selected. This color displays in the bar under the bucket icon on the button.

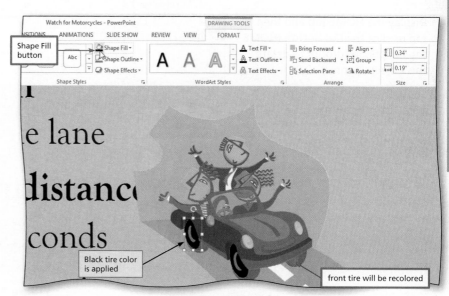

Figure 3–24

5

- Change the right front tire color to black (Figure 3–25).

Figure 3–25

Other Ways

1. Press and hold or right-click object, tap or click Fill button below shortcut menu

2. Press and hold or right-click object, tap or click Format Shape on shortcut menu, tap or click Fill & Line icon

To Delete a Clip Object

1 INSERT & ADD EFFECTS | 2 MODIFY PLACEHOLDERS | 3 MODIFY & COPY ILLUSTRATIONS
4 ADD MEDIA | 5 ANIMATE SLIDE CONTENT | 6 CUSTOMIZE SLIDE ELEMENTS

With the car tires' color changed, you want to delete the pink and purple background objects and the highway objects. *Why? These objects clutter the slide and are not necessary elements of the clip.* The following steps delete these objects.

1

- Tap or click the background in any area where the pink color displays to select this object (Figure 3–26).

Can I select multiple objects so I can delete them simultaneously?
Yes. While pressing the SHIFT key, tap or click the unwanted elements to select them.

Figure 3–26

- Display the HOME tab and then tap or click the Cut button (HOME tab | Clipboard group) to delete this object (Figure 3–27).

Q&A Should the purple background object display on the slide?
Yes. It is part of the car clip. You will remove it in the next step.

Figure 3–27

- Tap or click the purple background to select this object.
- Tap or click the Cut button to delete this object.

- Tap or click the mauve highway to select this object (Figure 3–28).
- Tap or click the Cut button to delete this object.

Q&A Should the white highway stripes display on the slide?
Yes. They are part of the car clip. You will remove them in the next step.

Figure 3–28

5

- If using a mouse, click one white highway stripe, press the SHIFT key, and then click the second white highway stripe to select both objects (Figure 3–29).
- If using a touch screen, select one stripe, tap the Cut button to delete this object, and then select the other stripe and tap the Cut button again.
- If using a mouse, click the Cut button to delete these objects.

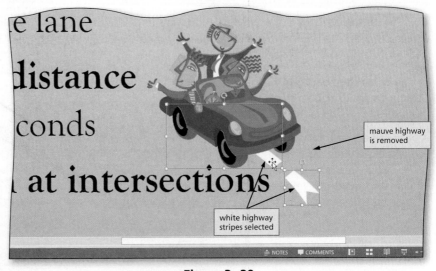

Figure 3–29

To Regroup Objects

When you ungrouped the car clip, you eliminated the embedding data or linking information that tied all the individual pieces together. If you attempt to move or size this clip now, you might encounter difficulties because it consists of hundreds of objects and is no longer one unified piece. Dragging or sizing affects only a selected object, not the entire collection of objects, so you must use caution when objects are not completely regrouped. All of the ungrouped objects in the car clip must be regrouped. *Why? So they are not accidentally moved or manipulated.* The following steps regroup these objects into one object.

- If necessary, select the clip, tap or click the DRAWING TOOLS FORMAT tab and then tap or click the Group button (DRAWING TOOLS FORMAT tab | Arrange group) to display the Group menu (Figure 3–30).

- Tap or click Regroup to recombine all the clip objects.

Figure 3–30

- Use the Zoom slider to change the zoom level to 74%.

- Increase the car's size by dragging one of the corner sizing handles outward until the illustration is the size shown in Figure 3–31 and then move the illustration to the location shown in the figure (Figure 3–31).

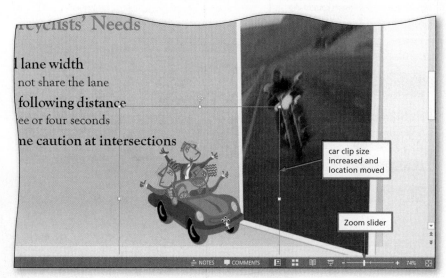

Figure 3–31

Other Ways

1. Press and hold or right-click clip, point to Group on shortcut menu, tap or click Regroup

To Copy a Clip from One Slide to Another

The car clip on Slide 2 also can display in its modified form on the title slide. You first must copy it using the Office Clipboard and then paste it in the desired location. ***Why?*** *The **Office Clipboard** is a temporary storage location that can hold a maximum of 24 text or graphics items copied from any Office program.* The same procedure of copying and pasting objects works for copying and pasting text from one placeholder to another. The following steps copy this slide element from Slide 2 to Slide 1.

- With the car illustration selected, display the HOME tab and then tap or click the Copy button (HOME tab | Clipboard group) (Figure 3–32).

2
- Display Slide 1 and then tap or click the Paste button (HOME tab | Clipboard group) to insert the car illustration into the title slide.

Q&A
Is the clip deleted from the Office Clipboard when I paste it into the slide?
No.

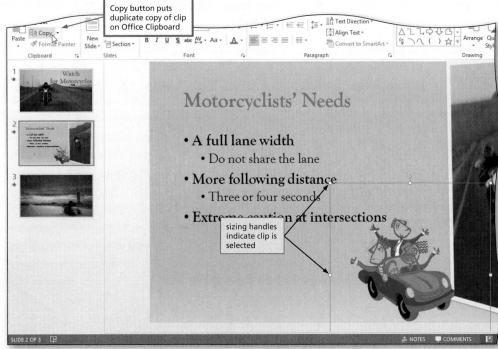

Figure 3–32

3
- Increase the car size by dragging one of the corner sizing handles outward until the car is the size shown in Figure 3–33. Drag the car to the location shown in this figure.

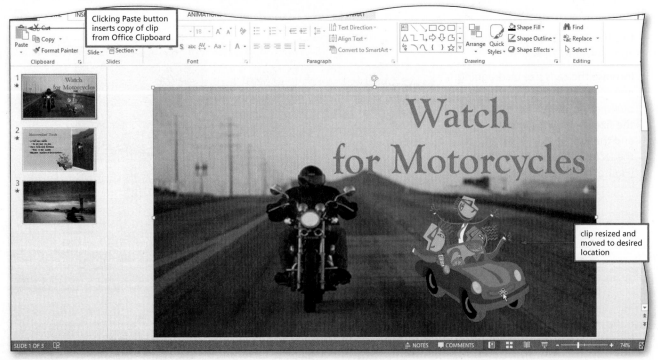

Figure 3–33

Break Point: If you wish to take a break, this is a good place to do so. Be sure to save the Watch for Motorcycles file again and then you can quit PowerPoint. To resume at a later time, start PowerPoint, open the file called Watch for Motorcycles, and continue following the steps from this location forward.

Adding Media to Slides

Media files can enrich a presentation if they are used correctly. Movie files can be produced with a camera and editing software, and sound files can come from the Office. com Clip Art collection, files stored on your computer, or an audio track on a CD. To hear the sounds, you need a sound card and speakers or headphones on your system.

Once an audio or video clip is inserted into a slide, you can specify options that affect how the file is displayed and played. For example, you can have the video play automatically when the slide is displayed, or you can tap or click the video frame when you are ready to start the playback. You also can have the video fill the entire slide, which is referred to as **full screen**. If you decide to play the slide show automatically and have it display full screen, you can drag the video frame to the gray area off the slide so that it does not display briefly before going to full screen. You can select the Loop until Stopped option to have the video repeat until you tap or click the next slide, or you can choose to not have the video frame display on the slide until you tap or click the slide.

If your video clip has recorded sounds, the volume controls give you the option to set how loudly this audio will play. They also allow you to mute the sound so that your audience will hear no background noise or music.

In the following pages, you will perform these tasks:

1. Insert a video file into Slide 3.
2. Trim the video file to shorten the play time.
3. Add video options that determine the clip's appearance and playback.
4. Insert an audio file into Slide 1.
5. Add audio options that determine the clip's appearance and playback.
6. Add a video style to the Slide 3 clip.
7. Resize the video.

BTW

Using Codecs
Video and audio content developers use a codec (**co**mpressor/**dec**ompressor) to reduce the file size of digital media. The reduced file size helps transfer files across the Internet quickly and smoothly and helps save space on storage media. Your computer can play any compressed file if the specific codec used to compress the file is available on your computer. If the codec is not installed or is not recognized, your computer attempts to download this file from the Internet. Many codex files are available to download from the Internet at no cost.

To Insert a Video File

1 INSERT & ADD EFFECTS | 2 MODIFY PLACEHOLDERS | 3 MODIFY & COPY ILLUSTRATIONS
4 ADD MEDIA | 5 ANIMATE SLIDE CONTENT | 6 CUSTOMIZE SLIDE ELEMENTS

Slide 3 has another photo of a motorcyclist, and you have a video clip of a person mounting a motorcycle, putting the bike into gear, and riding out of the scene. You want to use a majority of the clip and eliminate a few seconds from the end. PowerPoint allows you to insert this clip into your slide and then trim the file. *Why? Just a portion will play when you preview the clip or run the slide show.* This clip is available on the Data Files for Students. See the inside back cover of this book for instructions on downloading the Data Files for Students, or contact your instructor for more information about accessing the required file. The following steps insert this video clip into Slide 3.

- Display Slide 3 and then display the INSERT tab. Tap or click the Video button (INSERT tab | Media group) to display the Video menu (Figure 3–34).

Figure 3–34

2

- Tap or click 'Video on My PC' on the Video menu to display the Insert Video dialog box.

- If the list of files and folders for Chapter 3 is not displayed in the Insert Video dialog box, navigate to the location where the files are located.

- Tap or click Motorcycle Rider to select the file (Figure 3–35).

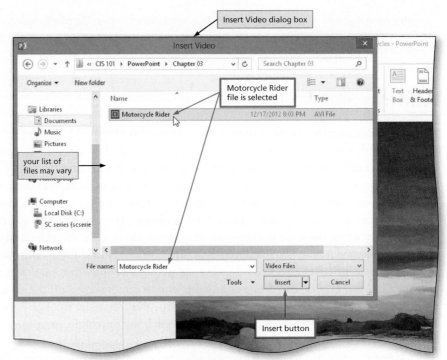

Figure 3–35

3

- Tap or click the Insert button (Insert Video dialog box) to insert the video clip into Slide 3 (Figure 3–36).

Q&A Can I adjust the color of a video clip?
Yes. You can correct the brightness and contrast, and you also can recolor a video clip using the same methods you learned in this chapter to color a photo.

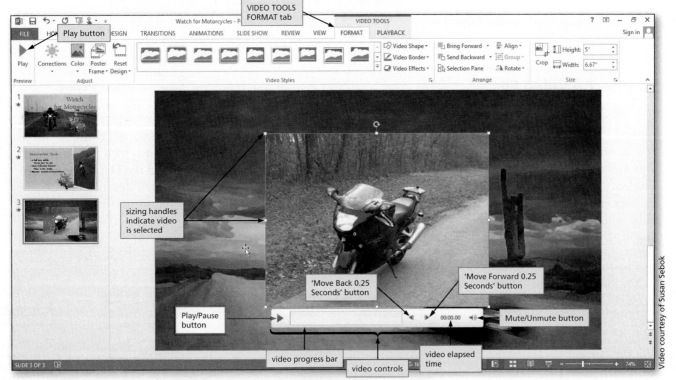

Figure 3–36

Video courtesy of Susan Sebok

To Trim a Video File

Why? The Motorcycle Rider video has a running time of slightly more than 14 seconds. Near the end of the clip, the motorcyclist rides out of the frame, so you delete a few seconds from that portion of the file. PowerPoint's **Trim Video** feature allows you to trim the beginning and end of your clip by designating your desired Start Time and End Time. These precise time measurements are accurate to one-thousandth of a second. The start point is indicated by a green marker, and the end point is indicated by a red marker. The following steps trim the Motorcycle Rider video clip.

- With the video clip selected on Slide 3, tap or click the Play/Pause button to play the entire video.

Q&A Can I play the video by tapping or clicking the Play button in the Preview group?
Yes. This Play button plays the entire clip. You may prefer to tap or click the Play/Pause button displayed in the video controls to stop the video and examine one of the frames.

- Tap or click PLAYBACK on the ribbon to display the VIDEO TOOLS PLAYBACK tab. Tap or click the Trim Video button (VIDEO TOOLS PLAYBACK tab | Editing group) to display the Trim Video dialog box (Figure 3–37).

Figure 3–37

- Point to the end point, which is indicated by the red marker on the right side, so that the pointer changes to a two-headed arrow.

- Slide or drag the red marker to the left until the End Time is 00:13:365 (Figure 3–38).

Q&A Can I specify the start or end times without dragging the markers?
Yes. You can enter the time in the Start Time or End Time boxes, or you can tap or click the Start Time or End Time box arrows. You also can tap or click the Next Frame and Previous Frame buttons (Trim Video dialog box).

How would I indicate a start point if I want the clip to start at a time other than at the beginning of the clip?
You would drag the green marker to the right until the desired time displays in the Start Time box.

Figure 3–38

3

- Tap or click the Play/Pause button (Trim Video dialog box) to review the shortened video clip.

- Tap or click the OK button to set the Start Time and End Time and to close the Trim Video dialog box.

Other Ways

1. Press and hold or right-click clip, tap or click Trim on shortcut menu

To Add Video Options

Once the video clip is inserted into Slide 3, you can specify that the video plays automatically when the slide is displayed. ***Why?*** *When you are giving your presentation, you do not want to click the mouse or tap the screen to start the video.* You also can adjust the volume of the sound recorded on the file. The following steps add the option of playing the video full screen automatically and also decrease the volume of the motorcycle engine.

- If necessary, tap or click PLAYBACK on the ribbon to display the VIDEO TOOLS PLAYBACK tab. Tap or click the Start arrow (VIDEO TOOLS PLAYBACK tab | Video Options group) to display the Start menu (Figure 3–39).

Q&A What does the On Click option do?
The video clip would begin playing when a presenter taps or clicks the frame during the slide show.

Figure 3–39

- Tap or click Automatically in the Start menu to run the video clip automatically when the slide is displayed.

- Tap or click the 'Play Full Screen' check box (VIDEO TOOLS PLAYBACK tab | Video Options group) to place a check mark in it.

- Tap or click the Volume button (VIDEO TOOLS PLAYBACK tab | Video Options group) to display the Volume menu (Figure 3–40).

Figure 3–40

- Tap or click Medium on the Volume menu to set the audio volume.

Q&A Will the Mute option silence the video's background sounds?
Yes. Tap or click Mute if you do not want your audience to hear any recorded sounds.

To Insert an Audio File

If you have an active Internet connection, you can search Office.com to locate several motorcycle sounds in audio files that you can download and insert into your presentation. The following steps insert an audio clip into Slide 1. ***Why?*** *Avid motorcyclists enjoy hearing the sounds of their engines and often can identify a bike by the engine sounds it makes. A clip of a motorcycle engine adds interest to the start of your presentation when Slide 1 is displayed.*

- Display Slide 1 and then tap or click INSERT on the ribbon to display the INSERT tab.

- Tap or click the Audio button (INSERT tab | Media group) to display the Audio menu (Figure 3–41).

Figure 3–41

- Tap or click Online Audio on the Insert Audio menu to open the Insert Audio dialog box.

- With the insertion point in the Office.com Clip Art area, type **motorcycle** in the search text box (Figure 3–42).

- Tap or click the Search button (the magnifying glass) or press the ENTER key so that Office.com will search for and display all audio clips having the keyword, motorcycle.

Figure 3–42

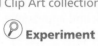

- If you are using a mouse, point to the 1200cc Passby clip to display the total time of the clip and to hear a preview of this file (Figure 3–43).

Q&A
What if the 1200cc Passby audio clip is not shown in my Office.com Clip Art dialog box?
Select a similar clip. Your clips may be different depending on the clips included in the Office.com Clip Art collection.

Experiment

- If you are using a mouse, point to other audio clips to hear the sounds and to view the clips' length.

- Tap or click the 1200cc Passby clip to select the clip (Figure 3–44).

Figure 3–43

Figure 3–44

5

• Tap or click the Insert button in the dialog box to insert that file into Slide 1 (Figure 3–45).

Q&A Why does a sound icon display on the slide?
The icon indicates an audio file is inserted.

Do the audio control buttons have the same functions as the video control buttons that displayed when I inserted the Motorcycle Rider clip?
Yes. The controls include playing and pausing the sound, moving back or forward 0.25 seconds, audio progress, elapsed time, and muting or unmuting the sound.

Figure 3–45

6

• Drag the sound icon to the lower-left corner of the slide (Figure 3–46).

Q&A Must I move the icon on the slide?
No. Although your audience will not see the icon when you run the slide show, it is easier for you to see the audio controls in the dark area of this slide.

Figure 3–46

To Add Audio Options

1 INSERT & ADD EFFECTS | 2 MODIFY PLACEHOLDERS | 3 MODIFY & COPY ILLUSTRATIONS
4 ADD MEDIA | 5 ANIMATE SLIDE CONTENT | 6 CUSTOMIZE SLIDE ELEMENTS

Once an audio clip is inserted into a slide, you can specify options that control playback and appearance. As with the video options you applied to the Motorcycle Rider clip, the audio clip can play either automatically or when tapped or clicked, it can repeat the clip while a particular slide is displayed, and you can drag the sound icon off the slide and set the volume. The following steps add the options of starting automatically, playing until the slide no longer is displayed, and hiding the sound icon on the slide. *Why? You do not want to tap or click the screen to start the sound, so you do not need to see the icon. In addition, you want the engine sound to repeat while the slide is displayed to coordinate with the motorcycle picture prominently shown and to keep the audience's attention focused on the topic of listening for motorcycles while operating a vehicle.*

1

• If necessary, tap or click PLAYBACK on the ribbon to display the AUDIO TOOLS PLAYBACK tab. Tap or click the Start arrow (AUDIO TOOLS PLAYBACK tab | Audio Options group) to display the Start menu (Figure 3–47).

2

• Tap or click Automatically in the Start menu.

Figure 3–47

Q&A Does the On Click option function the same way for an audio clip as On Click does for a video clip?
Yes. If you were to select On Click, the sound would begin playing only after the presenter taps or clicks Slide 1 during a presentation.

- Tap or click the 'Loop until Stopped' check box (AUDIO TOOLS PLAYBACK tab | Audio Options group) to place a check mark in it.

Q&A What is the difference between the 'Loop until Stopped' and the 'Play Across Slides' option?

The audio clip in the 'Loop until Stopped' option repeats for as long as one slide is displayed. In contrast, the 'Play Across Slides' option would play the clip only once, but it would continue to play while other slides in the presentation are displayed. Once the end of the clip is reached, the sound would end and not repeat.

- Tap or click the 'Hide During Show' check box (AUDIO TOOLS PLAYBACK tab | Audio Options group) to place a check mark in it (Figure 3–48).

Q&A Why would I want the icon to display during the show?

If you had selected the On Click option, you would need to find this icon on the slide and tap or click it to start playing the clip.

Can I adjust the sound's volume?

Yes. You can adjust the volume or mute the sound by clicking the Volume button (AUDIO TOOLS PLAYBACK tab | Audio Options group) or by clicking the Mute/Unmute button on the Media Controls bar and using the volume slider.

Figure 3–48

To Add a Video Style

1 INSERT & ADD EFFECTS | 2 MODIFY PLACEHOLDERS | 3 MODIFY & COPY ILLUSTRATIONS
4 ADD MEDIA | 5 ANIMATE SLIDE CONTENT | 6 CUSTOMIZE SLIDE ELEMENTS

The video styles are similar to the photo styles you applied in Chapter 2 and include various shapes, angles, borders, and reflections. The following steps apply a video style to the Motorcycle Rider clip on Slide 3. *Why? The Motorcycle Rider video clip on Slide 3 displays full screen when it is playing, but you decide to increase the visual appeal of the clip when it is not playing by applying a video style.*

- Display Slide 3 and select the video frame. Tap or click FORMAT on the ribbon to display the VIDEO TOOLS FORMAT tab (Figure 3–49).

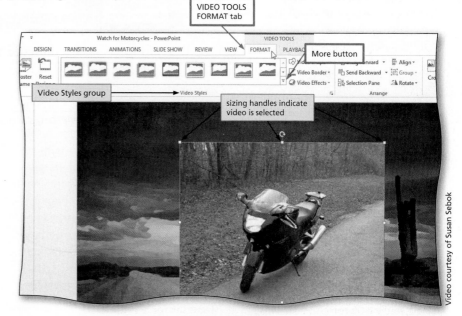

Video courtesy of Susan Sebok

Figure 3–49

2

- With the video frame selected, tap or click the More button in the Video Styles gallery (VIDEO TOOLS FORMAT tab | Video Styles group) (shown in Figure 3–49) to expand the gallery.

- If you are using a mouse, point to Canvas, Gray in the Intense area of the Video Styles gallery (third style in the second row) to display a live preview of that style applied to the video frame on the slide (Figure 3–50).

🔍 **Experiment**

- If you are using a mouse, point to various photo styles in the Video Styles gallery and watch the style of the video frame change in the document window.

Figure 3–50

3

- Tap or click Canvas, Gray in the Video Styles gallery to apply the style to the selected video (Figure 3–51).

Q&A

Can I preview the movie clip?
Yes. Point to the clip and then tap or click the Play button on the ribbon (Preview group) or the Play/Pause button on the video controls below the video.

Can I add a border to a video style?
Yes. You add a border using the same method you learned in Chapter 2 to add a border to a photo. Tap or click the Video Border button (VIDEO TOOLS FORMAT tab | Video Styles group) and then select a border line weight and color.

Figure 3–51

Other Ways

1. Tap or click Format Video on shortcut menu, tap or click Video icon, tap or click VIDEO, tap or click Presets button

BTW

PowerPoint Help

At any time while using PowerPoint, you can find answers to questions and display information about various topics through PowerPoint Help. Used properly, this form of assistance can increase your productivity and reduce your frustrations by minimizing the time you spend learning how to use PowerPoint. For instruction about PowerPoint Help and exercises that will help you gain confidence in using it, read the Office and Windows chapter at the beginning of this book.

To Resize a Video

The default Motorcycle Rider frame size can be changed. You resize a video clip in the same manner that you resize photos and illustrations. The following steps will increase the Motorcycle Rider video using a sizing handle. *Why? You want to fill some space on the left side of the slide.*

- With the video selected, drag the lower-left corner sizing handle diagonally outward until the frame is resized to approximately 5.89" × 7.86".

- Drag the clip to the location shown in Figure 3–52.

Figure 3–52

Break Point: If you wish to take a break, this is a good place to do so. Be sure to save the Watch for Motorcycles file again and then you can quit PowerPoint. To resume at a later time, start PowerPoint, open the file called Watch for Motorcycles, and continue following the steps from this location forward.

Animating Slide Content

BTW
Animation Effect Icon Colors
Animation effects allow you to control how objects enter, move on, and exit slides. Using a traffic signal analogy may help you remember the sequence of events. Green icons indicate when the animation effect starts on the slide. Yellow icons represent the object's motion; use them with caution so they do not distract from the message you are conveying to your audience. Red icons indicate when the object stops appearing on a slide.

Animation includes special visual and sound effects applied to text or other content. You already are familiar with one form of animation: transitions between slides. To add visual interest and clarity to a presentation, you can animate various parts of an individual slide, including pictures, shapes, text, and other slide elements. For example, each paragraph on the slide can spin as it is displayed. Individual letters and shapes also can spin or move in various motions. PowerPoint has a variety of built-in animations that will fade, wipe, or fly-in text and graphics.

Custom Animations

You can create your own **custom animations** to meet your unique needs. Custom animation effects are grouped in categories: entrance, exit, emphasis, and motion paths. **Entrance** effects, as the name implies, determine how slide elements first appear on a slide. **Exit** animations work in the opposite manner as entrance effects: They determine how slide elements disappear. **Emphasis** effects modify text and objects

BTW
Certification
The Microsoft Office Specialist (MOS) program provides an opportunity for you to obtain a valuable industry credential — proof that you have the PowerPoint 2013 skills required by employers. For more information, visit the Certification resource on the Student Companion Site located on www.cengagebrain.com. For detailed instructions about accessing available resources, visit www.cengage.com/ct/studentdownload or see the inside back cover of this book.

displayed on the screen. For example, letters may darken or increase in font size. The entrance, exit, and emphasis animations are grouped into categories: Basic, Subtle, Moderate, and Exciting. You can set the animation speed to Very Fast, Fast, Medium, Slow, or Very Slow.

The Slide 2 illustration shows three people in a car. When the slide is displayed, the audience will see this car enter from the upper-left corner, move diagonally across the slide and stop below the bulleted list, rock slightly, and then continue down the slide toward the lower-right corner.

In the following pages, you will perform these tasks:

1. Apply an entrance effect to the car illustration and then change the direction.
2. Apply emphasis and exit effects.
3. Change the exit effect direction.
4. Preview the animation sequence.
5. Modify the entrance, emphasis, and exit effects' timing.
6. Animate text paragraphs.

To Animate an Illustration Using an Entrance Effect

1 INSERT & ADD EFFECTS | 2 MODIFY PLACEHOLDERS | 3 MODIFY & COPY ILLUSTRATIONS
4 ADD MEDIA | 5 ANIMATE SLIDE CONTENT | 6 CUSTOMIZE SLIDE ELEMENTS

The car you modified will not appear on Slide 1 when you display the slide. Instead, it will enter the slide from the upper-left corner. **Why?** *To give the appearance it is driving toward the motorcycle photo.* It will then continue downward until it reaches the lower-left side of the photo. Entrance effects are colored green in the Animation gallery. The following step applies an entrance effect to the car illustration.

- Display Slide 2, select the car clip, and then tap or click ANIMATIONS on the ribbon to display the ANIMATIONS tab.

- If you are using a mouse, click the Fly In animation in the Animation gallery (ANIMATIONS tab | Animation group) to display a live preview of this animation and to apply this entrance animation to the car illustration; if you are using a touch screen, tap Fly In animation to apply this entrance animation to the car illustration (Figure 3–53).

Q&A Are more entrance animations available?
Yes. Tap or click the More button in the Animation gallery to see additional animations. You can select one of the 13 entrance animations that are displayed, or you can tap or click the More Entrance Effects command to expand the selection. You can tap or click any animation to see a preview of the effect.

Why does the number 1 appear in a box on the left side of the clip?
The 1 is a sequence number and indicates Fly In is the first animation that will appear on the slide when you tap or click the slide.

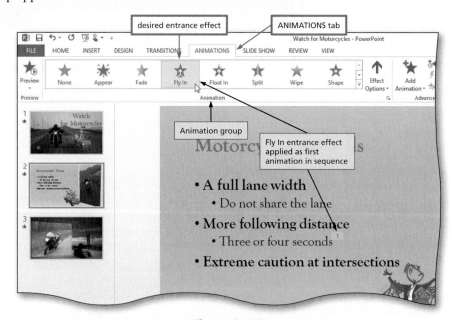

Figure 3–53

To Change Animation Direction

1 INSERT & ADD EFFECTS | 2 MODIFY PLACEHOLDERS | 3 MODIFY & COPY ILLUSTRATIONS
4 ADD MEDIA | 5 ANIMATE SLIDE CONTENT | 6 CUSTOMIZE SLIDE ELEMENTS

Why? *By default, the illustration appears on the slide by entering from the bottom edge, and you want it to enter from the top left.* You can modify this direction and specify that it enters from another side or from a corner. The following steps change the car entrance animation direction to the upper-left corner.

1
- Tap or click the Effect Options button (ANIMATIONS tab | Animation group) to display the Direction gallery (Figure 3–54).

Q&A Why does a pink box appear around the From Bottom arrow? From Bottom is the default entrance direction applied to the animation.

2
- Tap or click the From Top-Left arrow to apply this direction to the entrance animation.

Q&A Can I change this entrance effect? Yes. Repeat Step 1 to select another direction.

Figure 3–54

To Animate an Illustration Using an Emphasis Effect

1 INSERT & ADD EFFECTS | 2 MODIFY PLACEHOLDERS | 3 MODIFY & COPY ILLUSTRATIONS
4 ADD MEDIA | 5 ANIMATE SLIDE CONTENT | 6 CUSTOMIZE SLIDE ELEMENTS

Why? *The car will enter the slide from the upper-left corner and stop beside the motorcycle photo. You then want it to rock slightly.* PowerPoint provides several effects that you can apply to a picture once it appears on a slide. These movements are categorized as emphasis effects, and they are colored yellow in the Animation gallery. You already have applied an entrance effect to the car, so you want to add another animation to this illustration. The following steps apply an emphasis effect to the car after the entrance effect.

1
- Select the car illustration and then tap or click the Add Animation button (ANIMATIONS tab | Advanced Animation group) to display the Animation gallery (Figure 3–55).

Q&A Are more emphasis effects available in addition to those shown in the Animation gallery? Yes. To see additional emphasis effects, tap or click 'More Emphasis Effects' in the lower portion of the Animation gallery. The effects are arranged in the Basic, Subtle, Moderate, and Exciting categories.

Figure 3–55

2

- Tap or click Teeter (third effect in the first Emphasis row) to see a preview of this animation and to apply this emphasis effect to the car illustration (Figure 3–56).

Q&A

Do I need to use both an entrance and an emphasis effect, or can I use only an emphasis effect?
You can use one or the other effect, or both effects.

Why does the number 2 appear in a box below the number 1 on the left side of the illustration?
The 2 in the numbered tag indicates a second animation is applied in the animation sequence.

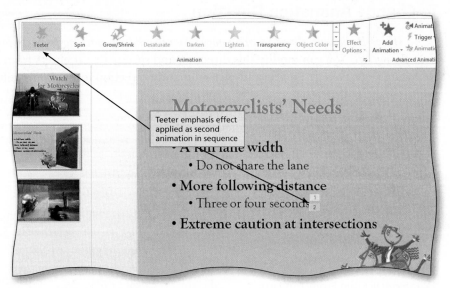

Figure 3–56

To Animate an Illustration Using an Exit Effect

1 INSERT & ADD EFFECTS | 2 MODIFY PLACEHOLDERS | 3 MODIFY & COPY ILLUSTRATIONS
4 ADD MEDIA | 5 ANIMATE SLIDE CONTENT | 6 CUSTOMIZE SLIDE ELEMENTS

The animated car will enter the slide from the upper-left corner, stop beside the motorcycle photo, and then teeter. It then will continue across the slide and exit in the lower-right corner. To continue this animation sequence, you first need to apply an exit effect. As with the entrance and emphasis effects, PowerPoint provides a wide variety of effects that you can apply to remove an illustration from a slide. These exit effects are colored red in the Animation gallery. You already have applied the Fly In entrance effect, so you will apply the Fly Out exit effect. ***Why?*** *It would give continuity to the animation sequence.* The following steps add this exit effect to the car illustration after the emphasis effect.

1

- Select the car illustration and then tap or click the Add Animation button (ANIMATIONS tab | Advanced Animation group) again to display the Animation gallery.

- Scroll down to display all the exit effects in the gallery (Figure 3–57).

Q&A

Are more exit effects available in addition to those shown in the Animation gallery?
Yes. To see additional exit effects, tap or click 'More Exit Effects' in the lower portion of the Animation gallery. The effects are arranged in the Basic, Subtle, Moderate, and Exciting categories.

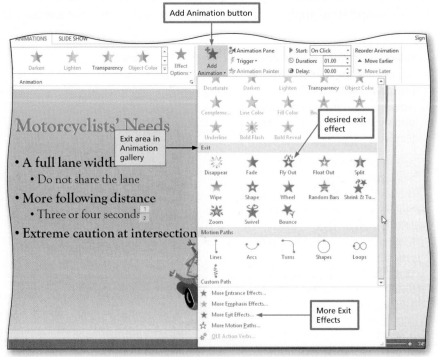

Figure 3–57

2

- Tap or click Fly Out to see a preview of this animation and to add this exit effect to the sequence of car illustration animations (Figure 3–58).

Q&A

How can I tell that this exit effect has been applied?

The Fly Out effect is displayed in the Animation gallery (ANIMATIONS tab | Animation group), and the number 3 is displayed to the left of the car illustration.

How can I delete an animation effect?

Tap or click the number associated with the animation you wish to delete and then press the DELETE key.

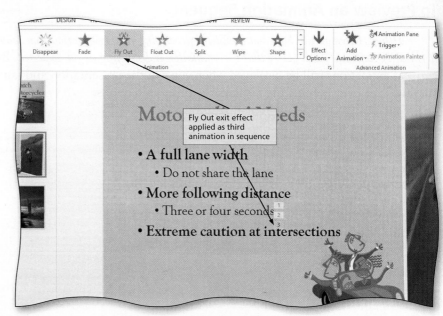

Figure 3–58

To Change Exit Animation Direction

The default direction for a picture to exit a slide is To Bottom. In this presentation, you want the car to exit in the lower-right corner. *Why? To give the impression it is continuing down an invisible highway.* The following steps change the exit animation direction from To Bottom to To Bottom-Right.

1 Tap or click the Effect Options button (ANIMATIONS tab | Animation group) to display the Direction gallery (Figure 3–59).

2 Tap or click the To Bottom-Right arrow to apply this direction to the exit animation effect.

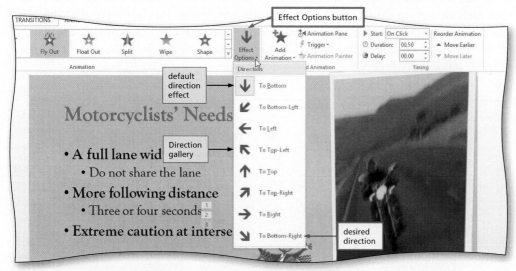

Figure 3–59

To Preview an Animation Sequence

Why? *Although you have not completed developing the presentation, you should view the animation you have added to check for continuity and verify that the animation is displaying as you expected.* By default, the entrance, emphasis, and exit animations will be displayed when you run the presentation and tap or click the slide. The following step runs the presentation and displays the three animations.

• Tap or click the Preview button (ANIMATIONS tab | Preview group) to view all the Slide 1 animations (Figure 3–60).

Q&A
Why does a red square appear in the middle of the circle on the Preview button when I tap or click that button? The red square indicates the animation sequence is in progress. Ordinarily, a green arrow is displayed in the circle.

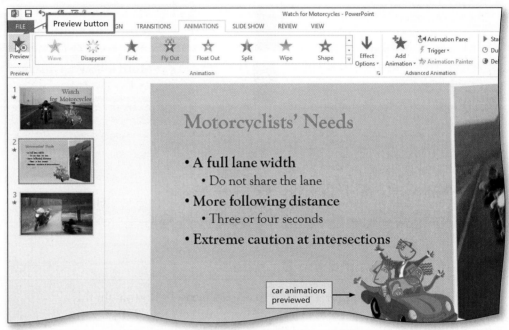

Figure 3–60

To Modify Entrance Animation Timing

The three animation effects are displayed quickly. To create a dramatic effect, you can change the timing. The default setting is to start each animation with a tap or click, but you can change this setting so that the entrance effect is delayed until a specified number of seconds has passed. The following steps modify the start, delay, and duration settings for the entrance animation. ***Why?*** *You want the slide title text to display and then, a few seconds later, the car to start to drive down the slide slowly.*

• Tap or click the tag numbered 1 on the left side of the car illustration and then tap or click the Start arrow (ANIMATIONS tab | Timing group) to display the Start menu (Figure 3–61).

Figure 3–61

● Tap or click After Previous to change the start option.

Q&A Why did the numbered tags change from 1, 2, 3 to 0, 1, 2?
The first animation now occurs automatically without a tap or click. The first and second taps or clicks now will apply the emphasis and exit animations.

What is the difference between the With Previous and After Previous settings?
The With Previous setting starts the effect simultaneously with any prior animation; the After Previous setting starts the animation after a prior animation has ended. If the prior animation is fast or a short duration, it may be difficult for a viewer to discern the difference between these two settings.

● Tap or click the Duration up arrow (ANIMATIONS tab | Timing group) several times to increase the time from 00.50 second to 02.00 seconds (Figure 3–62).

● Tap or click the Preview button to view the animations.

Q&A What is the difference between the duration time and the delay time?
The duration time is the length of time in which the animation occurs; the delay time is the length of time that passes before the animation begins.

Can I type the speed in the Duration box instead of tap or clicking the arrow to adjust the speed?
Yes. Typing the numbers allows you to set a precise timing.

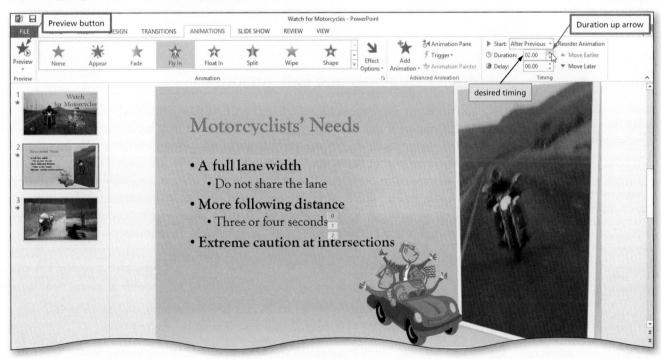

Figure 3–62

4

• Tap or click the Delay up arrow (ANIMATIONS tab | Timing group) several times to increase the delay time from 00.00 seconds to 04.00 seconds (Figure 3–63).

• Tap or click the Preview button to view the animations.

◄ | Can I adjust the delay time I just set?
Q&A | Yes. Tap or click the Delay up or down arrows and run the slide show to display Slide 1 until you find the time that best fits your presentation.

Figure 3–63

To Modify Emphasis and Exit Timings

BTW

Distributing a Document
Instead of printing and distributing a hard copy of a document, you can distribute the document electronically. Options include sending the document via email; posting it on cloud storage (such as SkyDrive) and sharing the file with others; posting it on a social networking site, blog, or other website; and sharing a link associated with an online location of the document. You also can create and share a PDF or XPS image of the document, so that users can view the file in Acrobat Reader or XPS Viewer instead of in PowerPoint.

Now that the entrance animation settings have been modified, you then can change the emphasis and exit effects for the car illustration. The emphasis effect can occur once the entrance effect has concluded, and then the exit effect can commence. With gravity's effect, the car should be able to roll more quickly down the lower part of the slide, so you will shorten the duration of the exit effect compared with the duration of the entrance effect. The animation sequence should flow without stopping, so you will not change the default delay timing of 00.00 seconds. The following steps modify the start and duration settings for the emphasis and exit animations.

1 Tap or click the tag numbered 1, which represents the emphasis effect, on the left side of the car illustration.

2 Tap or click the Start arrow (ANIMATIONS tab | Timing group) to display the Start menu and then tap or click After Previous to change the start option.

3 Tap or click the Duration up arrow (ANIMATIONS tab | Timing group) several times to increase the time to 03.00 seconds.

4 Tap or click the tag numbered 1, which now represents the exit effect, tap or click the Start arrow, and then tap or click After Previous.

⑤ Tap or click the Duration up arrow several times to increase the time to 04.00 seconds.

⑥ Preview the Slide 2 animation (Figure 3–64).

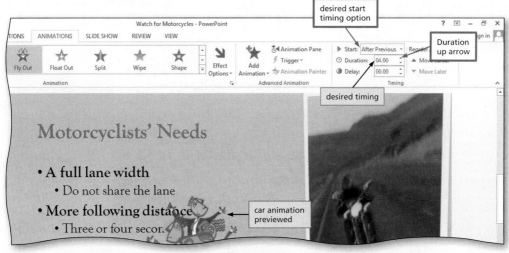

Figure 3–64

To Animate Content Placeholder Paragraphs

1 INSERT & ADD EFFECTS | 2 MODIFY PLACEHOLDERS | 3 MODIFY & COPY ILLUSTRATIONS
4 ADD MEDIA | **5 ANIMATE SLIDE CONTENT** | **6 CUSTOMIZE SLIDE ELEMENTS**

The car illustration on Slide 2 has one entrance, one emphasis, and one exit animation. You decide to add similar animations to the five bulleted paragraphs in the Slide 2 content placeholder. *Why? For a special effect, you can add several emphasis animations to one slide element.* The following steps add one entrance and one emphasis animation to the bulleted list paragraphs.

①

• Double-tap or click the Slide 2 content placeholder border so that it displays as a solid line (Figure 3–65).

Figure 3–65

②

• Tap or click the More button (shown in Figure 3–65) in the Animation group (ANIMATIONS tab | Animation group) to expand the Animation gallery (Figure 3–66).

Figure 3–66

3

- Tap or click the Fade entrance effect in the Animation gallery (second effect in first row) to add and preview this animation.

- Change the Start option to With Previous.

- Change the Duration time to 02.00 seconds (Figure 3–67).

Q&A Do I need to change the delay time?
No. The paragraphs can start appearing on the slide when the car exit effect is beginning.

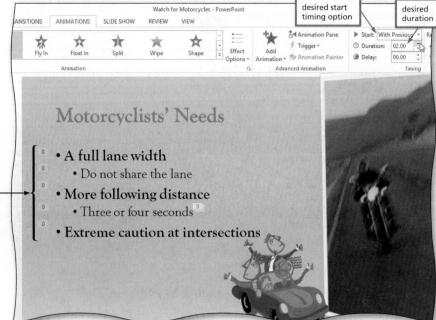

Figure 3–67

4

- Tap or click the Add Animation button (ANIMATIONS tab | Advanced Animation group) and then tap or click the Font Color emphasis animation effect (last effect in the third row).

- Change the Start option to After Previous.

- Preview the Slide 2 animation.

5

- Tap or click the Add Animation button and then click the Underline emphasis animation effect (the first effect in the fourth row), as shown in Figure 3–66.

Q&A Why do the animation effects display differently in the Animation gallery on my screen?
The width of the Animation gallery and the order of the animations may vary, especially if you are using a tablet.

- Change the Start option to With Previous (Figure 3–68).

Q&A Why is a second set of animation numbered tags starting with 0 displaying on the left side of the content placeholder?
They represent the three animations associated with the paragraphs in that placeholder.

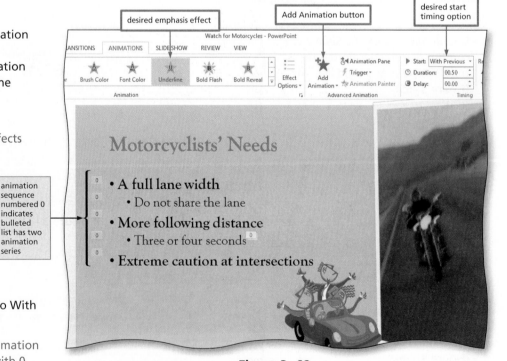

Figure 3–68

Customizing Slide Elements

PowerPoint's varied themes and layouts help give presentations a unified and aesthetically pleasing look. You may, however, desire to modify the default settings to give your slides a unique quality. One of the easier methods of developing a custom show is to change a theme for one or more slides, not an entire presentation. Similarly, you can change the variant for one or more slides to give a coordinating look to the slides in your deck. One other method of altering your slides slightly is to change the default colors associated with a particular theme.

The animated elements on Slide 2 help emphasize the need for drivers to pay particular attention to motorcyclists. Changing the theme colors for that slide to red calls even more attention to the importance of following the guidelines expressed in the bulleted list.

To Change the Theme and Variant on One Slide

1 INSERT & ADD EFFECTS | 2 MODIFY PLACEHOLDERS | 3 MODIFY & COPY ILLUSTRATIONS
4 ADD MEDIA | 5 ANIMATE SLIDE CONTENT | 6 CUSTOMIZE SLIDE ELEMENTS

The Office theme applied to the presentation is appropriate for this topic. The font and placeholder locations are simple and add variety without calling attention to the design elements. The following steps change the theme and variant for Slide 2. *Why? To call attention to the important material in the bulleted list on Slide 2, you can apply an equally effective theme that has a few design elements. You then can modify this new theme by changing the variant on one slide.*

- With Slide 2 displaying, display the DESIGN tab and then tap or click the More button (DESIGN tab | Themes group) to expand the Theme gallery (Figure 3–69).

🔍 Experiment

- If you are using a mouse, point to various document themes in the Themes gallery and watch the colors and fonts change on Slide 2.

Figure 3–69

- Press and hold or right-click the Retrospect theme (seventh theme in the first row) to display a shortcut menu (Figure 3–70).

Figure 3–70

3

- Tap or click 'Apply to Selected Slides' to apply the Retrospect theme to Slide 2.
- Press and hold or right-click the gray variant (third variant in the row) to display a shortcut menu (Figure 3–71).

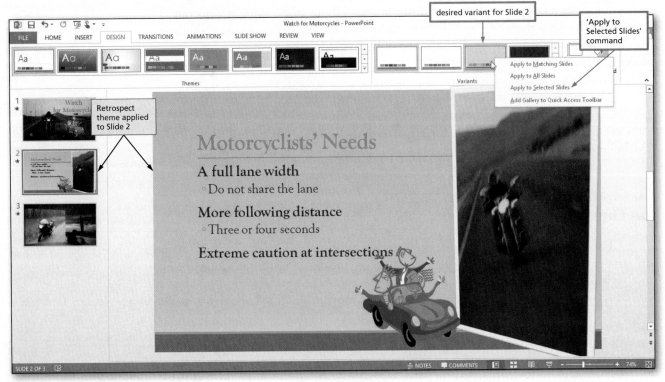

Figure 3–71

4

- Tap or click 'Apply to Selected Slides' to apply the gray variant to Slide 2 (Figure 3–72).

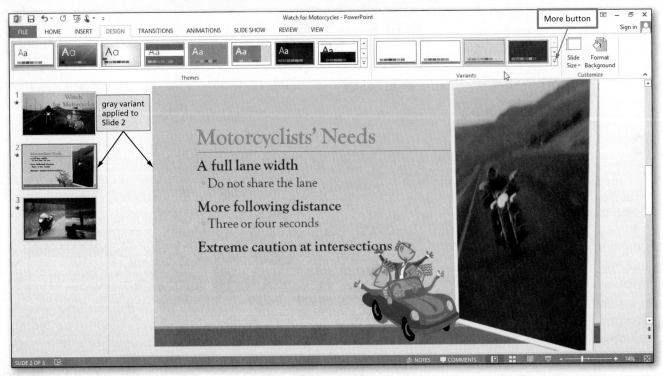

Figure 3–72

To Change the Theme Colors

Every theme has 10 standard colors: two for text, two for backgrounds, and six for accents. The following steps change the theme colors for the Watch for Motorcycles slides. *Why? You can change the look of your presentation and add variety by applying the colors from one theme to another theme.*

1

- Tap or click the More button (shown in Figure 3–72 on the previous page) in the Variants group to expand the gallery.
- Tap or point to Colors in the menu to display the Colors gallery (Figure 3–73).

🔍 Experiment

- If you are using a mouse, point to various color rows in the gallery and watch the colors change on Slide 2.

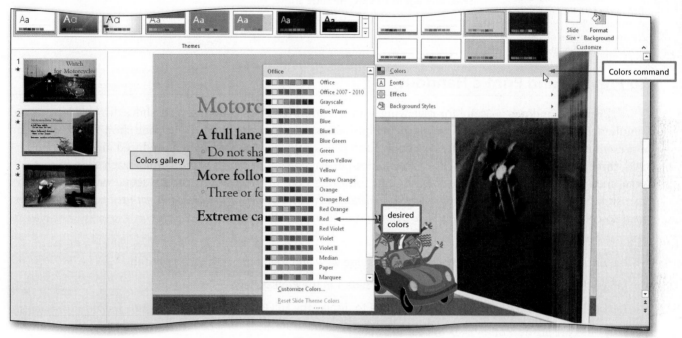

Figure 3–73

2

- Tap or click Red in the gallery to change the Slide 2 colors (Figure 3–74).

Figure 3–74

To Run a Slide Show with Media

All changes are complete, so you now can view the Watch for Motorcycles presentation. The following steps start Slide Show view.

1 Tap or click the 'Start from Beginning' button to display the title slide and listen to the motorcycle engine sound. Allow the audio clip to repeat several times.

2 Tap the screen or press the SPACEBAR to display Slide 2. Watch the car and bulleted list animations.

3 Tap the screen or press the SPACEBAR to display Slide 3. Watch the video clip.

4 Tap the screen or press the SPACEBAR to end the slide show and then tap or press the SPACEBAR again to exit the slide show.

To Preview and Print a Handout

1 INSERT & ADD EFFECTS | 2 MODIFY PLACEHOLDERS | 3 MODIFY & COPY ILLUSTRATIONS
4 ADD MEDIA | 5 ANIMATE SLIDE CONTENT | **6 CUSTOMIZE SLIDE ELEMENTS**

Printing handouts is useful for reviewing a presentation. You can analyze several slides displayed simultaneously on one page. Additionally, many businesses distribute handouts of the slide show before or after a presentation so attendees can refer to a copy. Each page of the handout can contain reduced images of one, two, three, four, six, or nine slides. The three-slides-per-page handout includes lines beside each slide so that your audience can write notes conveniently. The following steps preview and print a presentation handout with two slides per page. *Why? Two of the slides are predominantly pictures, so your audience does not need full pages of those images. The five bulleted paragraphs on Slide 2 can be read easily on one-half of a sheet of paper.*

1
- Tap or click FILE on the ribbon to open the Backstage view and then tap or click the Print tab.
- Tap or click the Previous Page button to display Slide 1 in the Print gallery.
- Tap or click 'Full Page Slides' in the Settings area to display the Full Page Slides gallery (Figure 3–75).

Q&A Why does the preview of my slide appear in color?
Your printer determines how the preview appears. If your printer is capable of printing color images, the preview will appear in color.

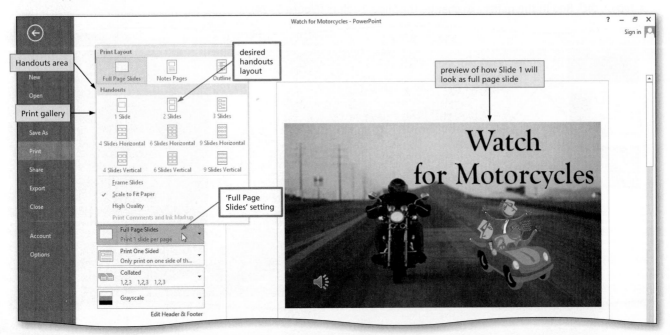

Figure 3–75

2

- Click 2 Slides in the Handouts area to select this option and display a preview of the handout (Figure 3–76).

Q&A The current date displays in the upper-right corner of the handout, and the page number displays in the lower-right corner of the footer. Can I change their location or add other information to the header and footer?

Yes. Click the Edit Header & Footer link at the bottom of the Print gallery, click the Notes and Handouts tab (Header and Footer dialog box), and then decide what content to include on the handout page.

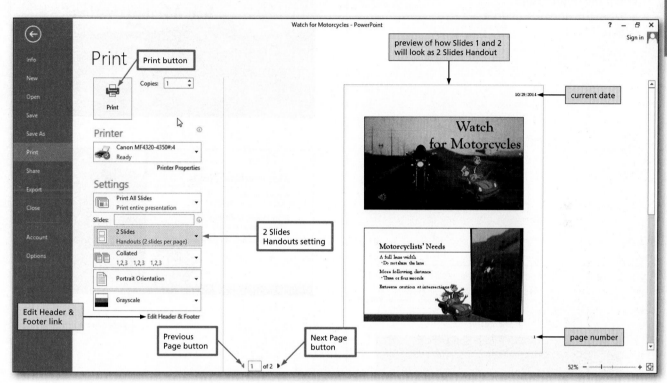

Figure 3–76

BTW

Conserving Ink and Toner

If you want to conserve ink or toner, you can instruct PowerPoint to print draft quality documents by tapping or clicking FILE on the ribbon to open the Backstage view, tapping or clicking Options in the Backstage view to display the PowerPoint Options dialog box, tapping or clicking Advanced in the left pane (PowerPoint Options dialog box), sliding or scrolling to the Print area in the right pane, placing a check mark in the 'Use draft quality' check box, and then tapping or clicking the OK button. Then, use the Backstage view to print the document as usual.

3

- Click the Next Page and Previous Page buttons to display previews of the two pages in the handout.

- Click the Print button in the Print gallery to print the handout.

- When the printer stops, retrieve the printed handout (Figure 3–77).

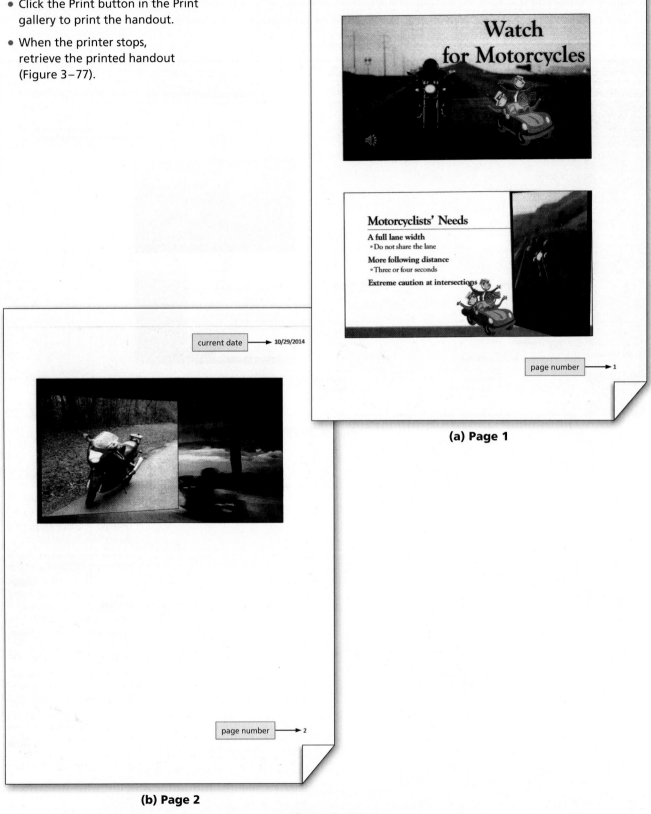

(a) Page 1

(b) Page 2

Figure 3–77

To Save the Presentation, Sign Out of a Microsoft Account, and Exit PowerPoint

You have made several changes to the presentation since you last saved it. Thus, you should save it again. The following steps save the presentation, sign out of your Microsoft account, and exit PowerPoint.

1 Tap or click the Save button on the Quick Access Toolbar.

2 If you wish to sign out of your Microsoft account, open the Backstage view, tap or click the Account tab to display the Account gallery, and then tap or click the Sign out link, which displays the Remove Account dialog box. If a Can't remove Windows accounts dialog box appears instead of the Remove Account dialog box, click the OK button and skip the remaining steps.

3 Tap or click the Yes button (Remove Account dialog box) to sign out of your Microsoft account on this computer.

4 Tap or click the Back button in the upper-left corner of the Backstage view to return to the document.

5a If you have one PowerPoint presentation open, tap or click the Close button on the right side of the title bar to close the open document and exit PowerPoint.

5b If you have multiple PowerPoint presentations open, press and hold or right-click the PowerPoint app button on the taskbar and then tap or click 'Close all windows' on the shortcut menu, or press ALT+F4 to close all open presentations and exit PowerPoint.

BTW
Quick Reference
For a table that lists how to complete the tasks covered in this book using touch gestures, the mouse, ribbon, shortcut menu, and keyboard, see the Quick Reference Summary at the back of this book, or visit the Quick Reference resource on the Student Companion Site located on www.cengagebrain.com. For detailed instructions about accessing available resources, visit www.cengage.com/ct/studentdownload or see the inside back cover of this book.

Chapter Summary

In this chapter you have learned how to adjust photo colors and effects, modify placeholders, modify and copy illustrations, add and format media, animate slide content, customize slides, and print a handout. The items listed below include all the new PowerPoint skills you have learned in this chapter, with the tasks grouped by activity.

Add Media to Increase Interest and Visual Appeal
Insert a Video File (PPT 167)
Trim a Video File (PPT 169)
Add Video Options (PPT 170)
Insert an Audio File (PPT 170)
Add Audio Options (PPT 172)
Add a Video Style (PPT 173)
Resize a Video (PPT 175)

Adjust Photo Colors and Effects
Color a Photo (PPT 150)
Add an Artistic Effect to a Photo (PPT 152)
Change the Stacking Order (PPT 153)

Animate Slide Content Using Effects and Timing
Change Views (PPT 157)
Animate an Illustration Using an Entrance Effect (PPT 176)
Change Animation Direction (PPT 177)
Animate an Illustration Using an Emphasis Effect (PPT 177)
Animate an Illustration Using an Exit Effect (PPT 178)

Preview an Animation Sequence (PPT 180)
Modify Entrance Animation Timing (PPT 180)
Animate Content Placeholder Paragraphs (PPT 183)

Customize Slide Colors and Themes
Change the Theme and Variant on One Slide (PPT 185)
Change the Theme Colors (PPT 187)

Modify Illustrations to Create Unique Clips
Ungroup an Illustration (PPT 160)
Change the Color of a Clip Object (PPT 161)
Delete a Clip Object (PPT 163)
Regroup Objects (PPT 165)
Copy a Clip from One Slide to Another (PPT 166)

Modify Placeholders to Customize Slide Appearance
Resize a Placeholder (PPT 154)
Align Paragraph Text (PPT 154)
Move a Placeholder (PPT 155)
Delete a Placeholder (PPT 156)
Add a Text Box (PPT 156)
Preview and Print a Handout (PPT 188)

What decisions will you need to make when creating your next presentation?

Use these guidelines as you complete the assignments in this chapter and create your own slide show decks outside of this class.

1. Determine if adjusting photo colors and effects can increase visual appeal.

   a) Change color saturation.

   b) Change tones.

   c) Recolor the image.

2. Vary paragraph alignment.

   a) Themes dictate whether paragraph text is aligned left, center, or right in a placeholder, but you can modify these design decisions when necessary. Moving placeholders and changing paragraph alignment can help create a unique slide.

   b) Different effects are achieved when text alignment shifts in a presentation.

3. Use multimedia selectively.

   a) Locate video, music, and sound files that are appropriate for your audience and that you have permission to use.

   b) Use media files only when necessary, however, because they draw the audience's attention away from the presenter and toward the slides.

   c) Using too many multimedia files can be overwhelming.

4. Use animation sparingly.

   a) PowerPoint audience members usually take notice the first time an animation is displayed on the screen, so be certain the animation will help focus on the precise points being presented during a particular time of the presentation.

   b) Avoid using animation for the sake of using animation. Use animation only when necessary to add emphasis.

   c) Animation overuse annoys and desensitizes audience members.

   d) Carefully decide how text or a slide element enters and exits a slide and how it is displayed once it is present on the slide.

5. Use handouts to organize your speech and to distribute to audiences.

   a) Determine if a handout with two slides per page will help unify your message when you distribute copies to an audience.

Apply Your Knowledge

Reinforce the skills and apply the concepts you learned in this chapter.

Resizing a Photo by Entering Exact Measurements, Formatting a Video Border, Moving a Placeholder, and Animating a Photo and Title Using an Entrance Effect

Note: To complete this assignment, you will be required to use the Data Files for Students. Visit www.cengage.com/ct/studentdownload for detailed instructions or contact your instructor for information about accessing the required files.

Instructions: Run PowerPoint. Open the presentation, Apply 3-1 Trees, from the Data Files for Students.

The six slides in the presentation, shown in Figure 3–78, discuss the importance of pruning trees and the methods used to prune the trees. The document you open is composed of slides containing photos, illustrations, and a video. You will apply artistic effects or modify some of these graphic elements. You also will move placeholders. In addition, you will animate photos and a title using an entrance effect.

Perform the following tasks:

1. On the title slide, color the photo by selecting Saturation: 200% from the Color Saturation area (the fifth effect), and apply the Paint Brush artistic effect (the third effect in the second row) to the photo, as shown in Figure 3–78a. Increase the photo size to 6.47" × 9.73" and apply the Soft Edge Oval picture style (the sixth style in the third row). Then apply the Float In Entrance effect, change the duration to 3.00, and change the start timing setting to With Previous. Move the photo to the top of the slide, as shown in the figure.

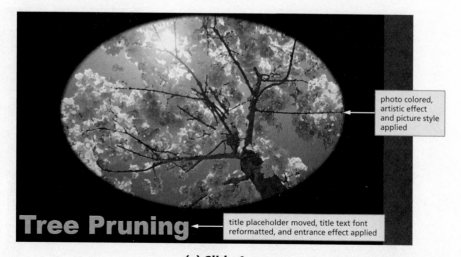

photo colored, artistic effect and picture style applied

title placeholder moved, title text font reformatted, and entrance effect applied

(a) Slide 1

Figure 3–78 (Continued)

Continued >

Apply Your Knowledge *continued*

2. Change the title font to Arial Black, increase the font size to 60 point, and then change the font color to Light Green (the fifth color in the Standard Colors row). Move the title placeholder to the lower-left corner of the slide as shown in the figure. Apply the Fly In from Top Right Entrance effect to the title text font and change the duration to 2.00. Change the start timing setting to After Previous.

3. On Slide 2, change the title text font to Arial Black and then change the font color to Dark Blue (the ninth color in the Standard Colors row). Use the Format Painter to format the title text font on Slides 3 through 6 with the same features as the title text font on Slide 2. Increase the size of the list font on Slide 2 to 24 point, change the font color to Dark Blue and then bold this text. Move the list placeholder to the lower-right area of the slide, as shown in Figure 3–78b.

4. Increase the size of the illustration to approximately 3.42" × 3.17", apply the Thick Matte, Black picture style (the first style in the second row), and then move the illustration to the location shown in the figure.

5. On Slide 3, increase the left and right placeholder text fonts to 28 point, and bold them. Change the font color in the left placeholder to Green (the sixth color in the Standard Colors) and change the font color in the right placeholder to Blue (the eighth color in the Standard Colors), as shown in Figure 3–78c.

6. On Slide 3, change the Drop Shadow Rectangle picture style to the Metal Frame picture style (the third style in the first row), and change the picture border color to Gold, Accent 5 (the ninth color in the first Theme Colors row) on both photos. Apply the Fly In from Left Entrance effect to the left photo, change the duration to 1.25, and change the start timing setting to After Previous. Apply the Fly In from the Right Entrance effect to the right photo, change the duration to 1.25, and then change the start timing setting to With Previous.

7. On Slide 4, increase the size of the video to 5.3" × 9.41" and move the video to the location shown in Figure 3–78d. Add a 6 pt Red, Accent 2 border (the sixth color in the first Theme Colors row) and then apply an Offset Diagonal Bottom Right Video Effect (the first effect in the Outer Shadow area) to the video, as shown in Figure 3–78d.

8. Increase the size of the photo to approximately 3.76" × 4.69" on Slide 5. Apply the Double Frame, Black picture style (the seventh style in the first row) to the photo, and then move the photo to the location shown in Figure 3–78e. Also move the list placeholder to the lower-right area of the slide as shown.

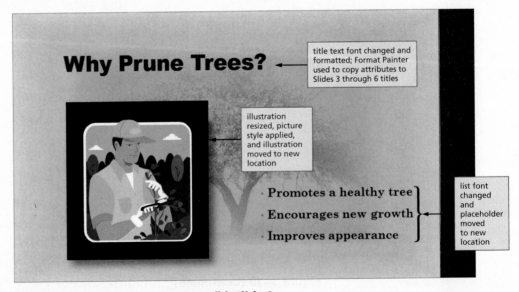

(b) Slide 2

Figure 3–78

(c) Slide 3

(d) Slide 4

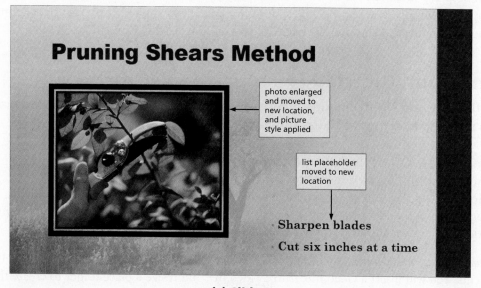

(e) Slide 5

Figure 3–78 (Continued)

Continued >

Apply Your Knowledge *continued*

9. On Slide 6, increase the font size of the subtitle text font to 32 point, change the font color to Red, Accent 2 (the sixth color in the first Theme Colors row), center the text and then move this placeholder so it is centered under the title text font, as shown in Figure 3–78f.

10. On Slide 6, increase the size of the illustration to approximately 5.53" × 4.24", apply the Reflected Bevel, Black picture style (the fourth style in the fourth row), and change the color to Red, Accent color 2 Light (the third effect in the third row in the Recolor area). Move the illustration to the location shown in the figure.

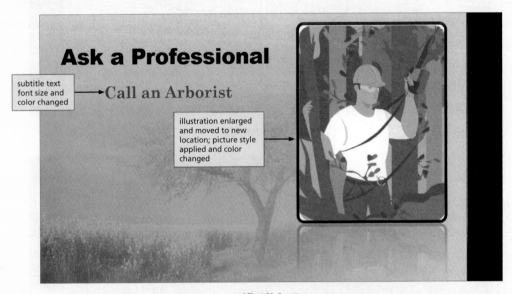

(f) Slide 6

Figure 3–78 (Continued)

11. If requested by your instructor, add your father's first name as a second line under the subtitle.

12. Apply the Wind transition in the Exciting category to Slides 2, 5, and 6. Change the duration to 3.50 seconds.

13. Save the presentation using the file name, Apply 3-1 Tree Pruning.

14. Submit the revised document in the format specified by your instructor.

15. ✴ In Step 2, you moved the title placeholder to the bottom of the title slide and changed the color. How did this style improve the slide? On Slide 3, you applied entrance effect animations to the two photos and changed the placeholder text fonts to different colors. Why?

Extend Your Knowledge

Extend the skills you learned in this chapter and experiment with new skills. You may need to use Help to complete the assignment.

Changing Theme Colors, Inserting a Video File, Trimming a Video File, Resizing a Placeholder, and Inserting an Audio File

Note: To complete this assignment, you will be required to use the Data Files for Students. Visit www.cengage.com/ct/studentdownload for detailed instructions or contact your instructor for information about accessing the required files.

Instructions: Run PowerPoint. Open the presentation, Extend 3-1 Tortoise, from the Data Files for Students. You will insert a video file, trim a video file, and resize a placeholder to create the presentation shown in Figure 3–79.

Perform the following tasks:

1. Change the theme variant to Green and choose the Sand texture fill (the third texture in the second row) to format the background on all slides. Also change the transparency to 33%.

2. On Slide 1, change the title text font to Cooper Black, increase the size to 80 point, and add the Small Caps font effect. Hint: Font effects are located in the Font dialog box (HOME tab | Font group). Also change the font color to Green, Accent 2, Darker 50% (the sixth color in the sixth Theme Colors row) and then center the text. Decrease the size of the title placeholder to approximately 1.33" × 5.49" and move this placeholder to the left side of the slide, as shown in Figure 3–79a.

3. Increase the text font size of the subtitle text font to 40 point, and center the text. Decrease the size of the subtitle placeholder to approximately 0.66" × 5.24" and move this placeholder under the title placeholder, as shown in the figure.

4. Increase the size of the photo to approximately 7.49" × 5.01", apply the Soft Edge Rectangle picture effect (the sixth effect in the first row), and then move the photo to the right side of the slide, as shown in Figure 3–79a.

5. On Slide 1, change the volume to low on the audio file (Gentle Nature), start it automatically, play across slides, and hide during the show.

6. Slide 2, change the title text font to Cooper Black, decrease the font size to 40 point, change the font color to Green, Accent 2, Darker 50% (the sixth color in the sixth Theme Colors row), and align the text left. Use the Format Painter to apply these attributes to the title text font on Slides 3 and 4. Apply the Bevel Perspective Level, White picture style (the third style in the fourth row) to the photo and move it to the upper-right corner of the slide, as shown in Figure 3–79b.

7. Copy the turtle illustration from Slide 4 and paste it on Slide 2 and move to the location shown. Apply the Fly Out To Right Exit effect to the illustration and change the duration to 4.00. Change the start timing setting to After Previous. Delete the turtle illustration from Slide 4.

8. On Slide 3, align the title font to the top of the placeholder. Hint: placeholder alignments are located on the Align Text dialog box (HOME tab | Paragraph group). Move the title placeholder to the top of the slide, as shown in Figure 3–79c.

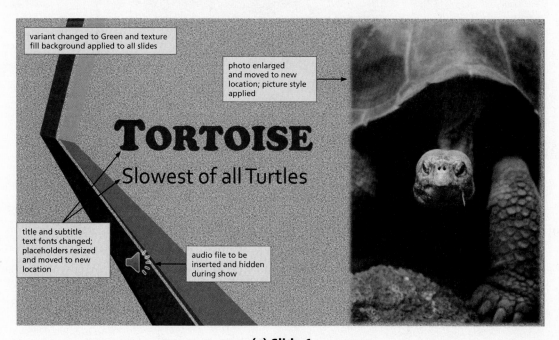

(a) Slide 1

Figure 3–79 (Continued)

Continued >

Extend Your Knowledge *continued*

variant to be changed to Green and texture fill background applied

title text font to be changed and formatted; Format Painter used to copy attributes to Slides 3 and 4 titles

A Land Animal

- Shells are dome shaped and very heavy
- They hide in their shells for protection
- Hibernate underground in cool weather

photo to be enlarged and moved to upper-right corner of slide; picture style to be applied

illustration to be copied from Slide 4 to this location and exit effect to be applied

(b) Slide 2

variant changed to Green and texture fill background applied

Move Slowly on Land

attributes from Slide 2 title applied

video file inserted, resized, and trimmed; video style applied; and video border color and weight changed

Video courtesy of Susan Sebok

(c) Slide 3
Figure 3–79

9. Insert the video file, Turtle, from the Data Files for Students. Resize this video file to approximately 6.34" × 8.45" and move the video to the location shown in the figure. Apply the Moderate Frame, Black video style (the second style in the first row in the Moderate area). Change the color of the border to Lime, Accent 1 (the fifth color in the first Theme Colors row) and change the border weight to 6 pt. Trim the video so that the Start Time is 00:09.650 and the End Time is 00:39.755. Start this video automatically.

10. On Slide 4, increase the size of the photo and apply the Reflected Bevel, Black picture style (the fourth style in the fourth row) to the photo, as shown in Figure 3–79d.

(d) Slide 4
Figure 3–79 (Continued)

11. Apply the Fly In From Right Entrance effect to the title text font and change the duration to 5.00. Change the start timing setting to After Previous. Delete the turtle illustration from Slide 4.

12. If requested by your instructor, insert a text box on Slide 4 under the turtle picture and add the name of your current or previous pet.

13. Apply an appropriate transition to all slides.

14. Save the presentation using the file name, Extend 3-1 Slow Tortoise.

15. Submit the revised document in the format specified by your instructor.

16. ✳ In this assignment, you inserted an audio file to play across the slides. How did this enhance the presentation?

Analyze, Correct, Improve

Analyze a presentation, correct all errors, and improve it.

Correcting Formatting, Coloring a Photo, Changing Animation Direction, and Inserting and Moving a Text Box

Note: To complete this assignment, you will be required to use the Data Files for Students. Visit www.cengage.com/ct/studentdownload for detailed instructions or contact your instructor for information about accessing the required files.

Instructions: Run PowerPoint. Open the presentation, Analyze 3-1 Bulb Flowers, from the Data Files for Students. This presentation contains five slides and explains how to plant bulb flowers. Modify the slides by making the indicated corrections and improvements.

1. Correct

a. Change the variant to green (the third one), as shown in Figure 3–80 on the next page.

b. Decrease the font size of the Slide 1 title text font to 66 point and change the font color to Yellow (the fourth color in the Standard Colors).

c. On Slide 1, change the volume of the audio file to low and hide during show.

Continued >

Analyze, Correct, Improve *continued*

d. If requested by your instructor, change your first name on Slide 1 to your grandmother's first name.

e. On Slides 2 and 3, adjust the photo sizes and move them so they do not overlap text and are the appropriate dimensions for the slide content.

f. On all slides, adjust text font sizes and text font colors so they are the appropriate size and enhance the presentation.

2. Improve

a. On Slide 1, change the Color Saturation of the photo to Saturation: 200% (the fifth color in the first row).

b. On Slides 2 and 3, change the picture style for all photos to Reflected Rounded Rectangle (the fifth style in the first row).

c. On Slide 4, change the picture border to Lavender, Accent 4 (the eighth color in the first Theme Colors row) on the photo and then change the border weight to 6 pt.

d. On Slides 4 and 5, change the From Bottom Left Entrance effect to the From Bottom Right Entrance effect on the titles.

e. Increase the size of the video on Slide 5 so that it is as large as possible and move it so it is aligned above the caption. Change the volume on the video to Medium on Slide 5. Also change the video option to start automatically.

f. Save the presentation using the file name, Analyze 3-1 – Planting Bulb Flowers.

g. Submit the revised document in the format specified by your instructor.

3. ✸ Which errors existed in the starting file? How did changing the picture styles help? When you adjusted the photo sizes, how did you determine their final sizes?

Figure 3–80

In the Labs

Design and/or create a presentation using the guidelines, concepts, and skills presented in this chapter. Labs 1 and 2, which increase in difficulty, require you to create solutions based on what you learned in the chapter; Lab 3 requires you to create a solution, which uses cloud and web technologies, by learning and investigating on your own from general guidance.

Lab 1: Changing the Stacking Order, Adding Audio Options to an Audio File, and Animating a Photo, Illustration, and Title Using Entrance Effects

Problem: Open the presentation, Lab 3-1 Kangaroos, from the Data Files for Students. You are studying Australia in your Geography class and on a recent vacation you visited a zoo that had kangaroos. You thought it would be interesting to put together a presentation for your class about some of the unique things about kangaroos like how long a joey stays in its mother's pouch. Create the slides shown in Figure 3–81.

Note: To complete this assignment, you will be required to use the Data Files for Students. Visit www.cengage.com/ct/studentdownload for detailed instructions or contact your instructor for information about accessing the required files.

Instructions: Perform the following tasks:

1. On Slide 1, increase the size of the photo, and apply the Soft Edge Oval picture style (the sixth style in the third row), and move the photo to the location shown in Figure 3–81a.

2. Apply the Grow and Turn entrance effect to the title text font. Change the start timing option to With Previous and the duration to 03.50 seconds.

3. Increase the size of the kangaroo illustration and bring the illustration to the front of the photo. Apply the Bounce entrance effect to the illustration and change the start timing option to After Previous and the duration to 03.50 seconds, as shown in Figure 3–81a.

4. Select the audio file, Happiness Music, on Slide 1 and change the volume to low, start Automatically, play across slides and loop until stopped. Also hide this audio file during the show.

5. On Slide 2, increase the size of the kangaroo illustration so that it measures approximately 3.27" × 5.24" and apply the Bounce entrance effect. Change the start timing option to With Previous and the duration to 03.00. Move the illustration to the lower-right corner of the slide, as shown in Figure 3–81b on the next page.

(a) Slide 1

Figure 3–81 (Continued)

Continued >

In the Labs *continued*

6. On Slide 3, apply the Simple Frame, Black picture styles (the second style in the second row) to both photos. Apply the Orange, Accent 6 fill (the last color in the first Theme Colors row) to each rounded rectangle shape. Also change the font color in these shapes to Black and then bold them, as shown in Figure 3–81c.

7. On Slide 4, change the size of the video so that it measures approximately 6.53" × 8.9", and move the video to the location shown in Figure 3–81d. Change the video style to the Beveled Perspective Left (the first style in the first Intense area row), change the border color to Orange, Accent 1 (the fifth color in the first Theme Colors row), and then change the border weight to 10 pt, as shown in the figure. Have the video start Automatically.

8. Trim the end of the video by leaving the Start Time at 00:00 and changing the End Time to 00:33.394.

9. On Slide 5, apply the Bevel Rectangle picture style (the seventh style in the third row) to the koala photo, apply the Bevel Perspective picture style (the first style in the fourth row) to the opossum photo. Move the two photos to the locations shown, and bring the opossum picture forward, as shown in Figure 3–81e.

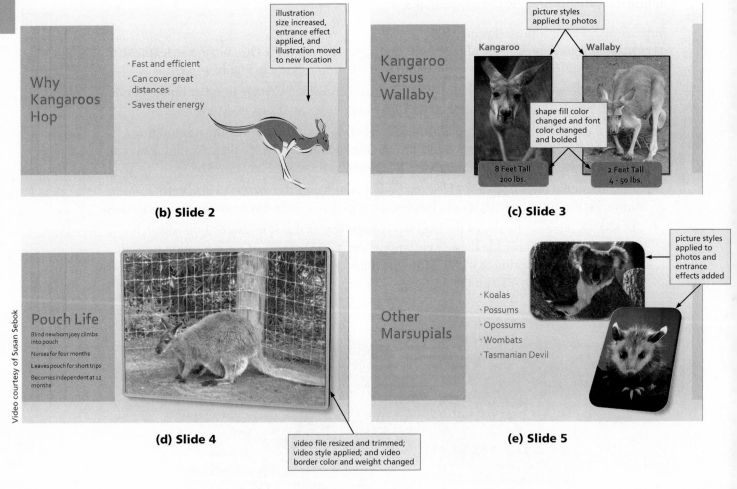

(b) Slide 2

(c) Slide 3

(d) Slide 4

(e) Slide 5

Figure 3–81

10. Apply the Fade entrance effect to the two photos. Change the start timing option to After Previous and the duration to 02.50.

11. If requested by your instructor, insert a text box on Slide 5 and add the name of the street where you lived as a child.

12. Save the presentation using the file name, Lab 3-1 Kangaroos and Wallabies.

13. Submit the document in the format specified by your instructor.

14. ☀ On Slide 1, why did you bring the kangaroo illustration to the front of the photo? Why did you trim the end of the video instead of the beginning of the video on Slide 4?

Lab 2: Ungrouping a Clip, Changing the Color of a Clip Object, Deleting a Clip Object, and Regrouping Objects

Problem: On your recent vacation in Mexico, you saw a muster of peafowl residing on the resort grounds. You found them to be very tame and interesting. And you were especially amazed at the beautiful plumage of the male peafowl or peacock. You belong to the local Audubon Society, and next month it is your turn to make a presentation. You thought the members would enjoy seeing a presentation of the peafowl you saw during your vacation. You decide to create the presentation shown in Figure 3–82.

Note: To complete this assignment, you will be required to use the Data Files for Students. Visit www.cengage.com/ct/studentdownload for detailed instructions or contact your instructor for information about accessing the required files.

Instructions: Perform the following tasks:

1. Open the presentation, Lab 3-2 Peacocks, from the Data Files for Students.

2. On Slide 1, apply the Rotated, White, picture style (the third style in the third row) to the photo. Increase the size of the photo so that it measures approximately 7.02" × 4.61" and move the photo to the location shown in Figure 3–82a.

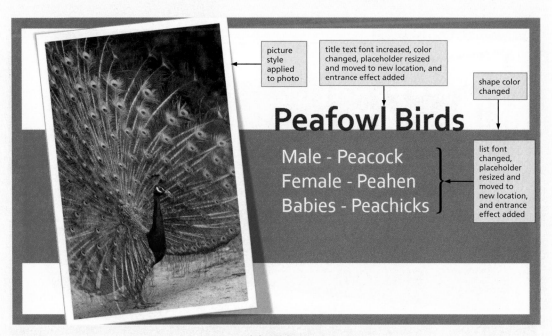

(a) Slide 1
Figure 3–82 (Continued)

Continued >

In the Labs *continued*

3. Increase the title text font to 60 point, and change the color of the title text font to Purple (the tenth color in the Standard Colors). Decrease the size of the title placeholder to approximately 1.11" × 6.33" and position the title on top of the rectangle, as shown in the figure. Apply the Fly In From Left entrance effect to the title, change the start timing option to After Previous, and change the duration to 03.00.

4. Change the color of the purple rectangular shape on Slide 1 to Turquoise, Accent 1 (the fifth color in the first Theme Colors row).

5. Increase the subtitle text font to 36 point, decrease the size of the subtitle placeholder to approximately 1.78" × 5.93", and move the placeholder to the position shown in the figure.

6. Apply the Fly In From Left entrance effect to the first line of the subtitle, change the start timing option to After Previous and the duration to 02.25. Apply the Fly In From Left entrance effect to the second line of the subtitle and then change the start timing option to After Previous and the duration to 02.25. Apply the same animation settings to the third line of the subtitle text.

7. On Slide 2, increase the size of the video to approximately 5.57" × 7.42", apply the Canvas, White video style (the fourth style in the second row in the Intense area) to the video, change the video border color to Turquoise, Accent 1 (the fifth color in the first Theme colors row), and then change the border weight to 6 pt, as shown in Figure 3–82b. Trim the video so that the Start Time is 00:01.147. Change the volume to Low, and start the video automatically. Move the video to the left side of the slide, as shown in the figure.

8. Apply the Soft Edge Oval picture style (the sixth style in the third row) to the photo, enlarge it, and move it to the bottom-right corner of the slide as shown.

9. On Slide 3, select the peacock illustration and zoom in to the three oval spots at the end of the peacock's feathers. Ungroup this illustration. Select the green oval spot on the left feather and change the color to Turquoise, Accent 3 (the seventh color in the first Shape Fill Theme Colors row). Regroup the clip, as shown in Figure 3–82c on the next page.

10. Change the volume on the audio file to low, play across slides, and hide during the show.

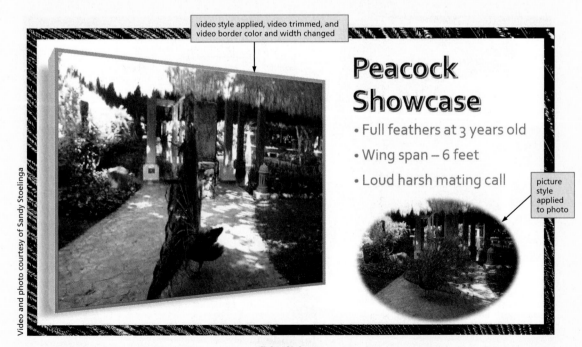

(b) Slide 2

Figure 3–82

(c) Slide 3

(d) Slide 4

Figure 3–82

11. On Slide 4, apply the Reflected Rounded Rectangle picture style (the fifth style in the first row) to the upper-right photo and apply the Bevel Rectangle picture style (the seventh style in the third row) to the photo at bottom-center of the slide, as shown in Figure 3–82d on the next page.

12. Apply the Appear entrance effect to the two photos. Change the start timing option to After Previous.

13. If requested by your instructor, insert a text box at the lower-right corner of Slide 3 and type the color of your eyes in the text box.

14. Change the transition to Fade in the Subtle category to all slides. Change the duration to 3.00 seconds.

Continued >

In the Labs *continued*

15. Save the presentation using the file name, Lab 3-2 Peacock Plumage.

16. Submit the revised document in the format specified by your instructor.

17. ✸ In Step 4, you changed the color of the rectangle shape from purple to turquoise. How did that color change improve the title slide? Why did you change the volume on the audio file to low?

Lab 3: Expand Your World: Cloud and Web Technologies
Inserting Video Files from the Web

Problem: The Watch for Motorcycles presentation you created in the chapter has a video you inserted from the Data Files for Students. The rider in this video demonstrated proper riding techniques and had appropriate riding attire. Many organizations promoting motorcycle safety have created videos and posted them to online websites. PowerPoint allows you to insert online videos easily in a manner similar to how you inserted the Motorcycle Rider file. You are going to search for and then insert one of these online videos into the Watch for Motorcycles presentation.

Note: To complete this assignment, you will be required to use the Data Files for Students. Visit www.cengage.com/ct/studentdownload for detailed instructions or contact your instructor for information about accessing the required files.

Instructions:

1. Open the Watch for Motorcycles file, insert a new Slide 4 with the Title and Content layout, and then type **Safety Tips** as the title text. Use the Format Painter to copy the font formatting from Slide 2 to the new Slide 4 title. Center this title text.

2. Format the Slide 4 background with a gradient or texture fill.

3. Tap or click the Insert Video icon in the content placeholder to display the Insert Video dialog box. If necessary, tap or click the YouTube button at the bottom on the dialog box to add that website to the list of file locations.

4. Tap or click the YouTube search box and then type **motorcycle safety tips** as the search text.

5. When the search results are displayed, browse the video frames and tap or click one that appears to fit the theme of this presentation. View the title of the video, its length, and its source in the lower-left corner of the dialog box. Then, tap or click the View Larger (magnifying glass) icon in the lower-right corner of the video frame to view a preview of the video.

6. Tap or click the Insert button to insert the video on Slide 4.

7. Add a style to the video and then resize the frame. Start this file automatically during the presentation and have it play full screen, if possible.

8. If requested to do so by your instructor, add the city where you were born to the Slide 4 title text.

9. Save the presentation using the file name, Lab 3-3 Watch for Motorcycles Expanded.

10. Submit the assignment in the format specified by your instructor.

11. ✸ What criteria did you use to select a particular YouTube video? What decisions did you make to choose a background format?

Consider This: Your Turn

Apply your creative thinking and problem-solving skills to design
and implement a solution.

1. Design and Create a Presentation about Canal Locks

Personal

Part 1: Your family belongs to a small boat club with 10 members. The club has planned a canal cruise next summer. Everyone knows there are different water levels on this canal. As the president of your club, you were asked to get all the information necessary about how the 10 boats will pass through the locks. Some of the members of your club have admitted they know very little about canal or river locks. Last summer when you went to one of the lock sites, you took a video and asked the person manning the locks some questions. You learned that the locks are manned 24 hours a day between May and October. He explained how the locks are similar to a flight of stairs. There are two sets of gates (top and bottom) and the chamber where your boat enters. The gates close and water is added or drained to meet the next level. Use the concepts and techniques presented in this chapter to prepare a presentation with a minimum of four slides that explores this subject. Select a suitable theme, add media including the video named Locks Video available in the Data Files for Students and search for an appropriate audio file to add interest to your presentation. The presentation should also contain photos and illustrations. The Data Files for Students contains five photos and illustrations called Locks1, Locks2, Locks3, Locks4, and Locks5. You can add your own digital photos or videos or photos from Office.com if they are appropriate for this topic. Apply picture styles and effects. Add a title slide and closing slide to complete your presentation. Submit your assignment in the format specified by your instructor.

Part 2: You made several decisions while creating the presentation in this assignment: where to place text, how to format the text (for example, font, font size, and adding font effects), which graphical image(s) to use, what styles and effects to apply, where to position the graphical image, how to format the graphical images, and which shapes to use to add interest to the presentation. What was the rationale behind each of these decisions? When you reviewed the document, what further revisions did you make and why? Where would you recommend showing this slide show?

2. Design and Create a Presentation about Garter Snakes

Professional

Part 1: You work part-time as a teacher's assistant in an elementary school science class. The teacher decided that a garter snake would make an excellent reptile addition to the classroom. She assigned you the task of getting a garter snake and setting up its habitat. You learned that they are harmless and non-venomous, they eat bugs and small rodents, they can grow to between 1 foot (0.3048 m) and 2 feet (0.6096 m) long. They can help control mice or insect problems. You will need a container with a secure lid, preferably a glass aquarium. You decide to put together a presentation to teach the class about garter snakes and how to care for them. Use the concepts and techniques presented in this chapter to create a presentation with at least four slides. Select a suitable theme and then include a title slide, photos, illustrations, and an audio file to add interest to the presentation. The Data Files for Students contains a video called Snake1 and five photos and illustrations called Snake2, Snake3, Snake4, Snake5, and Snake6. One or more of the illustrations can be ungrouped, and you can change the color to add some visual interest to the presentation. Submit your assignment in the format specified by your instructor.

Part 2: You made several decisions while creating the presentation in this assignment: where to place text, how to format the text (such as font and font size), which graphical image(s) to use, what styles and effects to apply, where to position the graphical images, and which shapes to use to add interest to the presentation. What was the rationale behind each of these decisions? When you reviewed the document, what further revisions did you make and why? Where would you recommend showing this slide show?

Consider This: Your Turn *continued*

3. Design and Create a Presentation about Bird Watching
Research and Collaboration

Part 1: Millions of people across the country enjoy watching birds. Some belong to clubs, and some join bird watching tours in their cities and also in other states and countries. Some plan holidays and family trips around the migration habits of their favorite birds. It is an inexpensive hobby and a good reason to get some exercise outdoors and enjoy nature. The activity is very relaxing and is a great social activity. You have decided to start a bird watching club with some of your friends and neighbors. There are 12 members of your club, so you divide into three groups of four members. One group will go to the library and do some research on the various species of birds in your area. The second group will research what kind of binoculars are best for beginners. The third group will take some video and photos at the local nature center so that you can put together a presentation about bird watching to share with your new club members. After gathering all the information and photos about bird watching, use the concepts and techniques presented in this chapter to prepare a presentation with a minimum of four slides that explore the subject of bird watching. Select a suitable theme, include a title slide, bulleted lists, shapes, and WordArt. The Data Files for Students contains one video called Bird Watching and six photos and illustrations called Birds1, Birds2, Birds3, Birds4, Birds5, and Birds6. Change the color for at least one photo. Apply a transition in the Subtle area to all slides and increase the duration. Submit your assignment in the format specified by your instructor.

Part 2: ✸ You made several decisions while creating the presentation in this assignment: where to place text, how to format the text (such as font, font size, and where to use WordArt), which image(s) to use, what styles and effects to apply, where to position the images, which styles to use, and which shapes to use to add interest to the presentation. What was the rationale behind each of these decisions? When you reviewed the document, what further revisions did you make and why? Where would you recommend showing this slide show?

Learn Online

Reinforce what you learned in this chapter with games, exercises, training, and many other online activities and resources.

Student Companion Site Reinforcement activities and resources are available at no additional cost on www.cengagebrain.com. Visit www.cengage.com/ct/studentdownload for detailed instructions about accessing the resources available at the Student Companion Site.

 SAM Put your skills into practice with SAM! If you have a SAM account, go to www.cengage.com/ sam2013 to access SAM assignments for this chapter.

4 | Creating and Formatting Information Graphics

Microsoft product screenshots used with permission from Microsoft Corporation.

Objectives

You will have mastered the material in this chapter when you can:

- Insert a SmartArt graphic
- Insert images from a file into a SmartArt graphic
- Format a SmartArt graphic
- Convert text to a SmartArt graphic
- Create and format a chart
- Rotate a chart

- Change the chart title and legend
- Separate a pie chart slice
- Create and format a table
- Insert a symbol in a table
- Change table text alignment and orientation
- Add an image to a table

4 | Creating and Formatting Information Graphics

Introduction

Audiences generally focus first on the visual elements displayed on a slide. Graphical elements increase **visual literacy**, which is the ability to examine and assess these images. They can be divided into two categories: images and information graphics. Images are the illustrations and photos you have used in Chapters 1, 2, and 3, and information graphics are tables, charts, graphs, and diagrams. Both sets of visuals help audience members interpret and retain material, so they should be designed and presented with care.

Project — Presentation with SmartArt, a Chart, and a Table

BTW
Value of Using Information Graphics
Audience members recall more material during a presentation when clear graphics, including SmartArt, charts, and tables, are displayed visually and then explained verbally. When the audience views graphics and listens to a speaker, they become engaged in the presentation. They tune out distractions, which ultimately increases their retention of the material being presented.

The National Audubon Society coordinates the Great Backyard Bird Count every February and a Christmas Bird Count every December. During these events, thousands of volunteers count and categorize every bird they see in the field and at feeders. You joined a local Audubon Society chapter a few months ago and bought a bird feeder to hang in your backyard, some different types of birdseed, and binoculars. You have been counting the number and types of birds that have visited your feeder, and you want to prepare a presentation for your Audubon chapter members that chronicles your experiences. The project in this chapter follows visual content guidelines and uses PowerPoint to create the presentation shown in Figure 4–1. The slide show uses several visual elements to help audience members understand how you are attracting birds to your backyard feeder. The first two slides are enhanced with SmartArt graphics and pictures. The three-dimensional pie chart on Slide 3 depicts a count of the number of times four birds visited your feeder in one day, and the five-column table on Slide 4 lists the types of seeds preferred by four birds.

FILE   HOME   INSERT   DESIGN   TRANSITIONS   ANIMATIONS   SLIDE SHOW   REVIEW   VIEW

SmartArt

(a) Slide 1 (Title slide with SmartArt enhanced with photos)

(b) Slide 2 (SmartArt enhanced with photos)

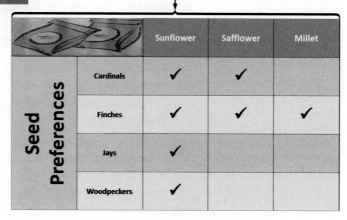

(c) Slide 3 (3-D chart)

(d) Slide 4 (Five-column chart)

Figure 4–1

For an introduction to Windows and instruction about how to perform basic Windows tasks, read the Office and Windows chapter at the beginning of this book, where you can learn how to resize windows, change screen resolution, create folders, move and rename files, use Windows Help, and much more.

Roadmap

In this chapter, you will learn how to create the slides shown in Figure 4–1 on the previous page. The following roadmap identifies general activities you will perform:

1. INSERT and MODIFY a SMARTART graphic.
2. ADD SMARTART STYLES and EFFECTS.
3. CONVERT TEXT TO a SMARTART graphic and FORMAT the content.
4. CREATE a CHART to show proportions.
5. FORMAT a CHART by changing style and layout.
6. CREATE a TABLE to compare and contrast data.
7. CHANGE TABLE content STYLE and ALIGNMENT.

At the beginning of step instructions throughout the chapter, you will see an abbreviated form of this roadmap. The abbreviated roadmap uses colors to indicate chapter progress: gray means the chapter is beyond that activity; blue means the task being shown is covered in that activity, and black means that activity is yet to be covered. For example, the following abbreviated roadmap indicates the chapter would be showing a task in the 5 FORMAT CHART activity.

1 INSERT & MODIFY SMARTART | 2 ADD SMARTART STYLES & EFFECTS | 3 CONVERT TEXT TO SMARTART & FORMAT
4 CREATE CHART | 5 FORMAT CHART | 6 CREATE TABLE | 7 CHANGE TABLE STYLE & ALIGNMENT

Use the abbreviated roadmap as a progress guide while you read or step through the instructions in this chapter.

To Run PowerPoint and Open and Save a Presentation

If you are using a computer to step through the project in this chapter and you want your screens to match the figures in this book, you should change your screen's resolution to 1366×768. For information about how to change a computer's resolution, refer to the Office and Windows chapter at the beginning of this book.

The following steps, which assume Windows 8 is running, use the Start screen or the search box to run PowerPoint based on a typical installation. You then will open a file located on the Data Files for Student. Visit www.cengage.com/ct/studentdownload for detailed instructions or ask your instructor for information about accessing the required files. For a detailed example of the procedure summarized below, refer to the Office and Windows chapter. The following steps run PowerPoint, open the Birding presentation, and save the file with a new name.

One of the few differences between Windows 7 and Windows 8 occurs in the steps to run PowerPoint. If you are using Windows 7, click the Start button, type **PowerPoint** in the 'Search programs and files' box, click PowerPoint 2013, and then, if necessary, maximize the PowerPoint window. For detailed steps to run PowerPoint in Windows 7, refer to the Office and Windows chapter at the beginning of this book. For a summary of the steps, refer to the Quick Reference located at the back of this book.

1 Scroll the Start screen for a PowerPoint 2013 tile. If your Start screen contains a PowerPoint 2013 tile, tap or click it to run PowerPoint and then proceed to Step 5; if the Start screen does not contain the PowerPoint 2013 tile, proceed to the next step to search for the PowerPoint app.

2 Swipe in from the right edge of the screen or point to the upper-right corner of the screen to display the Charms bar and then tap or click the Search charm on the Charms bar to display the Search menu.

3 Type **PowerPoint** as the search text in the Search box and watch the search results appear in the Apps list.

4 Tap or click PowerPoint 2013 in the search results to run PowerPoint.

5 Tap or click FILE on the ribbon and then tap or click the Open tab in the Backstage view.

6 If the Birding file is displayed in the Recent Presentations list, tap or click the file name to open the file and display the opened presentation in the PowerPoint window; then,

proceed to Step 10. If the Birding file is not displayed in the Recent Presentations list, proceed to the next step to locate the file.

7 Tap or click Computer, SkyDrive, or another location in the left pane and then navigate to the location of the file to be opened.

8 Tap or click Birding to select the file to be opened.

9 Tap or click the Open button (Open dialog box) to open the selected file and display the opened presentation.

10 If the PowerPoint window is not maximized, tap or click the Maximize button on its title bar.

11 Tap or click the Save button on the Quick Access Toolbar, which depending on settings, will display either the Save As gallery in the Backstage view or the Save As dialog box.

12 To save on a hard disk or other storage media on your computer, proceed to Step 12a. To save on SkyDrive, proceed to Step 12b.

12a If your screen opens the Backstage view and you want to save on storage media on your computer, tap or click Computer in the left pane, if necessary, to display options in the right pane related to saving on your computer. If your screen already displays the Save As dialog box, proceed to Step 14.

12b If your screen opens the Backstage view and you want to save on SkyDrive, tap or click SkyDrive in the left pane to display SkyDrive saving options or a Sign In button. If your screen displays a Sign In button, tap or click it and then sign in to SkyDrive.

13 Tap or click the Browse button in the right pane to display the Save As dialog box associated with the selected save location (i.e., Computer or SkyDrive).

14 Type **Backyard Birding** in the File name box to change the file name. Do not press the ENTER key.

15 Navigate to the desired save location.

16 Tap or click the Save button (Save As dialog box).

Creating and Formatting a SmartArt Graphic

An illustration often can help convey relationships between key points in your presentation. Microsoft Office 2013 includes **SmartArt graphics**, which are visual representations of your ideas. The SmartArt layouts have a variety of shapes, arrows, and lines to correspond to the major points you want your audience to remember.

You can create a SmartArt graphic in two ways: Select a type and then add text and pictures or convert text or pictures already present on a slide to a graphic. Once the SmartArt graphic is present, you can customize its look. Table 4–1 lists the SmartArt types and their uses.

Table 4–1 SmartArt Graphic Layout Types and Purposes	
Type	**Purpose**
List	Show non-sequential information
Process	Show steps in a process or timeline
Cycle	Show a continual process
Hierarchy	Create an organizational chart
Relationship	Illustrate connections
Matrix	Show how parts relate to a whole
Pyramid	Show proportional relationships with the largest component at the top or bottom
Picture	Include a placeholder for pictures within the graphic
Office.com	Use SmartArt available on the Office.com website

If you are using your finger on a touch screen and are having difficulty completing the steps in this chapter, consider using a stylus. Many people find it easier to be precise with a stylus than with a finger. In addition, with a stylus you see the pointer. If you still are having trouble completing the steps with a stylus, try using a mouse.

BTW
Building Speaker Confidence
Using information graphics in a presentation should give you confidence as a presenter because they support your verbal message and help reinforce the message you are trying to convey. As you rehearse your speech, keep in mind that your audience will be studying these visual elements during your actual presentation and will not be focusing on you.

© 2014 Cengage Learning

To Insert a SmartArt Graphic

Several SmartArt graphics have placeholders for one or more pictures, and they are grouped in the Picture category. The Circular Picture Callout graphic is appropriate for this presentation. *Why? It has one large area for a picture and three other areas for smaller pictures. These images would allow you to insert pictures of a bird feeder and several common birds seen in backyards, which would create interest among birders and people considering participating in this hobby.* The following steps insert the Circular Picture Callout SmartArt graphic on Slide 1.

1

- With Slide 1 selected, display the INSERT tab and then tap or click the SmartArt button (INSERT tab | Illustrations group) to display the Choose a SmartArt Graphic dialog box.

- Tap or click Picture in the left pane to display the Picture gallery.

- Tap or click the Circular Picture Callout graphic (the second graphic in the first row) to display a preview of this graphic in the right pane (Figure 4–2).

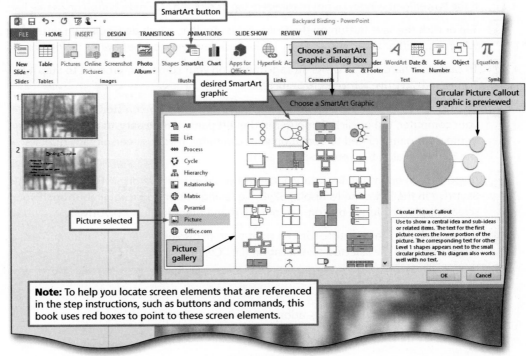

Figure 4–2

2

- Tap or click the OK button to insert this SmartArt graphic on Slide 1 (Figure 4–3).

- If necessary, tap or click the Text Pane button (SMARTART TOOLS DESIGN tab | Create Graphic group) or the arrow icon in the center-left edge of the graphic to open the Text Pane if it does not display automatically.

 Can I click either the Text Pane button or the arrow icon to close the Text Pane? Yes.

Figure 4–3

Text Pane

The **Text Pane** assists you in creating a graphic because you can direct your attention to developing and editing the message without being concerned with the actual graphic. The Text Pane consists of two areas: The top portion has the text that will appear in the SmartArt graphic and the bottom portion gives the name of the graphic and suggestions of what type of information is best suited for this type of visual. Each SmartArt graphic has an associated Text Pane with bullets that function as an outline and map directly to the image. You can create new lines of bulleted text and then indent and demote these lines. You also can check spelling. Table 4–2 shows the keyboard shortcuts you can use with the Text Pane.

Table 4–2 Text Pane Keyboard Shortcuts	
Activity	**Shortcut**
Indent text	TAB or ALT+SHIFT+RIGHT ARROW
Demote text	SHIFT+TAB or ALT+SHIFT+LEFT ARROW
Add a tab character	CTRL+TAB
Create a new line of text	ENTER
Check spelling	F7
Merge two lines of text	DELETE at the end of the first text line
Display the shortcut menu	SHIFT+F10
Switch between the SmartArt drawing canvas and the Text Pane	CTRL+SHIFT+F2
Close the Text Pane	ALT+F4
Switch the focus from the Text Pane to the SmartArt graphic border	ESC

© 2014 Cengage Learning

To Enter Text in a SmartArt Graphic

1 INSERT & MODIFY SMARTART | **2** ADD SMARTART STYLES & EFFECTS | **3** CONVERT TEXT TO SMARTART & FORMAT
4 CREATE CHART | **5** FORMAT CHART | **6** CREATE TABLE | **7** CHANGE TABLE STYLE & ALIGNMENT

Why? *You want to add text that shows the topic of the presentation and labels the images you will add on this slide. The Circular Picture Callout graphic has placeholders for text that can supplement the visuals. The following steps insert four lines of text in the Text Pane and in the corresponding SmartArt shapes on Slide 1.*

- If necessary, position the insertion point beside the first bullet in the Text Pane. Type **Backyard Bird Watching** in the first bullet paragraph and then tap the second bullet line or press the DOWN ARROW key to move the insertion point to the second bullet paragraph (Figure 4–4).

Figure 4–4

- Type **Woodpecker** in the second bullet paragraph and then tap the third bullet line or press the DOWN ARROW key to move the insertion point to the third bullet paragraph.

- Type **Robin** in the third bullet paragraph and then tap the fourth bullet line or press the DOWN ARROW key to move the insertion point to the fourth bullet paragraph.

- Type **Cardinal** in the fourth bullet paragraph. Do not press the DOWN ARROW or ENTER keys (Figure 4–5).

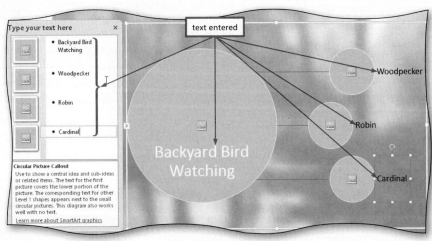

Figure 4–5

Q&A I mistakenly pressed the DOWN ARROW OR ENTER key. How can I delete the bullet paragraph I just added?
Press the BACKSPACE key to delete the paragraph.

> **Other Ways**
>
> 1. Press and hold or right-click SmartArt graphic, tap or click Show Text Pane on shortcut menu, enter text in Text Pane

To Format Text Pane Characters

1 INSERT & MODIFY SMARTART | 2 ADD SMARTART STYLES & EFFECTS | 3 CONVERT TEXT TO SMARTART & FORMAT
4 CREATE CHART | 5 FORMAT CHART | 6 CREATE TABLE | 7 CHANGE TABLE STYLE & ALIGNMENT

Once the desired characters are entered in the Text Pane, you can change the font size and apply formatting features, such as bold, italic, and underlined text. *Why? Changing the font and adding effects can help draw the audience members to the varied slide content and coordinate with the visual content.* The following steps format the text by changing the font and bolding the letters.

- With the Text Pane open, drag through all four bullet paragraphs to select the text and display the mini toolbar.

Q&A If my Text Pane no longer is displayed, how can I get it to appear?
Tap or click the control, which is the tab with a left-pointing arrow, on the left side of the SmartArt graphic.

- Display the Font gallery and change the font to Papyrus.

- Bold the text (Figure 4–6).

Q&A These formatting changes did not appear in the Text Pane. Why?
Not all the formatting changes are evident in the Text Pane, but they appear in the corresponding shape.

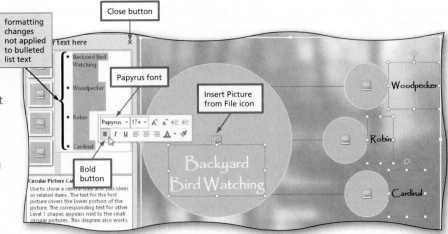

- Tap or click the Close button in the SmartArt Text Pane so that it no longer is displayed.

Figure 4–6

To Insert a Picture from a File into a SmartArt Graphic

1 INSERT & MODIFY SMARTART | 2 ADD SMARTART STYLES & EFFECTS | 3 CONVERT TEXT TO SMARTART & FORMAT

4 CREATE CHART | 5 FORMAT CHART | 6 CREATE TABLE | 7 CHANGE TABLE STYLE & ALIGNMENT

The picture icons in the middle of the four circles in the Circular Picture Callout SmartArt graphic indicate that the shapes are designed to hold images. These images can add a personalized touch to your presentation. *Why? The purpose of this presentation is to show the wide variety of birds that visit backyard feeders, and audience members would be familiar with the birds shown in these SmartArt circles.* You can select files from the Office.com collection or from images you have obtained from other sources, such as a photograph taken with your digital camera. The following steps insert images located on the Data Files for Students into the large SmartArt circle.

- Tap or click the Insert Picture from File icon in the SmartArt large circle picture placeholder (shown in Figure 4–6) to display the Insert Pictures dialog box.

- Tap or click the Browse button in the From a file area to display the Insert Picture dialog box.

- If necessary, navigate to the desired photo location (in this case, the Chapter 04 folder in the PowerPoint folder in the CIS 101 folder) and then click Feeder1 to select the file (Figure 4–7).

Q&A What if the photo is not in the CIS 101 folder?
Use the same process, but be certain to select the location containing the photo in the file list.

Figure 4–7

- Tap or click the Insert button (Insert Picture dialog box) to insert the Feeder1 picture into the SmartArt large circle picture placeholder (Figure 4–8).

Figure 4–8

Other Ways

1. Tap or click Shape Fill button (SMARTART TOOLS FORMAT tab | Shape Styles group), tap or click Picture

2. Press and hold or right-click SmartArt shape, tap or click Fill button, tap or click Picture

To Insert Additional Pictures from a File into a SmartArt Graphic

The Feeder1 photo fills the left shape in the SmartArt graphic, and you want to insert additional bird photos in the three circles in the right portion of the graphic. These images are located on the Data Files for Students. The following steps insert photos into the three smaller SmartArt graphic circles.

1 Tap or click the Insert Picture from File icon in the top circle to the left of the word, Woodpecker, to display the Insert Pictures dialog box.

2 Tap or click the Browse button in the From a file area, scroll down and then tap or click Woodpecker in the list of picture files, and then tap or click the Insert button (Insert Picture dialog box) to insert the photo into the top-right SmartArt circle picture placeholder.

3 Tap or click the center Insert Picture from File icon to the left of the word, Robin, click the Browse button in the Insert Pictures dialog box, and then insert the photo with the file name, Robin, into the placeholder.

4 Tap or click the bottom Insert Picture from File icon to the left of the word, Cardinal, and then insert the photo with the file name, Cardinal, into the placeholder (Figure 4–9).

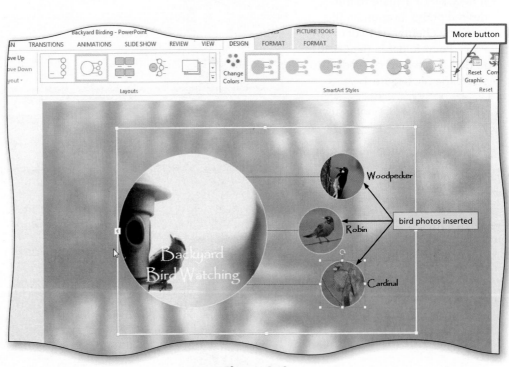

Figure 4–9

To Apply a SmartArt Style

1 INSERT & MODIFY SMARTART | **2 ADD SMARTART STYLES & EFFECTS** | **3 CONVERT TEXT TO SMARTART & FORMAT**
4 CREATE CHART | **5 FORMAT CHART** | **6 CREATE TABLE** | **7 CHANGE TABLE STYLE & ALIGNMENT**

You can change the look of your SmartArt graphic easily by applying a **SmartArt style**. *Why? You can use these professionally designed effects to customize the appearance of your presentation with a variety of shape fills, edges, shadows, line styles, gradients, and three-dimensional styles.* The following steps add the Polished style to the Circular Picture Callout SmartArt graphic.

①

- With the SmartArt graphic still selected, tap or click the SmartArt Styles More button (SMARTART TOOLS DESIGN tab | SmartArt Styles group) (shown in Figure 4–9) to expand the SmartArt Styles gallery (Figure 4–10).

Q&A How do I select the graphic if it no longer is selected?
Tap or click the graphic anywhere except the pictures you just added.

Figure 4–10

②

- If you are using a mouse, point to the Polished style in the 3-D area (the first style in the first 3-D row) in the SmartArt Styles gallery to display a live preview of this style (Figure 4–11).

🔍 Experiment

- If you are using a mouse, point to various styles in the SmartArt Styles gallery and watch the Circular Picture Callout graphic change styles.

③

- Tap or click Polished to apply this style to the graphic.

Figure 4–11

Other Ways

1. Press and hold or right-click SmartArt graphic in an area other than a picture, tap or click Style button

To Change SmartArt Color

1 INSERT & MODIFY SMARTART | 2 ADD SMARTART STYLES & EFFECTS | 3 CONVERT TEXT TO SMARTART & FORMAT
4 CREATE CHART | 5 FORMAT CHART | 6 CREATE TABLE | 7 CHANGE TABLE STYLE & ALIGNMENT

Another modification you can make to your SmartArt graphic is to change its color. As with the WordArt Style gallery, PowerPoint provides a gallery of color options you can preview and evaluate. The following steps change the SmartArt graphic color to a Colorful range. *Why? The styles in the Colorful range have different colors for the text and other slide elements. The birds in your SmartArt are very vibrant, so you want SmartArt elements that coordinate with these colors.*

1

- With the SmartArt graphic still selected, tap or click the Change Colors button (SMARTART TOOLS DESIGN tab | SmartArt Styles group) to display the Change Colors gallery (Figure 4–12).

Figure 4–12

2

- If you are using a mouse, point to Dark 2 Outline in the Primary Theme Colors area (the second color) to display a live preview of these colors (Figure 4–13).

Experiment

- If you are using a mouse, point to various colors in the Change Colors gallery and watch the shapes change colors.

Figure 4–13

3

- Tap or click Dark 2 Outline to apply this color variation to the graphic (Figure 4–14).

Figure 4–14

Other Ways

1. Press and hold or right-click SmartArt graphic in an area other than a picture, tap or click Color button

To Resize a SmartArt Graphic

When you view the completed graphic, you may decide that individual shapes or the entire piece of art needs to be enlarged or reduced. If you change the size of one shape, the other shapes also may change size to maintain proportions. Likewise, the font size may change in all the shapes if you increase or decrease the font size of one shape. On Slide 1, you want to change the SmartArt graphic size. *Why? A larger graphic size will fill the empty space on the slide and add readability.* All the shapes will enlarge proportionally when you adjust the graphic's height and width. The following step resizes the SmartArt graphic.

1

- With the SmartArt graphic still selected, drag the upper-left sizing handle to the upper-left corner of the slide.

- Drag the lower-right sizing handle to the lower-right corner of the slide, as shown in Figure 4–15.

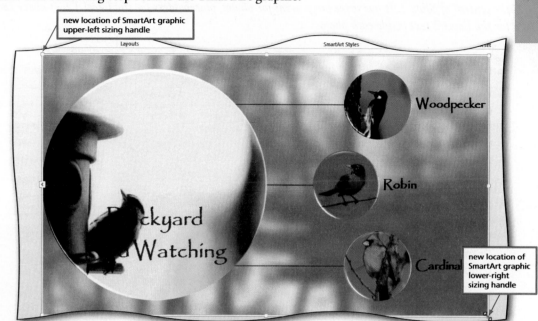

Figure 4–15

Other Ways

1. Press and hold or right-click SmartArt graphic, tap or click Size and Position on shortcut menu

To Move a Text Box

Why? The text box in the large SmartArt circle is covering the bird. The letters would be more readable if they were displayed in the white space in the circle. The following step moves the text box.

1

- Tap or click any of the letters in the large SmartArt circle to select the text box.

- Drag an edge of the text box upward to the location shown in Figure 4–16.

Figure 4–16

To Convert Text to a SmartArt Graphic

You quickly can convert small amounts of slide text and pictures into a SmartArt graphic. Once you determine the type of graphic, such as process or cycle, you then have a wide variety of styles from which to choose in the SmartArt Graphic gallery. As with other galleries, you can point to the samples and view a live preview if you are using a mouse. The following steps convert the six bulleted text paragraphs on Slide 2 to the Titled Picture Blocks graphic, which is part of the Picture category. *Why? This SmartArt style is a good match for the content of Slide 2. It has three large areas for photos, placeholders for the Level 1 text above each photo, and placeholders for the Level 2 text beside each photo.*

1
- Display Slide 2.
- With the HOME tab displayed, select the six bulleted list items and then tap or click the 'Convert to SmartArt' button (HOME tab | Paragraph group) to display the SmartArt Graphics gallery (Figure 4–17).

Figure 4–17

2
- Tap or click 'More SmartArt Graphics' in the SmartArt Graphics gallery to display the Choose a SmartArt Graphic dialog box.
- Tap or click Picture in the left pane to display the Picture gallery.
- Tap or click the Titled Picture Blocks graphic (the first graphic in the fourth row) to display a preview of this graphic in the right pane (Figure 4–18).

Figure 4–18

3
- Tap or click the OK button (Choose a SmartArt Graphic dialog box) to apply this shape and convert the text (Figure 4–19).

Q&A How can I edit the text that displays in the three shapes? You can tap or click the text and then make the desired changes. Also, if you display the Text Pane on the left side of the graphic, you can tap or click the text you want to change and make your edits.

Figure 4–19

Other Ways

1. Tap or click Convert to SmartArt on shortcut menu

To Insert Pictures from a File into a SmartArt Graphic

The picture icon in each of the three blue boxes in the SmartArt graphic indicates the shape is designed to hold an image. In this presentation, you will add images located on the Data Files for Students. The following steps insert photos into the SmartArt graphic.

1 Tap or click the Insert Picture from File icon in the left blue box under the word, Binoculars, to display the Insert Pictures dialog box.

2 Tap or click the Browse button in the From a file area, tap or click Binoculars in the list of picture files, and then tap or click the Insert button (Insert Picture dialog box) to insert the picture into the left SmartArt square picture placeholder.

3 Tap or click the Insert Picture from File icon in the center blue box under the word, Birdhouse, to display the Insert Pictures dialog box, click the Browse button to display the Insert Picture dialog box, and then insert the picture with the file name, Birdhouse, into the placeholder.

4 Tap or click the Insert Picture from File icon in the right blue box under the word, Feeder, and then insert the picture with the file name, Feeder2, into the placeholder (Figure 4–20).

BTW

The Ribbon and Screen Resolution
PowerPoint may change how the groups and buttons within the groups appear on the ribbon, depending on the computer's screen resolution. Thus, your ribbon may look different from the ones in this book if you are using a screen resolution other than 1366 × 768.

Figure 4–20

To Add a SmartArt Style to the Graphic

To enhance the appearance of the group of squares, you can add a three-dimensional style. The following steps add the Inset style to the Titled Picture Blocks graphic.

1 With the SmartArt graphic still selected, display the SMARTART TOOLS DESIGN tab and then tap or click the SmartArt Styles More button (SMARTART TOOLS DESIGN tab | SmartArt Styles) to expand the SmartArt Styles gallery.

2 Tap or click Inset in the 3-D area (the second graphic in the first 3-D row) to apply this style to the graphic (Figure 4–21).

Figure 4–21

To Change the SmartArt Color

Adding more colors to the SmartArt graphic would enhance its visual appeal. The following steps change the SmartArt graphic color to a Colorful range.

1 With the SmartArt graphic still selected, tap or click the Change Colors button (SMARTART TOOLS DESIGN tab | SmartArt Styles group) to display the Change Colors gallery.

2 Tap or click Colorful Range – Accent Colors 4 to 5 (the fourth color in the Colorful row) to apply this color variation to the graphic (Figure 4–22).

Figure 4–22

To Resize a SmartArt Graphic

Although white space on a slide generally is good to have, Slide 2 has sufficient space to allow the SmartArt graphic size to increase slightly. When you adjust the graphic's height and width, all the squares will enlarge proportionally. The following step resizes the SmartArt graphic.

1 With the SmartArt graphic still selected, drag the top-left sizing handle to the left edge of the slide and then drag the bottom-right sizing handle diagonally to the bottom-right edge of the slide (Figure 4–23).

Q&A Can I drag other sizing handles to resize the graphic?
You can drag the upper-right and lower-left sizing handles. If you drag the middle-left handle, however, you will display the Text Pane.

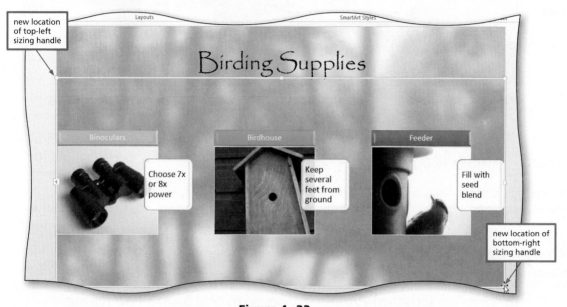

Figure 4–23

To Format SmartArt Graphic Text

1 INSERT & MODIFY SMARTART | 2 ADD SMARTART STYLES & EFFECTS | 3 CONVERT TEXT TO SMARTART & FORMAT
4 CREATE CHART | 5 FORMAT CHART | 6 CREATE TABLE | 7 CHANGE TABLE STYLE & ALIGNMENT

The text in the three rectangles above the photos can be reformatted. You can select all three rectangles and then change the text. ***Why?*** *Changing the size, color, and other aspects will make the text more readable.* For consistency and efficiency, it is best to format the same items on a slide simultaneously. These rectangles are separate items in the SmartArt graphic. If you have a mouse, you select these objects by selecting one rectangle, pressing and holding down the SHIFT key, and then selecting the second and third rectangles. The following steps simultaneously bold and underline the rectangle text and then change the font color to Yellow and increase the font size.

1

 Tap or click the rectangle labeled Binoculars to select it. If you are using a mouse, press and hold down the SHIFT key and then click the Birdhouse and Feeder rectangles (Figure 4–24).

Figure 4–24

- Display the HOME tab and then tap or click the Bold button (HOME tab | Font group).

- Tap or click the Underline button (HOME tab | Font group) to add an underline to the text.

- Click the Font Color arrow and then click Yellow (the fourth color in the Standard Colors row) to change the font color to Yellow.

- Click the Increase Font Size button several times to increase the font size to 24 point (Figure 4–25).

Figure 4–25

 Can I make other formatting changes to the graphics' text?

Yes. You can format the text by making any of the modifications in the Font group.

- If you are using a touch screen, repeat Step 2 for the Birdhouse and Feeder rectangles.

To Save an Existing Presentation with the Same File Name

You have made several modifications to the presentation since you last saved it. Thus, you should save it again. The following step saves the presentation again. For an example of the step listed below, refer to the Office and Windows chapter at the beginning of this book.

1 Tap or click the Save button on the Quick Access Toolbar to overwrite the previously saved file.

Break Point: If you wish to take a break, this is a good place to do so. Be sure to save the Backyard Birding file again and then you can exit PowerPoint. To resume at a later time, run PowerPoint, open the file called Backyard Birding, and continue following the steps from this location forward.

Adding a Chart to a Slide and Formatting

Practically every yard is a potential feeding area for wild birds. Attracting birds to a feeder is accomplished by providing food, water, nesting materials, and a safe haven away from natural predators. Some bird species remain in one geographical area all year while others stop to feed while migrating to and from colder and warmer climates. The chart on Slide 3, shown in Figure 4–1c on page PPT 211, shows the proportion of four birds that commonly visit backyard feeders.

Microsoft Excel and Microsoft Graph

PowerPoint uses one of two programs to develop a chart. It opens Microsoft Excel if that software is installed on your system. If Excel is not installed, PowerPoint opens Microsoft Graph and displays a chart with its associated data in a table called a datasheet. Microsoft Graph does not have the advanced features found in Excel. In this chapter, the assumption is made that Excel has been installed. When you start to create a chart, Excel opens and displays a chart in the PowerPoint slide. The default chart type is a **Clustered Column chart**. The Clustered Column chart is appropriate when comparing two or more items in specified intervals, such as comparing how inflation has risen during the past 10 years. Other popular chart types are line, bar, and pie. You will use a pie chart in Slide 3.

The figures for the chart are entered in a corresponding **Microsoft Excel worksheet**, which is a rectangular grid containing vertical columns and horizontal rows. Column letters display above the grid to identify particular **columns**, and row numbers display on the left side of the grid to identify particular **rows**. **Cells** are the intersections of rows and columns, and they are the locations for the chart data and text labels. For example, cell A1 is the intersection of column A and row 1. Numeric and text data are entered in the **active cell**, which is the one cell surrounded by a heavy border. You will replace the sample data in the worksheet by typing entries in the cells, but you also can import data from a text file, import an Excel worksheet or chart, or paste data obtained from another program. Once you have entered the data, you can modify the appearance of the chart using menus and commands.

In the following pages, you will perform these tasks:

1. Insert a chart and then replace the sample data.
2. Change the line and shape outline weights.
3. Change the chart layout.
4. Resize the chart and then change the title and legend font size.
5. Rotate the chart.
6. Separate a pie slice.
7. Insert a text box and format text.

CONSIDER THIS

How can I choose an appropriate chart type?
General adult audiences are familiar with bar and pie charts, so those chart types are good choices. Specialized audiences, such as engineers and architects, are comfortable reading scatter and bubble charts.

Common chart types and their purposes are as follows:

• Column — Vertical bars compare values over a period of time.

• Bar — Horizontal bars compare two or more values to show how the proportions relate to each other.

• Line — A line or lines show trends, increases and decreases, levels, and costs during a continuous period of time.

• Pie — A pie chart divides a single total into parts to illustrate how the segments differ from each other and the whole.

• Scatter — A scatterplot displays the effect on one variable when another variable changes.

In general, three-dimensional charts are more difficult to comprehend than two-dimensional charts. The added design elements in a three-dimensional chart add clutter and take up space. Also, legends help keep the chart clean, so use them prominently on the slide.

To Insert a Chart

The next step in developing the presentation is to insert a pie chart. *Why? The pie chart is a useful tool to show proportional amounts. In this presentation, you want to show how many birds visited a feeder during a period of time, and the slices of pie will show that cardinals visited your feeder approximately twice as often as other types of birds.* The following steps insert a chart with sample data into Slide 3.

1
- Tap or click the New Slide button (HOME tab | Slides group) to add Slide 3 to the presentation (Figure 4–26).

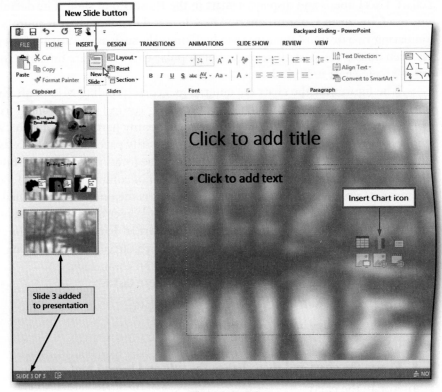

Figure 4–26

2
- Tap or click the Insert Chart icon in the content placeholder to display the Insert Chart dialog box.

- Tap or click Pie in the left pane to display the Pie gallery and then tap or click the 3-D Pie button to select that chart type.

- If you are using a mouse, point to the 3-D chart to see a large preview of this type (Figure 4–27).

Q&A
Can I change the chart type after I have inserted a chart?
Yes. Tap or click the Change Chart Type button in the Type group on the CHART TOOLS DESIGN tab to display the Change Chart Type dialog box and then make another selection.

Figure 4–27

3

- Tap or click the OK button (Insert Chart dialog box) to start the Microsoft Excel program and open a worksheet tiled on the top of the Backyard Birding presentation (Figure 4–28).

Q&A What do the numbers in the worksheet and the chart represent?
Excel places sample data in the worksheet and charts the sample data in the default chart type.

Figure 4–28

Other Ways

1. Tap or click Chart button (INSERT tab | Illustrations group)

How do I locate credible sources to obtain information for the graphic?

At times, you are familiar with the data for your chart or table because you have conducted in-the-field, or primary, research by interviewing experts or taking measurements. Other times, however, you must gather the data from secondary sources, such as magazine articles, newspaper articles, or web-sites. General circulation magazines and newspapers, such as *Newsweek* and the *Wall Street Journal,* use experienced journalists and editors to verify their information. Also, online databases, such as EBSCOhost, OCLC FirstSearch, LexisNexis Academic, and NewsBank contain articles from credible sources.

Some sources have particular biases, however, and they present information that supports their causes. Po-litical, religious, and social publications and websites often are designed for specific audiences who share a common point of view. You should, therefore, recognize that data from these sources can be skewed.

If you did not conduct the research yourself, you should give credit to the source of your information. You are acknowledging that someone else provided the data and giving your audience the opportunity to obtain the same materials you used. Type the source at the bottom of your chart or table, especially if you are distributing handouts of your slides. At the very least, state the source during the body of your speech.

CONSIDER THIS

BTW
Preparation Time
Be certain to begin developing a presentation well in advance of assignment deadlines when incorporating information graphics. Create a schedule so that you have adequate time to prepare clear visuals. Developing a presentation incorporating SmartArt, charts, and tables generally requires extra preparation time because you need to gather data from reputable and current sources to incorporate into these visual elements.

To Replace Sample Data

1 INSERT & MODIFY SMARTART | 2 ADD SMARTART STYLES & EFFECTS | 3 CONVERT TEXT TO SMARTART & FORMAT
4 CREATE CHART | 5 FORMAT CHART | 6 CREATE TABLE | 7 CHANGE TABLE STYLE & ALIGNMENT

The next step in creating the chart is to replace the sample data, which will redraw the chart. *Why? The worksheet displays sample data in two columns and five rows, but you want to change this data to show the specific bird names and the number of times they visited your feeder.* The first row and left column contain text labels and will be used to create the chart title and legend. A **legend** is a box that identifies each slice of the pie chart and coordinates with the colors assigned to the slice categories. The other cells contain numbers that are used to determine the size of the pie slices. The steps on the next page replace the sample data in the worksheet.

1

- Tap or click cell B1, which is the intersection of column B and row 1, to select it.

Q&A Why did my pointer change shape?

The pointer changes to a block plus sign to indicate a cell is selected.

- Type **Backyard Feeder Bird Sightings** in cell B1 to replace the sample chart title (Figure 4–29).

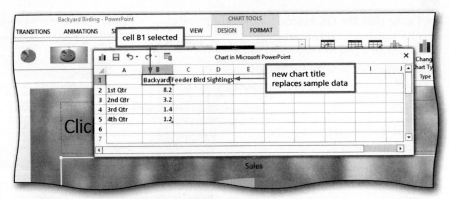

Figure 4–29

2

- Tap or click cell A2 to select that cell.

- Type **Jays** in cell A2 (Figure 4–30).

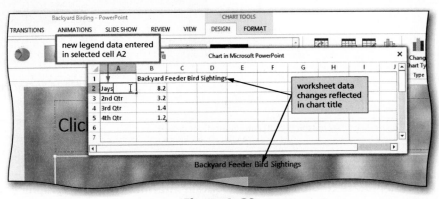

Figure 4–30

3

- Move the pointer to cell A3.

- Type **Cardinals** in cell A3 and then move the pointer to cell A4.

- Type **Finches** in cell A4 and then move the pointer to cell A5.

- Type **Woodpeckers** in cell A5 and then press the ENTER key (Figure 4–31).

Figure 4–31

- Tap or click cell B2, type 24 in that cell, and then move the pointer to cell B3.

- Type 40 in cell B3 and then move the pointer to cell B4.

- Type 10 in cell B4 and then move the pointer to cell B5.

- Type 6 in cell B5.

- Tap cell B6 or press the ENTER key (Figure 4–32).

Q&A Why do the slices in the PowerPoint pie chart change locations?
As you enter data in the Excel worksheet, the chart slices rotate to reflect these new figures.

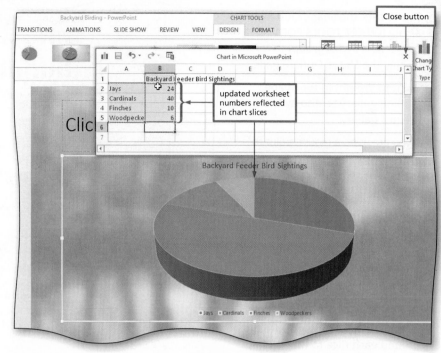

Figure 4–32

5

- Close Excel by tapping or clicking its Close button.

Q&A Can I open the Excel spreadsheet once it has been closed?
Yes. Tap or click the chart to select it and then tap or click the Edit Data button (CHART TOOLS DESIGN tab | Data group).

To Change the Shape Outline Weight

1 INSERT & MODIFY SMARTART | 2 ADD SMARTART STYLES & EFFECTS | 3 CONVERT TEXT TO SMARTART & FORMAT
4 CREATE CHART | 5 FORMAT CHART | 6 CREATE TABLE | 7 CHANGE TABLE STYLE & ALIGNMENT

The chart has a thin white outline around each pie slice and around each color square in the legend. You can change the weight of these lines. *Why? A thicker line can accentuate each slice and add another strong visual element to the slide.* The following steps change the outline weight.

- Tap or click the center of the pie chart to select it and display the sizing handles around each slice.

- Tap or click the CHART TOOLS FORMAT tab to display the CHART TOOLS FORMAT ribbon (Figure 4–33).

Figure 4–33

- Tap or click the Shape Outline arrow (CHART TOOLS FORMAT tab | Shape Styles group) to display the Shape Outline gallery.

- Point to Weight in the Shape Outline gallery to display the Weight gallery.

- If you are using a mouse, point to 4½ pt to display a live preview of this outline line weight (Figure 4–34).

 Experiment

- If you are using a mouse, point to various weights on the submenu and watch the border weights on the pie slices change.

Figure 4–34

- Tap or click 4½ pt to increase the border around each slice to that width.

Other Ways

1. Press and hold or right-click chart, choose Chart Area in Chart Elements box on shortcut menu, tap or click Outline button, tap or click Weight

---

To Change the Shape Outline Color

1 INSERT & MODIFY SMARTART | 2 ADD SMARTART STYLES & EFFECTS | 3 CONVERT TEXT TO SMARTART & FORMAT
4 CREATE CHART | 5 FORMAT CHART | 6 CREATE TABLE | 7 CHANGE TABLE STYLE & ALIGNMENT

Why? *At this point, it is difficult to see the borders around the legend squares and around each pie slice because they are white.* You can change this color to add contrast to each slice and legend color square. The following steps change the border color.

- Tap or click the Shape Outline arrow (CHART TOOLS FORMAT tab | Shape Styles group) to display the Shape Outline gallery.

- If you are using a mouse, point to Green (the sixth color in the Standard Colors row) to display a live preview of that border color on the pie slice shapes and legend squares (Figure 4–35).

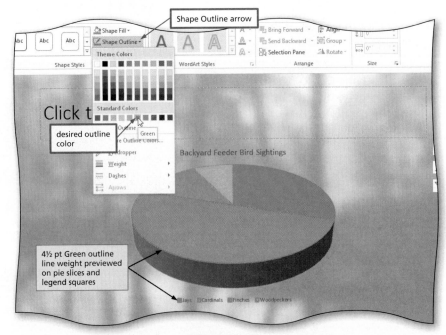 **Experiment**

- If you are using a mouse, point to various colors in the Shape Outline gallery and watch the border colors on the pie slices change.

Figure 4–35

- Tap or click Green to add green borders around each slice and also around the color squares in the legend.

Other Ways

1. Press and hold or right-click chart, choose Chart Area in Chart Elements box on shortcut menu, tap or click Outline button, tap or click desired color

To Change a Chart Layout

1 INSERT & MODIFY SMARTART | 2 ADD SMARTART STYLES & EFFECTS | 3 CONVERT TEXT TO SMARTART & FORMAT
4 CREATE CHART | 5 FORMAT CHART | 6 CREATE TABLE | 7 CHANGE TABLE STYLE & ALIGNMENT

Once you have selected a chart type, you can modify the look of the chart elements by changing its layout. The various layouts move the legend above or below the chart, or they move some or all of the legend data directly onto the individual chart pieces. For example, in the pie chart type, seven different layouts display various combinations of percentages and identifying information on the chart, and show or do not show the chart title. The following steps apply a chart layout with a title and legend that displays on the pie slices. *Why? Your data consists of bird names and counts, so you need a layout that shows the proportion of each bird's visits to your feeder along with a chart title.*

- With the chart still selected, tap or click the CHART TOOLS DESIGN tab to display the CHART TOOLS DESIGN ribbon and then tap or click the Quick Layout button to display the Quick Layout gallery.

- If you are using a mouse, point to Layout 5 (the second chart in the second row) to display a live preview of that style on the pie slice shapes (Figure 4–36).

- Tap or click Layout 5 in the Quick Layout gallery to apply the selected layout to the chart.

Figure 4–36

To Resize a Chart

1 INSERT & MODIFY SMARTART | 2 ADD SMARTART STYLES & EFFECTS | 3 CONVERT TEXT TO SMARTART & FORMAT
4 CREATE CHART | 5 FORMAT CHART | 6 CREATE TABLE | 7 CHANGE TABLE STYLE & ALIGNMENT

You resize a chart the same way you resize a SmartArt graphic or any other graphical object. When designing a slide, you may want to delete the slide title text placeholder. *Why? Removing the title text placeholder increases the white space on the slide, so you are able to enlarge the chart and aid readability. In addition, the chart layout displays a title that provides sufficient information to describe the chart's purpose.* The following steps delete the title text placeholder and resize the chart to fill Slide 3.

- If you are using a touch screen, press and hold on a border of the title placeholder and then tap Delete on the shortcut menu to remove the placeholder.

- If you are using a mouse, click a border of the title placeholder so that it displays as a solid line and then press the DELETE key to remove the placeholder.

2

- Select the chart and then drag the upper-left sizing handle to the upper-left corner of the slide.

- Drag the lower-right sizing handle to the lower-right corner of the slide (Figure 4–37).

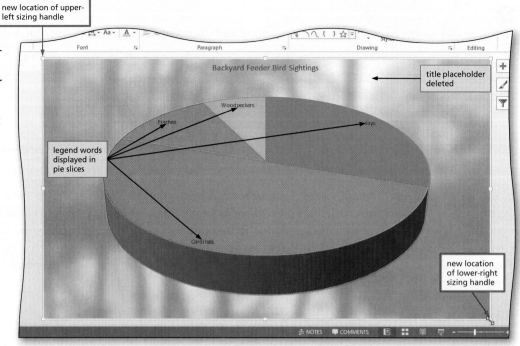

Figure 4–37

To Change the Title and Legend Font and Font Size

1 INSERT & MODIFY SMARTART | 2 ADD SMARTART STYLES & EFFECTS | 3 CONVERT TEXT TO SMARTART & FORMAT

4 CREATE CHART | 5 FORMAT CHART | 6 CREATE TABLE | 7 CHANGE TABLE STYLE & ALIGNMENT

Depending upon the complexity of the chart and the overall slide, you may want to increase the font size of the chart title and legend. ***Why?*** *The larger font size increases readability.* The following steps change the font size of both of these chart elements.

1

- Tap or click the chart title, Backyard Feeder Bird Sightings, to select the text box.

- Tap or click the Increase Font Size button (HOME tab | Font group) repeatedly until the font size is 48 point.

- Select all the text in the text box and then change the font to Papyrus (Figure 4–38).

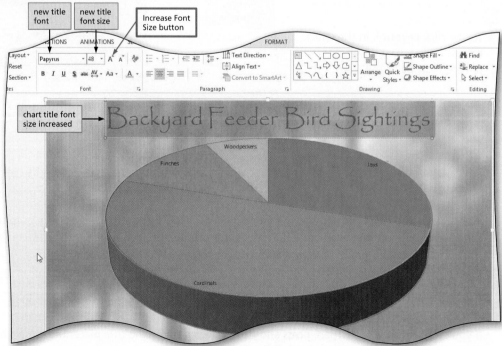

Figure 4–38

2

- Tap or click one of the legends to select all the legends simultaneously.

- Tap or click the Increase Font Size button (HOME tab | Font group) repeatedly until the font size of the legend text is 20 point.

- Change the legend font to Papyrus.

- Click the Bold button (HOME tab | Font group) to bold the legend text (Figure 4–39).

Figure 4–39

1 INSERT & MODIFY SMARTART | 2 ADD SMARTART STYLES & EFFECTS | 3 CONVERT TEXT TO SMARTART & FORMAT
4 CREATE CHART | 5 FORMAT CHART | 6 CREATE TABLE | 7 CHANGE TABLE STYLE & ALIGNMENT

To Rotate a Chart

Excel determines where each slice of pie is positioned in the chart. You may desire to have a specific slice display in a different location, such as at the top or bottom of the circle. You can rotate the entire chart clockwise until a particular part of the chart displays where you desire. A circle's circumference is 360 degrees, so if you want to move a slice from the top of the chart to the bottom, you would rotate it halfway around the circle, or 180 degrees. Similarly, if you a want a slice to move one-quarter of the way around the slide, you would rotate it either 90 degrees or 270 degrees. The steps on the next page rotate the chart so that the gray Finches slice displays at the bottom of the chart. *Why? Finches visit your feeder infrequently, so you want to call attention to the fact that you saw several finches when you were participating in the bird counting activity.*

BTW

Applying a Chart Style
Each chart type has a variety of styles that can change the look of the chart. To apply a style, select the entire chart area, tap or click a white space near the chart, tap or click the More button (CHART TOOLS DESIGN tab | Chart Styles group) to display the Chart Styles gallery, and then select a style.

1

- Click the gray Finches slice of the pie chart to select it. Tap or click the CHART TOOLS FORMAT tab to display the CHART TOOLS FORMAT ribbon.

- Tap or click the Format Selection button (CHART TOOLS FORMAT tab | Current Selection group) to display the Format Data Point pane (Figure 4–40).

Figure 4–40

2

- Tap or click the 'Angle of first slice' slider and drag it to the right until 200 is displayed in the 'Angle of first slice' box to rotate the Finches slice 200 degrees to the right (Figure 4–41).

Q&A Can I move the slider in small increments so that I can get a precise angle degree easily?
Yes. Tap or click the up or down arrows in the 'Angle of first slice' box to move the slider in one-degree increments or select the box and type the desired degree.

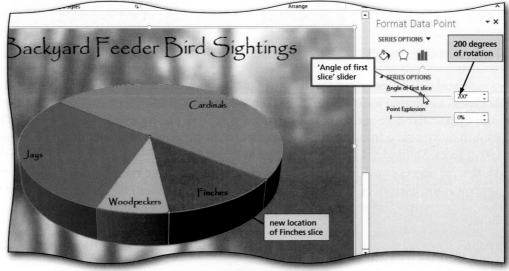

Figure 4–41

Other Ways

1. Press and hold or right-click selection, tap or click 'Format Data Point' on shortcut menu

To Separate a Pie Slice

Why? At times, you may desire to draw the viewers' attention to a particular area of the pie chart. To add this emphasis, you can separate, or explode, one or more slices. For example, you can separate the green Finches slice of the chart to stress that it was unusual to see so many Finches at this time of the year. The following steps separate a chart slice.

- Tap or click the Point Explosion slider and drag it to the right until 15 is displayed in the Point Explosion box to separate the slice from the pie chart (Figure 4–42).

Q&A Can I move the slider in small increments so that I can get a precise percentage easily?
Yes. Tap or click the up or down arrows in the Point Explosion box to move the slider in one-percent increments or select the box and type the desired percentage.

Figure 4–42

- Tap or click the Close button in the Format Data Point pane to close the pane.

Q&A Can I specify a precise position where the chart will display on the slide?
Yes. Press and hold or right-click the edge of the chart, tap or click 'Format Chart Area' on the shortcut menu, tap or click 'Size & Properties' in Format Chart Area task pane, enter measurements in the Position section, and then specify from the Top Left Corner or the Center of the slide.

Other Ways

1. Press and hold or right-click selection, tap or click Format Data Point on shortcut menu, set Point Explosion percentage

To Insert a Text Box and Format Text

A text box can contain information that is separate from the title or content placeholders. You can place this slide element anywhere on the slide and format the letters using any style and effect. You also can change the text box shape by moving the sizing handles. The steps on the next page insert a text box, add text, and then format these characters. *Why? You want to add an interesting fact about cardinals.*

• If you are using a mouse, display the INSERT tab, click the Text Box button (INSERT tab | Text group), and then click below the Cardinals label (Figure 4–43).

• If you are using a touch screen, display the INSERT tab and then tap the Text Box button (INSERT tab | Text group) to display the text box in the center of the slide.

Figure 4–43

• If necessary, tap or click the text box and then type **Seven states have the cardinal as their state bird** in the text box (Figure 4–44).

Figure 4–44

• Select the text in the text box and then change the font to Papyrus and increase the font size to 16 point.

• Drag the text box on top of the Cardinals slice (Figure 4–45).

Q&A

Can I change the shape of the text box?

Yes. Drag the sizing handles to the desired dimensions.

Figure 4–45

Break Point: If you wish to take a break, this is a good place to do so. Be sure to save the Backyard Birding file again and then you can exit PowerPoint. To resume at a later time, run PowerPoint, open the file called Backyard Birding, and continue following the steps from this location forward.

Adding a Table to a Slide and Formatting

One effective method of organizing information on a slide is to use a **table,** which is a grid consisting of rows and columns. You can enhance a table with formatting, including adding colors, lines, and backgrounds, and changing fonts.

In the following pages, you will perform these tasks:

1. Insert a table and then enter data and symbols.
2. Apply a table style.
3. Add borders and an effect.
4. Resize the table.
5. Merge cells and then display text in the cell vertically.
6. Add an image.
7. Align text in cells.
8. Format table data.

Tables

The table on Slide 4 (shown in Figure 4–1d on page PPT 211) contains information about the types of seeds that different birds prefer. This data is listed in five columns and five rows. The intersections of these rows and columns are **cells**.

To begin developing this table, you first must create an empty table and insert it into the slide. You must specify the table's **dimension**, which is the total number of rows and columns. This table will have a 5 × 5 dimension: the first number indicates the number of columns and the second specifies the number of rows. You will fill the cells with data pertaining to the types of seeds that attract specific birds. Then you will format the table using a table style.

BTW

Clearing Table Formatting
The table you create on Slide 4 has five columns and five rows. Many times, however, you may need to create larger tables and then enter data into many cells. In these cases, experienced PowerPoint designers recommend clearing all formatting from the table so that you can concentrate on the numbers and letters and not be distracted by the colors and borders. To clear formatting, click the Clear Table command at the bottom of the Table Styles gallery (TABLE TOOLS DESIGN tab | Table Styles group). Then, add a table style once you have verified that all table data is correct.

To Insert an Empty Table

1 INSERT & MODIFY SMARTART | 2 ADD SMARTART STYLES & EFFECTS | 3 CONVERT TEXT TO SMARTART & FORMAT
4 CREATE CHART | 5 FORMAT CHART | 6 CREATE TABLE | **7 CHANGE TABLE STYLE & ALIGNMENT**

Your next task in developing the presentation is to insert an empty table. The following steps insert a table with five columns and five rows into Slide 4. *Why? The first row will contain the column headings, and the additional rows will have information about four types of birds. The five columns will contain the table title and the birds' seed preferences.*

- Add a new slide to the presentation (Figure 4–46).

Figure 4–46

- Tap or click the Insert Table icon in the content placeholder to display the Insert Table dialog box.

- Tap or click the up arrow to the right of the 'Number of rows' box three times so that the number 5 appears in the box (Figure 4–47).

Figure 4–47

- Tap or click the OK button (Insert Table dialog box) to insert the table into Slide 4 (Figure 4–48).

Figure 4–48

Other Ways

1. Tap or click Table button (INSERT tab | Tables group), drag to select columns and rows, click or press ENTER

To Enter Data in a Table

1 INSERT & MODIFY SMARTART | 2 ADD SMARTART STYLES & EFFECTS | 3 CONVERT TEXT TO SMARTART & FORMAT
4 CREATE CHART | 5 FORMAT CHART | 6 CREATE TABLE | **7 CHANGE TABLE STYLE & ALIGNMENT**

Before formatting or making any changes in the table style, you enter the data in the table. *Why? It is easier to see formatting and style changes applied to existing data.* The second column will have the four bird types, and the three columns to the right of the bird names will contain data with check mark symbols representing the type of seed each bird prefers. The next step is to enter data in the cells of the empty table. To place data in a cell, you tap or click the cell and then type text. The following steps enter the data in the table.

- Tap or click the second cell in the second column to place the insertion point in this cell. Type **Cardinals** and then tap the cell below or press the DOWN ARROW key to advance the insertion point to the next cell in this column.

Figure 4–49

- Type **Finches** and then advance the insertion point to the next cell in this column.

- Type **Jays** and then advance the insertion point to the next cell in this column.

- Type **Woodpeckers** and tap the empty cell to the right or press the TAB key (Figure 4–49).

Q&A

What if I pressed the ENTER key after filling in the last cell?
Tap or click the BACKSPACE key.

How would I add more rows to the table?
If you are using a mouse, press the TAB key when the insertion point is positioned in the bottom-right cell. If you are using a touch screen, press and hold the bottom-right cell, tap Insert on the shortcut menu, and then tap Insert Rows Below.

2

- Tap or click the third cell in the first row to place the insertion point in this cell. Type **Sunflower** and then advance the insertion point to the adjacent right cell in this row.

- Type **Safflower** and then advance the insertion point to the adjacent right cell.

- Type **Millet** as the cell content (Figure 4–50).

Q&A How do I correct cell contents if I make a mistake?
Tap or click the cell and then correct the text.

Figure 4–50

To Insert a Symbol

1 INSERT & MODIFY SMARTART | 2 ADD SMARTART STYLES & EFFECTS | 3 CONVERT TEXT TO SMARTART & FORMAT
4 CREATE CHART | 5 FORMAT CHART | 6 CREATE TABLE | **7 CHANGE TABLE STYLE & ALIGNMENT**

The data in tables frequently consists of words. At times, however, the cells can contain characters and pictures that depict specific meanings. *Why? Audience members easily can identify these images, such as mathematical symbols and geometric shapes.* You can add illustrations and photos to the table cells and also can insert special symbols. Many symbols are found in the Webding and Wingding fonts. You insert symbols, such as mathematical characters and dots, by changing the font using the Symbol dialog box. The following steps insert a check mark symbol in several table cells.

1

- Tap or click the second cell in the third column to place the insertion point in this cell.

- Display the INSERT tab.

- Tap or click the Symbol button (INSERT tab | Symbols group) to display the Symbol dialog box (Figure 4–51).

Q&A What if the symbol I want to insert already appears in the Symbol dialog box?
You can tap or click any symbol shown in the dialog box to insert it in the slide.

Figure 4–51

Why does my 'Recently used symbols' list display different symbols from those shown in Figure 4–51?
As you insert symbols, PowerPoint places them in the 'Recently used symbols' list.

2

- Tap or click the Symbol dialog box title bar and then drag the dialog box to the lower-left edge of the slide so that the some of the content in the second column in the table is visible.

3

- If Wingdings is not the font displayed in the Font box, tap or click the Font arrow (Symbol dialog box) and then drag or scroll to Wingdings and tap or click this font.

- Drag or scroll down until the last row of this font is visible.

- Tap or click the check mark symbol shown in Figure 4–52.

As you insert symbols, PowerPoint places them in the Recently used symbols list. Your list will differ.

Figure 4–52

4

- Tap or click the Insert button (Symbol dialog box) to place the check mark symbol in the selected table cell (Figure 4–53).

Q&A Why is the Symbol dialog box still open?
The Symbol dialog box remains open, allowing you to insert additional symbols in the selected cell.

5

- Tap or click the Close button (Symbol dialog box).

Figure 4–53

To Copy a Symbol

1 INSERT & MODIFY SMARTART | 2 ADD SMARTART STYLES & EFFECTS | 3 CONVERT TEXT TO SMARTART & FORMAT
4 CREATE CHART | 5 FORMAT CHART | 6 CREATE TABLE | 7 CHANGE TABLE STYLE & ALIGNMENT

The Seed Preferences chart will contain check marks for the types of seeds that the four birds prefer. To add the check marks to specific cells, you would need to repeat the process you used to insert the first check mark. Rather than inserting this symbol from the Symbol dialog box, you can copy the symbol and then paste it in the appropriate cells. *Why? This process can be accomplished more quickly with copy and paste when using the same symbol multiple times.* The following steps copy the check mark symbol to cells in the Slide 4 table.

1

- Select the check mark symbol in the table, display the HOME tab, and then tap or click the Copy button (HOME tab | Clipboard group) to copy the check mark symbol to the Office Clipboard (Figure 4–54).

Figure 4–54

2

- Click the third cell in the third column to place the insertion point in this cell and then click the Paste button (HOME tab | Clipboard group) (Figure 4–55).

Q&A How do I delete the extra row that is displayed in the cell when I paste the symbol?

If you are using a touch screen, display the onscreen keyboard and press the BACKSPACE key. If you are using a regular keyboard, press the BACKSPACE key.

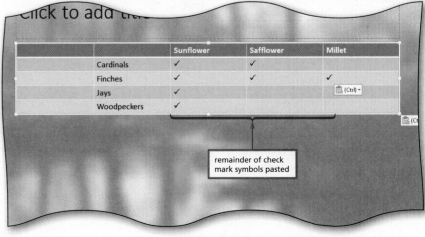

Figure 4–55

3

- Using Figure 4–56 as a guide, continue pasting the check mark symbols in the table cells.

BTW

Certification

The Microsoft Office Specialist (MOS) program provides an opportunity for you to obtain a valuable industry credential — proof that you have the PowerPoint 2013 skills required by employers. For more information, visit the Certification resource on the Student Companion Site located on www.cengagebrain.com. For detailed instructions about accessing available resources, visit www.cengage.com/ct/studentdownload or see the inside back cover of this book.

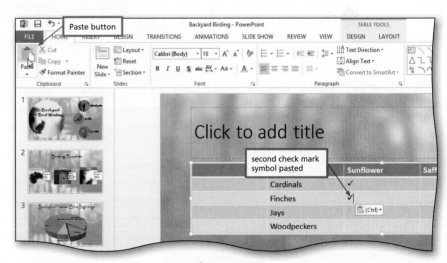

Figure 4–56

To Apply a Table Style

When you inserted the table, PowerPoint automatically applied a style. Thumbnails of this style and others are displayed in the Table Styles gallery. These styles use a variety of colors and shading and are grouped in the categories of Best Match for Document, Light, Medium, and Dark. The following steps apply a table style in the Best Match for Document area to the Slide 4 table. *Why? The styles in the Best Match for Document use the theme colors applied to the presentation, so they coordinate nicely with the colors you have been using in the first three slides in this presentation.*

1

- With the insertion point in the table, display the TABLE TOOLS DESIGN tab (Figure 4–57).

Figure 4–57

2

- Tap or click the More button in the Table Styles gallery (TABLE TOOLS DESIGN tab | Tables Styles group) to expand the Table Styles gallery.

- If you are using a mouse, point to Medium Style 2 – Accent 6 in the Medium area (the last style in the second Medium row) to display a live preview of that style applied to the table (Figure 4–58).

Experiment

- If you are using a mouse, point to various styles in the Table Styles gallery and watch the colors and format change on the table.

Figure 4–58

- Tap or click Medium Style 2 – Accent 6 in the Table Styles gallery to apply the selected style to the table (Figure 4–59).

Q&A Can I resize the columns and rows or the entire table?
Yes. To resize columns or rows, drag a **column boundary** (the border to the right of a column) or the **row boundary** (the border at the bottom of a row) until the column or row is the desired width or height. To resize the entire table, drag a **table sizing handle**.

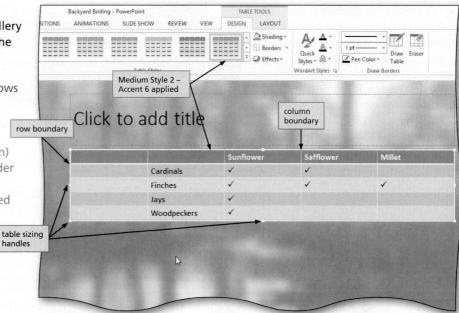

Figure 4–59

To Add Borders to a Table

1 INSERT & MODIFY SMARTART | 2 ADD SMARTART STYLES & EFFECTS | 3 CONVERT TEXT TO SMARTART & FORMAT
4 CREATE CHART | 5 FORMAT CHART | 6 CREATE TABLE | **7 CHANGE TABLE STYLE & ALIGNMENT**

The Slide 4 table does not have borders around the entire table or between the cells. The following steps add borders to the entire table. *Why? These details will give the chart some dimension and add to its visual appeal.*

- Tap or click the edge of the table so that the insertion point does not appear in any cell.
- Tap or click the Borders arrow (TABLE TOOLS DESIGN tab | Table Styles group) to display the Borders gallery (Figure 4–60).

Q&A Why is the button called No Border in the ScreenTip and Borders on the ribbon?
The ScreenTip name for the button will change based on the type of border, if any, present in the table. Currently no borders are applied.

Figure 4–60

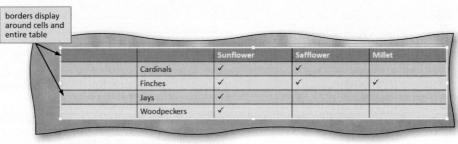

②

- Tap or click All Borders in the Borders gallery to add borders around the entire table and to each table cell (Figure 4–61).

Q&A

Why is the border color black?
PowerPoint's default border color is black. This color is displayed on the Pen Color button (TABLE TOOLS DESIGN tab | Draw Borders group).

Can I apply any of the border options in the Border gallery?
Yes. You can vary the look of your table by applying borders only to the cells, around the table, to the top, bottom, left or right edges, or a combination of these areas.

Figure 4–61

To Add an Effect to a Table

1 INSERT & MODIFY SMARTART | 2 ADD SMARTART STYLES & EFFECTS | 3 CONVERT TEXT TO SMARTART & FORMAT
4 CREATE CHART | 5 FORMAT CHART | 6 CREATE TABLE | 7 CHANGE TABLE STYLE & ALIGNMENT

Why? *Adding an effect will enhance the table design.* PowerPoint gives you the option of applying a bevel to specified cells so they have a three-dimensional appearance. You also can add a shadow or reflection to the entire table. The following steps add a shadow and give a three-dimensional appearance to the entire table.

①

- With the table selected, tap or click the Effects button (TABLE TOOLS DESIGN tab | Table Styles group) to display the Effects menu.

Q&A

What is the difference between a shadow and a reflection?
A shadow gives the appearance that light is falling on the table, which causes a shadow behind the graphic. A reflection gives the appearance that the table is shiny, so a mirror image appears below the actual graphic.

②

- If you are using a touch screen, tap Shadow to display the Shadow gallery.

- If you are using a mouse, point to Shadow to display the Shadow gallery (Figure 4–62).

Q&A

How do the shadows differ in the Outer, Inner, and Perspective categories?
The Outer shadows are displayed on the outside of the table, whereas the Inner shadows are displayed in the interior cells. The Perspective shadows give the illusion that a light is shining from the right or left side of the table or from above, and the table is casting a shadow.

Figure 4–62

❸

- If you are using a mouse, point to Offset Center in the Outer category (second shadow in the second row) to display a live preview of this shadow (Figure 4–63).

 Experiment

- If you are using a mouse, point to the various shadows in the Shadow gallery and watch the shadows change in the table.

Figure 4–63

❹

- Tap or click Offset Center to apply this shadow to the table.
- Tap or click outside the table so it no longer is selected (Figure 4–64).

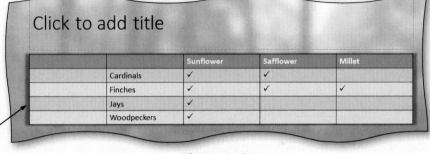

Figure 4–64

To Resize a Table

1 INSERT & MODIFY SMARTART | 2 ADD SMARTART STYLES & EFFECTS | 3 CONVERT TEXT TO SMARTART & FORMAT
4 CREATE CHART | 5 FORMAT CHART | 6 CREATE TABLE | **7 CHANGE TABLE STYLE & ALIGNMENT**

Why? *On Slide 4, you can remove the title text placeholder because the table will have the title, Seed Preferences, in the first column. If you resize the table to fill the slide it will be more readable.* You resize a table the same way you resize a chart, a SmartArt graphic, or any other graphical object. The following steps resize the table to fill Slide 4.

❶

- If you are using a touch screen, press and hold a border of the title placeholder and then tap Delete on the shortcut menu to remove the placeholder.

- If you are using a mouse, click a border of the title placeholder so that it displays as a solid line and then press the DELETE key to remove the placeholder (Figure 4–65).

Figure 4–65

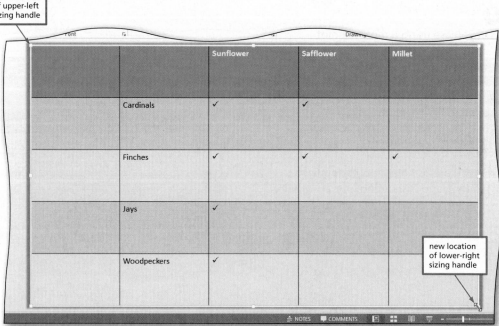

2

- Select the table and then drag the upper-left sizing handle diagonally to the upper-left corner of the slide.

- Drag the lower-right sizing handle diagonally to the lower-right corner of the slide (Figure 4–66).

Figure 4–66

To Merge Cells

1 INSERT & MODIFY SMARTART | 2 ADD SMARTART STYLES & EFFECTS | 3 CONVERT TEXT TO SMARTART & FORMAT
4 CREATE CHART | 5 FORMAT CHART | 6 CREATE TABLE | **7 CHANGE TABLE STYLE & ALIGNMENT**

You want to insert a picture of two birdseed bags in the area where the first two cells reside in the first row, so you need to make room for this illustration. In addition, you want to merge cells in the first column to fit a chart title. **Why?** *To provide space for graphics and text, you can merge two or more cells to create one large cell.* The Slide 4 table title will display vertically in the first column. The following steps merge two cells in the first table row into a single cell and merge four cells in the first column into a single cell.

- Drag through the first and second column cells in the first table row to select these two cells (Figure 4–67).

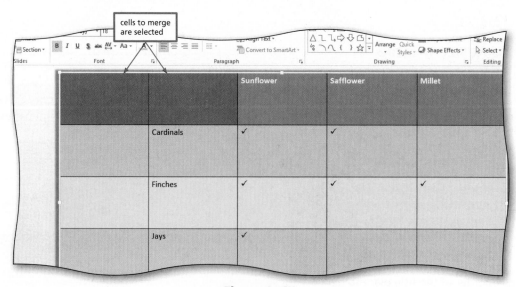

Figure 4–67

2

- Tap or click the TABLE TOOLS LAYOUT tab to display the TABLE TOOLS LAYOUT ribbon.

- Tap or click the Merge Cells button (TABLE TOOLS LAYOUT tab | Merge group) to merge the two cells into one cell (Figure 4–68).

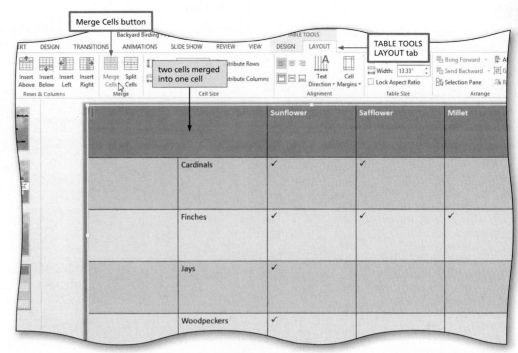

Figure 4–68

3

- Drag through the second, third, fourth, and fifth cells in the first table column to select these cells (Figure 4–69).

Figure 4–69

- Tap or click the Merge Cells button to merge these cells (Figure 4–70).

Q&A Could I have merged the four cells in the first column before merging the two cells in the first row? Yes.

BTW

Quick Reference
For a table that lists how to complete the tasks covered in this book using touch gestures, the mouse, ribbon, shortcut menu, and keyboard, see the Quick Reference Summary at the back of this book, or visit the Quick Reference resource on the Student Companion Site located on www.cengagebrain.com. For detailed instructions about accessing available resources, visit www.cengage.com/ct/studentdownload or see the inside back cover of this book.

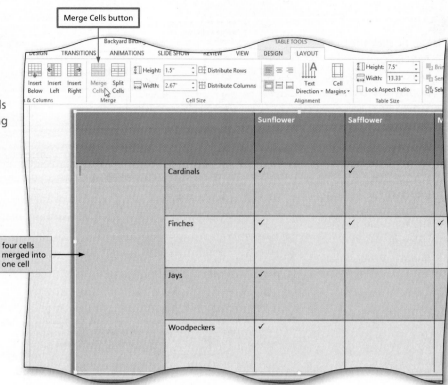

Figure 4–70

Other Ways

1. Press and hold or right-click selected cells, tap or click Merge Cells on shortcut menu

To Display Text in a Cell Vertically

1 INSERT & MODIFY SMARTART | 2 ADD SMARTART STYLES & EFFECTS | 3 CONVERT TEXT TO SMARTART & FORMAT
4 CREATE CHART | 5 FORMAT CHART | 6 CREATE TABLE | 7 CHANGE TABLE STYLE & ALIGNMENT

You want the Slide 4 table title to display vertically in the first column. **Why?** *To add variety to your slides, you can display text in a nonstandard manner.* By rotating text 270 degrees, you call attention to these letters. The default orientation of table cell text is horizontal. You can change this direction to stack the letters so they display above and below each other, or you can rotate the direction in 90-degree increments. The following steps rotate the text in the first column cell.

- With the TABLE TOOLS LAYOUT tab displayed and the column 1 cell selected, type **Seed Preferences** in the table cell.

- Tap or click the Text Direction button (TABLE TOOLS LAYOUT tab | Alignment group) to display the Text Direction gallery (Figure 4–71).

Experiment

- If you are using a mouse, point to the three other direction options in the Text Direction gallery and watch the text change in the cell.

Figure 4–71

2

- Tap or click 'Rotate all text 270°' to rotate the text in the cell (Figure 4–72).

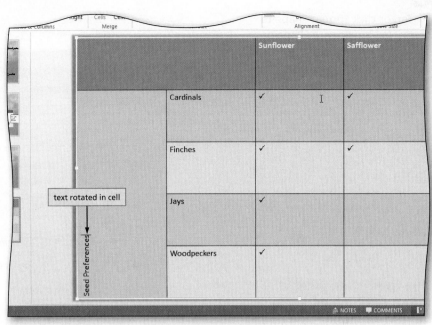

Figure 4–72

Other Ways

1. Press and hold or right-click selected cells, tap or click Format Shape on shortcut menu, tap or click TEXT OPTIONS tab, tap or click Textbox, tap or click Text direction arrow

To Add an Image to a Table

1 INSERT & MODIFY SMARTART | 2 ADD SMARTART STYLES & EFFECTS | 3 CONVERT TEXT TO SMARTART & FORMAT

4 CREATE CHART | 5 FORMAT CHART | 6 CREATE TABLE | **7 CHANGE TABLE STYLE & ALIGNMENT**

Another table enhancement you can make is to add a photo or illustration to a table cell. The following steps add a picture of birdseed bags to the upper-left table cell. *Why? This illustration is another graphical element that reinforces the purpose of the table.*

- Press and hold or right-click the first cell in the first row to display the shortcut menu and mini toolbar (Figure 4–73).

Figure 4–73

2

- Tap or click Format Shape to display the Format Shape pane and then, if necessary, tap or click FILL to expand the FILL section.

- Tap or click 'Picture or texture fill' to select this option (Figure 4–74).

Figure 4–74

3

- Tap or click the File button to display the Insert Picture dialog box.

- Tap or click the Seeds picture located on the Data Files for Students and then tap or click the Insert button (Insert Picture dialog box) to insert the Seeds picture into the table cell (Figure 4–75).

Figure 4–75

4

- Tap or click the Close button (Format Shape pane).

Other Ways

1. Press and hold or right-click selected cell, tap or click Shape Fill arrow on mini toolbar, tap or click Picture

To Align Text in Cells

The data in each cell can be aligned horizontally and vertically. You change the horizontal alignment of each cell in a similar manner as you center, left-align, or right-align text in a placeholder. You also can change the vertical alignment so that the data displays at the top, middle, or bottom of each cell. The following steps center the text both horizontally and vertically in each table cell. *Why? Having the text centered vertically and horizontally helps balance the cells by distributing the empty space evenly around the cell contents.*

1

- Tap or click the Select button (TABLE TOOLS LAYOUT tab |Table group) to display the Select menu (Figure 4–76).

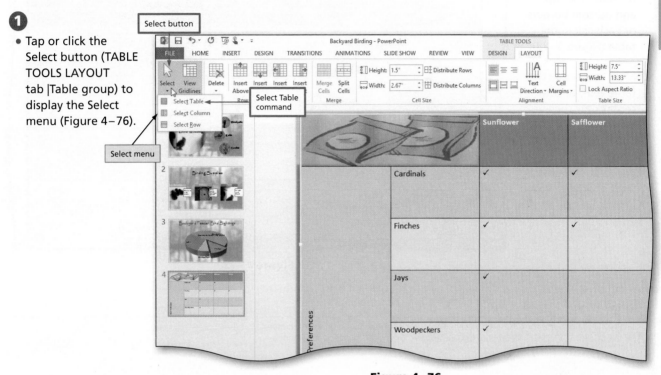

Figure 4–76

2

- Tap or click Select Table in the Select menu to select the entire table.

- Tap or click the Center button (TABLE TOOLS LAYOUT tab | Alignment group) to center the text between the left and right borders of each cell in the table (Figure 4–77).

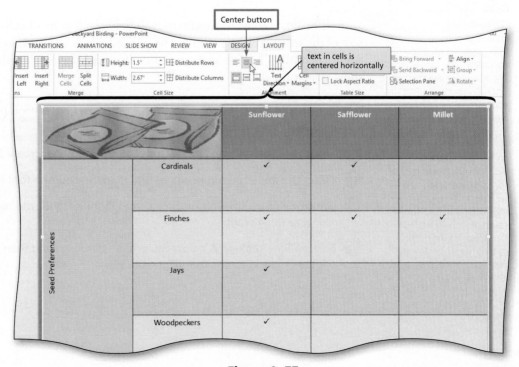

Figure 4–77

3

- Tap or click the Center Vertically button (TABLE TOOLS LAYOUT tab | Alignment group) to center the text between the top and bottom borders of each cell in the table (Figure 4–78).

Q&A Must I center all the table cells, or can I center only specific cells?
You can center as many cells as you desire at one time by selecting one or more cells.

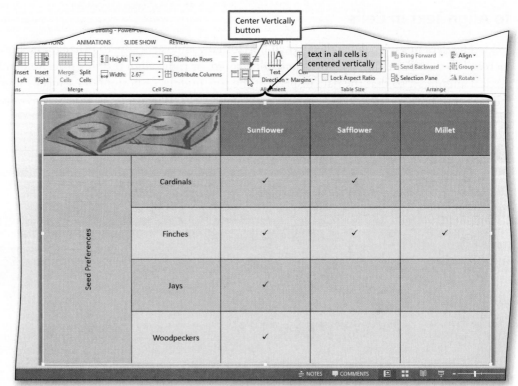

Figure 4–78

Other Ways

1. Press and hold or right-click selected cells, tap or click Format Shape on shortcut menu, tap or click TEXT OPTIONS tab, tap or click Textbox, tap or click Vertical alignment arrow

To Format Table Data

The final table enhancement is to bold the text in all cells and increase the font size of the title and the symbols. The entire table is selected, so you can bold all text simultaneously. The title and symbols will have different font sizes. The following steps format the data.

1 Display the HOME tab and then tap or click the Bold button (HOME tab | Font group) to bold all text in the table.

2 Select the table title text in the first column and then increase the font size to 60 point.

3 Select the three column headings and then increase the font size to 28 point.

4 Select the four cells with the bird names in the second column and then increase the font size to 24 point.

5 Select all the table cells below the column headings and then increase the font size of the check marks to 48 point (Figure 4–79).

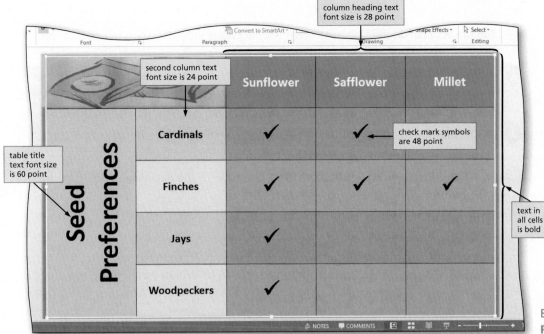

Figure 4–79

To Add a Transition between Slides

A final enhancement you will make in this presentation is to apply the Page Curl transition in the Exciting category to all slides and change the transition speed to 2.00. The following steps apply this transition to the presentation.

1 Apply the Page Curl transition in the Exciting category (TRANSITIONS tab | Transition to This Slide group) to all four slides in the presentation.

2 Change the transition speed from 01.25 to 02.00 for all slides.

To Print a Handout

With the completed presentation saved, you may want to print handouts. The following steps print a presentation handout with two slides per page.

1 Tap or click FILE on the ribbon to open the Backstage view and then tap or click the Print tab.

2 Tap or click 'Full Page Slides in the Settings area.

3 Click 2 Slides in the Handouts area to display a preview of the handout.

4 Verify that the printer listed on the Printer Status button will print a hard copy of the presentation.

5 Tap or click the Print button in the Print gallery to print the presentation (Figure 4–80 on the next page).

To Sign Out of a Microsoft Account

If you are signed in to a Microsoft account, you should sign out of the account from the Account gallery in the Backstage view before exiting PowerPoint. The following steps sign out of a Microsoft account from PowerPoint. For a detailed example of the procedure summarized below, refer to the Office and Windows chapter at the beginning of this book.

BTW
Printing Document Properties
To print document properties, tap or click FILE on the ribbon to open the Backstage view, tap or click the Print tab in the Backstage view to display the Print gallery, tap or click the first button in the Settings area to display a list of options specifying what you can print, tap or click Document Info in the list to specify you want to print the document properties instead of the actual document, and then tap or click the Print button in the Print gallery to print the document properties on the currently selected printer.

BTW
Conserving Ink and Toner
If you want to conserve ink or toner, you can instruct PowerPoint to print draft quality documents by tapping or clicking FILE on the ribbon to open the Backstage view, tapping or clicking Options in the Backstage view to display the PowerPoint Options dialog box, tapping or clicking Advanced in the left pane (PowerPoint Options dialog box), sliding or scrolling to the Print area in the right pane, placing a check mark in the 'Use draft quality' check box, and then tapping or clicking the OK button. Then, use the Backstage view to print the document as usual.

1. Tap or click FILE on the ribbon to open the Backstage view and then tap or click the Account tab to display the Account gallery.

2. Tap or click the Sign out link, which displays the Remove Account dialog box. If a Can't remove Windows accounts dialog box appears instead of the Remove Account dialog box, click the OK button and skip the remaining steps.

3. Tap or click the Yes button (Remove Account dialog box) to sign out of your Microsoft account.

4. Tap or click the Back button in the upper-left corner of the Backstage view to return to the presentation.

To Exit PowerPoint

This project now is complete. The following steps exit PowerPoint. For a detailed example of the procedure summarized below, refer to the Office and Windows chapter at the beginning of this book.

1. Tap or click the Close button on the right side of the title bar to close the open document and exit PowerPoint.

2. If a Microsoft PowerPoint dialog box appears, tap or click the Save button to save any changes made to the presentation.

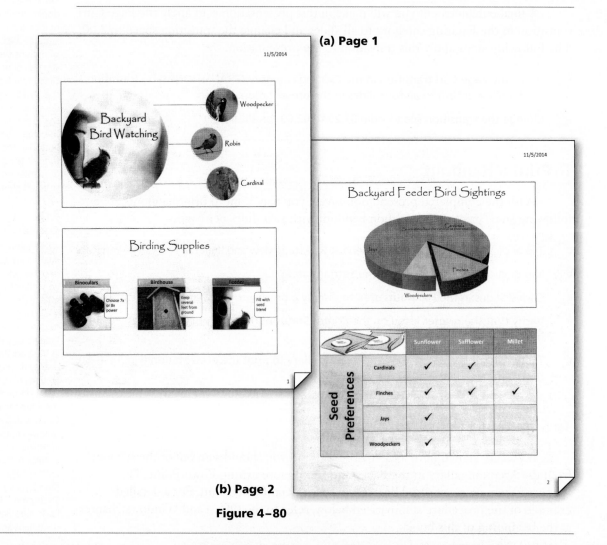

(a) Page 1

(b) Page 2

Figure 4–80

Chapter Summary

In this chapter you have learned how to insert a SmartArt graphic and then add a picture and text, convert text to a SmartArt graphic, create and format a chart and a table, change table text alignment and orientation, and insert symbols. The items listed below include all the new PowerPoint skills you have learned in this chapter.

Creating a Chart
Insert a Chart (PPT 228)
Replace Sample Data (PPT 229)

Creating a SmartArt Graphic
Insert a SmartArt Graphic (PPT 214)
Enter Text in a SmartArt Graphic (PPT 215)
Insert a Picture from a File into a SmartArt Graphic (PPT 217)
Convert Text to a SmartArt Graphic (PPT 222)

Creating a Table
Insert an Empty Table (PPT 239)
Enter Data in a Table (PPT 240)
Insert a Symbol (PPT 241)
Copy a Symbol (PPT 242)
Add an Image to a Table (PPT 251)

Formatting a Chart
Change the Shape Outline Weight (PPT 231)
Change the Shape Outline Color (PPT 232)
Change a Chart Layout (PPT 233)
Resize a Chart (PPT 233)

Change the Title and Legend Font and Font Size (PPT 234)
Rotate a Chart (PPT 235)
Separate a Pie Slice (PPT 237)
To Insert a Text Box and Format Text (PPT 237)

Formatting a SmartArt Graphic
Format Text Pane Characters (PPT 216)
Apply a SmartArt Style (PPT 218)
Change SmartArt Color (PPT 219)
Resize a SmartArt Graphic (PPT 221)
Move a Text Box (PPT 221)
Format SmartArt Graphic Text (PPT 225)

Formatting a Table
Apply a Table Style (PPT 244)
Add Borders to a Table (PPT 245)
Add an Effect to a Table (PPT 246)
Resize a Table (PPT 247)
Merge Cells (PPT 248)
Display Text in a Cell Vertically (PPT 250)
Align Text in Cells (PPT 253)

CONSIDER THIS

What decisions will you need to make when creating your next presentation?
Use these guidelines as you complete the assignments in this chapter and create your own slide show decks outside of this class.

1. Audiences recall visual concepts more quickly and accurately than when viewing text alone, so consider using graphics in your presentation.

   a) Decide the precise message you want to convey to your audience.

   b) Determine if a SmartArt graphic, chart, or table is the better method of presenting the information.

2. Choose an appropriate SmartArt layout.

   a) Determine which layout best represents the concept you are attempting to present. Some of the layouts, such as Matrix, Pyramid, and Relationship, offer outstanding methods of showing how ideas are connected to each other, while other layouts, such as Cycle, List, and Process, are best at showing steps to complete a task.

   b) Use Table 4–1 on page PPT 213 to help you select a layout.

3. Choose an appropriate chart type.

   a) Charts are excellent visuals to show relationships between groups of data, especially numbers.

   b) Decide which chart type best conveys the points you are attempting to make in your presentation. PowerPoint provides a wide variety of styles within each category of chart, so determine which one is most effective in showing the relationships.

4. Obtain information for the graphic from credible sources.

   a) Text or numbers should be current and correct.

   b) Verify the sources of the information.

   c) Be certain you have typed the data correctly.

   d) Acknowledge the source of the information on the slide or during your presentation.

5. Test your visual elements.

   a) Show your slides to several friends or colleagues and ask them to interpret what they see.

   b) Have your test audience summarize the information they perceive on the tables and charts and compare their analyses to what you are attempting to convey.

CONSIDER THIS

How should you submit solutions to questions in the assignments identified with a ✳ symbol?
Every assignment in this book contains one or more questions identified with a ✳ symbol. These questions require you to think beyond the assigned presentation. Present your solutions to the questions in the format required by your instructor. Possible formats may include one or more of these options: write the answer; create a document that contains the answer; present your answer to the class; discuss your answer in a group; record the answer as audio or video using a webcam, smartphone, or portable media player; or post answers on a blog, wiki, or website.

Apply Your Knowledge

Reinforce the skills and apply the concepts you learned in this chapter.

Converting Text to a SmartArt Graphic

Note: To complete this assignment, you will be required to use the Data Files for Students. Visit www.cengage.com/ct/studentdownload for detailed instructions or contact your instructor for information about accessing the required files.

Instructions: Run PowerPoint. Open the presentation, Apply 4-1 Emergency, from the Data Files for Students.

The slide in the presentation presents information about emergency evacuation plans. The document you open is a partially formatted presentation. You are to convert the list to SmartArt and format the graphic so the slide looks like Figure 4–81.

Perform the following tasks:

1. Move the WordArt title, Emergency Evacuation Plans, to the location shown in Figure 4–81.

2. Convert the list to SmartArt by applying the Vertical Block List (the second graphic in the seventh List area row). Change the colors to Colorful Range – Accent Colors 5 to 6 (the last color in the Colorful area). Apply the Inset 3-D Style (the second style in the first 3-D row).

3. Resize this SmartArt graphic to approximately 5.5" × 11" and move this SmartArt graphic to the area shown in Figure 4–81.

Figure 4–81

4. With the Text Pane open, select the three Level 1 bulleted lines, change the font to Bookman Old Style, decrease the font size to 36 point, change the font color to Black, Text 1 (the second color in the first Theme Colors row), and then bold and underline this text.

5. With the Text Pane open, select the eight Level 2 bulleted lines and then increase the font size to 26 point and bold this text.

6. Insert the Green marble texture (the fourth texture in the second row) to format the background. Change the transparency to 20%.

7. If requested by your instructor, add your grandfather's first name after the words, lot C, on the last line of the Level 2 bulleted list.

8. Apply the Comb transition in the Exciting category to the slide. Change the duration to 3.25 seconds.

9. Save the presentation using the file name, Apply 4-1 Emergency Evacuation Plans.

10. Submit the revised document in the format specified by your instructor.

11. ✳ In Step 2, you chose the Vertical Block List and changed the colors of the SmartArt graphic. How did this style improve the slide and increase the audience's attention of the content?

Extend Your Knowledge

Extend the skills you learned in this chapter and experiment with new skills. You may need to use Help to complete the assignment.

Changing the Chart Type and Style and Formatting a SmartArt Graphic

Note: To complete this assignment, you will be required to use the Data Files for Students. Visit www.cengage.com/ct/studentdownload for detailed instructions or contact your instructor for information about accessing the required files.

Instructions: Run PowerPoint. Open the presentation, Extend 4-1 Airplanes, from the Data Files for Students. You will format a chart by applying a type and style and then you will create a SmartArt graphic to create the presentation shown in Figure 4–82 on the next page.

Perform the following tasks:

1. Using Figure 4–82a as a guide, delete all the text in the bulleted list except for the last line, Total cost of flying lessons – $5,300, and remove the bullet from this text by tapping or pressing the BACKSPACE key one time. Change the size of the list placeholder to approximately 0.71" × 13.33". Increase the font size of this text to 28 point, bold the text, and then center it. Move the title text placeholder from the bottom edge of the slide to the top edge of the slide and then move the list placeholder to the bottom edge of the slide.

2. Change the chart type from a 3-D Pie chart to a Clustered Column chart, as shown in Figure 4–82a. *Hint:* Tap or click the chart to select it, then tap or click the Change Chart Type button (CHART TOOLS DESIGN tab | Type group), and then select the Clustered Column chart type.

3. Apply Style 9 (the first style in the second row) (CHART TOOLS DESIGN tab | Chart Styles group) and then change the layout to Layout 4 (the first layout in the second row). Increase the size of the chart to approximately 5.45" × 9.74" and then center the chart horizontally and vertically on Slide 1. *Hint:* To center the chart on the slide, click the Align button (CHART TOOLS FORMAT tab | Arrange group). Change the chart border color to Orange, Accent 5 (the ninth color in the first Theme Colors row) and then change the weight of the border to 6 pt. Delete the duplicate legend at the bottom of the chart by selecting the legend and then pressing the DELETE key.

Continued >

Extend Your Knowledge *continued*

(a) Slide 1

(b) Slide 2

Figure 4–82

4. On Slide 2 (Figure 4–82b), increase the size of the four outer circles of the SmartArt graphic to approximately 1.5" × 1.5". In the SmartArt Text Pane, type **Lift** as the first Level 2 text, type **Drag** as the second Level 2 text, type **Gravity** as the third Level 2 text, and type **Thrust** as the fourth Level 2 text. Select these four words in the SmartArt Text Pane and then bold them.

5. Increase the size of the center circle of the SmartArt graphic to approximately 2.11" × 2.11". Select the SmartArt graphic and then center it horizontally and vertically on the slide. Move the airplane illustration to the center circle of the SmartArt graphic.

6. Tap or click the SmartArt graphic to select it and then apply the Cartoon 3-D style (the third style in the first 3-D row) to the graphic. Select the four gray arrow shapes and then change the color to Orange, Accent 5 (the ninth color in the first Theme Colors row).

7. If requested by your instructor, insert a text box on Slide 2 in the lower-left area of the slide and add the name of the first school you attended.

8. Apply the Airplane transition in the Exciting category to both slides and then change the duration to 3.50 seconds.

9. Save the presentation using the file name, Extend 4-1 Learn to Fly a Plane.

10. Submit the revised document in the format specified by your instructor.

11. ✳ In this assignment, you deleted much text on the first slide. You also moved title and text placeholders. How did these edits enhance the presentation?

Analyze, Correct, Improve

Analyze a presentation, correct all errors, and improve it.

Modifying a Table by Adding an Image, Inserting a Symbol, and Formatting

Note: To complete this assignment, you will be required to use the Data Files for Students. Visit www.cengage.com/ct/studentdownload for detailed instructions or contact your instructor for information about accessing the required files.

Instructions: Run PowerPoint. Open the presentation, Analyze 4-1 Hurricane, from the Data Files for Students. This presentation contains one slide and gives the wind speeds of the various categories of hurricanes. Modify the slide by making the indicated corrections and improvements.

1. Correct

a. Use Table 4–3 to add the missing data for Category 1 hurricanes.

Table 4–3 Hurricane Winds					
	Category 1	**Category 2**	**Category 3**	**Category 4**	**Category 5**
Wind Speeds	74–95 mph (119–153 km/h)	96–110 mph (154–177 km/h)	111–129 mph (178–208 km/h)	130–156 mph (209–251 km/h)	> 157 mph > 252 km/h
Damage	Some	Extreme	Devastating	Catastrophic	Catastrophic

© 2014 Cengage Learning

Continued >

Analyze, Correct, Improve *continued*

b. Adjust text font sizes and text font colors shown in the figure so they are the appropriate size and enhance the presentation.

c. Move the WordArt shown in Figure 4–83 to center it above the table and then change the text fill color to Orange, Accent 6 (the last color in the first Theme Colors row).

d. Correct the spelling errors shown in the figure.

e. If requested by your instructor, insert a text box in the upper-right corner of the slide and type the year you graduated from high school in the text box.

2. Improve

a. Add the image, Hurricane Winds, available on the Data Files for Students, in the upper-left cell of the table. Delete the image shown in the lower-right corner of the slide, as shown in Figure 4–83.

b. Change the transparency of the background picture on the slide to 30%.

c. In the Category 5 column, delete the words, Greater than, and then insert the greater than symbol (>) on both text lines.

d. Apply the Convex Cell Bevel effect (the third effect in the second Bevel row) to the table.

e. Change the transition from Shred to Wind and then change the duration to 3.50 seconds.

f. Save the presentation using the file name, Analyze 4-1 Hurricane Winds.

g. Submit the revised document in the format specified by your instructor.

3. ✸ Which errors existed in the starting file? How did changing the font sizes and colors and adding the image help the audience focus on the slide content?

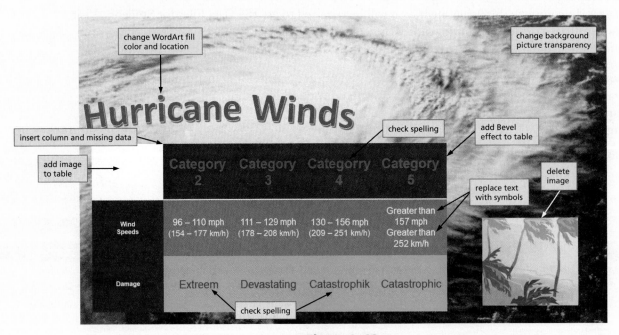

Figure 4–83

In the Labs

Design and/or create a presentation using the guidelines, concepts, and skills presented in this chapter. Labs 1 and 2, which increase in difficulty, require you to create solutions based on what you learned in the chapter; Lab 3 requires you to create a solution, which uses cloud and web technologies, by learning and investigating on your own from general guidance.

Lab 1: Inserting and Formatting SmartArt and Formatting a Table

Problem: Open the presentation, Lab 4-1 Wind Chill, from the Data Files for Students. You have an interest in meteorology and thought this topic would be appropriate for an informative speech assignment in your communication class. Create the slides shown in Figure 4–84.

(a) Slide 1

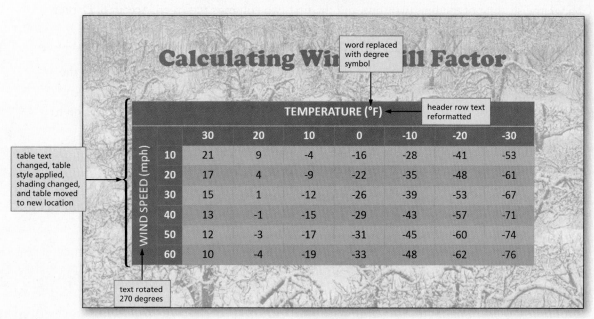

(b) Slide 2

Figure 4–84

Continued >

In the Labs *continued*

Note: To complete this assignment, you will be required to use the Data Files for Students. Visit www.cengage.com/ct/studentdownload for detailed instructions or contact your instructor for information about accessing the required files.

Instructions: Perform the following tasks:

1. On Slide 1, insert the Circular Picture Callout SmartArt graphic (the second graphic in the first Picture row), as shown in Figure 4–84a on the previous page.

2. In the SmartArt Text Pane, type **What to Wear Today?** as the top Level 1 text that will appear over the large circle on the left. Type **Wind Speed** as the second Level 1 text that will appear to the right of the first circle on the right, **Humidity** as the text for the middle circle, and **Air Temperature** for the third circle, as shown in the figure.

3. Insert the photo, Warm Clothes, from the Data Files for Students in the large circle on the left. Change the font color of the text in this circle to Black, Text 1, bold this text, and then move it to the location shown in the figure. In the three small circles, insert the pictures Windy, Humidity, and Air Temperature from the Data Files for Students, as shown in Figure 4–84a. Move the SmartArt graphic to the location shown on the slide.

4. Change the colors of the SmartArt graphic to Dark 1 Outline (the first color in the first Primary Theme Colors row). Apply the Cartoon style (the third style in the first 3-D row).

5. On Slide 2, change the font size of the table header text to 24 point, bold this text, and then center it in the header row, as shown in Figure 4–84b. Replace the word, Degrees, with the degree symbol.

6. For all cells other than the header row, change the font size to 22 point and then center all the text. Merge the cells in column 1, type **WIND SPEED (mph)** in the column, and then rotate all text 270°. Change the font size of this text to 24 point, change the font color to White, Background 1 (the first color in the first Theme Colors row), and then center it. Apply the Themed Style 1 – Accent 6 (the last style in the first Best Match for Document row) to the table. Change the font color of the first row under the header and the first two columns to White, Background 1 (the first color in the first Theme Colors row) and then bold this text. Change the shading of the first two rows and the first two columns to Green, Accent 6, Darker 25% (the last color in the fifth Theme Colors row).

7. Move the table to the location shown in the figure.

8. If requested by your instructor, add the name of your grade school after the header text in the table on Slide 2.

9. Apply the Fade transition in the Subtle category to both slides and then change the duration to 2.25 seconds.

10. Save the presentation using the file name, Lab 4-1 Wind Chill Factor.

11. Submit the document in the format specified by your instructor.

12. ✸ On Slide 1, you used the Circular Picture Callout SmartArt graphic. Why? Why did you select the style of the table on Slide 2?

Lab 2: Creating a Presentation with SmartArt and a Chart

Problem: You use your cell phone every day without a second thought about how it works. You use email at work and at home, you have a GPS in your car, and you watch television every evening. You decided to keep track for one week of how much you use these devices and depend on satellites. You thought it would be interesting to put the results of your study into a presentation shown in Figure 4–85 on the next page.

Note: To complete this assignment, you will be required to use the Data Files for Students. Visit www.cengage.com/ct/studentdownload for detailed instructions or contact your instructor for information about accessing the required files.

Instructions: Perform the following tasks:

1. Open the presentation, Lab 4-2 Satellites, from the Data Files for Students.

2. On Slide 1, insert the Bubble Picture List SmartArt graphic (the fourth graphic in the seventh Picture row). In the SmartArt Text Pane, insert the illustrations Satellite1, Satellite2, and Satellite3 from the Data Files for Students into the three picture boxes to the left of the Text area. Change the colors of the graphic to Gradient Loop – Accent 1 (the fourth color in the Accent 1 row) and then change the style to Flat Scene (the sixth style in the first 3-D row). Move the graphic to the upper-right area of the slide and resize it slightly, as shown in Figure 4–85a on the next page.

3. On Slide 2, insert the Hexagon Cluster SmartArt graphic (the third graphic in the seventh Picture row), as shown in Figure 4–85b on the next page. Tap or click the Add Shape button two times to add shapes to the graphic so that you have a total of ten shapes.

4. In the SmartArt Text Pane, insert the photo, Television, from the Data Files for Students in the first picture box and then type **Television** to the right of the photo. Insert the photo, Cell Phone, in the second picture box and then type **Cell Phone** to the right of the photo. Insert the photo, Email, in the third picture box and then type **Email** to the right of the photo. Insert the photo, Weather, in the fourth picture box and then type **Weather** to the right of the photo. Insert the photo, GPS, in the fifth picture box and then type **GPS** to the right of the photo.

5. Increase the size of the SmartArt graphic to approximately 7.42 × 10.99 and then move the graphic to the center of the slide, as shown in the figure. Change the colors of the SmartArt graphic to Gradient Range – Accent 1 (the third color in the Accent 1 row) and then change the style to Inset (the second style in the first 3-D row).

6. On Slide 3, insert a 3-D Pie chart (the second chart in the Pie area), as shown in Figure 4–85c on page PPT 267. Use the data in Table 4–4 to replace the sample data in the worksheet. Change the chart layout to Layout 1. Select the chart title text, Sales, and then press the DELETE key to delete this text.

Table 4–4 Personal Use	
Device	**Usage Amount**
Cell Phone	35%
Television	30%
GPS	10%
Weather	5%
Email	20%

© 2014 Cengage Learning

Continued >

In the Labs *continued*

(a) Slide 1

(b) Slide 2

Figure 4–85

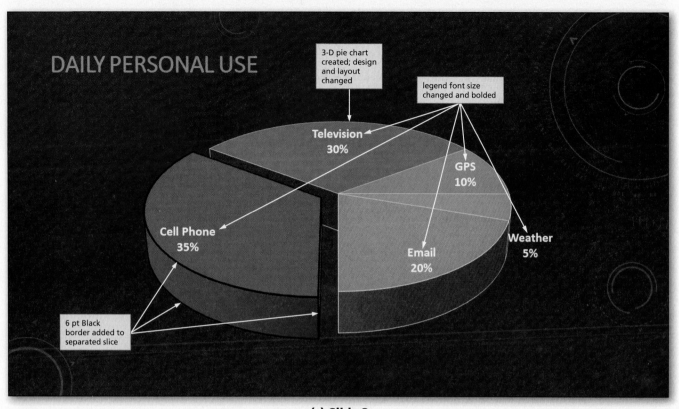

(c) Slide 3
Figure 4–85 (Continued)

7. Increase the legend font size to 18 point and then bold this text. Select the chart and rotate it approximately 180 degrees so that the pink slice is at the bottom-left of the chart, as shown in the figure. Separate the pink slice, which represents the average percentage of time you spend each day using your cell phone. Add a 6 pt border to this slice and then change the border color to Black, Background 1 (the first color in the first Theme Colors row).

8. Increase the size of the chart to 6.5" × 9.5" and then move it to the location shown on Slide 3.

9. If requested by your instructor, enter the name of the last TV program you watched as the second line of the subtitle on Slide 1.

10. Change the transition to Shape in the Subtle category to all slides. Change the duration to 3.00 seconds.

11. Save the presentation using the file name, Lab 4-2 Five Ways We Use Satellites.

12. Submit the revised document in the format specified by your instructor.

13. ✳ How did adding a SmartArt graphic without text to the title slide help the presentation?

Continued >

In the Labs *continued*

Lab 3: Expand Your World: Cloud and Web Technologies
Creating Charts and Graphs Using Websites

Problem: PowerPoint presents a wide variety of chart and table layouts, and you must decide which one is effective in presenting the relationships between data and indicating important trends. Several websites offer opportunities to create graphics that help explain concepts to your audience. Many of these websites are easy to use and allow you to save the chart or graph you create and then import it into your PowerPoint presentation.

Instructions:

1. Visit one of the following websites, or locate other websites that help you create a chart or graph: ChartGo (chartgo.com), Chartle (chartle.net), Rich Chart Live (richchartlive.com), Online Charts Builder (charts.hohli.com), or Lucidchart (lucidchart.com).

2. Create a chart using the same data you supplied for Slide 3 in the Backyard Birding presentation.

3. Save the new chart and then insert it into a new Slide 3 in the Backyard Birding presentation. Delete the original Slide 3 in the presentation.

4. If requested to do so by your instructor, add your grandmother's first name to the chart title.

5. Save the presentation using the file name, Lab 4-3 Alternate Backyard Birding.

6. Submit the assignment in the format specified by your instructor.

7. ✹ Which features do the websites offer that help you create charts and graphs? How does the graphic you created online compare to the chart you created using PowerPoint? How do the websites allow you to share your graphics using social networks?

✹ Consider This: Your Turn

Apply your creative thinking and problem-solving skills to design and implement a solution.

1. Design and Create a Presentation about Using Free Weights in Your Workouts
Personal

Part 1:   You have had a consistent and varied workout routine at your health club including yoga, cardio, and resistance training. One of your personal trainers suggested that you explore using free weights as part of your routine. Using free weights regularly can provide many benefits to your body, including improving muscle tone, increasing strength, improving balance, increasing energy level, and controlling weight. While machine-based exercises can be very effective, using free weights has the added benefits of doing more real-life movements and several different movements in one exercise. After doing some research about this topic, you decide to create a presentation to share with friends and, as suggested by your personal trainer, to present to others at your health club. Use the concepts and techniques presented in this chapter to prepare a presentation that explores this subject. Select a suitable theme and then use the data in Table 4–5 to create a pie chart showing how using free weights can benefit the body. The presentation can contain photos, illustrations, and videos. You can add your own digital photos or videos or photos from Office.com if they are appropriate for this topic. Apply chart styles and effects. Submit your assignment in the format specified by your instructor.

Table 4–5 Benefits of Using Free Weights	
Purpose	**Amount of Training**
Improve Muscle Tone	25%
Increase Strength	25%
Improve Balance	25%
Increase Energy	15%
Control Weight	10%

© 2014 Cengage Learning

Part 2: ☀ You made several decisions while creating the presentation in this assignment: where to place text, how to format the text (for example, font, font size, and font effects), which graphical image(s) to use, what chart styles and effects to apply, where to position the graphical images, how to format the graphical images, and which shapes to use to add interest to the presentation. What was the rationale behind each of these decisions? When you reviewed the document, what further revisions did you make and why? Where would you recommend showing this slide show?

2. Design and Create a Presentation about Parking at Your College
Professional

Part 1: You work part time in your campus safety office and are in charge of issuing parking permits each semester. You have gathered information on how many students, staff, and faculty need parking permits. Several parking spaces are available for campus visitors. Cars driven by students, faculty, and staff must be registered with your office. The parking decals are free and should be placed in plain view on the rear window. Drivers who change vehicles must register the new vehicle and receive a new decal. Three parking lots are available for students, two parking lots for faculty, and one lot for staff members. Because your campus has such a varied schedule, parking spaces are available at all times of the day. Use the concepts and techniques presented in this chapter to create a presentation describing the parking rules and lots. Select a suitable theme and use the data provided in Table 4–6 to create a table. Apply table styles and change colors where appropriate. The presentation can contain photos, illustrations, and videos. Add your own digital photos or videos or photos from Office.com if they are appropriate for this topic. Submit your assignment in the format specified by your instructor.

Table 4–6 Campus Parking Permits					
Semester	Five Day (M – F)	Seven Day (Sun. – Sat.)	Three Day (M-W-F)	Two Day (Tue. & Thurs.)	Handicap
Fall	575	850	648	482	50
Winter	525	780	635	450	40
Spring	635	880	750	535	58

© 2014 Cengage Learning

Part 2: ☀ You made several decisions while creating the presentation in this assignment: where to place text, how to format the text (such as font and font size), which graphical image(s) to use, which styles and effects to apply, where to position the graphical images, and which shapes to use to add interest to the presentation. What was the rationale behind each of these decisions? When you reviewed the document, what further revisions did you make and why? Where would you recommend showing this slide show?

Continued >

Consider This: Your Turn *continued*

3. Design and Create a Presentation about the Deepest Caves in the World
Research and Collaboration

Part 1: You enjoyed exploring caves, and some of your favorite family vacation memories are the times you and your family explored caves across the United States. You visited the Luchuguilla Cave in Carlsbad, New Mexico, several times. It is the deepest cave in the United States with the deepest part measuring 1,632 feet (497 meters). You and several of your friends who are also cavers are thinking about exploring caves outside of the United States. The deepest cave in the world, Krubera-Voronja, is in the western Caucasus mountains of the Georgian Republic; its depth has been recorded as 7,021 feet (2,140 meters). At least two other caves in that same country are among the top 10 deepest caves in the world. Your entire group would like to visit Georgia, a country nestled between Russia and Turkey on the Black Sea; however, you all agree that more research needs to be done before you make any definite plans. For your part of this prospective trip, you will research to locate the 10 deepest caves in the world. Two of your friends have experience planning travel and finding the best deals, so they will look into flights, hotels, and car rentals and learn about obtaining passports and other travel requirements. The remaining members of your group will research at the library or online to determine any restrictions for exploring these caves, if permits are needed, and if your group needs to schedule a specific time to explore the cave.

After using a variety of websites and books to gather information about traveling abroad to explore one of the world's deepest caves, you develop Table 4–7. Use this table to create a presentation using the concepts and techniques you learned in this chapter. Select a suitable theme, apply table styles, borders, and effects, and use at least three objectives found at the beginning of this chapter to develop the presentation. The Data Files for Students contains three photos called Caves1, Caves2, and Caves3, or you can use photos and illustrations from Office.com if they are appropriate for this topic.

Table 4–7 The World's Deepest Caves		
Cave	**Depth (ft)**	**Location (Country)**
Krubera-Voronja	7,021	Georgian Republic
Lamprechtsofen-Vogelshacht	5,354	Austria
Gouffre Mirolda	5,335	France
Reseau Jean Bernard	5,258	France
Torca del Cerro del Cuevon	5,210	Spain
Sarma	5,064	Georgian Republic
Shakta Vjacheslav Pantjukhina	4,948	Georgian Republic
Cehi 2	4,928	Slovenia
Sistema Cheve	4,870	Mexico
Sistema Huautla	4,840	Mexico

© 2014 Cengage Learning

Part 2: ☀ You made several decisions while creating the presentation in this assignment: where to place text, how to format the text (such as font, font size, and colors), which image(s) to use, what styles and effects to apply to a table, where to position the images, which styles to use, and which shapes to use to add interest to the presentation. What was the rationale behind each of these decisions? When you reviewed the document, what further revisions did you make and why? Where would you recommend showing this slide show?

Learn Online

Reinforce what you learned in this chapter with games, exercises, training, and many other online activities and resources.

Student Companion Site   Reinforcement activities and resources are available at no additional cost on www.cengagebrain.com. Visit www.cengage.com/ct/studentdownload for detailed instructions about accessing the resources available at the Student Companion Site.

 SAM   Put your skills into practice with SAM! If you have a SAM account, go to www.cengage.com/sam2013 to access SAM assignments for this chapter.

5 | Collaborating on and Delivering a Presentation

Microsoft product screenshots used with permission from Microsoft Corporation.

Objectives

You will have mastered the material in this chapter when you can:

- Combine PowerPoint files
- Accept and reject a reviewer's proposed changes
- Delete, reply to, and insert comments
- Reuse slides from an existing presentation
- Capture part of a slide using screen clipping
- Insert slide footer content

- Set slide size and presentation resolution
- Save files as a PowerPoint show
- Package a presentation for storage on a compact disc
- Save a presentation in a previous PowerPoint format
- Inspect and protect files
- Use presentation tools to navigate and annotate slide shows

5 | Collaborating on and Delivering a Presentation

Introduction

Often presentations are enhanced when individuals collaborate to fine-tune text, visuals, and design elements on the slides. A **review cycle** occurs when a slide show designer shares a file with multiple reviewers so they can make comments and changes to their copies of the slides and then return the file to the designer. A **comment** is a description that normally does not display as part of the slide show. It can be used to clarify information that may be difficult to understand, to pose questions, or to communicate suggestions. The designer then can display the comments, modify their content, and ask the reviewers to again review the presentation, and continue this process until the slides are satisfactory. Once the presentation is complete, the designer can protect the file so no one can open it without a password, remove comments and other information, and assure that slide content has not been altered. The designer also can save the presentation to a compact disc or as a PowerPoint show that will run without opening PowerPoint. In addition, a presenter can use PowerPoint's variety of tools to run the show effectively and emphasize various elements on the screen.

Project — Presentation with Comments, Inserted Slides, Protection, and Annotation

The seven slides in the Mayans presentation (Figure 5–1) give information and provide images of the San Gervasio ruins on the island of Cozumel, Mexico. All slides in the presentation were developed using versions of PowerPoint used prior to the current PowerPoint 2013. In these previous versions, the slides used a 4:3 width-to-height ratio, which was the proportion of standard monitors at that time. Today, however, most people use PowerPoint 2013's default 16:9 ratio, which is the proportion of most widescreen monitors and the default PowerPoint 2013 screen setting. You will change the slide size in your Mayans presentation after all the slides are created.

When you are developing a presentation, it often is advantageous to ask a variety of people to review your work in progress. These individuals can evaluate the wording, art, and design, and experts in the subject can check the slides for accuracy. They can add comments to the slides in specific areas, such as a paragraph, a graphic, or a table. You then can review their comments and use them to modify and enhance your work. You also can insert slides from other presentations into your presentation.

Once you develop the final set of slides, you can complete the file by removing any comments and personal information, adding a password so that unauthorized people cannot see the file contents without your permission, saving the file as a PowerPoint show so it runs automatically when you open a file, and saving the file to a compact disc.

When running your presentation, you may decide to show the slides nonsequentially. For example, you may need to review a slide you discussed already, or you may want to skip some slide and jump forward. You also may want to emphasize, or **annotate**, material on the slides by highlighting text or writing on the slides. You can save your annotations to review during or after the presentation.

Photo courtesy of Susan Sebok

theme changed to Trek

EXPLORE MAYAN RUINS

subtitle text from reviewer

WordArt from reviewer

San Gervasio: A cultural, spiritual, and political center

(a) Slide 1 (Title Slide Enhanced from Reviewer)

footer text → ← date added

SITE DEDICATED TO THE GODDESS IXCHEL

SmartArt graphic created by reviewer

Largest Mayan ruin site on Cozumel

Occupied from 300 A.D. to 16th century

Island's governmental and religious center

screen clipping from another presentation

MEXICO

slide number

(b) Slide 2 (SmartArt from Reviewer)

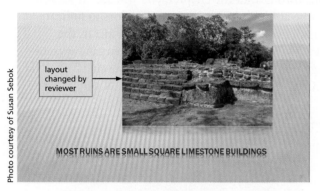

Photo courtesy of Susan Sebok

layout changed by reviewer

MOST RUINS ARE SMALL SQUARE LIMESTONE BUILDINGS

(c) Slide 3 (Enhanced from Reviewer)

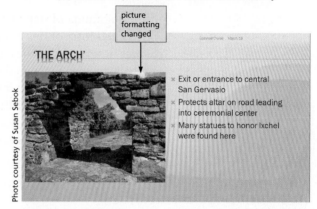

picture formatting changed

Photo courtesy of Susan Sebok

'THE ARCH'

× Exit or entrance to central San Gervasio
× Protects altar on road leading into ceremonial center
× Many statues to honor Ixchel were found here

(d) Slide 4 (Reused from Existing Presentation)

Photo courtesy of Susan Sebok

original theme retained

(e) Slide 5 (Reused from Existing Presentation)

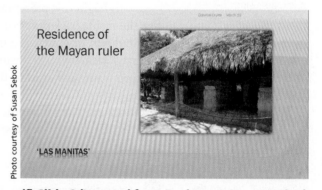

Photo courtesy of Susan Sebok

Residence of the Mayan ruler

'LAS MANITAS'

(f) Slide 6 (Inserted from Reviewer's Presentation)

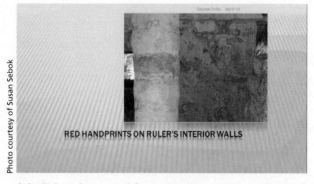

Photo courtesy of Susan Sebok

RED HANDPRINTS ON RULER'S INTERIOR WALLS

(g) Slide 7 (Inserted from Reviewer's Presentation)

Figure 5–1

Roadmap

In this chapter, you will learn how to create the slides shown in Figure 5–1 on the previous page. The following roadmap identifies general activities you will perform as you progress through this chapter:

1. COLLABORATE on a presentation by using comments.
2. SET SLIDE SIZE and SLIDE SHOW RESOLUTION.
3. SAVE and PACKAGE a PRESENTATION.
4. PROTECT and SECURE a PRESENTATION.
5. USE PRESENTATION TOOLS to navigate and annotate slides during a presentation.

At the beginning of step instructions throughout the chapter, you will see an abbreviated form of this roadmap. The abbreviated roadmap uses colors to indicate chapter progress: gray means the chapter is beyond that activity; blue means the task being shown is covered in that activity, and black means that activity is yet to be covered. For example, the following abbreviated roadmap indicates the chapter would be showing a task in the 4 PROTECT & SECURE PRESENTATION activity.

1 COLLABORATE | 2 SET SLIDE SIZE & SLIDE SHOW RESOLUTION | 3 SAVE & PACKAGE PRESENTATION
4 PROTECT & SECURE PRESENTATION | 5 USE PRESENTATION TOOLS

Use the abbreviated roadmap as a progress guide while you read or step through the instructions in this chapter.

To Run PowerPoint and Open and Save a Presentation

To begin this presentation, you will open a file from the Data Files for Students. See the inside back cover of this book for instructions on downloading the Data Files for Students, or contact your instructor for more information about accessing the required files. If you are using a computer to step through the project in this chapter and you want your screens to match the figures in this book, you should change your screen's resolution to 1366 × 768. For information about how to change a computer's resolution, refer to the Office and Windows chapter at the beginning of this book.

The following steps start PowerPoint and display formatting marks.

1 Run PowerPoint. If necessary, maximize the PowerPoint window.

2 Open the presentation, Mayans, located on the Data Files for Students.

3 Save the presentation using the file name, Mayans Final.

One of the few differences between Windows 7 and Windows 8 occurs in the steps to run PowerPoint. If you are using Windows 7, click the Start button, type **PowerPoint** in the 'Search programs and files' box, click PowerPoint 2013, and then, if necessary, maximize the PowerPoint window. For a summary of the steps to run PowerPoint in Windows 7, refer to the Quick Reference located at the back of this book.

CONSIDER THIS

What are some tips for collaborating successfully?

Working with your classmates can yield numerous benefits. Your peers can assist in brainstorming, developing key ideas, revising your project, and keeping you on track so that your presentation meets the assignment goals.

The first step when collaborating with peers is to define success. What, ultimately, is the goal? For example, are you developing a persuasive presentation to school administrators in an effort to fund a new club? Next, you can set short-term and long-term goals that help lead you to completing the project successfully. These goals can be weekly tasks to accomplish, such as interviewing content experts, conducting online research, or compiling an annotated bibliography. After that, you can develop a plan to finish the project by outlining subtasks that each member must accomplish. Each collaborator should inform the group members when the task is complete or if problems are delaying progress. When collaborators meet, whether in person or online, they should establish an agenda and have one member keep notes of topics discussed.

Collaborating on a Presentation

PowerPoint provides several methods to collaborate with friends or coworkers who can view your slide show and then provide feedback. When you **collaborate**, you work together on a document with other PowerPoint users who are cooperating jointly and assisting willingly with the endeavor. You can distribute your slide show physically to others by exchanging a compact disc or a flash drive. You also can share your presentation through the Internet by sending the file as an email attachment or saving the file to a storage location, such as Windows Live SkyDrive or a Microsoft Office SharePoint server.

In the following pages, you will follow these general steps to collaborate with Doug Cantlen, who has reviewed your Mayans presentation:

1. Combine (merge) presentations.
2. Print slides and comments.
3. Review and accept or reject changes.
4. Reply to a comment.
5. Insert a comment.
6. Delete a comment.

BTW
Q&As
For a complete list of the Q&As found in many of the step-by-step sequences in this book, visit the Q&A resource on the Student Companion Site located on www.cengagebrain.com. For detailed instructions about accessing available resources, visit www.cengage.com/ct/studentdownload or see the inside back cover of this book.

To Merge a Presentation

1 COLLABORATE | 2 SET SLIDE SIZE & SLIDE SHOW RESOLUTION | 3 SAVE & PACKAGE PRESENTATION
4 PROTECT & SECURE PRESENTATION | 5 USE PRESENTATION TOOLS

Why? *Doug Cantlen reviewed your Mayans presentation and made several comments, so you want to combine (merge) his changes with your file to see if they improve the original design and slide content.* Doug's changes to the initial presentation include converting the Slide 1 title text to WordArt and the Slide 2 bulleted list to a SmartArt graphic. A transition is added to all slides, the theme is changed, paragraphs are edited, and two slides are added. The following steps merge this reviewer's file with your Mayans Final presentation.

1

• With the Mayans Final presentation active, display the REVIEW tab (Figure 5–2).

Q&A Why do the slides have a different size than the slides I have seen in previous presentations?
The slides in the Mayans presentation use a 4:3 ratio, which was the default setting in PowerPoint versions prior to PowerPoint 2013.

Figure 5–2

- Tap or click the Compare button (REVIEW tab | Compare group) to display the Choose File to Merge with Current Presentation dialog box.

- With the list of files and folders on your USB flash drive displaying, tap or click Mayans - Doug to select the file name (Figure 5–3).

Figure 5–3

Photo courtesy of Susan Sebok

- Tap or click the Merge button (Choose File to Merge with Current Presentation dialog box) to merge Doug Cantlen's presentation with the Mayans presentation and to display the Comments pane and the Revisions pane (Figure 5–4).

Q&A How do I display the Comments pane if it does not display automatically?
Tap or click the Show Comments button (REVIEW tab | Comments group) or the COMMENTS button on the status bar to display or hide the Comments pane.

How do I display the Revisions pane if it does not display automatically?
Tap or click the Reviewing Pane button (REVIEW tab | Compare group) to display the Revisions pane.

Figure 5–4

Photo courtesy of Susan Sebok

- Tap or click the NOTES button on the status bar to hide the Notes pane.

Q&A If several reviewers have made comments and suggestions, can I merge their files, too?
Yes. Repeat Steps 1, 2, and 3. Each reviewer's initials display in a color-coded comment box.

To Print Comments

You can print each slide and the comments a reviewer has made before you begin to accept and reject each suggestion. *Why? As owner of the original presentation, you want to review the comments and modifications on a hard copy before making decisions about whether to accept these suggestions.* PowerPoint can print these slides and comments on individual pages. The following steps print the slides with comments.

- Open the Backstage view and then tap or click the Print tab to display the Print gallery.

- Tap or click 'Full Page Slides' in the Print gallery to display print layouts.

- If necessary, tap or click 'Print Comments and Ink Markup' to place a check mark by this option and turn on printing comment pages (Figure 5–5).

Q&A | If I want to print only the slides and not the comments, would I tap or click 'Print Comments and Ink Markup' to remove the check mark?
Yes. Tapping or clicking the command turns on and turns off printing the notes pages.

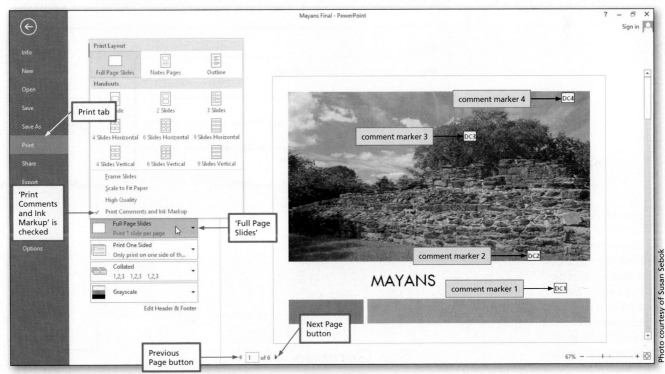

Figure 5–5

Photo courtesy of Susan Sebok

BTW

BTWs
For a complete list of the BTWs found in the margins of this book, visit the BTW resource on the Student Companion Site located on www.cengagebrain.com. For detailed instructions about accessing available resources, visit www.cengage.com/ct/studentdownload or see the inside back cover of this book.

2

- Tap or click the Next Page and Previous Page buttons to scroll through the previews of the three slides and the three comment pages.

- Tap or click the Print button to print the six pages (Figure 5–6).

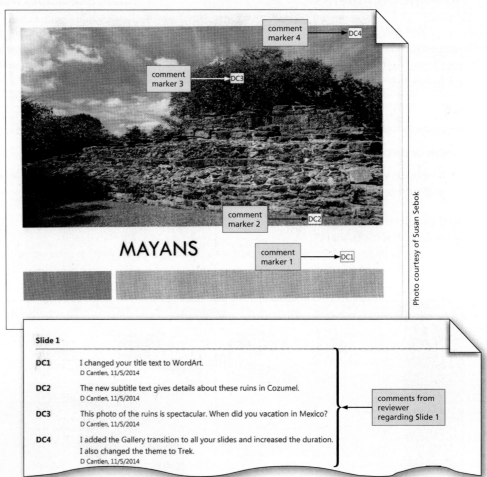

(a) Page 1 (Title Slide)

Photo courtesy of Susan Sebok

Slide 1

DC1	I changed your title text to WordArt. D Cantlen, 11/5/2014
DC2	The new subtitle text gives details about these ruins in Cozumel. D Cantlen, 11/5/2014
DC3	This photo of the ruins is spectacular. When did you vacation in Mexico? D Cantlen, 11/5/2014
DC4	I added the Gallery transition to all your slides and increased the duration. I also changed the theme to Trek. D Cantlen, 11/5/2014

comments from reviewer regarding Slide 1

(b) Page 2 (Comments from reviewer)

If you are using your finger on a touch screen and are having difficulty completing the steps in this chapter, consider using a stylus. Many people find it easier to be precise with a stylus than with a finger. In addition, with a stylus you see the pointer. If you still are having trouble completing the steps with a stylus, try using a mouse.

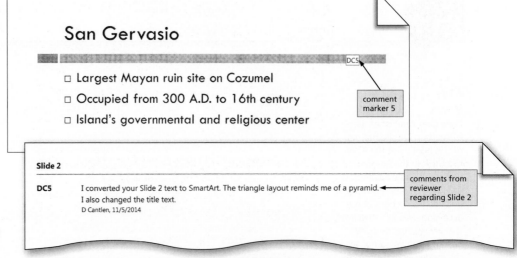

San Gervasio

DC5

☐ Largest Mayan ruin site on Cozumel

☐ Occupied from 300 A.D. to 16th century

☐ Island's governmental and religious center

comment marker 5

(c) Page 3 (Slide 2)

Slide 2

DC5	I converted your Slide 2 text to SmartArt. The triangle layout reminds me of a pyramid. I also changed the title text. D Cantlen, 11/5/2014

comments from reviewer regarding Slide 2

(d) Page 4 (Comments from reviewer)

Figure 5–6

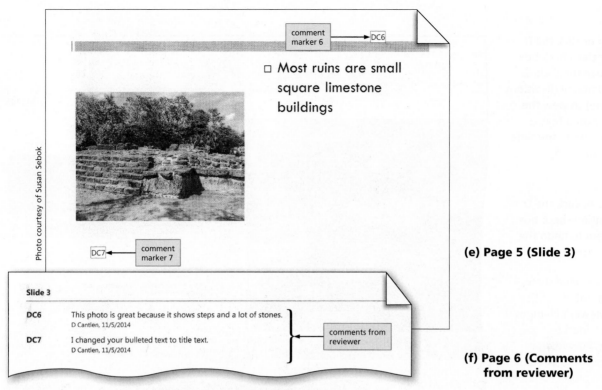

(e) Page 5 (Slide 3)

(f) Page 6 (Comments from reviewer)

Figure 5–6 (Continued)

Other Ways

1. Press CTRL+P, tap or click 'Full Page Slides' in the Print gallery, tap or click 'Print Comments and Ink Markup', tap or click Print button

To Preview the Presentation Changes

1 COLLABORATE | 2 SET SLIDE SIZE & SLIDE SHOW RESOLUTION | 3 SAVE & PACKAGE PRESENTATION
4 PROTECT & SECURE PRESENTATION | 5 USE PRESENTATION TOOLS

The reviewer made several changes to the overall presentation and then edited your three slides. You can preview his modifications to obtain an overview of his suggestions. *Why? Seeing his edits now can help you decide later whether to accept or reject each change as you step through each revision.* The changes that apply to the entire presentation are displayed in the Presentation Changes section of the Revisions pane, and changes to each individual slide are displayed in the Slide Changes section of this pane. Vertical rectangular icons indicate change markers, and horizontal rectangular icons represent comment markers. Each reviewer's revisions are color-coded. The following steps preview the merged presentation.

1

- If necessary, display the REVIEW tab. With Slide 1 displaying, tap or click the SLIDES tab in the Revisions pane to display a thumbnail of merged Slide 1 (Figure 5–7).

Figure 5–7

- Tap or click the D Cantlen check box above the Slide 1 thumbnail (Revisions pane) to view the proposed text changes in the slide (Figure 5–8).

- Tap or click the D Cantlen check box again to undo the changes.

Q&A Can I make some, but not all, of the reviewer's changes on Slide 1?
Yes. PowerPoint allows you to view each proposed change individually and then either accept or reject the modification.

Figure 5–8

How do I accept and evaluate criticism positively?

Receiving feedback from others ultimately should enhance your presentation. If several of your reviewers make similar comments, such as too much text appears on one slide or that a chart would help present your concept, then you should heed their criticism and modify your slides. Criticism from a variety of people, particularly if they are from different cultures or vary in age, gives a wide range of viewpoints. Some reviewers might focus on the font size, others on color and design choices, while others might single out the overall message. These individuals should evaluate and comment on your work, such as saying that the overall presentation is good or that a particular paragraph is confusing, and then give specific information of what elements are effective or how you can edit the paragraph.

When you receive these comments, do not get defensive. Ask yourself why your reviewers would have made these comments. Perhaps they lack a background in the subject matter. Or they may have a particular interest in this topic and can add their expertise.

To Review, Accept, and Reject Presentation Changes

1 COLLABORATE | 2 SET SLIDE SIZE & SLIDE SHOW RESOLUTION | 3 SAVE & PACKAGE PRESENTATION
4 PROTECT & SECURE PRESENTATION | 5 USE PRESENTATION TOOLS

Changes that affect the entire presentation are indicated in the Presentation Changes section of the Revisions pane. These changes can include transitions, color schemes, fonts, and backgrounds. They also can include slide insertions. Doug inserted three slides in his review; two have identical text and different photos of the Mayan ruler's dwelling, Las Manitas. After inserting these slides in the presentation, you can view each slide and then delete, or reject, a slide insertion. The following steps display and accept the reviewer's three slides and then delete one of the inserted slides. *Why? You want to see all the slides and then evaluate how they add value to the presentation. Two of the slides have similar photos of the Mayan ruler's dwelling, and you want to use the slide showing the exterior of the building instead of the interior.*

1

- Tap or click the DETAILS tab in the Revisions pane.

- Tap or click the first presentation change marker, Theme (1 - 3), in the Presentation Changes section of the Revisions pane to display the Theme box with an explanation of the proposed change for all slides in the presentation (Figure 5–9).

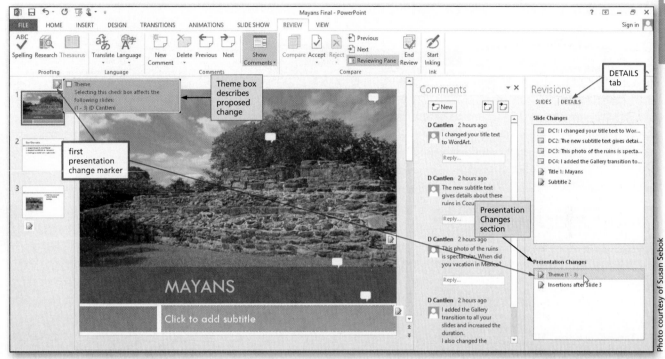

Figure 5–9

2

- Tap or click the Theme check box to view the new Trek theme on all slides (Figure 5–10).

Figure 5–10

Q&A

Can I also apply the change by tapping or clicking the Accept Change button (REVIEW tab | Compare group)?
Yes. Either method applies the Trek theme.

If I decide to not apply the new theme, can I reverse this change?
Yes. Tap or click the Reject Change button (REVIEW tab | Compare group) or tap or click the check box to remove the check and reject the reviewer's theme modification.

- Tap or click the second presentation change marker, Insertions after Slide 3, in the Presentation Changes section to display an insertion box with a list of the three proposed new slides to insert into the presentation, two with the title text, 'Las Manitas' and one with the title text, 'Red handprints on Ruler's interior walls' (Figure 5–11).

Q&A What is the significance of the check boxes in the insertion box?

You can tap or click the first check box to insert all three slides in your presentation. You can elect to insert one or two slides by tapping or clicking the check mark to the left of each slide title.

Figure 5–11

- Tap or click the 'All slides inserted at this position' check box to insert the three new slides (Figure 5–12).

Q&A Why do check marks appear in the Slide 4, 5, and 6 thumbnails in the Thumbnail pane and in the Presentation Changes section?

The check marks indicate you have applied the proposed change.

Figure 5–12

5

- Display Slide 4 and review the slide contents. Then, display Slide 5 and compare the photo on this slide to the photo on Slide 4.

- Display Slide 4 again and then read the comment Doug made about Slides 4 and 5 (Figure 5–13).

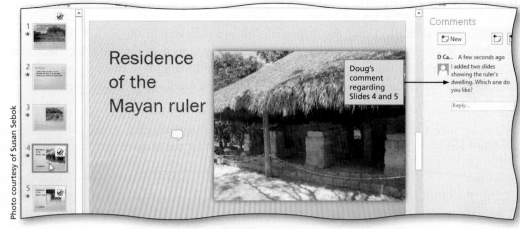

Figure 5–13

6

- Display Slide 5 and then tap or click the change marker on the Slide 5 thumbnail to display the insertion box (Figure 5–14).

Figure 5–14

7

- Tap or click the 'Inserted "'Las Manitas'"' check box to clear this check box and delete Slide 5 from the presentation (Figure 5–15).

Q&A If I decide to insert the original Slide 5, how can I perform this task?
Tap or click the change marker above the current Slide 5 to insert the slide you deleted.

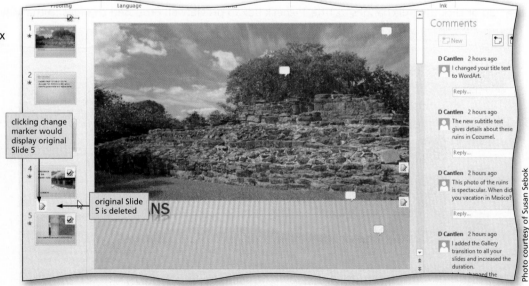

Figure 5–15

Other Ways

1. Tap or click Next Change or Previous Change buttons (REVIEW tab | Compare group), tap or click Accept Change button or Reject Change button

To Review, Accept, and Reject Slide Changes

Changes that affect only the displayed slide are indicated in the Slide Changes section of the DETAILS tab on the Revisions pane. A reviewer can modify many aspects of the slide, such as adding and deleting pictures and clips, editing text, and moving placeholders. The following steps display and accept the reviewer's revisions to Slide 1. *Why? You agree with the changes Doug suggested because they enhance your slides.*

1
- Display Slide 1 and then tap or click the slide change, 'Title 1: Mayans,' in the Slide Changes section to display the Title 1 box with Doug Cantlen's four proposed changes for the Mayans text in the rectangle (Figure 5–16).

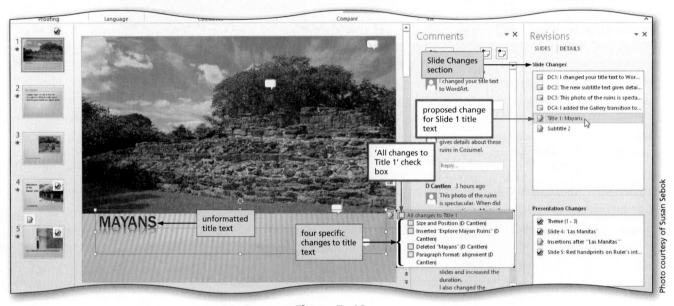

Figure 5–16

2
- Tap or click the 'All changes to Title 1' check box to preview all proposed changes to the Mayans text (Figure 5–17).

Figure 5–17

- Tap or click to uncheck the 'Paragraph format: alignment' check box to preview only the other changes to the title text, not the centered alignment (Figure 5–18).

Figure 5–18

Q&A Can I select any combination of the check boxes to modify the text in the rectangle?
Yes. You can tap or click the individual check boxes to preview the reviewer's modifications.

- Tap or click the slide change, Subtitle 2, in the Slide Changes section to display the insertion box showing the changes to the Slide 2 subtitle.

- Tap or click the 'All changes to Subtitle 2' check box to view the proposed changes (Figure 5–19).

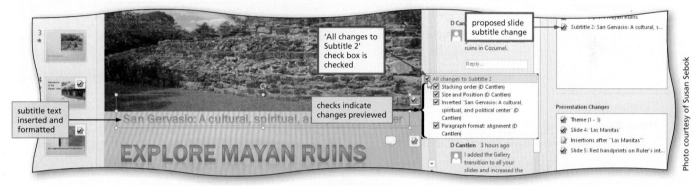

Figure 5–19

Other Ways

1. Tap or click Next Change or Previous Change buttons (REVIEW tab | Compare group), tap or click Accept Change button or Reject Change button

To Review Comments

1 COLLABORATE | 2 SET SLIDE SIZE & SLIDE SHOW RESOLUTION | 3 SAVE & PACKAGE PRESENTATION
4 PROTECT & SECURE PRESENTATION | 5 USE PRESENTATION TOOLS

Why? *You want to look at each comment before deciding to accept or reject the changes.* The Comments pane displays the reviewer's name above each comment, and an associated comment marker is displayed on the slide and in the Slide Changes section of the Revisions pane. The following steps review comments for Slide 1.

- Tap or click the DC1 comment in the Slide Changes section to select the comment and the associated comment marker on the slide (Figure 5–20).

Q&A Why does the number 1 display after the commenter's initials in the Slide Changes section of the Revisions pane?
The number indicates it is the first comment the reviewer inserted.

Figure 5–20

2

- Read the comment and then tap or click the Next button in the Comments pane to select the second comment and the associated comment marker on the slide (Figure 5–21).

Q&A | Can I tap or click the buttons on the REVIEW tab instead of the buttons in the Comments pane? Yes. Either method allows you to review comments.

3

- Tap or click the Next button to review the third comment and tap or click it again to review the fourth comment.

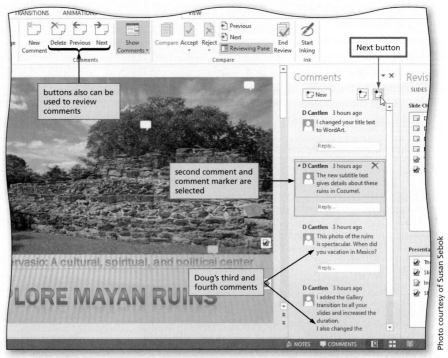

Figure 5–21

Other Ways
1. Tap or click Next button or Previous button (REVIEW tab | Comments group)

To Reply to a Comment

1 COLLABORATE \| 2 SET SLIDE SIZE & SLIDE SHOW RESOLUTION \| 3 SAVE & PACKAGE PRESENTATION
4 PROTECT & SECURE PRESENTATION \| 5 USE PRESENTATION TOOLS

Doug asked a question in his third comment. One method of responding is by replying to the comment he made. You want to provide feedback to him by responding to his query. **Why?** *Giving feedback helps the reviewer realize his efforts in improving the presentation were useful and encourages him to continue to participate in collaboration efforts.* The following steps reply to a comment on Slide 1.

1

- With Slide 1 displaying, select the third comment.

- Tap or click the Reply box to place the insertion point in the Reply box (Figure 5–22).

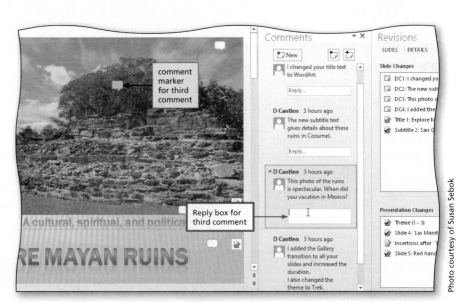

Figure 5–22

2

- Type I went to Mexico during Spring Break this past year. My cruise ship stopped in Cozumel, and I visited San Gervasio one afternoon. in the Reply box and then press the ENTER key (Figure 5–23).

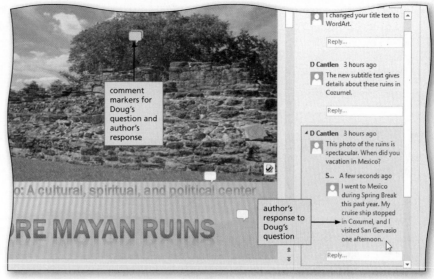

Photo courtesy of Susan Sebok

Figure 5–23

To Insert a Comment

1 COLLABORATE | 2 SET SLIDE SIZE & SLIDE SHOW RESOLUTION | 3 SAVE & PACKAGE PRESENTATION
4 PROTECT & SECURE PRESENTATION | 5 USE PRESENTATION TOOLS

Doug Cantlen's comments and changes greatly enhanced your slide show, and you would like to send him a copy of the revised presentation. *Why? He will be able to see what modifications you accepted. You also want to insert a comment to him on Slide 1 to thank him for taking the time to review your original slides.* The following steps insert a comment on Slide 1.

1

- With Slide 1 displaying, tap or click the Insert Comment button, which has the label New (Comments pane), to open a comment box in the Comments pane (Figure 5–24).

Q&A Why does my name differ from that shown in the figure, which is Stephanie?

The name reflects the information that was entered when Microsoft Office 2013 was installed on your computer.

Q&A Why is my comment box displayed at the top of the Comments pane?

Depending upon your computer, PowerPoint will display the new box either at the beginning or the end of the list of comments in the Comments pane.

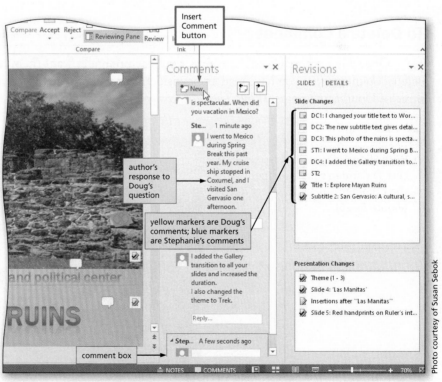

Photo courtesy of Susan Sebok

Figure 5–24

2

- Tap or click the comment box, type `I really appreciate the work you did to enhance my slides, Doug. Your comments and modifications are great.` in the box, and then press the ENTER key (Figure 5–25).

Q&A Can I move the comment on the slide?

Yes. Select the comment icon on the slide and then drag it to another location on the slide.

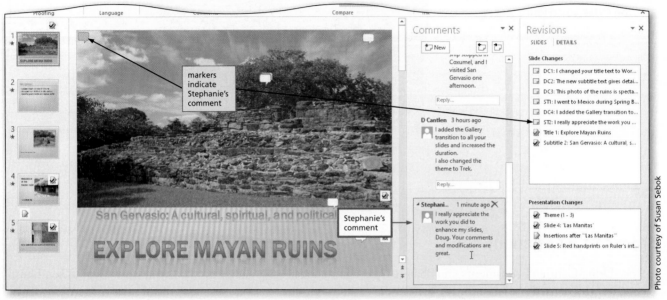

Figure 5–25

To Delete a Comment

Once you have reviewed comments, you may no longer want them to be a part of your slides. You can delete comments that you have read and considered as you are preparing your slides. The following steps delete three of Doug's comments. *Why? They are not necessary now because you have incorporated the changes into your initial presentation.*

1

- With Slide 1 displaying, tap or click D Cantlen's first comment in the Comments pane to select it (Figure 5–26).

Figure 5–26

2

- Tap or click the Delete button (Comments pane) to delete Doug's first comment and to select the new first comment, which previously was the second comment in the list (Figure 5–27).

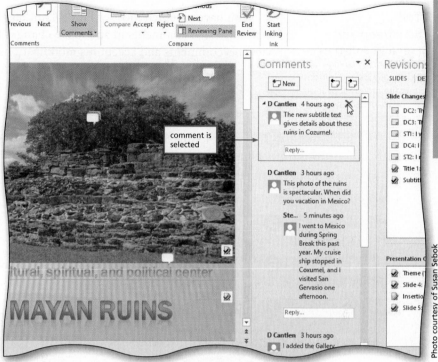

Figure 5–27

Photo courtesy of Susan Sebok

3

- Delete the selected comment about the new subtitle.

- Skip the next comment.

- Select the last D Cantlen comment and then delete this comment (Figure 5–28).

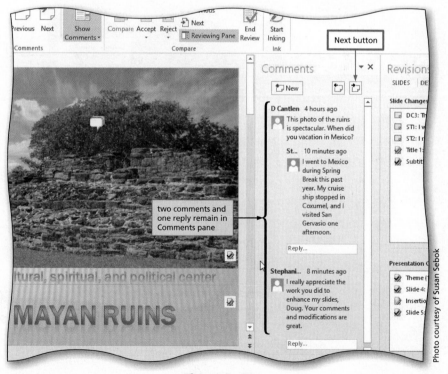

Figure 5–28

Photo courtesy of Susan Sebok

Other Ways

1. Tap or click Delete Comment button (REVIEW tab | Comments group)

To Review and Accept Slide Changes on the Remaining Slides

BTW

The Ribbon and Screen Resolution
PowerPoint may change how the groups and buttons within the groups appear on the ribbon, depending on the computer's screen resolution. Thus, your ribbon may look different from the ones in this book if you are using a screen resolution other than 1366 × 768.

You have accepted most of Doug Cantlen's presentation and Slide 1 changes. He also inserted comments in and made changes to other slides. The following steps review his comments and accept his modifications.

1 Tap or click the Next button (Comments pane) several times until Slide 2 displays.

2 Read the comment labeled DC5 and then delete this comment.

3 Tap or click the SLIDES tab in the Revisions pane to show a thumbnail of Slide 2 in the Revisions pane.

4 Tap or click the check box above the Slide 2 thumbnail (Revisions pane) to display a preview of the Slide 2 revisions.

5 Tap or click the Next button (Comments pane) to display Slide 3. Read and then delete the two comments on this slide.

6 Tap or click the check box above the Slide 3 thumbnail (Revisions pane) to display a preview of the Slide 3 revisions.

7 Tap or click the Next button (Comments pane) to display Slide 4. Read the comment and then type `I chose Slide 4 because it shows the exterior of the building.` as a reply.

8 Tap or click the Next button to display Slide 5 (Figure 5–29).

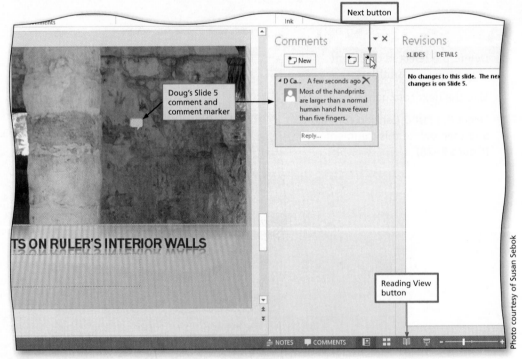

Figure 5–29

To Run the Revised Presentation in Reading View

1 COLLABORATE | 2 SET SLIDE SIZE & SLIDE SHOW RESOLUTION | 3 SAVE & PACKAGE PRESENTATION
4 PROTECT & SECURE PRESENTATION | 5 USE PRESENTATION TOOLS

Doug's changes modified the original presentation substantially, so it is a good idea to review the new presentation. The following steps review the slides in Reading view. *Why? This view helps you see large images of the slides so you can evaluate their content without needing to start Slide Show view.*

1

- Display Slide 1 and then tap or click the Reading View button on the status bar to display Slide 1 in this view (Figure 5–30).

2

- Tap or click the Next and Previous buttons to review the changes on each slide.

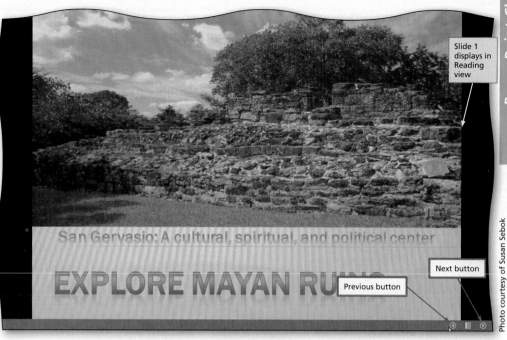

Figure 5–30

Photo courtesy of Susan Sebok

Other Ways

1. Tap or click Reading View button in Presentation Views group on VIEW tab

How should I give constructive criticism when I am reviewing a presentation?
If you are asked to critique a presentation, begin and end with positive comments. Give specific details about a few key areas that can be improved. Be honest, but be tactful. Avoid using the word, you. For example, instead of writing, "You need to give some statistics to support your viewpoint," write "I had difficulty understanding which departments' sales have declined in the past five months. Perhaps a chart with specific losses would help depict how dramatically revenues have fallen."

To End the Review and Hide Markup

1 COLLABORATE | 2 SET SLIDE SIZE & SLIDE SHOW RESOLUTION | 3 SAVE & PACKAGE PRESENTATION
4 PROTECT & SECURE PRESENTATION | 5 USE PRESENTATION TOOLS

You have analyzed all of the reviewer's proposed changes and replied to some of his questions. Your review of the merged presentation is complete, so you can accept and apply all the changes and then close the Comments and Revisions panes. You also can hide the comments that are present on Slide 1. *Why? You do not need to see the comments when you are developing the remainder of the presentation, so you can hide them.* The following steps end the review of the merged slides, close the Comments pane, and hide the comment markers.

1

- Tap or click the End Review button (REVIEW tab | Compare group) to display the Microsoft PowerPoint dialog box (Figure 5–31).

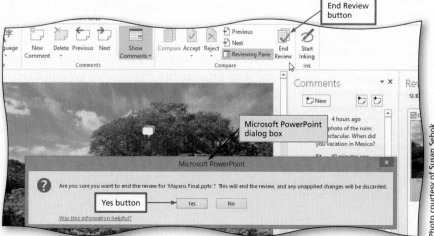

Photo courtesy of Susan Sebok

Figure 5–31

● Tap or click the Yes button (Microsoft PowerPoint dialog box) to apply the changes you accepted and discard the changes you rejected.

Q&A **Which changes are discarded?** You did not apply the centered title text on Slide 1 and did not insert Doug's proposed Slide 5.

● Tap or click the Show Comments arrow (REVIEW tab | Comments group) to display the Show Comments menu (Figure 5–32).

Figure 5–32

● Tap or click Comments Pane in the menu to close the Comments pane.

Q&A **Can I also close the Comments pane by tapping or clicking the Close button in that pane?** Yes.

● Tap or click the Show Comments arrow to display the Show Comments menu again (Figure 5–33).

Figure 5–33

● Tap or click Show Markup in the menu to hide comments on the slide.

SharePoint Servers

In a business environment, PowerPoint presentations can be stored on a centrally located Slide Library that resides on a server running Office SharePoint Server. These slide shows can be shared, reused, and accessed by many individuals who then can copy materials into their individual presentations. The Slide Library functions in much the same manner as your community library, for the SharePoint Server time stamps when an individual has borrowed a particular slide or presentation and then time stamps the slide or presentation when it is returned. If a particular slide in the Library has been updated, anyone who has borrowed that slide is notified that the content has changed. In this manner, people creating PowerPoint presentations can track the changes to presentations, locate the latest versions of slides, and check for slide updates.

Reusing Slides from an Existing Presentation

Occasionally you may want to insert a slide from another presentation into your presentation. PowerPoint offers two methods of obtaining these slides. One way is to open the second presentation and then copy and paste the desired slides. The second method is to use the Reuse Slides pane to view and then select the desired slides.

The PowerPoint presentation with the file name, Arch, has colorful pictures and useful text. It contains three slides, and you would like to insert two of these slides, shown in Figure 5–34, into your Mayans Final presentation. You would also like to use a part of one of the Arch slides in Slide 2 of your presentation.

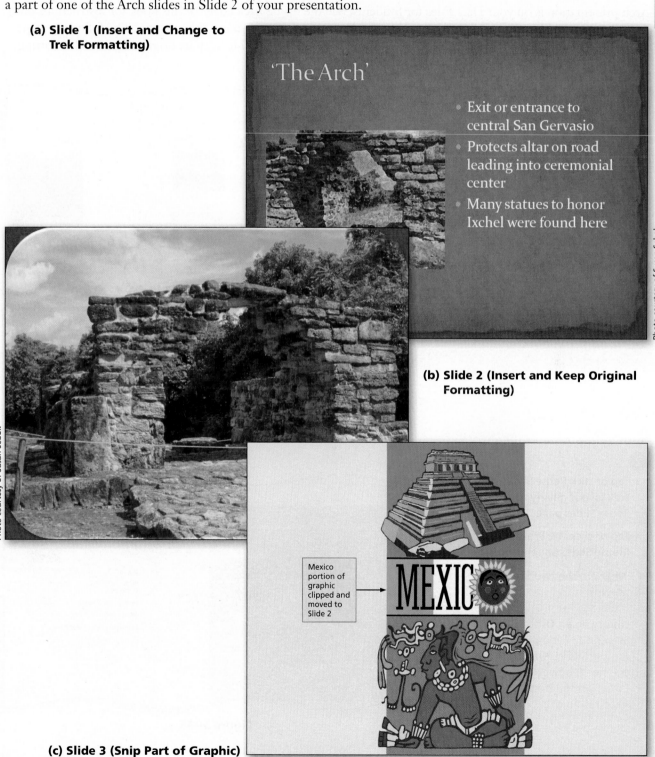

(a) Slide 1 (Insert and Change to Trek Formatting)

'The Arch'

- Exit or entrance to central San Gervasio
- Protects altar on road leading into ceremonial center
- Many statues to honor Ixchel were found here

Photo courtesy of Susan Sebok

Photo courtesy of Susan Sebok

(b) Slide 2 (Insert and Keep Original Formatting)

Mexico portion of graphic clipped and moved to Slide 2 →

MEXICO

(c) Slide 3 (Snip Part of Graphic)

Figure 5–34

To Reuse Slides from an Existing Presentation

You want to insert two slides from the Arch presentation in the Mayans Final presentation directly after Slide 3. PowerPoint converts inserted slides to the theme and styles of the current presentation, so the inserted slides will inherit the styles of the current Trek theme and Mayans Final presentation. However, you want the second slide to keep the source formatting of the Arch presentation, which uses the Paper theme. *Why?* *The Paper theme has a weathered look and reinforces the concept that the ruins are centuries old.* You also will need to add the Gallery transition to the second slide because you are not applying the Mayans Final formatting. The Arch presentation is on your Data Files for Students. See the inside back cover of this book for instructions on downloading the Data Files for Students, or contact your instructor for more information. The following steps add these two slides to your presentation, and specify that the second slide keep its original (source) formatting.

- Display Slide 3 and then display the HOME tab.

- Tap or click the New Slide arrow (Slides group) to display the Trek layout gallery (Figure 5–35).

Figure 5–35

- Tap or click Reuse Slides in the Trek layout gallery to display the Reuse Slides pane.

- Tap or click the Browse button (Reuse Slides pane) (Figure 5–36).

Q&A What are the two Browse options shown?

If the desired slides are in a Slide Library on an Office SharePoint Server, then you would tap or click Browse Slide Library. The slides you need, however, are on your Data Files for Students, so you need to tap or click Browse File.

Figure 5–36

3

- Tap or click Browse File to display the Browse dialog box.

- If necessary, navigate to the location of your Data Files for Students and then tap or click Arch to select the file (Figure 5–37).

Figure 5–37

4

- Tap or click the Open button (Browse dialog box) to display thumbnails of the three Arch slides in the Reuse Slides pane (Figure 5–38).

5

- Tap or click the 'The Arch' thumbnail to insert this slide into the Mayans Final presentation after Slide 3.

Q&A Can I insert all the slides in the presentation in one step instead of selecting each one individually? Yes. Press and hold or right-click any thumbnail and then tap or click Insert All Slides.

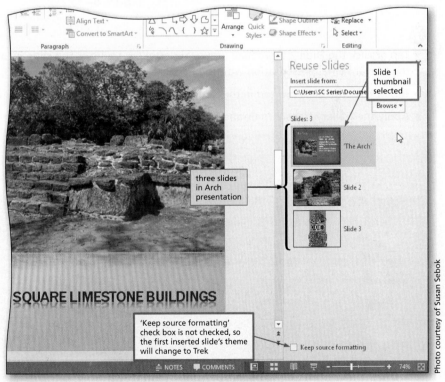

Figure 5–38

Photo courtesy of Susan Sebok

6

- Tap or click the 'Keep source formatting' check box at the bottom of the Reuse Slides pane to preserve the Arch presentation formatting with the Paper theme for the next slide that you will insert (Figure 5–39).

Q&A What would happen if I did not check this box?
PowerPoint would change the formatting to the characteristics found in the Trek theme.

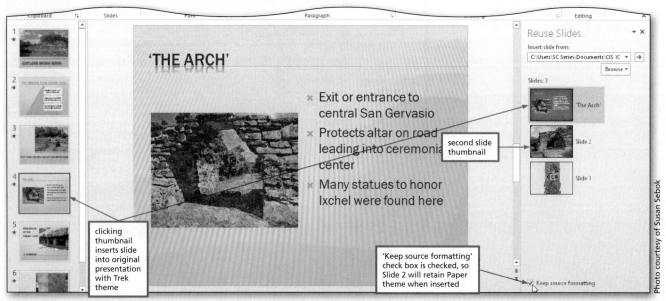

Figure 5–39

7

- Tap or click the Slide 2 thumbnail (Reuse Slides pane) to insert this slide into the presentation as the new Slide 5 in the Mayans Final presentation with the Paper theme retained (Figure 5–40).

- Tap or click the Close button in the Reuse Slides pane so that it no longer is displayed.

- Apply the Gallery transition (in the Exciting category) to Slide 5 and change the duration to 3.00.

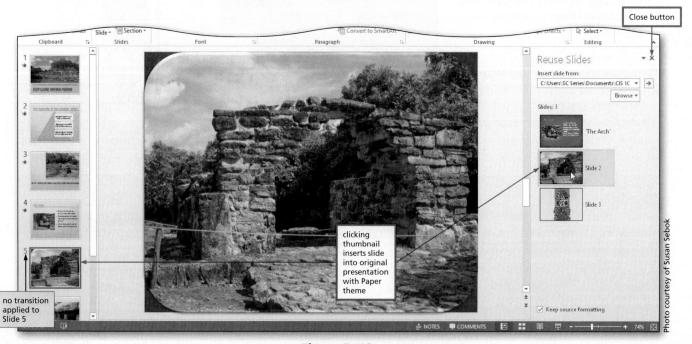

Figure 5–40

To Capture Part of a Screen Using Screen Clipping

At times you may be developing a presentation and need a portion of a clip or picture in another presentation. You can capture, or **snip**, part of an object on a slide in another presentation that is open. PowerPoint refers to this presentation as being available. The following steps snip part of an image on Slide 3 of the Arch presentation and paste it on Slide 2 in the Mayans Final presentation. *Why? This portion of the graphic has the word, Mexico, and you desire to place this snip on the Slide 2 triangle to reinforce the location of the Mayan ruins.*

- Open the Arch presentation from your Data Files for Students. Display Slide 3 of the Arch presentation.

- Display Slide 2 of the Mayans Final presentation.

- Display the INSERT tab and then tap or click the Screenshot button (INSERT tab | Images group) to display the Available Windows gallery (Figure 5–41).

Figure 5–41

- Tap or click Screen Clipping (Available Windows gallery) to display Slide 3 of the Arch presentation.

- When the white overlay displays on Slide 3, move the pointer to the upper-left point of the Mexico rectangle.

- Drag downward and to the right to select the Mexico rectangle (Figure 5–42).

Figure 5–42

- If you are using a mouse, release the mouse button.

- When the snip displays on Slide 2 of the Mayans Final presentation, drag the snip to the lower-left corner of the triangle (Figure 5–43).

Figure 5–43

Adding a Footer

Slides can contain information at the top or bottom. The area at the top of a slide is called a **header**, and the area at the bottom is called a **footer**. In general, footer content displays along the lower edge of a slide, but the theme determines where these elements are placed. As a default, no information is displayed in the header or footer. You can choose to apply only a header, only a footer, or both a header and footer. In addition, you can elect to have the header or footer display on single slides, all slides, or all slides except the title slide.

Slide numbers are one footer element. They help a presenter organize a talk. While few audience members are cognizant of this aspect of a slide, the presenter can glance at the number and know which slide contains particular information. If an audience member asks a question pertaining to information contained on a slide that had been displayed previously or is on a slide that has not been viewed yet, the presenter can jump to that slide in an effort to answer the question. In addition, the slide number helps pace the slide show. For example, a speaker could have the presentation timed so that Slide 4 is displaying three minutes into the talk.

PowerPoint gives the option of displaying the current date and time obtained from the system or a fixed date and time that you specify. In addition, you can add relevant information, such as your name, your school or business name, or the purpose of your presentation in the Footer area.

To Add a Footer with Fixed Information

1 COLLABORATE | 2 SET SLIDE SIZE & SLIDE SHOW RESOLUTION | 3 SAVE & PACKAGE PRESENTATION
4 PROTECT & SECURE PRESENTATION | 5 USE PRESENTATION TOOLS

To reinforce the fact that you visited ruins during a cruise to Cozumel in March, you can add this information in the Footer area. You also can add a slide number. The following steps add this text to all slides in the presentation except the title slide. *Why? In general, the footer text should not display on the title slide. In addition, the title slide has a large photo that extends to the top of the slide, so you do not want the footer text to overlap this content.*

1

- Display the INSERT tab.

- Tap or click the Header & Footer button (INSERT tab | Text group) to display the Header and Footer dialog box.

- If necessary, tap or click the Slide tab to display the Slide sheet (Figure 5–44).

Q&A Can I use this dialog box to add a header?

The slide theme determines the location of the placeholders at the top or bottom of the slide. The footer elements generally are displayed along the lower edge of the slide. Some themes, however, have the footer elements along the top edge, so they are considered header text.

Figure 5–44

2

- Tap or click 'Date and time' to select this check box.

- Tap or click Fixed to select this option. Type **March 19** in the Fixed box.

- Tap or click Slide number to select this check box.

- Tap or click Footer to select this check box.

- Type **Cozumel Cruise** in the Footer box.

- Tap or click the 'Don't show on title slide' check box to select the box (Figure 5–45).

Figure 5–45

Q&A What are the black boxes in the Preview section?

The black box in the top placeholder indicates where the footer text and fixed date will appear on the slide; the black box in the bottom placeholder indicates where the page number will appear.

What if I want the current date and time to appear?

Tap or click Update automatically in the 'Date and time' section.

3

- Tap or click the Apply to All button to display the date, footer text, and slide number on all slides except Slide 1.

Q&A When would I tap or click the Apply button instead of the Apply to All button?

Tap or click the Apply button when you want the header and footer information to appear only on the slide currently selected.

To Clear Formatting

1 COLLABORATE | 2 SET SLIDE SIZE & SLIDE SHOW RESOLUTION | 3 SAVE & PACKAGE PRESENTATION
4 PROTECT & SECURE PRESENTATION | 5 USE PRESENTATION TOOLS

PowerPoint provides myriad options to enhance pictures. You can, for example, format the images by recoloring, changing the color saturation and tone, adding artistic effects, and altering the picture style. After adding various effects, you may desire to reset the picture to its original state. *Why? The arch picture on Slide 4 has several formatting adjustments that obscure the photo, and now you want to see the original unformatted picture.* The following steps remove all formatting applied to the arch picture on Slide 4.

1
- Display Slide 4, select the arch picture, and then display the PICTURE TOOLS FORMAT tab (Figure 5–46).

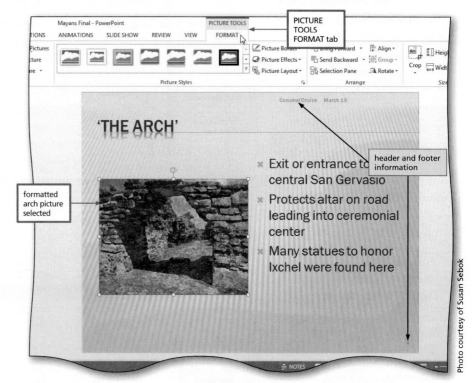

Figure 5–46

2
- Tap or click the Reset Picture button (FORMAT tab| Adjust group) to remove all formatting from the picture (Figure 5–47).

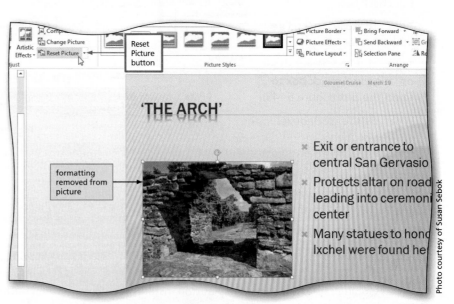

Figure 5–47

Other Ways

1. Press and hold or right-click picture, tap or click Format Picture, tap or click Picture icon (Format Picture pane), tap or click PICTURE CORRECTIONS, tap or click Reset

Break Point: If you wish to take a break, this is a good place to do so. Be sure to save the Mayans Final file again and then you can exit PowerPoint. To resume at a later time, start PowerPoint, open the file called Mayans Final, and continue following the steps from this location forward.

Changing Slide Size and Slide Show Resolution

Today's technology presents several options you should consider when developing your presentation. The on-screen show ratio determines the height and width proportions. The screen resolution affects the slides' clarity.

To Set Slide Size

1 COLLABORATE | 2 SET SLIDE SIZE & SLIDE SHOW RESOLUTION | 3 SAVE & PACKAGE PRESENTATION
4 PROTECT & SECURE PRESENTATION | 5 USE PRESENTATION TOOLS

Prior to PowerPoint 2013, PowerPoint set slides in a 4:3 size ratio, which is the proportion found on a standard monitor that is not widescreen. If you know your presentation will be viewed on a widescreen or you are using a widescreen display, you can change the slide size to optimize the proportions. The following steps change the default setting to 16:9 and then adjust the bulleted paragraphs on Slides 4 and 6. *Why? This 16:9 dimension is the proportion of most widescreen displays. When the slide width is changed, some of the words in the paragraphs are not spaced evenly. A good design principle is to keep all words in a prepositional phrase together on one line.*

- With Slide 4 displaying, display the DESIGN tab and then tap or click the Slide Size button (DESIGN tab | Customize group) to display the Slide Size gallery (Figure 5–48).

Figure 5–48

- Tap or click Widescreen (16:9) to change the slide size setting.

- On Slide 4, place the insertion point immediately before the word, San, in the first bulleted paragraph and then press SHIFT+ENTER to insert a line break.

- Place the insertion point immediately before the word, into, in the second bulleted paragraph and then press SHIFT+ENTER to insert a line break.

- Place the insertion point immediately before the word, were, in the third bulleted paragraph and then press SHIFT+ENTER to insert a line break.

Q&A | How do I adjust the second line in the bulleted paragraph if a space is displaying at the beginning of the line?
Delete the space at the beginning of the second line.

4

- Adjust the size of the Slide 4 photo so that it is approximately 4.88" × 6.5" and move it to the location shown in Figure 5–49.

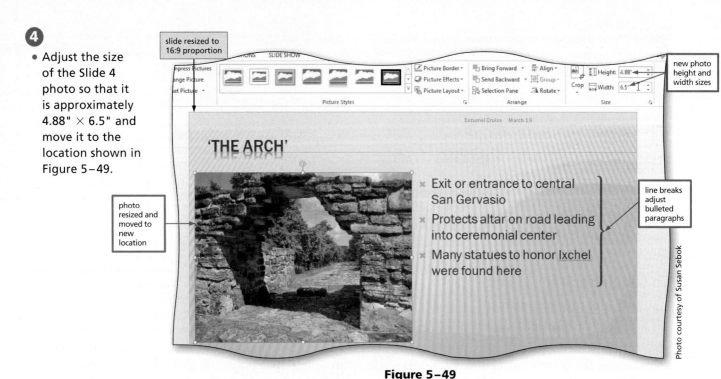

Figure 5–49

Photo courtesy of Susan Sebok

To Set Presentation Resolution

1 COLLABORATE | 2 SET SLIDE SIZE & SLIDE SHOW RESOLUTION | 3 SAVE & PACKAGE PRESENTATION
4 PROTECT & SECURE PRESENTATION | 5 USE PRESENTATION TOOLS

Screen, or presentation, resolution affects the number of pixels that are displayed on your screen. When screen resolution is increased, more information is displayed, but it is decreased in size. Conversely, when screen resolution is decreased, less information is displayed, but that information is increased in size. Throughout this book, the screen resolution has been set to 1366 × 768. The following steps change the presentation resolution to 800 × 600. *Why? You may need to run your presentation on a monitor that has a different resolution.*

1

- Display the SLIDE SHOW tab and then tap or click the 'Set Up Slide Show' button (SLIDE SHOW tab | Set Up group) to display the Set Up Show dialog box.

2

- If necessary, tap or click the Slide show monitor arrow in the Multiple monitors section and then choose Primary Monitor.

- Tap or click the Resolution arrow in the Multiple monitors section to display the Resolution list (Figure 5–50).

Photo courtesy of Susan Sebok

Figure 5–50

3

- Tap or click 800 × 600 to change the slide show resolution setting.

- If necessary, click the 'Use Presenter View' check box to clear the check box (Figure 5–51).

What is Presenter view?
When you use Presenter view, you control the slide show using one screen only you can see, but your audience views the slides on another main screen.

4

- Tap or click the OK button to close the Set Up Show dialog box and apply the new resolution to the slides.

Figure 5–51

Photo courtesy of Susan Sebok

Saving and Packaging a Presentation

PowerPoint 2013, PowerPoint 2010, and PowerPoint 2007 save files, by default, as a PowerPoint Presentation with a .pptx file extension. You can, however, select other file types that allow other computer users to view your slides if they do not have one of the newer PowerPoint versions installed. You also can save the file as a PowerPoint show so that it runs automatically when opened and does not require the user to have the PowerPoint program. Another option is to save one slide as an image that can be inserted into another program, such as Microsoft Word, or emailed.

If your computer has compact disc (CD) or digital video disc (DVD) burning hardware, the Package for CD option will copy a PowerPoint presentation and linked files onto a CD or DVD. Two types of CDs or DVDs can be used: recordable (CD-R or DVD-R) and rewritable (CD-RW or DVD-RW). You must copy all the desired files in a single operation if you use PowerPoint for this task because you cannot add any more files after the first set is copied. If, however, you want to add more files to the CD or DVD, you can use Windows Explorer to copy additional files. If you are using a CD-RW or DVD-RW with existing content, these files will be overwritten.

The **PowerPoint Viewer** is included when you package your presentation so you can show the presentation on another computer that has Microsoft Windows but does not have PowerPoint installed. The **PowerPoint Viewer** also allows users to view presentations created with PowerPoint 2003, 2000, and 97.

BTW
Considering Reviewers' Technology Limitations
People who receive copies of your presentation to review may not be able to open a PowerPoint 2013 file saved in the default .pptx format because they have a previous version of this software or may not have Internet access available readily. For these reasons, you need to know their software and hardware limitations and distribute your file or handouts accordingly.

To Save a File as a PowerPoint Show

Why? *To simplify giving a presentation in front of an audience, you may want your slide show to start running without having to start PowerPoint, open a file, and then tap or click the Slide Show button.* When you save a presentation as a **PowerPoint show (.ppsx)**, it automatically begins running when opened. The following steps save the Mayans Final file as a PowerPoint show.

- Open the Backstage view, display the Export tab, and then tap or click 'Change File Type' to display the Change File Type section.

- Tap or click PowerPoint Show in the Presentation File Types section (Figure 5–52).

Figure 5–52

- Tap or click the Save As button to display the Save As dialog box.

- Type **Mayans Final Show** in the File name box (Figure 5–53).

- Tap or click the Save button to close the Save As dialog box.

- Close both the current Mayans Final Show and Arch presentations.

Q&A Why do I want to close both presentations instead of using the current Mayans Final Show file? It is best to use the more current version of the presentation to complete the remaining tasks in this chapter. You no longer need the Arch presentation because you have inserted the slides and the screen clip.

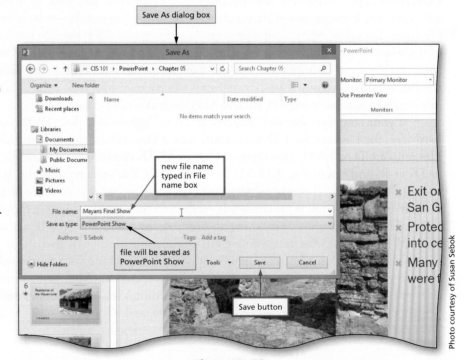

Photo courtesy of Susan Sebok

Figure 5–53

Other Ways

1. Tap or click FILE on ribbon, tap or click Save As in Backstage view, tap or click Browse button to locate save location, tap or click 'Save as type' arrow, select PowerPoint Show, tap or click Save button

To Save a Slide as an Image

To create visually interesting slides, you insert pictures, clips, and video files into your presentation. Conversely, you may want to insert a PowerPoint slide into another document, such as a file you created in Microsoft Word. *Why? A slide may have information that you want to share with an audience and include with other material that is not part of the PowerPoint presentation. You can save one slide as an image and then insert this file into another document.* The following steps save Slide 2 as a JPEG File Interchange Format image.

- Open the Mayans Final presentation from your Data Files for Students and then display Slide 2.

- Open the Backstage view, display the Export tab, and then tap or click 'Change File Type' to display the Change File Type section.

- Tap or click 'JPEG File Interchange Format' in the Image File Types section (Figure 5–54).

Figure 5–54

- Tap or click the Save As button to display the Save As dialog box.

- Type **Mayans SmartArt** in the File name box (Figure 5–55).

Figure 5–55

- Tap or click the Save button (Save As dialog box) to display the Microsoft PowerPoint dialog box (Figure 5–56).

- Tap or click the 'Just This One' button to save only Slide 2 as a file in JPEG (.jpg) format.

Figure 5–56

Other Ways

1. Tap or click FILE on ribbon, tap or click Save As in Backstage view, tap or click Browse button to locate save location, tap or click 'Save as type' arrow, select JPEG File Interchange Format, tap or click Save button

To Package a Presentation for Storage on a Compact Disc

1 COLLABORATE | 2 SET SLIDE SIZE & SLIDE SHOW RESOLUTION | **3 SAVE & PACKAGE PRESENTATION**
4 PROTECT & SECURE PRESENTATION | 5 USE PRESENTATION TOOLS

The Package for CD option will copy a PowerPoint presentation and linked files onto a CD or DVD. The following steps show how to save a presentation and related files to a CD or DVD using the Package for CD feature. **Why?** *The Package for CD dialog box allows you to select the presentation files to copy, linking and embedding options, and passwords to open and modify the files.*

- Insert a CD-RW or DVD-RW or a blank CD-R or DVD-R into your CD or DVD drive.
- Open the Backstage view, display the Export tab, and then tap or click 'Package Presentation for CD' (Figure 5–57).

Figure 5–57

- Tap or click the 'Package for CD' button in the Package Presentation for CD section to display the Package for CD dialog box.
- Delete the text in the 'Name the CD' box and then type **Mayans** in the box (Figure 5–58).

Q&A What if I want to add more files to the CD?
Tap or click the Add button and then locate the files you want to add to the CD.

Figure 5–58

- Tap or click the 'Copy to CD' button to begin packaging the presentation files and to display the Microsoft PowerPoint dialog box (Figure 5–59).

Q&A When would I copy the files to a folder instead of a CD?

If you want to copy your presentation to a network or to a storage medium other than a CD or DVD, click the 'Copy to Folder' button, enter a folder name and location, and then click the OK button.

Figure 5–59

- Tap or click the No button (Microsoft PowerPoint dialog box) to not include linked files and to display another Microsoft PowerPoint dialog box (Figure 5–60).

- Tap or click the Continue button (Microsoft PowerPoint dialog box) to continue copying the presentation to a CD without the comments added to the slides.

- When the files have been written, tap or click the No button (Microsoft PowerPoint dialog box) to not copy the files to another CD.

- Tap or click the Close button (Package for CD dialog box) to finish saving the presentation to a CD.

Figure 5–60

To View a PowerPoint Show Using the PowerPoint Viewer

When you arrive at a remote location, you will run the packaged presentation. The following steps explain how to run the presentation using the PowerPoint Viewer.

1 Insert your CD in the CD drive.

2 Accept the licensing agreement for the PowerPoint Viewer to open and run the slide show.

To Save a Presentation in a Previous PowerPoint Format

Prior to Microsoft Office 2007, PowerPoint saved presentations, by default, as a .ppt file type. The earlier versions of PowerPoint cannot open the .pptx type that PowerPoint 2013, 2010, and 2007 creates by default. The Microsoft website has updates and converters for users of these earlier versions of the program and also for other Microsoft Office software. The Microsoft Office Compatibility Pack for Word, Excel, and PowerPoint will open, edit, and save Office 2013, 2010, and 2007 documents. The following steps save the Mayans Final file as PowerPoint 97-2003 Presentation. *Why? You cannot assume that people who obtain a .pptx file from you have installed the Compatibility Pack, so to diminish frustration and confusion you can save a presentation as a .ppt type that will open with earlier versions of PowerPoint.*

- Open the Backstage view, display the Export tab, and then tap or click 'Change File Type'.

- Tap or click 'PowerPoint 97-2003 Presentation' in the Presentation File Types section (Figure 5–61).

Figure 5–61

- Tap or click the Save As button to display the Save As dialog box.

- Type **Mayans Final Previous Version** in the File name box (Figure 5–62).

- Tap or click the Save button (Save As dialog box) to save the Mayans Final presentation as a .ppt type and display the Microsoft PowerPoint Compatibility Checker.

Q&A Why does this Compatibility Checker dialog box display? PowerPoint is alerting you that the older file version will not keep some of the features used in the presentation. You will learn more about the Compatibility Checker in the next section of this chapter.

Figure 5–62

● Tap or click the Continue button (Microsoft PowerPoint Compatibility Checker) to continue to save the presentation.

5

● Close the current PowerPoint file and then open the Mayans Final presentation from your USB flash drive.

Q&A Why do I want to open this presentation instead of using the current file?
The current file is saved in a previous version of PowerPoint, so some features are not available when you run the final version of the slide show. It is best to use the more current version of the presentation to complete the remaining tasks in this chapter.

Other Ways

1. Tap or click FILE on ribbon, tap or click Save As in Backstage view, tap or click Browse button to locate save location, tap or click 'Save as type' arrow, select 'PowerPoint 97-2003 Presentation', tap or click Save button

---

Protecting and Securing a Presentation

When your slides are complete, you can perform additional functions to finalize the file and prepare it for distributing to other users or running on a computer other than the one used to develop the file. For example, the Compatibility Checker reviews the file for any feature that will not work properly or display on computers running a previous PowerPoint version. In addition, the Document Inspector locates inappropriate information, such as comments, in a file and allows you to delete these slide elements. You also can set passwords so only authorized people can distribute, view, or modify your slides. When the review process is complete, you can indicate this file is the final version.

To Identify Presentation Features Not Supported by Previous Versions

1 COLLABORATE | 2 SET SLIDE SIZE & SLIDE SHOW RESOLUTION | 3 SAVE & PACKAGE PRESENTATION
4 PROTECT & SECURE PRESENTATION | **5 USE PRESENTATION TOOLS**

PowerPoint 2013 has many new features not found in some previous versions of PowerPoint, especially versions older than PowerPoint 2007. For example, WordArt formatted with Quick Styles is an enhancement found only in PowerPoint 2013, 2010, and 2007. If you give your file to people who have a previous PowerPoint version installed on their computers, they will be able to open the file but may not be able to see or edit some special features and effects. The following steps run the Compatibility Checker. *Why? You can use the* **Compatibility Checker** *to see which presentation elements will not function in earlier versions of PowerPoint and display a summary of the elements in your Mayans Final presentation that will be lost if your file is opened in some earlier PowerPoint versions.*

1

● Open the Backstage view and then tap or click the 'Check for Issues' button in the Info tab to display the Check for Issues menu (Figure 5–63).

Figure 5–63

- Tap or click Check Compatibility to display the Microsoft PowerPoint Compatibility Checker dialog box.

- View the comments in the Summary section regarding the four features that are not supported by earlier versions of PowerPoint (Figure 5–64).

Q&A Why do the numbers 7, 1, 17, and 2 display in the Occurrences column in the right side of the Summary section?
The numbers indicate the number of times incompatible elements, such as the SmartArt graphic, appear in the presentation.

What happens if I tap or click the Help links in the Summary section?
PowerPoint will provide additional information about the particular incompatible slide element.

Figure 5–64

- Tap or click the OK button (Microsoft PowerPoint Compatibility Checker dialog box) to close the dialog box and return to the presentation.

To Remove Inappropriate Information

1 COLLABORATE | 2 SET SLIDE SIZE & SLIDE SHOW RESOLUTION | 3 SAVE & PACKAGE PRESENTATION
4 PROTECT & SECURE PRESENTATION | **5 USE PRESENTATION TOOLS**

As you work on your presentation, you might add information meant only for you to see. For example, you might write comments to yourself or put confidential information in the Notes pane. You would not want other people to access this information if you give a copy of the presentation file to them. You also added a comment and replied to Doug Cantlen's questions, and you may not want anyone other than him to view this information. The Document Inspector provides a quick and efficient method of searching for and deleting inappropriate information.

It is a good idea to make a duplicate copy of your file and then inspect this new second copy. *Why? If you tell the Document Inspector to delete content, such as personal information, comments, invisible slide content, or notes, and then decide you need to see those slide elements, quite possibly you will be unable to retrieve the information by using the Undo command.* The following steps save a duplicate copy of your Mayans Final presentation, run the Document Inspector on this new file, and then delete comments.

- Open the Backstage view, tap or click the Save As tab, and then tap or click the Browse button to open the Save As dialog box.

- Type **Mayans Final Duplicate** in the File name box.

- Tap or click the Save button to change the file name and save another copy of this presentation.

- Open the Backstage view and then tap or click the 'Check for Issues' button to display the Check for Issues menu (Figure 5–65).

Figure 5–65

3

- Tap or click Inspect Document to display the Document Inspector dialog box (Figure 5–66).

Q&A What information does the Document Inspector check? This information includes text in the Document Information Panel, such as your name and company. Other information includes details of when the file was last saved, objects formatted as invisible, graphics and text you dragged off a slide, presentation notes, and email headers.

Figure 5–66

4

- Tap or click the Inspect button to check the document and display the inspection results (Figure 5–67).

Figure 5–67

5

• Tap or click the Remove All button
in the Comments and Annotations
section of the inspection results to
remove the comments from the
presentation (Figure 5–68).

Q&A

Should I also remove the
document properties and personal
information?
You might want to delete this
information so that no identifying
information, such as your name,
is saved.

6

• Tap or click the Close button
(Document Inspector dialog box)
to close the dialog box.

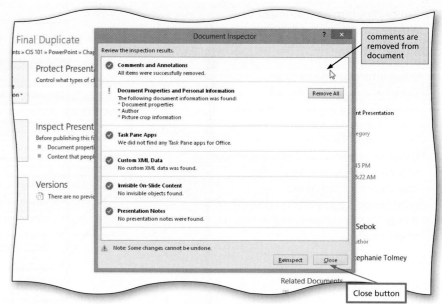

Figure 5–68

What types of passwords are best for security?
A password should be at least six characters and contain a combination of letters and numbers. Using both uppercase and
lowercase letters is advised. Do not use a password that someone could guess, such as your first or last name, spouse's or
child's name, telephone number, birth date, street address, license plate number, or Social Security number.

Once you develop this password, write it down in a secure place. Underneath your keyboard is not a secure place, nor is your
middle desk drawer.

To Set a Password

1 COLLABORATE | 2 SET SLIDE SIZE & SLIDE SHOW RESOLUTION | 3 SAVE & PACKAGE PRESENTATION
4 PROTECT & SECURE PRESENTATION | 5 USE PRESENTATION TOOLS

Why? *You can protect your slide content by using a password.* You can prohibit a user from modifying a file
without entering the password. The following steps set a password for the Mayans Final Duplicate file.

1

• With Backstage view open and
the Info tab displaying, tap or
click the Protect Presentation
button to display the Protect
Presentation menu (Figure 5–69).

Figure 5–69

- Tap or click 'Encrypt with Password' to display the Encrypt Document dialog box.

- Type **Mayan2Ruin** in the Password box (Figure 5–70).

Figure 5–70

- Tap or click the OK button to display the Confirm Password dialog box.

- Type **Mayan2Ruin** in the Reenter password box (Figure 5–71).

Q&A What if I forget my password?
You will not be able to open your file. For security reasons, Microsoft or other companies cannot retrieve a lost password.

4

- Tap or click the OK button in the Confirm Password dialog box.

Q&A When does the password take effect?
You will need to enter your password the next time you open your presentation.

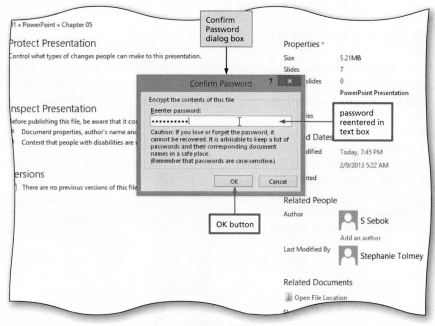

Figure 5–71

TO OPEN A PRESENTATION WITH A PASSWORD

To open a file that has been protected with a password, you would perform the following steps.

1. Display the Open dialog box, locate the desired file, and then tap or click the Open button to display the Password dialog box.

2. When the Password dialog box appears, type the password in the Password box and then tap or click the OK button to display the presentation.

To Change the Password or Remove Password Protection

To change a password that you added to a file or to remove all password protection from the file, you would perform the following steps.

1. Display the Open dialog box, locate the desired file, and then tap or click the Open button to display the Password dialog box.

2. When the Password dialog box appears, type the password in the Password box and then tap or click the OK button to display the presentation.

3. Open the Backstage view, tap or click Save As, and then browse to the desired Save location to display the Save As dialog box. Tap or click the Tools button and then tap or click General Options in the Tools list.

4. Select the contents of the 'Password to open' box or the 'Password to modify' box. To change the password, type the new password and then tap or click the OK button. When prompted, retype your password to reconfirm it, and then tap or click the OK button.

5. Tap or click the Save button and then tap or click the Yes button to resave the presentation.

To Mark a Presentation as Final

1 COLLABORATE | 2 SET SLIDE SIZE & SLIDE SHOW RESOLUTION | 3 SAVE & PACKAGE PRESENTATION
4 PROTECT & SECURE PRESENTATION | 5 USE PRESENTATION TOOLS

Why? *When your slides are completed, you may want to prevent others or yourself from accidentally changing the slide content or features.* If you use the **Mark as Final** command, the presentation becomes a read-only document. The following steps mark the presentation as a final (read-only) document.

1

- With Backstage view open and the Info tab displaying for the Mayans Final Duplicate file, tap or click the Protect Presentation button to display the Protect Presentation menu (Figure 5–72).

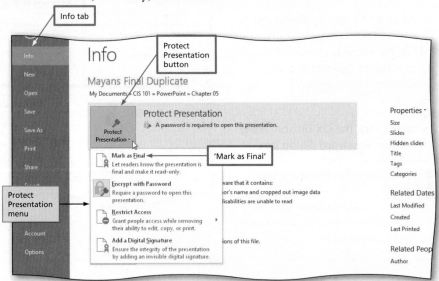

Figure 5–72

2

- Tap or click 'Mark as Final' to display the Microsoft PowerPoint dialog box indicating that the presentation will be saved as a final document (Figure 5–73).

Figure 5–73

- Tap or click the OK button (Microsoft PowerPoint dialog box) to save the file and to display another Microsoft PowerPoint dialog box with information about a final version of a document and indicating that the presentation is final (Figure 5–74).

Figure 5–74

Photo courtesy of Susan Sebok

Q&A | Can I turn off this read-only status so that I can edit the file?
Yes. Tap or click Mark as Final in the Protect Presentation menu to toggle off the read-only status.

- Tap or click the OK button (Microsoft PowerPoint dialog box). If an Information bar is displayed above the slide, tap or click the Edit Anyway button to allow changes to be made to the presentation.

Using Presentation Tools

When you display a particular slide and view the information, you may want to return to one of the other slides in the presentation. Jumping to particular slides in a presentation is called **navigating**. A set of keyboard shortcuts can help you navigate to various slides during the slide show. When running a slide show, you can press the F1 key to see a list of these keyboard controls. These navigational features are listed in Table 5–1.

Table 5–1 Slide Show Shortcuts

Keyboard Shortcut	Purpose
N ENTER SPACEBAR PAGE DOWN RIGHT ARROW DOWN ARROW	Perform the next animation or advance to the next slide
P BACKSPACE LEFT ARROW UP ARROW PAGE UP	Perform the previous animation or return to the previous slide
NUMBER FOLLOWED BY ENTER	Go to a specific slide number
B	Display a blank black slide
W	Display a blank white slide
S	Stop or restart an automatic presentation
ESC	End a presentation
E	Erase on-screen annotations
H	Go to the next slide if the next slide is hidden
T	Set new timings while rehearsing
R	Rerecord slide narration and timing
CTRL+P	Change the pointer to a pen
CTRL+A	Change the pointer to an arrow
CTRL+E	Change the pointer to an eraser
CTRL+M	Show or hide ink markup

© 2014 Cengage Learning

Delivering and Navigating a Presentation Using the Control Bar

When you begin running a presentation in full screen mode and move the pointer, a control bar is displayed with buttons that allow you to navigate to the next slide or previous slide, mark up the current slide, display slide thumbnails, zoom, or change the current display. When you move the mouse, the control bar is displayed in the lower-left corner of the slide; it disappears after the mouse has not been moved for three seconds. Table 5–2 describes the buttons on the control bar.

Table 5–2 Slide Show Control Bar Buttons	
Description	**Function**
Previous	Previous slide or previous animated element on the slide
Next	Next slide or next animated element on the slide
Pen and laser pointer tools	Shortcut menu for laser pointer, pen, highlighter, and eraser
See all slides	View thumbnails of all slides in presentation
Zoom into the slide	Zoom in on specific slide area
Options	Shortcut menu for slide navigation and screen displays. Also displays Presenter View on a single monitor.

© 2014 Cengage Learning

To Highlight Items on a Slide

1 COLLABORATE | 2 SET SLIDE SIZE & SLIDE SHOW RESOLUTION | 3 SAVE & PACKAGE PRESENTATION | 4 PROTECT & SECURE PRESENTATION | 5 USE PRESENTATION TOOLS

You tap or click the arrow buttons on the left side of the control bar to navigate backward or forward through the slide show. The 'Pen and laser pointer tools' button has a variety of functions, most often to emphasize aspects of slides or to make handwritten notes. The following steps highlight an item on a slide in Slide Show view. ***Why?*** *You want to call attention to the location of the Mayan ruins.*

1

- If necessary, display Slide 1 and then run the slide show.

- If the control bar is not visible in the lower-left corner of the slide, move the pointer on the slide.

- Tap or click 'Pen and laser pointer tools' on the control bar to display a menu (Figure 5–75).

Q&A Why is the slide displaying smaller than normal?
You changed the resolution to 800 × 600, so the slide size is reduced.

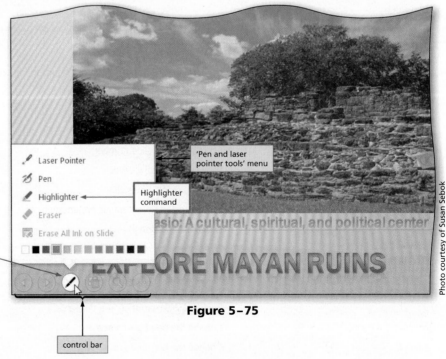

Photo courtesy of Susan Sebok

Figure 5–75

2
- Tap or click Highlighter and then drag over the words, San Gervasio, several times until all the letters are highlighted (Figure 5–76).

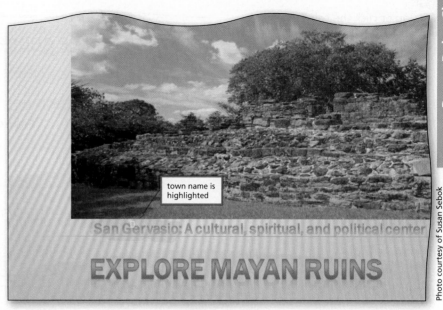

Photo courtesy of Susan Sebok

Figure 5–76

To Change Ink Color

1 COLLABORATE | 2 SET SLIDE SIZE & SLIDE SHOW RESOLUTION | 3 SAVE & PACKAGE PRESENTATION
4 PROTECT & SECURE PRESENTATION | 5 USE PRESENTATION TOOLS

Instead of Highlighter, you also can tap or click Pen to draw or write notes on the slides. *Why? The Pen tool is much thinner than the Highlighter, so you can write words or draw fine lines on the slides.* When the presentation ends, PowerPoint will prompt you to keep or discard the ink annotations. The following steps change the pointer to a pen and then change the color of ink during the presentation.

1
- Tap or click the Next button to display Slide 2. Tap or click the 'Pen and laser pointer tools' button on the control bar and then tap or click Pen on the menu.
- Tap or click the 'Pen and laser pointer tools' button on the control bar and then point to the color Green in the last row (Figure 5–77).

Figure 5–77

- Tap or click the color Green.
- Use your finger or drag the pointer around the title text to draw a circle around the word, Ixchel (Figure 5–78).

Figure 5–78

- Press and hold or right-click the slide to display the shortcut menu (Figure 5–79).

Figure 5–79

- Tap or click End Show to display the Microsoft PowerPoint dialog box (Figure 5–80).

- Tap or click the Discard button (Microsoft PowerPoint dialog box) to end the presentation without saving the annotations.

Figure 5–80

BTW

Certification

The Microsoft Office Specialist (MOS) program provides an opportunity for you to obtain a valuable industry credential — proof that you have the PowerPoint 2013 skills required by employers. For more information, visit the Certification resource on the Student Companion Site located on www.cengagebrain.com. For detailed instructions about accessing available resources, visit www.cengage.com/ct/ studentdownload or see the inside back cover of this book.

TO HIDE THE POINTER AND SLIDE SHOW CONTROL BAR

To hide the pointer and the control bar during the slide show, you would perform the following step.

1. Tap or click the Options button on the control bar, tap or click Arrow Options, and then tap or click Hidden.

To Constantly Display the Pointer and Slide Show Control Bar

By default, the pointer and control bar are set at Automatic, which means they are hidden after three seconds of no movement. After you hide the pointer and control bar, they remain hidden until you choose one of the other commands on the Options menu. They are displayed again when you move the mouse.

To keep the pointer and control bar displayed at all times during a slide show, you would perform the following step.

1. Tap or click the Options button on the control bar, tap or click Arrow Options, and then tap or click Visible.

To Save, Reset the Resolution, Print, and Exit PowerPoint

The presentation now is complete. The following steps reset the resolution to 1366 × 768, save the slides, print a handout, and then exit PowerPoint.

1 Tap or click the 'Set Up Slide Show' button (SLIDE SHOW tab | Set Up group), tap or click the Resolution arrow (Set Up Show dialog box), select 1366 × 768, and then click the OK button.

2 Save the presentation again with the same file name.

3 Print the slides as a handout using the 4 Slides Horizontal layout. If necessary, click 'Print Comments and Ink Markup' on the Print menu to deactivate the command and turn off printing comment pages (Figure 5–81).

4 Exit PowerPoint, closing all open documents.

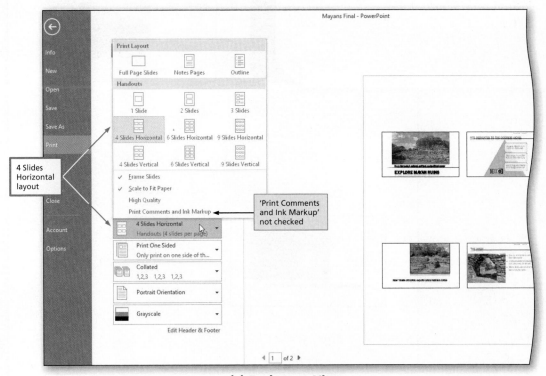

(a) Backstage View

Figure 5–81 (Continued)

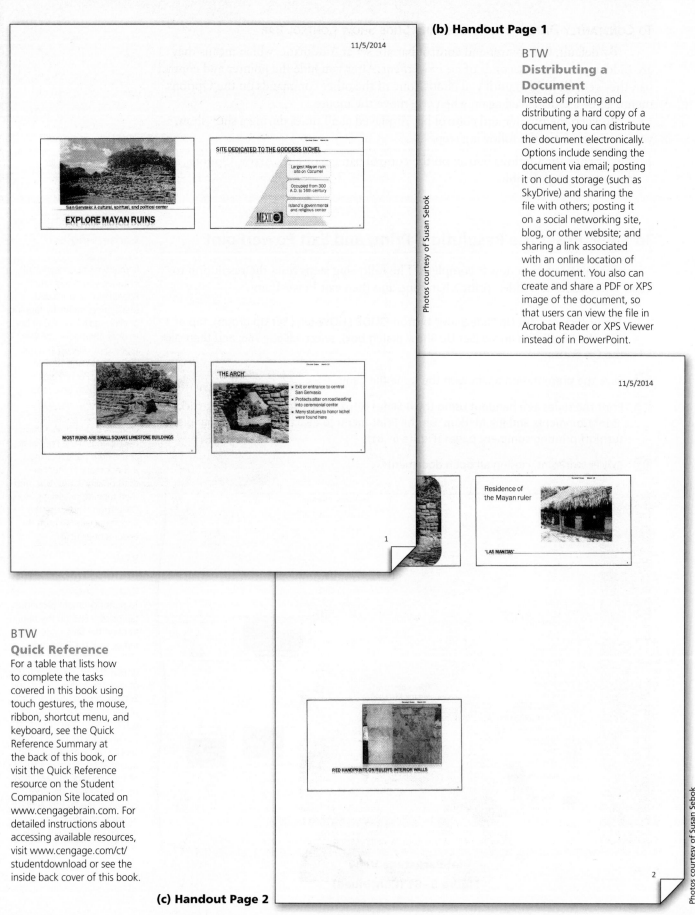

(b) Handout Page 1

(c) Handout Page 2

Figure 5–81

Photos courtesy of Susan Sebok

Chapter Summary

In this chapter you have learned how to merge presentations, review a reviewer's comments, and then review, accept, and reject proposed changes, as well as reply to and insert comments. You changed the slide size and presentation resolution, protected and secured the file with a password, checked compatibility, removed inappropriate information, and then saved the presentation in a variety of formats. Finally, you ran the presentation and annotated the slides with a highlighter and pen. The items listed below include all the new PowerPoint skills you have learned in this chapter.

Change Slide Size and Slide Show Resolution
Set Slide Size (PPT 303)
Set Presentation Resolution (PPT 304)

Combine and Review Presentations
Merge a Presentation (PPT 277)
Preview the Presentation Changes (PPT 281)
Review, Accept, and Reject Presentation Changes (PPT 282)
End the Review and Hide Markup (PPT 293)

Evaluate Comments
Print Comments (PPT 279)
Review Comments (PPT 287)
Reply to a Comment (PPT 288)
Insert a Comment (PPT 289)
Delete a Comment (PPT 290)

Evaluate Recommended Slide Changes
Review, Accept, and Reject Slide Changes (PPT 286)

Insert and Modify Slides from a Previous Presentation
Reuse Slides from an Existing Presentation (PPT 296)
Capture Part of a Screen Using Screen Clipping (PPT 299)
Add a Footer with Fixed Information (PPT 300)
Clear Formatting (PPT 302)

Protect and Secure a Presentation
Remove Inappropriate Information (PPT 312)
Set a Password (PPT 314)
Open a Presentation with a Password (PPT 315)
Change the Password or Remove Password Protection (PPT 316)
Mark a Presentation as Final (PPT 316)

Save and Package a Presentation Using Various Formats
Save a File as a PowerPoint Show (PPT 306)
Save a Slide as an Image (PPT 307)
Package a Presentation for Storage on a Compact Disc (PPT 308)
Save a Presentation in a Previous PowerPoint Format (PPT 310)
Identify Presentation Features Not Supported by Previous Versions (PPT 311)

Use Presentation Tools
Run the Revised Presentation in Reading View (PPT 292)
Highlight Items on a Slide (PPT 318)
Change Ink Color (PPT 319)
Hide the Pointer and Slide Show Control Bar (PPT 320)
Constantly Display the Pointer and Slide Show Control Bar (PPT 321)

What decisions will you need to make when creating your next presentation?
Use these guidelines as you complete the assignments in this chapter and create your own slide show decks outside of this class.

1. Develop a collaboration plan for group members to follow.
    a) Set an overall group goal.
    b) Set long-term and short-term goals.
    c) Identify subtasks that must be completed.
    d) Set a schedule.

2. Accept both positive and negative feedback.
    a) Realize that this criticism helps you to improve yourself and your work.
    b) Oral and written comments from others can help reinforce positive aspects and identify flaws.
    c) Seek comments from a variety of people who genuinely want to help you develop an effective presentation.

3. Give constructive criticism when asked to critique a presentation.
    a) Begin and end with positive comments.
    b) Give specific details about a few areas that can be improved.
    c) Be honest, but be tactful.

4. Select an appropriate password.
    a) A combination of letters and numbers is recommended.
    b) Avoid using words that someone knowing you could guess, such as your child's, best friend's, or pet's name.
    c) Keep your password confidential. Do not write it on a piece of paper, on a bulletin board, or under your keyboard.

PowerPoint Chapter 5

CONSIDER THIS

CONSIDER THIS

How should you submit solutions to questions in the assignments identified with a symbol?

Every assignment in this book contains one or more questions identified with a ❋ symbol. These questions require you to think beyond the assigned presentation. Present your solutions to the questions in the format required by your instructor. Possible formats may include one or more of these options: write the answer; create a document that contains the answer; present your answer to the class; discuss your answer in a group; record the answer as audio or video using a webcam, smartphone, or portable media player; or post answers on a blog, wiki, or website.

Apply Your Knowledge

Reinforce the skills and apply the concepts you learned in this chapter.

Inserting and Deleting Comments, Adding a Header and a Footer, Marking as Final, and Saving as a Previous Version

Note: To complete this assignment, you will be required to use the Data Files for Students. Visit www.cengage.com/ct/studentdownload for detailed instructions or contact your instructor for information about accessing the required files.

Instructions: Run PowerPoint. Open the presentation, Apply 5-1 A Healthy Heart, from the Data Files for Students.

The slides in the presentation present information about keeping your heart healthy. The document you open is a partially formatted presentation. You are to insert, edit (Reply) and delete a comment, add a header and a footer, mark the presentation as final, and save it as a previous version. Your presentation should look like Figure 5–82.

Perform the following tasks:

1. Increase the size of the heart illustration on Slide 1 to approximately 1.97" × 1.9" and move it to the location shown in Figure 5–82a.

2. On Slide 2 (Figure 5–82b), select the bulleted list, insert a new comment with the following text: **This bulleted list could be converted to a SmartArt graphic. I suggest using the Continuous Cycle graphic.** and then press the ENTER key. In the Reply box type: **I agree. I will create a new slide with this change.** as a reply to the comment.

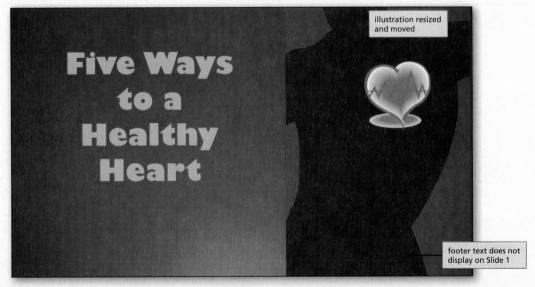

(a) Slide 1

Figure 5–82

(b) Slide 2

(c) Revised Slide 1

Figure 5–82 (Continued)

3. Duplicate Slide 2. On the new Slide 3 (Figure 5–82c), delete the comment. Delete the title text and the title placeholder.

4. On Slide 3 (Figure 5–82c), convert the bulleted list to the Continuous Cycle SmartArt graphic (the first graphic in the second Cycle row). Change the color to Colored Fill – Accent 6 (the second color in the Accent 6 row) and then change the style to Polished (the first style in the first 3-D row). Resize the SmartArt graphic to approximately 6" × 9.5" and then move it to the location shown on the slide. Move the illustration from the lower-right corner of the slide to the center of the SmartArt graphic, as shown in Figure 5–82c.

5. Display the Header and Footer dialog box and add the slide number and the automatic date and time. Type your name as the footer text. Do not show on title slide (Figure 5–82a).

6. If requested by your instructor, add your current or previous pet's name in the subtitle placeholder on Slide 1.

7. Apply the Fade transition in the Subtle category to all slides. Change the duration to 2.75 seconds.

8. Save the presentation using the file name, Apply 5-1 Five Ways to a Healthy Heart.

9. Inspect the document and remove all Comments and Annotations and Presentation Notes. Mark the presentation as final.

Continued >

Apply Your Knowledge *continued*

10. Save the presentation as a PowerPoint 97-2003 (.ppt) document using the name Apply 5-1 Maintain a Healthy Heart. Submit the revised document in the format specified by your instructor.

11. ✳ In Step 4, you converted the bulleted list to a SmartArt graphic and changed the colors and style of the graphic. How did this improve the presentation?

Extend Your Knowledge

Extend the skills you learned in this chapter and experiment with new skills. You may need to use Help to complete the assignment.

Changing Headers and Footers on Slides and Handouts, Inserting and Editing a Comment, and Saving a Slide as an Image

Note: To complete this assignment, you will be required to use the Data Files for Students. Visit www.cengage.com/ct/studentdownload for detailed instructions or contact your instructor for information about accessing the required files.

Instructions: Run PowerPoint. Open the presentation, Extend 5-1 Photography, from the Data Files for Students. You will change and add information to a footer on slides and handouts. You will add and change comments and save Slide 2 as an image.

Perform the following tasks:

1. Display the Header and Footer dialog box and then add your next birthday as the fixed date footer text on all slides. Type your school's name followed by the words, **Photography Club – meets every Friday at 3 p.m.** as the footer text. This footer text will be displayed in the area shown in Figure 5–83a.

2. Display the Notes and Handouts tab (Header and Footer dialog box) and then add the same date and footer text to the notes and handouts.

3. Increase the font size of the Slide 2 footer text to 11 point, bold and italicize this text, and then change the font color to Black, Text 1 (the second color in the first Theme Colors row). See Figure 5–83b for approximate placement of the footer.

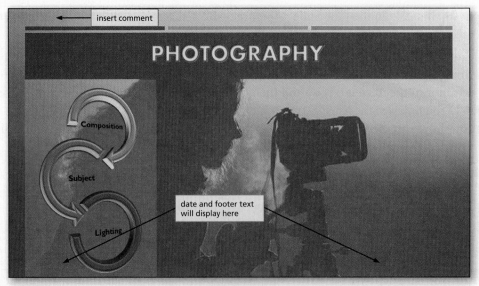

(a) Slide 1

Figure 5–83

(b) Slide 2

(c) Slide 3
Figure 5–83 (Continued)

4. Insert a comment on Slide 1 to remind yourself to ask the photography club president if you can use the image you made of Slide 2 to display on their bulletin board.

5. Edit the comment on Slide 3 by changing the words, two weeks, to the word, month.

6. If requested by your instructor, add the name of your home town after the words, Photography Club, in the footer on Slide 3 (Figure 5–83c).

7. Apply the Reveal transition in the Subtle category to all slides and then change the duration to 4.00 seconds.

8. Save the presentation using the file name, Extend 5-1 Photography Tips.

9. Save Slide 2 as a .jpg image with the file name, Extend 5-1 Photography Basics.

10. Submit the revised document in the format specified by your instructor.

11. ☀ In this assignment, you changed the font size and color of the footer text on Slide 2. Why? You saved Slide 2 as an image. What other slide could you have saved as an image and what use could it have?

Analyze, Correct, Improve

Analyze a presentation, correct all errors, and improve it.

Clearing Formatting and Applying an Artistic Effect, Changing Slide Show Resolution and Slide Size, and Correcting Headers and Footers

Note: To complete this assignment, you will be required to use the Data Files for Students. Visit www.cengage.com/ct/studentdownload for detailed instructions or contact your instructor for information about accessing the required files.

Instructions: Run PowerPoint. Open the presentation, Analyze 5-1 Fireplace, from the Data Files for Students. You work for a chimney maintenance service and your boss asked you to put some ideas together for a safety brochure to hand out to customers. Modify the slides by making the indicated corrections and improvements.

1. Correct

a. Change the design from Facet to Retrospect (the seventh design in the first row). Set the slide size to Widescreen (16:9). Change the slide show resolution to 800 × 600.

b. On Slide 1, adjust the size of the brown rectangle shape at the top of the slide so it fills the width of the slide, as shown in Figure 5–84a. Increase the size of the shape text to 54 point.

c. On Slide 2, adjust the width of the brown rectangle shape at the top of the slide so it fills the width of the slide, as shown in Figure 5–84b. Note: This figure shows the Standard (4:3) slide size, but your slide will display as Widescreen (16:9). Increase the size of the shape text to 44 point.

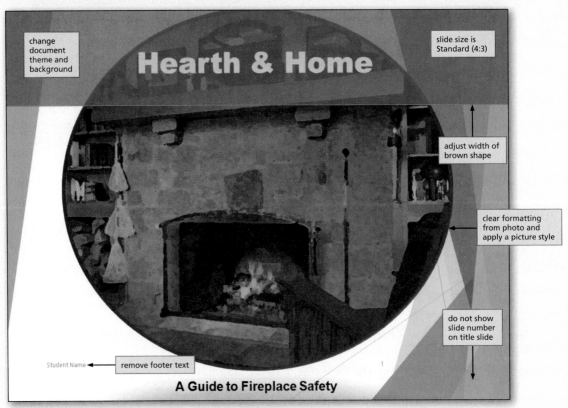

(a) Slide 1

Figure 5–84

(b) Slide 2
Figure 5–84

d. Change the size of the chimney sweep illustration to approximately 2.94" × 4" and then slightly adjust its location on the slide.

e. Display the Header and Footer dialog box, remove the student name from the footer, and do not show the slide number on the title slide.

f. If requested by your instructor, type the name of the high school you attended as the second Level 2 text in the SmartArt graphic under the word, Clean.

2. Improve

a. On Slide 1, clear the formatting from the photo, and then apply the Beveled Oval, Black picture style to the photo (the third style in the second row).

b. Change the background on both slides by inserting the Ice Blue, Background 2 (the third color in the first Theme Colors row) solid fill. Change the transparency to 20%.

c. Move the SmartArt graphic on Slide 2 (Figure 5–84b) so that the left edge of the top line of the graphic lines up with the left edge of the horizontal line on the slide.

d. Decrease the size of the Level 1 SmartArt graphic text to 24 point and then bold this text. Increase the size of the Level 2 SmartArt graphic text to 20 point.

e. Change the transition for both slides to Shape in the Subtle category and then change the duration to 3.00 seconds.

f. Save the presentation using the file name, Analyze 5-1 – Fireplace Safety.

g. Submit the revised document in the format specified by your instructor.

3. ✹ Which errors existed in the starting file? How did changing the font sizes help? How did clearing the format from the photo on Slide 1 make a difference?

In the Labs

Design and/or create a presentation using the guidelines, concepts, and skills presented in this chapter. Labs 1 and 2, which increase in difficulty, require you to create solutions based on what you learned in the chapter; Lab 3 requires you to create a solution, which uses cloud and web technologies, by learning and investigating on your own from general guidance.

Lab 1: Adding Comments to and Protecting a Presentation and Reusing (Inserting) a Slide

Problem: The garden center where you work is planning to host the second annual gardening event for kids from May through November. Your son and daughter attended the event last year, and they have been telling you what they learned at school about eating vegetables regularly. You decide to create a few slides about vegetables to add to the presentation you created last year for the garden center event. You add a comment, insert slides, and protect the presentation with a password before sending it to your boss for approval. When you run the presentation, you add annotations. The annotated slides are shown in Figures 5–85a and 5–85b. Create the slides shown in Figures 5–85a through 5–85d on page PPT 332.

Note: To complete this assignment, you will be required to use the Data Files for Students. Visit www.cengage.com/ct/studentdownload for detailed instructions or contact your instructor for information about accessing the required files.

Instructions: Perform the following tasks:
1. Open the presentation, Lab 5-1 Gardening for Kids, from the Data Files for Students.
2. On Slide 1, add a comment on the photo with the following text: `I suggest you enlarge this photo so it fills in from the top to the bottom of the slide and move it next to the horizontal shape on the right side of the slide` as shown in Figure 5–85a.
3. After Slide 2 (Figure 5–85b), keep the source formatting and then insert Slides 1 and 2 (which become the new Slides 3 and 4) from the Lab 5-1 Eat Your Veggies file located on the Data Files for Students, as shown in Figures 5–85c and 5–85d.
4. On Slide 1, change the title font to Gigi, increase the font size to 72 point, and then bold this text. Do not change the font color.

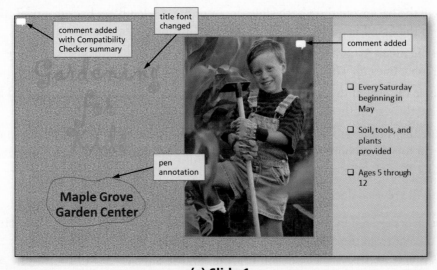

(a) Slide 1

Figure 5–85

5. On Slide 4, rotate the title text 270 degrees and then center the text. Increase the size of the SmartArt graphic to approximately 7.28" × 9.47" and move the graphic to the location shown in Figure 5–85d on the next page.

6. Run the Compatibility Checker to identify the presentation features not supported in previous PowerPoint versions. Summarize these features in a comment placed on Slide 1.

7. Protect the presentation with the password, veggies.

8. If requested by your instructor, add the name of the city in which you were born as the third line in the subtitle placeholder on Slide 1.

9. Apply the Uncover transition in the Subtle category to all slides and then change the duration to 2.50 seconds.

10. Save the presentation using the file name, Lab 5-1 Teaching Kids about Gardening.

11. Print the slides. In addition, print Slide 1 again.

12. Run the presentation. On Slide 1 (Figure 5–85a), tap or click the Pointer button, tap or click the Blue ink color (the tenth color in the Standard Colors row). Tap or click the Pen, draw a circle around the text, Maple Grove Garden Center. Tap or click the Next button on the toolbar, tap or click Highlighter, point to Light Green (the seventh color in the Standard Colors row), and then highlight the text, Join us every Saturday at 9 a.m., as shown in Figure 5–85b. Tap or click the Next button until you reach the end of the slide show. Save the annotations.

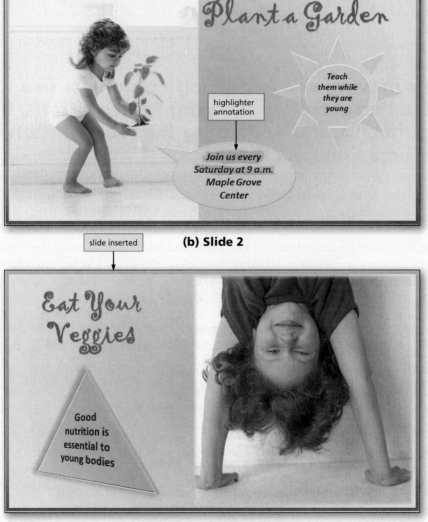

(b) Slide 2

(c) Slide 3 (Inserted Slide)

Figure 5–85 (Continued)

Continued >

In the Labs continued

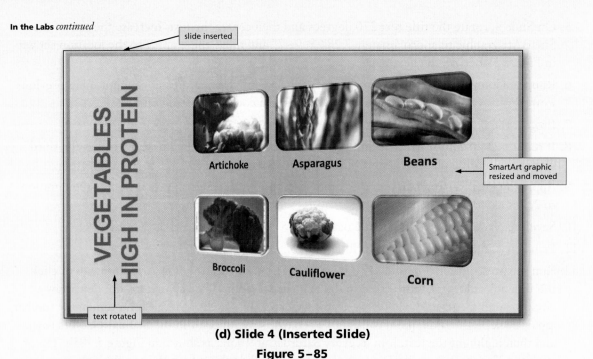

(d) Slide 4 (Inserted Slide)
Figure 5–85

13. Submit the document in the format specified by your instructor.

14. ✳ You reused two slides from another presentation. How did this help make your presentation more effective?

Lab 2: Reviewing and Accepting Comments in a Protected Presentation, Merging Presentations, Using Screen Clipping, and Packaging the Presentation for Storage on a Compact Disc

Problem: We all need at least 30 minutes of physical activity on most days. You have always enjoyed walking, and a friend invited you to join her walking club, Trailblazers. The group meets on Wednesday evenings and walks different trails every Saturday morning. You discovered that many walking trails exist in your area and volunteered to give a presentation about the health benefits of walking at the next meeting. You created a presentation of four slides and asked your friend if she would review the presentation by inserting comments and making revisions on the slides. Use her input to create the final presentation shown in Figures 5–86a through 5–86d on page PPT 334. In addition, use the Package for CD feature to distribute the presentation to members of the walking club.

Note: To complete this assignment, you will be required to use the Data Files for Students. Visit www.cengage.com/ct/studentdownload for detailed instructions or contact your instructor for information about accessing the required files.

Instructions: Perform the following tasks:
1. Open the presentation, Lab 5-2 Walking, from the Data Files for Students. The password is Walking.

2. Merge your friend's revised file, Lab 5-2 Walking2, located on the Data Files for Students. Accept the Theme presentation change so that the transition is added to all slides. Review all of your friend's comments on all four slides. Preview the slides, and then print the slides and the comments.

3. On Slide 1 (Figure 5–86a), accept all changes except the subtitle font color change.

(a) Slide 1

(b) Slide 2

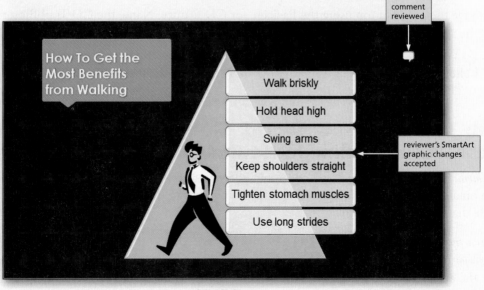

(c) Slide 3

Figure 5–86

Continued >

In the Labs *continued*

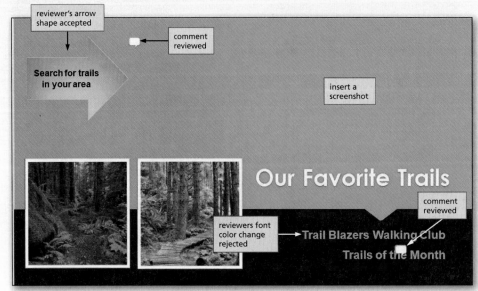

(d) Slide 4 (Inserted Slide)

Figure 5–86

4. On Slide 2 (Figure 5–86b), accept all the changes.

5. On Slide 3 (Figure 5–86c), accept the SmartArt graphic changes.

6. On Slide 4 (Figure 5–86d), accept all changes except the subtitle font color change.

7. Search the Internet for walking trails in your area. Insert a screenshot of one Web page on Slide 4. You may need to make the screenshot smaller.

8. On Slide 1, enhance the photo by applying the Reflected Rounded Rectangle Picture style (the fifth style in the first row).

9. Inspect the document and then remove all document properties and personal information.

10. If requested by your instructor, enter the name of the last TV program you watched as the second line of the subtitle on Slide 1.

11. Save the presentation using the file name, Lab 5-2 Walking for Good Health.

12. Mark the presentation as final.

13. Save the presentation using the Package for CD feature. Name the CD Trail Blazers. Submit the revised document and the CD in the format specified by your instructor.

14. ✳ Why did you add a granite texture to the title font on Slide 1? How did converting the bulleted list on Slide 3 to a SmartArt graphic improve the presentation?

Lab 3: Expand Your World: Cloud and Web Technologies
Researching Online Museums

Problem: In this chapter you learned about a few areas of the Mayan ruins in San Gervasio. You can obtain more information about the Mayans by visiting the websites of several museums worldwide that focus on natural history.

Instructions:

1. Visit one of the following websites, or locate other websites that contain information about the ancient Mayans: Institute of Maya Studies (instituteofmayastudies.org), London's Natural History Museum (nhm.ac.uk), Chicago's Field Museum (fieldmuseum.org), or Los Angeles County's Natural History Museum (nhm.org).

2. Locate information on the Mayan culture, such as where they traveled, how they built and organized their cities, what they ate, and how they developed a calendar.

3. Create at least two new slides and then insert them into your Mayan Final presentation. Use SmartArt or WordArt where appropriate and insert at least one photo from Office.com.

4. If requested to do so by your instructor, replace the words, Cozumel Cruise, in the footer with your high school mascot's name.

5. Save the presentation using the file name, Lab 5-3 Mayan Final History.

6. Submit the assignment in the format specified by your instructor.

7. ✸ Which features do the websites offer that help you create charts and graphs? How do the graphics you created online compare to the graphics you created using PowerPoint? How do the websites allow you to share your graphics using social networks?

✸ Consider This: Your Turn

Apply your creative thinking and problem-solving skills to design and implement a solution.

1. Design and Create a Presentation about How Climate Change Affects Polar Bears
Personal

Part 1:   The polar bear always has been one of your favorite animals. You heard about a female polar bear that swam for nine days and over 400 miles with her cub. This polar bear had to swim that far to survive and save her cub, and you believe that global warming is causing this situation. The world is getting warmer, especially over the last few decades. This warmth is causing sea ice to melt, resulting in rising sea levels and shrinking habitats, so polar bears and other animals are making these long, dangerous journeys every year. You want to do more research on this subject and decide to create a PowerPoint presentation about the polar bears' yearly swim. Use the concepts and techniques presented in this chapter to prepare a presentation. Select a suitable theme, add headers and footers, use WordArt or SmartArt graphics where appropriate, insert comments, and ask your friends to review your presentation before you make it final. The presentation can contain photos, illustrations, and videos. The Data Files for Students contains three photos and an illustration called Polar Bear 1, Polar Bear 2, Polar Bear 3, and Globe, or you can use photos and illustrations from Office.com if they are appropriate for this topic. Submit your assignment in the format specified by your instructor.

Part 2:   ✸ You made several decisions while creating the presentation in this assignment: where to place text, how to format the text (for example, font, font size, and font effects), what headers and footers to add, which graphical image(s) to use, where to position the graphical images to add interest to the presentation. What was the rationale behind each of these decisions? When you reviewed the document, what further revisions did you make and why? Where would you recommend showing this slide show?

2. Design and Create a Presentation about Traveling to Hawaii
Professional

Part 1:   You work for a travel agency, and your manager asked if you would create a PowerPoint presentation for a travel club whose members are visiting Hawaii for the first time. You are aware that Hawaii joined the U.S. in 1959 as our 50th state and is composed of six major islands. You decide to perform some online research to learn about Hawaiian history and obtain some helpful information for the travelers, such as weather, sights to see, and type of clothing to bring. After gathering information, you recommend the travel club members spend at least two weeks in Hawaii and visit three islands: Oahu (where the capital city, Honolulu, is located), Maui, and the big island of Hawaii. Use the concepts and techniques presented in this chapter to create a presentation.

Continued >

Consider This: Your Turn *continued*

Select a suitable theme, use WordArt and SmartArt graphics where appropriate, insert comments, and ask your manager to review your presentation before you make it final. The presentation could contain photos, illustrations, and videos. The Data Files for Students contains two photos and a map illustration called Hawaii 1, Hawaii 2, and Hawaii Map, or you can use photos and illustrations from Office.com if they are appropriate for this topic. Submit your assignment in the format specified by your instructor.

Part 2: ☀ You made several decisions while creating the presentation in this assignment: where to place text, how to format the text (such as font and font size), which graphical image(s) to use, which styles and effects to apply, where to position the graphical images, and which shapes to use to add interest to the presentation. What was the rationale behind each of these decisions? When you reviewed the document, what further revisions did you make and why? Where would you recommend showing this slide show?

3. Design and Create a Presentation about the Pioneers of Aviation

Research and Collaboration

Part 1: For your history class, you and two other students were assigned a project to create a presentation about the pioneers of aviation. Your part of the project is to find the names of these pioneers and gather some facts about them. You knew that Charles Lindbergh made the first nonstop trip from New York to Paris in a small single-engine plane, and you also knew a little about Amelia Earhart being the first female pilot to make this flight. You were surprised to find another pioneer of aviation, Otto Lilienthal, who successfully constructed and launched a glider, one of the earliest forms of a plane. Lilienthal built a large hill in Berlin and launched some of the different gliders he made from that location. He did not have to worry about the wind direction when he used this hill to launch his gliders. He died in 1896 in a glider when he lost control and fell to his death. Your professor located some websites about the Wright brothers and how they used Lilienthal's ideas to build a plane. Another classmate on your team volunteered to find photos that could be used in the presentation, and the third member of your team will visit an aviation museum that opened recently in your city. After coordinating all the information and photos, create a presentation using the concepts and techniques you learned in this chapter. Be certain to insert comments and then share your presentation with your team members to get their ideas and suggestions. Use at least three objectives found at the beginning of this chapter to develop the presentation. The Data Files for Students contains four photos called Female Pilot, Male Pilot, Glider, and Plane, or you can use photos and illustrations from Office.com if they are appropriate for this topic.

Part 2: ☀ You made several decisions while creating the presentation in this assignment: where to place text, how to format the text (such as font, font size, and colors), which image(s) to use, how to make use of headers and footers, how to add comments, using WordArt, shapes and SmartArt graphics, and which shapes to use to add interest to the presentation. What was the rationale behind each of these decisions? When you reviewed the document, what further revisions did you make and why? Where would you recommend showing this slide show?

Learn Online

Reinforce what you learned in this chapter with games, exercises, training, and many other online activities and resources.

Student Companion Site Reinforcement activities and resources are available at no additional cost on www.cengagebrain.com. Visit www.cengage.com/ct/studentdownload for detailed instructions about accessing the resources available at the Student Companion Site.

SAM Put your skills into practice with SAM! If you have a SAM account, go to www.cengage.com/sam2013 to access SAM assignments for this chapter.

6 Navigating Presentations Using Hyperlinks and Action Buttons

Microsoft product screenshots used with permission from Microsoft Corporation.

Objectives

You will have mastered the material in this chapter when you can:

- Create a presentation from a Microsoft Word outline
- Add hyperlinks to slides and objects
- Hyperlink to other Microsoft Office documents
- Add action buttons and action settings
- Display guides to position slide elements

- Set placeholder margins
- Create columns in a placeholder
- Change paragraph line spacing
- Format bullet size and color
- Change bullet characters to pictures and numbers
- Hide slides

6 | Navigating Presentations Using Hyperlinks and Action Buttons

Introduction

BTW
Developing Outlines
A formal outline can help you arrange slide content in multiple levels of major and supporting details. Before you can create this outline, however, you may attempt to develop your ideas by using a scratch outline, which is a rough sketch of the possible major points you would like to showcase and the order in which they might appear.

Many writers begin composing reports and documents by creating an outline. Others review their papers for consistency by saving the document with a new file name, removing all text except the topic headings, and then saving the file again. An outline created in Microsoft Word or another word-processing program works well as a shell for a PowerPoint presentation. Instead of typing text in PowerPoint, as you did in previous projects, you can import this outline, add visual elements such as clip art, photos, and graphical bullets, and ultimately create an impressive slide show. When delivering the presentation, you can navigate forward and backward through the slides using hyperlinks and action buttons to emphasize particular points, to review material, or to address audience concerns.

Project — Presentation with Action Buttons, Hyperlinks, and Formatted Bullet Characters

BTW
Defining Outline Levels
Imported outlines can have a maximum of nine outline levels, whereas PowerPoint outlines are limited to six levels (one for the title text and five for body paragraph text.) When you import an outline, all text in outline levels six through nine is treated as a fifth-level paragraph.

Speakers may elect to begin creating their presentations with an outline (Figure 6–1a) and then add formatted bullets and columns. When presenting these slides during a speaking engagement, they can run their PowerPoint slides nonsequentially depending upon the audience's needs and comprehension. Each of the three illustrations on the Exercise Motivation title slide (Figure 6–1b on page PPT 340) branches, or hyperlinks, to another slide in the presentation. Action buttons and hyperlinks on Slides 2, 3, and 4 (Figures 6–1c – 6–1e) allow the presenter to jump to Slide 5 (Figure 6–1f), slides in another presentation (Figures 6–1g and 6–1h on page PPT 341), or a Microsoft Word document (Figure 6–1i). The five resources on Slide 5 are hyperlinks that display specific exercise-related websites when tapped or clicked during a presentation. The slides in the presentation have a variety of embellishments, including a two-column list on Slide 4 that provides details of the benefits of exercise, formatted graphical bullets on Slides 2 and 5 in the shape of dumbbells and barbells, and a numbered list on Slide 3.

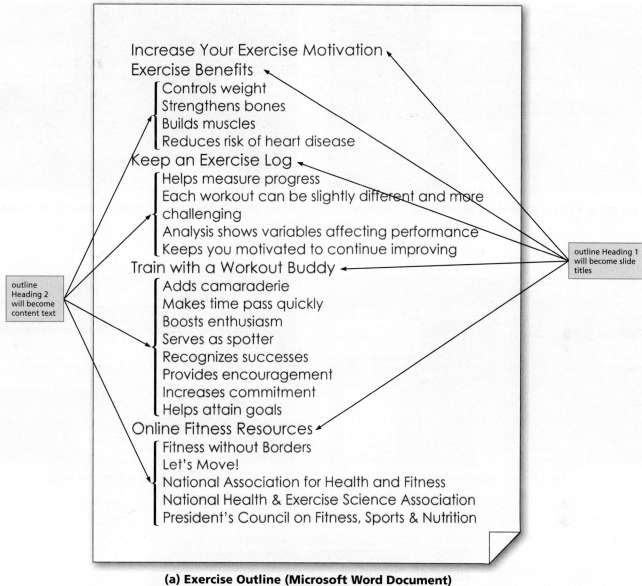

(a) Exercise Outline (Microsoft Word Document)

Figure 6–1

Roadmap

In this chapter, you will learn how to create the slides shown in Figure 6–1. The following roadmap identifies general activities you will perform as you progress through this chapter:

1. OPEN a Microsoft Word OUTLINE.

2. ADD ILLUSTRATION and TEXT HYPERLINKS.

3. ADD ACTION BUTTONS and HYPERLINKS.

4. POSITION ILLUSTRATIONS in content placeholders.

5. ALIGN PLACEHOLDER TEXT.

6. CONVERT and FORMAT BULLETS.

(b) Slide 1 (Title Slide with Illustration Hyperlinks)

(c) Slide 2 (Centered List with Graphical Bullets)

(d) Slide 3 (Numbered List)   **(e) Slide 4 (Two-Column List)**

(f) Slide 5 (Hyperlinks to Websites)

Figure 6–1 (Continued)

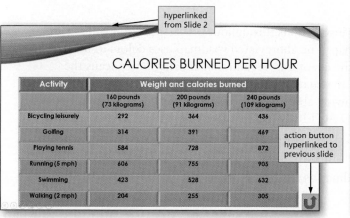

(g) Slide 1 (Hyperlinked from First Presentation)

(h) Slide 2 (Hyperlinked from First Presentation)

hyperlinked
from Slide 3

Workout Journal

Date:	Start time:	End time:
Location (home, gym)		
Goals (strength, build muscle, lose fat, increase endurance)		
Instructor (self, DVD, class)		
Workout type (mat, equipment)		
Intensity (easy, moderate, difficult)		
Focus (specific goals)		
Pre-workout meal		
Feelings before workout (energy level, breathing, mood)		
Feelings after workout		
Overall workout rating (1-10)		
Workout notes (insights, goals for next workout)		

(i) Workout Journal (Microsoft Word Document)

Figure 6–1 (Continued)

One of the few differences between Windows 7 and Windows 8 occurs in the steps to run PowerPoint. If you are using Windows 7, click the Start button, type **PowerPoint** in the 'Search programs and files' box, click PowerPoint 2013, and then, if necessary, maximize the PowerPoint window. For a summary of the steps to run PowerPoint in Windows 7, refer to the Quick Reference located at the back of this book.

At the beginning of step instructions throughout the chapter, you will see an abbreviated form of this roadmap. The abbreviated roadmap uses colors to indicate chapter progress: gray means the chapter is beyond that activity; blue means the task being shown is covered in that activity; and black means that activity is yet to be covered. For example, the following abbreviated roadmap indicates the chapter would be showing a task in the 3 ADD ACTION BUTTONS & HYPERLINKS activity.

1 OPEN OUTLINE | 2 ADD ILLUSTRATION & TEXT HYPERLINKS | 3 ADD ACTION BUTTONS & HYPERLINKS
4 POSITION ILLUSTRATIONS | 5 ALIGN PLACEHOLDER TEXT | 6 CONVERT & FORMAT BULLETS

Use the abbreviated roadmap as a progress guide while you read or step through the instructions in this chapter.

Creating a Presentation from a Microsoft Word Outline

An outline created in Microsoft Word or another word-processing program works well as a shell for a PowerPoint presentation. Instead of typing text in PowerPoint, you can import this outline, add visual elements such as pictures and graphical bullets, and ultimately create an impressive slide show.

In the following pages, you will follow these general steps to create a presentation from a Microsoft Word outline:

1. Add hyperlinks to illustrations and paragraphs.

2. Insert action buttons and then link them to other slides and files.

3. Align illustrations and text.

4. Create columns.

5. Change and format bullet characters.

BTW
Touch Screen Differences
The Office and Windows interfaces may vary if you are using a touch screen. For this reason, you might notice that the function or appearance of your touch screen differs slightly from this chapter's presentation.

To Run PowerPoint and Begin a New Presentation

To begin this project, you will run PowerPoint and then apply the Blank Presentation theme. If you are using a computer to step through the project in this chapter and you want your screens to match the figures in this book, you should change your screen's resolution to 1366 × 768. For information about how to change a computer's resolution, refer to the Office and Windows chapter at the beginning of this book.

The following steps start PowerPoint and apply a theme.

1 Start PowerPoint. If necessary, maximize the PowerPoint window.

2 Apply the Blank Presentation theme.

BTW
The Ribbon and Screen Resolution
PowerPoint may change how the groups and buttons within the groups appear on the ribbon, depending on the computer's screen resolution. Thus, your ribbon may look different from the ones in this book if you are using a screen resolution other than 1366 × 768.

Converting Documents for Use in PowerPoint

PowerPoint can produce slides based on an outline created in Microsoft Word, another word-processing program, or a webpage if the text was saved in a format that PowerPoint can recognize. Microsoft Word 2013, 2010, and 2007 files use the **.docx** file extension in their file names. Text originating in other word-processing programs for later use with PowerPoint should be saved in Rich Text Format (.rtf) or plain text (.txt). Webpage documents that use an HTML extension (.htm or .html) also can be imported.

PowerPoint automatically opens Microsoft Office files, and many other types of files, in the PowerPoint format. The **Rich Text Format (.rtf)** file type is used to transfer formatted documents between applications, even if the programs are running on different platforms, such as Windows and Macintosh. When you insert a Word or Rich Text Format document into a presentation, PowerPoint creates an outline structure based on heading styles in the document. A Heading 1 in a source document becomes a slide title in PowerPoint, a Heading 2 becomes the first level of content text on the slide, a Heading 3 becomes the second level of text on the slide, and so on.

If the original document contains no heading styles, PowerPoint creates an outline based on paragraphs. For example, in a .docx or .rtf file, for several lines of text styled as Normal and broken into paragraphs, PowerPoint turns each paragraph into a slide title.

To Open a Microsoft Word Outline as a Presentation

1 OPEN OUTLINE | 2 ADD ILLUSTRATION & TEXT HYPERLINKS | 3 ADD ACTION BUTTONS & HYPERLINKS
4 POSITION ILLUSTRATIONS | 5 ALIGN PLACEHOLDER TEXT | 6 CONVERT & FORMAT BULLETS

Why? *Instead of typing text for each of the five PowerPoint slides, you can open a Microsoft Word outline and have PowerPoint create the slides automatically.* The text for the Exercise Motivation presentation is contained in a Word file that is saved in the Rich Text Format (RTF). The following steps open this Microsoft Word outline located on the Data Files for Students as a presentation in PowerPoint. Visit www.cengage.com/ct/studentdownload for detailed instruction or contact your instructor for more information about accessing the file.

- Open the Backstage view, display the Open dialog box, and then navigate to the desired file location (in this case, the Chapter 06 folder in the PowerPoint folder in the CIS 101 folder) so that you can open the Exercise Outline file in that location.
- Tap or click the File Type arrow to display the File Type list (Figure 6–2).

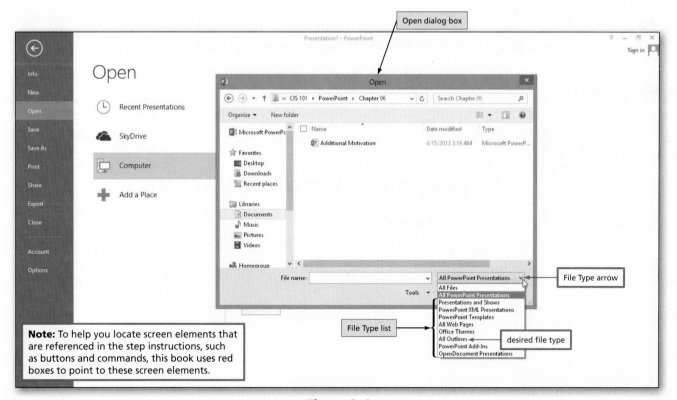

Note: To help you locate screen elements that are referenced in the step instructions, such as buttons and commands, this book uses red boxes to point to these screen elements.

Figure 6–2

2

- Tap or click All Outlines to select this file type.
- Tap or click Exercise Outline to select the file (Figure 6–3).

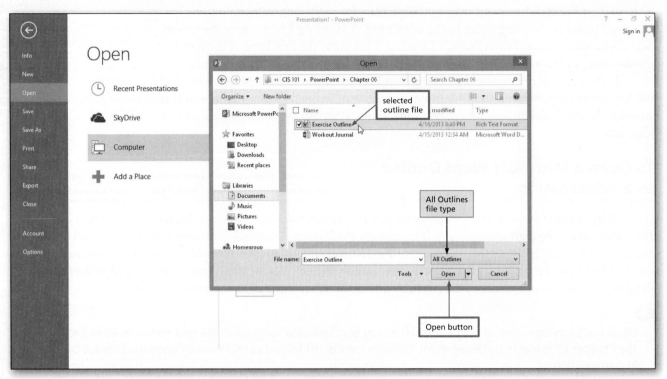

Figure 6–3

3

- Tap or click the Open button to create the five slides in your presentation (Figure 6–4).

Figure 6–4

4

- Display the VIEW tab and then tap or click the Outline View button (VIEW tab | Presentation Views group) to view the outline in the Thumbnail pane (Figure 6–5).

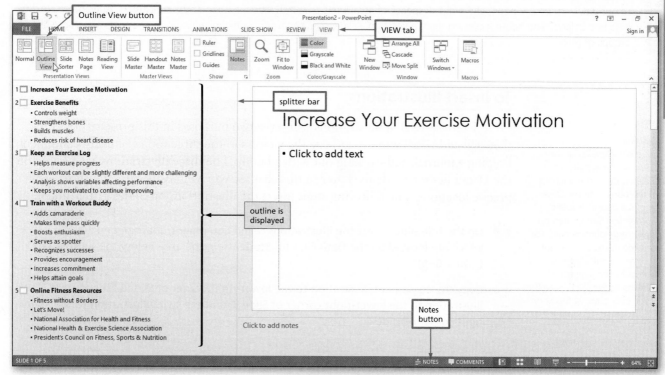

Figure 6–5

Q&A Do I need to see the text as an outline in the Thumbnail pane now?

No, but sometimes it is helpful to view the content of your presentation in this view before looking at individual slides.

Do I need to change to Normal view to navigate between slides?

No, you can tap or click the slide number in Outline view to navigate to slides.

Can I change the width of the Thumbnail pane?

Yes. Tap or click the splitter bar and drag it to the left or right to reduce or increase the width of the Thumbnail pane.

Other Ways

1. Tap or click New Slide arrow (HOME tab | Slides group), tap or click Slides from Outline, tap or click File Type arrow, tap or click All Outlines, tap or click Exercise Outline, tap or click Insert button, delete first blank slide

---

To Change the Slide 1 Layout and Change the Document Theme

When you created the new slides from the Word outline, PowerPoint applied the Title and Text slide layout to all slides. You want to apply the Title Slide layout to Slide 1 to introduce the presentation. The following steps change the Slide 1 slide layout and change the theme to Vapor.

1 With Slide 1 displaying, display the HOME tab, tap or click the Layout button (HOME tab | Slides group), and then tap or click Title Slide to apply that layout to Slide 1.

2 Apply the Vapor Trail document theme (shown in Figure 6–6 on the following page).

3 If necessary, tap or click the Notes button on the status bar to close the Notes pane.

BTW

Widening the Thumbnail Pane
If the Thumbnail pane is hidden or you need to display more of the outline text, widen the pane by dragging the right border. Work in Outline view when you want to make global edits, get an overview of the presentation, change the sequence of bullets or slides, or apply formatting changes.

Think threes.

Speechwriters often think of threes as they plan their talks and PowerPoint presentations. The number three is considered a symbol of balance, as in an equilateral triangle that has three 60-degree angles, the three meals we eat daily, or the three parts of our day — morning, noon, and night. A speech generally has an introduction, a body, and a conclusion. Audience members find balance and harmony seeing three objects on a slide, so whenever possible, plan visual components on your slides in groups of three.

To Insert Illustrations

BTW

Q&As

For a complete list of the Q&As found in many of the step-by-step sequences in this book, visit the Q&A resource on the Student Companion Site located on www.cengagebrain.com. For detailed instructions about accessing available resources, visit www.cengage.com/ct/studentdownload or see the inside back cover of this book.

Exercise-related illustrations will serve two purposes in this presentation. First, they will add visual interest and cue the viewers to the three topics of using equipment, keeping a journal, and working out with a buddy. The three illustrations are located on the Data Files for Students. Later in this chapter, you will position the illustrations in precise locations. The following steps insert the illustrations on Slides 1, 2, 3, and 4.

1 On the title slide, insert the illustrations called Equipment, Journal, and Swim, which are located on the Data Files for Students, in the area below the subtitle box (Figure 6–6).

2 Copy the equipment illustration to the lower-right corner of Slide 2, the journal illustration to the lower-right corner of Slide 3, and the swim illustration to the lower-right corner of Slide 4.

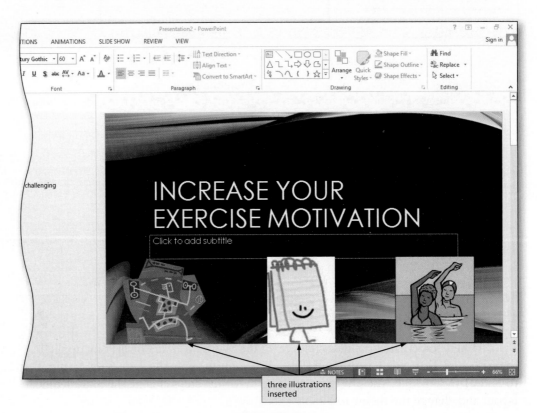

Figure 6–6

To Save the Presentation

With all five slides created, you should save the presentation. The following steps save the slides.

1 Tap or click the Save button on the Quick Access Toolbar, which, depending on settings, will display either the Save As gallery in the Backstage view or the Save As dialog box.

2 Save the presentation in the desired location (in this case, the PowerPoint folder in the CIS 101 folder [or your class folder]) using **Exercise Motivation** as the file name.

CONSIDER THIS

Choose outstanding hyperlink images or text.

Good speakers are aware of their audiences and know their speech material well. They have rehearsed their presentations and know where the hypertext is displayed on the slides. During a presentation, however, they sometimes need to divert from their planned material. Audience members may interrupt with questions, the room may not have optimal acoustics or lighting, or the timing may be short or long. It is helpful, therefore, to make the slide hyperlinks as large and noticeable to speakers as possible. The presenters can glance at the slide and receive a visual cue that it contains a hyperlink. They then can decide whether to tap or click the hyperlink to display a webpage.

Adding Hyperlinks and Action Buttons

Speakers sometimes skip from one slide to another in a presentation in response to audience needs or timing issues. In addition, if Internet access is available, they may desire to display a webpage during a slide show to add depth to the presented material and to enhance the overall message. When presenting the Exercise Motivation slide show and discussing exercise information on Slides 1, 2, 3, or 4, a speaker might want to skip to the last slide in the presentation and then access a website for further specific health information. Or the presenter may be discussing information on Slide 5 and want to display Slide 1 to begin discussing a new topic.

One method of jumping nonsequentially to slides is by tapping or clicking a hyperlink or an action button on a slide. A **hyperlink**, also called a **link**, connects one slide to a webpage, another slide, a custom show consisting of specific slides in a presentation, an email address, or a file. A hyperlink can be any element of a slide. This includes a single letter, a word, a paragraph, or any graphical image such as a picture, shape, or graph.

BTW

BTWs

For a complete list of the BTWs found in the margins of this book, visit the BTW resource on the Student Companion Site located on www.cengagebrain.com. For detailed instructions about accessing available resources, visit www.cengage.com/ct/studentdownload or see the inside back cover of this book.

To Add a Hyperlink to an Illustration

1 OPEN OUTLINE | 2 ADD ILLUSTRATION & TEXT HYPERLINKS | 3 ADD ACTION BUTTONS & HYPERLINKS
4 POSITION ILLUSTRATIONS | 5 ALIGN PLACEHOLDER TEXT | 6 CONVERT & FORMAT BULLETS

Why? *In the Exercise Motivation presentation, each piece of clip art on Slide 1 will link to another slide in the same presentation.* When you point to a hyperlink, the pointer becomes the shape of a hand to indicate the text or object contains a hyperlink. The steps on the next page create the first hyperlink for the equipment illustration on Slide 1.

1

- Display Slide 1, select the equipment illustration, and then display the INSERT tab.

- Tap or click the Hyperlink button (INSERT tab | Links group) to display the Insert Hyperlink dialog box.

- If necessary, tap or click the 'Place in This Document' button in the Link to area.

- Tap or click '2. Exercise Benefits' in the 'Select a place in this document' area (Insert Hyperlink dialog box) to select and display a preview of this slide (Figure 6–7).

Q&A Could I also have selected the Next Slide link in the 'Select a place in this document' area? Yes. Either action would create the hyperlink to Slide 2.

Figure 6–7

2

- Tap or click the OK button (Insert Hyperlink dialog box) to insert the hyperlink.

Q&A I tapped or clicked the equipment illustration, but Slide 2 did not display. Why? Hyperlinks are active only when you run the presentation, not when you are creating it in Normal, Reading, or Slide Sorter view.

Other Ways

1. Using touch screen, press and hold clip, tap More button on shortcut menu, tap Hyperlink, if necessary tap 'Place in This Document', tap slide, tap OK button

2. Using mouse, right-click clip, click Hyperlink, select slide, click OK button

3. Select clip, press CTRL+K, select slide, press ENTER

To Add Hyperlinks to the Remaining Slide 1 Illustrations

The hyperlink for the equipment clip is complete. The next task is to create the hyperlinks for the other two illustrations on Slide 1.

1 On Slide 1, tap or click the journal illustration.

2 Tap or click the Hyperlink button, if necessary tap or click 'Place in This Document', and then tap or click '3. Keep an Exercise Log' to select this slide as the hyperlink. Tap or click the OK button.

3 Tap or click the swim illustration, tap or click the Hyperlink button, and then tap or click '4. Train with a Workout Buddy'. Tap or click the OK button.

To Add a Hyperlink to a Paragraph

1 OPEN OUTLINE | 2 ADD ILLUSTRATION & TEXT HYPERLINKS | 3 ADD ACTION BUTTONS & HYPERLINKS
4 POSITION ILLUSTRATIONS | 5 ALIGN PLACEHOLDER TEXT | 6 CONVERT & FORMAT BULLETS

If you are connected to the Internet when you run the presentation, you can tap or click each hyperlinked paragraph, and your browser will open a new window and display the corresponding webpage for each hyperlink. By default, hyperlinked text is displayed with an underline and in a color that is part of the color scheme. The following steps create a hyperlink for the first paragraph on Slide 5. *Why? Each second-level paragraph will be a hyperlink to a fitness organization's webpage.*

1
- Display Slide 5 and then select the second-level paragraph that appears first, Fitness without Borders, to select the text.

- Display the Insert Hyperlink dialog box and then tap or click the 'Existing File or Web Page' button in the Link to area (Figure 6–8).

Figure 6–8

2
- Type **www.fitnesswithout borders.org** in the Address box (Figure 6–9).

3
- Tap or click the OK button to insert the hyperlink.

Q&A Why is this paragraph now underlined and displaying a new font color?
The default style for hyperlinks is underlined text. The Vapor Trail built-in theme hyperlink color is orange, so PowerPoint formatted the paragraph to that color automatically.

Figure 6–9

Other Ways

1. Using touch screen, press and hold selected text, tap More button on shortcut menu, tap Hyperlink, tap Existing File or Web Page, type address, tap OK button

2. Using mouse, right-click selected text, click Hyperlink, click Existing File or Web Page, type address, click OK button

3. Select text, press CTRL+K, click Existing File or Web Page, type address, press ENTER

BTW
Customizing Screen Tips
You can create a custom ScreenTip that displays when you hover your mouse over a hyperlink. Click the ScreenTip button (Insert Hyperlink dialog box), type the desired ScreenTip text (Set Hyperlink ScreenTip dialog box), and then click the OK button.

To Add Hyperlinks to the Remaining Slide 5 Paragraphs

The hyperlink for the second-level paragraph that appears first is complete. The next task is to create the hyperlinks for the other second-level paragraphs on Slide 5.

1 Select the second-level paragraph that appears second, Let's Move.

2 Display the Insert Hyperlink dialog box and then type `www.letsmove.gov` in the Address box. Tap or click the OK button.

3 Select the third paragraph, National Association for Health and Fitness, display the Insert Hyperlink dialog box, type `www.physicalfitness.org` in the Address box, and then tap or click the OK button.

4 Select the fourth paragraph, National Health & Exercise Science Association, display the Insert Hyperlink dialog box, type `www.nhesa.org` in the Address box, and then tap or click the OK button.

5 Select the fifth paragraph, President's Council on Fitness, Sports & Nutrition, display the Insert Hyperlink dialog box, type `www.fitness.gov` in the Address box, and then tap or click the OK button (Figure 6–10).

Q&A I tapped or clicked the hyperlink, but the webpage did not display. Why?
As with the hyperlinks associated with the illustrations on Slide 1, hyperlinks associated with text are active only when you run the presentation.

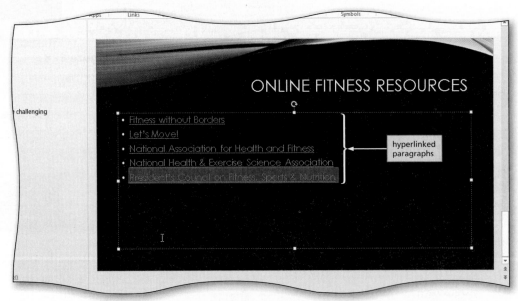

Figure 6–10

BTW
Using Action Buttons
The action buttons have images representing their functions, such as a right-pointing arrow representing moving forward to the next slide. These buttons are useful when using a touch screen or when a keyboard is not present, such as when a presentation is run at a kiosk. Slide designers also type specific years or descriptive words, such as True or False, on action buttons that link to slides with corresponding information. Be imaginative when developing your own presentations and creating buttons that have a specific meaning for your intended audience.

Action Buttons

PowerPoint provides 12 built-in action buttons. An **action button** is a particular type of hyperlink that has a built-in function. Each action button performs a specific task, such as displaying the next slide, providing help, giving information, or playing a sound. In addition, the action button can activate a hyperlink that allows users to jump to a specific slide in the presentation. The picture on the action button indicates the type of function it performs. For example, the button with the house icon represents the home slide, or Slide 1. To achieve a personalized look, you can customize an action button with a photograph, piece of clip art, logo, text, or any graphic you desire. Table 6–1 describes each of the built-in action buttons.

Table 6–1 Built-In Action Buttons

Button Name	Image	Description
Back or Previous	◁	Returns to the previous slide displayed in the same presentation.
Forward or Next	▷	Jumps to the next slide in the presentation.
Beginning	◁|	Jumps to Slide 1. This button performs the same function as the Home button.
End	|▷	Jumps to the last slide in the presentation.
Home	🏠	Jumps to Slide 1. This button performs the same function as the Beginning button.
Information	ⓘ	Does not have any predefined function. Use it to direct a user to a slide with details or facts.
Return	↵	Returns to the previous slide displayed in any presentation. For example, you can place it on a hidden slide or on a slide in a custom slide show and then return to the previous slide.
Movie	🎞	Does not have any predefined function. You generally would use this button to jump to a slide with an inserted video clip.
Document	📄	Opens a program other than PowerPoint. For example, you can open Microsoft Word or Microsoft Excel and display a page or worksheet.
Sound	🔊	Does not have any predefined function. You generally would use this button to jump to a slide with an inserted audio clip.
Help	?	Does not have any predefined function. Use it to direct a user to a slide with instructions or contact information.
Custom	☐	Does not have any predefined function. You can add a clip, picture, graphic, or text and then specify a unique purpose.

© 2014 Cengage Learning

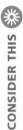

CONSIDER THIS

Customize action buttons for a unique look.

PowerPoint's built-in action buttons have icons that give the presenter an indication of their function. Designers frequently customize these buttons with images related to the presentation. For example, in a grocery store presentation, the action buttons may have images of a coupon, dollar sign, and question mark to indicate links to in-store coupons, sale items, and the customer service counter. Be creative when you develop your own presentations and attempt to develop buttons that have specific meanings for your intended audience.

To Insert an Action Button

1 OPEN OUTLINE | 2 ADD ILLUSTRATION & TEXT HYPERLINKS | **3 ADD ACTION BUTTONS & HYPERLINKS**
4 POSITION ILLUSTRATIONS | 5 ALIGN PLACEHOLDER TEXT | 6 CONVERT & FORMAT BULLETS

In the Exercise Motivation slide show, the action buttons on Slides 2, 3, and 4 hyperlink to the last slide, Slide 5. You will insert and format the action button shape on Slide 2 and copy it to Slides 3 and 4, and then create a link to Slide 5. ***Why?*** *You will be able to display Slide 5 at any point in the presentation by tapping or clicking the action button.* When you tap or click the action button, a sound will play. This sound will vary depending upon which slide is displayed. The steps on the next page insert an action button on Slide 2 and link it to Slide 5.

- Display Slide 2 and then tap or click the Shapes button (INSERT tab | Illustrations group) to display the Shapes gallery.

- If you are using a mouse, scroll down and then point to the 'Action Button: End' shape in the Action Buttons area (fourth image) (Figure 6–11).

Figure 6–11

- Tap or click the 'Action Button: End' shape.

- Tap or click the lower-left corner of the slide to insert the action button and to display the Action Settings dialog box.

- If necessary, tap or click the Mouse Click tab (Action Settings dialog box) (Figure 6–12).

Q&A Why is Last Slide the default hyperlink setting?
The End shape establishes a hyperlink to the last slide in a presentation.

Figure 6–12

3

- Tap or click the Play sound check box and then tap or click the Play sound arrow to display the Play sound list (Figure 6–13).

Figure 6–13

4

- Tap or click Whoosh in the Play sound list to select that sound (Figure 6–14).

Q&A I did not hear the sound when I selected it. Why not?
The Whoosh sound will play when you run the slide show and tap or click the action button.

5

- Tap or click the OK button to apply the hyperlink setting and sound to the action button and to close the Action Settings dialog box.

Figure 6–14

To Size an Action Button

The action button size can be decreased to make it less obvious on the slide. The following step resizes the selected action button.

1 With the action button still selected, display the DRAWING TOOLS FORMAT tab and then size the action button so that it is approximately 1" × 1". If necessary, move the action button to the lower-left corner of the slide, as shown in Figure 6–15.

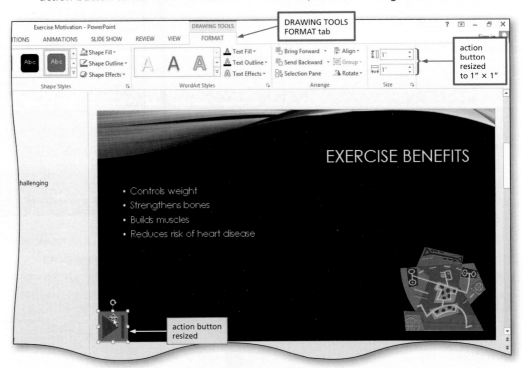

Figure 6–15

To Change an Action Button Fill Color

1 OPEN OUTLINE | 2 ADD ILLUSTRATION & TEXT HYPERLINKS | 3 ADD ACTION BUTTONS & HYPERLINKS
4 POSITION ILLUSTRATIONS | 5 ALIGN PLACEHOLDER TEXT | 6 CONVERT & FORMAT BULLETS

You can select a new action button fill color to coordinate with slide elements. The following steps change the fill color from Red to Light Blue. **Why?** *The action button's Red interior color does not coordinate well with the equipment illustration on the slide. A light blue color will match this illustration and the design in the upper-right corner of the slide.*

1

- With the action button still selected, tap or click the Shape Fill arrow (DRAWING TOOLS FORMAT tab | Shape Styles gallery) to display the Shape Fill gallery (Figure 6–16).

Figure 6–16

- Point to Light Blue (seventh color from left in Standard Colors row) to display a live preview of that fill color on the action button (Figure 6–17).

Experiment

- If you are using a mouse, point to various colors in the Shape Fill gallery and watch the fill color change in the action button.

- Tap or click Light Blue to apply this color to the action button.

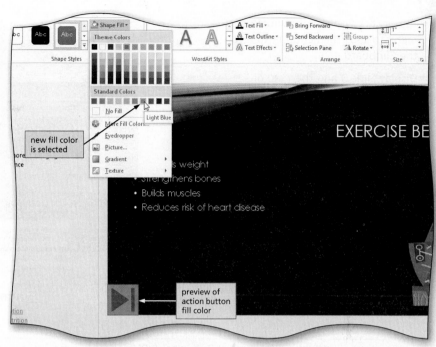

Figure 6–17

Other Ways

1. Using touch screen, press and hold action button, tap Fill on shortcut menu, tap desired color

2. Using mouse, right-click action button, click Format Shape on shortcut menu, click FILL on SHAPE OPTIONS tab (Format Shape pane), click Fill Color button, click desired color

To Copy an Action Button

1 OPEN OUTLINE | 2 ADD ILLUSTRATION & TEXT HYPERLINKS | 3 ADD ACTION BUTTONS & HYPERLINKS
4 POSITION ILLUSTRATIONS | 5 ALIGN PLACEHOLDER TEXT | 6 CONVERT & FORMAT BULLETS

The Slide 2 action button is formatted and positioned correctly. You can copy this shape to Slides 3 and 4. *Why? Copying the formatted shape saves time and ensures consistency.* The following steps copy the Slide 2 action button to the next two slides in the presentation.

- Press and hold or right-click the action button on Slide 2 to display a shortcut menu (Figure 6–18).

Q&A Why does my shortcut menu have different commands?
Depending upon where you pressed or right-clicked, you might see a different shortcut menu. As long as this menu displays the Copy command, you can use it. If the Copy command is not visible, click the slide again to display another shortcut menu.

Figure 6–18

- Tap or click Copy on the shortcut menu to copy the action button to the Clipboard.

- Display Slide 3 and then tap or click the Paste button (HOME tab | Clipboard group) to paste the action button in the lower-left corner of Slide 3 (Figure 6–19).

- Display Slide 4 and then tap or click the Paste button to paste the action button in the lower-left corner of Slide 4.

Figure 6–19

Other Ways

1. Copy button (HOME tab | Clipboard group), Paste button (HOME tab | Clipboard group)

2. CTRL+C to copy, CTRL+V to paste

To Edit an Action Button Action Setting

1 OPEN OUTLINE | 2 ADD ILLUSTRATION & TEXT HYPERLINKS | 3 ADD ACTION BUTTONS & HYPERLINKS
4 POSITION ILLUSTRATIONS | 5 ALIGN PLACEHOLDER TEXT | 6 CONVERT & FORMAT BULLETS

When you copied the action button, PowerPoint retained the settings to hyperlink to the last slide and to play the Whoosh sound. The following steps edit the Slide 3 and Slide 4 hyperlink sound settings. *Why? For variety, you want to change the sounds that play for the Slide 3 and Slide 4 action buttons.*

- With the action button still selected on Slide 4, display the INSERT tab and then tap or click the Action button (INSERT tab | Links group) shown in Figure 6–21 to display the Action Settings dialog box.

- Tap or click the Play sound arrow to display the Play sound menu (Figure 6–20).

Figure 6–20

- Tap or click Breeze in the Play sound list to select the Breeze sound to play when the action button is tapped or clicked (Figure 6–21).

- Tap or click the OK button (Action Settings dialog box) to apply the new sound setting to the Slide 4 action button.

Figure 6–21

- Display Slide 3, select the action button, and then tap or click the Action button (INSERT tab | Links group) to display the Action Settings dialog box.

- Tap or click the Play sound arrow to display the Play sound menu.

- Tap or click Typewriter in the Play sound list (Figure 6–22).

- Tap or click the OK button (Action Settings dialog box) to apply the new sound setting to the Slide 3 action button.

Figure 6–22

To Hyperlink to Another PowerPoint File

While hyperlinks are convenient tools to navigate through the current PowerPoint presentation or to webpages, they also allow you to open a second PowerPoint presentation and display a particular slide in that file. Slide 2 in your presentation provides information about the health benefits from exercising. When displaying this slide during a speech, you desire to show some useful information about how many calories are burned when exercising for a specific period of time. The first slide in another presentation, Additional Exercise Motivation, has a table listing the number of calories a person weighing 160 pounds, 200 pounds, and 240 pounds burns while participating in six popular activities for an hour. The following steps hyperlink the equipment illustration on Slide 2 to the first slide in the second presentation. *Why? The hyperlink offers a convenient method of moving from one presentation to another. A speaker has the discretion to use the hyperlink depending upon the audience's interest in the topic and time considerations.*

- Display Slide 2 and then select the equipment illustration.

- If necessary, display the INSERT tab and then tap or click the Action button (INSERT tab | Links group) to display the Action Settings dialog box.

- Tap or click Hyperlink to in the 'Action on click' area and then tap or click the Hyperlink to arrow to display the Hyperlink to menu (Figure 6–23).

Figure 6–23

- Scroll down and then tap or click 'Other PowerPoint Presentation' to display the Hyperlink to Other PowerPoint Presentation dialog box.

- Tap or click Additional Motivation to select this file as the hyperlinked presentation (Figure 6–24).

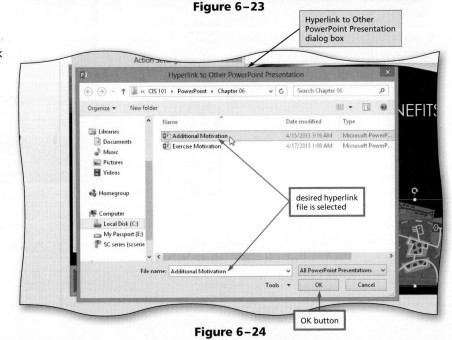

Figure 6–24

③

- Tap or click the OK button to display the Hyperlink to Slide dialog box (Figure 6–25).

Q&A What are the two items listed in the Slide title area?
They are the title text of the two slides in the Additional Motivation file.

Figure 6–25

④

- Tap or click the OK button (Hyperlink to Slide dialog box) to hyperlink the first slide in the Additional Motivation presentation to the equipment illustration (Figure 6–26).

⑤

- Tap or click the OK button (Action Settings dialog box) to apply the new action setting to the Slide 2 illustration.

Figure 6–26

Other Ways

1. Select illustration, tap or click Hyperlink button (INSERT menu | Links group), tap or click Existing File or Web Page (Link to: area), browse to and select desired file, tap or click OK button

To Hyperlink to a Second Slide in Another PowerPoint File

BTW
Verifying Hyperlinks
Always test your hyperlinks prior to giving a presentation. Web addresses change frequently, so if your hyperlinks are to websites, be certain your Internet connection is working, the websites are active, and that the content on these pages is appropriate for your viewers. If your hyperlinks direct PowerPoint to display specific slides and to open files, click the hyperlinks to verify your desired actions are followed and that the files exist.

Another slide in the Additional Motivation presentation has information regarding how to avoid injuries while exercising. This slide might be useful to display during a presentation when a speaker is discussing the information on Slide 4, which describes working out with a partner. A workout partner could serve as a spotter during some training, especially during weight training, so this person might offer advice about techniques that could prevent a potentially dangerous and unhealthy situation. If the speaker has time to discuss the material and the audience needs to know these specific body fat percentages, he could tap or click the swim illustration on Slide 4 and then hyperlink to Slide 2 in the second presentation. The following steps hyperlink Slide 4 to the second slide in the Additional Motivation presentation.

1 Display Slide 4, select the swim illustration, and then tap or click the Action button (INSERT tab | Links group) to display the Action Settings dialog box.

2 Tap or click Hyperlink to in the 'Action on click' area, tap or click the Hyperlink to arrow, and then scroll down and tap or click 'Other PowerPoint Presentation' in the Hyperlink to menu.

3 Tap or click Additional Motivation in the Hyperlink to Other PowerPoint Presentation dialog box to select this file as the hyperlinked presentation and then tap or click the OK button.

4 Tap or click 2. Prevent Workout Injuries (Hyperlink to Slide dialog box) (Figure 6–27).

5 Tap or click the OK button (Hyperlink to Slide dialog box) to hyperlink the second slide in the Additional Motivation presentation to the swim illustration.

6 Tap or click the OK button (Action Settings dialog box) to apply the new action setting to the Slide 4 illustration.

Figure 6–27

To Hyperlink to a Microsoft Word File

Personal trainers recommend their student keep a current record of all exercises performed during a session. A convenient form for recording these details is located on the Data Files for Students. The file, Workout Journal, was created using Microsoft Word, and it would be useful to display this document when discussing the information on Slide 3 of your presentation. *Why?* *The training log can serve as a reminder of goals set and achieved, particular difficulties encountered during the workout, and training times.* PowerPoint allows a speaker to hyperlink to other Microsoft Office documents in a similar manner as linking to another PowerPoint file. The following steps hyperlink the journal illustration on Slide 3 to the Microsoft Word document with the file name, Workout Journal.

1
- Display Slide 3, select the journal illustration, and then tap or click the Action button (INSERT tab | Links group) to display the Action Settings dialog box.

- Tap or click Hyperlink to, tap or click the Hyperlink to arrow to display the Hyperlink to menu, and then scroll down to the end of the Hyperlink to list and point to Other File (Figure 6–28).

Figure 6–28

2
- Tap or click Other File to display the Hyperlink to Other File dialog box, scroll down, and then tap or click Workout Journal to select this file as the hyperlinked document (Figure 6–29).

Figure 6–29

3

- Tap or click the OK button (Hyperlink to Other File dialog box) to hyperlink this file to the journal illustration action button (Figure 6–30).

4

- Tap or click the OK button (Action Settings dialog box) to apply the new action setting to the Slide 3 illustration.

Figure 6–30

To Insert and Format Action Buttons on the Hyperlinked File

BTW
Showing a Range of Slides
If your presentation consists of many slides, you may want to show only a portion of them in your slide show. For example, if your 30-slide presentation is designed to accompany a 30-minute speech and you are given only 10 minutes to present, you may elect to display only the first 10 slides. Rather than have the show end abruptly after Slide 10, you can elect to show a range of slides. To specify this range, display the SLIDE SHOW tab, tap or click the Set Up Slide Show button, and then specify the starting and ending slide numbers in the From and To boxes in the Show slides area (Set Up Show dialog box).

The action buttons on Slide 2 and Slide 3 hyperlink to slides in the Additional Motivation file. While running the presentation, if you tap or click an action button that opens and then displays either Slide 1 or Slide 2, you may need to review this slide and then return to the previous slide displayed in the first presentation. The Return action button performs this function. The following steps open the Additional Motivation file and then insert and format the Return action button on both slides.

1 In the Backstage view, tap or click the Open command to display the Open pane, navigate to the location of the Data Files for Students, tap or click the File Type arrow to display the File Type list, and then tap or click All PowerPoint Presentations to select this file type.

2 Open the Additional Motivation file located on the Data Files for Students.

3 With Slide 1 displaying, tap or click the Shapes button (INSERT tab | Illustrations group), and then scroll down and tap or click the Action Button: Return shape (seventh image).

4 Insert the action button in the lower-right corner of the slide.

5 When the Action Settings dialog box is displayed, hyperlink the action button to Slide 2 in the Exercise Motivation presentation.

6 Size the action button so that it is approximately 0.7" × 0.7".

7 Change the action button fill color to Orange (third color in Standard Colors row).

8 Copy the action button to the same location on Slide 2 (Figure 6–31). Display the Action Settings dialog box and then hyperlink this action button to Slide 4 (Train with a Workout Buddy) in the Exercise Motivation presentation.

9 Save the file using the same file name.

10 Close the Additional Motivation file.

Return action button is hyperlinked to previous slide (Slide 4) and formatted

Figure 6–31

Break Point: If you wish to take a break, this is a good place to do so. Be sure to save the Exercise Motivation file again and then you can quit PowerPoint. To resume at a later time, start PowerPoint, open the file called Exercise Motivation, and continue following the steps from this location forward.

Positioning Slide Elements

At times you may desire to arrange slide elements in precise locations. PowerPoint provides useful tools to help you position shapes and objects on slides. **Drawing guides** are two straight dotted lines, one horizontal and one vertical. When an object is close to a guide, its corner or its center (whichever is closer) **snaps**, or aligns precisely, on top of the guide. You can drag a guide to a new location to meet your alignment requirements. Another tool is the vertical or horizontal **ruler**, which can help you drag an object to a precise location on the slide. The center of a slide is 0.00 on both the vertical and the horizontal rulers.

Aligning and Distributing Objects

If you display multiple objects, PowerPoint can **align** them above and below each other (vertically) or side by side (horizontally). The objects, such as SmartArt graphics, clip art, shapes, boxes, and WordArt, can be aligned relative to the slide so that they display along the top, left, right, or bottom borders or in the center or middle of the slide. They also can be aligned relative to each other, meaning that you position either the first or last object in the desired location and then command PowerPoint to move the remaining objects in the series above, below, or beside it. Depending on the alignment option that you tap or click, objects will move straight up, down, left, or right, and might cover an object already located on the slide. Table 6–2 on the next page describes alignment options.

BTW

Measurement System
The vertical and horizontal rulers display the units of measurement in inches by default. This measurement system is determined by the settings in Microsoft Windows. You can change the measurement system to centimeters by customizing the numbers format in the Clock, Language, and Region area of the Control Panel.

Table 6–2 Alignment Options	
Alignment	**Action**
Left	Aligns the edges of the objects to the left
Center	Aligns the objects vertically through the centers of the objects
Right	Aligns the edges of the objects to the right
Top	Aligns the top edges of the objects
Middle	Aligns the objects horizontally through the middles of the objects
Bottom	Aligns the bottom edges of the objects
to Slide	Aligns one object to the slide

BTW
Displaying Slides
The slides in this presentation have important information about exercising properly. Your audience needs time to read and contemplate the advice you are providing in the content placeholders, so you must display the slides for a sufficient amount of time. Some public speaking experts recommend each slide in a presentation should display for at least one minute so that audience members can look at the material, focus on the speaker, and then refer to the slide again.

One object remains stationary when you align objects relative to each other by their edges. For example, Align Left aligns the left edges of all selected objects with the left edge of the leftmost object. The leftmost object remains stationary, and the other objects are aligned relative to it. Objects aligned to a SmartArt graphic are aligned to the leftmost edge of the SmartArt graphic, not to the leftmost shape in the SmartArt graphic. Objects aligned relative to each other by their middles or centers are aligned along a horizontal or vertical line that represents the average of their original positions. All of the objects might move.

Smart Guides appear automatically when two or more shapes are in spatial alignment with each other, even if the shapes vary in size. To evenly space multiple objects horizontally or vertically, you **distribute** them. PowerPoint determines the total length between either the outermost edges of the first and last selected object or the edges of the entire slide. It then inserts equal spacing among the items in the series. You also can distribute spacing by using the Size and Position dialog box, but the Distribute command automates this task.

BTW
Drawing Guides and Touch Screens
If you are using a touch screen, you may not be able to change the position of the drawing guides. In addition, the measurements indicating the position of the guides are not displayed.

To Display Slide Thumbnails in the Thumbnail Pane

The major slide elements are inserted on all slides, and you next will arrange these essential features. It is easier to move and align these elements when the main Slide pane is large. The following step changes the view from Outline View to Normal view.

1 Display the VIEW tab and then tap or click the Normal button (VIEW tab | Presentations Views group) to display the slide thumbnails in the Thumbnail pane.

2 If the Notes pane is displayed, tap or click the Notes button on the status bar to close the Notes pane.

To Display the Drawing Guides

1 OPEN OUTLINE | 2 ADD ILLUSTRATION & TEXT HYPERLINKS | 3 ADD ACTION BUTTONS & HYPERLINKS
4 POSITION ILLUSTRATIONS | 5 ALIGN PLACEHOLDER TEXT | 6 CONVERT & FORMAT BULLETS

Why? *Guides help you align objects on slides.* Using a mouse, when you point to a guide and then press and hold the mouse button, PowerPoint displays a box containing the exact position of the guide on the slide in inches. An arrow is displayed below the guide position to indicate the vertical guide either left or right of center. An arrow also is displayed to the right of the guide position to indicate the horizontal guide either above or below center. The following step displays the guides.

- Display Slide 2 of the Exercise Motivation presentation and then tap or click the Guides check box (VIEW tab | Show group) to display the horizontal and vertical guides (Figure 6–32).

Figure 6–32

Other Ways

1. Using touch screen, press and hold area of slide other than a placeholder or object, tap More button on shortcut menu, tap Grid and Guides arrow, tap Guides

2. Using mouse, right-click area of slide other than a placeholder or object, point to Grid and Guides on shortcut menu, click Guides

3. Press ALT+F9 to toggle guides on/off

To Position an Illustration Using Guides

1 OPEN OUTLINE | 2 ADD ILLUSTRATION & TEXT HYPERLINKS | 3 ADD ACTION BUTTONS & HYPERLINKS
4 POSITION ILLUSTRATIONS | 5 ALIGN PLACEHOLDER TEXT | 6 CONVERT & FORMAT BULLETS

The three illustrations on Slides 2, 3, and 4 should be displayed in precisely the same location. *Why? They will appear static as you transition from one slide to the next during the slide show.* The following steps position the illustration on Slide 2.

- If you are using a mouse, position the mouse pointer on the horizontal guide in a blank area of the slide so that the pointer changes to a double-headed arrow and then drag the horizontal guide to 0.75 inches below the center. Do not release the mouse button (Figure 6–33).

Q&A Why does 0.75 display when I hold down the mouse button?
The ScreenTip displays the horizontal guide's position. A 0.00 setting means that the guide is precisely in the middle of the slide and is not above or below the center, so a .75 setting indicates the guide is ¾-inch below the center line.

Figure 6–33

2

- Release the mouse button to position the horizontal guide at 0.75, which is the intended location of the illustration's top border.

- If you are using a mouse, position the mouse pointer on the vertical guide in a blank area of the slide so that the pointer changes to a double-headed arrow and then drag the vertical guide to 3.75 inches right of the center to position the vertical guide.

- Drag the illustration so the upper-left corner touches the intersection of the vertical and horizontal guides to position the illustration in the desired location (Figure 6–34).

Figure 6–34

Q&A | Can I add guides to help me align multiple objects?
Yes. Position the pointer over one guide and then press the CTRL key. When you drag your pointer, a second guide appears.

To Position the Slide 4 and Slide 3 Illustrations

The illustrations on Slide 4 and Slide 3 should be positioned in the same location as the Slide 2 illustration. The guides will display in the same location as you display each slide, so you easily can align similar objects on multiple slides. The following steps position the illustrations on Slide 4 and Slide 3.

1 Display Slide 4 and then drag the illustration so the upper-left corner of the swim illustration touches the intersection of the guides.

2 Display Slide 3 and use the guides to position the journal illustration (Figure 6–35).

Figure 6–35

To Hide Guides

The three illustrations on Slides 2, 3, and 4 are positioned in the desired locations, so the guides no longer are needed. The following step hides the guides.

 If necessary, display the VIEW tab and then tap or click the Guides check box (VIEW tab | Show group) to clear the check mark.

Other Ways

1. Using touch screen, press and hold area of slide other than a placeholder or object, tap More button on shortcut menu, tap Grid and Guides arrow, tap Guides to turn off guides

2. Using mouse, right-click area of slide other than a placeholder or object, click Grid and Guides on shortcut menu, click Guides to turn off guides

3. Press ALT+F9 to toggle guides on/off

To Display the Rulers

1 OPEN OUTLINE | 2 ADD ILLUSTRATION & TEXT HYPERLINKS | 3 ADD ACTION BUTTONS & HYPERLINKS
4 POSITION ILLUSTRATIONS | 5 ALIGN PLACEHOLDER TEXT | 6 CONVERT & FORMAT BULLETS

Why? *To begin aligning the three Slide 1 objects, you need to position either the left or the right object.* The vertical or horizontal **ruler** can help you drag an object to a precise location on the slide. The center of a slide is 0.00 on both the vertical and the horizontal rulers. The following step displays the rulers.

- If necessary, display the VIEW tab and then tap or click the Ruler check box (VIEW tab | Show group) to display the vertical and horizontal rulers (Figure 6–36).

Figure 6–36

Other Ways

1. Using touch screen, press and hold area of slide other than a placeholder or object, tap More button on shortcut menu, tap Ruler

2. Using mouse, right-click area of slide other than a placeholder or object, click Ruler

To Align Illustrations

Why? *The three illustrations on Slide 1 will look balanced if the bottom edges are aligned.* One method of creating this orderly appearance is by dragging the borders to a guide. Another method that is useful when you have multiple objects is to use one of PowerPoint's align commands. On Slide 1, you will position the far left illustration of the equipment and then align its bottom edge with those of the journal and swim illustrations. The following steps align the Slide 1 illustrations.

- Display Slide 1 and then position the pointer over the face in the equipment illustration.

- Drag the illustration so that the face is positioned approximately 3½ inches left of the center and approximately 2 inches below the center (Figure 6–37).

Figure 6–37

- Position the pointer over the eyes in the journal illustration.

- Drag the journal illustration so the eyes are positioned at the center of the slide (0 inches) and approximately 2½ inches below the center (Figure 6–38).

Q&A Why do the Smart Guides appear if the Guides box is not checked?
Smart Guides are displayed automatically when you move slide content. They are not affected by whether the Guides box is checked.

Figure 6–38

- Position the pointer over the pink cap in the swim illustration.

- Drag the swim illustration so the cap is positioned approximately 3½ inches right of the center and approximately 2 inches below the center (Figure 6–39).

Figure 6–39

To Distribute Illustrations

1 OPEN OUTLINE | 2 ADD ILLUSTRATION & TEXT HYPERLINKS | 3 ADD ACTION BUTTONS & HYPERLINKS
4 POSITION ILLUSTRATIONS | 5 ALIGN PLACEHOLDER TEXT | 6 CONVERT & FORMAT BULLETS

Now that the three Slide 1 illustrations are aligned along their bottom edges, you can have PowerPoint place the same amount of space between the first and second illustrations and the second and third illustrations. You have two distribution options: Align to Slide spaces all the selected objects evenly across the entire width of the slide; Align Selected Objects spaces only the middle objects between the fixed right and left objects. The following steps use the Align to Slide option. *Why? This option will distribute the Slide 1 illustrations horizontally to fill some of the space along the bottom of the slide.*

- Select the three Slide 1 illustrations, display the PICTURE TOOLS FORMAT tab, and then tap or click the Align button (PICTURE TOOLS FORMAT tab | Arrange group) to display the Align menu.

- If necessary, tap or click Align to Slide so that PowerPoint will adjust the spacing of the illustrations evenly between the slide edges and then tap or click the Align button to display the Align menu again (Figure 6–40).

Figure 6–40

● Tap or click
Distribute
Horizontally to
adjust the spacing
(Figure 6–41).

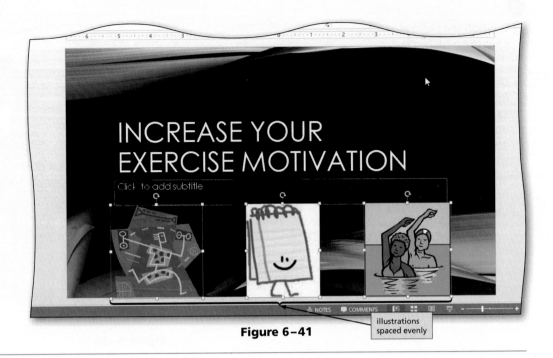

Figure 6–41

illustrations
spaced evenly

BTW
Saving the
Presentation
as an Outline
You began this project by
opening a Microsoft Word
outline, and you can save the
presentation as an outline
to use in a word processor
or another PowerPoint
project. An outline is saved
in Rich Text Format (.rtf)
and contains only text. To
save the presentation as an
outline, open the Backstage
view, tap or click the Save As
tab, navigate to the save
location and type a file name
in the File name box (Save As
dialog box), tap or click the
'Save as type' arrow and
select Outline/RTF in the
'Save as type' list, and then
tap or click the Save button.

To Hide Rulers

The three illustrations on Slide 1 are positioned in the desired locations, so the rulers no longer need to display. The following step hides the rulers.

 Display the VIEW tab and then tap or click the Ruler check box (VIEW tab | Show group) to remove the check mark.

Hiding a Slide

Slides 2, 3, and 4 present a variety of health information with hyperlinks. Depending on the audience's needs and the time constraints, you may decide not to display one or more of these slides. If need be, you can use the **Hide Slide** command to hide a slide from the audience during the normal running of a slide show. When you want to display the hidden slide, press the H key. No visible indicator displays to show that a hidden slide exists. You must be aware of the content of the presentation to know where the hidden slide is located.

When you run your presentation, the hidden slide does not display unless you press the H key when the slide preceding the hidden slide is displaying. For example, if you choose to hide Slide 4, then Slide 4 will not display unless you press the H key when Slide 3 displays in Slide Show view.

To Hide a Slide

1 OPEN OUTLINE | 2 ADD ILLUSTRATION & TEXT HYPERLINKS | 3 ADD ACTION BUTTONS & HYPERLINKS
4 POSITION ILLUSTRATIONS | 5 ALIGN PLACEHOLDER TEXT | 6 CONVERT & FORMAT BULLETS

Slide 4 discusses the benefits of training with a partner. As the presenter, you decide whether to show Slide 4. *Why? If time permits, or if the audience requires information on this subject, you can display Slide 4.* When you hide a slide in Slide Sorter view, a slashed rectangle surrounds the slide number, which indicates the slide is hidden. The following steps hide Slide 4.

- Tap or click the Slide Sorter view button on the status bar to display the slide thumbnails.

- Tap or click SLIDE SHOW on the ribbon to display the SLIDE SHOW tab and then tap or click the Slide 4 thumbnail to select it (Figure 6–42).

Figure 6–42

- Tap or click the Hide Slide button (SLIDE SHOW tab | Set Up group) to hide Slide 4 (Figure 6–43).

Q&A How do I know that Slide 4 is hidden?
The slide number has a slash through it to indicate Slide 4 is a hidden slide.

What if I decide I no longer want to hide a slide?
Repeat Steps 1 and 2. The Hide Slide button is a toggle; it either hides or displays a slide.

Figure 6–43

- Tap or click the Normal view button to display Slide 4.

Other Ways

1. Using touch screen, press and hold desired slide in Slide Sorter view or Normal view Thumbnail pane, tap Hide on shortcut menu

2. Using mouse, right-click desired slide in Slide Sorter view or Normal view Thumbnail pane, click Hide Slide on shortcut menu

Break Point: If you wish to take a break, this is a good place to do so. Be sure to save the Exercise Motivation file again and then you can quit PowerPoint. To resume at a later time, start PowerPoint, open the file called Exercise Motivation, and continue following the steps from this location forward.

Modifying Placeholder Text Settings

BTW
Certification
The Microsoft Office Specialist (MOS) program provides an opportunity for you to obtain a valuable industry credential — proof that you have the PowerPoint 2013 skills required by employers. For more information, visit the Certification resource on the Student Companion Site located on www.cengagebrain.com. For detailed instructions about accessing available resources, visit www.cengage.com/ct/studentdownload or see the inside back cover of this book.

The PowerPoint design themes specify default alignment of and spacing for text within a placeholder. For example, the text in most paragraphs is **left-aligned**, so the first character of each line is even with the first character above or below it. Text alignment also can be horizontally **centered** to position each line evenly between the left and right placeholder edges; **right-aligned**, so that the last character of each line is even with the last character of each line above or below it; and **justified**, where the first and last characters of each line are aligned and extra space is inserted between words to spread the characters evenly across the line.

When you begin typing text in most placeholders, the first paragraph is aligned at the top of the placeholder with any extra space at the bottom. You can change this default **paragraph alignment** location to position the paragraph lines centered vertically between the top and bottom placeholder edges, or you can place the last line at the bottom of the placeholder so that any extra space is at the top.

The design theme also determines the amount of spacing around the sides of the placeholder and between the lines of text. An internal **margin** provides a cushion of space between text and the top, bottom, left, and right sides of the placeholder. **Line spacing** is the amount of vertical space between the lines of text in a paragraph, and **paragraph spacing** is the amount of space above and below a paragraph. PowerPoint adjusts the line spacing and paragraph spacing automatically to accommodate various font sizes within the placeholder.

Long lists of items can be divided into several **columns** to fill the placeholder width and maximize the slide space. Once you have created columns, you can adjust the amount of space between the columns to enhance readability.

To Center Placeholder Text

1 OPEN OUTLINE | 2 ADD ILLUSTRATION & TEXT HYPERLINKS | 3 ADD ACTION BUTTONS & HYPERLINKS
4 POSITION ILLUSTRATIONS | 5 ALIGN PLACEHOLDER TEXT | 6 CONVERT & FORMAT BULLETS

By default, all placeholder text in the Vapor Trail document theme is left-aligned. You want the text to be centered, or placed with equal space horizontally between the left and right placeholder edges. *Why? Changing the alignment adds variety to the slide deck.* The following steps center the text in the content placeholders on Slides 2, 3, 4, and 5.

● Display Slide 2 and then select the four paragraphs in the content placeholder (Figure 6–44).

Figure 6–44

● Tap or click the Center button on the mini toolbar (shown in Figure 6–44) to center these paragraphs (Figure 6–45).

● Repeat Steps 1 and 2 to center the paragraph text in the content placeholders on Slides 3, 4, and 5.

Figure 6–45

Other Ways

1. Tap or click Center button (HOME tab | Paragraph group)	2. Using mouse, right-click selected text, click Paragraph on shortcut menu, click Alignment arrow (Paragraph dialog box), click Centered, click OK button	3. Tap or click Paragraph Dialog Box Launcher (HOME tab | Paragraph group), tap or click Alignment arrow (Paragraph dialog box), tap or click Centered, tap or click OK button	4. Press CTRL+E

To Align Placeholder Text

The Vapor Trail document theme aligns the text paragraphs at the top of the content placeholders. This default setting can be changed easily so that the paragraphs are aligned in the center or at the bottom of the placeholder. The following steps align the paragraphs vertically in the center of the content placeholders on Slides 2, 3, 4, and 5. *Why? The slides have a large amount of blank space, so centering the paragraphs vertically will fill some of this area and increase readability.*

- With the Slide 5 paragraphs still selected, display the HOME tab and then tap or click the Align Text button (HOME tab | Paragraph group) to display the Align Text gallery.

- If you are using a mouse, point to Middle in the Align Text gallery to display a live preview of the four paragraphs aligned in the center of the content placeholder (Figure 6–46).

 Experiment

- If you are using a mouse, point to the Bottom option in the gallery to see a preview of that alignment.

Figure 6–46

- Tap or click Middle in the Align Text gallery to align the paragraphs vertically in the center of the content placeholder (Figure 6–47).

Q&A What is the difference between centering the paragraphs in the placeholder and centering the text? Tapping or clicking the Align Text button and then tapping or clicking Middle moves the paragraphs up or down so that the first and last paragraphs are equal distances from the top and bottom placeholder borders. The Center button, on the other hand, moves the paragraphs left or right so that the first and last words in each line are equal distances from the left and right box borders.

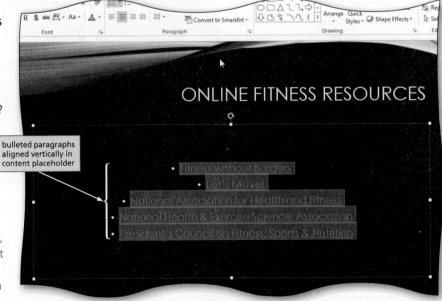

Figure 6–47

- Repeat Steps 1 and 2 to center the paragraph text in the middle of the content placeholders on Slides 2, 3, and 4.

To Change Paragraph Line Spacing

The vertical space between paragraphs is called **line spacing**. PowerPoint adjusts the amount of space based on font size. Default line spacing is 1.0, which is considered single spacing. Other preset options are 1.5, 2.0 (double spacing), 2.5, and 3.0 (triple spacing). You can specify precise line spacing intervals between, before, and after paragraphs in the Indents and Spacing tab of the Paragraph dialog box. The following steps increase the line spacing of the content paragraphs from single (1.0) to double (2.0) on Slides 2, 3, and 5. *Why? The additional space helps fill some of the area on the slide and also helps your audience read the paragraph text more easily.*

- With the HOME tab displayed, display Slide 2 and select the four content paragraphs.

- Tap or click the Line Spacing button (HOME tab | Paragraph group) to display the Line Spacing gallery.

- If you are using a mouse, point to 2.0 in the Line Spacing gallery to display a live preview of this line spacing (Figure 6–48).

Experiment

- If you are using a mouse, point to each of the line spacing options in the gallery to see a preview of that line spacing.

- Tap or click 2.0 in the Line Spacing gallery to change the line spacing to double.

Figure 6–48

- Repeat Steps 1 and 2 to change the line spacing to 2.0 for the paragraph text in the content placeholders on Slides 3 and 5. Do not change the line spacing on Slide 4.

Q&A Why is the line spacing not changing on Slide 4?
These content placeholder paragraphs will be changed into columns, so spacing is not a design concern at this time.

- Move the journal illustration on Slide 3 slightly downward so that it does not overlap the text in the second bulleted paragraph.

Other Ways

1. Using mouse, right-click selected text, click Paragraph on shortcut menu, click Line Spacing arrow (Paragraph dialog box), click Double, click OK button

2. Tap or click Paragraph Dialog Box Launcher (HOME tab | Paragraph group), tap or click Line Spacing arrow (Paragraph dialog box), tap or click Double, tap or click OK button

To Create Columns in a Placeholder

Why? The list of health risks in the Slide 4 placeholder is lengthy and lacks visual appeal. You can change these items into two, three, or more columns and then adjust the column widths. The following steps change the placeholder elements into columns.

- Display Slide 4 and then tap or click the content placeholder to select it.

- With the HOME tab displayed, tap or click the Columns button (HOME tab | Paragraph group) to display the Columns gallery.

- If you are using a mouse, point to Two Columns in the Columns gallery to display a live preview of the text in the first column (Figure 6–49).

🔎 Experiment

- If you are using a mouse, point to each of the column options in the gallery to see a preview of the text displaying in various columns.

Q&A
Why doesn't the content display in two columns if I selected two columns?
Because all the text fits in the first column in the placeholder.

Figure 6–49

- Tap or click Two Columns to create two columns of text.

- Drag the bottom sizing handle up to the location shown in Figure 6–50.

Q&A
Why is the bottom sizing handle between the fourth and fifth paragraphs?
Eight benefits are listed in the content placeholder, so dividing the paragraphs in two groups of four will balance the layout.

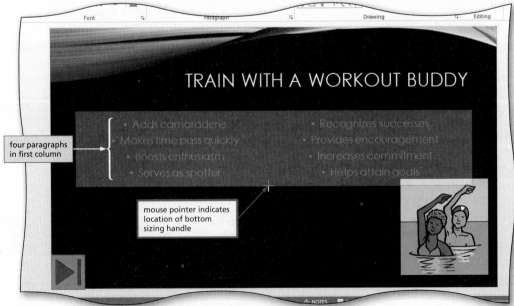

Figure 6–50

3

- Lift your finger or release the mouse button to resize the content placeholder and create the two columns of text.

To Adjust Column Spacing

Why? *The space between the columns in the placeholder can be increased to make room for the swim illustration, which you want to move between the columns.* The following steps increase the spacing between the columns.

1

• With the placeholder selected, tap or click the Columns button and then tap or click More Columns.

• Tap or click the Spacing box up arrow (Columns dialog box) until 3.5" is displayed (Figure 6–51).

Figure 6–51

2

• Tap or click the OK button to increase the spacing between the columns (Figure 6–52).

Q&A Can I change the paragraphs back to one column easily? Yes. Tap or click the Columns button and then tap or click One Column.

Figure 6–52

To Format the Content Placeholder

To add interest to the Slide 4 content placeholder, apply a Quick Style and then move the swim illustration from the lower-right corner to the space between the columns. The following steps apply a green Subtle Effect style to the placeholder and then change the illustration location.

BTW
Quick Reference
For a table that lists how to complete the tasks covered in this book using touch gestures, the mouse, ribbon, shortcut menu, and keyboard, see the Quick Reference Summary at the back of this book, or visit the Quick Reference resource on the Student Companion Site located on www.cengagebrain.com. For detailed instructions about accessing available resources, visit www.cengage.com/ct/studentdownload or see the inside back cover of this book.

1 With the placeholder selected, tap or click the Quick Styles button (HOME tab | Drawing group) to display the Quick Styles gallery.

2 Tap or click Subtle Effect – Orange, Accent 2 (third style in fourth row).

3 Move the swim illustration from the lower-right corner to the area between the two columns so that a vertical Smart Guide is displayed in the center of the illustration and a horizontal Smart Guide is displayed below the illustration (Figure 6–53).

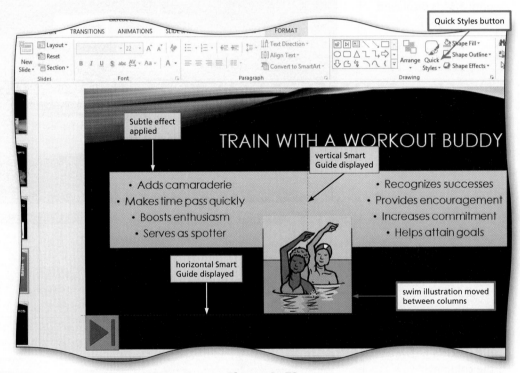

Figure 6–53

To Enter a Line Break

1 OPEN OUTLINE | 2 ADD ILLUSTRATION & TEXT HYPERLINKS | 3 ADD ACTION BUTTONS & HYPERLINKS
4 POSITION ILLUSTRATIONS | 5 ALIGN PLACEHOLDER TEXT | 6 CONVERT & FORMAT BULLETS

Why? *The second paragraph in Slide 3 in your presentation is lengthy and appears above the journal illustration. Separating the paragraph after the word, different, can emphasize the fact that journal serves two separate functions for each workout: showing differences and challenges.* If you press the ENTER key at the end of a line, PowerPoint automatically applies paragraph formatting, which could include indents and bullets. To prevent this formatting from occurring, you can press SHIFT+ENTER to place a **line break** at the end of the line, which moves the insertion point to the beginning of the next line. The following steps place a line break before the word, and, on Slide 3.

- Display Slide 3 and then place the insertion point before the word, and, in the second paragraph (Figure 6–54).

Figure 6–54

❷

- If you are using a touch screen, tap the Touch Keyboard button on the taskbar to display the touch keyboard.

- Press SHIFT+ENTER to insert a line break character and move the words, and more challenging, to the third line in the placeholder (Figure 6–55).

- If you are using a touch screen, close the touch keyboard.

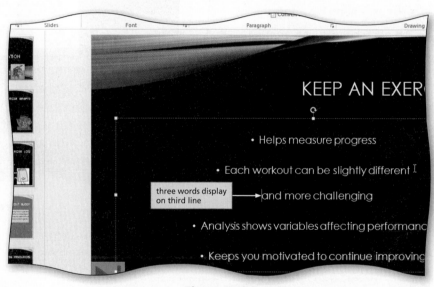

Figure 6–55

Modifying Bullets

PowerPoint allows you to change the default appearance of bullets in a slide show. The document themes determine the bullet character. A **bullet character** is a symbol, traditionally a closed circle, that sets off items in a list. It can be a predefined style, a variety of fonts and characters displayed in the Symbol gallery, or a picture from a file or from Office.com. You may want to change a bullet character to add visual interest and variety. Once you change the bullet character, you also can change its size and color.

If desired, you can change every bullet in a presentation to a unique character. If your presentation has many bulleted slides, however, you would want to have a consistent look on all slides by making the bullets a similar color and size.

To customize your presentation, you can change the default slide layout bullets to numbers by changing the bulleted list to a numbered list. PowerPoint provides a variety of numbering options, including Arabic and Roman numerals. These numbers can be sized and recolored, and the starting number can be something other than 1 or I. In addition, PowerPoint's numbering options include upper- and lowercase letters.

BTW
Distributing a Document
Instead of printing and distributing a hard copy of a document, you can distribute the document electronically. Options include sending the document via email; posting it on cloud storage (such as SkyDrive) and sharing the file with others; posting it on a social networking site, blog, or other website; and sharing a link associated with an online location of the document. You also can create and share a PDF or XPS image of the document, so that users can view the file in Acrobat Reader or XPS Viewer instead of in PowerPoint.

To Change a Bullet Character to a Picture

Why? *The plain bullet characters for the Vapor Trail document theme do not add much visual interest and do not relate to the topic of exercise.* One method of modifying these bullets is to use a relevant picture. The following steps change the first paragraph bullet character to a dumbbells picture, which is located on the Data Files for Students.

- With the HOME tab still displaying, display Slide 2 and then select all four content placeholder paragraphs.

 Can I insert a different bullet character in each paragraph?
Yes. Select only a paragraph and then perform the steps below for each paragraph.

- Tap or click the Bullets arrow (HOME tab | Paragraph group) to display the Bullets gallery (Figure 6–56).

 Why is an orange box displayed around the three characters?
They are the default first-level bullet characters for the Vapor Trail document theme.

Experiment

- If you are using a mouse, point to each of the bullets displayed in the gallery to see a preview of the characters.

Figure 6–56

- Tap or click Bullets and Numbering to display the Bullets and Numbering dialog box (Figure 6–57).

 Why are my bullets different from those displayed in Figure 6–57?
The bullets most recently inserted are displayed as the first items in the dialog box.

Figure 6–57

- Tap or click the Picture button (Bullets and Numbering dialog box) to display the Insert Pictures dialog box (Figure 6–58).

Figure 6–58

- Tap or click the Browse button (Insert Pictures dialog box) to display the Insert Picture dialog box.

- If necessary, navigate to the location of the Data Files for Students.

- Tap or click Dumbbells to select the file (Figure 6–59).

Figure 6–59

- Tap or click the Insert button (Insert Picture dialog box) to insert the Dumbbells picture as the paragraph bullet character (Figure 6–60).

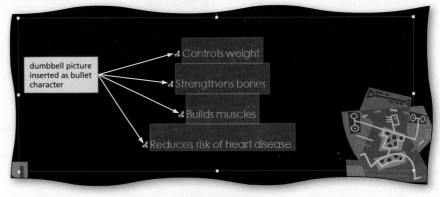

Figure 6–60

Other Ways

1. Using mouse, right-click paragraph, point to Bullets on shortcut menu, click Bullets and Numbering

To Change a Bullet Character to a Symbol

Why? *For variety and to add a unique characteristic to the presentation, another bullet change you can make is to insert a symbol as the character.* Symbols are found in several fonts, including Webdings, Wingdings, Wingdings 2, and Wingdings 3. The following steps change the bullet character on Slide 5 to a barbell symbol in the Webdings font.

- Display Slide 5, select all five hyperlinked paragraphs, tap or click the Bullets arrow (HOME tab | Paragraph group), and then tap or click Bullets and Numbering to display the Bullets and Numbering dialog box (Figure 6–61).

Figure 6–61

- Tap or click the Customize button (Bullets and Numbering dialog box) to display the Symbol dialog box (Figure 6–62).

Q&A Why is a symbol selected?
That symbol is the default bullet for the first-level paragraphs in the Vapor Trail document theme.

Figure 6–62

- Tap or click the Font arrow (Symbol dialog box), scroll down, and then tap or click Webdings.

- Scroll down to locate the barbell symbol.

- Tap or click the barbell symbol (shown in Figure 6–63) to select it.

Q&A Why does my dialog box have more rows of symbols and different fonts from which to choose?

The rows and fonts displayed depend upon how PowerPoint was installed on your system and the screen you are viewing.

What is the character code that is displayed in the Symbol dialog box?

Each character in each font has a unique code. If you know the character code, you can type the number in the Character code box to display that symbol. The character code for the barbell symbol in the Webdings font is 134.

Figure 6–63

- Tap or click the OK button (Symbol dialog box) to display the barbell bullet in the Bullets and Numbering dialog box (Figure 6–64).

Figure 6–64

- Tap or click the OK button (Bullets and Numbering dialog box) to insert the barbell symbol as the paragraph bullet (Figure 6–65).

Figure 6–65

To Change Bullet Size

Bullets have a default size determined by the document theme. **Bullet size** is measured as a percentage of the text size and can range from 25 to 400 percent. The following steps change the barbell symbol size. *Why?* *It is difficult to see the symbol, so increasing its size draws attention to the visual element and helps reinforce the exercising theme in the slide deck.*

- With the Slide 5 paragraphs still selected, tap or click the Bullets arrow (HOME tab | Paragraph group) and then tap or click Bullets and Numbering in the Bullets gallery to display the Bullets and Numbering dialog box.

- Set the size in the Size box to 150 (Figure 6–66).

Figure 6–66

- Tap or click the OK button to increase the barbell bullet size to 150 percent of its original size (Figure 6–67).

Figure 6–67

To Change the Size of Other Bullet Characters

For consistency, the bullet character on Slide 2 should have a similar size as that on Slide 5. The following steps change the size of the dumbbell bullets.

1. Display Slide 2 and then select the four paragraphs in the content placeholder.

2. Display the Bullets and Numbering dialog box, increase the bullet size to 150% of text, and then tap or click the OK button (Figure 6–68).

Figure 6–68

To Format Bullet Color

1 OPEN OUTLINE | 2 ADD ILLUSTRATION & TEXT HYPERLINKS | 3 ADD ACTION BUTTONS & HYPERLINKS
4 POSITION ILLUSTRATIONS | 5 ALIGN PLACEHOLDER TEXT | 6 CONVERT & FORMAT BULLETS

A default **bullet color** is based on the eight colors in the design theme. Additional standard and custom colors also are available. The following steps change the barbell bullet color to Orange. *Why? This color coordinates with the design at the top of the slide and provides a bright contrast to the black slide background.*

1

- Display Slide 5, select the five hyperlinked paragraphs, display the Bullets and Numbering dialog box, and then tap or click the Color button (Bullets and Numbering dialog box) to display the Color gallery (Figure 6–69).

Figure 6–69

2

- Tap or click the color Orange in the Standard Colors area to change the bullet color to Orange (third color in the Standard Colors area) (Figure 6–70).

Figure 6–70

3

- Tap or click the OK button to apply the color Orange to the barbell bullets (Figure 6–71).

Figure 6–71

Other Ways

1. Using mouse, right-click paragraph, point to Bullets on shortcut menu, click Bullets and Numbering, select color

To Change a Bullet Character to a Number

1 OPEN OUTLINE | 2 ADD ILLUSTRATION & TEXT HYPERLINKS | 3 ADD ACTION BUTTONS & HYPERLINKS
4 POSITION ILLUSTRATIONS | 5 ALIGN PLACEHOLDER TEXT | **6 CONVERT & FORMAT BULLETS**

PowerPoint allows you to change the default bullets to numbers. The process of changing the bullet characters is similar to the process of adding bullets to paragraphs. The following steps change the first-level paragraph bullet characters on Slide 3 to numbers. *Why? Numbers help to show steps in a sequence and also help guide a speaker during the presentation when referring to specific information in the paragraphs.*

1

- Display Slide 3 and then select all content paragraphs.

- With the HOME tab still displaying, tap or click the Numbering arrow (HOME tab | Paragraph group) to display the Numbering gallery.

- If you are using a mouse, point to the 1) 2) 3) numbering option in the Numbering gallery to display a live preview of these numbers (Figure 6–72).

 Experiment

- If you are using a mouse, point to each of the numbers in the Numbering gallery to watch the numbers change on Slide 3.

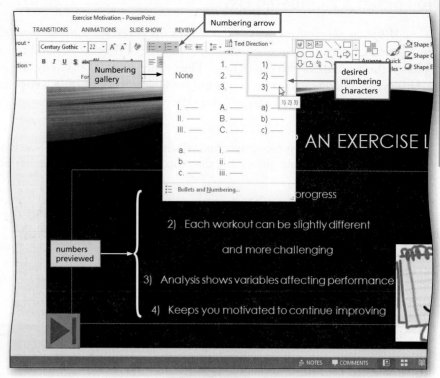

Figure 6–72

2

- Tap or click the 1) 2) 3) numbering option to insert these numbers as the first-level paragraph characters (Figure 6–73).

Q&A How do I change the first number in the list?
Tap or click Bullets and Numbering at the bottom of the Numbering gallery and then tap or click the up or down arrow in the Start at box to change the number.

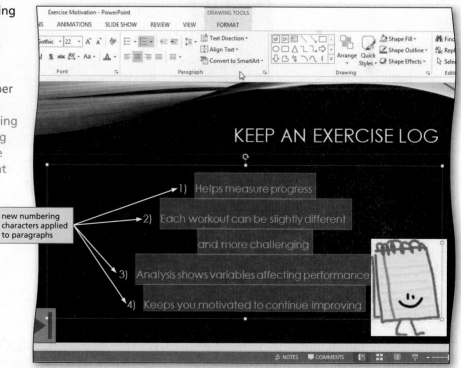

Figure 6–73

Other Ways

1. Using mouse, right-click paragraph, point to Numbering on shortcut menu, select numbering characters

To Format a Numbered List

Why? *To add emphasis, you can increase the size of the new numbers inserted in Slide 3.* As with bullets, numbering characters are measured as a percentage of the text size and can range from 25 to 400 percent. The color of these numbers also can change. The original color is based on the eight colors in the design theme. Additional standard and custom colors are available. The following steps change the size and colors of the numbers to 125 percent and Orange, respectively.

- With the Slide 3 content paragraphs still selected, tap or click the Numbering arrow (HOME tab | Paragraph group) to display the Numbering gallery and then tap or click Bullets and Numbering to display the Bullets and Numbering dialog box.

- Change the numbers' size to 125%.

- Tap or click the Color button (Bullets and Numbering dialog box) to display the color gallery and then tap or click Orange (third color in the Standard Colors area) to change the numbers' font color (Figure 6–74).

- Tap or click the OK button to apply the new numbers' font size and color.

Figure 6–74

Other Ways

1. Using mouse, right-click paragraph, point to Numbering on shortcut menu, click Bullets and Numbering, click up or down Size arrow until desired size is displayed, click Color button, select color, click OK button

To Remove Bullet Characters

The training benefits listed in the two Slide 4 columns are preceded by a bullet character. The following steps remove the bullet characters from the items in the two columns on Slide 4. *Why? The slide may appear less cluttered if you remove the bullets.*

1

- Display Slide 4, select all the text in the two columns, and then tap or click the Bullets arrow (HOME tab | Paragraph group).

Q&A What should I do if I tapped or clicked the Bullets button instead of the Bullets arrow?

If the paragraphs are bulleted, tapping or clicking the Bullets button removes the bullets. Tap or click the Bullets button again to display the bullets.

- If you are using a mouse, point to the None option in the Bullets gallery to display a live preview of how the slide will appear without bullets (Figure 6–75).

2

- Tap or click the None option to remove the bullet characters on Slide 4.

Q&A Would I use the same technique to remove numbers from a list?

Yes. The None option also is available in the Numbering gallery.

Figure 6–75

Consider the audience's interests.

As audience members start to view your presentation, they often think about their personal needs and wonder, "How will this presentation benefit me?" As you may have learned in your psychology classes, Maslow's hierarchy of needs drives much of your behavior, starting with basic sustenance and moving on to safety, belonging, ego-status, and self-actualization. Audience members cannot move to the next higher level of needs until their current level is satisfied. For example, an individual must first satisfy his needs of hunger and thirst before he can consider partaking in leisure time activities. Your presentations must meet the requirements of your audience members; otherwise, these people will not consider your talk as benefiting their needs. Having hyperlinks and action buttons can help you tailor a presentation to fulfill the audience's satisfaction level.

CONSIDER THIS

Running a Slide Show with Hyperlinks and Action Buttons

The Exercise Motivation presentation contains a variety of useful features that provide value to an audience. The graphics should help viewers understand and recall the information being presented. The hyperlinks on Slide 5 show useful websites that give current exercise information. In addition, the action button allows a presenter to jump to Slide 5 while Slides 2 or 3 are being displayed. If an audience member asks a question or if the presenter needs to answer specific questions regarding training with friends when Slide 3 is displaying, the information on the hidden Slide 4 can be accessed immediately by pressing the H key.

To Run a Slide Show with Hyperlinks, Action Buttons, and a Hidden Slide

Running a slide show that contains hyperlinks and action buttons is an interactive experience. A presenter has the option to display slides in a predetermined sequence or to improvise based on the audience's reaction and questions. When a presentation contains hyperlinks and the computer is connected to the Internet, the speaker can tap or click the links to command the default browser to display the websites. The following steps run the Exercise Motivation presentation.

1 Tap or click Slide 1. Tap or click the Slide Show button on the status bar to run the slide show and display Slide 1.

2 Tap or click the equipment illustration to display Slide 2. If a PowerPoint Security Notice dialog box is displayed, click the Yes button to continue running the presentation.

3 On Slide 2, tap or click the equipment illustration to link to the first slide in the Additional Motivation presentation.

4 Tap or click the Return action button on the first slide to return to Slide 2 in the Exercise Motivation presentation.

5 Press the ENTER key to display Slide 3. Tap or click the journal illustration to run Microsoft Word and open the Workout Journal file. View the information and then tap or click the Close button on the title bar to exit Word and return to Slide 3.

6 Press the H key to display Slide 4. Tap or click the swim illustration to link to the second slide in the Additional Motivation presentation. Tap or click the Return action button on the second slide to return to Slide 4 in the Exercise Motivation presentation.

7 Press the ENTER key to display Slide 5. Tap or click the first hyperlink to start your browser and access the Fitness without Borders webpage. If necessary, maximize the webpage window when the page is displayed. Tap or click the Close button on the webpage title bar to close the browser.

8 Continue using the hyperlinks and action buttons and then end both presentations.

To Save, Print, and Exit PowerPoint

The presentation now is complete. You should save the slides, print a handout, and then exit PowerPoint.

1 Save the Exercise Motivation presentation again with the same file name.

2 Print the presentation as a handout with two slides per page (Figure 6–76).

3 Exit PowerPoint, closing all open documents.

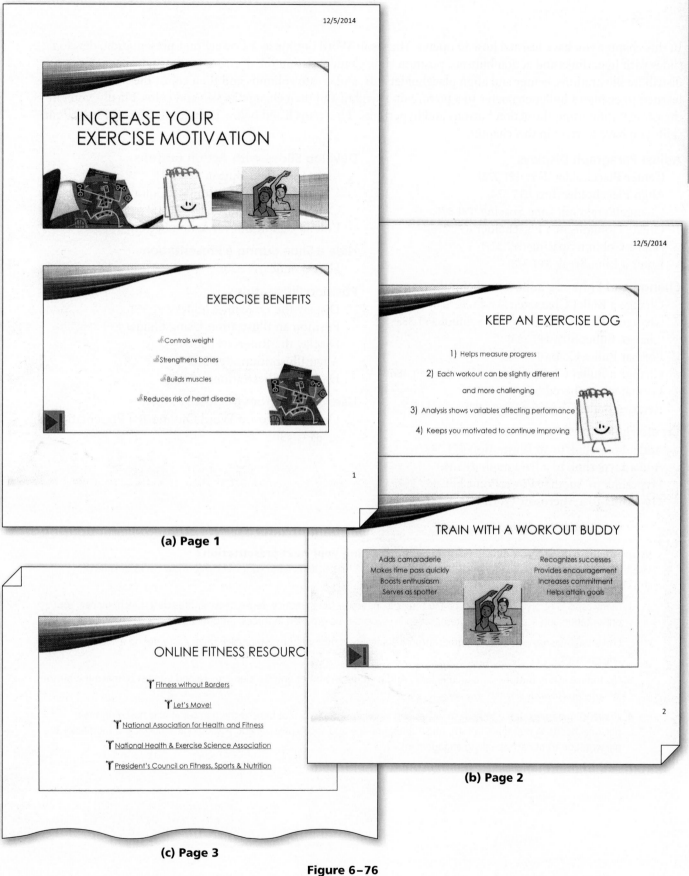

(a) Page 1

(b) Page 2

(c) Page 3

Figure 6-76

Chapter Summary

In this chapter you have learned how to open a Microsoft Word outline as a PowerPoint presentation, develop slides with hyperlinks and action buttons, position slide elements using the drawing guides and rulers, align and distribute illustrations, center and align placeholder text, and create columns and then adjust the width. You then learned to change a bullet character to a picture or a symbol and then change its size and color. Finally, you ran the presentation using the action buttons and hyperlinks. The items listed below include all the new PowerPoint skills you have learned in this chapter.

Adjust Paragraph Displays
Center Placeholder Text (PPT 372)
Align Placeholder Text (PPT 374)
Change Paragraph Line Spacing (PPT 375)
Create Columns in a Placeholder (PPT 376)
Adjust Column Spacing (PPT 377)
Enter a Line Break (PPT 378)

Change and Enhance Bullets and Numbering
Change a Bullet Character to a Picture (PPT 380)
Change a Bullet Character to a Symbol (PPT 382)
Change Bullet Size (PPT 384)
Format Bullet Color (PPT 385)
Change a Bullet Character to a Number (PPT 386)
Format a Numbered List (PPT 388)
Remove Bullet Characters (PPT 388)

Create Hyperlinks
Add a Hyperlink to an Illustration (PPT 347)
Add a Hyperlink to a Paragraph (PPT 349)
Hyperlink to Another PowerPoint File (PPT 358)
Hyperlink to a Microsoft Word File (PPT 361)

Develop Slides with Action Buttons
Insert an Action Button (PPT 351)
Change an Action Button Fill Color (PPT 354)
Copy an Action Button (PPT 355)
Edit an Action Button Action Setting (PPT 356)

Hide a Slide during a Presentation
Hide a Slide (PPT 370)

Position Illustrations
Display the Drawing Guides (PPT 364)
Position an Illustration Using Guides (PPT 365)
Display the Rulers (PPT 367)
Align Illustrations (PPT 368)
Distribute Illustrations (PPT 369)

Use Content from Microsoft Word
Open a Microsoft Word Outline as a Presentation (PPT 343)

CONSIDER THIS

What decisions will you need to make when creating your next presentation?
Use these guidelines as you complete the assignments in this chapter and create your own slide show decks outside of this class.

1. Many aspects of our lives are grouped in threes: sun, moon, stars; reduce, reuse, recycle; breakfast, lunch, dinner. Your presentation and accompanying presentation likewise can be grouped in threes: introduction, body, and conclusion.

2. Make the hypertext graphics or letters large so a speaker is prompted to tap or click them easily during a speaking engagement.

3. Customize action buttons for a unique look. Add pictures and other graphic elements to add interest or make the button less obvious to your viewers.

4. Audience members desire to hear speeches and view presentations that benefit them in some way based on their personal needs. A presenter, in turn, must determine the audience's physical and psychological needs and then tailor the presentation to fit each speaking engagement.

How should you submit solutions to questions in the assignments identified with a ✳ symbol?
Every assignment in this book contains one or more questions identified with a ✳ symbol. These questions require you to think beyond the assigned presentation. Present your solutions to the questions in the format required by your instructor. Possible formats may include one or more of these options: write the answer; create a document that contains the answer; present your answer to the class; discuss your answer in a group; record the answer as audio or video using a webcam, smartphone, or portable media player; or post answers on a blog, wiki, or website.

Apply Your Knowledge

Reinforce the skills and apply the concepts you learned in this chapter.

Revising a Presentation with Action Buttons, Bullet Styles, and Hidden Slides

Note: To complete this assignment, you will be required to use the Data Files for Students. Visit www.cengage.com/ct/studentdownload for detailed instructions or contact your instructor for information about accessing the required files.

Instructions: Run PowerPoint. Open the presentation, Apply 6-1 Knee, from the Data Files for Students.

The slides in the presentation present information about the knee. The document you open is a partially formatted presentation. You are to change the theme variant, add a picture style, insert action buttons, and hide slides. Your presentation should look like Figure 6–77 on the next page.

Perform the following tasks:

1. Change the Ion Boardroom theme variant from purple to blue (the third color variant).

2. On Slide 1, apply the WordArt style, Pattern Fill – Lime, Accent 1, 50%, Hard Shadow – Accent 1 (the third style in the fourth row), to the title text and add the Off Axis 1 Right 3-D Rotation text effect (the second rotation in the second Parallel row) to this text. Apply the Rotated, White picture style to the photo (the third style in the third row) as shown in Figure 6–77a.

3. On Slide 2 (Figure 6–77b), hyperlink each arrow shape to the corresponding slide. For example, the Femur arrow shape should hyperlink to Slide 3 (Figure 6–77c). The Patella arrow shape should hyperlink to Slide 4 (Figure 6–77d), and the Tibia arrow shape should hyperlink to Slide 5 (Figure 6–77e).

4. On Slide 3 (Figure 6–77c), insert a Home action button and hyperlink it to Slide 2. Change the action button fill color to Blue, and then change the transparency to 60%. Do not play a sound. Size the button so that it is approximately 0.75" × 0.75" and then move it to the location shown in Figure 6–77c. Copy this action button to Slides 4 and 5.

5. On Slides 3 through 5, add Star Bullets to the content text paragraphs and then increase the size of the bullets to 125% of text as shown in the figures.

6. Hide Slides 3, 4, and 5.

7. If requested by your instructor, add the street you grew up on in the subtitle placeholder on Slide 1.

8. Change the transition from Cut to Cover for all slides. Change the duration to 2.25 seconds.

9. Save the presentation using the file name, Apply 6-1 Knee Anatomy.

10. Submit the revised document in the format specified by your instructor.

11. ✳ In this presentation, you used action buttons between the names and photos of parts of the knee. Why? Why did you hide Slides 3, 4, and 5? How did this improve the presentation?

Continued >

Apply Your Knowledge *continued*

(a) Slide 1

(b) Slide 2

(c) Slide 3

(d) Slide 4

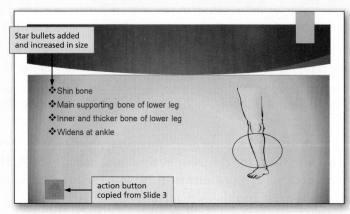

(e) Slide 5

Figure 6–77

Extend Your Knowledge

Extend the skills you learned in this chapter and experiment with new skills. You may need to use Help to complete the assignment.

Inserting a Photo into an Action Button and Changing a Bullet Character to a Picture
Note: To complete this assignment, you will be required to use the Data Files for Students. Visit www.cengage.com/ct/studentdownload for detailed instructions or contact your instructor for information about accessing the required files.

Instructions: Run PowerPoint. Open the presentation, Extend 6-1 Exercise, from the Data Files for Students. You will insert hyperlinks on Slide 2; insert action buttons on Slides 3, 4, and 5; and change the bullet characters to pictures on Slides 3, 4, and 5, as shown in Figure 6–78.

Perform the following tasks:

1. On Slide 1 (Figure 6–78a), add the Arch Up text effect (the first effect in the Follow Path row in the Transform area) to the title WordArt and then change the color of the text to Orange, Accent 2 (the sixth color in the first Theme Colors row). Change the color of the subtitle text to Yellow (the fourth color in the Standard Colors row). *Note:* The subtitle text placeholder

(a) Slide 1 **(b) Slide 2**

(c) Slide 3 **(d) Slide 4**

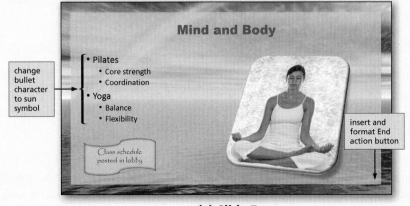

(e) Slide 5

Figure 6–78

Continued >

Extend Your Knowledge *continued*

is displayed above the title text placeholder in this layout. Change the subtitle text paragraph alignment to Distributed by selecting the text, displaying the HOME tab, tapping or clicking the Paragraph Dialog Box Launcher button (HOME tab | Paragraph group), tapping or clicking the Alignment arrow, and then tapping or clicking Distributed.

2. On Slide 2 (Figure 6–78b on the previous page), hyperlink each picture to the corresponding slide. For example, the Aerobics photo should hyperlink to Slide 3 (Figure 6–78c). The other two photos should hyperlink to Slides 4 and 5 (Figures 6–78d and 6–78e), respectively.

3. On Slide 3 (Figure 6–78c), insert a Custom action button in the lower-right area of the slide and hyperlink it to Slide 2. Change the size to approximately .75" × .75". Format this shape by inserting the photo, Aerobics, located on the Data Files for Students. Change the transparency of the photo to 50%. Copy and paste this action button on Slide 4 and move the banner slightly up and to the left so that it does not overlap the action button.

4. On Slide 4 (Figure 6–78d), format the action button by inserting the photo, Cycling, located on the Data Files for Students.

5. On Slide 5 (Figure 6–78e), insert an End action button in the lower-right corner of the slide, change the size to approximately .75" × .75", hyperlink it to End Show, and then change the transparency to 50%.

6. On Slides 3 and 4, change the bullet character for the level one only text to the Blue Weight illustration located on the Data Files for Students, and then increase the size of the bullets to 165%. Remove the bullet characters for the level two text on Slides 3 and 4. On Slide 5, change the bullet character for all levels of text to the sun symbol, which is a Wingdings 2 font and has the character code 237. Increase the size of the bullet to 150% and then change the color to Orange (the third color in the Standard Colors row).

7. If requested by your instructor, add the year you graduated from high school before the word, Class, in the shape on Slide 5 (Figure 6–78e).

8. Apply the Uncover transition in the Subtle category to all slides and then change the duration to 3.25 seconds.

9. Save the presentation using the file name, Extend 6-1 Exercise Classes.

10. Submit the revised document in the format specified by your instructor.

11. ✸ In Step 1, you changed the look of the title and subtitle fonts by adding a text effect, changing colors, and moving the text. How did this enhance your title slide? What did adding action buttons add to the presentation?

Analyze, Correct, Improve

Analyze a presentation, correct all errors, and improve it.

Modifying Text and Line Spacing in a Placeholder

Note: To complete this assignment, you will be required to use the Data Files for Students. Visit www.cengage.com/ct/studentdownload for detailed instructions or contact your instructor for information about accessing the required files.

Instructions: Run PowerPoint. Open the presentation, Analyze 6-1 Baseball Bats, from the Data Files for Students. You coach a little league baseball team. During registration, information is displayed about the upcoming season such as opening day events and concession stand schedules. The little league board members thought it would be interesting to have other information about baseball on display. You decide to create a presentation about why aluminum baseball bats are preferred over wood. Modify the slide by making the indicated corrections and improvements.

1. Correct

a. Delete the photo in the upper-right corner of the slide, shown in Figure 6–79. Increase the size of the remaining photo to 3.44" × 12.63" and move the photo to the upper-left corner of the slide. With the photo still selected, choose the Send to Back arrangement option.

b. Increase the first line of the title text font to 66 point. Increase the second line of the title text font to 36 point, and change the color to Blue (the eighth color in the Standard Colors row).

c. Change the bulleted text font to Arial, increase the size of the font to 24 point, and then change the line spacing from 1.5 to 1.0.

d. Correct the spelling errors.

e. If requested by your instructor, insert a box in the lower-right corner of the slide and type your mobile phone number in the box.

2. Improve

a. Change the variant to green (the third one).

b. Apply the Crisscross Etching artistic effect to the photo (the third effect in the fourth row).

c. Change both lines of the title text paragraph alignment to Distributed.

d. Change the Filled Round Bullets to Arrow Bullets, change the color to Blue (the eighth color in the Standard Colors row), and then increase the size of the bullets to 150% of the text size.

e. Remove the Vortex transition.

f. Save the presentation using the file name, Analyze 6-1 Aluminum Baseball Bats.

g. Submit the revised document in the format specified by your instructor.

3. ✳ Which errors existed in the starting file? How did changing the font sizes help? How did deleting one photo and enlarging the remaining photo improve the look of the slide?

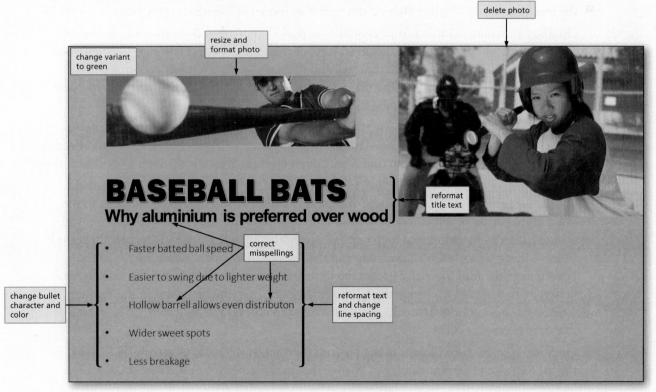

Figure 6–79

In the Labs

Design and/or create a presentation using the guidelines, concepts, and skills presented in this chapter. Labs 1 and 2, which increase in difficulty, require you to create solutions based on what you learned in the chapter; Lab 3 requires you to create a solution, which uses cloud and web technologies, by learning and investigating on your own from general guidance.

Lab 1: Creating Columns in a Box, Increasing the Size of Bullets, Inserting Hyperlinks, Using Guides, and Formatting Bullets

Problem: Your garden club is participating in the local annual home and garden show. You were asked to create a presentation for the show. Members of the club are starting to plant flowers, vegetables, and herbs to sell at the show. You decide to do your presentation on ladybugs and how they can help gardeners. Some of the plants that your club is selling, like fennel, dill, and cilantro, for example, attract ladybugs. You also found information about the Lost Ladybug Project, conducted by the Agricultural Research Service (ARS), South Dakota State University, and Cornell University. You will use hyperlinks in your presentation to share information about this project. You create the presentation shown in Figure 6–80.

Note: To complete this assignment, you will be required to use the Data Files for Students. Visit www.cengage.com/ct/studentdownload for detailed instructions or contact your instructor for information about accessing the required files.

Instructions: Perform the following tasks:

1. Open the presentation, Lab 6-1 Ladybugs, from the Data Files for Students.

2. Create a background for all slides by inserting the photo called, Ladybug1, from the Data Files for Students. Change the transparency to 25% on Slide 1, as shown in Figure 6–80a. Change the transparency to 75% for Slides 2 through 6, as shown in Figures 6–80b through 6–80f.

3. On Slide 1, change the title text placeholder vertical alignment to Bottom. Increase the title text size to 52 point, change the text to all caps, change the color to Dark Red (the first color in the Standard Colors row), bold this text, and then apply the Tight Reflection, touching reflection effect (the first one in the first Reflection Variations row) to the title text. Increase the subtitle text size to 28 point, and italicize this text, as shown in Figure 6–80a.

4. On Slide 2 (Figure 6–80b), increase the title text font size to 32 point, change the color to Dark Red (the first color in the Standard Colors row), and then bold this text. Use the Format Painter to format the title text on Slides 3 through 6 (Figures 6–80c through 6–80f) with the same features as the title text on Slide 2.

5. Insert the illustration called Ladybug2 from the Data Files for Students and move it to the lower-right corner of Slide 2, as shown in Figure 6–80b. With the ladybug illustration still selected, insert a hyperlink and then copy and paste the website from Slide 6 as the hyperlink address. Insert a box below the ladybug and then type, **Have you seen me?** , in the box. Change the font to Arial, increase the font size to 20 point, and then bold, italicize, and underline this text. Also, change the font color to Dark Red (the first color in the Standard Colors), as shown in the figure. Increase the size of the paragraph bullets to 125% of text, as shown in Figure 6–80b.

6. On Slide 3, create two columns in the box and then adjust the column spacing to 1". Change the list font size to 20 point and then change the line spacing to 1.5. Increase the size of the

(a) Slide 1

(b) Slide 2

(c) Slide 3

(d) Slide 4

(e) Slide 5

(f) Slide 6

Figure 6–80

paragraph bullets to 125% of text. Also, increase the size of the content placeholder so that the paragraphs in the columns display as shown in Figure 6–80c. Copy and paste the ladybug illustration from Slide 4, decrease the size of the illustration, and then move it to the location shown in the figure. Create hyperlinks for the two words in the box, Pronotum and Elytra, to Slide 4, as shown in the figure. (If spell check prompts you to correct the spelling of these two words, ignore the options shown.)

Continued >

In the Labs *continued*

7. On Slide 4, change the color of the shape fill of the eight callout shapes to White, Background 1, Darker 25% (the first color in the fourth Theme Colors row), change the shape outline color to Dark Red, Accent 1 (the fifth color in the Theme Colors row), and then change the outline weight to 1½ pt, as shown in Figure 6–80d on the previous page.

8. Insert a Return action button in the lower-right corner of Slide 4 and then hyperlink the button to the Last Slide Viewed, which will be Slide 3 when you run the presentation. Change the color of this action button to Gold, Background 2 (the third color in the Theme Colors), and change the transparency to 50%, as shown in Figure 6–80d. Hide this slide.

9. On Slide 5, select the four bulleted paragraphs in the left placeholder and convert this text to the Segmented Cycle SmartArt graphic (the second graphic in the second Cycle row). Apply the Colorful – Accent Colors (the first color in the Colorful row) and then apply the 3-D Sunset Scene (the second style in the second 3-D row) to the SmartArt graphic. Display the ruler and then center the SmartArt graphic vertically at 0" and align the left edge of the SmartArt graphic with the left edge of the title text, as shown in Figure 6–80e.

10. Hide the ruler. Increase the size of the paragraph bullets to 125% of text.

11. On Slide 6, change the title text to two lines, as shown in Figure 6–80f. Increase the size of the photo to approximately 6.17" × 5.1", apply the Drop Shadow Rectangle picture style (the fourth style in the first row), add the Mosaic Bubbles artistic effect (the fourth effect in the third row), and then move the photo to the location shown in the figure.

12. Create two columns in the text placeholder, adjust the column spacing to 0.25", and adjust the height of the box so that three items appear in each column. Change the line spacing in the bottom rectangle shape to 1.5. Change the three round bullet characters in the rectangle shape to the 1. 2. 3. Numbering format. Change the numbering color to Dark Red (the first color in the Standard Colors row) and then move the rectangle shape up slightly and align it with the title text, as shown in Figure 6–80f.

13. If requested by your instructor, add your high school mascot as the second line of the subtitle text on Slide 1.

14. Apply the Orbit transition in the Dynamic Content category to all slides and then change the duration to 2.50 seconds.

15. Save the presentation using the file name, Lab 6-1 Likeable Ladybugs.

16. Submit the document in the format specified by your instructor.

17. ✳ In Step 5, you added a hyperlink to the ladybug illustration and linked it to a website. Why? You added hyperlinks to only two of the bulleted text on Slide 3 and linked them to Slide 4 showing the ladybug anatomy. Why only two?

Lab 2: Opening a Microsoft Word Outline as a Presentation, Inserting Hyperlinks to Other Office Documents, Using Rulers and Guides, Entering Line Breaks, and Formatting Bullets

Problem: You work at a building supply company and several times a year, they offer home building project workshops to customers. The fall workshops will be about choosing the right wood for home projects. Your manager gave you a Microsoft Word outline with the details of the workshops. You also received a list of attendees in a Microsoft Excel file. You created a presentation of six slides as shown in Figure 6–81b and Figures 6–81d through 6–81h on pages PPT 402 and 403.

Note: To complete this assignment, you will be required to use the Data Files for Students. Visit www.cengage.com/ct/studentdownload for detailed instructions or contact your instructor for information about accessing the required files.

Instructions: Perform the following tasks:

1. Run PowerPoint and then open the Microsoft Word Outline, Lab 6-2 Powell Wood Workshops (Figure 6–81a on the next page), from the Data Files for Students, as a presentation. Change the Slide 1 layout to Title Slide.

2. On all slides, change the background to the Oak texture fill and change the transparency to 48%. Display the rulers and guides. If you are using a mouse, move the horizontal guide to 3.25" below center and move the horizontal guide to 5.75" left of center. To add a second vertical guide, right-click or press and hold a blank area of the slide, select Grid and Guides, and then tap or click Add Vertical Guide. Move the new vertical guide to 5.75" right of center.

3. On Slide 1, insert the illustration called Saw1 from the Data Files for Students. Move the illustration so that the right edge is aligned with the right Smart Guide and the bottom edge of the illustration is positioned at 3.25" below center. Apply the Drop Shadow Rectangle picture style to the illustration (the fourth effect in the first row), as shown in Figure 6–81b.

4. Move the subtitle text placeholder to the upper-left area of the slide, change the subtitle font to Comic Sans MS, and then bold this text. Create a hyperlink for the text, October Workshops, to the Excel document, Lab 6-2 Workshop Attendees (Figure 6–81c), located on the Data Files for Students.

5. On Slide 1, apply the Fill – Gray-25%, Background 2, Inner Shadow WordArt style (the fifth style in the third row) to the title text, and then apply the Slant Up text effect (the first effect in the last Warp row under Transform) to the title text. Change the text outline color to Blue (the eighth color in the Standard Colors row), and then change the text outline weight to 4½ pt. Change the size of the title text placeholder to approximately 4.98" × 6.58" and, if necessary, insert a line break before the word, Your. Move the placeholder so that the left edge lines up with the left Smart Guide and the bottom edge is at 3.25" below center (the same bottom edge as the illustration).

6. On Slide 2, change the title font to Comic Sans MS, decrease the font size to 32 point, change the font color to Blue (the eighth color in the Standard Colors row), and then apply a text shadow to the text. Use the Format Painter to format the title text on Slides 3 through 6 with the same features as the title text on Slide 2. Also, change the title font text on Slides 2 through 6 to uppercase, as shown in Figure 6–81b and Figures 6–81d through 6–81h on page PPT 403.

7. On Slide 2, insert the illustration called Wood from the Data Files for Students and position the illustration so that the bottom edge is at 3.25" below center. Also, center the illustration so that the center lines up with 0" on the vertical guide as shown in Figure 6–81d.

8. On Slide 3, insert a line break after the dash in the title and then delete the space before the word, OCTOBER, in the second line. Change the line spacing for the title to 1.0. Insert the photos called Kitchen Cabinets and Floor from the Data Files for Students and apply the Beveled Oval, Black picture style (the third style in the second row) to both photos. Resize the left photo to 2.51" × 4.33" and the right photo to 4.84" × 6.18". Using the same ruler and guides as in Step 5, align and position the photos on the slide, as shown in Figure 6–81e.

9. On Slide 4, insert a line break after the dash in the title and then delete the space before the word, OCTOBER, in the second line. Change the line spacing for the title to 1.0. Insert the photos called Table1, Table2, and Table3 from the Data Files for Students. Apply the Bevel Rectangle picture style (the last style in the third row) to all three photos. Use the Smart Guides to align the three photos to the slide and then distribute these images horizontally.

Continued >

In the Labs continued

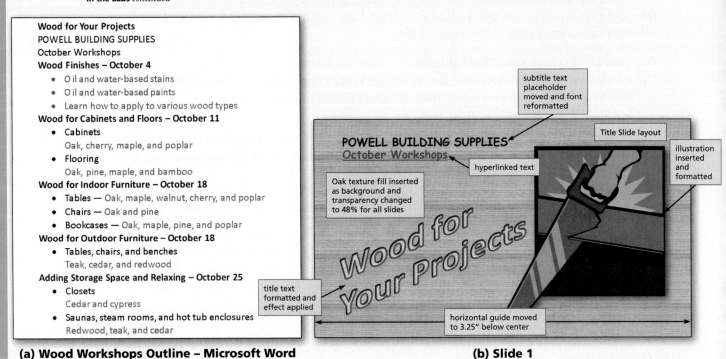

Wood for Your Projects
POWELL BUILDING SUPPLIES
October Workshops
Wood Finishes – October 4
- Oil and water-based stains
- Oil and water-based paints
- Learn how to apply to various wood types

Wood for Cabinets and Floors – October 11
- Cabinets
  Oak, cherry, maple, and poplar
- Flooring
  Oak, pine, maple, and bamboo

Wood for Indoor Furniture – October 18
- Tables — Oak, maple, walnut, cherry, and poplar
- Chairs — Oak and pine
- Bookcases — Oak, maple, pine, and poplar

Wood for Outdoor Furniture – October 18
- Tables, chairs, and benches
  Teak, cedar, and redwood

Adding Storage Space and Relaxing – October 25
- Closets
  Cedar and cypress
- Saunas, steam rooms, and hot tub enclosures
  Redwood, teak, and cedar

(a) Wood Workshops Outline – Microsoft Word Document

subtitle text placeholder moved and font reformatted

Title Slide layout

illustration inserted and formatted

POWELL BUILDING SUPPLIES
October Workshops

hyperlinked text

Oak texture fill inserted as background and transparency changed to 48% for all slides

Wood for Your Projects

title text formatted and effect applied

horizontal guide moved to 3.25" below center

(b) Slide 1

	Name	October 4 · Wood	October 11 · Kitchens	October 18 · Furniture	October 25 · Closets, etc.
1	Powell Building Supplies - Attendees - October Wood Seminars				
3 Ascot	Robert	✓		✓	
4 Amers	Erick	✓			✓
5 Bloom	Calista	✓	✓		✓
6 Conners	Jamie	✓	✓		✓
7 Cranz	William	✓	✓	✓	✓
8 Cravens	Joe	✓	✓	✓	
9 Dawson	Evelyn	✓	✓	✓	
10 Dawson	Miriam	✓	✓		✓
11 Evans	Joshua	✓	✓		✓
12 Flamer	Nicholas	✓			✓
13 Foster	Benjamin	✓	✓		✓
14 Hope	Christopher	✓	✓		
15 Jones	Brian	✓	✓	✓	✓
16 Linde	Jack	✓		✓	
17 Morgan	Bill	✓		✓	
18 O'Hehirr	Joey	✓		✓	
19 Roberts	John	✓		✓	
20 Smith	Mark	✓		✓	✓
21 Shuler	Kenneth	✓			✓
22 Williams	Zac	✓	✓	✓	✓

(c) Workshop Attendees – Microsoft Excel file

Figure 6–81

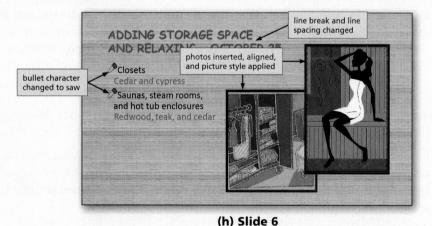

Figure 6–81 (Continued)

Once the photos are distributed horizontally, use the Arrange list to Align Bottom at 3.25" below center, as shown in Figure 6–81f.

10. On Slide 5, insert a line break after the dash in the title and then delete the space before the word, OCTOBER, in the second line. Change the line spacing for the title to 1.0. Insert the photos called Bench and Patio from the Data Files for Students. Apply the Soft Edge Rectangle picture style (the sixth style in the first row) to both photos. Use the Smart Guides to align the two photos to the slide and align the bottom of the photos at 3.25" below center, as shown in Figure 6–81g.

Continued >

In the Labs *continued*

11. On Slide 6, insert a line break after the word, SPACE, in the title and then delete the space before the word, AND, in the second line. Change the line spacing for the title to 1.0. Insert a line break after the word, rooms, in the third paragraph of the text and then delete the space before the word, and, in the second line. Insert the illustrations called Closet and Sauna from the Data Files for Students. Adjust the sizes of the illustrations and overlap them so they do not cover the text on the slide. Align Middle the sauna illustration and then use the Smart Guide to position it at the right side of the slide. Move the closet illustration to the location shown in Figure 6–81h on the previous page, aligning the bottom at 3.25" below center. Hide the rulers and guides.

12. Change the bullet character for all the level 1 text on Slides 2 through 6 to the illustration called Saw, located on the Data Files for Students, and increase the size of the bullets to 150%, as shown in Figures 6–81d through 6–81h on the previous page.

13. If requested by your instructor, enter your hair color after the word, paints, in the second text paragraph on Slide 2.

14. Apply the Window transition in the Dynamic Content category to all slides and then change the duration to 3.00 seconds.

15. Save the presentation using the file name, Lab 6-2 Powell Wood Workshops.

16. Submit the document in the format specified by your instructor.

17. ✺ Why did you add a wood background to all slides and why did you choose a 48% transparency? Did changing the bullet characters to pictures add interest to the presentation?

Lab 3: Expand Your World: Cloud and Web Technologies
Using Google Docs to Upload and Edit Files

Problem: You have begun creating a presentation at school for an upcoming informative speech that you were assigned to deliver next week. You did not have time to finish the slides at school, so you need to complete the slide deck at home. You do not have PowerPoint on your home computer, but you do have an Internet connection. You also have a Google account, so at school you upload your PowerPoint presentation to Google Drive so you can view and edit it later from home.

Notes:
- You will use a Google account, which you can create at no cost, to complete this assignment. If you do not have a Google account and do not want to create one, read this assignment without performing the instructions.
- To complete this assignment, you will be required to use the Data Files for Students. Visit www.cengage.com/ct/studentdownload for detained instructions or contact your instructor for information about accessing the required files.

Instructions: Perform the following tasks:
1. In PowerPoint, open the presentation, Lab 6-3 World Mythology in PowerPoint, from the Data Files for Students. Review the slides so that you are familiar with their contents and formats. If desired, print the slides so that you easily can compare them to the Google Docs converted file. Close the presentation.

2. Run a browser. Search for the text, google docs, using a search engine. Visit several websites to learn about Google Docs and Google Drive. Navigate to the Google website. If you do not have a Google account and you want to create one, tap or click the SIGN UP button and follow the instructions. If you do not have a Google account and you do not want to create one, read the remaining instructions without performing them. If you have a Google account, sign in to your account.

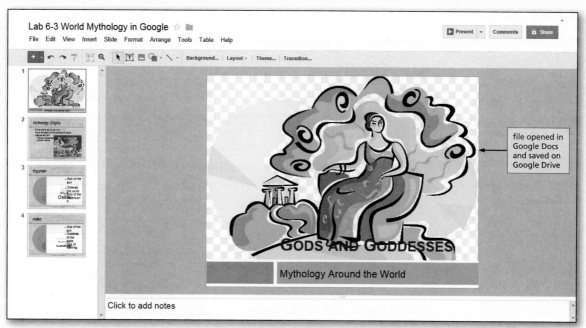

Figure 6–82

3. If necessary, tap or click Drive to display Google Drive. Tap or click the Upload, or similar, button and then follow the instructions to navigate to the location of the file, Lab 6-3 World Mythology in PowerPoint, and then upload the file.

4. Rename the file on Google Drive to Lab 6-3 World Mythology in Google. Open the file in Google Docs (Figure 6–82). What differences do you see between the PowerPoint document and the Google Docs converted document? Modify the document in Google Docs so that it looks appealing. If requested by your instructor, replace the name, Carl Rowly, in the footer, with the name of your favorite grade school teacher. Download the revised document to your local storage media, changing its format to Microsoft PowerPoint. Submit the document in the format requested by your instructor.

5. ✷ What is Google Drive? What is Google Docs? Answer the question posed in #4. Do you prefer using Google Docs or PowerPoint? Why?

✷ Consider This: Your Turn

Apply your creative thinking and problem-solving skills to design and implement a solution.

1. Design and Create a Presentation about Preparing for a Job Interview
Personal

Part 1: You and several of your college friends have been searching for jobs for some time. You meet occasionally to share ideas and information. You decide to do a presentation about preparing for a job interview to share with your friends. You have learned that body language is very important during a job interview. Some of the mistakes people make during an interview are: slouching (poor posture), crossing arms, nodding excessively, breaking eye contact, fidgeting, having hands in pockets or behind the back, staring intently, rolling eyes, and having unusual facial expressions. You can find other information about preparing for a job interview such as resume writing, proper attire, rules for following up after a job interview, and adding a hyperlink to a resume written using Microsoft Word and then using that document in the interview. Use the concepts and techniques presented in this chapter to prepare a presentation. Select a suitable theme, and use WordArt or

Continued >

Consider This: Your Turn *continued*

SmartArt graphics where appropriate. The presentation can contain photos, illustrations, and videos. You can use photos and illustrations from Office.com if they are appropriate for this topic. Submit your assignment in the format specified by your instructor.

Part 2: ☀ You made several decisions while creating the presentation in this assignment: where to place text, how to format the text (for example, font, font size, font effects, and line spacing), which graphical image(s) to use, where to use action buttons and hyperlinks, when to change bullet characters, and where to position the graphical images to add interest to the presentation. What was the rationale behind each of these decisions? When you reviewed the document, what further revisions did you make and why? Where would you recommend showing this slide show?

2. Design and Create a Presentation about Supplies Needed for Painting and Staining Wood
Professional

Part 1: After you completed the presentation in Lab 2 about the upcoming fall workshops that your employer is hosting, you realized that the most popular workshop is the one about wood finishes. The attendees will need supplies including an assortment of paints and stains, polyurethanes, paint brushes, scrapers, sandpaper, cloths, cleaning solutions, thinners, and removers. Powell Building Supplies sells everything the attendees will need and will be furnishing these items for the October 4 workshop. You decide to put together a presentation listing all these supplies that also can be used as a handout at the workshop. You also will create a slide listing the tools that Powell rents in case the participants need them when they work on their projects at home. You also can insert a hyperlink to the file, Lab 6-2 Workshop Attendees, on the Data Files for Students, so that all the names of the participants will be available and can be included in the handout. The presentation could contain photos, illustrations, and videos. The Data Files for Students contains five illustrations called Wood Stain, Painting, Painting2, Paint Can, and Wood Finishing, or you can use photos and illustrations from Office.com if they are appropriate for this topic. Use columns and create bullets related to this topic to add interest to the presentation. Submit your assignment in the format specified by your instructor.

Part 2: ☀ You made several decisions while creating the presentation in this assignment: where to place text, how to format the text (such as font and font size), which graphical image(s) to use, which styles and effects to apply, where to position the graphical images, and which shapes to use to add interest to the presentation. What was the rationale behind each of these decisions? When you reviewed the document, what further revisions did you make and why? Where would you recommend showing this slide show?

3. Design and Create a Presentation about the T. rex Dinosaur
Research and Collaboration

Part 1: For your world history class, you and two other students were assigned a project to create a presentation about the Tyrannosaurus Rex (T. rex) dinosaur. Tyrannosaurus means tyrant lizard. At about 40 feet (12 meters) long and about 15 to 20 feet (4.6 to 6 meters) tall, the T. rex was one of the largest meat-eating dinosaurs that ever lived. If it roamed the earth today, its bite could dent a car. The largest, most complete, best preserved T. rex is in The Field Museum in Chicago and she is named Sue. Her 67-million-year-old skeleton was presented to the public in May 2000. She was discovered in the badlands of South Dakota by a team of paleontologists headed by Sue Hendrickson. One member of your team will visit the Chicago museum website (fieldmuseum.org/sue) and gather information about Sue. Another member of your team has visited the Dinosaur National Monument located on the Colorado and Utah border and will gather information from its website (nps.gov/dino/index.htm). You will develop a Microsoft Word outline with the information gathered by you and your teammates. Use at least three objectives found at the beginning of this chapter to develop the presentation. Include hyperlinks to the two websites named above. The

Data Files for Students contains five photos called Dinosaur1, Dinosaur2, Dinosaur3, Dinosaur4, and Dinosaur5, or you can use photos and illustrations from Office.com if they are appropriate for this topic.

Part 2: ✺ You made several decisions while creating the presentation in this assignment: where to place text, how to format the text (such as font, font size, and colors), which image(s) to use, formatting bullets, inserting action buttons and hyperlinks, using WordArt and SmartArt graphics, and which shapes to use to add interest to the presentation. What was the rationale behind each of these decisions? When you reviewed the document, what further revisions did you make and why? Where would you recommend showing this slide show?

Learn Online

Reinforce what you learned in this chapter with games, exercises, training, and many other online activities and resources.

Student Companion Site   Reinforcement activities and resources are available at no additional cost on www.cengagebrain.com. Visit www.cengage.com/ct/studentdownload for detailed instructions about accessing the resources available at the Student Companion Site.

SAM   Put your skills into practice with SAM! If you have a SAM account, go to www.cengage.com/sam2013 to access SAM assignments for this chapter.

7 | Creating a Self-Running Presentation Containing Animation

Microsoft product screenshots used with permission from Microsoft Corporation.

Objectives

You will have mastered the material in this chapter when you can:

- Remove a photo background
- Crop and compress a photo
- Animate slide content with entrance, emphasis, and exit effects
- Add and adjust motion paths
- Reorder animation sequences
- Associate sounds with animations

- Control animation timing
- Animate SmartArt graphics and charts
- Insert and animate a text box
- Animate bulleted lists
- Rehearse timings
- Set slide show timings manually

7 | Creating a Self-Running Presentation Containing Animation

Introduction

One method used for disseminating information is a **kiosk**. This freestanding, self-service structure is equipped with computer hardware and software and is used to provide information or reference materials to the public. Some have a touch screen or keyboard that serves as an input device and allows users to select various options so they can browse or find specific information. Advanced kiosks allow customers to place orders, make payments, and access the Internet. Many kiosks have multimedia devices for playing sound and video clips.

Various elements on PowerPoint slides can have movement to direct the audience's attention to the point being made. For example, each paragraph in a bulleted list can fade or disappear after being displayed for a set period of time. Each SmartArt graphic component can appear in sequence. A picture can grow, shrink, bounce, or spin, depending upon its relationship to other slide content. PowerPoint's myriad animation effects allow you to use your creativity to design imaginative and distinctive presentations.

BTW

Animation Types
The transitions you have been applying between slides in a presentation are one type of PowerPoint animations. In this chapter you will use another type of animation to move or change elements on the slide. Animation is effective in adding interest to slide content and to call attention to important content. As a caution, however, resist the urge to add animation simply for the sake of animation when it does not have purpose on a particular slide.

BTW

Icon Colors for Animation Effects
Using a traffic signal analogy may help you remember the sequence of events as you apply animation effects to control how objects enter, move on, and exit slides. Green icons indicate when the animation effect starts on the slide. Yellow icons represent the object's motion; use them with caution so they do not distract from the message you are conveying to your audience. Red icons indicate when the object stops appearing on a slide.

Project — Presentation with Adjusted Pictures, Animated Content, and Slide Timings

Butterflies capture nature lovers' attention. People of all ages marvel at their beauty, grace, and delicate wings. Their name may have originated from the British, who watched yellow brimstone butterflies in the meadows and compared the form to butter flying. The title slide (Figure 7–1a) has animated title text and a butterfly that moves and turns through the flowers. The second slide (Figure 7–1b) shows butterflies that flutter gracefully through a garden. The third slide (Figure 7–1c) uses animated SmartArt to explain the metamorphosis from an egg to a caterpillar, chrysalis (or pupa), and adult butterfly. The next slide is an animated chart that shows some of the common butterflies in the local area (Figure 7–1d). One method of increasing the number of butterflies in your area is to develop a backyard habitat that attracts and protects these insects. Gardeners need to provide a variety of plants because adult butterflies need the nectar from flowers and adult females lay their eggs on plants that provide food for the emerging caterpillars. The last slide (Figure 7–1e) has two lists that describe the plants that attract butterflies and are easy to grow in a variety of gardening environments and an upward-rolling credit line to urge people to visit a local nursery to purchase some of these plants.

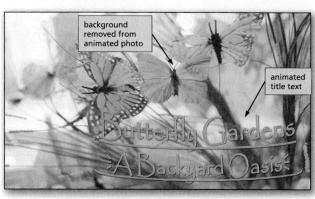

(a) Slide 1 (Title Slide with Animated WordArt and Photo)

(b) Slide 2 (Animated Illustrations with Motion Path and Sound)

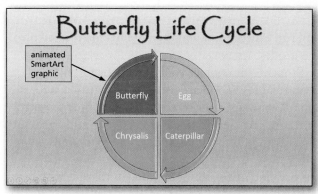

(c) Slide 3 (Animated SmartArt)

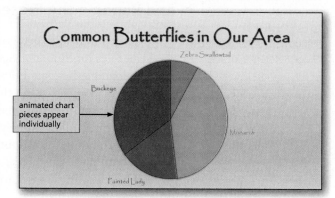

(d) Slide 4 (Animated Chart)

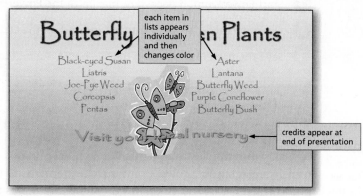

(e) Slide 5 (Animated List and Credits)

Figure 7–1

Roadmap

In this chapter, you will learn how to create the slides shown in Figure 7–1. The following roadmap identifies general activities you will perform as you progress through this chapter:

1. MODIFY PHOTOS by removing the background, cropping, and compressing.
2. ADD ENTRANCE, EMPHASIS, and EXIT ANIMATIONS to photos and text.
3. ANIMATE BOXES, SMARTART, and CHARTS.
4. CHANGE TRANSITION EFFECT options.
5. SET slide show TIMINGS.

One of the few differences between Windows 7 and Windows 8 occurs in the steps to run PowerPoint. If you are using Windows 7, click the Start button, type **PowerPoint** in the 'Search programs and files' box, click PowerPoint 2013, and then, if necessary, maximize the PowerPoint window. For a summary of the steps to run PowerPoint in Windows 7, refer to the Quick Reference located at the back of this book.

At the beginning of step instructions throughout the chapter, you will see an abbreviated form of this roadmap. The abbreviated roadmap uses colors to indicate chapter progress: gray means the chapter is beyond that activity; blue means the task being shown is covered in that activity; and black means that activity is yet to be covered. For example, the following abbreviated roadmap indicates the chapter would be showing a task in the 3 ANIMATE BOXES, SMARTART, & CHARTS activity.

1 MODIFY PHOTOS | 2 ADD ENTRANCE, EMPHASIS, & EXIT ANIMATIONS
3 ANIMATE BOXES, SMARTART, & CHARTS | 4 CHANGE TRANSITION EFFECTS | 5 SET TIMINGS

Use the abbreviated roadmap as a progress guide while you read or step through the instructions in this chapter.

To Run PowerPoint, Open a Presentation, and Rename the Presentation

To begin this project, you will run PowerPoint and then open a file located on the Data Files for Students. See the inside back cover of this book for instructions on downloading the Data Files for Students, or contact your instructor for more information about accessing the required files. If you are using a computer to step through the project in this chapter and you want your screens to match the figures in this book, you should change your screen's resolution to 1366×768. For information about how to change a computer's resolution, refer to the Office and Windows chapter at the beginning of this book.

The following steps start PowerPoint, open a presentation, and save it with a different name.

1 Start PowerPoint. If necessary, maximize the PowerPoint window.

2 Open the presentation, Butterfly, located on the Data Files for Students.

3 Save the presentation using the file name, Animated Butterflies.

BTW
Touch Screen Differences
The Office and Windows interfaces may vary if you are using a touch screen. For this reason, you might notice that the function or appearance of your touch screen differs slightly from this chapter's presentation.

Adjusting and Cropping a Photo

At times you may desire to emphasize one section of a photo and eliminate distracting background content. PowerPoint includes formatting tools that allow you to edit photos. The **Remove Background** command isolates the foreground from the background, and the **Crop** command removes content along the top, bottom, left, or right edges. Once you format the photo to include only the desired content, you can **compress** the image to reduce the file size.

To Remove a Background

1 MODIFY PHOTOS | 2 ADD ENTRANCE, EMPHASIS, & EXIT ANIMATIONS
3 ANIMATE BOXES, SMARTART, & CHARTS | 4 CHANGE TRANSITION EFFECTS | 5 SET TIMINGS

The title slide in the Animated Butterflies presentation has a photo of a yellow butterfly with green leaves in the background. You want to eliminate the leaves. *Why? To direct the viewers' attention to the butterfly.* The PowerPoint Background Removal feature makes it easy to eliminate extraneous aspects. When you click the Remove Background button, PowerPoint attempts to select the foreground of the photo and overlay a magenta marquee selection on this area. You then can adjust the marquee shape and size to contain all foreground photo components you want to keep. The following steps remove the background from the butterfly photo.

1

- With the title slide displaying, zoom the slide to 130%. Use the vertical and horizontal scroll bars to adjust the slide so the entire yellow butterfly photo in the foreground is visible.

- Tap or click the butterfly to select it. Tap or click the PICTURE TOOLS FORMAT tab.

- Tap or click the Remove Background button (PICTURE TOOLS FORMAT tab | Adjust group) to display the BACKGROUND REMOVAL tab and a marquee selection area.

Figure 7–2

- Tap or click and drag the center handle on the right side of the background removal lines toward the butterfly's right wing (Figure 7–2).

Q&A How does PowerPoint determine the area to display within the marquee?
Microsoft Research software engineers developed the algorithms that determine the portions of the photo in the foreground.

2

- Tap or click the Keep Changes button (BACKGROUND REMOVAL tab | Close group) to discard the unwanted photo background (Figure 7–3).

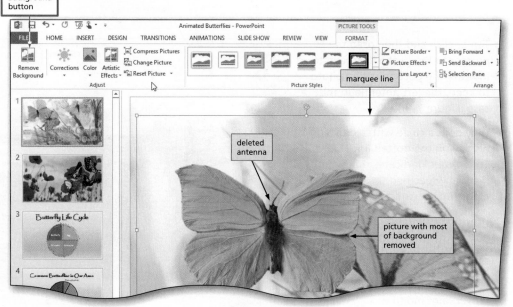

Figure 7–3

To Refine Background Removal

Why? In many cases, the Remove Background command discards all the undesired photo components. Occasionally, however, some desired pieces are discarded when the background is integrated closely with the foreground photo. In the title slide butterfly photo, for example, the butterfly's left antenna was removed along with the background. Tools on the BACKGROUND REMOVAL tab allow you to mark specific areas to keep and to remove. The following steps mark the left antenna as an area to keep.

1

● Tap or click the Remove Background button (shown in Figure 7–3 on the previous page) to display the BACKGROUND REMOVAL tab and the marquee selection area.

● Tap or click the 'Mark Areas to Keep' button (BACKGROUND REMOVAL tab | Refine group) and then position the pointer at the end of the left antenna (Figure 7–4).

Why did my pointer change shape? The pointer changed to a pencil to indicate you are about to draw on a precise area of the photo.

I am using a touch screen and am having difficulty positioning the pointer. What should I do? Zoom your screen to increase the level of detail you need. Using a mouse also might help with this task.

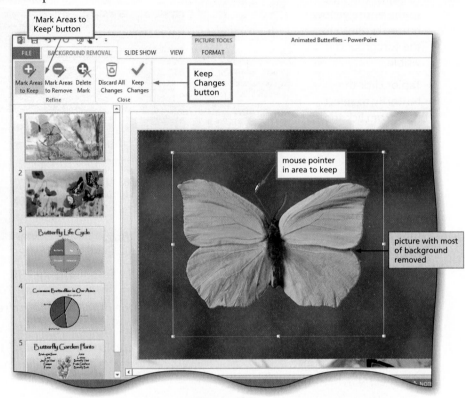

Figure 7–4

2

● Tap or click and then drag the pointer to the butterfly's head to indicate the portion of the photo to keep, the left antenna in this case (Figure 7–5).

Why does a circle with a plus sign display on the dotted line? That symbol indicates that you manually specified the addition of a portion of the background.

Why does some of the background remain on my photo? The location where you drew your background removal line determines the area that PowerPoint modifies.

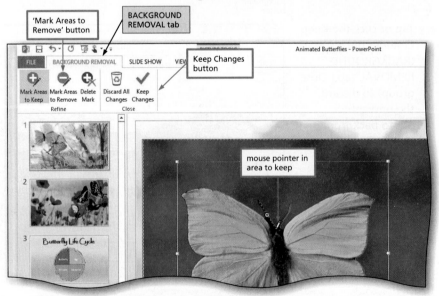

Figure 7–5

What if my butterfly still has both antennae or it does not have either antenna? You may need to make several passes to remove all of the unwanted background or add the desired photo elements.

❸

- Tap or click the Keep Changes button (BACKGROUND REMOVAL tab | Close group) to review the results of your background refinements.

Q&A Some of the green leaves still are displayed. Can I delete this piece of the background?
Yes. In the next step, you will instruct PowerPoint to delete any necessary area that was added.

❹

- Tap or click the Remove Background button again, tap or click the 'Mark Areas to Remove' button (BACKGROUND REMOVAL tab | Refine group), and then position the pointer on the green background between the antenna and the left wing.

- Tap or click and then drag the pointer to the butterfly's head (Figure 7–6).

Q&A I mistakenly removed the butterfly when I tried to remove some of the background. How can I keep the butterfly in the photo?
You can mark part of the butterfly as an area to keep and then delete the background again.

If I marked an area with a line and now want to delete it, can I reverse my action?
Yes. Tap or click the Delete Mark button (BACKGROUND REMOVAL tab | Refine group) and then tap or click the line to remove it. You also can press CTRL+Z immediately after you draw the line.

'Mark Areas to Remove' button

area marked to remove

mouse pointer dragged to butterfly's head

Figure 7–6

❺

- Tap or click the Keep Changes button to review the results of your background refinement.

Q&A If I want to see the original photo at a later time, can I display the components I deleted?
Yes. If you tap or click the Discard All Changes button (BACKGROUND REMOVAL tab | Close group), all the deleted pieces will reappear.

To Crop a Photo

1 MODIFY PHOTOS | 2 ADD ENTRANCE, EMPHASIS, & EXIT ANIMATIONS

3 ANIMATE BOXES, SMARTART, & CHARTS | 4 CHANGE TRANSITION EFFECTS | 5 SET TIMINGS

The Remove Background command deleted the green background components from your view, but they still remain in the photo. You can remove the unnecessary background from the edges of the butterfly. *Why? You will not need to display the background in this presentation, so the photo should contain only the element that will be shown.* When you crop a picture, you trim the vertical or horizontal sides so that the most important area of the photo is displayed. Any picture file type except animated GIF can be cropped. The steps on the next page crop the title slide butterfly photo.

- With the butterfly photo still selected, tap or click the Crop button (PICTURE TOOLS FORMAT tab | Size group) to display the cropping handles on the photo.

- If you are using a mouse, position the pointer over the center cropping handle on the right side of the photo (Figure 7–7).

Q&A | Why did my pointer change shape?
The pointer changed to indicate you are about to crop a photo.

Figure 7–7

- Drag the center cropping handle inward so that the right edge of the marquee is beside the butterfly's right wing.

- Drag the center cropping handles on the left, upper, and lower edges of the cropping lines inward to frame the photo (Figure 7–8).

Q&A | Does cropping actually cut the photo's edges?
No. Although you cannot see the cropped edges, they exist until you save the file.

Figure 7–8

- Tap or click an area of the slide other than the photo to crop the edges.

Q&A | Can I change the crop lines?
If you have not saved the file, you can undo your crops by tapping or clicking the Undo button on the Quick Access Toolbar, tapping or clicking clicking the Reset Picture button (PICTURE TOOLS FORMAT tab | Adjust group), or pressing CTRL+Z. If you have saved the file, you cannot undo the crop.

Other Ways

1. Press and hold or right-click photo, tap or click Crop on shortcut menu

To Compress a Photo

Photos inserted into slides greatly increase the total PowerPoint file size. PowerPoint automatically compresses photo files inserted into slides by eliminating details, generally with no visible loss of quality. You can increase the compression and, in turn, decrease the file size if you instruct PowerPoint to compress a photo you have cropped so you can save space on a storage medium such as a hard disk, USB flash drive, or optical disk. Although these storage devices generally have a large storage capacity, you might want to reduce the file size. *Why? A smaller size reduces the download time from an FTP server or website. Also, some Internet service providers restrict an attachment's file size.*

The photo on the title slide is cropped and displays only the butterfly. You will not need any of the invisible portions of the photo, so you can delete them permanently and reduce the photo file size. The following steps compress the size of the title slide butterfly photo.

- Tap or click the butterfly photo to display the PICTURE TOOLS FORMAT tab. Tap or click the Compress Pictures button (PICTURE TOOLS FORMAT tab | Adjust group) to display the Compress Pictures dialog box (Figure 7–9).

Q&A Should I apply an artistic effect prior to or after compressing a picture?
Compress a picture and then apply the artistic effect.

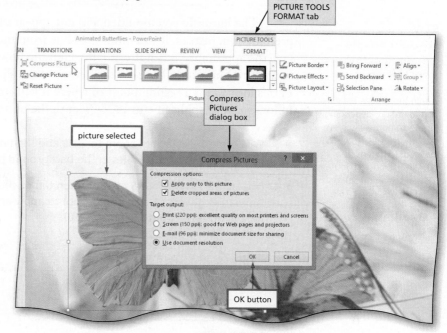

- Tap or click the OK button (Compress Pictures dialog box) to delete the cropped portions of this photo and compress the image.

Q&A Can I undo the compression?
Yes, as long as you have not saved the file after compressing the photo.

Figure 7–9

Animating Slide Content

The Slide 1 background photo shows a flower garden. When the presentation begins, the audience will view these flowers and then see a butterfly enter from the upper-right corner, move across the slide, pulse slightly at the center of the slide, and then continue toward the upper-left corner. To create this animation on the slide, you will use entrance, emphasis, and exit effects.

If you need to move objects on a slide once they are displayed, you can define a **motion path**. This predefined movement determines where an object will be displayed and then travel. Motion paths are grouped into the Basic, Lines & Curves, and Special categories. You can draw a **custom path** if none of the predefined paths meets your needs.

BTW
Q&As
For a complete list of the Q&As found in many of the step-by-step sequences in this book, visit the Q&A resource on the Student Companion Site located on www.cengagebrain.com. For detailed instructions about accessing available resources, visit www.cengage.com/ct/studentdownload or see the inside back cover of this book.

Use animation sparingly.

PowerPoint audience members usually take notice the first time an animation is displayed on the screen. When the same animation effect is applied throughout a presentation, the viewers generally become desensitized to the effect unless it is highly unusual or annoying. Resist the urge to use animation effects simply because PowerPoint provides the tools to do so. You have options to decide how text or a slide element enters and exits a slide and how it is displayed once it is present on the slide; your goal, however, is to use these options wisely. Audiences soon tire of a presentation riddled with animations, causing them to quickly lose their impact.

To Animate a Photo Using an Entrance Effect

BTW

The Ribbon and Screen Resolution
PowerPoint may change how the groups and buttons within the groups appear on the ribbon, depending on the computer's screen resolution. Thus, your ribbon may look different from the ones in this book if you are using a screen resolution other than 1366 × 768.

The butterfly you modified will not appear on Slide 1 when you begin the presentation. Instead, it will enter the slide from the upper-right corner of the slide to give the appearance it is fluttering through the flowers. It then will continue moving downward until it reaches near the center of the slide, so you need to move the photo to this location as a resting point of where it will stop moving temporarily. The following steps apply an entrance effect to the butterfly photo.

1 With Slide 1 displaying, zoom to 74% and then move the yellow butterfly photo between the two butterflies in the background photo.

2 Display the ANIMATIONS tab and then tap or click the Fly In animation in the Animation gallery (Animation group) to apply and preview this entrance animation for the butterfly photo (Figure 7–10).

Figure 7–10

To Change Animation Direction

By default, the photo appears on the slide by entering from the bottom edge. You can modify this direction and specify that it enters from another side or from a corner. The following steps change the butterfly photo entrance animation direction to the upper-right corner.

1 Tap or click the Effect Options button (ANIMATIONS tab | Animation group) to display the Direction gallery (Figure 7–11).

2 Tap or click the 'From Top-Right' arrow in the Direction gallery to apply this direction to the entrance animation and show a preview.

Figure 7–11

To Animate a Photo Using an Emphasis Effect

The butterfly will enter the slide from the upper-right corner and stop in the center of the slide. You then want it to fade out and in, or pulse, slightly to give the impression that it is moving its wings. PowerPoint provides several effects that you can apply to a picture once it appears on a slide. These movements are categorized as emphasis effects, and they are colored yellow in the Animation gallery. You already have applied an entrance effect to the butterfly photo, so you want to add another animation to this photo. The following steps apply an emphasis effect to the butterfly photo after the entrance effect.

1 With the butterfly photo still selected, tap or click the Add Animation button (ANIMATIONS tab | Advanced Animation group) to expand the Animation gallery (Figure 7–12 on the next page).

2 Tap or click Pulse in the Emphasis section to apply this emphasis effect to the butterfly photo.

BTW
BTWs
For a complete list of the BTWs found in the margins of this book, visit the BTW resource on the Student Companion Site located on www.cengagebrain.com. For detailed instructions about accessing available resources, visit www.cengage.com/ct/studentdownload or see the inside back cover of this book.

Figure 7–12

To Animate a Photo Using an Exit Effect

BTW
Numbered
Animation Events
A number is displayed next to an object you animate. Each time you assign an animation effect to an object, a new number is displayed. These effects are numbered in the sequence you apply the animations.

The animated butterfly photo will enter the slide from the upper-right corner, stop in the center of the slide, and then pulse. It then will continue across the slide toward the upper-left corner. To continue this animation sequence, you need to apply an exit effect. As with the entrance and emphasis effects, PowerPoint provides a wide variety of effects that you can apply to remove a picture from a slide. These exit effects are colored red in the Animation gallery. You already have applied the Fly In entrance effect, so the Fly Out exit effect would give continuity to the animation sequence. The following steps add this exit effect to the butterfly photo after the emphasis effect.

1 With the butterfly photo still selected, tap or click the Add Animation button again to expand the Animation gallery. Scroll down to display the Exit section (Figure 7–13).

2 Tap or click Fly Out in the Exit section to add this exit effect to the sequence of butterfly photo animations.

Figure 7–13

To Change Exit Animation Direction

The default direction for a photo to exit a slide is To Bottom. In this presentation, you want the butterfly to exit in the upper-left corner to give the impression it is continuing to fly through the flower bed. The following step changes the exit animation direction from To Bottom to To Top-Left.

1 Tap or click the Effect Options button to display the Direction gallery and then tap or click the 'To Top-Left' arrow to apply this direction to the exit animation effect.

To Preview an Animation Sequence

Although you have not completed developing the presentation, you should view the animation you have added. By default, the entrance, emphasis, and exit animations will be displayed when you run the presentation and tap the screen or click the mouse. The following step runs the presentation and displays the three animations.

1 Tap or click the Preview button (ANIMATIONS tab | Preview group) to view all the Slide 1 animations.

To Modify Entrance Animation Timing

The three animation effects are displayed quickly. To create a dramatic effect, you can change the timing so that the background photo displays and then, a few seconds later, the butterfly starts to fly through the flowers slowly. The default setting is to start each animation with a mouse click, but you can change this setting so that the entrance effect is delayed until a specified number of seconds has passed. The following steps modify the start, delay, and duration settings for the entrance animation.

1 Tap or click the 1 numbered tag on the left side of the butterfly photo and then tap or click the Start arrow (ANIMATIONS tab | Timing group) to display the start timing menu.

2 Tap or click After Previous to change the start timing setting.

3 Using a mouse, click the Duration up arrow (ANIMATIONS tab | Timing group) several times to increase the time from 00.50 second to 05.00 seconds. Using a touch screen, tap the Duration box and replace the 00.50 time with 05.00 seconds.

4 Using a mouse, click the Delay up arrow (ANIMATIONS tab | Timing group) several times to increase the time from 00.00 seconds to 04.00 seconds (Figure 7–14). Using a touch screen, change the Delay time from 00.00 seconds to 04.00 seconds.

5 Tap or click the Preview button to view the animations.

BTW

Selecting Individual Animations
Selecting individual animations may be difficult when using a touch screen because your finger may be too big to select a small item that is located close to other items. If you encounter this problem, try using a stylus or open the Animation pane to select an animation.

Figure 7–14

To Modify Emphasis and Exit Timings

BTW
Developing Animations
You can add the parts of the animation in any order and then change the sequence. Many slide designers, however, develop the animation using the sequence in which the elements will display on the slide in an effort to save time and help organize the animation sequence.

Now that the entrance animation settings have been modified, you can change the emphasis and exit effects for the butterfly photo. The emphasis effect can occur once the entrance effect has concluded, and then the exit effect can commence. With gravity's effect, the butterfly should not be able to glide as quickly up through the flowers, so you will increase the duration of the exit effect compared with the duration of the entrance effect. The animation sequence should flow without stopping, so you will not change the default delay timing of 00.00 seconds. The following steps modify the start and duration settings for the emphasis and exit animations.

1 Tap or click the 1 sequence number, which now represents the emphasis effect, on the left side of the butterfly photo, tap or click the Start arrow, and then tap or click After Previous to change the start timing option setting.

2 Increase the duration time to 03.00 seconds.

3 Tap or click the 1 sequence number, which now represents the exit effect, and then change the Start timing to After Previous.

4 Increase the duration time to 06.00 seconds (Figure 7–15).

5 Preview the Slide 1 animation.

Figure 7–15

To Animate Title Text Placeholder Paragraphs

The butterfly photo on Slide 1 has one entrance, one emphasis, and one exit animation, and you can add similar animations to the two paragraphs in the Slide 1 title text placeholder. For a special effect, you can add several emphasis animations to one slide element. The following steps add one entrance and two emphasis animations to the title text paragraphs.

1 Tap or click the Slide 1 title text placeholder to select it.

2 If you are using a mouse, double-click the border so that it displays as a solid line.

③ Tap or click the More button in the Animation gallery (ANIMATIONS tab | Animation group) to expand the Animation gallery.

④ Tap or click the Random Bars entrance effect in the Animation gallery to add this animation.

⑤ Change the start timing option to With Previous.

⑥ Change the duration time to 02.00 seconds.

⑦ Tap or click the Add Animation button and then tap or click the Font Color Emphasis animation effect.

⑧ Change the start timing option to After Previous.

⑨ Tap or click the Add Animation button and then tap or click the Underline emphasis animation effect.

⑩ Change the start timing option to With Previous (Figure 7–16).

Figure 7–16

To Change Animation Order

1 MODIFY PHOTOS | 2 ADD ENTRANCE, EMPHASIS, & EXIT ANIMATIONS
3 ANIMATE BOXES, SMARTART, & CHARTS | 4 CHANGE TRANSITION EFFECTS | 5 SET TIMINGS

Two title slide elements have animations: the butterfly photo and the title text placeholder. PowerPoint applies the animations in the order you created them, so on this slide the butterfly photo animations will appear first and then the title text placeholder animation will follow. You can reorder animation elements. *Why? You may decide one set of animations should appear before another set or you also can reorder individual animation elements within an animation group.* In this presentation, you decide to display the title text placeholder animation first, and then you decide that the Underline emphasis effect should appear before the Font Color emphasis effect. The steps on the next page reorder the two animation groups on the slide and then reorder the Font Color and Underline emphasis effects.

1

- Select the Slide 1 title text placeholder border so that it displays as a solid line. Tap or click the Animation Pane button (ANIMATIONS tab | Advanced Animation group) to display the Animation Pane (Figure 7–17).

Why are the three Rectangle effects shaded in the Animation Pane?

The shading corresponds to the three animation effects that you applied to the title text placeholder. The green star indicates the entrance effect, the A with the multicolor underline indicates the Font Color emphasis effect, and the black B indicates the Underline emphasis effect.

Why do I see a different number after the Rectangle label?

PowerPoint numbers slide elements consecutively, so you may see a different number if you have added and deleted photos, text, and other graphics. You will rename these labels in a later set of steps.

Figure 7–17

2

- Tap or click the up button in the Animation Pane three times to move the three Rectangle animations above the Picture animations (Figure 7–18).

- Tap or click the Play Selected button (Animation Pane) to see the reordered animation.

Q&A

Can I tap or click the Move Earlier button (ANIMATIONS tab | Timing group) on the ribbon instead of the up button in the Animation Pane?

Yes. Either button will change the animation order.

Figure 7–18

3

- In the Animation Pane, tap or click the second Rectangle label representing the Font Color animation to select it and then tap or click the down button to move this animation below the Rectangle label representing the Underline animation (Figure 7–19).

- Tap or click the Play From button (Animation Pane) to see the reordered text placeholder animation beginning with the font color change and the butterfly animations.

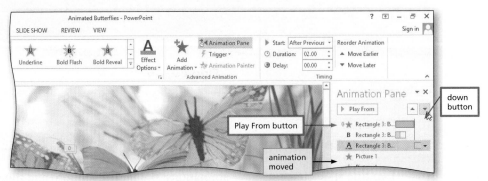

Figure 7–19

Q&A

Can I tap or click the Move Later button (ANIMATIONS tab | Timing group) on the ribbon instead of the down button in the Animation Pane?

Yes. Either button will change the animation order.

Can I view the Animation Pane at any time when I am adding and adjusting animation effects?

Yes. Tap or click the Animation Pane button (ANIMATIONS tab | Advanced Animation group) to display the Animation Pane.

To Rename Slide Objects

The two animated title slide elements are listed in the Animation Pane as Rectangle and Picture. You can give these objects meaningful names. *Why? So that you can identify them in the animation sequence.* The following steps rename the animated Slide 1 objects.

- Display the HOME tab and then tap or click the Select button (HOME tab | Editing group) to display the Select menu (Figure 7–20).

- Tap or click Selection Pane in the Select menu to display the Selection pane.

Figure 7–20

- Tap or click the Picture label in the Selection pane and then tap or click the label again to place the insertion point in the box (Figure 7–21).

Q&A What does the Picture label represent on three animations?
It indicates that the green entry, yellow emphasis, and red exit animations are applied to a picture, in this case the butterfly photo.

Figure 7–21

- Delete the text and then type **Butterfly** in the Picture box.

- Tap or click the Rectangle label in the Selection pane, tap or click the label again, delete the text, and then type **Title Text** in the Rectangle box (Figure 7–22).

Q&A What does the Rectangle label represent on three animations?
It indicates that the green entry and two emphasis animations are applied to the title text placeholder.

Figure 7–22

- Tap or click the Close button on the Selection pane.

- Tap or click the Close button on the Animation pane.

Break Point: If you wish to take a break, this is a good place to do so. Be sure to save the Animated Butterflies file again and then you can quit PowerPoint. To resume at a later time, start PowerPoint, open the file called Animated Butterflies, and continue following the steps from this location forward.

To Insert a Text Box and Format Text

1 MODIFY PHOTOS | 2 ADD ENTRANCE, EMPHASIS, & EXIT ANIMATIONS
3 ANIMATE BOXES, SMARTART, & CHARTS | 4 CHANGE TRANSITION EFFECTS | 5 SET TIMINGS

Slide 2 contains three elements that you will animate. First, you will add a text box, format and animate text, and add a motion path and sound. Next, you will add an entrance effect and custom motion path to a butterfly illustration. Finally, you will animate one butterfly and copy the animation to the other butterflies using the Animation Painter. The first sequence will be a text box in the lower-left corner of the slide. The following steps add a text box to Slide 2.

1

- Display Slide 2 and then display the INSERT tab.

- Tap or click the Text Box button (INSERT tab | Text group).

- If you are using a mouse, position the pointer in the red flower in the lower-left corner of the slide (Figure 7–23), then click the slide.

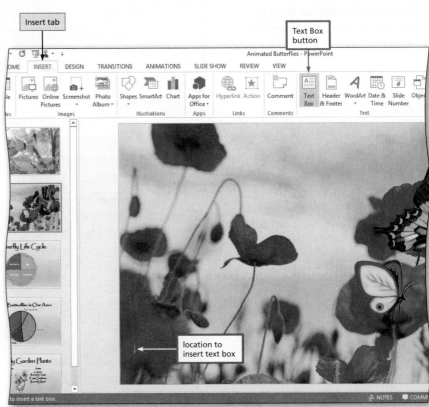

Figure 7–23

2

- Type **Admire the Beauty** in the box. If you are using a touch screen, move the box to the position shown in Figure 7–24 and adjust the size of the box as needed to display the text on one line.

Figure 7–24

- Display Slide 1, position the pointer in the second line of the title text placeholder, and then double-click the Format Painter button (HOME tab | Clipboard group) (Figure 7–25).

Q&A
I am using a touch screen and cannot use the Format Painter for this task. What should I do?
You many need to change the formatting manually.

- Display Slide 2 and then triple-click the inserted box to apply the Slide 1 title text format to the text in the box.

- Press the ESC key to turn off the Format Painter feature.

Figure 7–25

- Display the DRAWING TOOLS FORMAT tab, tap or click the Text Effects button (DRAWING TOOLS FORMAT tab | WordArt Styles group), and then apply the Can Down WordArt text effect (fourth effect in the fourth row of the Warp section of the Transform gallery) to the words in the box (Figure 7–26). If necessary, move the box so that all the letters display as shown in the figure.

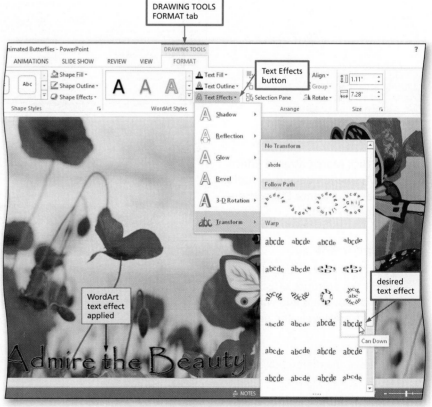

Figure 7–26

To Animate a Text Box Using
an Entrance Effect

Boxes can have the same animation effects applied to pictures and placeholders, and slide designers often use entrance, emphasis, and exit animations. *Why? These effects can add interest to slides, and the default timings can be changed to synchronize with the slide content.* The 13 effects shown in the Entrance section of the Animation gallery are some of the more popular choices; PowerPoint provides many more effects that are divided into the Basic, Subtle, Moderate, and Exciting categories. The following steps add an entrance effect to the text box.

1

- If necessary, tap or click the box to select it and then display the ANIMATIONS tab.

- Tap or click the More button in the Animation gallery (ANIMATIONS tab | Animation group) to expand the Animation gallery (Figure 7–27).

Figure 7–27

2

- Tap or click More Entrance Effects in the Animation gallery to display the Change Entrance Effect dialog box (Figure 7–28).

Experiment

- If you are using a mouse, click some of the entrance effects in the various areas and watch the effect preview in the box on Slide 2.

Q&A

Can I move the dialog box so that I can see the effect preview?
Yes. Drag the dialog box title bar so that the dialog box does not cover the box.

Figure 7–28

3

- Tap or click Fade in the Subtle section (Figure 7–29).

Q&A Why do I see a preview of the effects when I tap or click their names?

The Preview Effect box is selected. If you do not want to see previews, click the box to deselect it.

Figure 7–29

4

- Tap or click the OK button (Change Entrance Effect dialog box) to apply the Fade entrance effect to the text.

- Change the start timing option to With Previous.

- Change the duration to 03.00 seconds (Figure 7–30).

Q&A Can I remove an animation?

Yes. Tap or click None (ANIMATIONS tab | Animation group). You may need to tap or click the More button to see None.

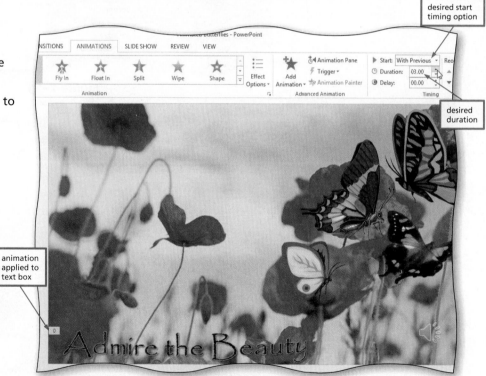

Figure 7–30

To Animate a Text Box by Applying a Motion Path

Why? One of the more effective methods of animating slide objects is to use a motion path to predetermine the route *the object will follow.* In your presentation, the text box will move from the left side of the slide to the right side in a curving motion that simulates a butterfly's flight through the flower garden. The following steps apply a motion path to the Slide 2 text box.

1

- With the Slide 2 text box still selected, tap or click the Add Animation button (ANIMATIONS tab | Advanced Animation group) to expand the Animation gallery.

- Scroll down until the Motion Paths section is visible (Figure 7–31).

Figure 7–31

2

- Tap or click the Arcs motion path to apply the animation to the box.

- Change the start timing option to After Previous.

- Change the duration to 05.00 seconds (Figure 7–32).

Are more motion paths available in addition to those shown in the Animation gallery? Yes. To see additional motion paths, click More Motion Paths in the lower portion of the Animation gallery. The motion paths are arranged in the Basic, Lines & Curves, and Special categories.

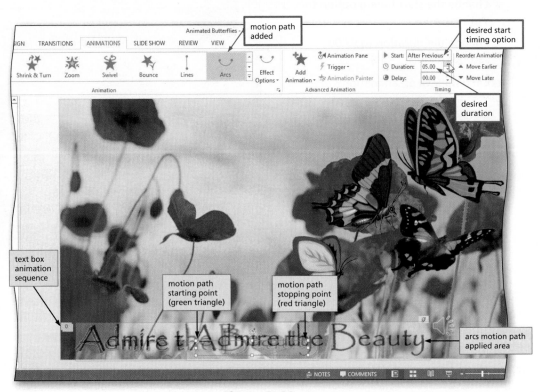

Figure 7–32

To Adjust a Motion Path

The Arcs motion path moves the box in the correct directions, but the path can be extended to move across the entire width of the slide. The green triangle in the middle of the word, the, indicates the starting point, and the red triangle after the word, Beauty, indicates the stopping point. You would like to move the starting point toward the left edge and the stopping point toward the right edge. ***Why?*** *This increased distance provides the maximum animation effect on the slide.* The following steps move the starting and stopping points on the Slide 2 box and then reverse the direction of the arc.

- Tap or click the slide to clear the selected text. With the motion path selected in the box, drag the red stopping point to the location shown in Figure 7–33.

Q&A
My entire motion path moved. How can I move only the red stopping point arrow?
Be certain your pointer is a two-headed arrow and not a four-headed arrow.

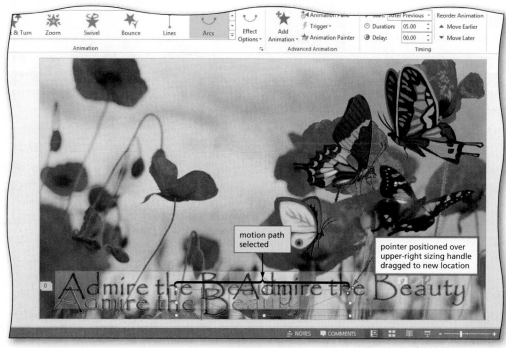

Figure 7–33

2

- Drag the green starting point to the location shown in Figure 7–34.

- Preview the custom animation (Figure 7–34).

Q&A
My animation is not exactly like the path shown in Figure 7–34. Can I change the path?
Yes. Continue adjusting the starting and stopping points and playing the animation until you are satisfied with the effect.

Figure 7–34

3

- Tap or click the Effect Options button (ANIMATIONS tab | Animation group) to display the Effect Options gallery (Figure 7–35).

4

- Tap or click Up in the Direction section to reverse the direction from Down to Up.

- Preview the custom animation.

Figure 7–35

To Associate a Sound with an Animation

1 MODIFY PHOTOS | 2 ADD ENTRANCE, EMPHASIS, & EXIT ANIMATIONS
3 ANIMATE BOXES, SMARTART, & CHARTS | 4 CHANGE TRANSITION EFFECTS | 5 SET TIMINGS

Why? *Sounds can enhance a presentation if used properly, and they can be linked to other animations on the slide.* Slide 2 already has an inserted harp-like musical sound. The following step associates the sound with the box on Slide 2.

1

- Tap or click the sound icon on Slide 2 and then tap or click the Play button (ANIMATIONS tab | Animation group).

- Change the start timing option to With Previous (Figure 7–36).

- Display the AUDIO TOOLS PLAYBACK tab and then tap or click 'Loop until Stopped' to select the check box.

Figure 7–36

To Draw a Custom Motion Path

Why? *Although PowerPoint supplies a wide variety of motion paths, at times they may not fit the precise animations your presentation requires. In that situation, you can draw a custom path that specifies the unique movement your slide element should make.* Slide 2 has clips of several butterflies. You can animate a butterfly to fly to several flowers. No preset motion path presents the exact motion you want to display, so you will draw your own custom path.

Drawing a custom path requires some practice and patience. A mouse is required to perform this task, and you click the mouse to begin drawing the line. If you want the line to change direction, such as to curve, you click again. When you have completed drawing the path, you double-click to end the line. The following steps draw a custom motion path.

1

- Select the colorful butterfly illustration in the upper-right corner of the slide. Apply the Fade entrance effect and then change the start timing option to After Previous.

- Click the Add Animation button and then scroll down until the entire Motion Paths section is visible (Figure 7–37).

Q&A Can I draw a custom motion path when using a touch screen?

No. You must use a mouse to perform this task.

Figure 7–37

2

- Click Custom Path in the Motion Paths gallery to add this animation.

- Click the Effect Options button (ANIMATIONS tab | Animation group) to display the Type gallery (Figure 7–38).

Figure 7–38

3

- Click Curve in the Type gallery and then position the pointer directly in front of the colorful butterfly's antennae.

Q&A Why did I need to change the option from Scribble to Curve?
Your custom motion path will select particular flowers on the slide, and the Curve type will create rounded edges to connect the lines you draw. The Scribble option would draw only straight lines, so the butterfly would not have smooth turns as it flew from one flower to the next.

- Click to indicate where the curve will start and then move the pointer to the location shown in Figure 7–39, which is where the curve will change direction.

Figure 7–39

4

- Click to position the pointer at the single flower near the center of the slide, and then click to indicate the end of this direction of travel.

- Position the pointer at the top of the green leaf above the word, Admire, and then click to indicate the end of this curve (Figure 7–40).

Figure 7–40

5

- Position the pointer on the black dot in the center of the small flower in the left edge of the slide and then double-click to indicate the end of the motion path and preview the animation.

- Change the start timing option to With Previous and the duration setting to 07.00 seconds (Figure 7–41).

Q&A If my curve is not correct, can I delete it?
Yes. Select the motion path, press the DELETE key, and then repeat the previous steps.

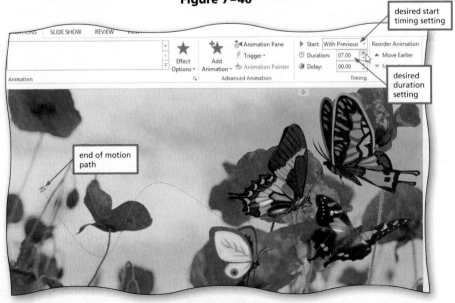

Figure 7–41

To Use the Animation Painter to Animate an Illustration

At times, you may desire to apply the same animation effects to several objects on a slide. On Slide 2, for example, you want to animate the three butterflies with identical entrance, emphasis, and exit effects. As with the Format Painter that is used to duplicate font and paragraph attributes, the Animation Painter copies animation effects. Using the Animation Painter can save time. *Why? It duplicates numerous animations quickly and consistently.* The following steps animate one butterfly and then use the Animation Painter to copy these effects to three other butterflies.

1

- Select the butterfly with the green wings in the upper-right corner of the slide and then apply the Fly In entrance effect.

- Tap or click the Effect Options button and then change the direction to From Top-Left.

- Change the start timing option to With Previous and the duration to 06.00 seconds (Figure 7–42).

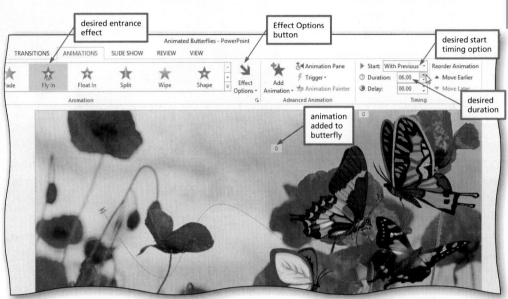

Figure 7–42

2

- With the butterfly still selected, add the Pulse emphasis effect, change the start timing option to After Previous, and then change the duration to 01.00 seconds (Figure 7–43).

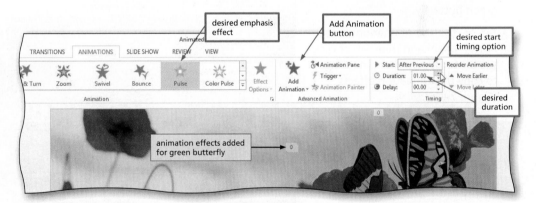

Figure 7–43

3

- Add the Fade exit effect, change the start timing option to After Previous, and then change the duration to 03.00 seconds (Figure 7–44).

 Can I copy the animation to an object on another slide?

Yes. Once you establish the desired animation effects, you can copy them to any object that can be animated on any slide.

Figure 7–44

4

- Tap or click the green butterfly with the animation effects to select it and then tap or click the Animation Painter button (ANIMATIONS tab | Advanced Animation group).

- If you are using a mouse, position the pointer over the brown butterfly that is located near the center of the slide (Figure 7–45).

Q&A Why did my pointer change shape?
The pointer changed shape by displaying a paintbrush to indicate that the Animation Painter function is active.

Figure 7–45

5

- Tap or click the brown butterfly to apply the same entrance, emphasis, and exit animation effects as those added to the green butterfly.

- Tap or click the Animation Painter button again and then tap or click the butterfly with the pink wings to copy the animation effects (Figure 7–46).

- Preview the animation effects.

Q&A Can I copy the animation to more than one object simultaneously?
No. Unlike using the Format Painter, you must click the Animation Painter button each time you want to copy the animation to an object on the slide.

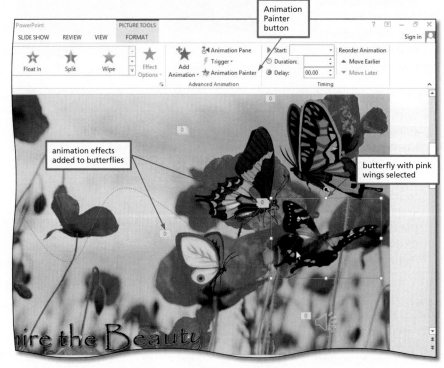

Figure 7–46

Break Point: If you wish to take a break, this is a good place to do so. Be sure to save the Animated Butterflies file again and then you can quit PowerPoint. To resume at a later time, start PowerPoint, open the file called Animated Butterflies, and continue following the steps from this location forward.

To Animate a SmartArt Graphic

1 MODIFY PHOTOS | 2 ADD ENTRANCE, EMPHASIS, & EXIT ANIMATIONS
3 ANIMATE BOXES, SMARTART, & CHARTS | 4 CHANGE TRANSITION EFFECTS | 5 SET TIMINGS

The Slide 3 SmartArt graphic shows the four stages in a butterfly's life. You can add animation to each shape representing one stage. *Why? This animation emphasizes each stage in a butterfly's life cycle and helps the audience concentrate on each component.* While you can add a custom animation to each shape in the cycle, you also can use one of PowerPoint's built-in animations to simplify the animation procedure. The following steps apply an entrance animation effect to the Segmented Cycle diagram.

- Display Slide 3, select the SmartArt graphic, and then display the Animation gallery (Figure 7–47).

- Select the Shape entrance effect.

Figure 7–47

To Change a SmartArt Graphic Animation Sequence

1 MODIFY PHOTOS | 2 ADD ENTRANCE, EMPHASIS, & EXIT ANIMATIONS
3 ANIMATE BOXES, SMARTART, & CHARTS | 4 CHANGE TRANSITION EFFECTS | 5 SET TIMINGS

By default, all SmartArt graphic components enter the slide simultaneously. You can modify this entrance sequence setting. *Why? Each element will enter one at a time and build a clockwise sequence.* The steps on the next page change the sequence for the SmartArt animation to One by One.

1
- Tap or click the Effect Options button to display the Effect Options gallery (Figure 7–48).

Q&A Can I reverse the order of individual shapes in the SmartArt sequence? No. You can reverse the order of the entire SmartArt graphic but not individual shapes within the sequence.

Figure 7–48

2
- Tap or click One by One in the Sequence section to change the animation order.
- Change the start timing option to After Previous, the duration to 4.00 seconds, and the delay to 01.00 second (Figure 7–49).

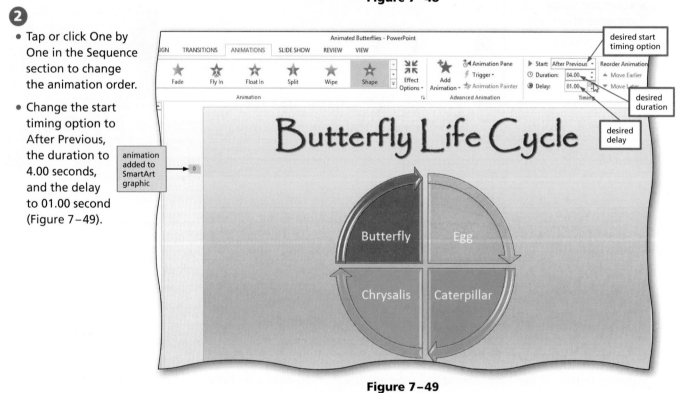

Figure 7–49

To Animate a Chart

1 MODIFY PHOTOS | 2 ADD ENTRANCE, EMPHASIS, & EXIT ANIMATIONS
3 ANIMATE BOXES, SMARTART, & CHARTS | 4 CHANGE TRANSITION EFFECTS | 5 SET TIMINGS

The chart on Slide 4 depicts specific butterflies that commonly appear in a particular region of the country. You can animate the slices of the pie chart. *Why?* *So that each slice enters the slide individually and the audience's attention is drawn to each type of butterfly.* As with the SmartArt animation, PowerPoint gives you many options to animate the chart data. The following steps animate the Slide 4 chart slices.

1

- Display Slide 4 and then tap or click an edge of the chart so that the frame is displayed. Display the Animation gallery (Figure 7–50).

Q&A

An outer white frame is displayed rather than the black chart frame shown in Figure 7–50. What should I do?
Tap or click the chart edge again.

2

- Tap or click the Fly In entrance effect, change the start timing option to After Previous, change the duration to 02.00 seconds, and change the delay to 02.50 seconds.

Figure 7–50

3

- Tap or click the Effect Options button to display the Effect Options gallery (Figure 7–51).

4

- Tap or click By Category to change the chart animation so that each slice appears individually and to preview the animation.

Figure 7–51

To Animate a List

The two lists on Slide 5 give recommended plants that can attract butterflies. Each item in the placeholder is a separate paragraph. You can have each paragraph in the left list enter the slide individually. *Why? To add interest during a presentation.* When the entire list has displayed, the list can disappear and then each paragraph in the right list can appear. The following steps animate the Slide 5 paragraph lists.

1

- Display Slide 5 and then select the five items in the left text placeholder.

- Apply the Shape entrance animation effect, change the duration to 03.00 seconds, and change the delay to 01.50 seconds. If necessary, change the start timing option to After Previous (Figure 7–52).

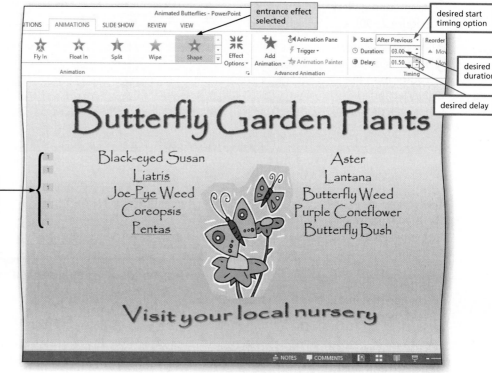

Figure 7–52

2

- Tap or click the Effect Options button to display the Effect Options gallery (Figure 7–53).

3

- Change the Shapes from Circle to Diamond.

- Tap or click the Effect Options button again and then change the Direction to Out.

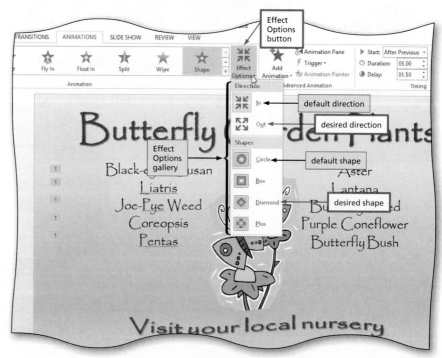

Figure 7–53

Select colors for dimming text.

After paragraphs of text are displayed, you can change the color, or dim the text, to direct the audience's attention to another area of the slide. Choose the dimming colors carefully. For example, use cool colors, such as blue, purple, and turquoise, as backgrounds so that the audience focuses on the next brighter, contrasting color on the slide. Avoid using light blue because it often is difficult to see, especially against a dark background. In addition, use a maximum of three colors unless you have a compelling need to present more variety.

To Dim Text after Animation

1 MODIFY PHOTOS | 2 ADD ENTRANCE, EMPHASIS, & EXIT ANIMATIONS
3 ANIMATE BOXES, SMARTART, & CHARTS | 4 CHANGE TRANSITION EFFECTS | 5 SET TIMINGS

As each item in the list is displayed, you may desire to have the previous item removed from the screen or to have the font color change, or **dim**. PowerPoint provides several options for you to alter this text by specifying an After Animation effect. The following steps dim each item in the left placeholder list by changing the font color to Purple. *Why? The color, purple, coordinates with the purple color in the illustration.*

1

- If necessary, select the five paragraphs in the left placeholder and then tap or click the Animation Pane button (ANIMATIONS tab | Advanced Animation group) to display the Animation Pane with all paragraphs selected.

- Tap or click the Animation Order list arrow to the right of Pentas to display the Animation Order menu (Figure 7–54).

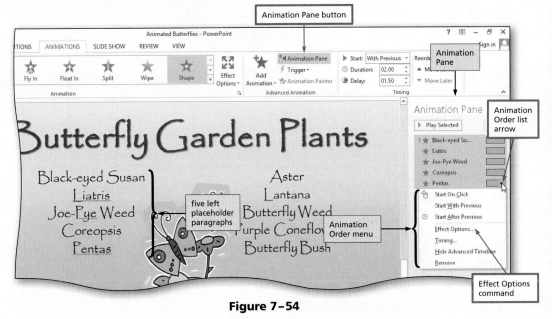

Figure 7–54

2

- Tap or click Effect Options on the Animation Order list to display the Diamond dialog box.

- Tap or click the After animation arrow to display the After animation menu (Figure 7–55).

Figure 7–55

- Tap or click the color purple (last color in the row of colors) to select this color for the dim effect (Figure 7–56).

- Tap or click the OK button (Diamond dialog box) to apply the dim effect to the five items in the left placeholder on Slide 5.
- Close the Animation pane.

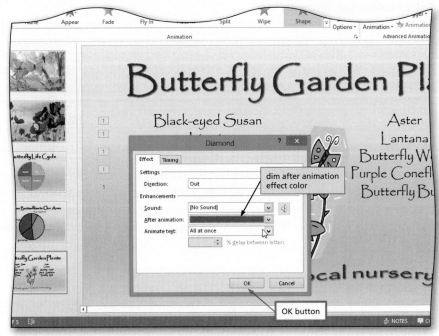

Figure 7–56

To Use the Animation Painter to Copy Animations

1 MODIFY PHOTOS | 2 ADD ENTRANCE, EMPHASIS, & EXIT ANIMATIONS
3 ANIMATE BOXES, SMARTART, & CHARTS | 4 CHANGE TRANSITION EFFECTS | 5 SET TIMINGS

All animations have been applied to the left placeholder paragraphs. You now can copy these animations to the five items in the right text placeholder. The following steps use the Animation Painter to copy the animation. *Why? Copying the animation saves time and ensures consistency between the left and right paragraphs.*

- Tap or click the flower name, Black-eyed Susan, in the left text placeholder and then tap or click the Animation Painter button (Figure 7–57).

Q&A Can I place the insertion point in any word in the left text placeholder instead of the first item in the list?
Yes. All the paragraphs have the same animation effect applied, so you can click any word in the list.

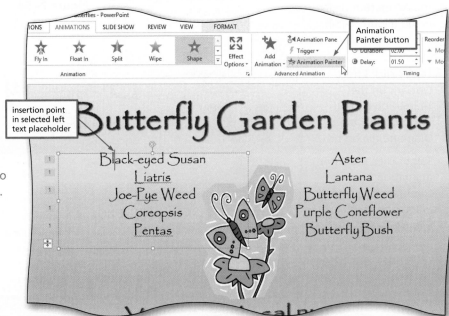

Figure 7–57

2

- Tap or click the word, Aster, in the right list to copy the animations in the left list to the five words in the right list.

Can I tap or click any word in the right text placeholder instead of the first item in the list?
Yes. You can click any word in the list to copy the animation effect to all words.

- Select the five words in the list in the right placeholder if necessary, change the start timing option to After Previous, and then change the duration to 03.00 seconds, and the delay to 01.50 seconds (Figure 7–58).

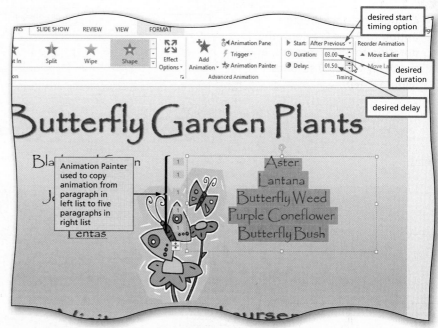

Figure 7–58

To Create Credits

1 MODIFY PHOTOS | 2 ADD ENTRANCE, EMPHASIS, & EXIT ANIMATIONS
3 ANIMATE BOXES, SMARTART, & CHARTS | 4 CHANGE TRANSITION EFFECTS | 5 SET TIMINGS

Many motion pictures use rolling credits at the end of the movie to acknowledge the people who were involved in the filmmaking process or to provide additional information about the actors or setting. You, too, can use a credit or closing statement at the end of your presentation. *Why? You can use credits to thank individuals or companies who helped you develop your slide show or to leave your audience with a final thought.* The following steps display text as an ascending credit line on Slide 5.

1

- With Slide 5 displaying, tap or click the box with the words, Visit your local nursery, at the bottom of the slide to select it.

- Display the Animation gallery and then tap or click More Entrance Effects to display the Change Entrance Effect dialog box.

- Scroll down to display the Exciting section (Figure 7–59).

2

- Tap or click the Credits entrance animation effect in the Exciting section to see a preview of the animation effect.

- Tap or click the OK button (Change Entrance Effect dialog box) to apply the effect.

Figure 7–59

• Change the start timing option to After Previous, the duration to 18.00 seconds, and the delay to 02.00 seconds (Figure 7–60).

• Preview the animation.

Figure 7–60

To Use the Eyedropper to Format Text

1 MODIFY PHOTOS | 2 ADD ENTRANCE, EMPHASIS, & EXIT ANIMATIONS

3 ANIMATE BOXES, SMARTART, & CHARTS | 4 CHANGE TRANSITION EFFECTS | 5 SET TIMINGS

Why? *A slide can look cohesive when the shapes, pictures, and text have identical colors.* The eyedropper tool can ensure precise color matching. This tool is new to PowerPoint 2013; it is not, however, available when using a touch screen. The eyedropper allows you to select any color on the slide to match. The eyedropper is available on several menus, including Shape Fill, Font Color, Shape Outline, Text Outline, Picture Variations, and Glow Colors. After you select the eyedropper, move the pointer to any area of the slide to see a live preview of the color. If you hover over a particular area, a ScreenTip is displayed with the color name and its RGB (red, green, and blue) color coordinates. If many colors are intertwined on the slide, press the ENTER key or the SPACEBAR to select the desired color. The following steps color the text in the text box at the bottom of the slide with the pink color in the butterfly illustration.

BTW

Selecting Text Animation Options

Multi-level bulleted list paragraphs can have animation effects that help direct the audience's attention. For example, you can animate the second-level paragraphs so they are displayed individually along with any associated third-level paragraphs. To specify a text animation option, display the Animation Pane, tap or click an animation you want to manipulate in the list, tap or click this animation's list arrow to display a menu, tap or click Effect Options in the list, and then tap or click the Text Animation tab. If desired, you can tap or click the Group Text arrow and select a paragraph level, such as 2nd level, in the list. Tap or click the Automatically after check box and enter a time if you want the next bulleted paragraph to appear after a specific number of seconds. In addition, tap or click the 'In reverse order' check box to build the paragraphs from the bottom to the top of the slide.

BTW

Eyedropper Tool and Touch Screens

The eyedropper tool is not available on touch screens.

1

- Display the HOME tab and then select all the text in the text box at the bottom of the slide.

Q&A Can I select several slide elements to color simultaneously? Yes. Press CTRL and then tap or click the objects you desire to color.

- Click the Font Color arrow to display the Font menu (Figure 7–61).

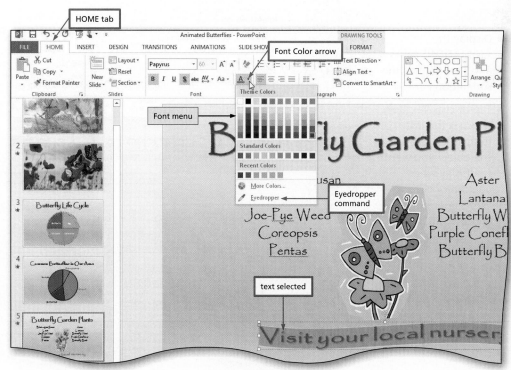

Figure 7–61

2

- Click Eyedropper and then place the pointer over the Pink wings on the right butterfly (Figure 7–62).

Q&A Can I cancel using the eyedropper without selecting a color? Yes. Press the ESC key.

3

- Click the wing to apply the Pink color to the selected text box text.

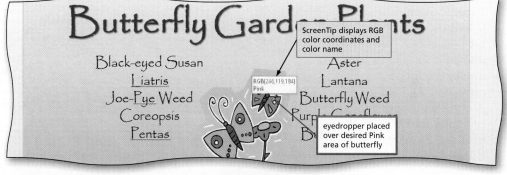

Figure 7–62

To Trigger an Animation Effect

1 MODIFY PHOTOS | 2 ADD ENTRANCE, EMPHASIS, & EXIT ANIMATIONS

3 ANIMATE BOXES, SMARTART, & CHARTS | 4 CHANGE TRANSITION EFFECTS | 5 SET TIMINGS

If you select the 'On Click' start timing option and run the slide show, PowerPoint starts the animation when you tap or click any part of the slide or press the SPACEBAR. You may, however, want the option to play an animation in a particular circumstance. *Why? You may have an animated sequence ready to show if time permits or if you believe your audience needs time to understand a process and would understand the concept more readily if you revealed one part of a SmartArt graphic at a time.* A **trigger** specifies when an animation or other action should occur. It is linked to a particular component of a slide so that the action occurs only when you click this slide element. For example, you can trigger an animation effect to start when you click a shape or other object that has the animation applied, or you can trigger an animation effect to begin playing at the start of, or sometime during, an audio or video clip. If you click any other part of the slide, PowerPoint will display the next slide in the presentation. The steps on the next page set the butterfly illustration on Slide 5 as the trigger to play music.

1

- Display the ANIMATIONS tab and then display the Animation Pane.

- Tap or click TextBox, which is the last item in the list, as the object you want to display when you tap or click the trigger object (Figure 7–63).

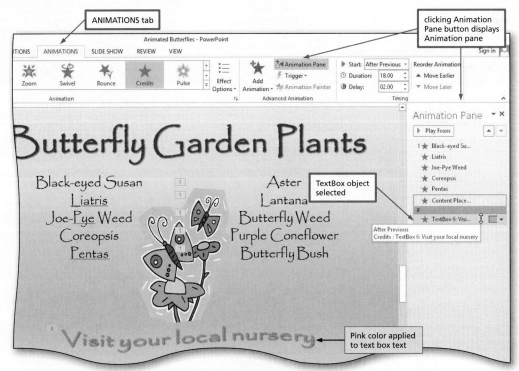

Figure 7–63

2

- Tap or click the Trigger button (ANIMATIONS tab | Advanced Animation group) to display the Trigger menu and then tap or click 'On Click of' to display the list of Slide 5 elements (Figure 7–64).

3

- Tap or click Title 1, which is the title text, as the object that will trigger the animation when clicked.

- Close the Animation pane.

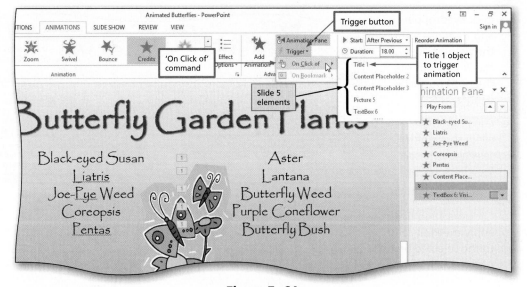

Figure 7–64

To Modify a Transition Effect

1 MODIFY PHOTOS | 2 ADD ENTRANCE, EMPHASIS, & EXIT ANIMATIONS
3 ANIMATE BOXES, SMARTART, & CHARTS | 4 CHANGE TRANSITION EFFECTS | 5 SET TIMINGS

The Box transition will be applied to the five slides in this presentation. The default rotation is From Right, so the current slide turns to the left while the new slide appears from the right side of the screen. You can change the Box rotation so that the current slide moves to the bottom of the screen and the new slide appears from the top. *Why? You want the transition effect to be consistent with the butterflies entering the slides from the upper-left and upper-right edges of the slide.* The following steps apply the Box transition and then modify the Transition Effect for all slides in the presentation.

- Display the TRANSITIONS tab and then apply the Box transition (in the third row of the Exciting category) to all slides in the presentation.

- Tap or click the Effect Options button (TRANSITIONS tab | Transition to This Slide group) to display the Effect Options gallery (Figure 7–65).

Q&A Are the same four effects available for all transitions?
No. The transition effects vary depending upon the particular transition selected.

Figure 7–65

- Tap or click the From Top effect to change the rotation.

- Tap or click the 'Apply To All' button (TRANSITIONS tab | Timing group) to set the From Top transition effect for all slides in the presentation (Figure 7–66).

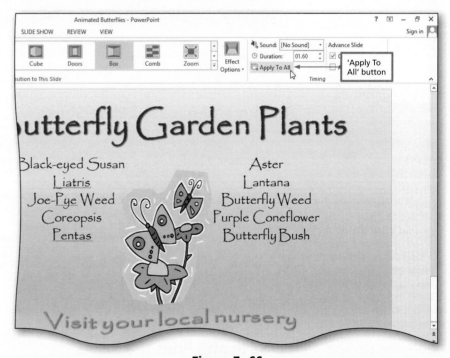

Figure 7–66

To Apply a Transition to a Single Slide

1 MODIFY PHOTOS | 2 ADD ENTRANCE, EMPHASIS, & EXIT ANIMATIONS
3 ANIMATE BOXES, SMARTART, & CHARTS | 4 CHANGE TRANSITION EFFECTS | 5 SET TIMINGS

The final slide in the presentation acquaints viewers with specific plants that attract butterflies and urges them to visit a nursery to see this foliage. You can change the transition for this one slide. *Why? To emphasize the variety of plants and possibility of creating a butterfly garden.* The following step applies the Curtains transition to Slide 5.

• With Slide 5 and the TRANSITIONS tab displaying, display the Transitions gallery and then tap or click the Curtains transition in the Exciting category to select this effect for Slide 5 and to see a preview (Figure 7–67).

Figure 7–67

To Run an Animated Slide Show

All changes are complete. You now can view the Animated Butterflies presentation. The following steps run the slide show.

1 Tap or click the 'Start From Beginning' button in the Quick Access toolbar to start the presentation and display the title slide.

2 As each slide is displayed, review the information.

3 When Slide 5 is displayed and the list of plants is displayed, click the title text to trigger the text box to display.

To Save and Print the Slides

The presentation now is complete. You should save the slides and print a handout.

1 Save the Animated Butterflies presentation again with the same file name.

2 Print the presentation as a handout with two slides per page (Figure 7–68).

(a) Page 1

(b) Page 2

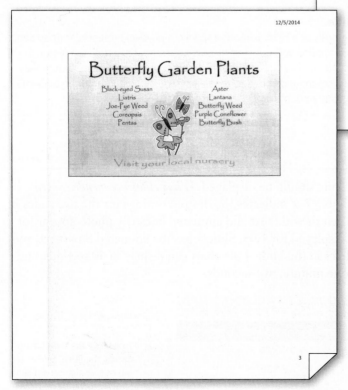

(c) Page 3

BTW
Printing Document Properties
To print document properties, tap or click FILE on the ribbon to open the Backstage view, tap or click the Print tab in the Backstage view to display the Print gallery, tap or click the first button in the Settings area to display a list of options specifying what you can print, tap or click Document Info in the list to specify you want to print the document properties instead of the actual document, and then tap or click the Print button in the Print gallery to print the document properties on the currently selected printer.

Figure 7–68

BTW
Conserving Ink and Toner
If you want to conserve ink or toner, you can instruct PowerPoint to print draft quality documents by tapping or clicking FILE on the ribbon to open the Backstage view, tapping or clicking Options in the Backstage view to display the PowerPoint Options dialog box, tapping or clicking Advanced in the left pane (PowerPoint Options dialog box), sliding or scrolling to the Print area in the right pane, placing a check mark in the 'Use draft quality' check box, and then tapping or clicking the OK button. Then, use the Backstage view to print the document as usual.

BTW
Certification
The Microsoft Office Specialist (MOS) program provides an opportunity for you to obtain a valuable industry credential — proof that you have the PowerPoint 2013 skills required by employers. For more information, visit the Certification resource on the Student Companion Site located on www.cengagebrain.com. For detailed instructions about accessing available resources, visit www.cengage.com/ct/studentdownload or see the inside back cover of this book.

Preparing for a Self-Running Presentation

In previous slide shows, you clicked to advance from one slide to the next. Because all animations have been added to the slides in the presentation, you now can set the time each slide is displayed on the screen. You can set these times in one of two ways. The first method is to specify each slide's display time manually. The second method is to use PowerPoint's **rehearsal feature**, which allows you to advance through the slides at your own pace, and the amount of time you view each slide is recorded. You will use the second technique in this chapter and then adjust the fourth slide's timing manually.

When you begin rehearsing a presentation, the Rehearsal toolbar is displayed. The **Rehearsal toolbar** contains buttons that allow you to start, pause, and repeat viewing the slides in the slide show and to view the times for each slide as well as the elapsed time. Table 7–1 describes the buttons on the Rehearsal toolbar.

Table 7–1 Rehearsal Toolbar Buttons		
Button Name	**Image**	**Description**
Next	➡	Displays the next slide or next animated element on the slide.
Pause Recording	❚❚	Stops the timer. Tap or click the Next or Pause Recording button to resume timing.
Slide Time	0:00:00	Indicates the length of time a slide has been displayed. You can enter a slide time directly in the Slide Time box.
Repeat	↺	Clears the Slide Time box and resets the timer to 0:00:00.
Elapsed Time	0:00:00	Indicates slide show total time.

© 2014 Cengage Learning

CONSIDER THIS

Give your audience sufficient time to view a slide.
The presentation in this chapter is designed to run continuously at a kiosk without a speaker's physical presence. Your audience, therefore, must read or view each slide and absorb the information without your help as a narrator. Be certain to give them time to read the slide and grasp the concept you are presenting. They will become frustrated if the slide changes before they have finished viewing and assimilating the material. As you set the slide timings, read each slide aloud and note the amount of time that elapses. Add a few seconds to this time and use this amount for the total time the slide is displayed.

To Rehearse Timings

1 MODIFY PHOTOS | 2 ADD ENTRANCE, EMPHASIS, & EXIT ANIMATIONS
3 ANIMATE BOXES, SMARTART, & CHARTS | 4 CHANGE TRANSITION EFFECTS | 5 SET TIMINGS

You need to determine the length of time each slide should be displayed. *Why? Audience members need sufficient time to read the text and watch the animations.* Table 7–2 indicates the desired timings for the five slides in the Butterflies presentation. Slide 1 is displayed and then the title text and animated butterfly photo appear for 25 seconds. The Slide 2 title text, sound, and clip are displayed for 1:05. Slide 3 has the animated SmartArt, and it takes 45 seconds for the elements to display. The slices in the Slide 4 pie chart can display in 40 seconds, and the two lists and rolling credit on Slide 5 display for one minute, five seconds.

Table 7–2 Slide Rehearsal Timings		
Slide Number	**Display Time**	**Elapsed Time**
1	0:00	0:25
2	1:05	1:30
3	0:45	2:15
4	0:40	2:55
5	1:05	4:00

© 2014 Cengage Learning

BTW
Discarding Slide Timings
To remove the slide timings, display the SLIDE SHOW tab, tap or click the Record Slide Show arrow (SLIDE SHOW tab | Set Up group), tap or point to Clear, and then click 'Clear Timings on All Slides'.

The following steps add slide timings to the slide show.

1

- Display Slide 1 and then tap or click Slide Show on the ribbon to display the SLIDE SHOW tab (Figure 7–69).

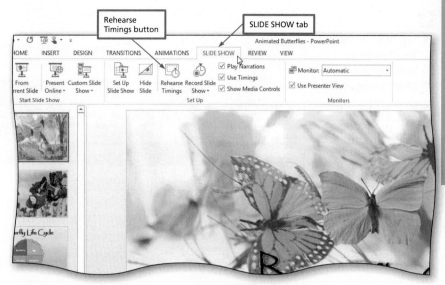

Figure 7–69

2

- Tap or click the Rehearse Timings button (SLIDE SHOW tab | Set Up group) to start the slide show and the counter (Figure 7–70).

Figure 7–70

3

- When the Elapsed Time displays 0:25, tap or click the Next button to display Slide 2.

- When the Elapsed Time displays 1:30, tap or click the Next button to display Slide 3.

- When the Elapsed Time displays 2:15, tap or click the Next button to display Slide 4.

- When the Elapsed Time displays 2:55, tap or click the Next button to display Slide 5.

- When the Elapsed Time displays 4:00, tap or click the Next button to display the Microsoft PowerPoint dialog box (Figure 7–71).

Figure 7–71

- Tap or click the Yes button to keep the new slide timings with an elapsed time of 4:00.

- Review each slide's timing displayed in the lower-left corner in Slide Sorter view (Figure 7–72).

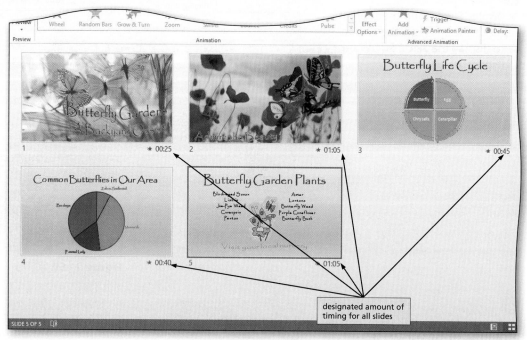

Figure 7–72

To Adjust Timings Manually

1 MODIFY PHOTOS | 2 ADD ENTRANCE, EMPHASIS, & EXIT ANIMATIONS
3 ANIMATE BOXES, SMARTART, & CHARTS | 4 CHANGE TRANSITION EFFECTS | 5 SET TIMINGS

Why? If the slide timings need adjustment, you manually can change the length of time each slide is displayed. In this presentation, you decide to display Slide 4 for 30 seconds instead of 40 seconds. The following step decreases the Slide 4 timing.

- In Slide Sorter view, display the TRANSITIONS tab and then select Slide 4.

- Change the 'Advance Slide After' setting (TRANSITIONS tab | Timing group) to 00:30.00 (Figure 7–73).

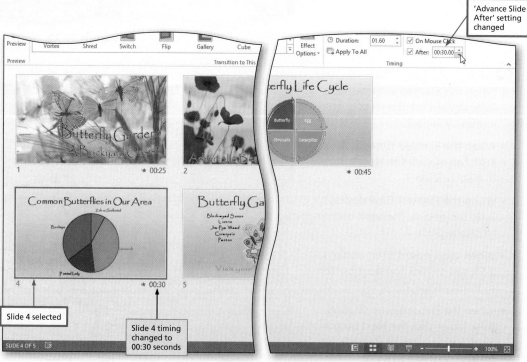

Figure 7–73

To Create a Self-Running Presentation

Why? The Butterflies presentation can accompany a speech, but it also can run unattended at nature centers and nurseries. When the last slide in the presentation is displayed, the slide show **loops**, or restarts, at Slide 1. PowerPoint has the option of running continuously until the user presses the ESC key. The following steps set the slide show to run in this manner.

- Display the SLIDE SHOW tab and then tap or click the 'Set Up Slide Show' button (SLIDE SHOW tab | Set Up group) to display the Set Up Show dialog box.

- Tap or click 'Browsed at a kiosk (full screen)' in the Show type section (Figure 7–74).

- Tap or click the OK button to apply this show type.

Figure 7–74

To Run an Animated Slide Show

All changes are complete. You now can view the presentation. The following steps run the slide show.

1 Tap or click the From Beginning button (SLIDE SHOW tab | Start Slide Show group) to start the presentation.

2 As each slide automatically is displayed, review the information.

3 When Slide 1 is displayed again, press the ESC key to stop the presentation.

To Save and Exit PowerPoint

The presentation now is complete. You should save the slides with a new file name and then exit PowerPoint.

1 Save the Animated Butterflies presentation with the file name, Automatic Butterflies.

2 Exit PowerPoint, closing all open documents.

BTW

Stopping Slide Shows with a Touch Screen
It may not be possible to stop an animated slide show when using a touch screen, unless you can display a touch keyboard that includes an ESC key.

BTW

Quick Reference
For a table that lists how to complete the tasks covered in this book using touch gestures, the mouse, ribbon, shortcut menu, and keyboard, see the Quick Reference Summary at the back of this book, or visit the Quick Reference resource on the Student Companion Site located on www.cengagebrain. com. For detailed instructions about accessing available resources, visit www.cengage. com/ct/studentdownload or see the inside back cover of this book.

Chapter Summary

In this chapter you have learned how to remove a background from a photo and then crop and compress the image. You then applied entrance, emphasis, and exit effects to slide content and created a custom animation using a motion path. Also, you inserted and animated a text box and associated a sound with this text. You animated a SmartArt graphic, a chart, and two lists. Then, you set timing so that the slide show runs automatically. The items listed below include all the new PowerPoint skills you have learned in this chapter.

Animate and Format Text
Insert a Text Box and Format Text (PPT 426)
Animate a Text Box Using an Entrance
    Effect (PPT 428)
Dim Text after Animation (PPT 441)
Use the Eyedropper to Format Text (PPT 444)

Animate Slide Objects
Use the Animation Painter to Animate an
    Illustration (PPT 435)
Animate a SmartArt Graphic (PPT 437)
Animate a Chart (PPT 438)
Animate a List (PPT 440)
Use the Animation Painter to Copy
    Animations (PPT 442)

Create Motion Paths
Animate a Text Box by Applying a
    Motion Path (PPT 430)
Adjust a Motion Path (PPT 431)
Draw a Custom Motion Path (PPT 433)

Modify Animation Effects
Change Animation Order (PPT 423)
Rename Slide Objects (PPT 425)
Associate a Sound with an Animation (PPT 432)
Change a SmartArt Graphic Animation
    Sequence (PPT 437)
Create Credits (PPT 443)
Trigger an Animation Effect (PPT 445)
Modify a Transition Effect (PPT 446)
Apply a Transition to a Single Slide (PPT 447)

Modify Photos
Remove a Background (PPT 412)
Refine Background Removal (PPT 414)
Crop a Photo (PPT 415)
Compress a Photo (PPT 417)

Set Slide Show Timings
Rehearse Timings (PPT 450)
Adjust Timings Manually (PPT 452)
Create a Self-Running Presentation (PPT 453)

CONSIDER THIS

What decisions will you need to make when creating your next presentation?

Use these guidelines as you complete the assignments in this chapter and create your own slide show decks outside of this class.

1. Do not use animation merely for the sake of using animation. Prior to using an animation effect, think about why you need it and how it will affect your presentation.

2. The dimming effect, which changes the color of text paragraphs after they display on a slide, can be used effectively to emphasize important points and to draw the audience's attention to another area of the slide. Select dimming colors that suit the purpose of the presentation.

3. On average, an audience member will spend only eight seconds viewing a basic slide with a simple graphic or a few words. They need much more time to view charts, graphs, and SmartArt graphics. When you are setting slide timings, keep this length of time in mind, particularly when the presentation is viewed at a kiosk without a speaker's physical presence.

How should you submit solutions to questions in the assignments identified with a ✳ symbol?
Every assignment in this book contains one or more questions identified with a ✳ symbol. These questions require you to think beyond the assigned presentation. Present your solutions to the questions in the format required by your instructor. Possible formats may include one or more of these options: write the answer; create a document that contains the answer; present your answer to the class; discuss your answer in a group; record the answer as audio or video using a webcam, smartphone, or portable media player; or post answers on a blog, wiki, or website.

Apply Your Knowledge

Reinforce the skills and apply the concepts you learned in this chapter.

Applying Entrance and Emphasis Effects, Animating a SmartArt Graphic, Drawing a Custom Motion Path, Animating a Text Box by Applying a Motion Path, and Adjusting a Motion Path

Note: To complete this assignment, you will be required to use the Data Files for Students. Visit www.cengage.com/ct/studentdownload for detailed instructions or contact your instructor for information about accessing the required files.

Instructions: Run PowerPoint. Open the presentation, Apply 7-1 Kale, from the Data Files for Students.

The slides in this presentation present information about the health benefits of eating kale. The document you open is a partially formatted presentation. You are to add entrance and emphasis effects to text, an illustration, and a SmartArt graphic. You will draw a custom motion path, animate a text box by applying a motion path, and adjust the motion path. Your presentation should look like Figures 7–75a and 7–75b on the next page.

Perform the following tasks:

1. On Slide 1, increase the size of the photo in the upper-left corner of the slide to 5.06" × 7.18", apply the Soft Edge Oval picture style (sixth style in the third row), and then move the photo to the location shown in Figure 7–75a.

2. Apply the 'Fly In From Top' entrance effect to the kale seed packet, change the start timing option from On Click to After Previous, and then change the duration to 2.25 seconds.

3. Convert the bulleted text on Slide 1 to the Vertical Accent List SmartArt graphic (the fourth graphic in the seventh List row). Change the font to Arial and increase the font size to 28 point. Increase the size of the SmartArt graphic to approximately 6.02" × 6.45", change the color to the Gradient Loop – Accent 1 color (the fourth color in the Accent 1 row), apply the Brick Scene style (the fifth style in the first 3-D row), and then move the graphic to the upper-right area of the slide, as shown in Figure 7–75a.

4. Apply the 'Fly In From Bottom-Right' entrance effect to the SmartArt graphic. Add the 'One by One' effect option, do not change the start timing option, and then change the duration to 2.00 seconds. Add another animation to the kale seed packet by drawing a custom motion path. Draw the path so the seed packet moves down to the right area of the slide and ends up to the left of the text box. Apply the Shapes motion path to the text box and select the Equal Triangle effect. Change the start timing option to After Previous and change the duration to 2.25 seconds. To adjust this motion path, select the text box, select the bottom-center sizing handle of the triangle, and then move it up to just above the green bar on the bottom of the slide.

5. On Slide 2 (Figure 7–75b), select the title and apply the Zoom entrance effect, animate text by word, and change the delay between words to 100%. Change the start timing option from On Click to After Previous and then change the duration to 0.75 seconds.

Continued >

Apply Your Knowledge *continued*

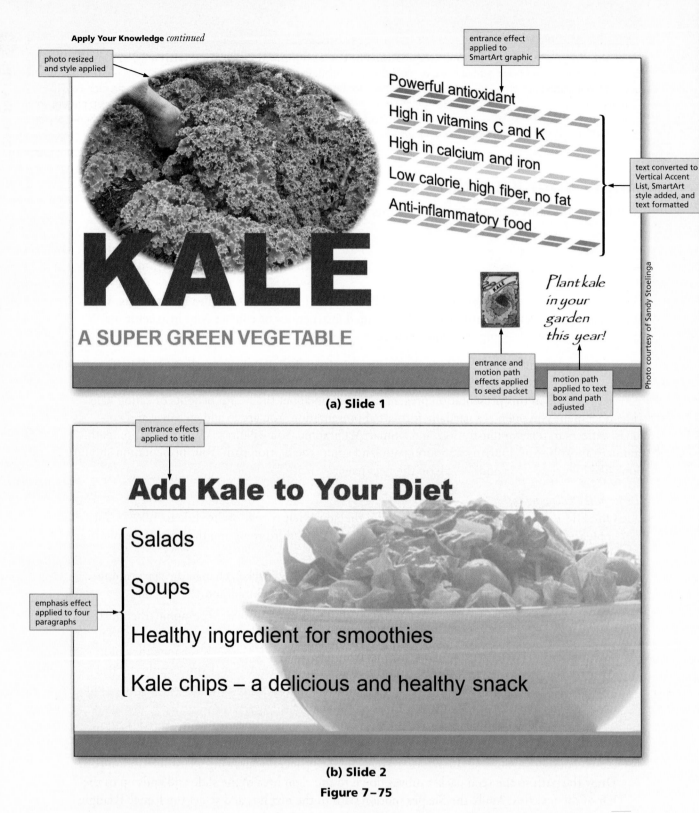

(a) Slide 1

(b) Slide 2

Figure 7–75

6. Apply the Brush Color emphasis effect to the four paragraphs in the content placeholder. Choose the By word effect option and then change the color to Black (the second color in the Theme Colors). Change the start timing option to After Previous and then change the duration to 2.50 seconds.

7. If requested by your instructor, add your grandmother's first name in the lower-right text box after the word, year, on Slide 1.

8. Save the presentation using the file name, Apply 7-1 Plant Kale in Your Garden.

9. Submit the revised document in the format specified by your instructor.

10. ✳ In this presentation, you converted text to a SmartArt graphic on Slide 1. How will adding animation to the graphic help when you are giving this presentation?

Extend Your Knowledge

Extend the skills you learned in this chapter and experiment with new skills. You may need to use Help to complete the assignment.

Changing and Reordering Animation, Adding Sound to Animation, Copying Animation Using the Animation Painter, Compressing a Photo, and Cropping a Photo to a Shape

Note: To complete this assignment, you will be required to use the Data Files for Students. Visit www.cengage.com/ct/studentdownload for detailed instructions or contact your instructor for information about accessing the required files.

Instructions: Run PowerPoint. Open the presentation, Extend 7-1 Horses, from the Data Files for Students. You will change, reorder, and add sound to animation, copy animation using the Animation Painter, and crop a photo to a shape, as shown in Figure 7–76.

Perform the following tasks:

1. On Slide 1 (Figure 7–76a), add the Chevron Up text effect (the first effect in the second Warp row) to the title WordArt and then change the color of the text to Orange, Accent 1 (the fifth color in the Theme Colors). Delete the subtitle text placeholder. Using the guides, position the title so that it is centered horizontally on the slide and the bottom edge of the title placeholder is 3.25" below center.

2. Apply the Reflected Bevel, Black picture style (the fourth style in the fourth row) to the photo, compress the photo, and then center the photo on the slide. Turn off the guides.

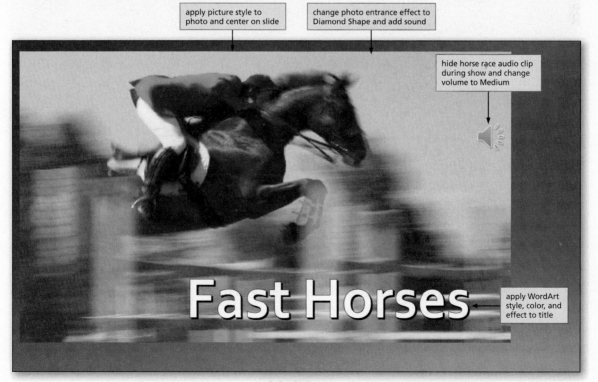

apply picture style to photo and center on slide

change photo entrance effect to Diamond Shape and add sound

hide horse race audio clip during show and change volume to Medium

apply WordArt style, color, and effect to title

(a) Slide 1
Figure 7–76

Continued >

Extend Your Knowledge *continued*

(b) Slide 2

(c) Slide 3

Figure 7–76 (Continued)

3. Change the 'Grow & Turn' entrance effect on the photo to the Shape entrance effect. Change the effect option to the Diamond shape. Change the start timing option from On Click to With Previous, the duration to 2.50 seconds, and add the Applause sound that is included with PowerPoint. (*Hint:* In the Animation pane, select the photo, display the Animation Order menu, click Effect Options, display the Sound list in the Enhancements section, and then select the sound.) Reorder this entrance effect animation, Picture 3, so that it precedes the horse race audio clip. Have the horse race audio clip, which is next to the horse's head on the slide, hide during the show and change the volume to Medium.

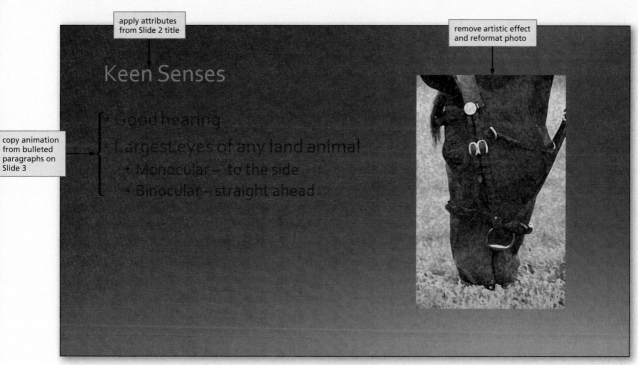

apply attributes
from Slide 2 title

remove artistic effect
and reformat photo

copy animation
from bulleted
paragraphs on
Slide 3

Keen Senses

• Good hearing
• Largest eyes of any land animal
  • Monocular – to the side
  • Binocular – straight ahead

(d) Slide 4

Figure 7–76 (Continued)

4. On Slide 2 (Figure 7–76b), change the title font to Arial, the color of the text to Blue, and the font size to 44 point. Center the title and then bold it. Use the Format Painter to apply these same attributes to the title text on Slides 3 and 4 (Figures 7–76c and 7–76d).

5. Apply the Fade entrance effect to the light yellow rectangle on Slide 2. Change the start timing option to After Previous, the duration to 2.00 seconds, and the delay to .50 second.

6. On Slide 3 (Figure 7–76c), insert the White Horse photo located on the Data Files for Students. Crop the photo to fill a Regular Pentagon shape. Change the weight of the border to 3 pt, change the border color to Orange (the third color in the Standard Colors), and then move the photo to the right side of the slide. You may need to use Help to learn how to crop to a shape.

7. Apply the 'Brush Color By Paragraph' emphasis effect to the four bulleted paragraphs in the content placeholder on Slide 3 and then change the color to Orange (the third color in the Standard Colors). Change the start timing option from On Click to After Previous and the duration to 1.50 seconds. Use the Animation Painter to apply this same animation to the four paragraphs in the text placeholder on Slide 4 (Figure 7–76d).

8. On Slide 4 (Figure 7–76d), remove the artistic effect from the photo. Increase the size of the photo to 7.5" × 5", apply the Bevel Perspective picture style (first style in the fourth row) to the photo, and, if necessary, move it to the right so it does not cover the bulleted text. Select the title text and then change the alignment to left.

9. If requested by your instructor, add the name of your current or previous pet as the fifth bulleted paragraph on Slide 4.

10. Save the presentation using the file name, Extend 7-1 Fast Horses.

11. Submit the revised document in the format specified by your instructor.

12. ✺ In Step 3, you changed the entrance effect for the photo. Is this new entrance effect more effective? Why or why not? Did adding the applause sound help the animation? In Step 5, did adding the fade entrance effect to the rectangle add visual interest to the slide?

Analyze, Correct, Improve

Analyze a presentation, correct all errors, and improve it.

Note: To complete this assignment, you will be required to use the Data Files for Students. Visit www.cengage.com/ct/studentdownload for detailed instructions or contact your instructor for information about accessing the required files.

Instructions: Run PowerPoint. Open the presentation, Analyze 7-1 Earth, from the Data Files for Students. Earth Day began in 1970 and is celebrated worldwide every year on April 22. You put together a short two-slide presentation about this special day to remind people what they can do to help make their Earth greener. Modify the slides by making the indicated corrections and improvements.

1. Correct

a. Remove the Ripple transition and then change the layout for Slide 1 (Figure 7–77) to Title Slide and Title Only for Slide 2.

b. Cut and paste the tree illustration from Slide 1 (Figure 7–77) to Slide 2.

c. On Slide 1, change the title text font to Nyala and the size to 54 point. Align the text at top of the placeholder and then bold this text. Change the font size of the text, April 22, to 36 point. Change the font of the first line of subtitle text, Since 1970, to Arial and then change the font size to 24 point. Note: The second and third lines in the placeholder will be used to add to sun shapes later in the exercise.

d. Increase the size of the photo on Slide 1 to approximately 7.5" × 4.46" and align center on the slide. Copy and paste the photo two times. Align the second photo left and align the third photo right. Distribute the second and third photos vertically on the slide so that all three photos are covering the entire slide.

e. On Slide 1, change the Fly In entrance effect on the left photo to the Dissolve Out exit effect. Remove the animation from the center photo. Change the Fly In entrance effect on the right photo to the Dissolve Out exit effect. Change the start timing option to After Previous, the duration to 2.00 seconds, and the delay to .50 second on the left and right photos.

f. On Slide 2, increase the size of the SmartArt graphic to approximately 5.21" × 10.42" and then move it to the upper-right area of the slide.

g. Move the tree illustration to the lower-left area of the slide. The left edge of the tree branches can hang off the left side of the slide. If necessary, reduce the size of the tree illustration so it is not covering the lower-left text box in the SmartArt graphic. Move the title placeholder down and to the right so that the text is not hidden by the tree trunk.

h. If requested by your instructor, insert a text box in the lower-right corner of Slide 2 and type your home address in the box.

2. Improve

a. Change the variant to green (the second variant).

b. On Slide 1, insert a sun shape, adjust the size to approximately 3.54" × 3.54", change the shape fill color to Yellow (the fourth color in the Standard Colors), and cut and paste the second line, We can all do our part, from the content placeholder to the shape. Change the font size to 18 point and then bold this text. Move this shape to the lower-left area of the slide. Copy and paste the sun shape and cut and paste the third line, to make our Earth greener, from the content placeholder to the second shape. Move this shape to the right area of the slide and then distribute it vertically. Apply the 'Horizontal Blinds As One Object' entrance effect to both sun shapes. Change the start timing option to After Previous and the duration to 2.50 seconds. Move the title and subtitle placeholders up to allow room for the sun shape.

c. On Slide 2, apply the 'Appear One by One' entrance effect to the SmartArt graphic. Change the start timing option to After Previous and the duration to 1.00 second.

d. Change the title font on Slide 2 to Nyala, change the size to 48 point, and then bold this text.

e. Apply the Window transition in the Dynamic Content category to both slides, add the Wind sound, change the duration to 2.00 seconds, and then advance the slide after 3.00 seconds.

f. Save the presentation using the file name, Analyze 7-1 Earth Day.

g. Submit the revised document in the format specified by your instructor.

3. ✳ Which errors existed in the starting file? How did changing the layout of the slides help present the message? You changed the animation on the photo on Slide 1 and you animated the SmartArt graphic on Slide 2. How did these animations improve the presentation?

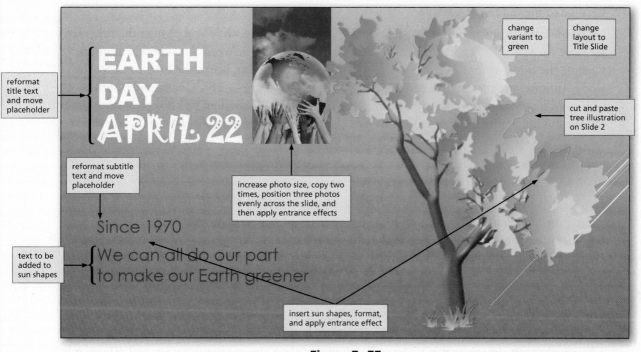

Figure 7–77

In the Labs

Design and/or create a presentation using the guidelines, concepts, and skills presented in this chapter. Labs 1 and 2, which increase in difficulty, require you to create solutions based on what you learned in the chapter; Lab 3 requires you to create a solution, which uses cloud and web technologies, by learning and investigating on your own from general guidance.

Lab 1: Using the Eyedropper to Match Colors, Removing a Background from a Photo, Cropping a Photo, Animating a SmartArt Graphic, and Creating Credits

Problem: You work at the local library part time, and the owner of the new antique auto museum asked if he could display a poster on the community bulletin board about the museum's upcoming grand opening. He gave you a PowerPoint document and asked you to edit it, if necessary, and to

Continued >

In the Labs *continued*

print the first two slides to post on the bulletin board. After looking at the presentation, you decide to change some of the animation and add some of your creative touches. In addition to displaying the first two slides on the bulletin board, the presentation will run on a kiosk in the main area of the library. You will remove and add animation, use the eyedropper to match colors, remove a background, and crop a photo. You create the presentation in Figure 7–78.

Note: To complete this assignment, you will be required to use the Data Files for Students. Visit www.cengage.com/ct/studentdownload for detailed instructions or contact your instructor for information about accessing the required files.

Instructions: Perform the following tasks:

1. Open the presentation, Lab 7-1 Antique Auto, from the Data Files for Students.

2. Change to the red theme variant.

3. Move the auto illustration on Slide 1 to the left side of the slide while you change the title text. Remove the Wave entrance effect from the title text. Change the word, Automobile, to Auto. Change the title text font to Impact, increase the size to 72 point, break the first line after the word, Antique, and then right align the text, as shown in Figure 7–78a. Change the subtitle font to Arial, increase the size to 36 point, bold the text, and then align right. Increase the size of the auto illustration to approximately 3.14" × 5.08" and then move it to the location shown.

4. With the subtitle text still selected, use the eyedropper to match the Dark Red color on the door of the car. Then, select the title text and use the eyedropper to match the Blue-Gray color on the side of the car's convertible top, as shown in Figure 7–78a.

5. Apply the 'Fly In From Left' entrance effect to the photo. Change the start timing option to After Previous, change the duration to 2.00 seconds, add the Voltage sound, and select the highest volume level. Select the car horn audio clip located in the lower-left area of Slide 1, change the volume to high, and hide during the show. Apply the Zoom entrance effect to the subtitle text. Change the start timing option to After Previous and then change the duration to 2.00 seconds.

6. On Slide 2 (Figure 7–78b), select the title text and use the eyedropper to match the Dark Red color on the front of the car above the grill. Apply the Zoom entrance effect to the title text. Change the start timing option to After Previous and then change the duration to 2.50 seconds. Animate text By word and then change the delay between words to 100%. Select the four bulleted paragraphs and then apply the Bold Reveal emphasis effect. Change the start timing option to After Previous and then change the duration to 1.50 seconds. Change the After animation color to Black, animate text By word, and then change the delay between words to 0.5 second.

7. Crop the car illustration on the right side to the middle of the driver's door. Apply the Reflected Rounded Rectangle picture style (the fifth style in the first row) to the photo, as shown in Figure 7–78b.

8. On Slide 3, select the blue car (in the middle of the slide) and then apply the 'Fly Out To Right' exit effect. Change the start timing option to After Previous and then change the duration to 1.50 seconds. Add a 'Fly In From Left' entrance effect to the blue car. Change the start timing option to After Previous and then change the duration to 1.50 seconds. With the blue car selected, use the Animation Painter to apply the same animation to the black/green car, gray/yellow car, and the multicolored car. Note: These four cars are on the left side of the slide facing to the right, as shown in Figure 7–78c on page PPT 464.

9. Select the pink car in the upper-right area of the slide and then apply the 'Fly In From Top-Right' entrance effect. Change the start timing option to After Previous and then change the duration to 1.50 seconds. Select the red car on the right side of the slide and then apply the 'Fly In From Top-Left' entrance effect. Change the start timing option to After Previous and the duration to 1.50 seconds. Preview the animations. In the Animation Pane, you can reorder any of these animations.

(a) Slide 1

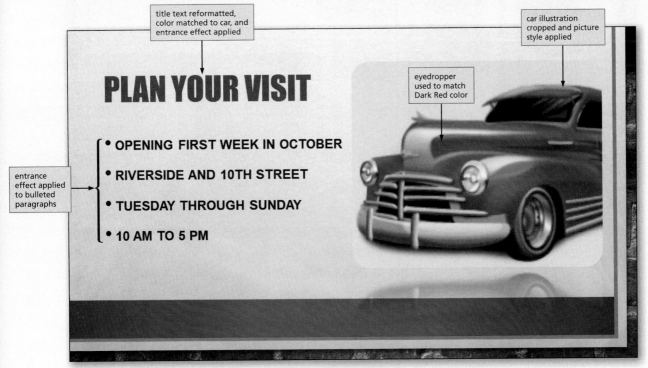

(b) Slide 2

Figure 7–78

Continued >

In the Labs *continued*

(c) Slide 3

(d) Slide 4

Figure 7–78 (Continued)

10. On Slide 4 (Figure 7–78d), remove the background from the photo. Note: You will need to use the 'Mark Areas to Keep' and the 'Mark Areas to Remove' tools on the right side of the photo around the tire of the car.

11. Change the title font color to Dark Red (the first color in the Standard Colors) and then right-align this text. Move the title placeholder up slightly, as shown in the figure.

12. Convert the bulleted text on Slide 4 to the Descending Block List SmartArt graphic (the third graphic in the eighth List row). Increase the size of the graphic to 7.27" × 11.1". Change the color to Colored Fill – Accent 2 (the second color in the Accent 2 row) and then apply the Inset 3-D style (the second style in the first 3-D row) to the SmartArt graphic. Change the font to Arial and the font size to 28 point and then bold this text. Move the graphic to the area shown in the figure. Adjust the size of the photo to approximately 3.95" × 5.94" and move it to the lower-left area of the slide, as shown in Figure 7 – 78d.

13. Apply the Fly In From Bottom entrance effect to the SmartArt graphic and then change the sequence to One by One. Change the start timing option to After Previous and then change the duration to 2.00 seconds. Insert a text box at the bottom of Slide 4 and then type **Visit Al's Antique Auto Museum** on the first line and **OUR CARS WILL DRIVE YOU CRAZY** on the second line. Change the font to MV Boli, change the size of the font to 44 point, change the line spacing to 3.0, bold this text, and then center it. Resize the text box so that it is the same width as the slide. Apply the Credits entrance effect to this text and then animate text 'All at Once'. Change the start timing option to After Previous, and then change the duration to 5.00 seconds.

14. If requested by your instructor, add the city or county in which you were born as the third bulleted paragraph on Slide 2.

15. Apply the Doors transition in the Exciting category to Slide 3 only and then change the duration to 4.50 seconds.

16. Save the presentation using the file name, Lab 7-1 Antique Auto Museum.

17. Submit the document in the format specified by your instructor.

18. ✷ Why did you remove the Wave entrance effect from the title text? Why did you crop the car photo on Slide 2? How did using the eyedropper tool to match colors help improve the presentation?

Lab 2: Creating a Self-Running Presentation, Renaming a Slide Object, Adding a Trigger to an Animation, Animating a List, Animating a Chart, Applying a Transition to a Single Slide, and Modifying a Transition Effect

Problem: You work for a computer repair business. Occasionally, your company offers seminars to your clients. Many of your clients have brought their computers to your office after they have had issues with viruses, scammers, and computer hacking. You decide to create a presentation to use for a seminar titled Protecting Your Computer from Hackers. You create a presentation with four slides, as shown in Figures 7 – 79a through 7 – 79d on the next page and on page PPT 467.

Note: To complete this assignment, you will be required to use the Data Files for Students. Visit www.cengage.com/ct/studentdownload for detailed instructions or contact your instructor for information about accessing the required files.

Instructions: Perform the following tasks:

1. Run PowerPoint and then open the presentation, Lab 7-2 Computer, from the Data Files for Students, and then add the Ion theme with the green variant.

2. On Slide 1, increase the size of the title text placeholder to approximately 3.64" × 11.06" so that the title text is on one line and then center the text. Apply the WordArt style, Fill – Gold, Accent 3, Sharp Bevel (the fifth style in the second row). Apply the Transform text effect, Arch

Continued >

In the Labs *continued*

Up (the first effect in the Follow Path row), to this text, as shown in Figure 7–79a. Apply the Shape entrance effect to the WordArt title. Choose the Out direction, change the start timing option to After Previous, and then change the duration to 2.00 seconds.

3. Remove the background from the dog photo, increase the size of the photo to 3.77" × 6.63", and then move it to the location shown in Figure 7–79a. Apply the 'Fly In' entrance effect to this photo and then change the direction to From Right. Change the start

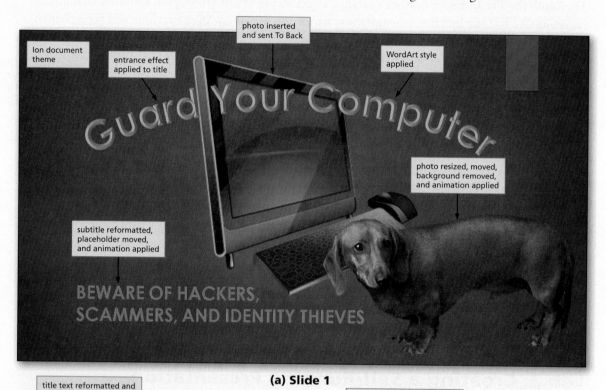

photo inserted and sent To Back

Ion document theme

entrance effect applied to title

WordArt style applied

photo resized, moved, background removed, and animation applied

subtitle reformatted, placeholder moved, and animation applied

(a) Slide 1

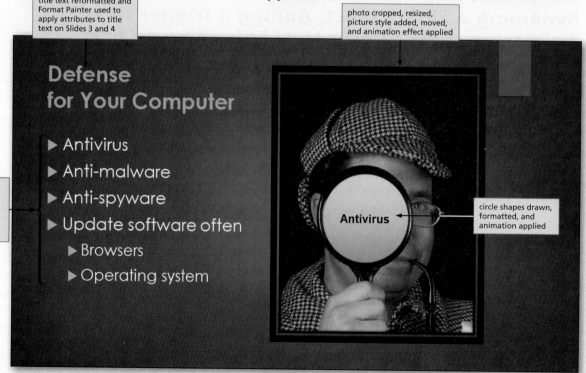

title text reformatted and Format Painter used to apply attributes to title text on Slides 3 and 4

photo cropped, resized, picture style added, moved, and animation effect applied

entrance effect applied to bulleted paragraphs and Animation Painter used to apply same animation to Slide 3

circle shapes drawn, formatted, and animation applied

(b) Slide 2

Figure 7–79

apply attributes
from Slide 2 title

Create Strong Passwords

▶ Minimum of 14 characters

apply animation
from Slide 2
bulleted
paragraphs

▶ Mix letters, numbers, and symbols

▶ Use different passwords

▶ Keep secret

animation applied
to block shapes,
and sound added

(c) Slide 3

apply attributes
from Slide 2 title

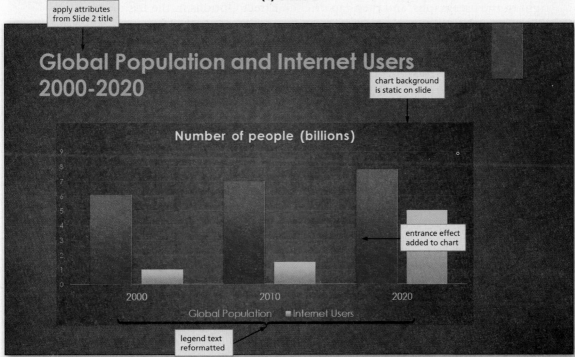

Global Population and Internet Users 2000-2020

chart background
is static on slide

Number of people (billions)

entrance effect
added to chart

2000   2010   2020

Global Population ■ Internet Users

legend text
reformatted

(d) Slide 4

Figure 7–79 (Continued)

timing option to After Previous and then change the duration to 3.00 seconds. Open the Animation pane and the Selection pane. Change the name of this picture to Dog in the Selection pane. Trigger the dog photo to appear on the click of the Subtitle. Close both the Animation and Selection panes.

4. Insert the photo, Computer, which is available on the Data Files for Students. Move the photo to the location shown in Figure 7–79a and then send this photo To Back.

Continued >

5. Change the subtitle font size to 30 point, change the color to Red (the second color in the Standard colors), and then bold this text. Move the subtitle placeholder down to the location shown in the figure. Apply the Strips Right Down entrance effect to the subtitle. Change the start timing option to After Previous and then change the duration to 2.25 seconds.

6. On Slide 2 (Figure 7–79b on page PPT 466), change the title text font size to 36 point, change the font color to Gold, Accent 3 (the seventh color in the Theme Colors), and then bold this text. Use the Format Painter to apply these same attributes to the title text on Slides 3 and 4, as shown in Figures 7–79b through 7–79d on the previous page.

7. Crop the photo on Slide 2. *Hint:* Move the lower-right corner handle up to the left until only the man's three fingers and a small area of the white pipe are visible in the lower-right corner of the photo. Change the size of the photo to approximately 5.89" × 4.5" and then apply the Double Frame, Black picture style (last effect in the first row). Move the photo to the location shown in Figure 7–79b. Apply the Fade entrance effect to the photo. Change the start timing option to After Previous, change the duration to 3.25 seconds, and then change the delay to 1.00 seconds.

8. On Slide 2, apply the Wipe entrance effect to the bulleted text, change the direction to From Left, tap or click the Effect Options button again, and then tap or click By Paragraph in the Sequence section. Display the Animation Pane, tap or click the list arrow to the right of the paragraphs, and then tap or click Effect Options in the list to display the Wipe dialog box. Tap or click the Animate text arrow in the Enhancements section, select By word, and then change the '% delay between letters' to 15%. In the Wipe dialog box, tap or click the Text Animation tab, tap or click the Group text arrow, and then select 'By 1st Level Paragraphs'. Tap or click the OK button to close the Wipe dialog box. Change the start timing option to After Previous and then change the duration to 2.00 seconds. Use the Animation Painter to apply these same animations to the bulleted text on Slide 3 (Figure 7–79c).

9. On Slide 2, select the Oval shape (the second shape in the Basic Shapes area) and while holding down the SHIFT key, draw a circle 2" × 2". Change the shape style to Subtle Effect – Purple, Accent 6 (the seventh style in the fourth row). Type **Antivirus** in the shape. Change the font to Arial, bold this text, and then change the font size to 20 point. Copy and paste this shape two times. Change the text in the second shape to **Anti-malware** and then change the text in the third shape to **Anti-spyware.** Select the Antivirus shape and then apply the Appear entrance effect. Change the start timing option to After Previous and then change the duration to 2.00 seconds. Add the Disappear exit effect and then change the duration to 2.00 seconds. Use the Animation Painter to apply this animation first to the Anti-malware shape and then to the Anti-spyware shape. Move the Anti-spyware shape on top of the photo centered in the magnifying glass. Move the Anti-malware shape to the same location and then Bring it Forward. Move the Antivirus shape to the same location and then Bring it to Front. Preview this animation. Each of the three shapes should appear and disappear from the center of the magnifying glass in this order: Antivirus, Anti-malware, and Anti-spyware.

10. On Slide 3 (Figure 7–79c), apply the Fly In entrance effect to the first block (letter A) on the password illustration and then change the direction to From Top-Right. Change the start timing option to After Previous, change the duration to 1.00 second, and add the Typewriter sound. Use the Animation Painter to apply this animation to the other five blocks.

11. On Slide 4, change the chart color to Color 2 (the second row in the Colorful area) and then change the chart style to Style 8 (the eighth style in the first row), as shown in Figure 7–79d.

Apply the Fly In entrance effect to the chart, keep the direction to From Bottom, and then select the By Element in Category Sequence. Keep the On Click start timing option but change the duration to 1.50 seconds. With the chart still selected, select the first animation box next to the chart and delete it. This action will display the chart background on the slide before the animation starts.

12. Increase the font size of the Horizontal (Category) Axis text and the legend text at the bottom of the chart to 16 point, as shown in Figure 7–79d on page PPT 467.

13. If requested by your instructor, enter the name of the last movie you saw as the fifth bulleted paragraph on Slide 3.

14. Apply the Cube transition in the Exciting section to Slide 4 only, select the From Left effect option, and then change the duration to 2.00 seconds.

15. Rehearse the presentation and then set the slide timings to 22 seconds for Slide 1, 30 seconds for Slides 2 and 3, and 34 seconds for Slide 4. Set the show type as 'Browsed at a kiosk.'

16. Save the presentation using the file name, Lab 7-2 Guard Your Computer.

17. Submit the document in the format specified by your instructor.

18. ✷ Did you have difficulty removing the background from the dog photo on Slide 1? How did removing the background help the slide? Why did you remove the first animation from the chart on Slide 4?

Lab 3: Expand Your World: Cloud and Web Technologies
Locating and Inserting Animated GIF Files

Problem: In this chapter you animated a photo, illustrations, a SmartArt object, a chart, and text. Some objects, however, already have animation applied when inserted into a PowerPoint slide or other file, such as a website. These animated GIF files generally are simple pictures with a limited number of colors. As noted in this chapter, animated GIFs cannot be cropped.

GIF, or Graphics Interchange Format, images were introduced in 1987 and are used frequently. They may or may not be animated. Many websites provide a variety of free and low-cost animated GIFs, and some offer information creating animated GIF files. Care must be taken, however, to visit and download files from reputable sources so that malware is not embedded in the image. You can use a search engine or another search tool to locate recommended or popular resources.

Instructions:

1. Visit one of the following websites, or locate other websites that contain animated GIFs: GIFS. net, GIFanimations, or Animation Factory.

2. Locate files that could enhance your Animated Butterflies presentation. Some websites have collections of butterflies and flowers that could be useful.

3. Download at least two animated GIFs and then insert them into your Animated Butterflies presentation.

4. If requested to do so by your instructor, insert the name of your favorite grade school teacher in the footer.

5. Save the presentation using the file name, Lab 7-3 GIF Animated Butterflies.

6. Submit the assignment in the format specified by your instructor.

7. ✷ Why did you select these particular images for your slides? Do the animated GIF images enhance or detract from your presentation? Where might you use GIF files other than in PowerPoint slides?

✺ Consider This: Your Turn

Apply your creative thinking and problem-solving skills to design and implement a solution.

---

1. Design and Create a Presentation about Home Gardening
Personal

Part 1: Regardless of what climate you live in, you must follow important steps when planting a garden. With the interest in eating more organic foods, gardening has become very popular. If you are going to start from seeds, you need to start your seedlings at least a month in advance of when you want to plant them outdoors. Cardboard egg cartons make great containers for seedlings. Once your seedlings are ready to transplant, you can cut apart the egg carton and plant them right in the ground. You also will need to check your supplies in advance and clean and repair your garden tools. If you live in an area where the temperature fluctuates, you need to take precautions about frost killing your plants. In the Midwest, for example, frost dates can extend into late May. You can search online to find the average last frost date. If frost is predicted, cover your plants with light tarps or fabric. Before planting, prepare your soil and add homemade compost to give your plants a great start. Composting is easy. Look online or get a book from your library to learn how to make compost. Use the concepts and techniques presented in this chapter to prepare a presentation with these gardening tips. Select a suitable theme and use WordArt or SmartArt graphics where appropriate. The presentation can contain photos, illustrations, and videos. Delete backgrounds, crop photos, and add animation to add interest to your presentation. You can use personal photos and videos or search on Office.com for graphical images. Submit your assignment in the format specified by your instructor.

Part 2: ✺ You made several decisions while creating the presentation in this assignment: where to place text, how to format the text (for example, font, font size, and font effects), which graphical image(s) to remove backgrounds and crop, where to use animation, and where to position the graphical images to add interest to the presentation. What was the rationale behind each of these decisions? When you reviewed the document, what further revisions did you make and why? Where would you recommend showing this slide show?

2. Design and Create a Presentation about Penguins
Professional

Part 1: You work at the penguin exhibit at an aquatic animal center. The center is fortunate to have one of the largest varieties of penguins, and they feature Little Blue, Crested, and Emperor penguins. The exhibit is fairly new, and you have been assigned the task of developing a presentation for visitors. These aquatic, flightless birds (sometimes referred to as "flippered flyers") can swim in excess of 12 mph (20 kph) and can stay under water 15 to 20 minutes. They are nearsighted on land; however, they have exceptional vision under water. They eat a diet of krill, fish, and squid. The largest penguin (Emperor) can grow up to 3 feet 7 inches tall (1.1 m) and can weigh up to 75 lbs. (35 kg). The smallest penguin (Little Blue) can grow to 16 inches tall (40 cm) and weighs about 2.2 lbs. (1 kg). Your presentation could contain photos, illustrations, and videos. The Data Files for Students contains five photos called Penguin1, Penguin2, Penguin3, Penguin4, and Penguin5, or you can use photos and illustrations from Office.com if they are appropriate for this topic. Crop, remove backgrounds from photos, and add animation to add interest to your presentation. Submit your assignment in the format specified by your instructor.

Part 2: ✺ You made several decisions while creating the presentation in this assignment: where to place text, how to format the text (such as font and font size), which graphical image(s) to use, which styles and effects to apply, where to position the graphical images, and what animation to add. What was the rationale behind each of these decisions? When you reviewed the document, what further revisions did you make and why? Where would you recommend showing this slide show?

3. Design and Create a Presentation about Color and Personalities

Research and Collaboration

Part 1:   In your biology class, you are studying color and how it affects personalities. A person's favorite color can reveal many traits. Researchers have found people have two responses to color. The first response is physical. For example, the color red can make people feel warm, and the color orange can boost energy. The second response is emotional. The color yellow can make people feel happy. A favorite color also can reveal many personality traits and have a deeper meaning. People who like purple usually are very creative and are good leaders. The color blue represents patience and compassion. People who choose the color brown are very responsible and dependable. Your instructor has divided your class into two groups. Each group will research and gather a list of personality traits related to four colors. Then each group will determine the classmates' favorite colors and see if they match the personalities that researchers determined. Once all the data is collected, create a PowerPoint presentation using at least three objectives found at the beginning of this chapter. You may want to take digital photos of your classmates so that you can match their photos with shapes filled with their favorite colors. You can use photos and illustrations from Office.com if they are appropriate for this topic.

Part 2:   ☀ You made several decisions while creating the presentation in this assignment: where to place text, how to format the text (such as font, font size, and colors), which image(s) to use, where to crop and remove backgrounds from photos, and which animations to use for graphic elements. What was the rationale behind each of these decisions? When you reviewed the presentation, what further revisions did you make and why? Where would you recommend showing this slide show?

Learn Online

Reinforce what you learned in this chapter with games, exercises, training, and many other online activities and resources.

Student Companion Site   Reinforcement activities and resources are available at no additional cost on www.cengagebrain.com. Visit www.cengage.com/ct/studentdownload for detailed instructions about accessing the resources available at the Student Companion Site.

SAM   Put your skills into practice with SAM! If you have a SAM account, go to www.cengage.com/sam2013 to access SAM assignments for this chapter.

8 | Customizing a Template and Handouts Using Masters

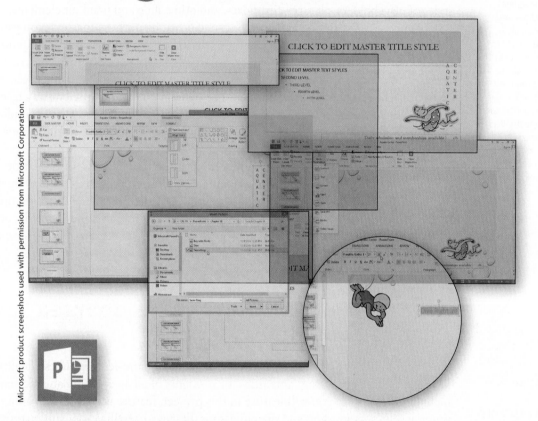

Objectives

You will have mastered the material in this chapter when you can:

- Apply slide and font themes to a slide master

- Change a slide master background

- Add a background style and graphic to a slide master

- Insert a placeholder into a slide layout

- Apply a Quick Style to a placeholder

- Change text direction and character spacing

- Hide background graphics on individual slides

- Apply a fill to a text box and change transparency

- Rename a slide master

- Save a slide master as a template

- Create handouts using the handout master

- Create speaker notes using the notes master

8 | Customizing a Template and Handouts Using Masters

Introduction

PowerPoint provides a variety of designs and layouts to meet most presenters' needs. At times, however, you may need a different set of colors, fonts, placeholders, or graphics to display throughout a presentation. PowerPoint allows you to customize the master layouts for slides, handouts, and speaker notes. These masters specify the precise locations and styles of placeholders, pictures, text boxes, and other slide and handout elements.

Once you determine your custom specifications in these masters, you can save the file as a template so that you can reuse these key elements as a starting point for multiple presentations. This unique **template** is a set of special slides you create and then use to create similar presentations. A template consists of a general master slide layout that has elements common to all the slide layouts. One efficient way to create similar presentations is to create a template, save the template, open the template, and then save the slides as a different PowerPoint presentation each time a new presentation is required.

Templates help speed and simplify the process of creating a presentation, so many PowerPoint designers create a template for common presentations they develop frequently. Templates can have a variable number of slide layouts depending upon the complexity of the presentation. A simple presentation can have a few slide layouts; for example, the Aquatic Center presentation will have three slide layouts. A more complex template can have many slide masters and layouts.

Project — Presentation with Customized Slide, Handout, and Notes Masters

The community pool has evolved into full-fledged aquatic centers. These facilities offer a wide variety of events and amenities for residents of all ages. Many aquatic centers, including the facility you will feature in this project, feature water slides, wading pools, water aerobics, swimming and diving lessons, lifeguard certification, and birthday parties. The project in this chapter (Figure 8–1) promotes these components. All three slides are created by starting with a template file that contains two basic slide elements: the Aquatic Center's name on a formatted placeholder and an illustration of a man floating. The overall template, called the **slide master** (Figure 8–1a), is formatted with a theme, customized title and text fonts, and customized footer placeholders for the slide layouts. The title slide layout (Figure 8–1b) is used to create Slide 1 (Figure 8–1c), which introduces audiences to the Aquatic Center. Similarly, the blank slide layout (Figure 8–1d) is used for Slide 2 (Figure 8–1e), which promotes the new water slide. The title and content layout (Figure 8–1f on page PPT 476) is used to create the text and graphic on Slide 3 (Figure 8–1g). In addition, the custom handout master

(Figure 8–1h on the next page) is used to create a handout with a diver illustration and header and footer text (Figure 8–1i). Likewise, the custom notes master (Figure 8–1j on page PPT 477) is used to create speaker notes pages (Figures 8–1k, 8–1l, and 8–1m).

(a) Slide Master

(b) Title Slide Layout (Master)

(c) Slide 1 (Title Slide Layout)

(d) Blank Layout (Master)

(e) Slide 2 (Blank Layout)

Figure 8–1

(f) Title and Content Layout (Master)

(g) Slide 3 (Title and Content Layout)

(h) Handout Master

(i) Handout

Figure 8–1 (Continued)

(j) Notes Master

(k) Speaker Notes – Page 1

(l) Speaker Notes – Page 2

(m) Speaker Notes – Page 3

Figure 8–1 (Continued)

Roadmap

In this chapter, you will learn how to create the slides shown in Figure 8–1 on pages PPT 475 through PPT 477. The following roadmap identifies general activities you will perform as you progress through this chapter:

1. CUSTOMIZE SLIDE MASTERS by changing the theme fonts and background.
2. FORMAT and ARRANGE slide master FOOTERS.
3. INSERT and FORMAT GRAPHICS and TEXT BOXES.
4. RENAME and DELETE SLIDE LAYOUTS.
5. CUSTOMIZE HANDOUT and NOTES MASTERS.
6. USE a CUSTOM TEMPLATE to create a new presentation.

At the beginning of step instructions throughout the chapter, you will see an abbreviated form of this roadmap. The abbreviated roadmap uses colors to indicate chapter progress: gray means the chapter is beyond that activity; blue means the task being shown is covered in that activity, and black means that activity is yet to be covered. For example, the following abbreviated roadmap indicates the chapter would be showing a task in the 3 INSERT & FORMAT GRAPHICS & TEXT BOXES activity.

1 CUSTOMIZE SLIDE MASTERS | 2 FORMAT & ARRANGE FOOTERS | **3 INSERT & FORMAT GRAPHICS & TEXT BOXES**
4 RENAME & DELETE SLIDE LAYOUTS | 5 CUSTOMIZE HANDOUT & NOTES MASTERS | 6 USE CUSTOM TEMPLATE

Use the abbreviated roadmap as a progress guide while you read or step through the instructions in this chapter.

To Run PowerPoint and Create and Save a Blank Presentation

If you are using a computer to step through the project in this chapter and you want your screens to match the figures in this book, you should change your screen's resolution to 1366 × 768. For information about how to change a computer's resolution, refer to the Office and Windows chapter at the beginning of this book.

The following steps, which assume Windows 8 is running, use the Start screen or the search box to run PowerPoint based on a typical installation. You may need to ask your instructor how to run PowerPoint on your computer. For a detailed example of the procedure summarized below, refer to the Office and Windows chapter.

1 Scroll the Start screen for a PowerPoint 2013 tile. If your Start screen contains a PowerPoint 2013 tile, tap or click it to run PowerPoint and then proceed to Step 5; if the Start screen does not contain the PowerPoint 2013 tile, proceed to the next step to search for the PowerPoint app.

2 Swipe in from the right edge of the screen or point to the upper-right corner of the screen to display the Charms bar and then tap or click the Search charm on the Charms bar to display the Search menu.

3 Type **PowerPoint** as the search text in the Search box and watch the search results appear in the Apps list.

4 Tap or click PowerPoint 2013 in the search results to run PowerPoint.

5 Tap or click the Blank Presentation thumbnail on the PowerPoint start screen to create a blank presentation and display it in the PowerPoint window.

6 If the PowerPoint window is not maximized, tap or click the Maximize button on its title bar to maximize the window.

One of the few differences between Windows 7 and Windows 8 occurs in the steps to run PowerPoint. If you are using Windows 7, tap or click the Start button, type **PowerPoint** in the 'Search programs and files' box, tap or click PowerPoint 2013, and then, if necessary, maximize the PowerPoint window. For a summary of the steps to run PowerPoint in Windows 7, refer to the Quick Reference located at the back of this book.

To Save a Presentation with a New File Name

You should save the presentation on your hard disk, SkyDrive, or a location that is most appropriate to your situation.

The following steps assume you already have created folders for storing your files, for example, a CIS 101 folder (for your class) that contains a PowerPoint folder (for your assignments). Thus, these steps save the presentation in the PowerPoint folder in the CIS 101 folder on your desired save location. For a detailed example of the procedure for saving a file in a folder or saving a file on SkyDrive, refer to the Office and Windows chapter at the beginning of this book.

1 Tap or click the Save button on the Quick Access Toolbar, which depending on settings, will display either the Save As gallery in the Backstage view or the Save As dialog box.

2 To save on a hard disk or other storage media on your computer, proceed to Step 2a. To save on SkyDrive, proceed to Step 2b.

2a If your screen opens the Backstage view and you want to save on storage media on your computer, tap or click Computer in the left pane, if necessary, to display options in the right pane related to saving on your computer. If your screen already displays the Save As dialog box, proceed to Step 4.

2b If your screen opens the Backstage view and you want to save on SkyDrive, tap or click SkyDrive in the left pane to display SkyDrive saving options or a Sign In button. If your screen displays a Sign In button, tap or click it and then sign in to SkyDrive.

3 Tap or click the Browse button in the right pane to display the Save As dialog box associated with the selected save location (i.e., Computer or SkyDrive).

4 Type `Aquatic Center` in the File name box to change the file name. Do not press the ENTER key after typing the file name because you do not want to close the dialog box at this time.

5 Navigate to the desired save location (in this case, the PowerPoint folder in the CIS 101 folder [or your class folder] on your computer or SkyDrive).

6 Tap or click the Save button (Save As dialog box) to save the document in the selected folder on the selected save location with the entered file name.

Customizing Presentation Slide Master Backgrounds and Fonts

PowerPoint has many template files with the file extension .potx. Each template file has three masters: slide, handout, and notes. A slide master has at least one layout; you have used many of these layouts, such as Title and Content, Two Content, and Picture with Caption, to create presentations. A **handout master** designates the placement of text, such as page numbers, on a sheet of paper intended to distribute to audience members. A **notes master** defines the formatting for speaker's notes.

Slide Master

If you select a document theme and want to change one of its components on every slide, you can override that component by changing the slide master. In addition, if you want your presentation to have a unique design, you might want to

BTW

The Ribbon and Screen Resolution
PowerPoint may change how the groups and buttons within the groups appear on the ribbon, depending on the computer's screen resolution. Thus, your ribbon may look different from the ones in this book if you are using a screen resolution other than 1366 × 768.

BTW
Q&As
For a complete list of the
Q&As found in many of
the step-by-step sequences
in this book, visit the Q&A
resource on the Student
Companion Site located on
www.cengagebrain.com. For
detailed instructions about
accessing available resources,
visit www.cengage.com/ct/
studentdownload or see the
inside back cover of this book.

create a slide master rather than attempt to modify a current document theme. A slide master indicates the size and position of text and object placeholders, font styles, slide backgrounds, transitions, and effects. Any change to the slide master results in changing that component on every slide in the presentation. For example, if you change the second-level bullet on the slide master, each slide with a second-level bullet will display this new bullet format.

One presentation can have more than one slide master. You may find two or more slide masters are necessary when your presentation reuses special slide layouts. In this Aquatic Center presentation, for example, one slide will have the title slide to introduce the overall concept, another will have a blank slide to showcase a new water slide, and a third slide will have a title and a bulleted list to give specific information about swim lessons. All slides will have an illustration of a man floating in a swim tube and the words, Aquatic Center, on the slide master.

CONSIDER THIS

Plan the slide master.

Using a new slide master gives you the freedom to specify every slide element. Like an artist with a new canvas or a musician with blank sheet music, your imagination permits you to create an appealing master that conveys the overall look of your presentation.

Before you start developing the master, give your overall plan some careful thought. The decisions you make at this point should be reflected on every slide. A presentation can have several master layouts, but you should change these layouts only if you have a compelling need to change them. Use the concepts you read throughout the chapters in this book to guide your decisions about fonts, colors, backgrounds, art, and other essential slide elements.

To Display a Slide Master

1 CUSTOMIZE SLIDE MASTERS | 2 FORMAT & ARRANGE FOOTERS | 3 INSERT & FORMAT GRAPHICS & TEXT BOXES
4 RENAME & DELETE SLIDE LAYOUTS | 5 CUSTOMIZE HANDOUT & NOTES MASTERS | 6 USE CUSTOM TEMPLATE

To begin developing the Aquatic Center slides, you need to display the slide master. *Why? The slide master allows you to customize the slide components and create a unique design.* The following steps display the slide master.

• Tap or click VIEW on the ribbon to display the VIEW tab (Figure 8–2).

Figure 8–2

- Tap or click the Slide Master button (VIEW tab | Master Views group) to display the SLIDE MASTER tab and the slide thumbnails in the Overview pane.

- If necessary, scroll up and then tap or click the Office Theme Slide Master layout (Figure 8–3).

Q&A

What are all the other thumbnails in the left pane below the slide master?
They are all the slide layouts associated with this slide master. You have used many of these layouts in the presentations you have developed in the exercises in this book.

Why is the layout given this name? The slide layout names begin with the theme applied to the slides. In this case, the default Office Theme is applied. The first slide layout in the list is called the master because it controls the colors, fonts, and objects that are displayed on all the other slides in the presentation.

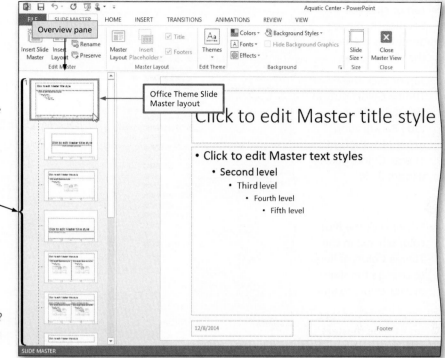

Figure 8–3

To Apply Slide and Font Themes to a Slide Master

1 CUSTOMIZE SLIDE MASTERS | 2 FORMAT & ARRANGE FOOTERS | 3 INSERT & FORMAT GRAPHICS & TEXT BOXES
4 RENAME & DELETE SLIDE LAYOUTS | 5 CUSTOMIZE HANDOUT & NOTES MASTERS | 6 USE CUSTOM TEMPLATE

You can change the look of an entire presentation by applying formats to the slide master in the same manner that you apply these formats to individual slides. In this presentation, you will change the slide theme to Droplet and the font colors to blue and green. ***Why?*** *The Droplet theme features water drops along the edges and colors that match the aquatic topic of this presentation.* The following steps apply a theme and change the font theme colors.

- With the slide master displaying, tap or click the Themes button (SLIDE MASTER tab | Edit Theme group) to display the Themes gallery.

- Scroll down to display the Droplet theme in the gallery (Figure 8–4).

Experiment

- If you are using a mouse, point to various themes in the Themes gallery and watch the colors and fonts change on the slide master.

Figure 8–4

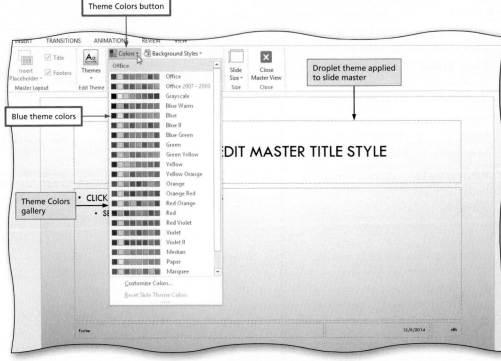

• Tap or click the Droplet theme to apply this theme to the slide master.

• Tap or click the Theme Colors button (SLIDE MASTER tab | Background group) to display the Theme Colors gallery (Figure 8–5).

• Tap or click the Blue color scheme in the Theme Colors gallery to change the slide master colors to Blue.

Q&A Can I insert another set of slide masters to give other slides in the presentation a unique look?

Yes. PowerPoint allows you to insert multiple masters into an existing presentation.

Figure 8–5

To Customize Theme Fonts

1 CUSTOMIZE SLIDE MASTERS | **2 FORMAT & ARRANGE FOOTERS** | **3 INSERT & FORMAT GRAPHICS & TEXT BOXES**
4 RENAME & DELETE SLIDE LAYOUTS | **5 CUSTOMIZE HANDOUT & NOTES MASTERS** | **6 USE CUSTOM TEMPLATE**

Each theme has a heading font and a body font applied to it. At times both fonts are the same, and other times, the heading font differs from the body font, but both fonts coordinate with each other. You can customize theme fonts by selecting your own combination of heading and body font and then giving the new theme font set a unique name. *Why? A particular font may match the tone of the presentation and help convey the message you are presenting.* The following steps apply a new heading and body font to the Droplet theme.

• Tap or click the Theme Fonts button (SLIDE MASTER tab | Background group) to display the Theme Fonts gallery (Figure 8–6).

Figure 8–6

• Tap or click Customize Fonts in the Theme Fonts gallery to display the Create New Theme Fonts dialog box.

• Tap or click the Heading font arrow and then scroll to display Garamond in the list (Figure 8–7).

Q&A Can I preview the fonts to see how they are displayed on the slide master?

No preview is available when using the Create New Theme Fonts dialog box. Once you select the font, however, PowerPoint will display text in the Sample box.

Figure 8–7

• Tap or click Garamond to apply that font as the new heading text font.

• Tap or click the Body font arrow and then scroll to display Franklin Gothic Book in the list (Figure 8–8).

Q&A What if the Garamond or Franklin Gothic Book fonts are not in my list of fonts?

Select fonts that resemble the fonts shown in Figure 8–8.

Figure 8–8

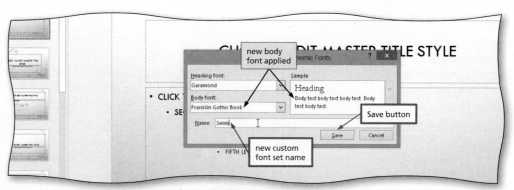

• Tap or click Franklin Gothic Book to apply that font as the new body text font.

• Select the text, Custom 1, in the Name text box and then type **Swim** to name the new font set (Figure 8–9).

Q&A Must I name this font set I just created?

No. If you name the set, however, you easily will recognize this combination in your font set if you want to use it in new presentations. It will display in the Custom area of the Fonts gallery.

Figure 8–9

• Tap or click the Save button (Create New Theme Fonts dialog box) to save this new font set with the name, Swim, and to display the font changes in the slide master.

BTW
**Touch Screen
Differences**
The Office and Windows
interfaces may vary if you are
using a touch screen. For this
reason, you might notice that
the function or appearance
of your touch screen differs
slightly from this chapter's
presentation.

To Save an Existing Presentation with the Same File Name

You have made several modifications to the presentation since you last saved it. Thus, you should save it again. The following step saves the presentation again. For an example of the step listed below, refer to the Office and Windows chapter at the beginning of this book.

 Tap or click the Save button on the Quick Access Toolbar to overwrite the previously saved file.

To Format a Slide Master Background and Apply a Quick Style

1 CUSTOMIZE SLIDE MASTERS | 2 FORMAT & ARRANGE FOOTERS | 3 INSERT & FORMAT GRAPHICS & TEXT BOXES
4 RENAME & DELETE SLIDE LAYOUTS | 5 CUSTOMIZE HANDOUT & NOTES MASTERS | 6 USE CUSTOM TEMPLATE

Once you have applied a theme to the slide master and determined the fonts for the presentation, you can further customize the presentation. *Why? Adding a unique background and customizing the colors can give your presentation a unique look that matches the message you are conveying.* The following steps format the slide master background and then apply a Quick Style.

• Tap or click the Background Styles button (SLIDE MASTER tab | Background group) to display the Background Styles gallery (Figure 8–10).

 Experiment

• If you are using a mouse, point to various styles in the Background Styles gallery and watch the backgrounds change on the slide master title text placeholder.

Figure 8–10

• Tap or click Background Style 2 (second style in first row) to apply this background to the slide master (Figure 8–11).

Figure 8–11

- Tap or click the slide master title text placeholder to select it.

- Display the HOME tab and then tap or click the Quick Styles button (HOME tab | Drawing group) to display the Quick Styles gallery (Figure 8–12).

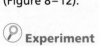 **Experiment**

- If you are using a mouse, point to various styles in the Quick Styles gallery and watch the background and borders change on the slide master title text placeholder.

Figure 8–12

- Tap or click the Subtle Effect – Turquoise, Accent 2 Quick Style (third style in the fourth row) to apply this style to the title text placeholder (Figure 8–13).

Figure 8–13

To Delete, Move, and Add Text to a Slide Master Footer

1 CUSTOMIZE SLIDE MASTERS | 2 FORMAT & ARRANGE FOOTERS | 3 INSERT & FORMAT GRAPHICS & TEXT BOXES
4 RENAME & DELETE SLIDE LAYOUTS | 5 CUSTOMIZE HANDOUT & NOTES MASTERS | 6 USE CUSTOM TEMPLATE

Slide numbers, the date and time, and footer text can be displayed anywhere on a slide, not just in the default footer placeholder locations. At times you may want to rearrange or delete these slide elements. *Why? These placeholders may interfere with other slide content, or you may not want to display information, such as a page number or the date.* The following steps delete one footer placeholder, move the footer placeholders, and then add footer text.

- With the slide master displaying, tap or click the border of the date footer placeholder to select it (Figure 8–14).

Figure 8–14

- If you are using a keyboard, press the DELETE key to delete the date placeholder.
- If you are using a touch screen, tap to select the date placeholder, then press and hold on the placeholder and tap Delete on the shortcut menu.

Q&A What should I do if the placeholder still is showing on the slide?

Be certain you tapped or clicked the placeholder border and not just the text. The border must display as a solid line before you can delete it.

3

- Tap or click the content footer placeholder and then drag it to the location where the date placeholder originally appeared (Figure 8–15).

Figure 8–15

4

- Display the INSERT tab, tap or click the Header & Footer button (INSERT tab | Text group), and then place a check mark in the Slide number check box.

- Place a check mark in the Footer check box and then type **Daily admission and memberships available** in the Footer text box.

- Place a check mark in the 'Don't show on title slide' check box (Figure 8–16).

Q&A Can I verify where the footer placeholders will display on the slide layout?

Yes. The black boxes in the bottom of the Preview area indicate the footer placeholders' locations.

Figure 8–16

5

- Tap or click the 'Apply to All' button (Header and Footer dialog box) to add the slide number and footer text to the slide master.

To Format Slide Master Footer Text

1 CUSTOMIZE SLIDE MASTERS | 2 FORMAT & ARRANGE FOOTERS | 3 INSERT & FORMAT GRAPHICS & TEXT BOXES

4 RENAME & DELETE SLIDE LAYOUTS | 5 CUSTOMIZE HANDOUT & NOTES MASTERS | 6 USE CUSTOM TEMPLATE

You can format footer text using the same font styles and text attributes available to title and subtitle text. *Why? Using the same font ensures continuity among the slide elements.* The following steps format the footer text.

1

• Display the HOME tab, select the content footer text, and then tap or click the Font arrow to display the Font gallery (Figure 8–17).

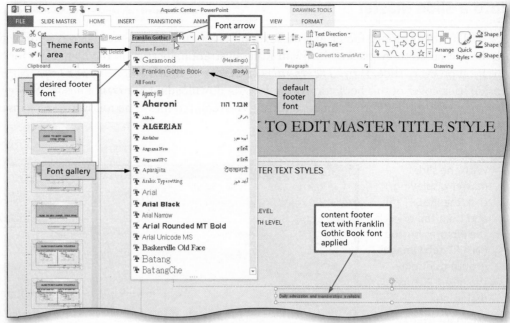

Figure 8–17

2

• Tap or click Garamond in the Theme Fonts section of the Font gallery (HOME tab | Font group) to change the footer font.

• Tap or click the Increase Font Size button several times to increase the font size from 10 to 18 point.

• Change the font color to Blue, Accent 1 (fifth color in the first row).

• Tap or click the Bold button to bold the text.

• Tap or click the Align Right button (HOME tab | Paragraph group) to move the footer text alignment to the right border of the placeholder.

• Use the Format Painter to apply the content footer placeholder formatting to the page number placeholder (Figure 8–18).

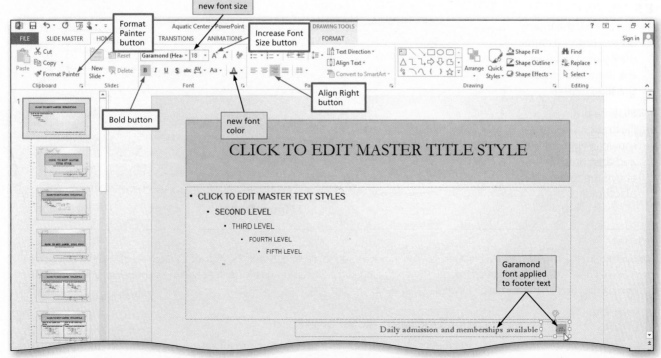

Figure 8–18

To Insert a Background Graphic into a Slide Master

The theme, fonts, footer, and background colors are set. The next step is to draw the viewers' attention to the presentation by placing the Swim Ring illustration, located on the Data Files for Students, in the same location on every slide. *Why? The repetition of this picture creates consistency and helps reinforce the message.* See the inside back cover of this book for instructions on downloading the Data Files for Students, or contact your instructor for more information on accessing the required files. The following steps insert a man floating in a swim ring illustration into the slide master.

- With the slide master displaying, click the INSERT tab and then tap or click the Pictures button (INSERT tab | Images group) to display the Insert Picture dialog box.

- Navigate to the location where your data files are stored (in this case, the PowerPoint Chapter 08 folder) and then tap or click Swim Ring to select the file name (Figure 8–19).

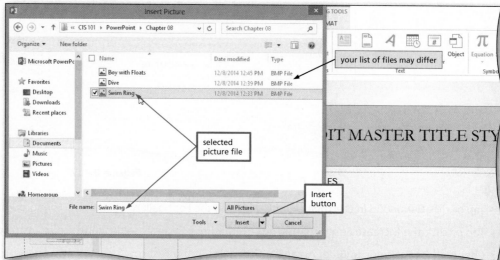

Figure 8–19

What if the picture is not in my data files folder?

Use the same process, but select the device containing the illustration. Another option is to locate this illustration or a similar one on Office.com. You may need to remove the illustration background to call attention to the swimmer.

- Tap or click the Insert button (Insert Picture dialog box) to insert the illustration into the slide master.

- Increase the illustration size, as shown in Figure 8–20, and then drag it above the footer placeholders.

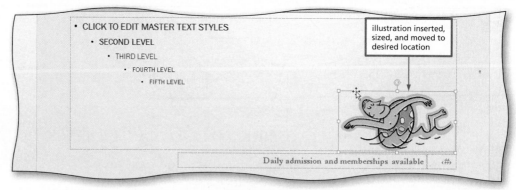

Figure 8–20

Break Point: If you wish to take a break, this is a good place to do so. Be sure to save the Aquatic Center file again and then you can exit PowerPoint. To resume at a later time, run PowerPoint, open the file called Aquatic Center using the steps below, and continue following the steps from this location forward.

TO OPEN A DOCUMENT FROM POWERPOINT

Earlier in this chapter, you saved your presentation using the file name, Aquatic Center. If you exit PowerPoint, you would need to open the Aquatic Center file from the PowerPoint folder in the CIS 101 folder and then continue following the steps in this chapter. For a detailed example of the procedure summarized below, refer to the Office and Windows chapter at the beginning of this book. To open a document from PowerPoint, you would follow these steps:

1. Tap or click FILE on the ribbon to open the Backstage view and then tap or click the Open tab in the Backstage view to display the Open gallery.

2. If the file you wish to open is displayed in the Recent Presentations list, tap or click the file name to open the file and display the opened presentation in the Power-Point window; then, skip the remaining steps. If the file you wish to open is not displayed in the Recent Presentations list, proceed to the next step to locate the file.

3. Tap or click Computer, SkyDrive, or another location in the left pane and then navigate to the location of the file to be opened (in this case, the PowerPoint folder in the CIS 101 folder).

4. Tap or click Aquatic Center to select the file to be opened.

5. Tap or click the Open button (Open dialog box) to open the selected file and display the opened presentation in the PowerPoint window.

BTW
BTWs
For a complete list of the BTWs found in the margins of this book, visit the BTW resource on the Student Companion Site located on www.cengagebrain.com. For detailed instructions about accessing available resources, visit www.cengage.com/ct/studentdownload or see the inside back cover of this book.

Adding and Formatting Placeholders

Each design theme determines where placeholders appear on individual layouts. The slide master has placeholders for bulleted lists, title text, pictures, and other graphical elements. At times, you may find that you need a specific placeholder for a design element not found on any of the slide master layouts. You can add a placeholder in Slide Master view for text, SmartArt, charts, tables, and other graphical elements.

To Insert a Placeholder into a Blank Layout

1 CUSTOMIZE SLIDE MASTERS | 2 FORMAT & ARRANGE FOOTERS | 3 INSERT & FORMAT GRAPHICS & TEXT BOXES
4 RENAME & DELETE SLIDE LAYOUTS | 5 CUSTOMIZE HANDOUT & NOTES MASTERS | 6 USE CUSTOM TEMPLATE

The words, Aquatic Center, will appear on the title slide, but you may desire to add these words to every text slide. **Why?** *Displaying this text in the same location on all slides helps emphasize the name and also provides a consistent, uniform look to the presentation.* One efficient method of adding this text is to insert a placeholder, type the words, and, if necessary, format the characters. The following steps insert a placeholder into the Blank Layout.

1
• In the Overview pane, scroll down and then tap or click the Blank Layout to display this layout.

• If necessary, display the SLIDE MASTER tab and then tap or click the Insert Placeholder arrow (SLIDE MASTER tab | Master Layout group) to display the Insert Placeholder gallery (Figure 8–21).

Q&A Why does the Insert Placeholder button on my screen differ from the button shown in Figure 8–21? The image on the button changes based on the type of placeholder content that was last inserted. A placeholder can hold any content, including text, pictures, and tables. If the last type of placeholder inserted was for SmartArt, for example, the Insert Placeholder button would display the SmartArt icon.

Figure 8–21

- Tap or click Text in the gallery. If you are using a mouse, the pointer changes to a crosshair.

Q&A Could I have inserted a Content placeholder rather than a Text placeholder?
Yes. The Content placeholder is used for any of the seven types of slide content: text, table, chart, SmartArt, picture, clip art, or media. In this project, you will insert text in the placeholder. If you know the specific kind of content you want to place in the placeholder, it is best to select that placeholder type.

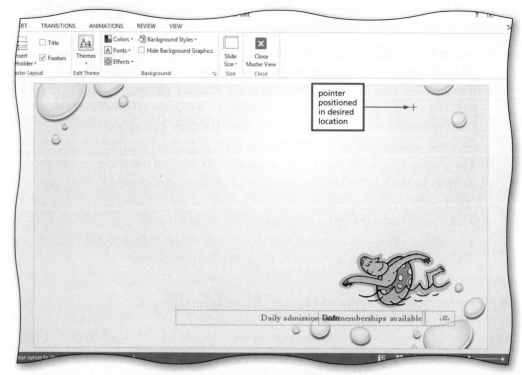

Figure 8–22

- Position your finger or the pointer at the upper-right area of the layout (Figure 8–22).

- Tap or click to insert the new placeholder into the Blank Layout (Figure 8–23).

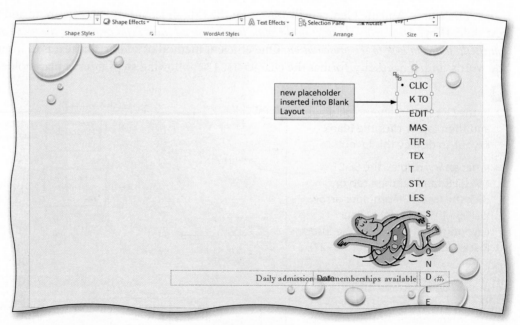

Figure 8–23

To Add and Format Placeholder Text

Now that the text placeholder is positioned, you can add the desired text and then format the characters. You will need to delete the second-, third-, fourth-, and fifth-level bullets in this placeholder. *Why? The placeholders are not used in this presentation.* The following steps add and format the words in the new Blank Layout placeholder.

- Tap or click inside the new placeholder and then select all the text in the placeholder (Figure 8–24).

Figure 8–24

- If you are using a keyboard, press the DELETE key to delete all the selected text in the placeholder. If you are using a touch screen, display the touch keyboard then tap the Backspace key to delete the selected text.

- Display the HOME tab and then tap or click the Bullets button (HOME tab | Paragraph group) to remove the bullet from the placeholder.

- Type **Aquatic Center** in the placeholder.

- Drag the bottom sizing handle down until it is above the Swim Tube illustration, as shown in Figure 8–25.

Figure 8–25

3

- Tap or click the Text Direction button (HOME tab | Paragraph group) to open the Text Direction gallery (Figure 8–26).

 Experiment

- If you are using a mouse, point to various directions in the Text Direction gallery and watch the two words in the placeholder change direction on the layout.

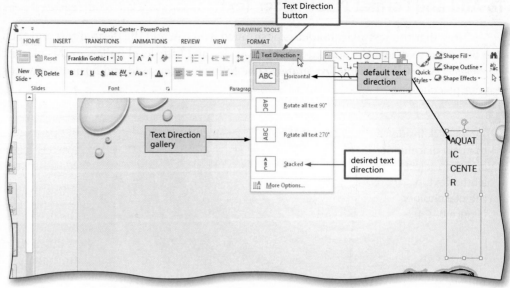

Figure 8–26

4

- Tap or click Stacked to display the text vertically.
- Tap or click the Align Text button (HOME tab | Paragraph group) to display the Align Text gallery (Figure 8–27).

 Experiment

- If you are using a mouse, point to the Center and Right icons in the Align Text gallery and watch the two words in the placeholder change alignment on the layout.

Figure 8–27

5

- Tap or click Center to display the text in the middle of the placeholder (Figure 8–28).

Q&A

What is the difference between the Center button in the Paragraph group and the Center button in the Align gallery?

For the Stacked text layout, the Center button in the Paragraph group positions the text between the top and bottom borders of the placeholder. The Center button in the Align gallery centers the text between the left and right borders.

Figure 8–28

6

- Press and hold or right-click the text in the placeholder to display the mini toolbar and shortcut menu, tap or click the Font arrow on the mini toolbar, and then select Garamond in the Theme Fonts area of the Font gallery.

- Tap or click the Bold button to bold the text.

- Tap or click the Font Color button to change the font color to Blue, Accent 1 (fifth color in the first row) (Figure 8–29).

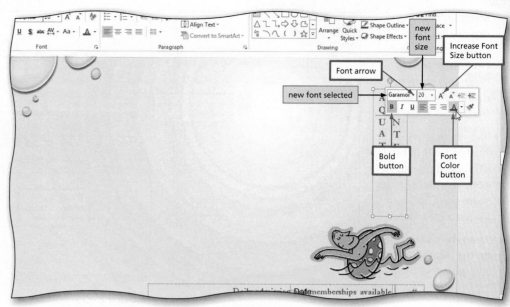

Figure 8–29

To Cut a Placeholder and Paste It into a Slide Master

1 CUSTOMIZE SLIDE MASTERS | 2 FORMAT & ARRANGE FOOTERS | 3 INSERT & FORMAT GRAPHICS & TEXT BOXES
4 RENAME & DELETE SLIDE LAYOUTS | 5 CUSTOMIZE HANDOUT & NOTES MASTERS | 6 USE CUSTOM TEMPLATE

The new formatted placeholder appears only on the Blank Layout. If you selected any other layout in your presentation, such as Two Content or Title Only, this placeholder would not display. This placeholder should appear on all text slides. *Why? Repeating this placeholder will provide consistency throughout the presentation.* You are not given the opportunity to insert a placeholder into the slide master, but you can paste a placeholder that you copied or cut from another slide. The following steps cut the new placeholder from the Blank Layout and paste it into the slide master.

1

- With the HOME tab displaying, tap or click the new placeholder border and then tap or click the Cut button (HOME tab | Clipboard group) to delete the placeholder from the layout and copy it to the Clipboard (Figure 8–30).

 Why did I tap or click the Cut button instead of the Copy button?

Tapping or clicking the Cut button deletes the

 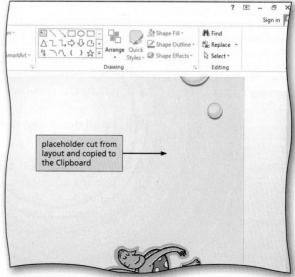

Figure 8–30

placeholder. Tapping or clicking the Copy button keeps the original placeholder on the slide, so if you paste the placeholder on the slide master, a second, identical placeholder would display on the Blank Layout.

• Scroll up and then tap or click the Droplet Slide Master thumbnail in the Overview pane to display the slide master.

• Tap or click the Paste button (HOME tab | Clipboard group) to copy the placeholder from the Clipboard to the slide master.

• Drag the placeholder to the location shown in Figure 8–31.

Figure 8–31

Break Point: If you wish to take a break, this is a good place to do so. Be sure to save the Aquatic Center file again and then you can exit PowerPoint. To resume at a later time, run PowerPoint, open the file called Aquatic Center, and continue following the steps from this location forward.

To Insert an Illustration and a Text Box into a Blank Layout

BTW
Inserting Objects into the Slide Master
In this project you will add a placeholder, text box, and pictures to the layout. You can, however, insert other objects, including clip art and video and audio files. Corporations often insert their company logos into a slide master.

One slide in the completed presentation will feature the Aquatic Center's new events. The content on this slide can vary depending upon the occasion; it might be photographs of children enrolled in swimming classes, teens participating in weekend activities, or adults swimming laps. To ensure continuity when publicizing the Aquatic Center promotions and facilities, you can insert another illustration into the Blank Layout and then add and format a text box. This layout includes the Aquatic Center placeholder you inserted into the slide master. The following steps insert an illustration and a text box into the Blank Layout and then add text in the text box.

1 Scroll down and then tap or click the Blank Layout thumbnail in the Overview pane.

2 Display the INSERT tab, insert the Dive illustration from the Data Files for Students into the Blank Layout and then move the illustration to the location shown in Figure 8–32. You may need to increase the size of the illustration slightly to match the illustration shown in the figure.

❸ Display the INSERT tab and then tap or click the Text Box button (INSERT tab | Text group). If you are using a mouse, insert a new text box in a blank area in the center of the slide layout. (If you are using a touch screen, the text box will be inserted automatically.)

❹ Type `Dive Right In!` as the text box text, change the font color to Lime, Accent 6 (last color in first row), and then increase the font size to 24 point (Figure 8–32).

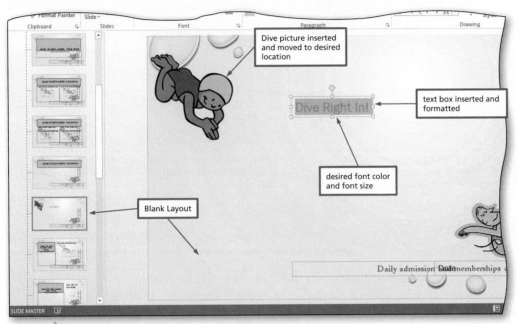

Figure 8–32

To Change Character Spacing

1 CUSTOMIZE SLIDE MASTERS | 2 FORMAT & ARRANGE FOOTERS | 3 INSERT & FORMAT GRAPHICS & TEXT BOXES
4 RENAME & DELETE SLIDE LAYOUTS | 5 CUSTOMIZE HANDOUT & NOTES MASTERS | 6 USE CUSTOM TEMPLATE

Now that the text is added, you can change the spacing between the letters in the placeholder. The amount of space, called **character spacing**, can be increased or decreased from the Normal default in one of four preset amounts: Very Tight, Tight, Loose, or Very Loose. In addition, you can specify a precise amount of space in the Character Spacing tab of the Font dialog box. In this presentation, you will move the text box below the Dive illustration and stretch the letters. ***Why?*** *You want to associate the text box with the illustration, so moving them together along the left side of the slide shows the relationship between the female diver and the words in the text box. In addition, the letters in the text box can be stretched to fit the length of the diver.* The following steps increase the character spacing in the text box.

❶

- With the text in the new text box selected, tap or click the Character Spacing button (HOME tab | Font group) to display the Character Spacing gallery (Figure 8–33).

🔍 **Experiment**

- If you are using a mouse, point to the spacing options in the gallery and watch the characters in the placeholder change.

Figure 8–33

● Tap or click Very Loose in the gallery to change the character spacing in the text box. If necessary, adjust the size of the text box to fit the text on one line (Figure 8–34).

Figure 8–34

Other Ways

1. Tap or click Font dialog box launcher (HOME tab | Font group), tap or click Character Spacing tab (Font dialog box), select Expanded or Condensed in Spacing box and point size in By text box

2. Press and hold or right-click text, tap or click Character Spacing tab (Font dialog box), select Expanded or Condensed in Spacing box and point size in By text box

To Apply a Fill to a Text Box and Increase Transparency

1 CUSTOMIZE SLIDE MASTERS | 2 FORMAT & ARRANGE FOOTERS | 3 INSERT & FORMAT GRAPHICS & TEXT BOXES
4 RENAME & DELETE SLIDE LAYOUTS | 5 CUSTOMIZE HANDOUT & NOTES MASTERS | 6 USE CUSTOM TEMPLATE

Now that the text is added, you can format the text box. A **fill** refers to the formatting of the interior of a shape. The fill can be a color, picture, texture, pattern, or the presentation background. If a color fill is desired, you can increase the transparency so that some of the background color or pattern mixes with the fill color. The following steps apply a green fill to the text box on the Blank Layout and increase the transparency. *Why? The green color is part of the Blue theme colors and also coordinates well with the blue text.*

● Tap or click the text inside the Dive Right In text box to remove the selection from the letters.

● Tap or click the Shape Fill arrow (HOME tab | Drawing group) to display the Shape Fill gallery.

🔍 **Experiment**

● If you are using a mouse, point to various colors in the Shape Fill gallery and watch the placeholder background change.

● Tap or click Blue, Accent 1 (fifth color in the first row) to fill the text box.

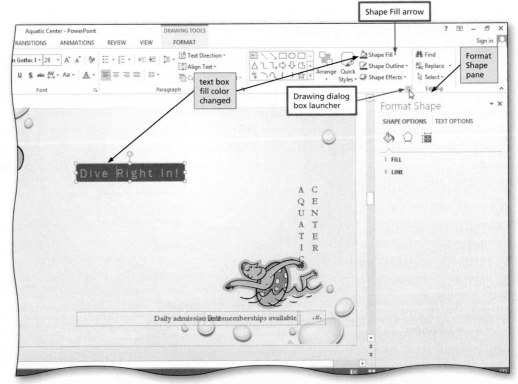

Figure 8–35

● Tap or click the Drawing dialog box launcher (HOME tab | Drawing group) to display the Format Shape pane (Figure 8–35).

- If necessary, tap or click FILL to display the FILL section.

- Tap or click the Transparency slider in the FILL section and drag it to the right until 25% is displayed in the Transparency text box (Figure 8–36).

 Experiment

- If you are using a mouse, drag the Transparency slider to the left and right, and watch the text box background change.

Figure 8–36

Other Ways

1. Enter percentage in Transparency text box

2. Using mouse, click Transparency up or down arrow

To Change a Text Box Internal Margin

1 CUSTOMIZE SLIDE MASTERS | 2 FORMAT & ARRANGE FOOTERS | 3 INSERT & FORMAT GRAPHICS & TEXT BOXES
4 RENAME & DELETE SLIDE LAYOUTS | 5 CUSTOMIZE HANDOUT & NOTES MASTERS | 6 USE CUSTOM TEMPLATE

Each placeholder and text box has preset internal margins, which are the spaces between the border and the contents of the box. The default left and right margins are 0.1", and the default top and bottom margins are 0.05". In this project, you will drag the text box below the diver illustration, so you want to change the margins. *Why? You want the text to align as closely as possible against the top and bottom borders of the box and the left and right margins to have a slight space between the border and the first and last letters.* The following steps change all four text box margins.

1

- Tap or click the 'Size & Properties' Shape Option (Format Shape pane).

- If necessary, click TEXT BOX to display the TEXT BOX section.

2

- Increase the Left margin setting to 0.4".

- Increase the Right margin setting to 0.4".

- Decrease the Top margin setting to 0".

- Decrease the Bottom margin setting to 0" (Figure 8–37).

Q&A Must I change all the margins?
No. You can change one, two, three, or all four internal margins depending upon the placeholder shape and the amount of text entered.

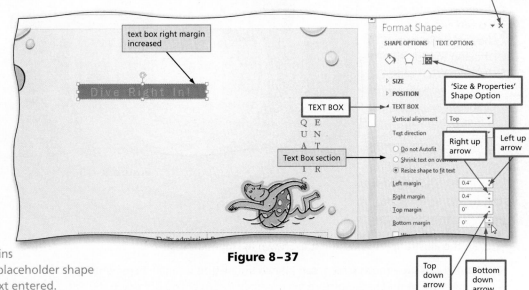

Figure 8–37

3

- Tap or click the Close button (Format Shape pane).

To Rotate a Picture and a Text Box

Why? *To balance the pictures on the slide, you can move the Dive illustration and the Dive Right In! text box. For a dramatic effect, you can change the orientation of the picture and the placeholder on the slide by rotating them.* Dragging the green **rotation handle** above a selected object allows you to rotate an object in any direction. The following steps move and rotate the Dive picture and the Dive Right In! text box.

1

- Tap or click the Dive illustration to select it.

- If you are using a mouse, position the pointer over the rotation handle so that it changes to a Free Rotate pointer (Figure 8–38).

Q&A I selected the picture, but I cannot see the rotation handle. Why?
The rotation handle may not be visible at the top of the slide layout. Drag the picture downward, and the rotation handle will appear.

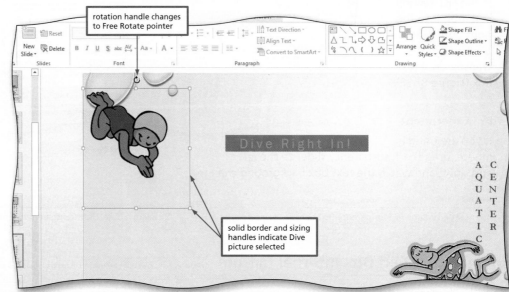

Figure 8–38

2

- Drag the rotation handle counterclockwise so that it is displayed as shown in Figure 8–39.

Q&A I am using a touch screen and am having difficulty moving the rotation handle. What can I do?
When moving small items on a slide, it may be easier to use a mouse or a stylus instead of attempting to make adjustments using your fingers.

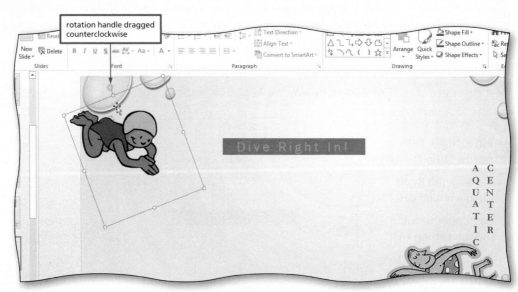

Figure 8–39

3

- Drag the illustration to position it as shown in Figure 8–40.

Q&A If I am not using a touch screen, can I move the picture in small increments?
Yes. To move or nudge the picture in very small increments, hold down the CTRL key with the picture selected while pressing the UP ARROW, DOWN ARROW, RIGHT ARROW, or LEFT ARROW keys. You cannot perform this action using a touch screen.

4

- Tap or click the Dive Right In! text box to select it. If you are using a mouse, position the pointer over the rotation handle so that it changes to a Free Rotate pointer.

- Rotate the text box so that it is at the same angle as the diver.

- Drag the text box below the diver, as shown in Figure 8–40.

Figure 8–40

Other Ways

1. For text box, tap or click Rotate button (DRAWING TOOLS FORMAT tab | Arrange group), choose desired rotation

2. For picture, tap or click Rotate button (PICTURE TOOLS FORMAT tab | Arrange group), choose desired rotation

3. For picture, press and hold or right-click picture, tap or click Format Object on shortcut menu, tap or click 3-D ROTATION (Format Picture pane), set rotation to desired angle

4. For text box, press and hold or right-click text box, tap or click Format Shape on shortcut menu, tap or click Effects icon (Format Shape pane), tap or click 3-D ROTATION, set rotation to desired angle

To Hide and Unhide Background Graphics

1 CUSTOMIZE SLIDE MASTERS | 2 FORMAT & ARRANGE FOOTERS | 3 INSERT & FORMAT GRAPHICS & TEXT BOXES
4 RENAME & DELETE SLIDE LAYOUTS | 5 CUSTOMIZE HANDOUT & NOTES MASTERS | 6 USE CUSTOM TEMPLATE

The placeholder, text box, pictures, and other graphical elements are displayed on some slide master layouts and are hidden on others. You have the ability to change the default setting by choosing to hide or unhide the background graphics. The Title Slide Layout, by default, does not hide the background elements. You want to hide the Swim Ring illustration on the title slide. *Why? You want your audience to focus on the title text and not be distracted by any art on the slide.* The following steps hide the background graphics on the Title Slide Layout, which is the first layout below the Droplet Slide Master in the Overview pane.

- Scroll up, tap or click the Title Slide Layout to display it, and then display the SLIDE MASTER tab (Figure 8–41).

Figure 8–41

2

- Tap or click the Hide Background Graphics check box (SLIDE MASTER tab | Background group) to insert a check mark in it (Figure 8–42).

Q&A

If I decide to unhide the graphics, do I tap or click the same check box to make them appear?
Yes. The Hide Background Graphics check box is a toggle that displays and conceals the graphics.

Figure 8–42

To Rename a Slide Master and a Slide Layout

1 CUSTOMIZE SLIDE MASTERS | 2 FORMAT & ARRANGE FOOTERS | 3 INSERT & FORMAT GRAPHICS & TEXT BOXES
4 RENAME & DELETE SLIDE LAYOUTS | 5 CUSTOMIZE HANDOUT & NOTES MASTERS | 6 USE CUSTOM TEMPLATE

Once all the changes are made to a slide master and a slide layout, you may want to rename them with meaningful names that describe their functions or features. The new slide master name will be displayed on the status bar; the new layout name will be displayed in the Slide Layout gallery. The following steps rename the Droplet Slide Master, the Title Slide Layout, the Blank Layout, and the Title and Content Layout. *Why? Renaming the layouts gives meaningful names that reflect the purpose of the design.*

1

- Display the Droplet Slide Master and then tap or click the Rename button (SLIDE MASTER tab | Edit Master group) to display the Rename Layout dialog box.

- Delete the text in the Layout name text box and then type **Aquatic** in the text box (Rename Layout dialog box) (Figure 8–43).

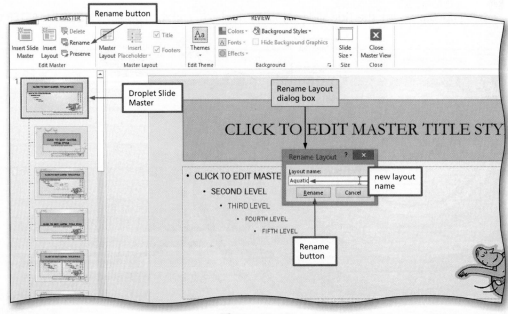

Figure 8–43

2

- Tap or click the Rename button (Rename Layout dialog box) to give the layout the new name, Aquatic Slide Master.

3

- Display the Title Slide Layout, tap or click the Rename button, delete the text in the Layout name text box, and then type **Aquatic Title** as the new layout name (Figure 8–44).

Figure 8–44

4

- Tap or click the Rename button (Rename Layout dialog box) to rename the Title Slide layout.

- Scroll down and then tap or click the Blank Layout to display it, tap or click the Rename button, delete the text in the Layout name text box, and then type **Dive Right In** as the new layout name (Figure 8–45).

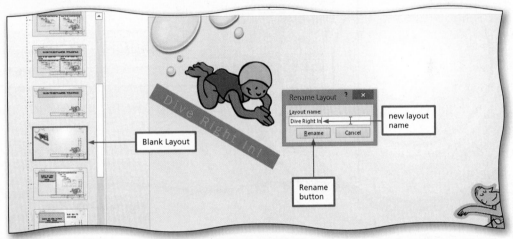

Figure 8–45

5

- Tap or click the Rename button (Rename Layout dialog box).

- Scroll up to display the Title and Content Layout, tap or click the Rename button, delete the text in the Layout name text box, and then type **Miscellaneous** as the new layout name (Figure 8–46).

6

- Tap or click the Rename button (Rename Layout dialog box).

Figure 8–46

To Delete a Slide Layout

You have made many changes to the slide master and two slide layouts. You will use these layouts and the Title and Content Layout, which is now called the Miscellaneous layout, when you close Master view and then add text, graphics, or other content to the presentation in Normal view. You can delete the other layouts in the Overview pane. *Why? You will not use them in this presentation.* The following steps delete slide layouts that will not be used to create the presentation.

- Tap or click the Section Header Layout in the Overview pane to select it (Figure 8–47).

Figure 8–47

2

- If you are using a keyboard, press and hold down the SHIFT key, if necessary scroll down to display the Title Only Layout, and then click the Title Only Layout to select four consecutive layouts. If you are using a touch screen, swipe to the right across each of the three layouts below the Title Only layout to select them (Figure 8–48).

Q&A

Why did I select only these four layouts?
The layout below the Title Only Layout is the Dive Right In Layout, and you will use that layout when you create Slide 2 in your presentation.

Figure 8–48

3

- Tap or click the Delete button (SLIDE MASTER tab | Edit Master group) to delete the four layouts.

- Tap or click the Content with Caption Layout (the layout below the Dive Right In layout), then select all layouts below it including the last layout, which is the Vertical Title and Text Layout, in the Overview pane (Figure 8–49).

Figure 8–49

4

- Tap or click the Delete button (SLIDE MASTER tab | Edit Master group) to delete the 10 layouts (Figure 8–50).

 Q&A Now that I have created this slide master, can I ensure that it will not be changed when I create future presentations?

Yes. Normally a slide master is deleted when a new design template is selected. To keep the original master as part of your presentation, you can preserve it by selecting the thumbnail and then tapping or clicking the Preserve button in the Edit Master group. An icon in the shape of a pushpin is displayed below the slide number to indicate the master is preserved. If you decide to unpreserve a slide master, select this thumbnail and then tap or click the Preserve button.

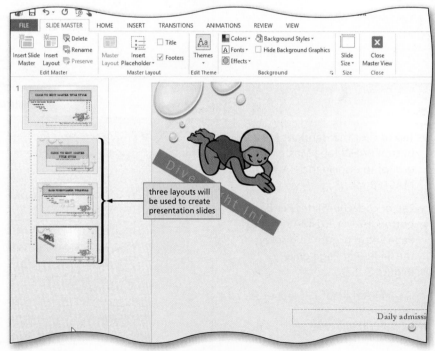

Figure 8–50

Other Ways

1. Tap or click Delete button (HOME tab | Slides group)
2. Press and hold or right-click selected slide, tap or click Delete Layout on shortcut menu
3. Press DELETE key on keyboard

Break Point: If you wish to take a break, this is a good place to do so. You can exit PowerPoint now. To resume at a later time, run PowerPoint and continue following the steps from this location forward.

BTW
**Formatting the
'Date and time'
Placeholder**
The 'Date and time' footer
can have a variety of formats.
If you tap or click the Update
automatically arrow, you can
choose among formats that
display the day, date, and time
in a variety of combinations.

Customizing Handout and Notes Masters

You have used PowerPoint's slide master template file to create unique slide layouts for the Aquatic Center presentation. PowerPoint also has master template files to create handouts and notes. If you are going to distribute handouts to your audience, you can customize the handout master so that it coordinates visually with the presentation slides and reinforces your message. In addition, if you are going to use speaker notes to guide you through a presentation, you can tailor the notes master to fit your needs.

To Customize a Handout Using a Handout Master

1 CUSTOMIZE SLIDE MASTERS | 2 FORMAT & ARRANGE FOOTERS | 3 INSERT & FORMAT GRAPHICS & TEXT BOXES
4 RENAME & DELETE SLIDE LAYOUTS | **5 CUSTOMIZE HANDOUT & NOTES MASTERS** | 6 USE CUSTOM TEMPLATE

When you created the Aquatic slide master, you specified the background, fonts, theme, and pictures for all slides. You likewise can create a specific handout master to determine the layout and graphics that will display on the printed page. *Why? You can customize handouts for a your audience's needs by moving, restoring, and formatting the header and footer placeholders; setting the page number orientation; adding graphics; and specifying the number of slides to print on each page.* The following steps use the handout master to create a custom handout.

1
- Display the VIEW tab (Figure 8–51).

Figure 8–51

2
- Tap or click the Handout Master button (VIEW tab | Master Views group) to display the HANDOUT MASTER tab.

- Tap or click the 'Slides Per Page' button (HANDOUT MASTER tab | Page Setup group) to display the Slides Per Page gallery (Figure 8–52).

Q&A Is 6 Slides the default layout for all themes?
Yes. If you have fewer than six slides in your presentation or want to display slide details, then choose a handout layout with 1, 2, 3, or 4 slides per sheet of paper.

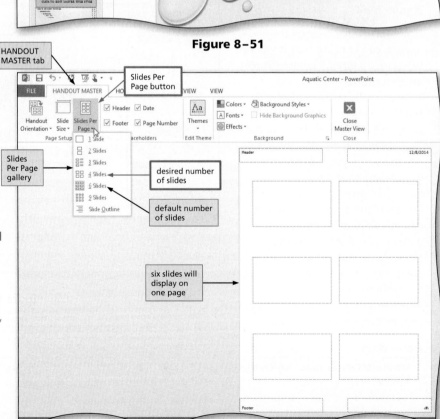

Figure 8–52

3

- Tap or click 4 Slides in the list to change the layout from 6 slides to 4 slides.

- Tap or click the Handout Orientation button (HANDOUT MASTER tab | Page Setup group) to display the Handout Orientation gallery (Figure 8–53).

Figure 8–53

4

- Tap or click Landscape in the gallery to display the page layout in landscape orientation (Figure 8–54).

Q&A How do I decide between portrait and landscape orientation?
If your slide content is predominantly vertical, such as an athlete running or a skyscraper in a major city, consider using the default portrait orientation. If, however, your slide content has long lines of text or pictures of four-legged animals, landscape orientation may be a more appropriate layout.

Figure 8–54

- Tap or click the Header placeholder and then type **Aquatic Center** as the header text.

- Tap or click the Footer placeholder and then type **New this year: Adult swimming lessons and aqua aerobics!** as the footer text.

- Drag the Footer placeholder above the page number placeholder (Figure 8–55).

Figure 8–55

- Tap or click the Theme Fonts button (HANDOUT MASTER tab | Background group) to display the Theme Fonts gallery (Figure 8–56).

- Tap or click Swim in the Custom area of the gallery to apply the Franklin Gothic Book font to the text in the placeholder.

Figure 8–56

8

- Display the INSERT tab, tap or click the Pictures button (INSERT tab | Images group), and then insert the Dive illustration located on the Data Files for Students.

- Rotate the Dive illustration counterclockwise, resize the picture so it is approximately 2.6" × 2.4", and then center it along the upper edge of the handout layout, as shown in Figure 8–57.

Figure 8–57

9

- Display the INSERT tab, tap or click the 'Header & Footer' button (INSERT tab | Text group), and then place a check mark in the 'Date and time' check box.

- Place a check mark in the Header check box.

- Place a check mark in the Footer check box (Figure 8–58).

10

- Tap or click the 'Apply to All' button (Header and Footer dialog box) to add the header and footer text and date to the handout master.

Figure 8–58

Q&A | Where will the header and footer display on the handout?
The black boxes in the preview area show where these placeholders are located.

To Customize a Notes Page
Using a Notes Master

If you type notes in the Notes pane, you can print them for yourself or for your audience. The basic format found in the Backstage view generally suffices for handouts, but you may desire to alter the layout using the notes master. *Why? You may desire to add graphics and rearrange and format the header, footer, and page number placeholders.* The following steps use the notes master to create a custom handout.

1

- Display the VIEW tab (Figure 8–59).

Figure 8–59

2

- Tap or click the Notes Master button (VIEW tab | Master Views group) to display the NOTES MASTER tab.

- Tap or click the Footer placeholder, delete the text, and then type **Open swim begins at noon daily** as the new footer text.

3

- Tap or click the Theme Fonts button to display the Theme Fonts gallery (Figure 8–60).

Figure 8–60

● Tap or click Swim in the Custom area of the Theme Fonts gallery to apply the Franklin Gothic Book font to the text in the header, footer, date, and page number placeholders.

● Tap or click the 'Notes Page Orientation' button (NOTES MASTER tab | Page Setup group) to display the 'Notes Page Orientation' gallery (Figure 8–61).

Figure 8–61

● Tap or click Portrait in the gallery to display the page layout in portrait orientation.

● Display the INSERT tab, tap or click the Pictures button, and then insert the Dive illustration located on the Data Files for Students.

● Resize the picture so that it is approximately 2" × 1.85".

● Move the picture so that it is centered between the two footer placeholders, as shown in Figure 8–62.

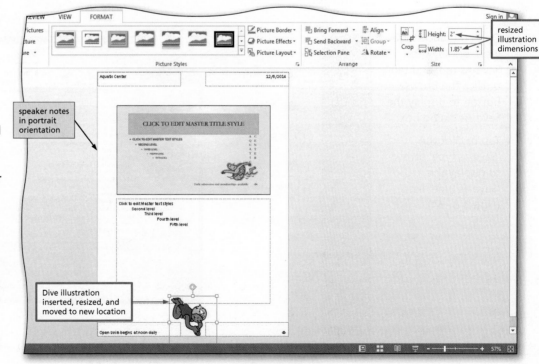

Figure 8–62

To Close Master View

You now can exit Master view and return to Normal view. *Why? All the changes to the slide master, handout master, and notes master are complete.* The following steps close Master view.

1
• Display the NOTES MASTER tab (Figure 8–63).

2
• Tap or click the 'Close Master View' button (NOTES MASTER tab | Close group) to exit Master view and return to Normal view.

Figure 8–63

To Save a Master as a Template

The changes and enhancements you have made to the Aquatic Center slide master, handout master, and notes master are excellent starting points for future presentations. The background text and graphics allow users to add text boxes, pictures, SmartArt, tables, and other elements depending upon the specific message that needs to be communicated to an audience. Saving a slide master as a template is convenient when you often reuse and modify presentations. *Why? You can save your slide layouts as a template to use for a new presentation and use the revised handout and notes masters to print unique pages.* The following steps save the Aquatic masters as a template.

1
• Open the Backstage view, display the Save As tab, and tap or click the Browse button to display the Save As dialog box.

• Tap or click the 'Save as type' arrow to display the 'Save as type' list (Figure 8–64).

Figure 8–64

- Tap or click 'PowerPoint Template' in the 'Save as type' list to change the save as type.

- Type **Aquatic Center Template** in the File name box (Figure 8–65).

- Tap or click the Save button (Save As dialog box) to save the Aquatic Center presentation as a template.

4

- Close the Aquatic Center Template file.

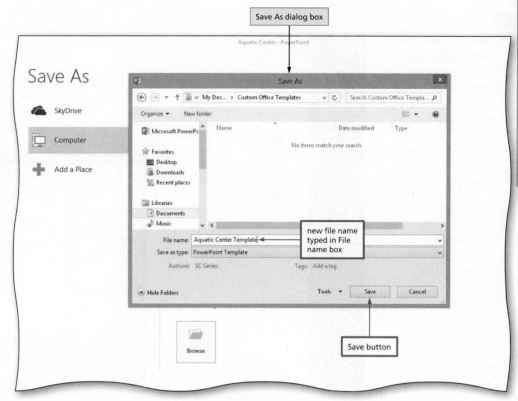

Figure 8–65

Break Point: If you wish to take a break, this is a good place to do so. You can exit PowerPoint now. To resume at a later time, run PowerPoint and continue following the steps from this location forward.

To Open a Template and Save a Presentation

1 CUSTOMIZE SLIDE MASTERS | 2 FORMAT & ARRANGE FOOTERS | 3 INSERT & FORMAT GRAPHICS & TEXT BOXES
4 RENAME & DELETE SLIDE LAYOUTS | 5 CUSTOMIZE HANDOUT & NOTES MASTERS | **6 USE CUSTOM TEMPLATE**

The Aquatic Center Template file you created is a convenient start to a new presentation. The graphical elements and essential slide content are in place; you then can customize the layouts for a specific need, such as a new event or special program. PowerPoint saves templates users create in a folder called 'Custom Office Templates' in the My Documents folder. The steps on the next page open the Aquatic Center Template file and save the presentation with the Aquatic Center name.

1

- Open the Backstage view, display the Open tab, tap or click the Computer button, and then tap or click the Custom Office Templates folder to display the Open dialog box (Figure 8–66).

Q&A

Can I select the Aquatic Center Template from the list of Recent Presentations instead of opening the Custom Office Templates folder? Yes. Either technique will locate the desired template.

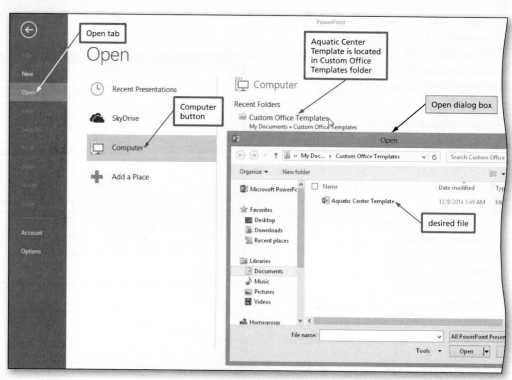

Figure 8–66

2

- Open the file, 'Aquatic Center Template'.

- Open the Backstage view, display the Save As tab, and then navigate to the location where your files are saved.

- Tap or click the 'Save as type' arrow to display the 'Save as type' list, and then tap or click PowerPoint Presentation in the 'Save as type' list to change the save as type.

- Tap or click Aquatic Center in the Save As dialog box to select the file (Figure 8–67).

Figure 8–67

3

- Tap or click the Save button (Save As dialog box) to display the Confirm Save As dialog box (Figure 8–68).

- Click the Yes button to replace the file.

Figure 8–68

To Add Text and Notes to the Title Slide

By default, the title slide layout, which was renamed Aquatic Title, is applied to the first slide. The following steps add text and speaker notes to Slide 1.

1 With the title slide displaying, type **Aquatic Center Programs and Events** as the title text and **Splish Splash - Have a Blast!** as the subtitle text.

2 If necessary, display the Notes pane. Tap or click the Notes pane and type **The Aquatic Center is open daily and offers community residents a variety of lessons, parties, and special events.** (Figure 8–69).

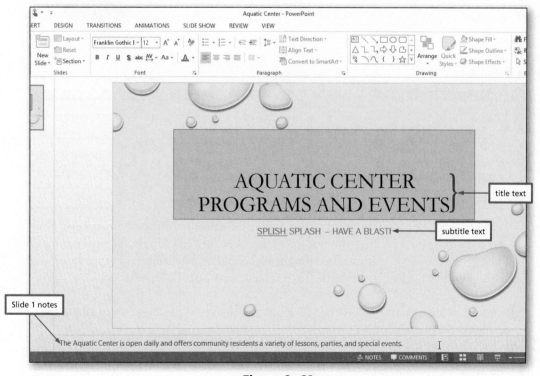

Figure 8–69

BTW
Distributing Notes Text
If you desire to share your notes with your audience, you can print the text with or without thumbnail images of the corresponding slides. Public speaking experts recommend distributing your notes before or after your presentation, not during your speech.

To Add Text and Notes to the Blank Layout

The second slide in your presentation will feature the new water slide. The Dive Right In slide layout, which is the new name for the Blank Layout, is designed so that you can add variable slide content below the diver illustration in the upper-left corner. The following steps add a text box and speaker notes to Slide 2. *Why? The text box will call attention to the water slide, and the speaker notes contain ideas that a presenter may want to discuss during a presentation.*

1 Insert a slide with the Dive Right In layout and then insert a text box between the two illustrations. Type **New three-chute** as the first line of text box text and then press or tap ENTER. Then type **150' water slide** as the second line of text.

2 Increase the text box font size to 54 point. Size the text box as shown in Figure 8–70 and then drag it to the location shown in the figure.

3 In the Notes pane, type **Community residents can enjoy a leisure pool with a zero-depth edge, a 50-meter pool with six lanes, and a wading pool with a tot slide.** (Figure 8–70).

Figure 8–70

To Add Text, Notes, and an Illustration to the Title and Content Layout

The third slide in your presentation will list details about the swim lessons. The Miscellaneous layout, which is the new name for the Title and Content slide layout, will allow you to insert text into the content placeholder. The following steps insert a slide and add text and a picture to the title and content placeholder.

1 Insert a slide with the Miscellaneous layout and then type **Swim Lessons** as the title text.

2 Type **Small class size (10 students maximum)** as the first content placeholder paragraph.

3 Type **Lifeguard training includes CPR certification** as the second paragraph.

④ Type `Parent / Tot swim prepares for lifetime of aquatic enjoyment` as the third paragraph.

⑤ Type `Morning, evening, and Saturday classes available` as the fourth paragraph.

⑥ In the Notes pane, type `Small class sizes allow instructors to give individualized attention, which helps students make progress and feel proud of their accomplishments.`

⑦ Insert the illustration with the file name, Boy with Floats, located on the Data Files for Students, increase its size to approximately 2.4" × 2.26", and then move the illustration to the lower-left corner of the slide (Figure 8–71).

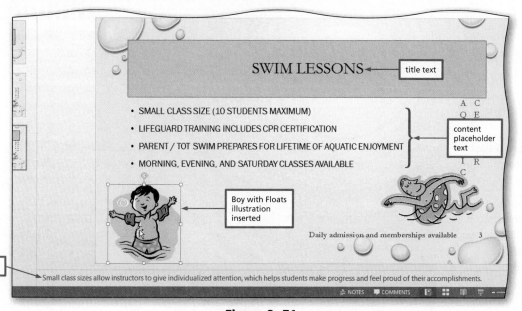

Figure 8–71

To Apply a Fill Color to a Slide

1 CUSTOMIZE SLIDE MASTERS | 2 FORMAT & ARRANGE FOOTERS | 3 INSERT & FORMAT GRAPHICS & TEXT BOXES
4 RENAME & DELETE SLIDE LAYOUTS | 5 CUSTOMIZE HANDOUT & NOTES MASTERS | 6 USE CUSTOM TEMPLATE

Earlier in this project, you formatted the interior of the Dive Right In! text box by applying a fill. In a similar manner, you can apply a fill to an entire slide by selecting a color from the Shape Fill gallery. If desired, you can increase the transparency to soften the color. The following steps apply a fill to Slide 3 and increase the transparency. **Why?** *Because the Dive Right In! text on Slide 2 is green, you can coordinate the Slide 3 fill color by changing the Slide 3 background to green and decrease the transparency so the letters can be read easily.*

①

• With Slide 3 displaying, press and hold or right-click anywhere on the blue background without a text box or illustration to display the shortcut menu (Figure 8–72).

Figure 8–72

- Tap or click Format Background on the shortcut menu to display the Format Background pane.

- With the FILL section displaying and the Solid fill option selected, tap or click the Color button to display the Fill Color gallery (Figure 8–73).

Q&A Can I experiment with previewing the background colors?
No live preview feature is available.

Figure 8–73

- Tap or click Lime, Accent 6 (last color in the first row) to change the slide background color.

- Tap or click the Transparency slider in the Fill Color area and drag it to the right until 15% is displayed in the Transparency text box (Figure 8–74).

 Experiment

- Drag the Transparency slider to the left and right, and watch the text box background change.

Q&A How can I delete a fill color if I decide not to apply one to my slide?
Any fill effect in the Format Background dialog box is applied immediately. If this dialog box is displayed, tap or click the Reset Background button. If you already have applied the fill color, you must tap or click the Undo button on the Quick Access Toolbar.

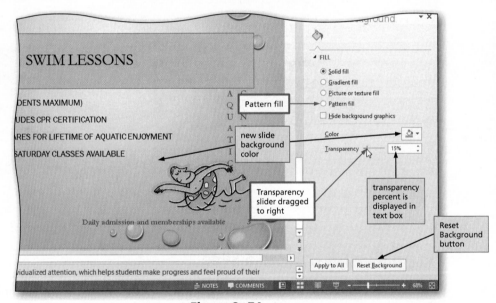

Figure 8–74

Other Ways

1. Enter percentage in Transparency text box   2. Using mouse, click Transparency up or down arrow

To Apply a Pattern to a Slide

1 CUSTOMIZE SLIDE MASTERS | 2 FORMAT & ARRANGE FOOTERS | 3 INSERT & FORMAT GRAPHICS & TEXT BOXES
4 RENAME & DELETE SLIDE LAYOUTS | 5 CUSTOMIZE HANDOUT & NOTES MASTERS | **6 USE CUSTOM TEMPLATE**

You add variety to a slide by making a **pattern fill**. This design of repeating horizontal or vertical lines, dots, dashes, or stripes can enhance the visual appeal of one or more slides in the presentation. If you desire to change the colors in the pattern, PowerPoint allows you to select the fill foreground and background colors by clicking the Color button and then choosing the desired colors. The following steps apply a pattern to Slide 3. **Why?** *The dots in this pattern coordinate with the water droplets in the slide background.*

1

- With the Format Background pane displaying, click Pattern fill to display the Pattern gallery and the 5% pattern on Slide 3 (Figure 8–75).

 Experiment

- Tap or click various patterns in the Pattern gallery and the 5% pattern on Slide 3.

Q&A How can I delete a pattern if I decide not to apply one to my slide?

If the Format Background pane is displayed, tap or click the Reset Background button. If you already have applied the pattern, you must tap or click the Undo button on the Quick Access Toolbar.

Figure 8–75

2

- Tap or click the 90% pattern (last color in second row) to apply this pattern to the Slide 3 background (Figure 8–76).

Q&A Can I apply this pattern to all the slides in the presentation?

Yes. You would tap or click the 'Apply to All' button in the Format Background pane.

3

- Tap or click the Close button to close the Format Background task pane.

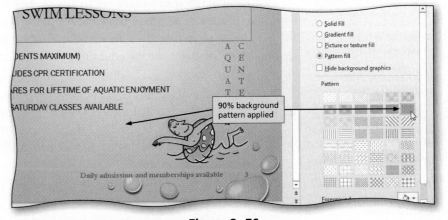

Figure 8–76

To Add a Slide Transition

A final enhancement you will make in this presentation is to apply the Ripple transition to all slides and then change the transition speed and effect option. The following steps apply a transition and effect to the presentation.

1 Display the TRANSITIONS tab and then apply the Ripple transition in the Exciting category to all three slides in the presentation.

2 Change the transition speed from 01.40 to 04.00.

3 Change the Effect Option from Center to From Top-Left.

Document Properties

PowerPoint helps you organize and identify your files by using **document properties**, which are the details about a file such as the project author, title, and subject. For example, a class name or presentation topic can describe the file's purpose or content.

Why would you want to assign document properties to a presentation?

Document properties are valuable for a variety of reasons:

• Users can save time locating a particular file because they can view a file's document properties without opening the presentation.

• By creating consistent properties for files having similar content, users can better organize their presentations.

• Some organizations require PowerPoint users to add document properties so that other employees can view details about these files.

The more common document properties are standard and automatically updated properties. **Standard properties** are associated with all Microsoft Office files and include author, title, and subject. **Automatically updated properties** include file system properties, such as the date you create or change a file, and statistics, such as the file size.

TO CHANGE DOCUMENT PROPERTIES

To change document properties, you would follow these steps.

1. Tap or click FILE on the ribbon to open the Backstage view and then, if necessary, tap or click the Info tab in the Backstage view to display the Info gallery.

2. If the property you wish to change is displayed in the Properties list in the right pane of the Info gallery, try to tap or click to the right of the property. If a text box appears to the right of the property, type the text for the property in the text box, and then tap or click the Back button in the upper-left corner of the Backstage view to return to the PowerPoint window. Skip the remaining steps.

3. If the property you wish to change is not displayed in the Properties list in the right pane of the Info gallery or you cannot change it in the Info gallery, tap or click the Properties button in the right pane to display the Properties menu, and then tap or click 'Show Document Panel' on the Properties menu to close the Backstage view and display the Document Information Panel in the PowerPoint presentation window.

Q&A Why are some of the document properties in my Document Information Panel already filled in?

The person who installed Office 2013 on your computer or network may have set or customized the properties.

4. Type the desired text in the appropriate property text boxes.

Q&A What if the property I want to change is not displayed in the Document Information Panel?

Tap or click the Document Properties button in the Document Information Panel and then tap or click Advanced Properties on the menu to display the Properties dialog box. If necessary, tap or click the Summary tab (Properties dialog box) to display the Summary sheet, fill in the appropriate text boxes, and then tap or click the OK button.

5. Tap or click the 'Close the Document Information Panel' button at the right edge of the Document Information Panel so that the panel no longer appears in the PowerPoint presentation window.

Printing a Presentation

After creating a presentation, you may want to print it. Printing a presentation enables you to distribute it to others in a form that can be read or viewed but typically not edited. It is a good practice to save a presentation before printing it, in the event you experience difficulties printing.

BTW
Printing Document Properties
To print document properties, tap or click FILE on the ribbon to open the Backstage view, tap or click the Print tab in the Backstage view to display the Print gallery, tap or click the first button in the Settings area to display a list of options specifying what you can print, tap or click Document Info in the list to specify you want to print the document properties instead of the actual document, and then tap or click the Print button in the Print gallery to print the document properties on the currently selected printer.

BTW
Conserving Ink and Toner
If you want to conserve ink or toner, you can instruct PowerPoint to print draft quality documents by tapping or clicking FILE on the ribbon to open the Backstage view, tapping or clicking Options in the Backstage view to display the PowerPoint Options dialog box, tapping or clicking Advanced in the left pane (PowerPoint Options dialog box), sliding or scrolling to the Print area in the right pane, placing a check mark in the 'Use draft quality' check box, and then tapping or clicking the OK button. Then, use the Backstage view to print the document as usual.

What is the best method for distributing a presentation?

The traditional method of distributing a presentation uses a printer to produce a hard copy. A **hard copy** or **printout** is information that exists on a physical medium such as paper. Hard copies can be useful for the following reasons:

• Some people prefer proofreading a hard copy of a presentation rather than viewing it on the screen to check for errors and readability.

• Hard copies can serve as a backup reference if your storage medium is lost or becomes corrupted and you need to recreate the presentation.

Instead of distributing a hard copy of a presentation, users can distribute the presentation as an electronic image that mirrors the original presentation's appearance. The electronic image of the presentation can be sent as an email attachment, posted on a website, or copied to a portable storage medium such as a USB flash drive. Two popular electronic image formats, sometimes called fixed formats, are PDF by Adobe Systems and XPS by Microsoft. In PowerPoint, you can create electronic image files through the Save As dialog box and the Export, Share, and Print tabs in the Backstage view. Electronic images of presentations, such as PDF and XPS, can be useful for the following reasons:

• Users can view electronic images of presentations without the software that created the original presentation (e.g., PowerPoint). Specifically, to view a PDF file, you use a program called Adobe Reader, which can be downloaded free from Adobe's website. Similarly, to view an XPS file, you use a program called XPS Viewer, which is included in the latest versions of Windows and Internet Explorer.

• Sending electronic presentations saves paper and printer supplies. Society encourages users to contribute to **green computing**, which involves reducing the electricity consumed and environmental waste generated when using computers, mobile devices, and related technologies.

To Print a Presentation

1 CUSTOMIZE SLIDE MASTERS | 2 FORMAT & ARRANGE FOOTERS | 3 INSERT & FORMAT GRAPHICS & TEXT BOXES
4 RENAME & DELETE SLIDE LAYOUTS | 5 CUSTOMIZE HANDOUT & NOTES MASTERS | 6 USE CUSTOM TEMPLATE

With the completed presentation saved, you may want to print it. *Why? Because this handout is being distributed, you will print a hard copy on a printer.* The following steps print a hard copy of the contents of the saved Aquatic Center presentation.

• Tap or click FILE on the ribbon to open the Backstage view.

• Tap or click the Print tab in the Backstage view to display the Print gallery.

Q&A How can I print multiple copies of my presentation?
Increase the number in the Copies box in the Print gallery.

What if I decide not to print the presentation at this time?
Tap or click the Back button in the upper-left corner of the Backstage view to return to the presentation window.

• Verify that the printer listed on the Printer Status button will print a hard copy of the presentation. If necessary, click the Printer Status button to display a list of available printer options and then click the desired printer to change the currently selected printer.

• Tap or click the Print button in the Print gallery to print the presentation on the currently selected printer.

• When the printer stops, retrieve the hard copy.

Q&A Do I have to wait until my presentation is complete to print it?
No, you can follow these steps to print a presentation at any time while you are creating it.

What if I want to print an electronic image of a presentation instead of a hard copy?
You would click the Printer Status button in the Print gallery and then select the desired electronic image option, such as Microsoft XPS Document Writer, which would create an XPS file.

Other Ways

1. Press CTRL+P, press ENTER

To Print a Handout Using the Handout Master

The handout master you created has header and footer text using the Franklin Gothic Book font, a revised location for the Footer placeholder, and the Swim Ring illustration in the lower-left corner. The following steps print a handout using the handout master.

1

- Open the Backstage view and then display the Print gallery.

2

- Tap or click the 'Full Page Slides' button in the Settings area to display the gallery (Figure 8–77).

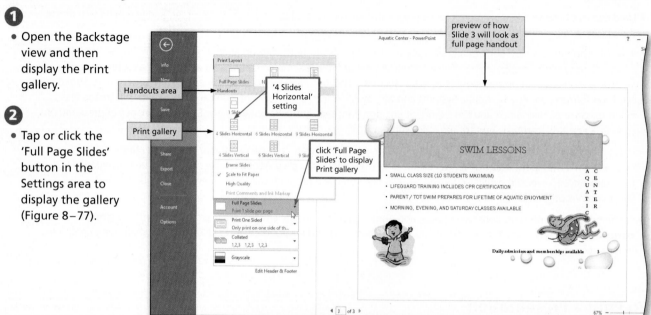

Figure 8–77

3

- Tap or click '4 Slides Horizontal' in the Handouts area.

- Tap or click Portrait Orientation in the Settings area to display the Orientation gallery (Figure 8–78).

Figure 8–78

- Tap or click Landscape Orientation to change the setting.

- Verify that '4 Slides Horizontal' is selected as the option in the Settings area and that the preview of Page 1 shows the header text, date, footer text, page number, Dive illustration, and three slides in landscape orientation.

- Tap or click the Print button in the Print Gallery to print the handout (Figure 8–79).

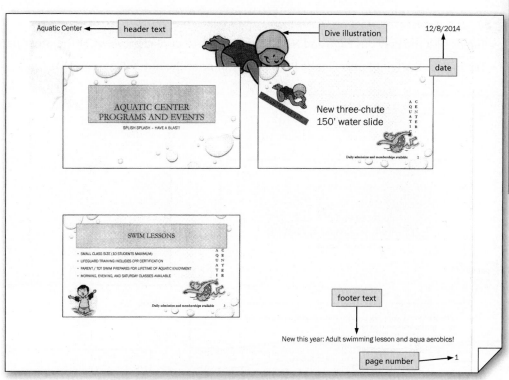

Figure 8–79 Handout in Landscape Orientation

To Print Speaker Notes Using the Notes Master

1 CUSTOMIZE SLIDE MASTERS | 2 FORMAT & ARRANGE FOOTERS | 3 INSERT & FORMAT GRAPHICS & TEXT BOXES
4 RENAME & DELETE SLIDE LAYOUTS | 5 CUSTOMIZE HANDOUT & NOTES MASTERS | 6 USE CUSTOM TEMPLATE

You also can print speaker notes while the Backstage view is displayed. The custom notes master you created has the same footer as the handout master, revised footer text using the Franklin Gothic Book font, the current date, and the resized Swim Ring illustration in the lower-right corner. The following steps print notes pages using the notes master.

1

- With the Backstage view open, display the Print gallery and then tap or click Notes Pages in the Print Layout area.

- Tap or click Landscape Orientation in the Settings area and then tap or click Portrait Orientation in the gallery to change the setting.

- If necessary, tap or click the Previous Page button to preview Slide 1.

- Verify that the page preview shows the header text, date, speaker notes, revised footer text, diver illustration, and page number in portrait orientation (Figure 8–80).

Figure 8–80

- Tap or click the Previous Page and Next Page buttons to display previews of the other pages.
- Tap or click the Print button in the Print gallery to print the notes (Figure 8–81).

Figure 8–81

To Sign Out of a Microsoft Account

If you are signed in to a Microsoft account and are using a public computer or otherwise wish to sign out of your Microsoft account, you should sign out of the account from the Account gallery in the Backstage view before exiting PowerPoint. Signing out of the account is the safest way to make sure that nobody else can access SkyDrive files or settings stored in your Microsoft account. The following steps sign out of a Microsoft account from PowerPoint. For a detailed example of the procedure summarized below, refer to the Office and Windows chapter at the beginning of this book.

1 If you wish to sign out of your Microsoft account, tap or click FILE on the ribbon to open the Backstage view and then tap or click the Account tab to display the Account gallery.

2 Tap or click the Sign out link, which displays the Remove Account dialog box. If a Can't remove Windows accounts dialog box appears instead of the Remove Account dialog box, click the OK button and skip the remaining steps.

Q&A Why does a Can't remove Windows accounts dialog box appear?
If you signed in to Windows using your Microsoft account, then you also must sign out from Windows, rather than signing out from within PowerPoint. When you are finished using Windows, be sure to sign out at that time.

3 Tap or click the Yes button (Remove Account dialog box) to sign out of your Microsoft account on this computer.

Q&A Should I sign out of Windows after signing out of my Microsoft account?
When you are finished using the computer, you should sign out of your account for maximum security.

4 Tap or click the Back button in the upper-left corner of the Backstage view to return to the presentation.

To Exit PowerPoint

This project now is complete. The following steps exit PowerPoint. For a detailed example of the procedure summarized below, refer to the Office and Windows chapter at the beginning of this book.

1a If you have one PowerPoint presentation open, tap or click the Close button on the right side of the title bar to close the open document and exit PowerPoint.

1b If you have multiple PowerPoint presentations open, press and hold or right-click the PowerPoint app button on the taskbar and then tap or click 'Close all windows' on the shortcut menu, or press ALT+F4 to close all open presentations and exit PowerPoint.

Q&A Could I press and hold or repeatedly click the Close button to close all open documents and exit PowerPoint?
Yes.

2 If a Microsoft PowerPoint dialog box appears, tap or click the Save button to save any changes made to the presentation since the last save.

BTW

Certification
The Microsoft Office Specialist (MOS) program provides an opportunity for you to obtain a valuable industry credential — proof that you have the PowerPoint 2013 skills required by employers. For more information, visit the Certification resource on the Student Companion Site located on www.cengagebrain.com. For detailed instructions about accessing available resources, visit www.cengage.com/ct/studentdownload or see the inside back cover of this book.

BTW

Quick Reference
For a table that lists how to complete the tasks covered in this book using touch gestures, the mouse, ribbon, shortcut menu, and keyboard, see the Quick Reference Summary at the back of this book, or visit the Quick Reference resource on the Student Companion Site located on www.cengagebrain.com. For detailed instructions about accessing available resources, visit www.cengage.com/ct/studentdownload or see the inside back cover of this book.

Chapter Summary

In this chapter you have learned how to customize master slide layouts by changing the slide and font themes, formatting the background and footers, and adding background graphics. You then inserted a placeholder, added and formatted text, applied a fill, and changed the internal margins. Also, you rotated a picture and a placeholder, displayed the background graphics, and renamed and deleted slide layouts. Then you customized the handout and notes masters by adding a picture and changing the layout orientation. You then saved the slide master as a template, opened this template, added slide content, and printed a handout and speaker notes pages. The items listed below include all the new PowerPoint skills you have learned in this chapter.

Change Slide Background Elements
Format a Slide Master Background and Apply a
    Quick Style (PPT 484)
Insert a Background Graphic into a Slide
    Master (PPT 488)
Hide and Unhide Background Graphics (PPT 499)
Apply a Fill Color to a Slide (PPT 515)
Apply a Pattern to a Slide (PPT 516)

Create and Use a Template
Save a Master as a Template (PPT 510)
Open a Template and Save a Presentation (PPT 511)

Customize and Print Handouts and Notes Using Masters
Customize a Handout Using a Handout
    Master (PPT 504)
Customize a Notes Page Using a Notes
    Master (PPT 508)
Print a Presentation (PPT 519)
Print a Handout Using the Handout
    Master (PPT 520)
Print Speaker Notes Using the Notes
    Master (PPT 521)

Customize Slide Masters
Display a Slide Master (PPT 480)
Apply Slide and Font Themes to a Slide
    Master (PPT 481)
Customize Theme Fonts (PPT 482)
Cut a Placeholder and Paste It into a Slide
    Master (PPT 493)
Rename a Slide Master and a Slide Layout (PPT 500)
Delete a Slide Layout (PPT 502)
Close Master View (PPT 510)

Insert and Format Placeholders
Delete, Move, and Add Text to a Slide Master
    Footer (PPT 485)
Format Slide Master Footer Text (PPT 486)
Insert a Placeholder into a Blank Layout (PPT 489)
Add and Format Placeholder Text (PPT 491)
Change Character Spacing (PPT 495)

Insert and Format Text Boxes
Apply a Fill to a Text Box and Increase
    Transparency (PPT 496)
Change a Text Box Internal Margin (PPT 497)
Rotate a Picture and a Text Box (PPT 498)

CONSIDER THIS

What decisions will you need to make when creating your next presentation?

Use these guidelines as you complete the assignments in this chapter and create your own slide show decks outside of this class.

1. **Plan the slide master.** Using a new slide master gives you the freedom to plan every aspect of your slide. Take care to think about the overall message you are trying to convey before you start PowerPoint and select elements for this master.

2. **Develop the slide master prior to creating presentation slides.** You can save time and create consistency when you design and build your master at the start of your PowerPoint session rather than after you have created individual slides.

3. **Decide how to distribute copies of slides.** Some audience members will desire printed copies of your slides. To conserve paper and ink, you may decide to limit the number of copies you print or to post the presentation electronically in a shared location for users to print the presentation if they so choose.

CONSIDER THIS

How should you submit solutions to questions in the assignments identified with a ☀ symbol?

Every assignment in this book contains one or more questions identified with a ☀ symbol. These questions require you to think beyond the assigned presentation. Present your solutions to the questions in the format required by your instructor. Possible formats may include one or more of these options: write the answer; create a document that contains the answer; present your answer to the class; discuss your answer in a group; record the answer as audio or video using a webcam, smartphone, or portable media player; or post answers on a blog, wiki, or website.

Apply Your Knowledge

Reinforce the skills and apply the concepts you learned in this chapter.

Applying a Slide Theme to a Slide Master, Creating a New Theme Font, and Changing the Title Layout

Note: To complete this assignment, you will be required to use the Data Files for Students. Visit www.cengage.com/ct/studentdownload for detailed instructions or contact your instructor for information about accessing the required files.

Instructions: Run PowerPoint. Open the presentation, Apply 8-1 Culinary, from the Data Files for Students.

The three slides in this presentation discuss careers available to culinary arts majors. The document you open is a partially formatted presentation. You will apply a slide theme to a slide master, create a new theme font, and change the slide master background. Your presentation should look like Figure 8–82 on the next page.

Perform the following tasks:

1. Display Slide Master view and select the Slide Master thumbnail. Change the document theme to Berlin, the colors to Red Violet, and then create a new Theme Font named Bouchet using Papyrus for the heading font and Verdana for the body font.

2. Select the Title Slide Layout (Figure 8–82a), select the title text, change the color to Pink, Accent 1 (the fifth color in the first Theme Colors row), and then align this text left. Select the subtitle text, change the font size to 32 point, align the text left, bold the text, and then apply the Fill – Indigo, Background 2, Inner Shadow WordArt style (the fifth style in the third row) to the subtitle text. Delete the slide number text box in the pink rectangle shape, type, **Since 1926,** on two lines in the pink rectangle shape, and then change the font size to 24 point. Create a background on the title slide layout by inserting the photo called Wine and Cheese, which is available on the Data Files for Students. Change the transparency to 50%, as shown in Figure 8–82a.

3. Select the Two Content Layout, select the title font and change the font color to Pink, Accent 1 (the fifth color in the first Theme Colors row). Close Slide Master view.

4. On Slide 1, type **Bouchet Academy** as the title and **Culinary Career Education** as the subtitle, as shown in Figure 8–82b.

5. On Slide 2, change the layout to Two Content. Apply the Bevel Rectangle picture style to the two photos (the seventh style in the third row) and move them to the location shown in Figure 8–82c.

6. On Slide 3, change the layout to Two Content. Increase the size of the photo to approximately 4.28" × 4.28", apply the Rotated, White picture style (the third style in the third row), and then move the photo to the location shown in Figure 8–82d.

7. If requested by your instructor, add the name of your high school mascot as the fourth bulleted paragraph on Slide 3.

8. Apply the Split transition and change the duration to 3.25 for all slides.

9. Save the presentation using the file name, Apply 8-1 Bouchet Academy.

10. Submit the revised document in the format specified by your instructor.

11. ✳ In this presentation, you created a new theme font in the Slide Master and named it Bouchet. Why? You also changed the theme colors to Red Violet. How did this improve the presentation?

Continued >

Apply Your Knowledge *continued*

(a) Title Slide Layout

(b) Slide 1

(c) Slide 2

(d) Slide 3

Figure 8–82

Extend Your Knowledge

Extend the skills you learned in this chapter and experiment with new skills. You may need to use Help to complete the assignment.

Adding a Background to a Slide Master, Adjusting Footer Content and Placeholders, Inserting and Renaming a Layout, and Applying a Quick Style to a Placeholder

Note: To complete this assignment, you will be required to use the Data Files for Students. Visit www.cengage.com/ct/studentdownload for detailed instructions or contact your instructor for information about accessing the required files.

Instructions: Run PowerPoint. Open the presentation, Extend 8-1 Early Childhood, from the Data Files for Students. You will add a background graphic to the slide master, adjust footer content and placeholders, insert and rename a layout, and apply a style to a placeholder, as shown in Figure 8–83 on page PPT 528.

Perform the following tasks:
1. Display Slide Master view and then select the Slide Master thumbnail. Add the slide number and the Fixed date 12/8/14 to the footer placeholders. *Hint*: You may need to use Help to learn how to insert the date into the footer. Delete the center text placeholder in the footer area. Move the 'Date' footer placeholder to the upper-right area of the slide master. Right-align the 'Date' placeholder text, change the color to Black, Text 1 (the second color in the first Theme Colors row), and then bold this text. Add a background texture fill style by selecting Bouquet from the preset textures (the fifth texture in the fourth row). Customize the theme fonts using Rockwell for the heading font and Arial for the body font, as shown in Figure 8–83a. Name the new font set, Childhood.

2. Select the Title Slide Layout, select the title text and the subtitle text and align the text left. Select the Title and Content Layout and apply the 90% Pattern fill to this layout.

3. Insert a layout and rename it Closing Slide (Figure 8–83b on the next page). Select the title text, change the font color to Purple (the tenth color in the Standard Colors row), and then center this text. Select the title text placeholder, change the fill to Blue, Accent 1 (the fifth color in the Theme Colors row), select the Subtle Effect – Blue, Accent 5 style (the sixth style in the fourth row), and then change the transparency to 75%. Close Slide Master view.

4. On Slide 1 (Figure 8–83c), apply the Soft Edge Oval picture style (the sixth style in the third row) to both photos. Move the photos to the right side of the slide with the photo of the twins positioned on top of the other photo. Move the title and subtitle text placeholders so the left edges are at 5.50" left of center. Move the subtitle text placeholder down so the bottom of the placeholder is at the bottom edge of the slide. Decrease the size of the blocks illustration to approximately 1.04" × 1.87" and move it below the title placeholder.

5. Select the title text, change the font color to Blue, Accent 1 (the fifth color in the first Theme Colors row), bold it, and then apply the Gray – 50%, 18 pt glow, Accent color 3 glow effect to the text (the third effect in the fourth Glow Variations row). Use Format Painter to apply these same attributes to the subtitle text. Use the Smart Guides to position the blocks illustration between the title and subtitle placeholders.

6. On Slide 2 (Figure 8–83d), change the layout to Two Content. Change the title font color to Purple (the last color in the Standard Colors row), and then bold the title text. Use Format Painter to apply this same attribute to the title text on Slide 3. Change the second line of the title text on Slide 2 to 36 point and then use the Format Painter to apply this same attribute to the second line of the title on Slide 3.

7. Convert the bulleted text on Slide 2 to the Step Up Process SmartArt graphic (the second graphic in the first Process row). Change the colors to Colorful Range – Accent Colors 5 to 6 (the fifth color in the Colorful row), change the style to Cartoon (the third style in the first 3-D row), and then increase the size of the SmartArt graphic to approximately 5.75" × 7.5". Insert the photo called Toddler 1, which is available on the Data Files for Students. Move the photo to the right side of the slide using the Smart Guide and apply the Reflected Rounded Rectangle picture style (the fifth style in the first row), as shown in Figure 8–83d.

8. On Slide 3 (Figure 8–83e), convert the bulleted text to the Stacked Venn SmartArt graphic (the second graphic in the last Relationship row). Change the colors to Colorful Range – Accent Colors 5 to 6 (the fifth color in the Colorful row), change the style to Powder (the fourth style in the first 3-D row), and then increase the size of the SmartArt graphic text to 16 point and bold it. Move the graphic to the position shown in the figure. Insert the photo called Toddler 2, which is available on the Data Files for Students. Apply the Perspective Shadow, White picture style (the fourth style in the third row), as shown in Figure 8–83e.

9. On Slide 4 (Figure 8–83f), change the layout to Closing Slide. Create a background by inserting the photo called Children Playing, which is available on the Data Files for Students.

10. If requested by your instructor, add the number of bones you have broken after the word, Skills, in the subtitle placeholder on Slide 1 (Figure 8–83c).

11. Apply the Cube transition in the Exciting category to all slides and then change the duration to 2.50 seconds.

12. Save the presentation using the file name, Extend 8-2 Early Childhood Motor Skills.

13. Submit the revised document in the format specified by your instructor.

14. ❋ In this presentation, you changed the background of some slides to Bouquet. Was this a good choice? Why? In the Slide Master, you inserted a layout and changed the title text placeholder fill color and applied a style. How did this help your presentation?

Continued >

STUDENT ASSIGNMENTS

Extend Your Knowledge *continued*

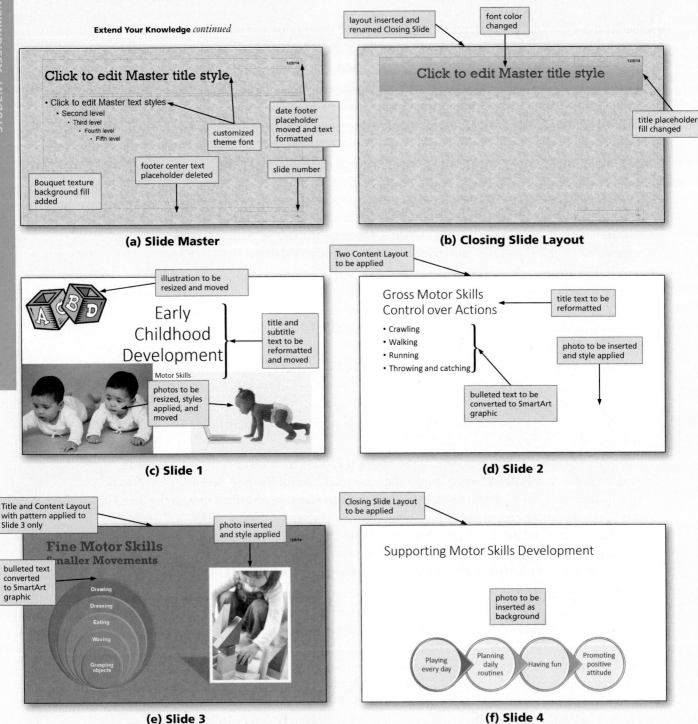

Figure 8–83

Analyze, Correct, Improve

Analyze a presentation, correct all errors, and improve it.

Changing a Font Theme and Background Style, Deleting a Placeholder and a Graphic, Hiding a Background Graphic on a Slide, and Rotating a Placeholder on a Slide Master

Note: To complete this assignment, you will be required to use the Data Files for Students. Visit www.cengage.com/ct/studentdownload for detailed instructions or contact your instructor for information about accessing the required files.

Instructions: Run PowerPoint. Open the presentation, Analyze 8-1 Rock Climbing, from the Data Files for Students. You are a rock climbing instructor and guide for PEAKS Rock Climbing

Company. Your boss asked you to prepare a presentation with information about your company to hand out to the next group of rock climbing students. Modify the slides by making the indicated corrections and improvements.

1. Correct

a. Display the Slide Master view (Figure 8–84a on the next page) and then select the Slide Master thumbnail. Change the background style from Style 10 to the Granite texture fill (second fill in third row). Change the theme font to Gil Sans MT. Delete the illustration in the lower-right corner of the slide. Close Slide Master view.

b. On Slide 1 (Figure 8–84b), cut the Peaks logo from the upper-left corner of the slide, display Slide Master view, select the Slide Master thumbnail and paste the logo and then move it to the lower-left corner of the Slide Master. Close Slide Master view.

c. On Slide 1 (Figure 8–84b), delete the photo and create a background by inserting the same photo, called Rock Climber, which is available on the Data Files for Students. Center both lines of the title text.

d. On Slide 2 (figure not shown), decrease the size of the photo to approximately 4.87" × 4.94", move it to the right side of the slide, and apply the Moderate Frame, Black picture style to the photo (the fifth style in the second row).

e. On Slide 3 (figure not shown), decrease the size of the text box so that it is not covering the logo. Move the rope photo to the upper-right corner of the slide, and move the shoes photo to the right and down slightly so it is not touching the text box. Apply the Rotated, White picture style to the shoes photo (the third style in the third row).

f. If requested by your instructor, add your mother's maiden name as the last bulleted paragraph on Slide 2.

2. Improve

a. Display the Slide Master view (Figure 8–84a) and select the Slide Master thumbnail. Delete the Date and Time, Slide number, and Footer placeholders because the Granite texture makes them difficult to view. Close Slide Master view.

b. On Slide 1, change the first line of the title font to Gil Sans Ultra Bold. Apply the WordArt style Gradient Fill – Gold, Accent 4, Outline – Accent 4 to the title (the third style in the second row). Change the text outline color to Black, Text 1 (the second color in the first Theme Colors row), and then change the outline weight to 3 pt. Change the second line of the title to Gil Sans Ultra Bold Condensed, and the size to 40 point.

c. Display the Slide Master view. Insert a new layout and rename it, Rotated Title. Move this new layout under the Slide Master. Insert a Picture placeholder in the right side of the slide. Insert a text placeholder in the center of the slide. Change the size of the title text placeholder to 1.45" × 7.5", rotate it left 90 degrees, and then change the shape fill color to Gray-50%, Accent 3 (the seventh color in the first Theme Colors row). Hide the background graphic on this layout and then move the Title placeholder to the left edge of the slide. Change character spacing to Very Loose and center the text. Close Slide Master view.

d. Change the layout on Slide 4 (figure not shown) to Rotated Title. Change the title font to Gil Sans Ultra Bold and change the font color to Dark Red (the first color in the Standard Colors row).

e. On Slides 2, 3, and 5, bold the title text (figures not shown).

f. On Slide 4, change the size of the bulleted text placeholder to approximately 3.12" × 5.2" and, if necessary, move the text placeholder to the left. Increase the size of the photo and move it to the right.

g. Change the Vortex transition to the Doors transition and then change the duration to 4.50 seconds for all slides.

h. Save the presentation using the file name, Analyze 8-1 Peaks Rock Climbing.

i. Submit the revised document in the format specified by your instructor. *Continued >*

Analyze, Correct, Improve *continued*

3. ☀ Which errors existed in the starting file? How did changing the fonts and font sizes help? How did creating a background with the rock climber photo on Slide 1 improve the look of the slide?

(a) Slide Master

(b) Slide 1

Figure 8–84

In the Labs

Design and/or create a presentation using the guidelines, concepts, and skills presented in this chapter. Labs 1 and 2, which increase in difficulty, require you to create solutions based on what you learned in the chapter; Lab 3 requires you to create a solution, which uses cloud and web technologies, by learning and investigating on your own from general guidance.

Lab 1: Deleting Slide Layouts, Rotating a Text Box and a Photo, Renaming a Slide Layout, Adding a Graphic, and Saving a Slide Master as a Template

Problem: You work for the town of Treesville in the parks and recreation division. Your director has decided to run weekly ads in the local newspaper highlighting the summer activities planned at Center Park. He has asked you to set up a template so that he can use it for future presentations about Center Park. He asked you to prepare the first week's ad and the ad for the annual July 4th fireworks event. You decide to do a PowerPoint presentation so that the ads also can run on a kiosk at the library and the town hall. You create the slide master template shown in Figure 8–85a, title slide layout and July 4th layout shown in Figures 8–85b and 8–85d. You create the two ads shown in Figures 8–85c and 8–85e.

Note: To complete this assignment, you will be required to use the Data Files for Students. Visit www.cengage.com/ct/studentdownload for detailed instructions or contact your instructor for information about accessing the required files.

Instructions: Perform the following tasks:

1. Open the presentation, Lab 8-1 Center Park, from the Data Files for Students.

2. Display Slide Master view. Delete all layouts except the Title Slide Layout, Title and Content Layout, and the Blank Layout. Select the Slide Master thumbnail. Create a background by inserting the photo called Park, which is available on the Data Files for Students. Delete all the placeholders except for the center footer text placeholder. Add the text, `Ad for week of:` in the center footer placeholder and change the font color to Black, Text 1. Close Slide Master view.

3. Select the Treesville logo and the WordArt on the Slide 1 and cut and paste it to the slide master. Close Slide Master view and then delete Slide 1. Click in the slide area to add the first slide with the new slide master. Save this file as a template and name it Center Park Template (Figure 8–85a).

4. Save the Center Park Template file as a presentation with the name, Lab 8-1 Treesville Summer Ads (Figures 8–85c and 8–85e).

5. Display Slide Master view and select the Title Slide Layout (Figure 8–85b). Delete all the placeholders except for the center footer placeholder. Insert a Rectangle shape in the lower-center area of the slide, type, **This Week in the Park**, in the shape, change the font size to 32 point, and then align the text to the top of the shape. Resize the shape to 5.93" × 13.33", change the transparency to 55%, and then move the shape so the bottom edge is at the bottom of the slide, as shown in Figure 8–85b. Close Slide Master view.

6. On Slide 1 (Figure 8–85c), change the layout to Title Slide. Insert the two photos called Volleyball and Carnival, and the illustration called Music, which are available on the Data Files for Students. Apply the Soft Edge Oval picture style (sixth style in the fourth row) to the Volleyball and Carnival photos. Insert a text box under the music illustration and type, **Enjoy music with DJ John every evening from 6 - 10 p.m.**, change the font size to 22 point, change the font color to Yellow (the fourth color in the Standard Colors row), and then center the text. Copy and paste this text box two times. Type **Volleyball tournaments!** in the second text box and type **Carnival - Fun for all ages!** in the third text box. Move these text boxes under the respective photos as shown in Figure 8–85c.

7. Display Slide Master view and select the Blank Layout. Insert the photo called Flag, which is available on the Data Files for Students. Adjust the size of the photo to approximately 2.59" × 2.07", rotate it -57 degrees, and then move it to the upper-right area of the slide. Insert a text box and type **Enjoy a day of family fun!** in the text box, increase the font size to 32 point, change the font color to White, Background 1 (the first color in the first Theme Colors row), and then center the text. Rotate the text box -34 degrees and then move it to the location shown in Figure 8–85d. Rename this layout, July 4th. Close Slide Master view.

8. Insert a new slide with the July 4th layout. Insert the two photos called Family and Fireworks, which are available on the Data Files for Students. Apply the Reflected Perspective Right picture style (the second style in the fourth row) to the Family photo and apply the Bevel Perspective Left, White picture

(a) Center Park Template

(b) Title Slide Layout

(c) Slide 1 – Ad1

(d) July 4th Layout – Ad2

Figure 8–85 (Continued) *Continued >*

In the Labs *continued*

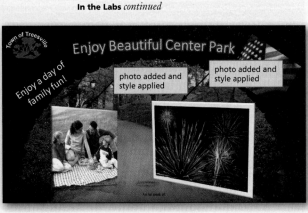

(e) Slide 2 – Ad2

Figure 8–85

style (the third style in the fourth row) to the Fireworks photo, and then move the photos to the locations shown in Figure 8–85e.

9. If requested by your instructor, add the time you were born after the word, tournaments in the left text box on Slide 1 (Figure 8–85c on the previous page).

10. Submit the document in the format specified by your instructor.

11. ✸ In Step 3, you saved the presentation as a template. Why? How did adding a shape with a transparent background to the title slide layout help your presentation?

Lab 2: Formatting a Slide Master Background, Inserting a Placeholder into a Blank Layout, Rotating a Text Box, Applying a Fill to a Text Box, Changing a Text Box Internal Margin, and Creating Handouts Using the Handout and Notes Masters

Problem: You are the public relations manager for a brand new office design company. There are two events coming up in your town. One is a local business seminar and the other is a job fair. Because your company is new to the area, you decide these events would be beneficial to introduce your company to the local market. You created a presentation with four slides, as shown in Figures 8–86c through 8–86f.

Note: To complete this assignment, you will be required to use the Data Files for Students. Visit www.cengage.com/ct/studentdownload for detailed instructions or contact your instructor for information about accessing the required files.

Instructions: Perform the following tasks:

1. Open the presentation, Lab 8-2 Jay Jones, from the Data Files for Students. Display Slide Master view. Select the Slide Master thumbnail. Create a background by using a solid fill, select the color Orange (the third color in the first Standard Colors row), and then change the transparency to 65%.

2. Display the Blank Layout. Insert a Text Placeholder on the right side of the slide and adjust the size to 7.5" × 1.35". Select all the text in the placeholder, remove the bullet, and type **Jay Jones Office Designers**, change the font to Castellar, increase the font size to 36 point, center this text, and then rotate all text 270 degrees. Apply the shape quick style Light 1 Outline, Colored Fill – Gray-50%, Accent 3 (the fourth style in the third row). Change the text box left internal margin to 0.2" and change the top internal margin to 1". The text should be on two lines as shown in Figure 8–86a. Cut and paste this placeholder to the Slide Master and move it to the right edge of the slide as shown in the figure.

3. With the Slide Master still open, insert the illustration called Logo, which is available on the Data Files for Students. Rotate the illustration left 90 degrees and move it to the top of the new text placeholder, as shown in Figure 8–86a.

4. Display the Title Slide Layout (Figure 8–86b) and delete the title placeholder. Align the subtitle placeholder to the bottom edge of the slide and change the size to 1.36" × 12".

Insert a Picture placeholder in the upper-left corner of the slide, change the size to 6.14" × 12", and then move it to the area shown in Figure 8–86b.

5. Display the Two Content Layout. Change the title font size to 48 point, the color to Purple (the tenth color in the Standard Colors row), and then bold this text. Close Slide Master view.

6. Select Slide 1 and change the layout to Title Slide. Insert the photo called JJ Office, which is available on the Data Files for Students. Select the subtitle text and bold the text. With the subtitle placeholder still selected, use the eyedropper to match the Purple color on the left side of the third floor of the office building, as shown in Figure 8–86c.

7. On Slides 2 through 4 (Figures 8–86d through 8–86f), adjust the sizes of the photos so they are not overlapping the titles or the text on the right side of the slides.

8. If requested by your instructor, type the name of the last TV program you watched as the fifth bulleted paragraph on Slide 4.

9. Apply the Doors transition in the Exciting category and then change the duration to 3.00 seconds for all slides.

10. Open the handout master, change the orientation to landscape. Type `Jay Jones Office Designers` as the header text. Delete the date in the upper-right header text box. Insert the JJ Office photo, change the size to 2.09" × 4.13", and then move it to the lower-right area of the handout master, as shown in Figure 8–86g. Close the Master View.

11. Open the notes master and then type `Jay Jones Office Designers` as the header text. Delete the date in the upper-right header text box. Insert the JJ Office photo, change the size to 1.2" × 2.38", and then move it to the right side of the notes master, as shown in Figure 8–86h. Close the Master View.

12. Save the presentation using the file name, Lab 8-2 Jay Jones Office Designers.

13. Submit the document in the format specified by your instructor.

14. ✹ Why did you add a background to all slides and why did you choose a 65% transparency? Did inserting a text placeholder with the company name and logo help the presentation? How?

(a) Slide Master

(b) Title Slide Layout

(c) Slide 1

(d) Slide 2

Figure 8–86 (Continued)

Continued >

In the Labs *continued*

(e) Slide 3

(f) Slide 4

(g) Handout Master

(h) Notes Master

Figure 8–86

Lab 3: Expand Your World: Cloud and Web Technologies
Linking to a YouTube Video

Problem: You have created a presentation and want to play a video from an online website, such as YouTube or a news or sports organization, while running a slide show. Some websites encourage users to share video clips, while others restrict users from performing this process. The videos are not downloaded and inserted, or **embedded**, in the file; instead, they are **linked** to the presentation so that when the slide show is running and an Internet connection is present, the user can click the Play button to begin watching the video. PowerPoint includes commands on the Insert Video dialog box to insert a video clip from YouTube and from other websites.

Note: You will need Internet access to complete this assignment. If you do not have Internet access, read this assignment without performing the instructions.

Instructions: Perform the following tasks:
1. Log on to your Microsoft Windows account. In PowerPoint, open the Aquatic Center presentation you created in this chapter. At the end of the presentation, insert one slide using the Miscellaneous layout and then add the title text, "Swimming Safety Tips" on Slide 4. Save the file with the new filename, Lab 8-3 Aquatic Center with Video.
2. With Slide 4 displaying, tap or click the Insert Video icon in the content placeholder to display the Insert Video dialog box.

3. If necessary, tap or click the YouTube icon in the 'Also insert from' area to display the YouTube search box. Tap or click the YouTube search text box, type `swimming safely` as the search text, and then tap or click the Search button (the magnifying glass) or press the ENTER key. Watch several videos on the website and then select one you desire to link to your PowerPoint presentation.

4. Tap or click the Insert button (Insert Video dialog box) to display the selected clip on Slide 4. Increase the clip size and then add a border and an effect.

5. If requested by your instructor, enter the name of the city or county in which you were born in the Notes pane.

6. ✹ Do videos add to the audience's ability to retain information presented during a presentation? Why did you select this specific video to display on Slide 4?

Consider This: Your Turn

Apply your creative thinking and problem-solving skills to design and implement a solution.

1. Design and Create a Presentation about Tornado Safety Awareness
Personal

Part 1:   There have been a lot of tornadoes reported all over the country. Some areas seem to have more tornadoes than others, but they can occur anywhere. Most tornadoes form from thunderstorms when two air masses (warm moist air and cool dry air) meet. A tornado can touch down to the ground from the storm and can produce wind speeds of up to 300 mph. The paths of tornadoes can be as wide as 50 miles. A funnel cloud is a cone-shaped rotating air column that extends down from the thunderstorm; if it touches the ground, it is called a tornado. If you hear about a tornado watch, tornadoes are possible in your area, and you should be alert and listen to the news. If you hear there is a tornado warning, a tornado could be close by and you should seek shelter right away. Your family does not have a plan if a tornado strikes. You decide to do a PowerPoint presentation to share with your family and friends. Information to include in your presentation is how to prepare ahead of time, such as putting together an emergency kit with food and water. You also should discuss what to do during a tornado. Use the concepts and techniques presented in this chapter to prepare a presentation. Select a suitable theme, and use WordArt or SmartArt graphics where appropriate. The presentation can contain photos, illustrations, and videos. You can use photos and illustrations from Office.com if they are appropriate for this topic. Submit your assignment in the format specified by your instructor.

Part 2:   ✹ You made several decisions while creating the presentation in this assignment: where to place text, how to format the text (such as font, font size, and colors), which image(s) to use, what shapes, WordArt, and SmartArt graphics to add to the slide master to make the presentation look professional and consistent. What was the rationale behind each of these decisions? When you reviewed the document, what further revisions did you make and why? Where would you recommend showing this slide show?

2. Design and Create a Presentation about Boxing for Fitness
Professional

Part 1:   As a personal trainer, you feel it is important to give your clients some variety in their workout routines. You enjoy boxing for fitness. It is a great full-body cardio workout and can be a lot of fun. It is a great way to burn calories. You decide to put together a presentation for the next open house at your fitness center. You want to give your clients and others information about boxing and what they may need to get started. Your fitness center has some of the equipment already such as heavy bags (for hitting), gloves in various sizes, and jump ropes for training.

Continued >

Consider This: Your Turn *continued*

The wraps that are worn under the gloves to cover the knuckles and prevent bruising and scrapes should be purchased by each individual. You also will mention some of the techniques used such as proper stance. You will describe the different punches like jabs, hooks, and uppercuts. The presentation could contain photos, illustrations, and videos. You can use your own photos and videos or use photos and illustrations from Office.com if they are appropriate for this topic. Customize your presentation by creating new layouts in the slide master to add interest to the presentation. Submit your assignment in the format specified by your instructor.

Part 2: ✳ You made several decisions while creating the presentation in this assignment: where to place text, how to format the text (such as font, font size, and colors), which image(s) to use, what shapes, WordArt, and SmartArt graphics to add to the slide master to make the presentation look professional and consistent. What was the rationale behind each of these decisions? When you reviewed the document, what further revisions did you make and why? Where would you recommend showing this slide show?

3. Design and Create a Presentation about Distracted Driving
Research and Collaboration

Part 1: Your criminal justice class is studying the effects of distracted driving. When you are driving any kind of vehicle, you need to have full concentration. Motorists continue to use cell phones despite the fact that the majority of states have banned texting while driving and several states now prohibit use of a phone without a hands-free device. Cell phone usage is not the only distraction while driving. Eating and drinking, applying make-up and nail polish, even listening to the radio or books on tape can distract you while you are driving. Your class has divided into three groups. One group will conduct a survey among students and non-students in the area about use of cell phones or other distracted behavior while driving. Another group will research the statistics from state to state and laws that have been passed regarding distracted driving. Your group will pull all the information together and create a PowerPoint presentation. Use at least three objectives found at the beginning of this chapter to develop the presentation. Print handouts and speaker notes for the class presentation. Customize a template for your school that may be used for other reports like this. You can use your own photos and videos or those available from Office.com if they are appropriate for this topic.

Part 2: ✳ You made several decisions while creating the presentation in this assignment: where to place text, how to format the text (such as font, font size, and colors), which image(s) to use, what shapes, WordArt, and SmartArt graphics to add to the slide master to make the presentation look professional and consistent. What was the rationale behind each of these decisions? When you reviewed the document, what further revisions did you make and why? Where would you recommend showing this slide show?

Learn Online

Reinforce what you learned in this chapter with games, exercises, training, and many other online activities and resources.

Student Companion Site   Reinforcement activities and resources are available at no additional cost on www.cengagebrain.com. Visit www.cengage.com/ct/studentdownload for detailed instructions about accessing the resources available at the Student Companion Site.

SAM   Put your skills into practice with SAM! If you have a SAM account, go to www.cengage .com/sam2013 to access SAM assignments for this chapter.

9 | Modifying a Presentation Using Graphical Elements

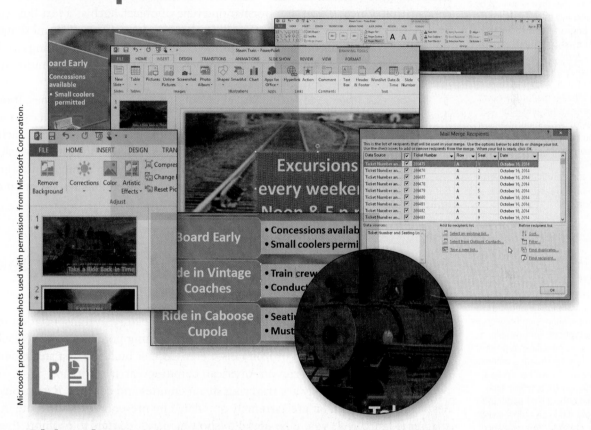

Microsoft product screenshots used with permission from Microsoft Corporation.

Objectives

You will have mastered the material in this chapter when you can:

- Change a text box outline color, weight, and style
- Set text box formatting as the default for new text boxes
- Apply a gradient, texture, pattern, and effects to a text box
- Convert WordArt to SmartArt
- Reorder SmartArt shapes
- Promote and demote SmartArt text

- Add and remove SmartArt shapes
- Convert a SmartArt graphic to text
- Customize the ribbon
- Combine and subtract shapes
- Create a handout by exporting files to Microsoft Word
- Save the presentation as a picture presentation

9 | Modifying a Presentation Using Graphical Elements

BTW
Identifying Shapes
Most objects in our world are composed of shapes: a circle, square, and triangle. Artists see objects as combinations of these shapes and begin their drawings by sketching these basic forms in proportion to each other. For example, a tree has the form of a circle for the branches and a rectangle for the trunk. A car has the form of a rectangle for the body, a smaller rectangle for the passenger compartment, and four circles for the wheels. Become observant of the relationships between objects in your world as you learn to use PowerPoint's drawing tools.

Introduction

PowerPoint's themes determine the default characteristics of slide objects. Colors, border weights and styles, fills, effects, and other formatting options give the slides a unique character. You can create your own designs for text boxes, shapes, lines, and other slide content, and then reuse these graphical objects throughout the presentation. Once you learn to format one type of object, such as a text box, you can use similar techniques to format other slide objects, such as SmartArt and shapes. One efficient way to create consistent graphical elements is to save your settings as the default. Then, when you insert the same objects later during the presentation design process, they will have the same characteristics as the initial element.

SmartArt graphics have individual layouts, styles, and color schemes. If one of these designs does not meet the specific needs of your slide content, you can modify the graphic by adding shapes, reordering the current shapes, and changing each element's size and location. You also can convert the SmartArt to text or to a shape if SmartArt is not the best method of conveying your ideas to an audience. PowerPoint's myriad formatting options allow you to tailor graphical elements to best fit your unique design needs.

BTW
Using Metaphorical Shapes
Use your imagination to use simple shapes and objects as metaphors. For example, a broken pencil can represent a stressful situation whereas a slice of cake can serve as imagery for a simple task. Make the shape large and bold, and use as few words as possible. Your audience should be able to understand and relate to the images without much explanation on the slides or from the speaker.

Project — Presentation with Customized Text Boxes, SmartArt, and Shapes

The invention of the steam locomotive changed the history of transportation forever. In the early 1800s, trains powered by steam were gaining popularity and replacing carts pulled by horses on wooden or iron rails. Peter Cooper built the first steam engine, called the Tom Thumb, to run on American common-carrier railroads.

Railroad buffs today are restoring steam engines and coaches. Excursions to destinations near and far are extremely popular. The presentation you create in this chapter (Figure 9–1) would be useful to show at visitor centers to promote these trips. All four slides are created by modifying a starting file that has a variety of content. The title slide (Figure 9–1a) contains a text box that is formatted with an outline style, a weight, and a color. These modifications are saved as the default settings for all other text boxes inserted into other slides. The second slide (Figure 9–1b) features a new colorful picture and a formatted text box. The text on Slide 3 (Figure 9–1c) is converted from WordArt to a SmartArt graphic. The layout, style, color, and shapes are changed and enhanced. The final slide (Figure 9–1d) has bulleted text converted from a SmartArt graphic; it also has a steam engine composed of formatted shapes. After the slides are created, you export the file to Microsoft Word to create a handout (Figures 9–1e and 9–1f) and then save the presentation as a picture presentation.

FILE   HOME   INSERT   DESIGN   TRANSITIONS   ANIMATIONS   SLIDE SHOW   REVIEW   VIEW

(a) Slide 1

formatted text box

picture changed from original presentation

pattern applied to inserted text box

(b) Slide 2

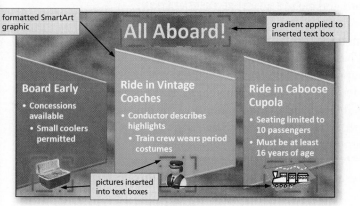

formatted SmartArt graphic

gradient applied to inserted text box

pictures inserted into text boxes

(c) Slide 3

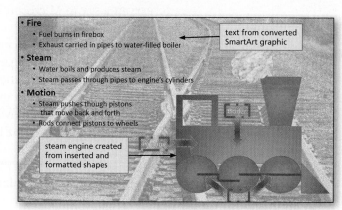

text from converted SmartArt graphic

steam engine created from inserted and formatted shapes

(d) Slide 4

notes are displayed beside slide thumbnails

(e) Microsoft Word Handout – Page 1

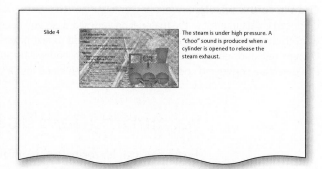

(f) Microsoft Word Handout – Page 2

Figure 9–1

Roadmap

In this chapter, you will learn how to create the slides shown in Figure 9–1 on the previous page. The following roadmap identifies general activities you will perform as you progress through this chapter:

1. INSERT and CUSTOMIZE TEXT BOXES by changing the weight, color, and style and by adding an effect, pattern, and fill.

2. CONVERT WORDART TO SMARTART and then FORMAT by changing bullet levels, the layout, and the shape.

3. INSERT and FORMAT SHAPES.

4. DRAW and FORMAT LINES.

5. CUSTOMIZE THE RIBBON by adding a new group and buttons.

6. EXPORT a FILE to Microsoft Word and CREATE a PICTURE PRESENTATION.

At the beginning of step instructions throughout the chapter, you will see an abbreviated form of this roadmap. The abbreviated roadmap uses colors to indicate chapter progress: gray means the chapter is beyond that activity; blue means the task being shown is covered in that activity, and black means that activity is yet to be covered. For example, the following abbreviated roadmap indicates the chapter would be showing a task in the 3 INSERT & FORMAT SHAPES activity.

1 INSERT & CUSTOMIZE TEXT BOXES | 2 CONVERT WORDART TO SMARTART & FORMAT | **3 INSERT & FORMAT SHAPES**
4 DRAW & FORMAT LINES | 5 CUSTOMIZE THE RIBBON | 6 EXPORT FILE & CREATE PICTURE PRESENTATION

Use the abbreviated roadmap as a progress guide while you read or step through the instructions in this chapter.

To Run PowerPoint and Save a File

If you are using a computer to step through the project in this chapter and you want your screens to match the figures in this book, you should change your computer's resolution to 1366 × 768. The following steps run PowerPoint and then save a file.

1 Run PowerPoint. If necessary, maximize the PowerPoint window.

2 Open the presentation, Train, located on the Data Files for Students.

3 Save the presentation using the file name, Steam Train.

One of the few differences between Windows 7 and Windows 8 occurs in the steps to run PowerPoint. If you are using Windows 7, tap or click the Start button, type **PowerPoint** in the 'Search programs and files' box, tap or click PowerPoint 2013, and then, if necessary, maximize the PowerPoint window. For a summary of the steps to run PowerPoint in Windows 7, refer to the Quick Reference located at the back of this book.

CONSIDER THIS

Choose colors wisely.

Color can create interest in the material on your slides, so you need to think about which colors best support the message you want to share with your audience. The color you add to text boxes signals that the viewer should pay attention to the contents. Orange, red, and yellow are considered warm colors and will be among the first colors your viewers perceive on your slide. Blue and green are considered cool colors, and they often blend into a background and are less obvious than the warm colors.

Formatting Text Boxes

Text boxes can be formatted in a variety of ways to draw attention to slide content. You can apply formatting, such as fill color, gradient, texture, and pattern. You can add a picture; change the outline color, weight, and style; and then set margins and alignment. Once you determine the desired effects for a text box, you can save these settings as a default to achieve consistency and save time. Then, each time you insert another text box, the same settings will be applied.

In the following pages, you will perform these tasks on Slide 1:

1. Insert a text box into Slide 1.
2. Type text into the text box.
3. Change the text box outline color.
4. Change the text box outline weight.
5. Change the text box outline style.
6. Apply a glow effect to the text box.
7. Change the text box text to WordArt.
8. Increase the WordArt font size and center the paragraph in the text box.
9. Set the text box formatting as the default for new text boxes.

Once the text box formatting is complete on Slide 1, you then will perform these tasks on Slide 2:

1. Insert a text box and enter text.
2. Apply a pattern to the text box.
3. Change the text box pattern foreground and background colors.
4. Change the Slide 2 picture.

You also will perform these tasks on Slide 3:

1. Insert a text box and enter text.
2. Apply a gradient to the text box.
3. Align the text box in the center of the slide.

To Insert a Text Box and Text

The default text box is displayed with the Calibri font and has no border, fill, or effects. To begin customizing the Steam Train presentation, you will insert a text box and then type the text that serves as the title to your presentation. The following steps insert a text box and enter text into the text box.

1 Display the INSERT tab, tap or click the Text Box button (INSERT tab | Text group), position the pointer in the grass below the engine's front wheel on Slide 1, and then tap or click to insert the new text box.

2 Type **Take a Ride Back in Time** as the text box text (Figure 9–2 on the next page).

Q&A
Do I need to position the text box in the precise location indicated in Figure 9–2?
No. You will reposition the text box later in this chapter after you have made the formatting changes.

Can I change the shape of the text box?
Yes. By default, a rectangular text box is inserted. If you want to use a different shape, select the text box, display the DRAWING TOOLS FORMAT tab, tap or click the Edit Shape button (DRAWING TOOLS FORMAT tab | Insert Shapes group), point to Change Shape in the list, and then tap or click the desired new shape.

BTW

The Ribbon and Screen Resolution
PowerPoint may change how the groups and buttons within the groups appear on the ribbon, depending on the computer's screen resolution. Thus, your ribbon may look different from the ones in this book if you are using a screen resolution other than 1366 × 768.

BTW

Q&As
For a complete list of the Q&As found in many of the step-by-step sequences in this book, visit the Q&A resource on the Student Companion Site located on www.cengagebrain.com. For detailed instructions about accessing available resources, visit www.cengage.com/ct/studentdownload or see the inside back cover of this book.

Figure 9–2

To Change a Text Box Outline Weight

1 INSERT & CUSTOMIZE TEXT BOXES | 2 CONVERT WORDART TO SMARTART & FORMAT | 3 INSERT & FORMAT SHAPES

4 DRAW & FORMAT LINES | 5 CUSTOMIZE THE RIBBON | 6 EXPORT FILE & CREATE PICTURE PRESENTATION

The first graphical change you will make to the text box is to increase the thickness of its border, which is called the outline. *Why? This thicker line is a graphical element that helps to call attention to the box.* The weight, or thickness, of the text box border is measured in points. The following steps increase the outline weight.

- Tap or click FORMAT on the ribbon to display the DRAWING TOOLS FORMAT tab.

- Tap or click the Shape Outline arrow (DRAWING TOOLS FORMAT tab | Shape Styles group) to display the Shape Outline gallery.

- Tap or click Weight in the Shape Outline gallery to display the Weight list (Figure 9–3).

Figure 9–3

- If you are using a mouse, point to 6 pt to display a live preview of this outline line weight (Figure 9–4).

 Experiment

- If you are using a mouse, point to various line weights on the Weight list and watch the border weights on the text box change.

- Tap or click 6 pt to add an outline around the text box.

Figure 9–4

To Change a Text Box Outline Color

1 INSERT & CUSTOMIZE TEXT BOXES | 2 CONVERT WORDART TO SMARTART & FORMAT | 3 INSERT & FORMAT SHAPES
4 DRAW & FORMAT LINES | 5 CUSTOMIZE THE RIBBON | 6 EXPORT FILE & CREATE PICTURE PRESENTATION

The default outline color in the Office Theme is black. In this project, you will change the outline color to blue. *Why? The majority of people state that blue is their favorite color. In addition, blue contrasts well with the black-and-white photo in the slide background.* The following steps change the text box outline color.

1

- With the text box still selected, tap or click the Shape Outline arrow (DRAWING TOOLS FORMAT tab | Shape Styles group) to display the Shape Outline gallery.

- If you are using a mouse, point to Blue in the Standard Colors area to display a live preview of that outline color on the text box (Figure 9–5).

 Experiment

- If you are using a mouse, point to various colors in the Shape Outline gallery and watch the border colors on the text box change.

2

- Tap or click Blue to change the text box border color.

Figure 9–5

To Change a Text Box Outline Style

The default outline style is a solid line. You can add interest by changing the style to dashes, dots, or a combination of dashes and dots. The following steps change the text box outline style to Long Dash Dot. *Why? The dashes in this pattern resemble the rails and the dots resemble the shorter railroad ties that anchor the rails.*

- Tap or click the Shape Outline arrow (DRAWING TOOLS FORMAT tab | Shape Styles group) to display the Shape Outline gallery.

- Tap or click Dashes to display the Dashes list.

- If you are using a mouse, point to Long Dash Dot to display a live preview of this outline style (Figure 9–6).

 Experiment

- Point to various styles in the Shape Outline gallery and watch the borders on the text box change.

- Tap or click Long Dash Dot to change the text box border style.

Figure 9–6

To Apply an Effect to a Text Box

PowerPoint provides a variety of visual effects to add to the text box. They include shadow, glow, reflection, and 3-D rotation. The following steps apply a glow effect to the text box. *Why? The background photo has a soft texture, so you can coordinate with this soft effect by adding a glow effect to the text box.*

- Tap or click the Shape Effects button (DRAWING TOOLS FORMAT tab | Shape Styles group) to display the Shape Effects gallery.

- Tap or click Glow to display the Glow gallery.

- If you are using a mouse, point to Blue, 18 pt glow, Accent color 1 (first color in the fourth row in the Glow Variations area) to display a live preview of this outline effect (Figure 9–7).

 Experiment

- If you are using a mouse, point to various effects in the Glow gallery and watch the glow effects change on the text box.

- Tap or click the Blue, 18 pt glow, Accent color 1 variation to apply the glow effect.

Figure 9–7

To Format Text Box Text

The text box outline color, width, line style, and effect are set, so you now can choose a font and font size that complement the formatting changes. A WordArt style can add visual interest to the text box. The following steps change the text box text to WordArt, change the font size, and center the text in the text box.

1 Select all the text box text, tap or click the WordArt Styles More button (DRAWING TOOLS FORMAT tab | WordArt Styles group) to expand the gallery, and then tap or click Pattern Fill – Blue, Accent 1, Light Downward Diagonal Outline - Accent 1 (fourth letter A in fourth row) to apply this style.

2 Increase the font size to 66 point.

3 Center the text in the text box. If necessary, drag the text box to the location shown in Figure 9–8.

Figure 9–8

BTW

Touch Screen Differences
The Office and Windows interfaces may vary if you are using a touch screen. For this reason, you might notice that the function or appearance of your touch screen differs slightly from this chapter's presentation.

BTW

Line Spacing Measurements
The lower part of each letter rests on an imaginary line called the baseline. The space between the baseline of one row of type and the baseline of the row beneath it is called line spacing. Typically, the line spacing is 120 percent of the font size. For example, if the font size is 10 point, the line spacing is 12 point so that two points of space are displayed between the lines.

To Set Text Box Formatting as the Default

1 INSERT & CUSTOMIZE TEXT BOXES | 2 CONVERT WORDART TO SMARTART & FORMAT | 3 INSERT & FORMAT SHAPES
4 DRAW & FORMAT LINES | 5 CUSTOMIZE THE RIBBON | 6 EXPORT FILE & CREATE PICTURE PRESENTATION

The text box you inserted and formatted has a variety of visual elements that work well with the steam engine picture and overall theme. You can insert text boxes with the same formatting into other slides in the presentation. *Why? To save time and ensure all the formatting changes are applied consistently, you can set the formatting of one text box as the default for all other text boxes you insert into the presentation.* The steps on the next page set the text box on Slide 1 as the default.

1

- Press and hold or right-click the text box outline to display the shortcut menu (Figure 9–9).

2

- Tap or click 'Set as Default Text Box' on the shortcut menu to set the text box formatting as the default for any new text boxes.

Q&A What should I do if the 'Set as Default Text Box' command is not displayed on the shortcut menu? Repeat Step 1 and be certain to tap or click the text box border, not the interior of the box.

Does setting the default text box affect all presentations or just the current one? Only the current presentation is affected.

Figure 9–9

BTW
Adding Contrast for Energy
The samples in the Color gallery columns range from light to dark. If you want your graphic to have a high level of energy, consider using colors at opposite ends of the columns to add a dramatic effect. The greater the contrast, the higher the energy. In contrast, if your goal is to give your graphic a peaceful feeling, use colors in the same row that have the same levels of intensity.

To Insert a Formatted Text Box and Enter Text

Any new text boxes you insert will have the same formatting you applied to the Slide 1 text box. You want to emphasize to your presentation viewers that train excursions are offered twice daily, so a text box on Slide 2 is a good place to state this information. The following steps insert a formatted text box into Slide 2 and enter text.

1 Display Slide 2, display the INSERT tab, and then tap or click the Text Box button.

2 Insert the text box into the center of the slide and then type **Excursions** as the first line of the text box text.

3 Press SHIFT+ENTER to insert a line break and then type **every weekend** as the second text box line.

4 Press SHIFT+ENTER to insert a line break and then type **Noon & 5 p.m.** as the third text box line.

5 If necessary, drag the text box to the location shown in Figure 9–10.

Figure 9–10

To Apply a Pattern to a Text Box

Why? A pattern fill can call attention to a text box. PowerPoint provides a Pattern gallery, allowing you to change the appearance of the text box with a variety of horizontal and vertical lines, dots, dashes, and stripes. If desired, you can change the default fill foreground and background colors. The following steps apply a pattern to the Slide 2 text box and change the foreground and background colors.

1

- Press and hold or right-click anywhere on the Slide 2 text box to display the shortcut menu (Figure 9–11).

Figure 9–11

2

- Tap or click Format Shape on the shortcut menu to display the Format Shape pane.

- If necessary, tap or click FILL to expand the FILL section. Tap or click Pattern fill to display the Pattern gallery and the 5% pattern on the text box (Figure 9–12).

Q&A Can I experiment with previewing the patterns on the text box?
No, the live preview function is not available.

Can the default pattern gallery color vary?
Yes. You may find that your default color is black rather than the shade of blue shown in the figure.

Figure 9–12

3

- Tap or click the Narrow vertical pattern (third pattern in fourth row) to apply this pattern to the Slide 2 text box.

Q&A How can I delete a pattern if I decide not to apply one to my slide?
If you already have applied the pattern, tap or click the Undo button on the Quick Access Toolbar.

- Scroll down the Format Shape pane and then tap or click the Foreground button to display the color gallery (Figure 9–13).

Figure 9–13

Q&A Can the default foreground color vary in the gallery?
Yes. You may find that your default color is black rather than the shade of blue shown in the figure.

4

- Tap or click Light Blue (seventh color in the Standard Colors row) to apply this color to the text box pattern and to display the Pattern gallery with the new foreground color.

- Tap or click the Background button to display a color gallery (Figure 9–14).

Figure 9–14

- Tap or click Dark Blue (ninth color in the Standard Colors row) to apply this color to the text box background and to display the Pattern gallery with the new background color (Figure 9–15).

6

- Tap or click the Close button to close the Format Shape pane.

Figure 9–15

To Apply a Gradient Fill to a Text Box

1 INSERT & CUSTOMIZE TEXT BOXES | 2 CONVERT WORDART TO SMARTART & FORMAT | 3 INSERT & FORMAT SHAPES
4 DRAW & FORMAT LINES | 5 CUSTOMIZE THE RIBBON | 6 EXPORT FILE & CREATE PICTURE PRESENTATION

Why? *A gradient fill is another type of format you can apply to create interest in a slide element.* It blends one color into another shade of the same color or another color. PowerPoint provides several preset gradients, or you can create your own custom color mix. The following steps insert a text box into Slide 3 and then apply a gradient fill.

1

- Display Slide 3, display the INSERT tab, and then insert a text box near the top of the slide.

- Type **All Aboard!** as the text box text, and if necessary, drag the text box to the location shown in Figure 9–16.

Figure 9–16

- Tap or click the
DRAWING TOOLS
FORMAT tab and
then tap or click
the Shape Fill arrow
(DRAWING TOOLS
FORMAT tab | Shape
Styles group) to
display the Shape
Fill gallery.

- Tap or click Gradient
to display the
Gradient gallery
(Figure 9–17).

 Experiment

- If you are using a
mouse, point to
various fills in the
Gradient gallery and
watch the interior of
the text box change.

Figure 9–17

- Tap or click From Center (second variation in the second row in the Dark Variations area) to apply the gradient fill.

To Center a Text Box

1 INSERT & CUSTOMIZE TEXT BOXES | 2 CONVERT WORDART TO SMARTART & FORMAT | 3 INSERT & FORMAT SHAPES
4 DRAW & FORMAT LINES | 5 CUSTOMIZE THE RIBBON | 6 EXPORT FILE & CREATE PICTURE PRESENTATION

The text box on Slide 3 will serve as the title. You could attempt to center it horizontally on the slide and use the rulers to aid you in this process. You also can use PowerPoint's align feature. *Why? Using the Align command is a more efficient method of centering the text box between the left and right edges of the slide.* You can align a slide element horizontally along the left or right sides or in the center of the slide, and you also can align an element vertically along the top, bottom, or middle of the slide. The following steps align the Slide 3 text box horizontally.

- With the Slide 3 text
box selected, tap
or click the Align
button (DRAWING
TOOLS FORMAT tab |
Arrange group) to
display the Align
menu (Figure 9–18).

Figure 9–18

2

- Tap or click Align Center to center the text box horizontally on the slide (Figure 9–19).

Q&A Can I position a text box in a precise location on a slide? Yes. With the text box selected, press and hold or right-click a border of the box to display the shortcut menu and then tap or click Format Shape on the shortcut menu to display the Format Shape pane. Tap or click the Size & Properties icon, and then tap or click POSITION and enter Horizontal position and Vertical position measurements. Specify if these measurements should be from the Top Left Corner or the Center of the text box and then tap or click the Close button (Format Shape pane).

Figure 9–19

To Change a Slide Picture

1 INSERT & CUSTOMIZE TEXT BOXES | 2 CONVERT WORDART TO SMARTART & FORMAT | 3 INSERT & FORMAT SHAPES
4 DRAW & FORMAT LINES | 5 CUSTOMIZE THE RIBBON | 6 EXPORT FILE & CREATE PICTURE PRESENTATION

PowerPoint allows you to change a picture on a slide easily. The following steps change the Slide 2 picture. *Why? The photograph on Slide 2 features crossing train tracks, but the background does not have much contrast or many rich colors. A more dramatic photograph of tracks is located on the Data Files for Students.*

1

- Display Slide 2, tap or click anywhere on the picture except the text box to select the picture, and then tap or click the PICTURE TOOLS FORMAT tab (Figure 9–20).

Figure 9–20

● Tap or click the Change Picture button (PICTURE TOOLS FORMAT tab | Adjust group) to display the Insert Pictures dialog box.

● Tap or click the Browse button and then navigate to the location where your Data Files for Students are stored (in this case, the PowerPoint folder in the CIS 101 folder [or your class folder] on your computer or SkyDrive).

Figure 9–21

● Tap or click Center Track to select the file name (Figure 9–21).

Q&A What if the picture is not in my Data Files for Students folder?
Use the same process, but select the device containing the photograph.
Another option is to locate this photograph or a similar one on Office.com.

3

● Tap or click the Insert button (Insert Picture dialog box) to change the Slide 2 picture. If necessary, drag the sizing handles to the borders of the slide (Figure 9–22).

Q&A What if I do not want to use this picture?
Tap or click the Undo button on the Quick Access Toolbar.

Figure 9–22

Break Point: If you wish to take a break, this is a good place to do so. Be sure to save the Steam Train file again and then you can exit PowerPoint. To resume at a later time, run PowerPoint, open the file called Steam Train, and continue following the steps from this location forward.

Manipulating SmartArt

Every SmartArt layout has a unique design and graphical elements. The shapes maximize vertical and horizontal space for text and pictures. When your presentation calls for special design needs or additional shapes, you can change the defaults that specify where each SmartArt element is displayed. You can add, subtract, and reorder shapes; promote and demote text; make a single shape smaller or larger; and change the SmartArt fill, outline, and colors.

In the following pages, you will perform these tasks on Slide 3:

1. Convert WordArt paragraphs to a SmartArt Target List.
2. Reorder two shapes in the SmartArt layout.
3. Reorder two bulleted paragraphs in a shape.
4. Promote and demote bulleted paragraphs.
5. Change the SmartArt layout and style.
6. Resize the entire SmartArt layout and shapes within the layout.
7. Apply pictures to SmartArt shapes.
8. Convert the SmartArt graphic to text.

CONSIDER THIS

Use keywords in SmartArt graphics.

Most SmartArt shapes have very limited space for text. You must, therefore, carefully choose each word you are going to display in the graphic. The text you select can serve as keywords, or a speaking outline. If you glance at the SmartArt when you are presenting the slide show in front of an audience, each word should prompt you for the main point you are going to make. These keywords should jog your memory if you lose your train of thought or are interrupted.

To Convert WordArt to SmartArt

1 INSERT & CUSTOMIZE TEXT BOXES | 2 CONVERT WORDART TO SMARTART & FORMAT | 3 INSERT & FORMAT SHAPES
4 DRAW & FORMAT LINES | 5 CUSTOMIZE THE RIBBON | 6 EXPORT FILE & CREATE PICTURE PRESENTATION

The bulleted paragraphs on Slide 3 are formatted as WordArt. Although WordArt can add visual interest, using a graphical element such as SmartArt can be even more effective in helping the audience to grasp essential concepts. ***Why?*** *SmartArt diagrams are creative means to show processes, lists, cycles, and other relationships.* PowerPoint suggests layouts that might fit the concept you are trying to present and then easily converts WordArt to SmartArt. The following steps convert WordArt to SmartArt.

1
- Display Slide 3, press and hold or right-click anywhere in the WordArt bulleted list paragraphs to display the shortcut menu, and then tap or click 'Convert to SmartArt' to display the SmartArt gallery.

Q&A
Does it matter where I place the cursor?
No. As long as the cursor is placed in the WordArt text, you will be able to convert the paragraphs to SmartArt.

Figure 9–23

- If you are using a mouse, point to Vertical Block List in the gallery to display a live preview of that layout applied to the WordArt paragraphs (Figure 9–23).

 Experiment

- If you are using a mouse, point to various graphics in the SmartArt gallery and watch the layouts change.

• Tap or click Vertical Block List in the SmartArt gallery to convert the WordArt to that layout.

Q&A | How is the text arranged in the Vertical Block List SmartArt layout?
The four first-level paragraphs are in the left column of the graphic and have a larger font size than the eight bulleted second-level paragraphs in the right column.

To Reorder SmartArt Shapes

1 INSERT & CUSTOMIZE TEXT BOXES | 2 CONVERT WORDART TO SMARTART & FORMAT | 3 INSERT & FORMAT SHAPES
4 DRAW & FORMAT LINES | 5 CUSTOMIZE THE RIBBON | 6 EXPORT FILE & CREATE PICTURE PRESENTATION

Now that the SmartArt layout is created, you can modify the graphic. One change you can make is to change the order of the shapes. You decide that two items in the graphic should be displayed in a different order. *Why? The caboose is at the end of a train, so it is fitting that the Ride in Caboose Cupola shape is displayed at the end of the list. You also decide that potential customers would be interested in knowing that the excursion is narrated, so you want to move the information in the second bulleted paragraph in the Ride in Vintage Coaches shape above the fact that the crew will be dressed in period costumes.* PowerPoint provides tools to move shapes and paragraphs in a vertical layout up or down. The following steps reorder the Ride in Caboose Cupola and Ride in Vintage Coaches shapes and the two bulleted paragraphs in the Ride in Vintage Coaches shape.

1

• Position the pointer in the Ride in Vintage Coaches shape and then tap or click to select it and the two bulleted paragraphs (Figure 9–24).

Q&A | Are both shapes selected even though the sizing handles are displayed only around the Ride in Vintage Coaches shape?
Yes. The Ride in Vintage Coaches shape is a first-level paragraph, and the two bulleted second-level paragraphs are associated with it. When a first-level paragraph is selected, any related paragraphs also are selected with it.

Figure 9–24

● With the SMARTART TOOLS DESIGN tab displaying, tap or click the Move Up button (SMARTART TOOLS DESIGN tab | Create Graphic group) to reorder the Ride in Vintage Coaches shape above the Ride in Caboose Cupola shape.

● Position the pointer in the bulleted paragraph, Train crew wears period costumes (Figure 9–25).

Figure 9–25

● Tap or click the Move Down button (SMARTART TOOLS DESIGN tab | Create Graphic group) to reorder the bulleted paragraph, Train crew wears period costumes, below the bulleted paragraph, Conductor describes highlights.

To Promote a SmartArt Bullet Level

1 INSERT & CUSTOMIZE TEXT BOXES | 2 CONVERT WORDART TO SMARTART & FORMAT | 3 INSERT & FORMAT SHAPES
4 DRAW & FORMAT LINES | 5 CUSTOMIZE THE RIBBON | 6 EXPORT FILE & CREATE PICTURE PRESENTATION

PowerPoint provides tools that allow you to promote and demote bulleted text. These tools function in the same manner as the Increase List Level and Decrease List Level buttons that change the indents for bulleted text.

Another change you want to make on Slide 3 is to promote the bulleted paragraph, 5% discount for groups of 10 or more, to the same level as the bullet above it. *Why? Because this fact may encourage people to attend the excursion.* The following steps promote the second bullet in the Purchase Tickets at Depot shape.

1

● Select the All Aboard! text box and drag it to the left so that it is positioned over the Purchase Tickets at Depot graphic.

● Position the pointer in the bulleted paragraph, 5% discount for groups of 10 or more, and then display the SMARTART TOOLS DESIGN tab (Figure 9–26).

Figure 9–26

2

● Tap or click the Promote button (SMARTART TOOLS DESIGN tab | Create Graphic group) to decrease the indent of the bulleted paragraph.

To Demote a SmartArt Bullet Level

The two bulleted items in the Board Early shape are second-level paragraphs, but you decide to demote the second paragraph, Small coolers permitted. You also want to demote the paragraph, Train crew wears period costumes. *Why? The fact that passengers are permitted to bring small coolers on board is not as important to emphasize as the fact that concessions are available. In addition, the fact that the crew is wearing costumes is secondary to the point that the excursion is narrated.* The following steps demote the second-level bulleted paragraphs.

1

- Position the pointer in the bulleted paragraph, Small coolers permitted (Figure 9–27).

Figure 9–27

2

- With the SMARTART TOOLS DESIGN tab displaying, tap or click the Demote button (SMARTART TOOLS DESIGN tab | Create Graphic group) to increase the indent of the bulleted paragraph.

- Position the pointer in the bulleted paragraph, Train crew wears period costumes, and then tap or click the Demote button to increase the indent of this paragraph (Figure 9–28).

Figure 9–28

TO ADD A SMARTART BULLET

If you need to add information to a SmartArt shape, you can create a new bulleted paragraph. This text would display below the last bulleted paragraph in the shape. If you wanted to add a SmartArt bullet, you would perform the following steps.

1. Select the SmartArt graphic shape where you want to insert the bulleted paragraph.
2. Tap or click the Add Bullet button (SMARTART TOOLS DESIGN tab | Create Graphic group) to insert a new bulleted paragraph below any bulleted text.

To Change the SmartArt Layout

1 INSERT & CUSTOMIZE TEXT BOXES | 2 CONVERT WORDART TO SMARTART & FORMAT | 3 INSERT & FORMAT SHAPES
4 DRAW & FORMAT LINES | 5 CUSTOMIZE THE RIBBON | 6 EXPORT FILE & CREATE PICTURE PRESENTATION

Once you begin formatting a SmartArt shape, you may decide that another layout better conveys the message you are communicating to an audience. PowerPoint allows you to change the layout easily. Any graphical changes that were made to the original SmartArt, such as moving shapes or promoting and demoting paragraphs, are applied to the new SmartArt layout. The following steps change the SmartArt layout to Trapezoid List. **Why?** *Most of the shapes and pictures in the presentation are composed of squares and rectangles, so you want to continue using similar shapes. In addition, the Trapezoid List shapes are placed in a consecutive horizontal order, much like the train coaches that are coupled together.*

- With the SMARTART TOOLS DESIGN tab displaying, tap or click the More button in the Layouts group to expand the Layouts gallery (Figure 9–29).

Q&A Can I select one of the layouts displaying in the Layouts group without expanding the layout gallery?
Yes. At times, however, you may want to display the gallery to view and preview the various layouts.

Figure 9–29

- If you are using a mouse, point to the Trapezoid List layout (last layout in the fifth row) to display a live preview of this SmartArt layout (Figure 9–30).

Experiment

- If you are using a mouse, point to various layouts in the gallery and watch the SmartArt layouts change.

Figure 9–30

Are additional layouts available other than those displayed in the gallery?

Yes. Tap or click More Layouts to display the Choose a SmartArt Graphic dialog box and then select another layout.

- Tap or click Trapezoid List to change the layout.

To Remove a SmartArt Shape

1 INSERT & CUSTOMIZE TEXT BOXES | 2 CONVERT WORDART TO SMARTART & FORMAT | **3 INSERT & FORMAT SHAPES**

4 DRAW & FORMAT LINES | 5 CUSTOMIZE THE RIBBON | 6 EXPORT FILE & CREATE PICTURE PRESENTATION

Now that the new SmartArt layout is created, you can modify the graphic. One change you can make is to delete elements. You decide to delete the first shape on Slide 2. *Why? The slide contains information about what passengers will experience during the excursion, so the facts about buying tickets and boarding are a different topic.* The following steps remove a SmartArt shape.

1

- Tap or click a border of the left SmartArt shape, Purchase Tickets at Depot, to select the entire shape (Figure 9–31).

2

- If you are using a keyboard, press the DELETE key to delete the left SmartArt shape.

- If you are using a touch screen, press and hold the SmartArt shape and then tap Delete on the shortcut menu.

Figure 9–31

BTW

BTWs
For a complete list of the BTWs found in the margins of this book, visit the BTW resource on the Student Companion Site located on www.cengagebrain.com. For detailed instructions about accessing available resources, visit www.cengage.com/ct/studentdownload or see the inside back cover of this book.

TO ADD A SMARTART SHAPE

You may add a new SmartArt shape to the layout if you need to display additional information. PowerPoint gives you the option of adding this shape above or below a selected shape or to the left or the right side of the shape. If you wanted to add a SmartArt shape, you would perform the following steps.

1. Select a SmartArt graphic shape near where you want to insert another shape.

2. Tap or click the Add Shape arrow (SMARTART TOOLS DESIGN tab | Create Graphic group) to display the Add Shape menu.

3. Tap or click the desired location for the new shape, which would be after, before, above, or below the selected shape.

To Resize a SmartArt Graphic by Entering an Exact Measurement

1 INSERT & CUSTOMIZE TEXT BOXES | 2 CONVERT WORDART TO SMARTART & FORMAT | 3 INSERT & FORMAT SHAPES

4 DRAW & FORMAT LINES | 5 CUSTOMIZE THE RIBBON | 6 EXPORT FILE & CREATE PICTURE PRESENTATION

Why? *The All Aboard text box overlaps the left SmartArt shape, so you need to make room for this element at the top of the slide by reducing the size of the entire SmartArt graphic.* You can resize a slide element by dragging the sizing handles or by specifying exact measurements for the height and width. The following steps resize the SmartArt graphic by entering an exact measurement.

- If necessary, select the entire SmartArt graphic by tapping or clicking an outer edge of the graphic at the edge of the slide (Figure 9–32).

Q&A How will I know the entire graphic is selected?
You will see the Text pane control and sizing handles around the outer edge of the SmartArt.

Figure 9–32

- Display the SMARTART TOOLS FORMAT tab and then change the setting in the Height box to 6" (Figure 9–33).

- Drag the SmartArt graphic downward so its lower edge is aligned with the lower edge of the slide.

Figure 9–33

Other Ways

1. Press and hold or right-click graphic, tap or click 'Size and Position' on shortcut menu, if necessary tap or click 'Size & Properties' icon (Format Shape pane), if necessary tap or click SIZE, enter graphic height and width values in boxes, close Format Shape pane

To Resize a SmartArt Graphic Shape

The entire SmartArt shape and the text box now are the proper proportions to display together on the slide. In addition to changing the height and width of the SmartArt graphic, you also can change the height and width of one individual SmartArt shape in the graphic. **Why?** *Passengers who ride the steam train excursions marvel at the vintage coaches and the quality of workmanship they have. To emphasize this unique feature, you want to make the center SmartArt shape larger than the others and deemphasize the Board Early and Ride in Caboose Cupola shapes.* The following steps resize the SmartArt graphic shapes.

1

- Tap or click the left SmartArt shape, Board Early, to select it.

- With the SMARTART TOOLS FORMAT tab displaying, tap or click the Smaller button (SMARTART TOOLS FORMAT tab | Shapes group) once to decrease the shape size (Figure 9–34).

Figure 9–34

2

- Tap or click the right shape, Ride in Caboose Cupola, to select it and then tap or click the Smaller button (Figure 9–35).

Figure 9–35

- Tap or click the center shape, Ride In Vintage Coaches, to select it and then tap or click the Larger button twice (Figure 9–36).

Figure 9–36

Other Ways

1. Press and hold or right-click graphic, tap or click 'Size and Position' on shortcut menu, if necessary tap or click 'Size & Properties' icon (Format Shape pane), if necessary tap or click SIZE, enter graphic height and width values in boxes, close Format Shape pane

---

To Apply a Picture to a Text Box

1 INSERT & CUSTOMIZE TEXT BOXES | 2 CONVERT WORDART TO SMARTART & FORMAT | 3 INSERT & FORMAT SHAPES
4 DRAW & FORMAT LINES | 5 CUSTOMIZE THE RIBBON | 6 EXPORT FILE & CREATE PICTURE PRESENTATION

Sufficient space exists in the lower halves of the three shapes to insert a picture. *Why? A picture helps to reinforce the written message and also calls attention to the major points being made in each of the three shapes.* For consistency with the slide title, you can insert a text box that has the default formatting and then add a picture. The following steps add a text box and then apply a picture into two SmartArt graphic shapes.

- Display the INSERT tab and then insert a text box below the bulleted paragraph, Train crew wears period costumes, in the middle SmartArt shape.

- Display the DRAWING TOOLS FORMAT tab and then tap or click the Shape Fill arrow (DRAWING TOOLS FORMAT tab | Shape Styles group) to display the Shape Fill gallery (Figure 9–37).

Figure 9–37

- Tap or click Picture in the Shape Fill gallery to display the Insert Pictures dialog box. Tap or click the Browse button and then navigate to the location where your Data Files for Students are stored (in this case, the PowerPoint folder in the CIS 101 folder [or your class folder] on your computer or SkyDrive).

- Tap or click Conductor to select the file name (Figure 9–38).

Figure 9–38

- Tap or click the Insert button (Insert Picture dialog box) to insert the Conductor picture into the text box. You will resize the text box in a later step.

- Insert a text box below the bulleted paragraph, Small coolers permitted, in the left SmartArt shape, display the Shape Fill gallery, and then insert the picture, Cooler.

- Insert a text box below the bulleted paragraph, Must be at least 16 years of age, in the right SmartArt shape, display the Shape Fill gallery, and then insert the picture, Caboose.

- Drag the left and right sizing handles of the boxes to size the three text boxes and then use the Smart Guides to align the lower edges of the pictures, as shown in Figure 9–39.

Figure 9–39

To Add a SmartArt Style to the Graphic and Change the Color

To enhance the appearance of the rectangles in the Trapezoid List layout, you can add a transparent three-dimensional style that allows some of the background to show through the graphic. You also can add more colors. The following steps add the Inset style and a Colorful range.

1 Select the entire SmartArt graphic, display the SMARTART TOOLS DESIGN tab, and then tap or click the More button in the SmartArt Styles group to expand the SmartArt Styles gallery.

2 Tap or click Inset in the 3-D area (second graphic in first row) to apply this style to the graphic.

3 Tap or click the Change Colors button (SMARTART TOOLS DESIGN tab | SmartArt Styles group) to display the Change Colors gallery.

4 Tap or click Colorful Range – Accent Colors 5 to 6 (fifth graphic in Colorful row) to apply this color variation to the graphic.

5 Select the All Aboard! text box, display the DRAWING TOOLS FORMAT tab, tap or click the Align button (DRAWING TOOLS FORMAT tab | Arrange group), and then tap or click Align Center to center the text box at the top of the slide (Figure 9–40).

BTW

Displaying Smart Guides
If the Smart Guides are not displayed when you are attempting to align objects, you may need to specify that PowerPoint should show them. Display the VIEW tab, tap or click the Show Group launcher, and then tap or click the 'Display Smart Guides when shapes are aligned' check box to select this option.

Figure 9–40

To Convert a SmartArt Graphic to Text

1 INSERT & CUSTOMIZE TEXT BOXES | 2 CONVERT WORDART TO SMARTART & FORMAT | 3 INSERT & FORMAT SHAPES
4 DRAW & FORMAT LINES | 5 CUSTOMIZE THE RIBBON | 6 EXPORT FILE & CREATE PICTURE PRESENTATION

Passengers often wonder how a steam engine operates, and the SmartArt graphic information on Slide 4 explains the basic principles. In a later portion of this chapter, you will supplement these details with a graphic pointing out the main components of a steam engine. At times, you may decide that SmartArt is not the optimal method of presenting information to an audience and instead want to depict the same concept using text. *Why? The SmartArt's visual elements may detract from the points being made, so the bulleted list might be useful for instructional purposes. In addition, it may take up so much room on the slide that other visual elements may not fit.* PowerPoint allows you to remove the shapes and change the text in the graphic to a bulleted list. The steps on the next page convert the SmartArt graphic to text.

1

- Display Slide 4 and then select the entire SmartArt graphic.

Q&A If one of the SmartArt shapes is selected, how do I select the entire graphic?
Be certain to tap or click the edge of the graphic. You will see sizing handles and the Text pane control when the SmartArt graphic is selected.

- Display the SMARTART TOOLS DESIGN tab and then tap or click the Convert button (SMARTART TOOLS DESIGN tab | Reset group) to display the Convert menu (Figure 9–41).

Figure 9–41

2

- Tap or click 'Convert to Text' to display the SmartArt text as nine bulleted list paragraphs (Figure 9–42).

Figure 9–42

- Position the bulleted list placeholder in the upper-left corner of the slide (Figure 9–43).

Figure 9–43

To Convert a SmartArt Graphic to Shapes

An alternative to changing a graphic to text is changing a graphic to shapes. In this manner, a shape can be moved, resized, or deleted independently of any other shape in the SmartArt. If you wanted to convert a SmartArt graphic to shapes, you would perform the following steps.

1. Select the entire SmartArt graphic.
2. Tap or click the Convert button (SMARTART TOOLS DESIGN tab | Reset group) to display the Convert menu.
3. Tap or click 'Convert to Shapes'.

> **BTW**
> **SmartArt in Handouts**
> SmartArt diagrams are composed of individual vector graphics. Some presenters decide to include these diagrams in a handout but not as part of a presentation so that audience members can study the relationships among the shapes after the presentation has concluded.

Break Point: If you wish to take a break, this is a good place to do so. Be sure to save the Steam Train file again and then you can exit PowerPoint. To resume at a later time, run PowerPoint, open the file called Steam Train, and continue following the steps from this location forward.

Inserting and Modifying Shapes

The items in the Shapes gallery provide a variety of useful shapes you can insert into slides. Diagrams with labels often help audiences identify the parts of an object. Text boxes with clear, large type and an arrow pointing to a precise area of the object work well in showing relationships between components. You also can use items in the Shapes gallery to create your own custom artwork.

A steam engine has several components: They include the firebox, which provides the heat; the boiler, where the water is heated until it forms steam; and the rods, which turn the wheels. These parts can be depicted with a variety of items found in the Shapes gallery. You also want to add text boxes and arrows to identify the components. At times, you may be unable to find a shape in the gallery that fits your specific needs. In those instances, you might find a similar shape and then alter it to your specifications.

> **BTW**
> **Vector Graphics**
> Geometric shapes, lines, arrows, and action buttons are vector graphics, which are drawn using mathematical formulas. The size, color, line width, starting and ending points, and other formatting attributes are stored as numeric values and are recalculated when you resize or reformat each shape. Most clip art and video games also use vector graphics.

BTW

Inserting Shapes
The Shapes gallery is displayed on two tabs: the DRAWING TOOLS FORMAT tab (Insert Shapes group) and the HOME tab (Drawing group). Shapes also are available if you display the INSERT tab and then tap or click the Shapes button (Illustrations group).

To Insert Shapes and an Arrow

You can draw parts of the steam engine with shapes located in the Shapes gallery: one rectangle for the rear of the engine, which contains the firebox and also the cab for the engineer and fireman; another rectangle for the boiler; circles for the wheels; a triangle for the pilot, also called the cow catcher, in the front; and a trapezoid for the stack. A cloud shape can represent the exhaust that has moved through the stack. In addition, the Notched Right Arrow shape can be inserted to serve as a leader line for labeling a steam engine part. The following steps insert six shapes and an arrow into Slide 4.

1 With Slide 4 displaying, tap or click the More button in the Shapes gallery (HOME tab | Drawing group) to display the entire Shapes gallery and then tap or click the Rectangle shape (first shape in the Rectangles area).

2 Position the pointer below the last bulleted paragraph and then tap or click to insert the Rectangle shape.

3 Display the Shapes gallery and then tap or click the Oval shape (second shape in the first Basic Shapes row).

4 Position the pointer below the Rectangle and then tap or click to insert the Oval shape.

5 Display the Shapes gallery, tap or click the Trapezoid shape (sixth shape in the first row in the Basic Shapes area), and then insert this shape to the right of the word, forth, in the bulleted list.

6 Display the Shapes gallery, tap or click the Cloud shape (eleventh shape in the third row in the Basic Shapes area), and then insert this shape above the Trapezoid shape.

7 Display the Shapes gallery, tap or click the Right Triangle shape (fourth shape in the first Basic Shapes row), and then insert this shape below the Trapezoid shape.

8 Display the Shapes gallery, tap or click the Notched Right Arrow shape (sixth shape in the second row in the Block Arrows area), and then insert this shape to the right of the Cloud shape (Figure 9–44).

Figure 9–44

To Resize and Move Shapes

The six shapes on Slide 4 are the default sizes, and they need to be proportioned to reflect accurate engine dimensions. If you are not using a touch screen, you can keep the resized shape proportions identical to the original shape by pressing the SHIFT key while tapping or clicking a sizing handle and then dragging the pointer inward or outward to decrease or increase the size. If you do not hold down the SHIFT key, you can elongate the height or the width to draw an object that is not identical to the shape shown in the Shapes gallery. If you want to alter the shape's proportions, drag one of the sizing handles inward or outward. The following steps resize the shapes and arrow.

① Select the rectangle and then drag the top-center sizing handle upward to the bulleted list and the bottom-center sizing handle downward to the center of the circle.

② With the rectangle selected, display the HOME tab, tap or click the Copy button (HOME tab | Clipboard group), and then tap or click the Paste button (HOME tab | Clipboard group).

③ Drag the new rectangle to the right and then position the pointer over the rotation handle and turn the rectangle to the right 90 degrees.

④ Drag the triangle to the lower-right side of the new rectangle and then drag the upper-right sizing handle diagonally to the lower left.

⑤ Drag the trapezoid to the upper-right edge of the new rectangle and then position the pointer over the rotation handle and turn the rectangle 180 degrees.

⑥ Drag the Cloud to the upper-left side of the Trapezoid.

⑦ With the HOME tab displaying, tap or click the Oval, tap or click the Copy button and then tap or click the Paste button twice. Position the two new ovals to the right of the first oval.

⑧ Use the Smart Guides to align the bottom of the ovals and the triangle (Figure 9–45).

Figure 9–45

To Apply a Fill to a Shape

The shapes on Slide 4 have light blue fill. You can change the shape fill using the same types of fills you used for the text boxes in this presentation. For example, you can apply a gradient, pattern, texture, or picture. *Why? Using similar fills among the slides adds consistency and gives a uniform look to the presentation.* The method of applying these fill effects is similar to the steps you used to format text boxes. The following steps apply fills to the shapes.

1

- Select the two rectangles and the triangle. Display the DRAWING TOOLS FORMAT tab, tap or click the Shape Fill arrow (DRAWING TOOLS FORMAT tab | Shape Styles group) to display the Shape Fill gallery, and then tap or click Gradient to display the Gradient gallery (Figure 9–46).

 Experiment

- If you are using a mouse, point to various gradients in the Gradient gallery and watch the interiors of the three shapes change.

Figure 9–46

2

- Tap or click More Gradients in the Gradient gallery to display the Format Shape pane.

- If necessary, display the FILL section. Tap or click Gradient fill to expand the gradient options and then tap or click the Preset gradients button to display the Preset gradients gallery (Figure 9–47).

Q&A Can I experiment with previewing the gradient colors?
No, the live preview feature is not available.

Figure 9–47

3

- Tap or click Bottom Spotlight - Accent 6 (last color in the fourth row in the Preset gradients gallery) to apply the gradient fill to the three shapes.

Q&A How can I delete a gradient fill if I decide not to apply one to the shape?

If you already have applied the pattern, you must tap or click the Undo button on the Quick Access Toolbar.

4

- Select the trapezoid and the three wheels, tap or click Gradient fill, and then tap or click the Preset gradients button (Figure 9–48).

Q&A Why did these four shapes fill with the green gradient fill when I tapped or clicked Gradient fill? PowerPoint recalls the last gradient you selected.

Figure 9–48

5

- Tap or click Radial Gradient – Accent 3 (third color in the fifth row) to apply this gradient to the shapes.

- Select the cloud and then tap or click 'Picture or texture fill' to display the 'Picture or texture fill' section (Figure 9–49).

Figure 9–49

Q&A Why did the cloud fill with a texture?

Depending on previous settings for shape fills, PowerPoint may insert a fill or change the Transparency when you click the 'Picture or texture fill' option button.

6

- Tap or click the Texture button to display the Texture gallery (Figure 9–50).

Figure 9–50

- Tap or click the White marble texture (fifth texture in the second row) to apply this texture to the cloud.

- If necessary, set the Transparency slider to 0%.

- Scroll down the Format Picture pane and then, if necessary, tap or click LINE to expand the LINE section. Tap or click the Color button to display the Color gallery (Figure 9–51).

Figure 9–51

- Tap or click Gray - 25%, Background 2 (third color in the first Theme Colors row) to apply this color to the cloud edges.

- Tap or click the Close button to close the Format Picture pane.

To Subtract a Shape

1 INSERT & CUSTOMIZE TEXT BOXES | 2 CONVERT WORDART TO SMARTART & FORMAT | 3 INSERT & FORMAT SHAPES
4 DRAW & FORMAT LINES | 5 CUSTOMIZE THE RIBBON | 6 EXPORT FILE & CREATE PICTURE PRESENTATION

The cab you drew does not have a window, but you easily can create one. *Why? Your engine will look more accurate with this element.* One method of creating this window is to overlap a new Rectangle shape and the current vertical rectangle shape and then subtract the area of the new rectangle. The result is a blank area that displays the slide background. The following steps insert a Rectangle shape and then subtract this object.

- Display the Shapes gallery, select the Rectangle shape in the Rectangles area (first shape), and then insert the shape into the cab portion of the engine.

- Size the shape so that each side is 0.7" and then use the Smart Guides to align the shape, as shown in Figure 9–52.

Figure 9–52

- If you are using a keyboard, click the vertical green rectangle to select it, press and hold down the CTRL key, and then click the square to select both shapes.

Can I perform this step using a touch screen?
No. You will need to use a keyboard to select multiple shapes.

- With the DRAWING TOOLS FORMAT tab displaying, tap or click the Merge Shapes button (DRAWING TOOLS FORMAT tab | Insert Shapes group) to display the Merge Shapes list (Figure 9–53).

Do I need to select the shapes in this order?
Yes. You first select the shape that you want to keep and then tap or click the shape that you want to delete.

Experiment

- If you are using a mouse, point to the commands in the Merge Shapes list and watch the results of the various merge commands.

Figure 9–53

- Tap or click Subtract in the Merge Shapes list to delete the green background behind the square shape.

To Merge Shapes

1 INSERT & CUSTOMIZE TEXT BOXES | 2 CONVERT WORDART TO SMARTART & FORMAT | 3 INSERT & FORMAT SHAPES
4 DRAW & FORMAT LINES | 5 CUSTOMIZE THE RIBBON | 6 EXPORT FILE & CREATE PICTURE PRESENTATION

The two rectangles forming the engine have a common vertical line where the two shapes intersect. You can eliminate this line if you merge the shapes. In addition, you can merge the triangular pilot shape with the rectangles. *Why? The three elements will appear seamless as part of the main structure of the engine.* The following steps merge the two rectangles and the triangle.

- Select the three green engine shapes (the two rectangles and the triangle). With the DRAWING TOOLS FORMAT tab displaying, tap or click the Merge Shapes button (DRAWING TOOLS FORMAT tab | Insert Shapes group) to display the Merge Shapes list (Figure 9–54).

How do I select the three engine shapes?
Hold down the CTRL key and then tap or click each shape.

Experiment

- If you are using a mouse, point to the commands in the Merge Shapes list and watch the results of the various merge commands.

Figure 9–54

- Tap or click Union (DRAWING TOOLS FORMAT tab | Insert Shapes group) to combine the green shapes.

Q&A Why am I using the Union command instead of the Combine command?
The Union command joins the shapes using the formatting of the top shape. The Combine command also joins shapes, but it deletes the area where the two shapes overlap.

To Draw a Line

1 INSERT & CUSTOMIZE TEXT BOXES | 2 CONVERT WORDART TO SMARTART & FORMAT | 3 INSERT & FORMAT SHAPES
4 DRAW & FORMAT LINES | 5 CUSTOMIZE THE RIBBON | 6 EXPORT FILE & CREATE PICTURE PRESENTATION

Why? *The shapes on Slide 4 comprise the main parts of a steam engine. To complete the drawing, you need to add the rods, which connect on one end to the wheels and on the other end to a piston.* Rods can be represented by a line shape. One type of rod is a straight bar, and this type of line is included in the Shapes gallery. Some other lines in the gallery are the Elbow Connector, Curve, Freeform, and Scribble. The lines and connectors have zero, one, or two arrowheads. The following steps draw a straight line without arrowheads and position this shape on Slide 4.

- Display the Shapes gallery and then point to the Line shape (first shape in the Lines area) (Figure 9–55).

Figure 9–55

- Tap or click the Line shape and then position the pointer on the right wheel to display the points (Figure 9–56).

Q&A What are the dots on the perimeter of the wheel?
The dots are called points. Every shape is formed by a series of points connected with lines that are straight or curved. If desired, you can drag a point to alter the shape's form.

Figure 9–56

3

- Position the pointer on the point at the 3 o'clock position on the right side of the wheel and then tap or click to insert one end of the line on this point.

- Drag the sizing handle at the other end of the line to the center of the middle wheel (Figure 9–57).

Figure 9–57

To Change a Line Weight and Color

1 INSERT & CUSTOMIZE TEXT BOXES | 2 CONVERT WORDART TO SMARTART & FORMAT | 3 INSERT & FORMAT SHAPES
4 DRAW & FORMAT LINES | 5 CUSTOMIZE THE RIBBON | 6 EXPORT FILE & CREATE PICTURE PRESENTATION

In this project, you changed a text box and shape outline color and weight. In a similar fashion, you can change line outline formatting. ***Why?*** *The line you drew on Slide 4 is thin, and the color does not display well against the wheels' gray background.* You can increase the line thickness and change its color to enhance the shape. The following steps change the line thickness and color.

1

- With the line selected, tap or click the Shape Outline arrow (DRAWING TOOLS FORMAT tab | Shape Styles group) and then tap or click Weight to display the Weight gallery.

- If you are using a mouse, point to 6 pt to see a preview of that weight applied to the line (Figure 9–58).

🔍 **Experiment**

- If you are using a mouse, point to various weights in the Weight gallery and watch the line thickness change.

Figure 9–58

- Tap or click 6 pt in the Weight gallery to apply that weight to the line.

- Tap or click the Shape Outline arrow again. If you are using a mouse, point to Blue-Gray, Text 2 (fourth color in the first Theme Colors area) to see a preview of that color applied to the line (Figure 9–59).

 Experiment

- If you are using a mouse, point to various colors in the Theme Colors gallery and watch the line color change.

Figure 9–59

- Tap or click Blue-Gray, Text 2 to apply that color to the line.

To Set Line Formatting as the Default

1 INSERT & CUSTOMIZE TEXT BOXES | 2 CONVERT WORDART TO SMARTART & FORMAT | 3 INSERT & FORMAT SHAPES
4 DRAW & FORMAT LINES | **5 CUSTOMIZE THE RIBBON** | 6 EXPORT FILE & CREATE PICTURE PRESENTATION

The line you inserted and formatted is one of two rods in the steam engine diagram. You can set these line attributes as the default for the other line you will draw in the presentation. *Why? Setting the default characters saves time when you add other lines because you do not need to repeat all the formatting steps. It also ensures consistency among the line shapes.* The following steps set the line shape on Slide 4 as the default.

- Press and hold or right-click the line to display the shortcut menu (Figure 9–60).

- Tap or click 'Set as Default Line' on the shortcut menu to set the line formatting as the default for any new lines.

Figure 9–60

To Draw an Additional Line

One more line is needed to connect the left wheel to the center wheel. A line with an elbow is the best shape to use in this instance. ***Why?*** *This shape has two bends, which is the shape of the rear rod. You could, instead, draw this rod using three lines and then connect these shapes, but the elbow already has the required components.* The following steps draw these lines.

- Display the Shapes gallery again. If you are using a mouse, point to the Elbow Connector (fourth line in the Lines area) (Figure 9–61).

Figure 9–61

- Tap or click the Elbow Connector, position the pointer in the center of the left wheel, and then tap or click to insert one end of the line at this location (Figure 9–62).

Figure 9–62

- Drag the sizing handle at the other end of the line near the center of the middle wheel, slightly below the straight line that connects the right and center wheels (Figure 9–63).

Figure 9–63

To Group and Size the Engine Objects

All the shapes comprising the engine are separate elements on the slide. You will need to move and enlarge the engine on the slide, so you easily can complete these tasks if you group all the components so they no longer are individual pieces. The following steps group all these shapes and then enlarge the entire engine shape.

1 Select all the engine shapes and the cloud and then display the PICTURE TOOLS FORMAT tab.

2 Tap or click the Group button (PICTURE TOOLS FORMAT tab | Arrange group) to display the Group list and then click Group in the list to combine all the shapes.

3 Size the engine object so that it is approximately 6" × 6.5" and then move it to the right side of the slide, as shown in Figure 9–64.

4 Position the pointer after the word, pistons, in the first bulleted list item below the word, Motion. If you are using a touch screen, display the onscreen keyboard.

5 Tap or press SHIFT+ENTER to insert a line break (Figure 9–64).

Figure 9–64

To Change a Shape Fill and Outline and Apply Effects

Earlier in this project, you changed a text box outline color, weight, and style. You also applied a glow effect to a text box. You, similarly, can change the outline formatting and effects for a shape. For consistency, you can enhance the arrow by using some of the same formatting changes that you applied to the text box. The following steps change the arrow shape outline and apply an effect.

1 Select the Notched Right Arrow, tap or click the Shape Fill arrow (DRAWING TOOLS FORMAT tab | Shape Styles group), display the Gradient gallery, and then tap or click From Center (second gradient in second row) in the Dark Variations area.

2 Tap or click the Shape Outline arrow (DRAWING TOOLS FORMAT tab | Shape Styles group), display the Weight gallery, and then tap or click 3 pt.

3 Display the Shape Outline gallery again and then tap or click Green (sixth color in the Standard Colors area) to change the shape border color.

4 Display the Shape Outline gallery again, display the Dashes gallery, and then tap or click Square Dot to change the border style.

5 Tap or click the Shape Effects button to display the Shape Effects gallery, display the Glow gallery, and then tap or click the Blue, 8 pt glow, Accent color 1 (first color in the second row in the Glow Variations area) to apply the glow effect (Figure 9–65).

BTW
Printing Document Properties
To print document properties, tap or click FILE on the ribbon to open the Backstage view, tap or click the Print tab in the Backstage view to display the Print gallery, tap or click the first button in the Settings area to display a list of options specifying what you can print, tap or click Document Info in the list to specify you want to print the document properties instead of the actual document, and then tap or click the Print button in the Print gallery to print the document properties on the currently selected printer.

Figure 9–65

To Set Shape Formatting as the Default

1 INSERT & CUSTOMIZE TEXT BOXES | 2 CONVERT WORDART TO SMARTART & FORMAT | 3 INSERT & FORMAT SHAPES
4 DRAW & FORMAT LINES | 5 CUSTOMIZE THE RIBBON | 6 EXPORT FILE & CREATE PICTURE PRESENTATION

The Notched Right Arrow shape you inserted and formatted complements the default text box you inserted on the slides in the presentation. You will use this shape on several parts of Slide 4 to help identify parts of the steam engine, so you can set its formatting as a default. *Why? To save time and ensure all the formatting changes are applied, you can set the formatting of one shape as the default for all other shapes you insert into the presentation.* The following steps set the arrow shape formatting on Slide 4 as the default.

1

- Press and hold or right-click the Notched Right Arrow shape to display the shortcut menu (Figure 9–66).

2
- Tap or click 'Set as Default Shape' on the shortcut menu to set the shape formatting as the default for any new shapes.

Figure 9–66

Use politically correct language.

Many companies have strict policies in order to prevent harassment in the workplace. These guidelines are developed to protect employees from adverse treatment based on race, religion, national origin, gender, or other personal traits. Keep these policies in mind as you label components on your slides. For example, some females may be offended if you refer to an adult woman as a "girl," or an older athlete may resent being labeled as an "aging" rather than as a "veteran" player.

To Label the Shapes

The final step in creating Slide 4 is to label the parts of the steam engine. The Notched Right Arrow shape and the text box are formatted as defaults, so the labeling process is easy to accomplish. The following steps insert text boxes and arrows into Slide 4 and then enter text in the text boxes.

1. With Slide 4 displaying, insert a text box into the railroad track on the left side of the engine, type **Rods** in the text box, decrease the font size to 24 point, and move the text box to the bottom edge of the center wheel. Use the Smart Guides to center the text box and the wheel.

2. Insert a text box into the railroad track on the left side of the engine, type **Boiler** in the text box, decrease the font size to 24 point, and move the text box between the engine cab and the stack. Use the Smart Guides to align this text box with the Rods text box.

3. Insert a text box, type **Firebox** in the text box, decrease the font size to 24 point, and move the text box to the left side of the engine. Use the Smart Guides to align the text box in the center of the slide and the center of the engine.

4. Drag the Notched Right arrow to the right of the Firebox text box. Display the DRAWING TOOLS FORMAT tab, tap or click the Bring Forward arrow (DRAWING TOOLS FORMAT tab | Arrange group), and then tap or click 'Bring to Front' to display the arrow on top of the engine.

5. Insert a Notched Right arrow. Rotate the arrow 90 degrees and then drag it below the Boiler text box.

6. Insert a Notched Right arrow. Rotate the arrow so it is pointing to the upper-right corner of the slide and then drag it to the right of the Rods text box.

7. Insert a Notched Right arrow. Rotate the arrow so it is pointing to the upper-left corner of the slide and then drag it to the left of the Rods text box (Figure 9–67).

Figure 9–67

To Customize the Ribbon

Many commands available in PowerPoint are not included on any of the tabs on the ribbon. You can, however, add such commands to the ribbon or to the Quick Access Toolbar. *Why? Many of these commands perform tasks you commonly repeat, so it would be convenient to have the buttons accessible in a group on the ribbon.* The following steps customize the ribbon by adding the 'Print Preview and Print' and 'Create Handouts in Microsoft Word' commands to the ribbon and then arranging their order in the group.

- With the HOME tab displaying, open the Backstage view and then tap or click Options to display the PowerPoint Options dialog box.

- Tap or click Customize Ribbon in the left pane to display the Customize the Ribbon pane (Figure 9–68).

Figure 9–68

- Tap or click the 'Choose commands from' arrow to display the 'Choose commands from' list (Figure 9–69).

Figure 9–69

● Tap or click
'Commands Not in
the Ribbon' in the
'Choose commands
from' list to display
a list of commands
that do not display
in the ribbon
(Figure 9–70).

Figure 9–70

● Scroll down and
then tap or click
'Create Handouts in
Microsoft Word' to
select this button.

● Tap or click Editing
in the Main Tabs
area under Home
to specify that the
'Create Handouts
in Microsoft Word'
button will be added
in a new group after
the Editing group
on the HOME tab
(Figure 9–71).

Figure 9–71

5

- Tap or click the New Group button to create a new group.

- Tap or click the Rename button and then type **Handouts** as the new group name in the Display name text box (Rename dialog box) (Figure 9–72).

Figure 9–72

6

- Tap or click the OK button (Rename dialog box) to rename the new group.

- Tap or click the Add button to add the 'Create Handouts in Microsoft Word' button to the Handouts group.

- Scroll down, tap or click 'Print Preview and Print' in the list of 'Commands Not in the Ribbon', and then tap or click the Add button to add the button to the Handouts group (Figure 9–73).

Figure 9–73

• Tap or click the
Move Up button
(PowerPoint Options
dialog box) to
move the 'Print
Preview and Print'
button above the
'Create Handouts
in Microsoft
Word' button
(Figure 9–74).

• Tap or click the OK
button to close
the PowerPoint
Options dialog box
and display the two
buttons in the new
Handouts group on
the HOME tab in the
ribbon.

Figure 9–74

To Create a Handout by Exporting a File to Microsoft Word

1 INSERT & CUSTOMIZE TEXT BOXES | 2 CONVERT WORDART TO SMARTART & FORMAT | 3 INSERT & FORMAT SHAPES
4 DRAW & FORMAT LINES | 5 CUSTOMIZE THE RIBBON | **6 EXPORT FILE & CREATE PICTURE PRESENTATION**

The handouts you create using Microsoft PowerPoint are useful to distribute to audiences. Each time
you need to create these handouts, however, you need to open the file in PowerPoint and then print from
the Backstage view. As an alternative, it might be convenient to save, or export, the file as a Microsoft Word
document if you are going to be using Microsoft Word to type a script or lecture notes. ***Why?*** *The handout
can have a variety of layouts; for example, the notes you type in the Notes pane can be displayed to the right of or beneath
the slide thumbnails, blank lines can be displayed to the right of or beneath the slide thumbnails, or just an outline can
be displayed.* The following steps use the 'Create Handouts in Microsoft Word' button you added to the new
Handouts group on the HOME tab to export the presentation to Microsoft Word and then create a handout.

• With the HOME
tab displaying,
tap or click the
'Create Handouts
in Microsoft Word'
button (HOME tab |
Handouts group)
to display the
'Send to Microsoft
Word' dialog box
(Figure 9–75).

Q&A How would I create
this handout if I
had not created the
Handouts group?
You would use the
Backstage view.

Figure 9–75

2

- Tap or click the OK button to save the file with the default 'Notes next to slides' layout.
- If the handout does not display in a new Microsoft Word window, tap or click the Microsoft Word program button on the Windows taskbar to see a live preview of the handout. If you print the handouts, they will resemble the pages shown Figure 9–76.

Slide 1

The first steam locomotive ran in the United Kingdom in 1804. Steam trains came to the United States in 1830. The first steamer, Tom Thumb, ran 26 miles round trip from Baltimore to Ellicott's Mill.

Slide 4

The steam is under high pressure. A "choo" sound is produced when a cylinder is opened to release the steam exhaust.

Slide 2

Steam locomotives pulled trains for more than 100 years. The last steam locomotive was retired in 1960. Today, many private groups have restored the steam engines and passenger cars and schedule excursions for rail buffs to enjoy.

Slide 3

The conductor, brakeman, and flagman traveled in the caboose when the train was moving. The raised lookout area on the top of the caboose is called the cupola. It allowed the conductor to peer out the window and fhve a bird-eye view of the length of the train.

(a) Page 1   **(b) Page 2**

Figure 9–76

3

- Save the presentation using the file name, Steam Engine Word Handout.
- Close the Word file and then exit Word.

Other Ways

1. Open Backstage view, display Export tab, tap or click Create Handouts, tap or click Create Handouts button

---

Work with a buddy.
Although you may believe you create your best work when you work alone, research shows that the work product generally improves when two or more people work together on a creative task. A classmate or team member at work can assist you in many ways. For example, this person can help you gather research for your graphics and bulleted text or provide feedback on the slides' clarity and readability. As you rehearse, a buddy can time your talk and identify the times when the presentation lacks interest. If a buddy attends your actual presentation, he can give objective feedback on the components that worked and those that can use revision for the next time you present the material.

CONSIDER THIS

To Save the Presentation as a Picture Presentation

Why? *If you are going to share your slides with other presenters and do not want them to alter the slide content, you can save each slide as a picture. When they run the slide show, each slide is one complete picture, so the text and shapes cannot be edited. You also can use an individual slide picture as a graphic on another slide or in another presentation.* The following steps save a copy of the presentation as a picture presentation.

1
- Open the Backstage view, display the Export tab, and then tap or click 'Change File Type' to display the 'Change File Type' gallery.

- Tap or click 'PowerPoint Picture Presentation' in the Presentation File Types area (Figure 9–77).

Figure 9–77

2
- Tap or click the Save As button to display the Save As dialog box.

- Type **Steam Train Picture Presentation** in the File name text box (Figure 9–78).

3
- Tap or click the Save button (Save As dialog box) to save the presentation as a picture presentation.

- Tap or click the OK button (Microsoft PowerPoint dialog box).

Figure 9–78

To Reset the Ribbon

Why? *Your work with the PowerPoint presentation is complete, so you can delete the group and buttons you added to the ribbon.* The following steps remove the Handouts group and the 'Print Preview and Print' and 'Create Handouts in Microsoft Word' commands from the HOME tab.

- Open the Backstage view, tap or click Options to display the PowerPoint Options dialog box, and then tap or click Customize Ribbon in the left pane to display the Customize the Ribbon pane.

- Tap or click the Reset button (PowerPoint Options dialog box) to display the Reset menu (Figure 9–79).

- Tap or click 'Reset all customizations'.

- Tap or click the Yes button (Microsoft Office dialog box) to delete all customizations.

Figure 9–79

- Tap or click the OK button (PowerPoint Options dialog box) to close the dialog box.

Q&A Do I need to remove the group and commands from the ribbon?

No. For consistency, the ribbon is reset after the added group and commands no longer are needed. If you share a computer with others, you should reset the ribbon.

To Save a Presentation and Exit PowerPoint

The presentation now is complete. You should save the presentation and then exit PowerPoint.

1 Save the Steam Train presentation again with the same file name.

2 Exit PowerPoint, closing all open documents.

BTW

Quick Reference

For a table that lists how to complete the tasks covered in this book using touch gestures, the mouse, ribbon, shortcut menu, and keyboard, see the Quick Reference Summary at the back of this book, or visit the Quick Reference resource on the Student Companion Site located on www.cengagebrain.com. For detailed instructions about accessing available resources, visit www.cengage.com/ct/studentdownload or see the inside back cover of this book.

Chapter Summary

In this chapter you have learned how to modify a presentation using text boxes, SmartArt, and shapes. You customized a text box, set it as the default, and then inserted new text boxes and applied formatting, including a texture, gradient, and pattern. You also converted WordArt to SmartArt and then formatted the shapes and bulleted paragraphs. Then you created a diagram from shapes, which had gradients and patterns applied. Finally, you saved the presentation as a picture presentation and exported the file to Microsoft Word to create a handout. The items listed below include all the new PowerPoint skills you have learned in this chapter.

Format Text Boxes and Change a Slide Picture
Change a Text Box Outline Weight (PPT 542)
Change a Text Box Outline Color (PPT 543)
Change a Text Box Outline Style (PPT 544)
Apply an Effect to a Text Box (PPT 544)
Set Text Box Formatting as the Default (PPT 545)
Apply a Pattern to a Text Box (PPT 547)
Apply a Gradient Fill to a Text Box (PPT 549)
Center a Text Box (PPT 550)
Change a Slide Picture (PPT 551)
Apply a Picture to a Text Box (PPT 561)

Create and Format SmartArt
Convert WordArt to SmartArt (PPT 553)
Reorder SmartArt Shapes (PPT 554)
Promote a SmartArt Bullet Level (PPT 555)
Demote a SmartArt Bullet Level (PPT 556)
Add a SmartArt Bullet (PPT 557)
Change the SmartArt Layout (PPT 557)
Remove a SmartArt Shape (PPT 558)
Add a SmartArt Shape (PPT 558)
Resize a SmartArt Graphic by Entering an Exact Measurement (PPT 559)

Resize a SmartArt Graphic Shape (PPT 560)
Convert a SmartArt Graphic to Text (PPT 563)
Convert a SmartArt Graphic to Shapes (PPT 565)

Draw and Insert Shapes, Lines, and Arrows
Apply a Fill to a Shape (PPT 568)
Subtract a Shape (PPT 570)
Merge Shapes (PPT 571)
Draw a Line (PPT 572)
Change a Line Weight and Color (PPT 573)
Set Line Formatting as the Default (PPT 574)
Draw an Additional Line (PPT 575)
Set Shape Formatting as the Default (PPT 577)

Customize the Ribbon
Customize the Ribbon (PPT 579)
Reset the Ribbon (PPT 585)

Create Handouts and Save the Presentation
Create a Handout by Exporting a File to Microsoft Word (PPT 582)
Save the Presentation as a Picture Presentation (PPT 584)

CONSIDER THIS

General Project Guidelines

When creating a PowerPoint presentation, the actions you perform and the decisions you make will affect the appearance and characteristics of the finished document. As you create a presentation with illustrations, such as the project shown in Figure 9–1 on page PPT 539, you should follow these general guidelines:

1. **Choose colors wisely.** The appropriate use of color can add interest and help audience members retain information. Used inappropriately, however, mismatched colors will generate confusion and create an impression of unprofessionalism.

2. **Use keywords in SmartArt graphics.** The words you type into your SmartArt graphic can serve as a prompt of the key points you want to make in the presentation.

3. **Use politically correct language.** When you type words into text boxes, be mindful of the terms you are using to identify the images.

4. **Work with a buddy.** As you develop your slide content and then rehearse the presentation, ask a friend or work associate to assist you with various tasks.

CONSIDER THIS

How should you submit solutions to questions in the assignments identified with a **symbol?**

Every assignment in this book contains one or more questions identified with a symbol. These questions require you to think beyond the assigned presentation. Present your solutions to the questions in the format required by your instructor. Possible formats may include one or more of these options: write the answer; create a document that contains the answer; present your answer to the class; discuss your answer in a group; record the answer as audio or video using a webcam, smartphone, or portable media player; or post answers on a blog, wiki, or website.

Apply Your Knowledge

Reinforce the skills and apply the concepts you learned in this chapter.

Applying an Effect to a Text Box, Inserting and Subtracting Shapes, Resizing a SmartArt Graphic Using Exact Measurements, and Reordering SmartArt Shapes

Note: To complete this assignment, you will be required to use the Data Files for Students. Visit www.cengage.com/ct/studentdownload for detailed instructions or contact your instructor for information about accessing the required files.

Instructions: Run PowerPoint. Open the presentation, Apply 9-1 Sun Corp, from the Data Files for Students.

The two slides in this presentation are for the Sun Corporation's announcement of its new management team. The document you open is a partially formatted presentation. You will apply an effect to a text box, insert and subtract shapes for a logo, reorder SmartArt shapes, and resize SmartArt to an exact measurement. Your presentation should look like Figure 9–80.

Perform the following tasks:

1. On Slide 1, select the title text placeholder and apply the Orange, 18 pt glow, Accent color 1 Glow effect (the first effect in the fourth Glow Variations row). Change the subtitle font to Arial, change the size to 32 point, change the font color to Gray-25%, Background 2, Darker 75% (the third color in the fifth Theme Colors row), bold, italicize, and then underline this text.

2. Insert a rectangle by using the Rectangle shape, (the first shape in the Rectangles row), resize the shape to 2.87" × 2.2", change the shape fill color to Orange, Accent 1, Lighter 40% (the fifth color in the fourth Theme Colors row), and then change the shape outline to No Outline. Move this shape to the left side of the title text placeholder as shown in Figure 9–80a.

3. Create a sun shape by inserting a 24-Point Star (the eleventh shape in the first Stars and Banners row), resize the shape to 1.5" × 1.5", and then copy and paste this shape three times. Move these four sun shapes on top of the rectangle shape that you created in Step 2. Position one at the top, bottom, left, and right, respectively so that about half of the sun shapes are off the edge of the rectangle shape. Use the Smart Guides to help you line them up.

4. Select the rectangle shape, hold down the CTRL key, select the four sun shapes, tap or click the Merge Shapes button, and then tap or click the Subtract command. Figure 9–80a shows the completed logo.

5. On Slide 2, select the shape labeled Sandra Smith on the organization chart and delete it. Select the shape labeled Ann Wilson and Promote up one level, as shown in Figure 9–80b. Change the Organization Chart SmartArt layout to the Picture Organization Chart (the second graphic in the first Hierarchy row) and resize it to 7.5" × 11.5".

(a) Slide 1

(b) Slide 2

Figure 9–80

Continued >

Apply Your Knowledge *continued*

6. Insert the photos of the six employees which are available from the Data Files for Students and named, Robert Jones, Sara Anders, John Winn, Sue Mills, Mae Smith, and Ann Wilson. Select the text in the shape labeled, Robert Jones, center this text, and then change the shape fill color to Orange, Accent 1 (the fifth color in the first Theme Colors row). Select all the text in the organization chart, change the font to Arial Narrow, change the font size to 20 point, and then bold this text.

7. Change the colors of the SmartArt graphic to Colorful Range – Accent Colors 2 to 3 (the second color in the Colorful area), and then apply the Cartoon 3-D style (the third style in the 3-D area). Center the SmartArt graphic on the slide as shown in the figure.

8. If requested by your instructor, add your birth year, birth city, and birth state as the second line of the subtitle on Slide 1.

9. Apply the Push transition and change the duration to 4.00 for all slides.

10. Save the presentation using the file name, Apply 9-1 Sun Corp Management.

11. Submit the revised document in the format specified by your instructor.

12. ✳ In this presentation, you created a logo by subtracting shapes. Did this enhance the presentation? How? You changed the layout of the SmartArt organization chart and added photos. How did this help your presentation?

Extend Your Knowledge

Extend the skills you learned in this chapter and experiment with new skills. You may need to use Help to complete the assignment.

Applying a Photo to a Shape, Changing a Text Box Outline Style, Applying a Pattern to a Text Box, Merging Shapes Using Union, and Setting Line Formatting as the Default

Note: To complete this assignment, you will be required to use the Data Files for Students. Visit www.cengage.com/ct/studentdownload for detailed instructions or contact your instructor for information about accessing the required files.

Instructions: Run PowerPoint. Open the presentation, Extend 9-1 Flower Shop, from the Data Files for Students. You will apply a photo to a shape, change text box outlines and fills, insert and merge shapes, and set line formatting as the default. Use Figures 9–81a and 9–81b as a guide.

Perform the following tasks:

1. On Slide 1, insert the Bevel shape (the first shape in the third Basic Shapes row). Resize the shape to approximately 5.26" × 4.51" and apply the tulip photo to the shape, as shown in Figure 9–81a. The photo, named Yellow Tulip, is available on the Data Files for Students. Move the shape so the left edge is approximately 1" from the left side of the slide and then center it vertically on the slide.

2. Insert a text box on the right side of Slide 1, type **Visit the Flower Pot** in the text box, change the font to MV Boli, change the font size to 66 point, apply the Gradient Fill – Gold, Accent 4, Outline – Accent 4 WordArt style (the third style in the second row) to the text, and then center the text. Change the size of the text box to 2.32"× 5.5" so that there are two words on each line, and then align the text in the middle of the text box. Change the border of the text box to the Square Dot dashes and then change the line weight to 3 pt.

3. Insert a second text box on the right side of Slide 1, type `Located outside the bookstore` in the text box, change the font size to 36 point, center the text, and then bold it. Adjust the size of the text box so that the text fits on two lines. Apply the Wide upward diagonal pattern to the text box. Move this text box so it is centered under the first text box. Select both text boxes and Distribute Vertically on the right side of the slide.

4. On Slide 2, change the square shape to a Trapezoid (the fifth shape in the first Basic Shapes row). *Hint:* You may need to use Help to learn how to change a shape. Center the trapezoid shape on top of the blue oval shape, move it down so that the bottom of the trapezoid shape is almost to the bottom of the oval shape, select both shapes, and then select Union under Merge Shapes. Change the shape fill color to Orange, Accent 2, Darker 25% (the sixth color in the fifth Theme Colors row). Select the green oval shape and apply the Walnut texture fill to this shape. Move this shape on top of the flower pot, and then select the flower pot and group these two shapes together. Move the flower pot to the bottom-center area of the slide, as shown in Figure 9–81b.

(a) Slide 1

(b) Slide 2

Figure 9–81

Continued >

Extend Your Knowledge *continued*

5. Create a flower shape by inserting a 7-Point Star shape, resize it to approximately 2" × 2", change the shape fill color to Yellow (the fourth color in the Standard Colors row), change the shape outline color to Purple (the last color in the Standard Colors row), and then change the outline weight to 6 pt. Type `The` in the shape, change the font size to 36 point, and then change the font color to Black, Text 1 (the second color in the first Theme Colors row). Duplicate the shape and then type `Pot` in the second shape. Move the two flower shapes to the location shown in Figure 9–81b on the previous page.

6. Select the left flower shape and duplicate it. With the flower shape selected, apply the Lock aspect ratio and then use one of the corner sizing handles to resize the shape to approximately 2.87" × 2.87". *Hint:* You may need to use Help to learn how to apply the Lock aspect ratio. Move this shape above the flower pot to the location indicated in the figure. Type `Flower` in the shape.

7. Insert a line from the bottom-center (yellow area) of the middle flower to the middle of the dark area on the top of the flower pot, change the line color to Green, Accent 6, Darker 25% (the last color in the fifth Theme Colors row), change the weight of the line to 10 pt. Set this line formatting as the default. Insert a line from each of the two small flowers to the dark area on the top of the flower pot. Select all three lines and send them backward. Approximate size and location of the center green line is shown in Figure 9–81b.

8. Insert a text box in the center of the flower pot and type `Open Daily: 9 to 5` on the first line, type `Fresh flowers` on the second line, and then type `Gift ideas` on the third line. Change the font to Arial Narrow, increase the font size as large as possible (approximately 22 points) so the top line does not break, center the text, and then bold it. Increase the width of the text box so the type fits on the flower pot, and if necessary, remove the shape fill and outline from the text box.

9. If requested by your instructor, type your mother's maiden name in place of the text, Gift Ideas, in the text box on Slide 2 (Figure 9–81b).

10. Apply the Blinds transition in the Exciting category to all slides and then change the duration to 3.50 seconds.

11. Save the presentation using the file name, Extend 9-1 The Flower Pot.

12. Submit the revised document in the format specified by your instructor.

13. ✸ In this presentation, you inserted a flower photo into the bevel shape. How did this improve the look of the slide? Why did you use the Lock aspect ratio when changing the size of the flower shape on Slide 2?

Analyze, Correct, Improve

Analyze a presentation, correct all errors, and improve it.

Changing a Background Photo, Applying a Fill to a Shape, Converting WordArt to SmartArt, and Resizing, Changing Line Weight, and Color of a Shape

Note: To complete this assignment, you will be required to use the Data Files for Students. Visit www.cengage.com/ct/studentdownload for detailed instructions or contact your instructor for information about accessing the required files.

Instructions: Run PowerPoint. Open the presentation, Analyze 9-1 Classes, from the Data Files for Students. The principal at the high school you work at asked you to prepare a presentation about the new adult classes that will be offered in the fall. Modify the slides by making the indicated corrections and improvements.

1. Correct

a. The photo used as the background on Slide 1 (Figure 9–82a) is outdated so you will change it to the photo called Classroom, shown in the figure, which is available on the Data Files for Students. Change the transparency to 0%. Delete the copy of the Classroom photo.

b. On Slide 1, increase the size of the top Wavy shape to approximately 2.14" × 8.85", change the border weight to 3 pt, change the shape fill color to Dark Blue (the ninth color in the Standard Colors row), and then change the transparency to 50%. Move this shape to the upper-left corner of the slide. Set this shape formatting as the Default.

c. Insert a Double Wave shape (the eighth shape in the second Stars and Banners row) across the width of the slide and copy and paste the text from the text box at the bottom of the slide into this shape. Change the height of the shape to 1.25". Delete the text box at the bottom of the slide.

d. On Slide 2 (Figure 9–82b), convert the WordArt bulleted text to the Vertical Block List SmartArt graphic (the second graphic in the seventh List row). Change the colors to Colorful Range – Accent Colors 4 to 5 (the fourth colors in the Colorful row). Select the five left shapes labeled with the days of the week, and then tap or click the Smaller button three times.

e. If requested by your instructor, type the name of your high school in place of Eagle Ridge on Slide 1 (Figure 9–82a).

(a) Slide 1

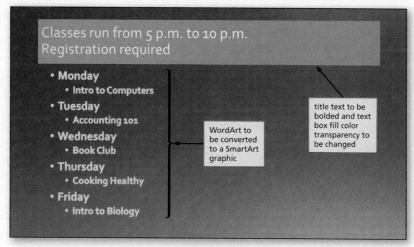

(b) Slide 2

Figure 9–82

Continued >

Analyze, Correct, Improve *continued*

2. Improve

 a. On Slide 1, change the border color on the two wavy shapes to Orange, Accent 1 (the fifth color in the first Theme Colors row).

 b. Change the font size of the text in the bottom shape to 40 point, apply the Fill – White, Text 1, Shadow WordArt style (the first style in the first row) to the text, and then bold this text. Move this shape to approximately .05" from the bottom of the slide.

 c. On Slide 2, bold the title text and with the title text placeholder still selected, change the blue fill color transparency to 50%.

 d. Apply the Metallic Scene style to the SmartArt graphic and then visually center the graphic on the slide.

 e. Change the Rotate transition to the Conveyor transition and then change the duration to 3.25 seconds for all slides.

 f. Save the presentation using the file name, Analyze 9-1 Adult Classes.

 g. Submit the revised document in the format specified by your instructor.

3. ✹ Which errors existed in the starting file? How did changing the shape fills and line weights help? How did changing the photo on Slide 1 improve the look of the slide?

In the Labs

Design and/or create a presentation using the guidelines, concepts, and skills presented in this chapter. Labs 1 and 2, which increase in difficulty, require you to create solutions based on what you learned in the chapter; Lab 3 requires you to create a solution, which uses cloud and web technologies, by learning and investigating on your own from general guidance.

Lab 1: Combining Shapes, Changing the Outline Style and Centering a Text Box, Converting a SmartArt Graphic to Text, Promoting a SmartArt Bullet Level, and Applying an Illustration to a Text Box

Problem: You are an instructor at the Dance Studio 9 school of dance. Your school is under new ownership, and the new owner has made some changes including a new name and moving to a new larger location. He asked you to create a new logo with the new name and create a PowerPoint presentation to promote an upcoming dance lesson special. You create the presentation shown in Figures 9–83a through 9–83d on page PPT 594.

Note: To complete this assignment, you will be required to use the Data Files for Students. Visit www.cengage.com/ct/studentdownload for detailed instructions or contact your instructor for information about accessing the required files.

Instructions: Perform the following tasks:

 1. Open the presentation, Lab 9-1 Dance, from the Data Files for Students. Customize the Ribbon by adding a group called Nudge to the HOME tab and then adding the Nudge Down, Nudge Left, Nudge Right, and the Nudge Up commands to this new group.

 2. Decrease the size of the illustration on Slide 1 to approximately 4.09" × 3.42", apply the Perspective Shadow, White picture style (the fourth style in the third row), change the color to Grayscale, and then change the picture border color to Gold, Accent 3 (the seventh color in the first Theme Colors row). Move the illustration to the upper-right area of the slide, as shown in Figure 9–83a.

3. *Note:* See Figure 9–83d on the next page for illustrations to assist you in creating the logo on Slide 1. Insert a Double Wave shape (the last shape in the second Stars and Banners row), resize to 2" × 4", and rotate the shape slightly to the left. With the shape still selected, copy and paste the shape two times. Select the HOME tab and locate the Nudge Group you added to the ribbon. Select the top shape, tap or click the Nudge Right button, and then the Nudge Down button 16 times each. Select the middle shape, tap or click the Nudge Right button, and then the Nudge Down button eight times each. See the upper-left illustration in Figure 9–83d.

4. Select the three shapes, and then merge them using the Combine command as shown in the upper-right illustration in Figure 9–83d. Add the text `Dance Studio 9` in the combined shape, change the font to Arial, change the font color to Black, Background 1 (the first color in the first Theme Colors row), and then bold this text. Change the shape fill color to White, Text 1, Darker 35% (the second color in the fifth Theme Colors row), as shown in the lower-left illustration in Figure 9–83d.

5. Apply the Triangle Down Transform text effect (the fourth effect in the first Warp row) to the text. Select the shape, and then apply the Olive Green, 11 pt glow, Accent color 4 Glow effect as shown in the lower-right illustration in Figure 9–83d. Apply the Preset 2 shape effect to the shape, resize it to approximately 2.5" × 5", and move the shape to the upper-left area of the Slide 1, as shown in Figure 9–83a.

6. Insert a text box on Slide 1, type `DANCERS OF ALL LEVELS WELCOME`, change the font size to 40 point, bold this text, center it, align the text in the middle of the text box, and then apply the Fill – White, Outline – Accent 2, Hard Shadow – Accent 2 WordArt style (the fourth style in the third row) to the text. Change the text box shape fill color to Black, Background 1, Lighter 25% (the first color in the fourth Theme Colors row), change the text box outline to the Round Dot Dashes, and then change the outline weight to 6 pt.

7. Change the size of the text box to 1.5" × 10", distribute the text box horizontally, and then align it to the bottom of the slide. Press the Nudge Up button 15 times to position the text box, as shown in Figure 9–83a. Copy and paste this text box to Slides 2 and 3, and position them as shown in Figure 9–83b and 9–83c.

8. On Slide 2 (Figure 9–83b), change the title text to, `NEW STUDENT SPECIALS`. Do not change the size of the text box. Change the SmartArt layout to the Vertical Block List (the second layout in the seventh List row). Change the color of the SmartArt graphic to Colored Fill – Accent 3 (the second color in the Accent 3 row), and then apply the Polished style (the first style in the first 3-D row).

9. Select the two left shapes that show the prices, and tap or click the Smaller button three times. Change the font size in these two shapes to 36 point, the font color to Black, Background 1 (the first color in the first Theme Colors row). In the top-right shape, demote the second and fourth bulleted paragraphs. In the bottom-right shape, demote the second bulleted paragraph, and then promote the fourth bulleted paragraph. Change the font size in the top-right and bottom-right shapes to 24 point, as shown in Figure 9–83b.

10. Insert a text box in the right area of the top-right and bottom-right shapes in the SmartArt graphic. In the top text box, insert the illustration called Dancing Shoes. In the bottom text box, insert the illustration called Music. Both illustrations are available from the Data Files for Students.

11. On Slide 3, change the title text to, `FEATURED DANCES`, as shown in Figure 9–83c. Do not change the size of the text box. Convert the SmartArt graphic to text. Change the bulleted list font size to 36 point, and then change the bullets to the Arrow bullets. Change the size of the text box to 3" × 5", and then change the shape fill to Gold, Accent 3 (the seventh color in the Theme Colors row). Change the bulleted list font color to Black, Background 1 (the first color in the first Theme Colors row). Move the bulleted list text box to the area shown in the figure. Apply the Soft Edge Oval picture style (the sixth style in the third row) to the illustration.

Continued >

In the Labs *continued*

12. If requested by your instructor, add the year of your birth after the word Waltz on Slide 3 (Figure 9–83c).

13. Apply the Shape transition in the Subtle category to all slides and then change the duration to 3.00 seconds.

14. Reset the ribbon. Save the presentation using the file name, Lab 9-1 Dance Studio 9. Submit the document in the format specified by your instructor.

15. ✳ Did the design of the new logo enhance the presentation? You added a Dashed Dot border to the title text boxes? Why? Did changing the SmartArt graphic to text help the presentation? Why?

(a) Slide 1

(b) Slide 2

(c) Slide 3

(d) Logo Diagram

Figure 9–83

Lab 2: Changing a Text Box Outline Weight and Style, Changing a Photo, Inserting Shapes and Combining Shapes, Setting Shape and Text Box Formatting as the Default, Reordering SmartArt Shapes, and Creating a Handout by Exporting a File to Microsoft Word

Problem: You are studying the anatomy of the human eye in your biology class. Your instructor has divided the class into several groups. Your group was instructed to prepare a PowerPoint presentation focusing on how we see and some tips on keeping your eyes healthy. One of the members in your group started designing a diagram of the eye using shapes, and asked if you would finish the diagram and add some creative touches to the presentation. You create a presentation with four slides, as shown in Figure 9–84a on the next page through 9–84d on page PPT 597.

Note: To complete this assignment, you will be required to use the Data Files for Students. Visit www.cengage.com/ct/studentdownload for detailed instructions or contact your instructor for information about accessing the required files.

Instructions: Perform the following tasks:

1. Open the presentation, Lab 9-2 Eyes, from the Data Files for Students.

2. On Slide 1, change the photo to Brown Eyes, which is available on the Data Files for Students. Resize the photo to approximately 4" × 6", change the picture style to the Rotated, White picture style, change the picture border color to Blue, Accent 4, Lighter 80% (the eighth color in the second Theme Colors row), and then move the photo to the upper-left area of the slide as shown in Figure 9–84a.

3. Change the title font text to Arial Black, increase the font size to 60 point, and then apply the Gradient Fill – Blue, Accent 4, Outline – Accent 4 WordArt style (the third style in the second row). Drag the left-center sizing handle to the left until the text is on one line, center the text, and then align the text in the middle of the text box. Add the Newsprint texture to the text box shape. Apply the Long Dash Dot Dot dashes outline to the shape, change the color to Blue, Accent 4, Lighter 40% (the eighth color in the fourth Theme Colors row), and then change the shape outline weight to 6 pt. Change the size of the text box to approximately 2" × 10", send it backward, and then move it so that the upper-left corner of the text box is behind the bottom-right edge of the photo, as shown in the figure.

4. On Slide 2, increase the size of the photo to 3.67" × 5.5" and then align the photo vertically on the right area of the slide, as shown in Figure 9–84b.

5. Insert the callout shape, Line Callout 1 (Border and Accent Bar) (second shape in the second Callouts row), change the shape outline color to Yellow (the fourth color in the first Standard Colors row), change the shape outline weight to 2¼ pt. Type a letter in the shape, highlight it, change the font to Arial Narrow, change the font size to 24 point, bold the text, and then change the font color to Yellow. Press and hold or right-click this shape and set it as the default shape.

6. On Slide 2, insert three callout shapes, type the text in each shape, move them to the locations shown, and then select the yellow sizing handle at the end of each line and move it on the eye diagram, as shown in Figure 9–84b. *Note:* For the Iris callout, you can flip the shape horizontally as shown.

7. Slide 3 is the eye diagram you will finish by adding shapes for the cornea and retina. Insert a Moon shape (the tenth shape in the third Basic Shapes row), select No Outline, resize it to 3.44" × 1.54", change the shape fill to White, Text 1 (the second color in the first Theme Colors row), and then duplicate the shape. Select the first shape, Send it to Back, and then move it to the left side of the blue diagram as shown in Figure 9–84c.

8. Select the second moon shape, rotate it horizontally, change the size to 2.94" × 0.76", and then change the shape fill color to Purple, Accent 5 (the ninth color in the first Theme Colors row). Insert a Right Arrow shape (the first shape in the first Block Arrows row), select No Outline, resize it to 0.87" × 1.25", and then change the shape fill color to Purple, Accent 5. Move this arrow shape to the right-center area of the purple moon, select both purple shapes and then merge them using the Union command. Move this purple shape to the inside of the blue circle shape lining it up at the right edge of the green line inside the circle shape, as shown in Figure 9–84c. You will not be able to merge these shapes. You can select the three shapes and then group them in case you need to move the eye diagram on the slide.

Continued >

In the Labs *continued*

9. For the callouts on Slide 3, insert a text box, change the shape fill and shape outline color to Black, Background 1 (the first color in the Theme Colors row), change the font to Arial, change the font size to 20 point, and then bold the text. Change the internal margins to 0.2" for the left and right margins, and 0.1" for the top and bottom margins. Set this text box formatting as the default. Create six text boxes, enter the text shown in the figure, adjust the size of each text box for even line distribution, and then move them to the locations shown in Figure 9–84c.

10. On Slide 3, insert an Arrow line (the second shape in the Lines row), change the shape outline color to Black, Background 1, and then change the weight of the line to 3 pt, and then set it as the default line. Insert a line from each of the six text boxes with the arrow pointing to the respective part on the diagram, as shown in Figure 9–84c. *Note:* Use the zoom to make it easier to position the callouts.

11. On Slide 4, center the title text and then bold it. Convert the WordArt bulleted text to the Varying Width List SmartArt graphic (the fourth graphic in the second List row), change the colors to Colorful Range – Accent Colors 5 to 6 (the fifth color group in the Colorful area), and then apply the Inset 3-D style (the second style in the first 3-D row) to the graphic. Reorder the SmartArt shapes so that the shape with the text, Get regular eye exams, is at the top, as shown in Figure 9–84d.

12. If requested by your instructor, add your eye color after the dash in the Iris callout on Slide 2.

13. Apply the Uncover transition in the Subtle category to all slides and then change the duration to 2.50 seconds.

14. Create a handout in Microsoft Word using the 'Blank lines next to slides' page layout, as shown in Figure 9–84e.

15. Save the presentation using the file name, Lab 9-2 Anatomy of the Eye.

16. Save the presentation as a picture presentation using the file name, Lab 9-2 Amazing Eyes.

17. Submit the document in the format specified by your instructor.

18. ✳ Did formatting the text box on Slide 1 improve the look of the slide? Was saving the formatting as the default for shapes, lines, and text boxes helpful? Why? Do you think your audience will be able to read the callouts on Slides 2 and 3? If not, how could you have improved the formatting?

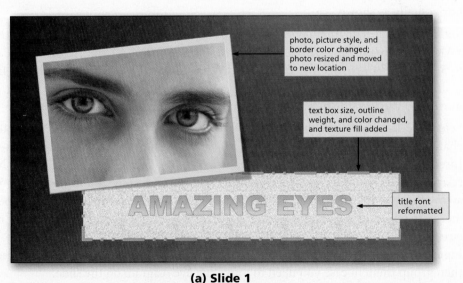

(a) Slide 1

Figure 9–84 (Continued)

(b) Slide 2

(c) Slide 3

6 Tips for Healthy Eyes

Get regular eye exams

Shield eyes from the sun

Give doctor your health history

Control air quality at home and work

Take breaks from computer

Eat healthy

title text centered and bolded

WordArt bulleted text converted to SmartArt graphic

SmartArt shapes reordered

(d) Slide 4

Figure 9–84 (Continued)

Continued >

In the Labs *continued*

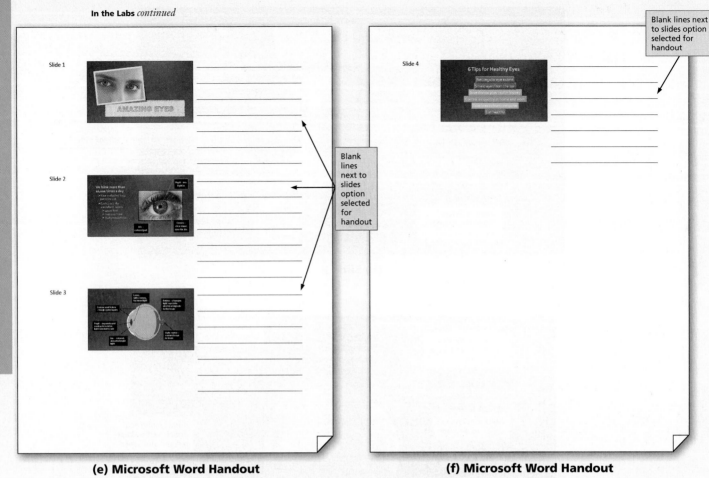

(e) Microsoft Word Handout   **(f) Microsoft Word Handout**

Figure 9–84

Lab 3: Expand Your World: Cloud and Web Technologies
Reviewing Google Images SmartArt

Problem: You want to add SmartArt to the presentation you have created to accompany a speech you are scheduled to deliver in your Earth science class on the topic of tidal waves. You need some ideas, so you browse the images on Google for ideas.

Note: You will need Internet access to complete this assignment. If you do not have Internet access, read this assignment without performing the instructions.

Instructions: Perform the following tasks:
1. In PowerPoint, open the file, Lab 9-3 Tidal Wave, located on the Data Files for Students. View Slides 2 and 3 to familiarize yourself with the content.
2. Open your browser and navigate to Google.com. Tap or click Images at the top of the screen to display the Google Images webpage. Tap or click the Google Images search text box, type **smartart** as the search text, and then tap or click the Search button (the magnifying glass) or press the ENTER key.
3. View several SmartArt images with designs that would be appropriate for the material on Slides 2 and 3 in your Tidal Wave presentation. Select two different designs and then convert the bulleted lists in the slides to these designs.
4. On Slide 1, replace the Student Name text with your name. If requested by your instructor, change the course number to the area code of the town where you were born.

5. Save the presentation with the file name, Lab 9-3 Tidal Wave SmartArt.

6. Submit the revised presentation in the format specified by your instructor.

7. ✳ Which SmartArt images on the Google Images webpage did you use as guides for your presentation? Why did you select these particular examples?

✳ Consider This: Your Turn

Apply your creative thinking and problem-solving skills to design and implement a solution.

1. Design and Create a Presentation about Underwater Hockey

Personal

Part 1: Most people are familiar with some of the more popular forms of hockey like ice, field, and roller hockey, but not many know about underwater hockey. Like other types of hockey, in underwater hockey two teams try to score goals with a puck or ball, into the opponent's net using a stick. Your son joined an underwater hockey league and has asked you to gather some information and create a presentation that he can use to share with his friends who have expressed an interest in the sport. Sometimes referred to as Octopush or water hockey, the sport is a non-contact sport played around the world beginning in the United Kingdom in the mid-1950s. The goals are set up on the bottom of a swimming pool and two teams with six players at a time play two 10-minute sessions, and four additional team players are ready to play as subs. There is equipment required such as a diving mask, snorkel, fins, a glove, and a short stick (not more than 350mm including the handle), and of course head and ear protection (usually a helmet). When the game starts and the puck is in place in the middle of the pool, players hold their breath and dive to the bottom of the pool to go after the puck and push it to the opponent's goal net. Play stops after a goal is scored, or when a referee calls time for a penalty. The puck is about the same size as an ice hockey puck, but is made of lead and weighs about 3 pounds. Use the concepts and techniques presented in this chapter to prepare a presentation. Select a suitable theme, and use shapes, WordArt, and SmartArt graphics where appropriate. The presentation can contain photos, illustrations, and videos. You can use photos and illustrations from Office.com if they are appropriate for this topic. Submit your assignment in the format specified by your instructor.

Part 2: ✳ You made several decisions while creating the presentation in this assignment: where to insert text boxes and shapes, what fills to use, how to format the text and text box backgrounds (such as font, font size, and colors), which image(s) to use, and what WordArt and SmartArt graphics to use to make the presentation look professional and consistent. What was the rationale behind each of these decisions? When you reviewed the document, what further revisions did you make and why? Where would you recommend showing this slide show?

2. Design and Create a Presentation about the Writing Process

Professional

Part 1: Your English composition instructor taught you how to compose an essay using the writing process. This theory stresses that writing is not a linear procedure because a good writer brainstorms ideas, selects one as a topic, performs some prewriting to generate essay details, organizes the major points, writes, and then revises. At any point in the essay, a writer can backtrack to repeat or refine a step. Once a draft is complete, it should be reviewed by a peer. The writer should then take the criticism and revise the rough draft at least once.

You work in your school's Writing Lab, and many students have come to you for help when composing their essays. After explaining the writing process verbally many times, you decide to develop a PowerPoint presentation that depicts this concept to show the students. The presentation should contain SmartArt, text boxes, and shapes to help explain the writing process. You may find examples in your English composition textbook or online. Submit your assignment in the format specified by your instructor.

Continued >

Consider this: Your Turn *continued*

Part 2: ✳ You made several decisions while creating the presentation in this assignment: where to insert text boxes and shapes, what fills to use, how to format the text and text box backgrounds (such as font, font size, and colors), which image(s) to use, and which SmartArt graphics to use to make the presentation look professional and consistent. What was the rationale behind each of these decisions? When you reviewed the document, what further revisions did you make and why? Where would you recommend showing this slide show?

3. Design and Create a Presentation about Clouds

Research and Collaboration

Part 1: In your meteorology class you are studying cloud formations. Clouds are grouped into four categories: Low clouds, middle clouds, high clouds, and vertically-developed clouds. The low clouds form below 6,500 feet and are primarily water droplets but can also contain ice or snow. Stratus clouds usually are a dull gray color and look like a blanket. Stratocumulus clouds are formed when stratus clouds break up. Nimbostratus clouds are darker than stratus clouds and bring rain or snow consistently for long periods of time. Middle clouds form at 6,500 to 20,000 feet and are primarily water droplets, but also can be ice crystals. Altocumulus clouds usually appear as layers of puffy clouds. Altostratus clouds appear as gray flat sheets that cover most of the sky and obscure the sun. High clouds form above 20,000 feet and are primarily ice crystals. Cirrus clouds spread across the sky and have a feathery appearance. Cirrocumulus clouds are wavy and rippled. Cirrostratus clouds spread in a thin sheet and give the sky a white appearance. Vertically-developed clouds grow to heights of more than 39,000 feet. Cumulus clouds look like cotton balls. Cumulonimbus clouds are cumulus clouds that have grown high into the atmosphere with dark bases, and can produce severe storms. Your class will be divided into four groups, and each group will gather information and photos about one category of clouds. Then you will meet to discuss what information to include in the PowerPoint presentation. Use at least three objectives found at the beginning of this chapter to develop the presentation. Some shapes in PowerPoint may help with your presentation, and a few lines, such as Freeform, can be used to draw and illustrate clouds. Print handouts and speaker notes for the class presentation. You can use your own photos and videos or those available from Office.com if they are appropriate for this topic.

Part 2: ✳ You made several decisions while creating the presentation in this assignment: where to insert text boxes and shapes, what fills to use, how to format the text and text box backgrounds (such as font, font size, and colors), which image(s) to use, and what WordArt and SmartArt graphics to use to make the presentation look professional and consistent. What was the rationale behind each of these decisions? When you reviewed the document, what further revisions did you make and why? Where would you recommend showing this slide show?

Learn Online

Reinforce what you learned in this chapter with games, exercises, training, and many other online activities and resources.

Student Companion Site Reinforcement activities and resources are available at no additional cost on www.cengagebrain.com. Visit www.cengage.com/ct/studentdownload for detailed instructions about accessing the resources available at the Student Companion Site.

SAM Put your skills into practice with SAM! If you have a SAM account, go to www.cengage.com/sam2013 to access SAM assignments for this chapter.

10 Developing a Presentation with Content from Outside Sources

Objectives

You will have mastered the material in this chapter when you can:

- Insert an object from a file
- Embed and edit a file
- Draw and format a table
- Resize, split, distribute, and arrange table columns and rows
- Insert and edit a linked Excel worksheet
- Switch chart rows and columns

- Change a chart type
- Apply a chart style
- Apply effects to chart elements
- Display chart elements
- Edit chart data
- Add a hyperlink to a table

10 | Developing a Presentation with Content from Outside Sources

BTW
Using Tables and Charts
Charts and tables can give meaning to the figures and facts you want to emphasize in your presentation. These tools help audiences understand abstract concepts and the relationships between sets of data. Present only one main idea in a chart or table. Overloading your slides with data may confuse your audience and defeat the purpose of these graphical elements.

Introduction

Adding visuals to a presentation could help audience members remember the important facts you want to share. Researchers have found that adding such graphics as tables, charts, graphs, and maps increases retention by more than 50 percent. Audiences also believe that speakers who include visuals in their presentations are more qualified and believable than speakers who do not have accompanying visuals. In addition, studies have shown that meeting times are reduced and decisions are reached more quickly when group members have seen visuals that help them reach a consensus.

PowerPoint has many features that allow you to insert visuals and then modify them directly on the slide. For example, you can embed a Microsoft Word document and then edit its text or replace its graphics. You can link an Excel worksheet with a PowerPoint slide so that when numbers are modified in the slide, the corresponding numbers on the worksheet also are updated. These tools help you work productively and generate slides with graphics that help your audience comprehend and remember your message.

Project — Presentation with Embedded and Linked Files and Formatted Table and Chart

BTW
First Impressions
Take care in designing an opening slide that meets the audience's expectations and generates interest in the remainder of the presentation. The first slide in your presentation sets the tone of your entire presentation. Before you say one word, your audience sees what you have projected on the screen and forms a first impression of whether the speech is going to be interesting, professional, and relevant.

A low-fat diet and exercise are two factors that can prevent and treat many chronic diseases, including heart disease, obesity, diabetes, and hypertension. Many fitness centers include wellness programs that focus on eating properly and monitoring cholesterol levels. They offer classes in meal proportions, nutrition, and cooking, and they also provide blood pressure checks and blood tests.

The presentation you create in this chapter (Figure 10–1) would be useful to show during a nutrition class at your local fitness center. You begin Slide 1 (Figure 10–1a) by inserting a flyer with graphics and text (Figure 10–1b). You then decide to emphasize the healthy aspect of learning to eat properly and monitor blood composition, so you edit the title text by adding the word, Healthy, directly onto the slide. The second slide (Figure 10–1c) includes a chart that you draw and enhance using PowerPoint's tools and graphical features. If you tap or click a cell in the chart when running the presentation, a hyperlinked Adobe PDF file that can be used to track food consumption (Figure 10–1d) displays. You insert the table on Slide 3 (Figure 10–1e) from a Microsoft Excel worksheet (Figure 10–1f) that contains the results of one blood draw. You will update this table with the results of a second blood draw, and these figures also will update the original Excel worksheet. Fitness center members have provided the results of their cholesterol tests, and this data was used to create the chart that is displayed on Slide 4 (Figure 10–1g on page PPT 604) and created in Microsoft Excel (Figure 10–1h). You then obtain the test results from a few more fitness center members, so you update the worksheet data that generated the chart, which, in turn, modifies the chart automatically.

Figure 10–1

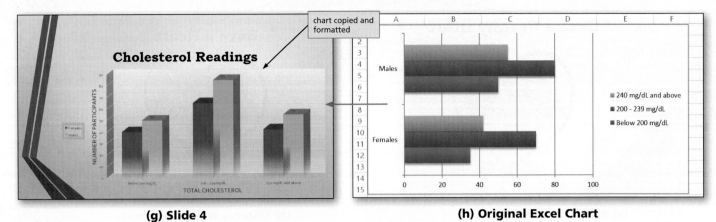

(g) Slide 4   **(h) Original Excel Chart**

Figure 10–1 (Continued)

Roadmap

In this chapter, you will learn how to create the slides shown in Figure 10–1 on this and the previous page. The following roadmap identifies general activities you will perform as you progress through this chapter:

1. INSERT AND EDIT a Microsoft WORD FILE by adding text.
2. DRAW TABLE ROWS AND COLUMNS and then erase lines and split columns and rows.
3. FORMAT a TABLE by adding shading, a gradient fill, and a cell bevel, and then distributing rows and resizing columns and rows.
4. INSERT AND EDIT a LINKED Excel WORKSHEET.
5. COPY, FORMAT and EDIT an Excel CHART by changing the type, colors, legend, labels, background, and data.

At the beginning of step instructions throughout the chapter, you will see an abbreviated form of this roadmap. The abbreviated roadmap uses colors to indicate chapter progress: gray means the chapter is beyond that activity; blue means the task being shown is covered in that activity, and black means that activity is yet to be covered. For example, the following abbreviated roadmap indicates the chapter would be showing a task in the 3 FORMAT TABLE activity.

1 INSERT & EDIT WORD FILE | 2 DRAW TABLE ROWS & COLUMNS | 3 FORMAT TABLE
4 INSERT & EDIT LINKED WORKSHEET | 5 COPY, FORMAT & EDIT CHART

Use the abbreviated roadmap as a progress guide while you read or step through the instructions in this chapter.

To Run PowerPoint, Choose a Theme and Variant, and Save a File

If you are using a computer to step through the project in this chapter and you want your screens to match the figures in this book, you should change your computer's resolution to 1366×768. The following steps run PowerPoint and then save a file.

1 Run PowerPoint, apply the Parallax theme, and then select the last variant (with the gray and red stripes). If necessary, maximize the PowerPoint window.

2 Save the presentation using the file name, Healthy Heart.

One of the few differences between Windows 7 and Windows 8 occurs in the steps to run PowerPoint. If you are using Windows 7, tap or click the Start button, type **PowerPoint** in the 'Search programs and files' box, tap or click PowerPoint 2013, and then, if necessary, maximize the PowerPoint window. For a summary of the steps to run PowerPoint in Windows 7, refer to the Quick Reference located at the back of this book.

BTW
The Ribbon and Screen Resolution
PowerPoint may change how the groups and buttons within the groups appear on the ribbon, depending on the computer's screen resolution. Thus, your ribbon may look different from the ones in this book if you are using a screen resolution other than 1366×768.

Use powerful words to accompany the text on your slides.
Carefully plan the speech that coordinates with the slides in your presentation. Use examples that substantiate the objects on the slides, and use familiar, precise words and terms that enlighten the audience. Do not include obvious material as filler because audience members will conclude that you are wasting their time with irrelevant information.

Inserting Graphics or Other Objects from a File

PowerPoint allows you to insert many types of objects into a presentation. You can insert clips, pictures, video and audio files, and symbols, and you also can copy and paste or drag and drop objects from one slide to another. At times you may want to insert content created with other Microsoft Office programs, such as a Word flyer, an Excel table or graph, a Paint graphic, or a document created with another Microsoft Windows-based application. The original document is called the **source**, and the new document that contains this object is called the **destination**. When you want to copy a source document object, such as a Word flyer, to a destination document, such as your PowerPoint slide, you can use one of three techniques.

- **Embedding** — An **embedded object** becomes part of the destination slide, but you edit and modify the contents using the source program's commands and features. In this project, for example, you will embed a Word document and then edit the text using Microsoft Word without leaving PowerPoint.

- **Linking** — Similar to an embedded object, a **linked object** also is created in another application and is stored in the **source file**, the original file in which the object was created. The linked object maintains a connection to its source and does not become part of the destination slide. Instead, a connection, or link, made between the source and destination objects gives the appearance that the objects are independent. In reality, the two objects work together so that when one is edited, the other is updated. If the original object is changed, the linked object on the slide also changes. In this project, for example, you will link a Microsoft Excel table and then edit the data using Excel. As the numbers in the table change, the numbers in the linked table on the PowerPoint slide also are updated to reflect those changes.

- **Copying and pasting** — An object that you copy from a source document and then paste in a destination document becomes part of the destination program. Any edits that you make are done using the destination software. When you paste the object, you have the options of embedding or linking the document. For example, if you copy a picture from a Word document, embed it into your slide, and then recolor or remove the background, those changes are made using PowerPoint's commands and do not affect the source object. In contrast, in this project you will copy an Excel chart and then paste it into a slide by linking the two documents. When you modify the object without leaving PowerPoint, any changes you make to the data in PowerPoint will be reflected in the original Excel source document.

The first two techniques described above are termed **object linking and embedding** (**OLE**, pronounced o-lay). This means of sharing material developed in various sources and then updating the files within a destination program is useful when you deliver presentations frequently that display current data that changes constantly. For example, your PowerPoint presentation may contain a chart reflecting current fitness center enrollment statistics, or you may include a table with the fitness center's membership totals for the previous year.

BTW
Touch Screen Differences
The Office and Windows interfaces may vary if you are using a touch screen. For this reason, you might notice that the function or appearance of your touch screen differs slightly from this chapter's presentation.

BTW
Q&As
For a complete list of the Q&As found in many of the step-by-step sequences in this book, visit the Q&A resource on the Student Companion Site located on www.cengagebrain.com. For detailed instructions about accessing available resources, visit www.cengage.com/ct/studentdownload or see the inside back cover of this book.

To Insert a File with Graphics and Text

The first object you will add to your presentation is a graphical flyer created in Microsoft Word. This flyer contains artwork and text developed as part of an advertising campaign for a class at the fitness center promoting lowering heart attack risks. You desire to use this document in your slide show. *Why? The heart image and text fit well with the topic of your presentation.* The following steps insert a Microsoft Word file with a graphic and text.

1

- Delete both the title and subtitle placeholders.

- Display the INSERT tab and then tap or click the Object button (INSERT tab | Text group) to display the Insert Object dialog box (Figure 10–2).

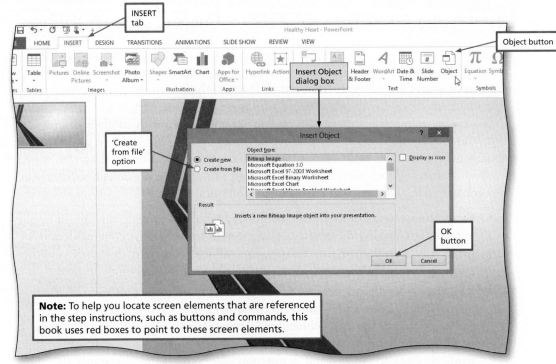

Figure 10–2

2

- Tap or click 'Create from file' (Insert Object dialog box) to display the File box.

- Tap or click the Browse button and then navigate to the location where your Data Files for Students are stored (in this case, the PowerPoint folder in the CIS 101 folder [or your class folder] on your computer or SkyDrive).

- Scroll down and then tap or click Heart Flyer to select the Microsoft Word file (Figure 10–3).

Figure 10–3

 What is the difference between the Create new and the 'Create from file' options?

The Create new option opens an application and allows you to develop an original object. In contrast, the 'Create from file' option prompts you to locate a file that already is created and saved so you can modify the object using the program that was used to create it.

3

- Tap or click the OK button (Browse dialog box) to insert the file name into the File box (Insert Object dialog box) (Figure 10–4).

Figure 10–4

4

- Tap or click the OK button (Insert Object dialog box) to display the Heart Flyer contents on Slide 1 (Figure 10–5).

Q&A Why did several seconds pass before this flyer was displayed on the slide?

PowerPoint takes more time to insert embedded and linked inserted objects than it takes to perform an ordinary cut-and-paste or copy-and-paste action. You must be patient while PowerPoint is inserting the object.

Figure 10–5

BTW

Importing Text Files

In this project you import a Microsoft Word file, but you also can import a text (.txt) file, which has alphanumeric characters with little or no visual formatting. To import a text file, perform the same steps you use to insert the Heart Flyer, but locate a file with the .txt file extension instead of the .docx file extension.

To Edit an Embedded File

The flyer provides an excellent graphic and text to use on Slide 1, but you want to edit the text by adding the word, Healthy. *Why?* *Adding the word, Healthy, emphasizes the need to adopt an overall lifestyle approach, which leads nicely to your slides that emphasize the benefits of a low-fat diet and regular blood tests.* PowerPoint allows you to edit an embedded file easily by opening the source program, which in this case is Microsoft Word. The following steps edit the Microsoft Word text.

1

● Double-tap or double-click the embedded heart object to run the Microsoft Word program and open the document on Slide 1 (Figure 10–6).

Figure 10–6

2

● Position the pointer directly before the letter H in the word, Heart, type **Healthy** as the insertion text, and then press the SPACE BAR (Figure 10–7).

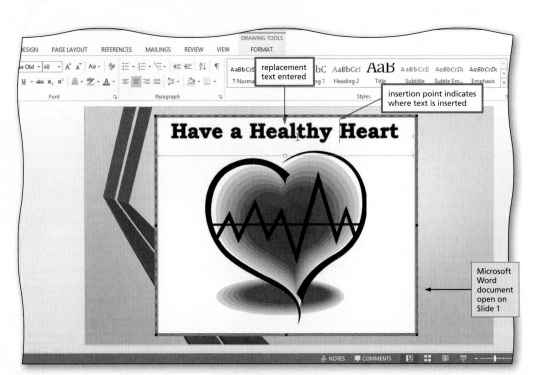

Figure 10–7

❸

• Tap or click outside the Word document to close Microsoft Word and display the edited flyer object on Slide 1.

• Display the DRAWING TOOLS FORMAT tab, size the object so that it is approximately 7.5" × 8.2", and then position the object as shown in Figure 10–8.

Q&A Does PowerPoint take more time to position embedded objects than copied objects?
Yes, you must be patient while PowerPoint responds to your touch, mouse, or arrow key movements.

How can I center the object precisely as shown in Figure 10–8?
If you are using a keyboard, you can use the ARROW keys to move the object in small increments.

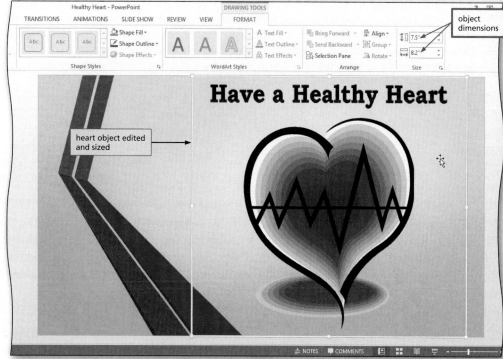

Figure 10–8

Other Ways

1. Press and hold or right-click Word object, tap or click Document Object on shortcut menu, tap or click Edit

---

Drawing and Adjusting a Table

Tables are useful graphical elements to present data organized in descriptive rows and columns. Each cell created from the intersection of a row and column has a unique location name and contains numeric or textual data that you can edit.

In the following pages, you will perform these tasks on Slide 2:

1. Draw a table.
2. Draw table rows.
3. Draw table columns.
4. Erase a table line.
5. Split a table column and row.
6. Add shading to a table.
7. Add a gradient fill to a table.
8. Add a cell bevel.
9. Distribute table rows.
10. Resize table columns and rows.
11. Center the table.

BTW

Drawing a Table Using a Tablet
In this project, you will create a table using PowerPoint's pencil pointer. This tool allows you to use a mouse and draw rows and columns. On a touch screen, however, the pencil pointer is not available. You may, therefore, use a mouse, stylus, or other pointing device to draw a table. Or, you can create a table by tapping the 'Add a Table' button (INSERT tab | Tables group) and then specifying the desired number of rows and columns.

CONSIDER THIS

Develop tables that are clear and meaningful.

Use a table to present complex material, but be certain the information makes useful comparisons. Tables generally are used to show relationships between sets of data. For example, they may show prices for grades of gasoline in three states, the number of in-state and out-of-state students who have applied for admission to various college programs, or the rushing and passing records among quarterbacks in a particular league. The units of measurement, such as dollars, specific majors, or yards, should be expressed clearly on the slides. The data in the rows and columns should be aligned uniformly. Also, the table labels should be meaningful and easily read.

To Draw a Table

1 INSERT & EDIT WORD FILE | 2 DRAW TABLE ROWS & COLUMNS | 3 FORMAT TABLE
4 INSERT & EDIT LINKED WORKSHEET | 5 COPY, FORMAT & EDIT CHART

PowerPoint allows you to insert a table in several ways. You can tap or click the Table button on the INSERT tab and either tap or click the Insert Table command or drag your finger or pointer to specify the number of rows and columns you need. You also can tap or click the Insert Table button in a content placeholder. Another method that allows flexibility is to draw the entire table. However, you must use a mouse or other pointing device to use the Draw Table command. The following steps draw a table on Slide 2. *Why? This method allows flexibility to draw the outer edges and then add the columns and rows.*

1

- Insert a new slide with the Title Only layout. Type **Sources of Fat and Cholesterol** as the title text.

- Change the title text font to Bookman Old Style and bold this text.

- Display the VIEW tab and then, if necessary, click the Ruler check box (VIEW tab | Show group) to display the horizontal and vertical rulers.

- Display the INSERT tab and then click the Table button (INSERT tab | Tables group) to display the Insert Table gallery (Figure 10–9).

Figure 10–9

- Click Draw Table and then position the pointer, which has the shape of a pencil, in the upper-left area below the slide title.

Q&A If I decide I do not want to draw a table, how can I change the pointer to the block arrow?
Press the ESC key.

- Drag the pencil pointer to the lower-right corner of the slide to draw the outer edges of the table (Figure 10–10).

3

- Release the mouse button to create the table frame.

Q&A Must my table be the same size or be positioned in the same location shown in the figure?
No. You will resize and reposition the table later in this project.

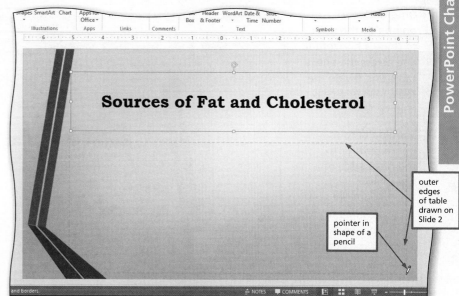

Figure 10–10

To Draw Table Rows

1 INSERT & EDIT WORD FILE | 2 DRAW TABLE ROWS & COLUMNS | 3 FORMAT TABLE
4 INSERT & EDIT LINKED WORKSHEET | 5 COPY, FORMAT & EDIT CHART

Once you draw the four sides of the table, you then can use the pointer as a pencil to draw lines for the columns and rows in the positions where you desire them to display. You could, therefore, draw columns having different widths and rows that are spaced in irregular heights. The following steps draw four lines to create five table rows. *Why? The first row will contain the column headings, and the remaining rows will list specific foods that contain the four types of fats: monounsaturated, polyunsaturated, saturated, and trans.* Note that you must use a mouse or other pointing device to draw table rows.

- With the TABLE TOOLS DESIGN tab displaying, click the Draw Table button (TABLE TOOLS DESIGN tab | Draw Borders group) to change the pointer to a pencil and then position the pencil pointer inside the table approximately 1" from the top table edge (Figure 10–11).

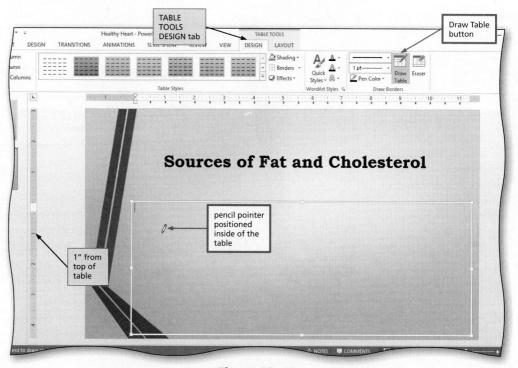

Figure 10–11

2

● Drag the pencil pointer to the right to draw a horizontal line across the entire table and divide the table into two cells (Figure 10–12).

Q&A Should I drag the pencil pointer to the right edge of the table?
No. PowerPoint will draw a complete line when you begin to move the pencil pointer in one direction.

If I drew the line in an incorrect location, how can I erase it?
Press the ESC key or CTRL+Z, tap or click the Undo button on the Quick Access Toolbar, or tap or click the Table Eraser button (TABLE TOOLS DESIGN tab | Draw Borders group) and then tap or click the line.

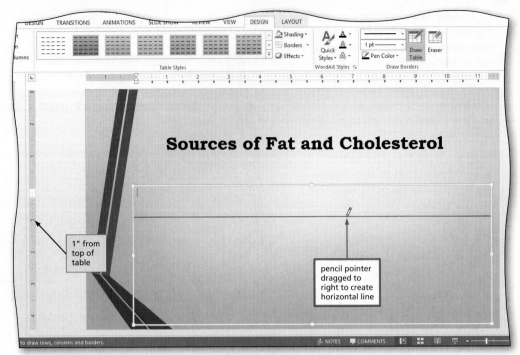

Figure 10–12

3

● Draw three additional horizontal lines, as shown in Figure 10–13.

Q&A How can I get my pencil pointer to reappear if it no longer is displaying?
Click the Draw Table button again.

Do I need to align the lines in the precise positions shown?
No. You will create evenly spaced rows later in this project.

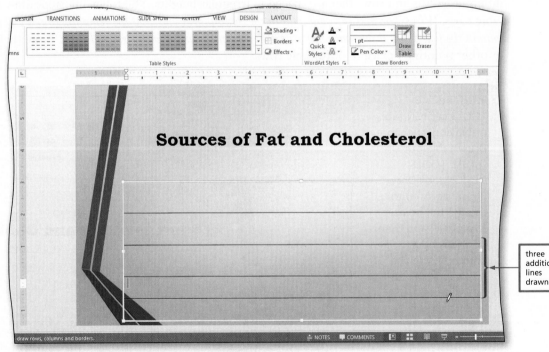

Figure 10–13

To Draw Table Columns

1 INSERT & EDIT WORD FILE | 2 DRAW TABLE ROWS & COLUMNS | 3 FORMAT TABLE
4 INSERT & EDIT LINKED WORKSHEET | 5 COPY, FORMAT & EDIT CHART

The pencil pointer is useful to draw table columns with varying widths. The two major categories in the table are the type of fats and the specific foods that contain high levels of these fats. The saturated row will be subdivided. *Why? You want to show an additional food item that has a high amount of that particular fat.* The following steps draw six vertical lines to create columns. Note that you must use a mouse or other pointing device to draw table columns.

1

- Position the pencil pointer inside the table approximately 2.5" from the left table edge (Figure 10–14).

  Can I change the line color?
Yes. Click the Pen Color button (TABLE TOOLS DESIGN tab | Draw Borders group) and then select a different color.

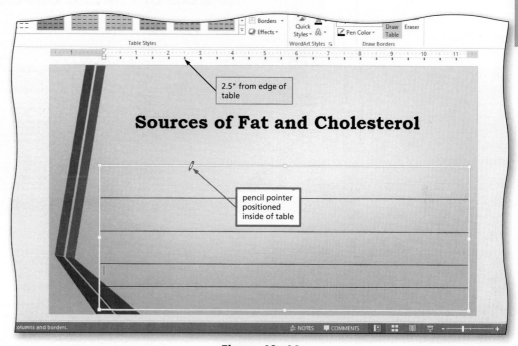

Figure 10–14

2

- Drag the pencil pointer down through all the horizontal lines to draw a vertical line that divides the table into 10 cells.

- Position the pencil pointer inside the second cell in the second row approximately 4.5" from the left table edge (Figure 10–15).

Figure 10–15

3

- Drag the pencil pointer down slightly to draw a vertical line in only that cell (Figure 10–16).

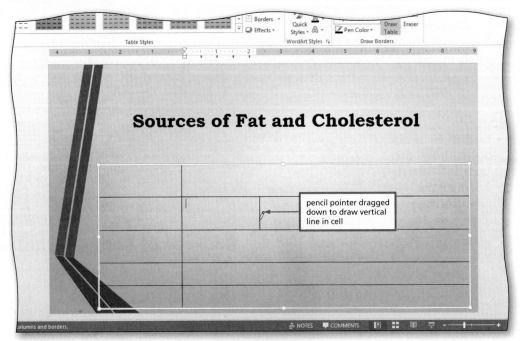

Figure 10–16

4

- Draw five additional vertical lines, as shown in Figure 10–17.

Q&A
Are vertical and horizontal lines the only types of lines I can draw?
No. You also can draw a diagonal line from one corner of a cell to another corner.

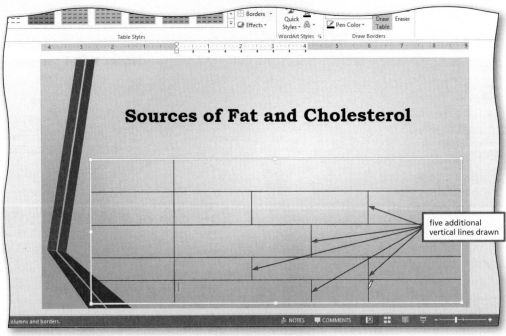

Figure 10–17

BTW

Checking for Accessibility Issues
As you develop tables and other slide elements, you may want to check the presentation for content that people with disabilities may be unable to read. To identify possible accessibility problems, display the Info tab in the Backstage view and notice if the message, Content that people with disabilities find difficult to read, is displayed next to the 'Check for Issues' button. If so, tap or click the 'Check for Issues' button and then tap or click Check Accessibility in the menu. The Accessibility Checker task pane will display issues that you can address.

To Erase a Table Line

PowerPoint supplies an eraser tool that allows you to delete vertical and horizontal lines in a table. This eraser is useful to delete unnecessary column lines. You must use a mouse or other pointing device to use the eraser tool. The following steps use the eraser to delete one vertical line in a row. *Why? You decide to include only two food items in the last row.*

- Click the Table Eraser button (TABLE TOOLS DESIGN tab | Draw Borders group).

- Position the pointer, which has the shape of an eraser, over the third line in the last row (Figure 10–18).

Figure 10–18

- Click the vertical line to erase it (Figure 10–19).

- Press the ESC key and then click inside the cell to change the pointer to the I-beam and display the insertion point.

- Display the VIEW tab and then click the Ruler check box (VIEW tab | Show group) to hide the horizontal and vertical rulers.

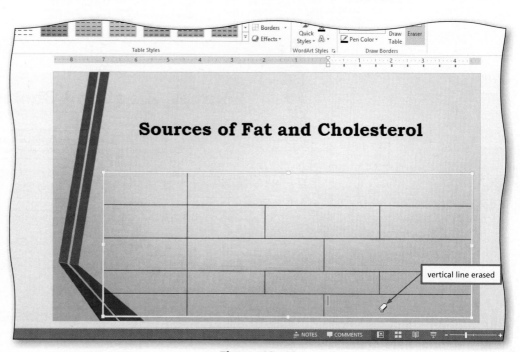

Figure 10–19

To Enter Data in a Table

Four major types of fats are found in food: monounsaturated, polyunsaturated, saturated, and trans. The table you created will list the fat types on the left side of each row and specific foods on the right side. The first row will label the two parts of the table. To place data in a cell, you tap or click the cell and then type text. The following steps enter data in the cells of the empty table.

1 Position the pointer in the upper-left cell of the table, type `Type` in the cell, and then press the TAB key or tap the next cell to advance the insertion point to the next cell.

2 Type `Frequently Found In...` in the upper-right cell and then tap the first cell in the second row or press the TAB key to advance the insertion point to the first cell in the second row.

3 Type `Monounsaturated` and then tap in the next cell or press the TAB key to advance the insertion point to the next cell. Type `Olive oil` and then advance the insertion point to the next cell. Type `Avocados` and advance the insertion point to the next cell. Type `Almonds` and then advance the insertion point to the first column of the third row.

4 In the third row, type `Polyunsaturated` in the first column, `Vegetable oil` in the second column, and `Soybeans` in the third column. Tap or press the TAB key to advance the insertion point to the first column of the fourth row.

5 In the fourth row, type `Saturated` in the first column, `Animal fat` in the second column, `Butter` in the third column, and `Chocolate` in the fourth column. Advance the insertion point to the first column of the fifth row.

6 In the fifth row, type `Trans` in the first column, `French fries` in the second column, and `Margarine` in the third column (Figure 10–20).

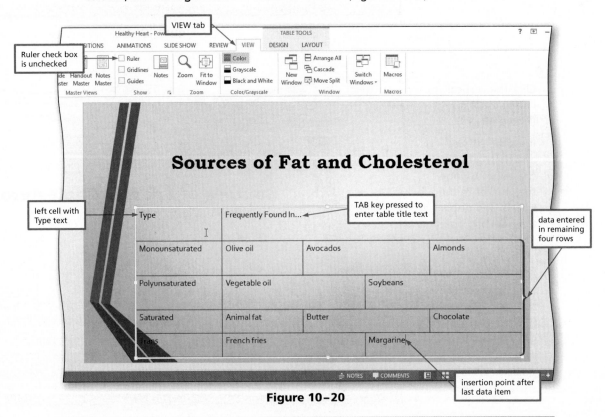

Figure 10–20

To Split a Table Column and Row

You easily can create additional table columns and rows by dividing current cells and rows. The following steps split a column and a row. *Why? You want to add another food in the Trans row. You also decide that it is important to note several foods that have high levels of cholesterol and want this information to be displayed as the last row in the table.*

1

- With the pointer positioned in the French fries cell, tap or click the TABLE TOOLS LAYOUT tab to display the TABLE TOOLS LAYOUT ribbon and then tap or click the Split Cells button (TABLE TOOLS LAYOUT tab | Merge group) to display the Split Cells dialog box (Figure 10–21).

Q&A Are the default numbers in the dialog box always 2 columns and 1 row?

Yes, but you can increase the numbers if you need to divide the cell into more than two halves or need to create two or more rows within one cell.

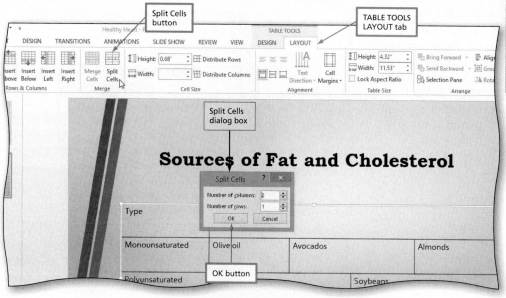

Figure 10–21

2

- Tap or click the OK button (Split Cells dialog box) to create a third cell in the Trans row.

- Tap or click the Select button (TABLE TOOLS LAYOUT tab | Table group) to display the Select menu (Figure 10–22).

Figure 10–22

- Tap or click Select Row in the Select menu to select the Trans row.

- With the TABLE TOOLS LAYOUT tab displaying, tap or click the Split Cells button (TABLE TOOLS LAYOUT tab | Merge group) to display the Split Cells dialog box (Figure 10–23).

Figure 10–23

- Decrease the number of columns from 2 to 1.

- Increase the number of rows from 1 to 2 (Figure 10–24).

Q&A
How many rows and columns can I create by splitting the cells? The maximum number varies depending upon the width and height of the selected cell.

- Tap or click the OK button (Split Cells dialog box) to create a row below the Trans row.

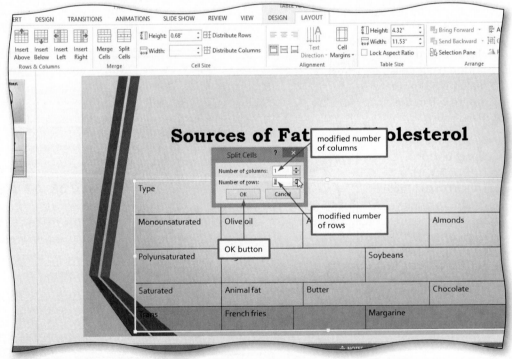

Figure 10–24

Other Ways

1. Right-click table, click Split Cells on shortcut menu, enter number of columns and rows, click OK button

To Enter Additional Data in a Table

With the additional row and column added to the table, you now can add the Cholesterol data in the inserted row and also add another food, Potato chips, to the new cell in the Trans row. The following steps enter data in the new cells.

1 Position the pointer in the first cell of the last row and then type `Cholesterol` in the cell. Advance the insertion point to the adjacent right column cell and then type `Eggs` and `Shrimp` and `Lobster` in the cells in this row.

2 Position the pointer in the new cell in the Trans row and then type `Potato chips` in the cell.

3 Drag the edges of the cells so the cell widths are similar to those in Figure 10–25. Use the Smart Guides to help align the cells vertically.

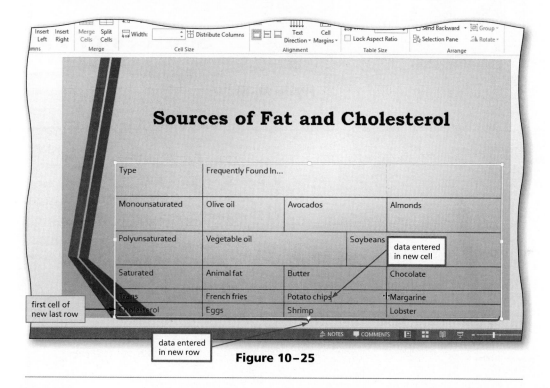

Figure 10–25

BTW
Customizing Table Formatting
PowerPoint applies a style to a table automatically based on the theme. To change this format, you can select a style in the Table Styles gallery, which presents several options to give a professional and colorful design and format. You, however, may desire to customize the layout by adding or modifying borders, the background color, or the font. To clear a style from a table, display the TABLE TOOLS DESIGN tab, tap or click the More button in the Table Styles group, and then tap or click Clear Table.

To Add Shading to a Table

You can format the table in several ways, including adding shading to color the background. The following steps add shading to the table. *Why? Shading makes the table more visually appealing and helps distinguish each cell.*

● Tap or click the Select button (TABLE TOOLS LAYOUT tab | Table group) to display the Select menu (Figure 10–26).

Figure 10–26

● Tap or click Select Table in the Select menu to select the entire table.

● Tap or click the TABLE TOOLS DESIGN tab and then tap or click the Shading arrow (TABLE TOOLS DESIGN tab | Table Styles group) to display the Shading gallery.

● If you are using a mouse, point to Red, Accent 1, Lighter 80% (fifth color in the second Theme Colors row) in the Shading gallery to display a live preview of that color applied to the table in the slide (Figure 10–27).

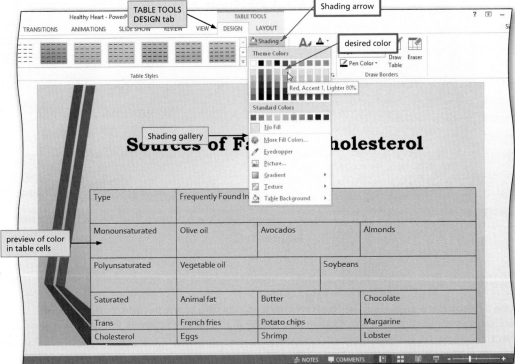

Figure 10–27

Experiment

● If you are using a mouse, point to various colors in the Shading gallery and watch the background of the table change.

● Tap or click Red, Accent 1, Lighter 80% in the Shading gallery to apply the selected color to the table.

To Add a Gradient Fill to a Table

Another enhancement you can make to the table is to add a gradient fill so that one shade of the red color gradually progresses to another shade of the same color. The following steps add a gradient fill to the table. *Why? Using a gradient fill is another method of calling attention to each individual table cell.*

1

- With the table still selected, tap or click the Shading arrow (TABLE TOOLS DESIGN tab | Table Styles group) again to display the Shading gallery.

- Tap or click Gradient to display the Gradient gallery.

- If you are using a mouse, point to Linear Diagonal – Bottom Right to Top Left (last gradient in the last row of the Variations area) to display a live preview of that gradient applied to the table in the slide (Figure 10–28).

Figure 10–28

Q&A What if my Gradient gallery shows Light and Dark variations?
Select the last gradient in the Light Variations area.

 Experiment

- If you are using a mouse, point to various gradients in the Gradient gallery and watch the background of the table change.

2

- Tap or click Linear Diagonal – Bottom Right to Top Left in the Shading gallery to apply the selected gradient to the table.

To Add a Cell Bevel

Why? Bevels modify the cell edges to give a 3-D effect, which makes each cell stand out. Some bevels give the appearance that the cell is protruding from the table, while others give the effect that the cell is depressed into the table. The steps on the next page add a bevel to the table cells.

- With the table still selected, tap or click the Effects button (TABLE TOOLS DESIGN tab | Table Styles group) to display the Effects menu.

- Tap or click Cell Bevel on the Effects menu to display the Cell Bevel gallery.

- If you are using a mouse, point to Cool Slant (rightmost bevel in the first row) to display a live preview of that bevel applied to the table in the slide (Figure 10–29).

🔍 **Experiment**

- If you are using a mouse, point to various bevel effects in the Bevel gallery and watch the table cells change.

2

- Tap or click Cool Slant in the Bevel gallery to apply the selected bevel effect to the table.

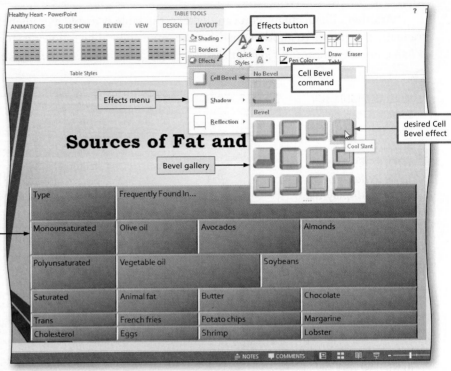

Figure 10–29

To Distribute Table Rows

1 INSERT & EDIT WORD FILE | 2 DRAW TABLE ROWS & COLUMNS | 3 FORMAT TABLE
4 INSERT & EDIT LINKED WORKSHEET | 5 COPY, FORMAT & EDIT CHART

At times you may desire the row heights to vary. In the Slide 2 table, however, you desire the heights of the rows to be uniform. To make each selected row the same height, you distribute the desired rows. The following steps distribute table rows. *Why? The horizontal lines you drew are not spaced equidistant from each other, and distributing the rows is an efficient manner of creating rows with the same height.*

1

- With the table still selected, display the TABLE TOOLS LAYOUT tab and then select the cells in the second, third, fourth, fifth, and sixth rows (Figure 10–30).

Figure 10–30

● Tap or click the Distribute Rows button (TABLE TOOLS LAYOUT tab | Cell Size group) to equally space these five rows vertically (Figure 10–31).

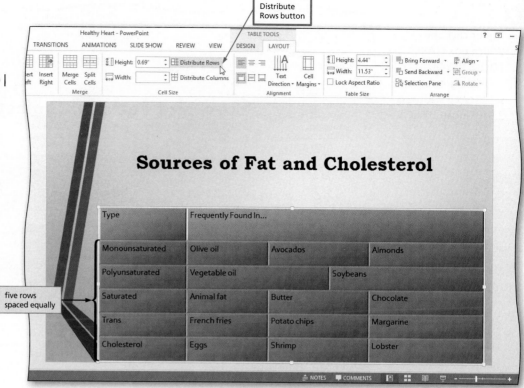

Figure 10–31

To Resize Table Columns and Rows

1 INSERT & EDIT WORD FILE | 2 DRAW TABLE ROWS & COLUMNS | 3 FORMAT TABLE
4 INSERT & EDIT LINKED WORKSHEET | 5 COPY, FORMAT & EDIT CHART

The first table row should have a height taller than the rows beneath it. In addition, the first column of the table should be somewhat narrower than the specific foods listed below the Frequently Found In... heading. *Why? You will increase the heading text font size in a later part of this project, so you need to leave sufficient room for these letters. In addition, each cell in the first column has only one word per row.* The following steps resize the table columns and rows.

● With the TABLE TOOLS LAYOUT tab displaying, position the insertion point in the Type cell in the first row.

● Tap or click the Height box (TABLE TOOLS LAYOUT tab | Cell Size group) and set the row height to 1" (Figure 10–32).

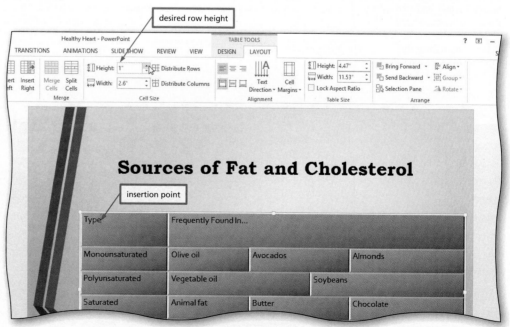

Figure 10–32

2

- Tap or click the Width box (TABLE TOOLS LAYOUT tab | Cell Size group) and set the cell width to 2.3" (Figure 10–33).

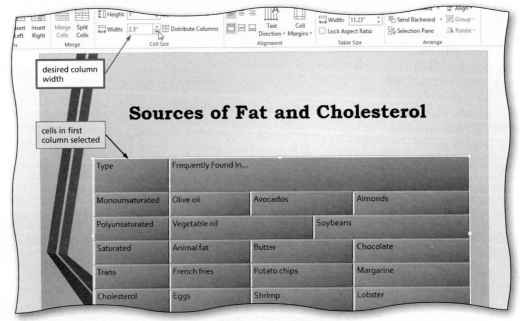

Figure 10–33

BTW

Positioning a Table or Other Slide Object
At times you might desire to place a table, text box, shape, or other element in a precise location on the slide. To specify a position, press and hold or right-click the object, tap or click Format Shape on the shortcut menu to display the Format Shape pane, tap or click 'Size & Properties' in the SHAPE OPTIONS tab, if necessary tap or click Position, and then enter the precise measurements of the horizontal and vertical distances from either the top-left corner or the center of the slide.

To Align Data in Cells

The next step is to change the alignment of the data in all the table cells. In addition to aligning text horizontally in a cell (left, center, or right), you can align it vertically within a cell (top, middle, or bottom). The following steps center data in the table both horizontally and vertically.

1 Select all the table cells and then tap or click the Center button (TABLE TOOLS LAYOUT tab | Alignment group) to center the text horizontally in the cells.

2 Tap or click the Center Vertically button (TABLE TOOLS LAYOUT tab | Alignment group) to center the contents of the cells vertically (Figure 10–34).

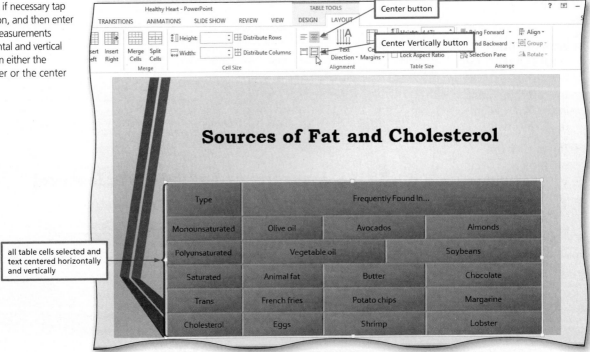

Figure 10–34

To Center a Table

Why? *The table should be positioned an equal distance between the left and right slide edges to balance this object in the slide.* To center the table, you align it in the middle of the slide. The following steps center the table horizontally.

- With the insertion point in the table, tap or click the Align button (TABLE TOOLS LAYOUT tab | Arrange group) to display the Align menu (Figure 10–35).

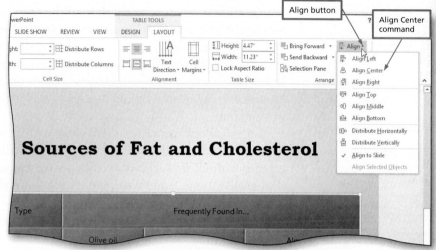

Figure 10–35

- Tap or click Align Center on the Align menu, so PowerPoint adjusts the position of the table evenly between the left and right sides of the slide. Adjust the table vertically on the slide so that it is displayed between the title text placeholder and the bottom edge of the slide.

To Format Table Data

The final table enhancements are to bold and increase the font size of the text in the first row and to change the font of all the table text. The following steps bold the text in the first row and then increase the font size and also change the font for all the table data.

① Select the first row, display the HOME tab, and then bold the text and increase the font size to 32 point.

② Select all the table text and then change the font to Bookman Old Style (Figure 10–36). If necessary, change the width of the columns so the words display with adequate spacing on the left and right sides.

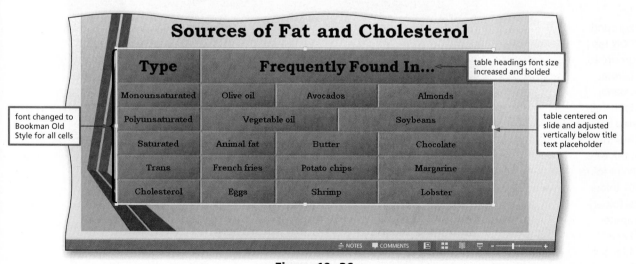

Figure 10–36

Break Point: If you wish to take a break, this is a good place to do so. Be sure to save the Healthy Heart file again and then you can exit PowerPoint. To resume at a later time, run PowerPoint, open the file called Healthy Heart, and continue following the steps from this location forward.

Inserting a Linked Excel Worksheet

Linked files maintain a connection between the source file and the destination file. When you select the **Link check box** in the Insert Object dialog box, the object is inserted as a linked object instead of an embedded object. Your PowerPoint presentation stores a representation of the original file and information about its location. If you later move or delete the source file, the link is broken, and the object will not be available. Consequently, if you make a presentation on a computer other than the one on which the presentation was created, and the presentation contains linked objects, be certain to include a copy of the source files. The source files must be stored in the exact location as originally specified when you linked them to your presentation.

PowerPoint associates a linked file with a specific application, which PowerPoint bases on the file extension. For example, if you select a source file with the file extension **.docx**, PowerPoint recognizes the file as a Microsoft Word file. Additionally, if you select a source file with the file extension **.xlsx**, PowerPoint recognizes the file as a Microsoft Excel file.

In the following pages, you will insert a linked Excel worksheet, align it on the slide, and then edit three cells.

To Insert a Linked Excel Worksheet

1 INSERT & EDIT WORD FILE | 2 DRAW TABLE ROWS & COLUMNS | 3 FORMAT TABLE
4 INSERT & EDIT LINKED WORKSHEET | **5 COPY, FORMAT & EDIT CHART**

The Lipid Profile Excel worksheet contains a table with data corresponding to measurements taken during a blood test. The first column lists four components of blood: total cholesterol, high-density lipoprotein (HDL) cholesterol, low-density lipoprotein (LDL) cholesterol, and triglycerides. The second column lists desired test results. The third column gives the results of one blood test taken on March 20. You can insert the results of a second blood test in the last column. When you insert the Lipid Profile chart, you can specify that it is linked from the PowerPoint slide to the Excel worksheet. *Why? Any edits made to specific cells are reflected in both the source and destination files.* The following steps insert and link the Microsoft Excel worksheet.

- Insert a new slide with the Blank layout.

- Tap or click the Format Background button (DESIGN tab | Customize group) to display the Format Background pane. Insert the Blood Cells picture located on your Data Files for Students (in this case, the Power Point folder in the CIS 101 folder [or your class folder] on your computer or SkyDrive) as a background for the new slide (Figure 10–37).

Blood Cells picture inserted as background

Figure 10–37

- Close the Format Background pane.
- Display the INSERT tab and then tap or click the Object button (INSERT tab | Text group) to display the Insert Object dialog box.
- Tap or click 'Create from file' (Insert Object dialog box) to display the File box (Figure 10–38).

Figure 10–38

- Tap or click the Browse button, navigate to the location of your Data Files for Students (in this case, the PowerPoint folder in the CIS 101 folder [or your class folder] on your computer or SkyDrive), and then scroll down and tap or click Lipid Profile to select the file name (Figure 10–39).

Figure 10–39

- Tap or click the OK button (Browse dialog box) to insert the file name into the File box (Insert Object dialog box).
- Tap or click the Link check box (Insert Object dialog box) to select the check box (Figure 10–40).

Figure 10–40

5

- Tap or click the OK button (Insert Object dialog box) to insert the Lipid Profile Excel worksheet into Slide 3.

- Display the DRAWING TOOLS FORMAT tab and change the worksheet height to 5.5" (Figure 10–41).

Q&A Why did the worksheet width change when I changed the height measurement?
The worksheet's width and height stay in proportion to each other, so when you change one dimension, the other dimension changes accordingly.

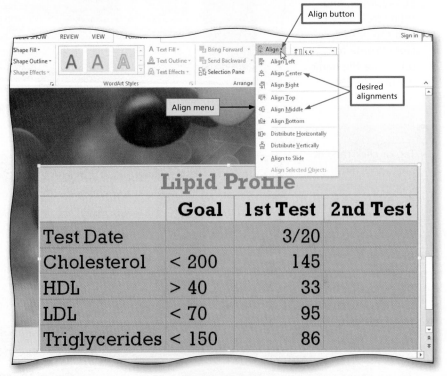

Figure 10–41

To Align a Worksheet

1 INSERT & EDIT WORD FILE | 2 DRAW TABLE ROWS & COLUMNS | 3 FORMAT TABLE
4 INSERT & EDIT LINKED WORKSHEET | 5 COPY, FORMAT & EDIT CHART

Why? *PowerPoint inserts the table on Slide 3 in a location that is not visually appealing, so you want to center it on the slide.* You can drag the table to a location, but you also can have PowerPoint precisely align the object horizontally in the left, center, or right areas of the slide, and vertically in the top, middle, or bottom of the slide. The following steps align the table horizontally and vertically on Slide 3.

1

- With the DRAWING TOOLS FORMAT tab displaying, tap or click the Align button (DRAWING TOOLS FORMAT tab | Arrange group) to display the Align menu (Figure 10–42).

Figure 10–42

- Tap or click Align Center on the Align menu to position the worksheet evenly between the left and right edges of the slide.

- Tap or click the Align button again to display the Align menu and then tap or click Align Middle to position the worksheet in the center of the slide (Figure 10–43).

Figure 10–43

To Edit a Linked Worksheet

1 INSERT & EDIT WORD FILE | 2 DRAW TABLE ROWS & COLUMNS | 3 FORMAT TABLE
4 INSERT & EDIT LINKED WORKSHEET | 5 COPY, FORMAT & EDIT CHART

Each table or worksheet cell is identified by a unique address, or **cell reference**, representing the intersection of a column and row. The column letter is first and is followed by the row number. For example, cell B6 is located at the intersection of the second column, B, and the sixth row. Three cells need updating. *Why? You have obtained test results from a blood test taken on December 6 and want to record this information.* The following steps edit cells in the linked table.

- Double-tap or double-click the table to open Microsoft Excel and display the worksheet.

- Tap or click the blank Test Date cell below the rightmost column, 2nd Test, to make cell D3 the active cell (Figure 10–44). If you are using a touch screen, display the onscreen keyboard.

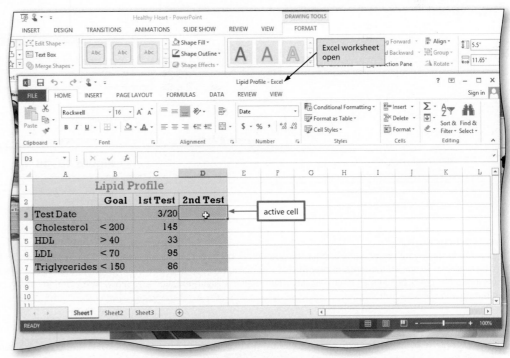

Figure 10–44

2

- Type **12/6** as the new test date and then tap or press the ENTER key to complete the entry and make cell D4 the active cell.

- Type **130** as the new cholesterol number and then tap or press the ENTER key to complete the entry and make cell D5 the active cell.

- Type **30** as the new HDL number, **85** as the new LDL number, and **90** as the new triglycerides number. Be certain to tap or press the ENTER key to complete the triglycerides entry in cell D7 (Figure 10–45). If you are using a touch screen, hide the onscreen keyboard.

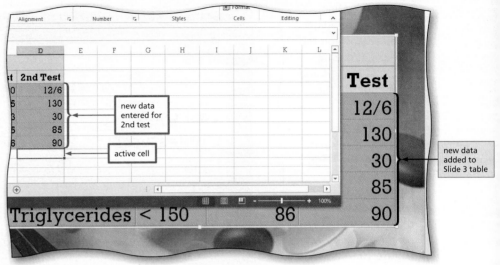

Figure 10–45

3

- Tap or click the Close button in the upper-right corner of the Microsoft Excel window to quit Excel (Figure 10–46).

- Tap or click the Save button (Microsoft Excel dialog box) to save your edited numbers in the worksheet.

Figure 10–46

BTW

Embedding Fonts

If you plan to show your presentation using a computer other than yours, consider embedding the fonts to ensure that the fonts on your slides will be available. To embed the fonts, display the Save As dialog box, tap or click the Tools button, tap or click Save Options, select the 'Embed fonts in the file' check box in the Preserve fidelity when sharing this presentation area (PowerPoint Options dialog box), and then tap or click the OK button and the Save button.

Break Point: If you wish to take a break, this is a good place to do so. Be sure to save the Healthy Heart file again and then you can exit PowerPoint. To resume at a later time, run PowerPoint, open the file called Healthy Heart, and continue following the steps from this location forward. Note: PowerPoint will prompt you to update the Excel file that you modified.

Copying and Modifying a Linked Excel Chart

The Microsoft Excel table you inserted into Slide 3 is a linked object. You added data to the table using the Microsoft Excel source program, and that change is reflected on the PowerPoint slide and in the original Excel document. Now you will insert and then modify a Microsoft Excel chart on Slide 4. This object will be linked, so any changes you make to the layout, legend, or background will be reflected in the destination object on the slide and in the original Excel worksheet.

In the following pages, you will perform these tasks on Slide 4:

1. Copy a chart from a file.
2. Align the chart.
3. Switch rows and columns.
4. Change the chart type.
5. Apply a style.
6. Display and format axis titles.
7. Format a legend.
8. Display and format chart labels.
9. Display gridlines.
10. Format the background.
11. Edit data.

BTW

Certification
The Microsoft Office Specialist (MOS) program provides an opportunity for you to obtain a valuable industry credential — proof that you have the PowerPoint 2013 skills required by employers. For more information, visit the Certification resource on the Student Companion Site located on www.cengagebrain. com. For detailed instructions about accessing available resources, visit www.cengage. com/ct/studentdownload or see the inside back cover of this book.

To Copy an Excel Chart

1 INSERT & EDIT WORD FILE | 2 DRAW TABLE ROWS & COLUMNS | 3 FORMAT TABLE
4 INSERT & EDIT LINKED WORKSHEET | **5 COPY, FORMAT & EDIT CHART**

The chart you want to insert into your slide show was created in Microsoft Excel. The file consists of two sheets: one for the chart and another for the numbers used to create the chart. The chart is on Sheet1. One method of placing this chart into a PowerPoint presentation is to copy this object from the Excel worksheet and then paste it into a slide. The following steps copy and link a chart from Sheet1 of the Microsoft Excel file using the destination formatting. *Why? Copying and linking allows you to modify the chart content easily. You want to use the destination formatting so the chart uses the Parallax theme colors and styles.*

1
- Insert a new slide with the Title Only layout. Type **Cholesterol Readings** as the title text, change the font to Bookman Old Style, and then bold this text.

- Tap or click the File Explorer app button on the taskbar to make the File folder window the active window. Navigate to the location where your Data Files for Students are stored (in this case, the PowerPoint folder in the CIS 101 folder [or your class folder] on your computer or SkyDrive). If necessary, scroll down to display the Cholesterol Readings file in the Name list (Figure 10–47).

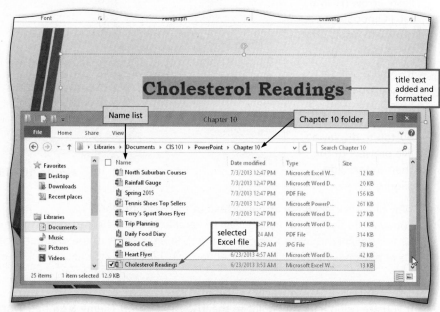

Figure 10–47

2

- Double-tap or double-click the Cholesterol Readings file to run Microsoft Excel and display the chart on Sheet1.

- Tap or click a blank area above the chart legend to select the entire chart and then display the HOME tab.

- Tap or click the Copy button (HOME tab | Clipboard group) to copy the chart to the Office Clipboard (Figure 10–48).

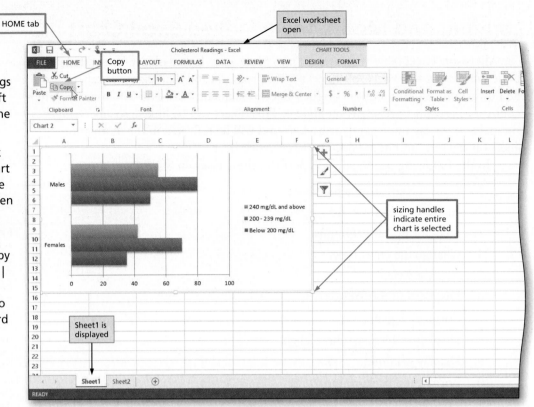

Figure 10–48

3

- Tap or click the PowerPoint app button on the taskbar to make the PowerPoint window the active window. With Slide 4 and the HOME tab displaying, click the Paste arrow (HOME tab | Clipboard group) to display the Paste Options gallery.

- If you are using a mouse, point to the 'Use Destination Theme & Link Data' button to display a live preview of the chart in the slide (Figure 10–49).

Figure 10–49

 Why did I click the Paste arrow instead of the Paste button?

You want to use the colors and style of Parallax theme (the destination theme), so you need to display the Paste Options gallery to make that choice and to link the chart to the original Excel worksheet. If you had clicked the Paste button, you would have embedded the chart using the Excel worksheet theme (the source theme).

Experiment

- If you are using a mouse, point to the 'Use Destination Theme & Embed Workbook' button in the Paste Options gallery to display a live preview of the chart with the Parallax theme applied.

- Tap or click the 'Use Destination Theme & Link Data' button to paste the chart into Slide 4.

- Display the CHART TOOLS FORMAT tab and then change the chart size to 5.5" × 11.5" (Figure 10–50).

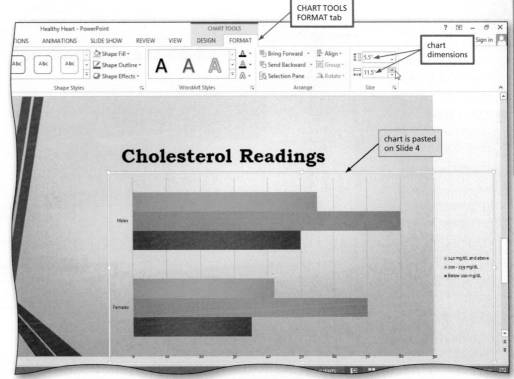

Figure 10–50

Other Ways

1. Press and hold or right-click Excel chart, tap or click Copy, exit Microsoft Excel, tap or click Paste arrow (HOME tab | Clipboard group), tap or click 'Use Destination Theme & Link Data'

To Align a Chart

1 INSERT & EDIT WORD FILE | 2 DRAW TABLE ROWS & COLUMNS | 3 FORMAT TABLE
4 INSERT & EDIT LINKED WORKSHEET | **5 COPY, FORMAT & EDIT CHART**

Why? *You aligned the table on Slide 3 horizontally and vertically. You, likewise, want to align the chart on Slide 4 so that it is displayed in an appropriate location on the slide.* Although you can drag the chart on the slide, you also can use PowerPoint commands to align the object horizontally in the left, center, or right areas of the slide, and vertically in the top, middle, or bottom of the slide. The following steps align the chart horizontally and vertically on Slide 4.

- With the chart selected and the CHART TOOLS FORMAT tab displaying, tap or click the Align button (CHART TOOLS FORMAT tab | Arrange group) to display the Align menu (Figure 10–51).

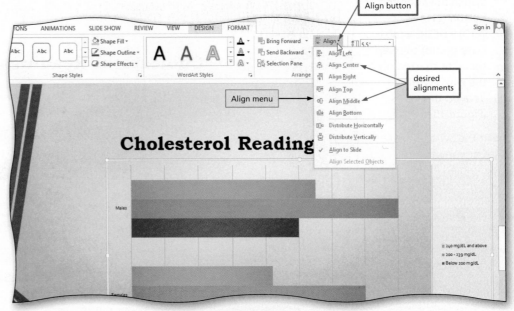

Figure 10–51

2

- Tap or click Align Right on the Align menu to position the chart along the right edge of the slide.

- Tap or click the Align button again to display the Align menu and then tap or click Align Bottom to position the chart at the lower edge of the slide (Figure 10–52).

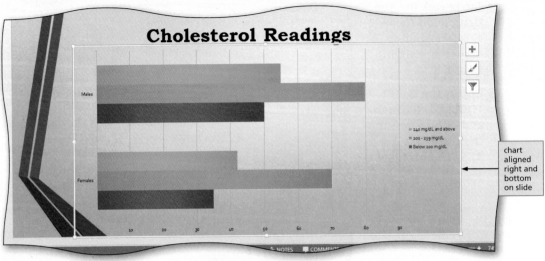

Figure 10–52

To Switch Rows and Columns in a Chart

1 INSERT & EDIT WORD FILE | 2 DRAW TABLE ROWS & COLUMNS | 3 FORMAT TABLE
4 INSERT & EDIT LINKED WORKSHEET | 5 COPY, FORMAT & EDIT CHART

Excel created the chart on Slide 4 (Sheet1 in the Excel file) based on the values in the worksheet on Sheet2 of the Excel file. The scale is based on the values in the **y-axis**, which also is called the **vertical axis** or **value axis**. The titles along the **x-axis**, also referred to as the **horizontal axis** or **category axis**, are derived from the top row of the Sheet2 worksheet and are displayed along the left edge of the chart. Each bar in the chart has a specific color to represent one of the three categories of cholesterol levels grouped by males and females. You can switch the data in the chart so that a male and female bar is displayed for each of the three cholesterol levels. *Why? In your presentation to fitness center members, you want to emphasize that males and females often have quite different cholesterol levels.* The following step switches the rows and columns in the chart.

1

- Display the CHART TOOLS DESIGN tab on the ribbon.

- Tap or click the Switch Row/Column button (CHART TOOLS DESIGN tab | Data group) to swap the data charted on the x-axis with the data on the y-axis (Figure 10–53).

Q&A If the Switch Row/Column button is dimmed, how can I switch the data? Be certain the Excel worksheet is open. The button is active only when the worksheet is open.

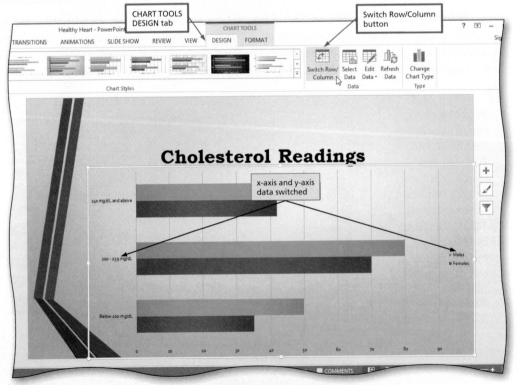

Figure 10–53

To Change the Chart Type

The bar chart represents data horizontally for each of the three cholesterol levels. You can change the chart appearance by selecting another type in the Insert Chart dialog box. The sample charts are divided into a variety of categories, including column, line, pie, and bar. The clustered column type that you want to use in the presentation is located in the Column area, which has seven layouts. The following steps change the chart to a 3-D Clustered Column chart type. ***Why?*** *The vertical bars help show the increase and decrease of cholesterol levels, and the 3-D effect adds an interesting visual element.*

1

- Tap or click the 'Change Chart Type' button (CHART TOOLS DESIGN tab | Type group) to display the Change Chart Type dialog box.

- Tap or click Column in the left pane (Change Chart Type dialog box) to display a Clustered Column thumbnail (Figure 10–54).

Figure 10–54

2

- Tap or click the 3-D Clustered Column button (fourth chart) to select this chart type and display a thumbnail with a 3-D effect (Figure 10–55).

 Q&A Can I see a larger preview of the chart?
If you are using a mouse, you can point to the chart to enlarge the preview.

3

- Tap or click the OK button (Change Chart Type dialog box) to change the chart type to 3-D Clustered Column.

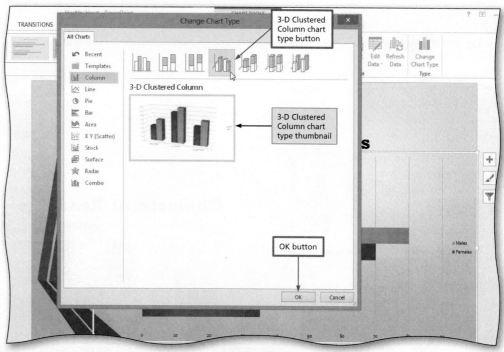

Figure 10–55

BTW
Displaying Gridlines
Gridlines can help you align charts, shapes, and other objects on slides. To show the gridlines, display the VIEW tab and then select the Gridlines check box (VIEW tab | Show group).

TO EXCLUDE DATA IN A CHART

If you have multiple categories (which display in the x-axis) or series (which display in the legend) of data and want to exclude one or more of them from displaying, you can instruct PowerPoint to exclude data elements. If you wanted to exclude a particular category or series, you would perform the following steps.

1. Tap or click the Chart Filters button (funnel icon) on the right side of the chart to display a pane with each data element.
2. Clear the check boxes of the elements you want to exclude on the chart.
3. To display an excluded data element, select the check box.

To Apply a Style to a Chart

Why? *You can modify the chart's appearance easily by selecting a predefined style.* The styles available in the Chart Styles gallery have a variety of colors and backgrounds and display in both 2-D and 3-D. The following steps apply a style to the chart.

- Tap or click the Chart Style button (paintbrush icon) on the right side of the chart area to display the Chart Style gallery with the STYLE tab displayed.
- If you are using a mouse, scroll down until the eighth style (Style 8) in the Chart Style gallery is displayed and then point to this style to see a live preview on Slide 4 (Figure 10–56).

Experiment

- If you are using a mouse, point to various chart styles and watch the layouts change.

- Tap or click Style 8 in the Chart Style gallery to apply the chart style to the chart.

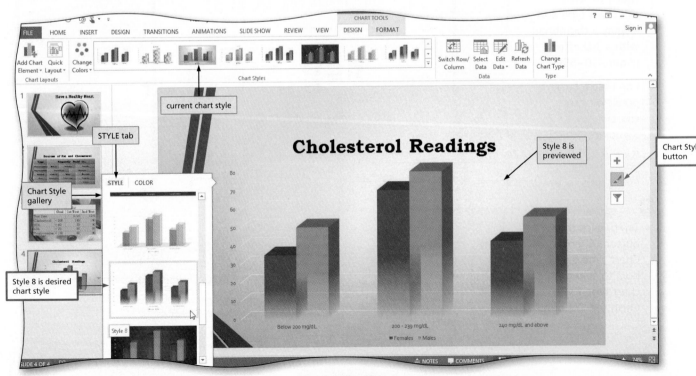

Figure 10–56

To Change Chart Colors

You can modify a chart's colors easily by selecting one of the color groups available in the Chart Color gallery. These colors are grouped in two categories: Colorful and Monochromatic. For a unique look, PowerPoint also allows you create a custom color combination. The following steps change the chart colors. *Why? The two columns in the chart have very similar colors, so you want to distinguish the Males columns from the Females columns by changing to a color scheme with more contrast.*

1

- With the Chart Style gallery still displaying, tap or click the COLOR tab at the top of the pane to display the Chart Color gallery (Figure 10–57).

Q&A | Why is a box surrounding the six colors in the first row in the Colorful section?
Those colors are currently applied to the chart.

Experiment

- If you are using a mouse, point to various color groups and watch the chart colors change.

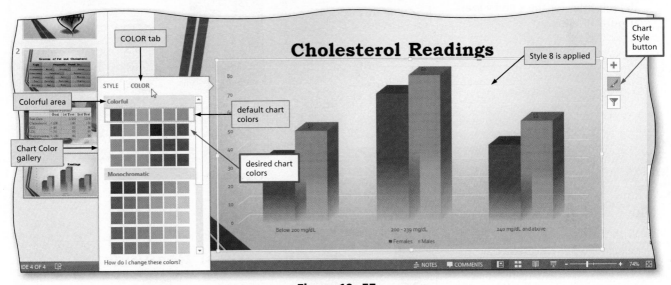

Figure 10–57

2

- Tap or click Color 2 (the second row in the Colorful area) to apply these colors to the chart.

- Tap or click the Chart Style button to the right of the chart to close the Chart Color gallery.

- Press and hold or right-click the Excel app button on the taskbar and then tap or click Close window to exit Excel.

Other Ways

1. Tap or click Change Colors button (CHART TOOLS DESIGN tab | Chart Styles group)

BTW
Quick Reference
For a table that lists how to complete the tasks covered in this book using touch gestures, the mouse, ribbon, shortcut menu, and keyboard, see the Quick Reference Summary at the back of this book, or visit the Quick Reference resource on the Student Companion Site located on www.cengagebrain.com. For detailed instructions about accessing available resources, visit www.cengage.com/ct/studentdownload or see the inside back cover of this book.

To Display and Format Axis Titles

The legend below the chart identifies the colors assigned to each of the bars. You can modify the default legend in a variety of ways, including moving its location, changing the fill and outline, adding an effect, and changing the font. The Chart Elements button on the right side of the chart area allows you to display or hide a chart element. When you click this button, the Chart Elements pane is displayed. A check mark appears in the check box for each chart element that is displayed. You can check and uncheck each chart element to display or hide axes, the chart title, labels, gridlines, and the legend. The following steps display the axis titles and then format the text. ***Why?*** *You want your audience to recognize that the y-axis represents the total number of people in the cholesterol sample and the x-axis represents the cholesterol categories.*

1
- Tap or click the Chart Elements button (plus sign icon) on the right side of the chart area to display the CHART ELEMENTS pane. Tap or click the Axis Titles check box to display the two default titles for the x and y axes (Figure 10–58).

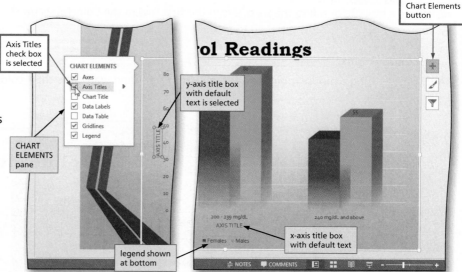

Figure 10–58

2
- With the default y-axis title box selected, type **Number of Participants** in the text box.
- Select the text and then increase the font size to 18 point and bold the text.

3
- Tap or click the x-axis title to select it, delete the default text, and then type **Total Cholesterol** as the replacement text.
- Select the text and then increase the font size to 18 point and bold the text (Figure 10–59).

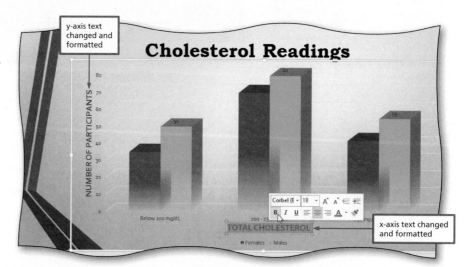

Figure 10–59

Other Ways

1. Tap or click Add Chart Element button (CHART TOOLS DESIGN tab | Chart Layouts group), tap or click Axis Titles

To Move a Chart Legend

The legend below the chart identifies the colors assigned to each of the bars. You can modify the default legend in a variety of ways, including moving its location, changing the fill and outline, adding an effect, and changing the font. The following steps move the legend to the left side of the chart. *Why? A blank area is available between the two vertical bars and the left side of the chart, and you believe the legend will be more effective there.*

- With the CHART ELEMENTS pane still displaying, position the pointer over the word, Legend, in the list to display an arrow and then tap or click this arrow to display the Legend menu (Figure 10–60).

- Tap or click Left to display the legend on the left side of the chart.

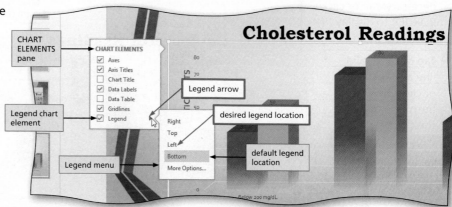

Figure 10–60

Other Ways

1. Tap or click Add Chart Element button (CHART TOOLS DESIGN tab | Chart Layouts group), tap or click Legend arrow

To Format a Chart Legend

You can modify the default legend in a variety of ways, including moving its location, changing the fill and outline, adding an effect, and changing the font. The following steps format the legend. *Why? Changing the line color and adding a glow help call attention to the legend.*

- With the CHART ELEMENTS pane still displaying, display the Legend menu (Figure 10–61).

Figure 10–61

2
- Tap or click More Options to display the Format Legend pane. Tap or click the 'Fill & Line' button and then, if necessary, tap or click BORDER to display the BORDER area.
- Tap or click Solid line and then tap or click the Color button to display the Color gallery (Figure 10–62).

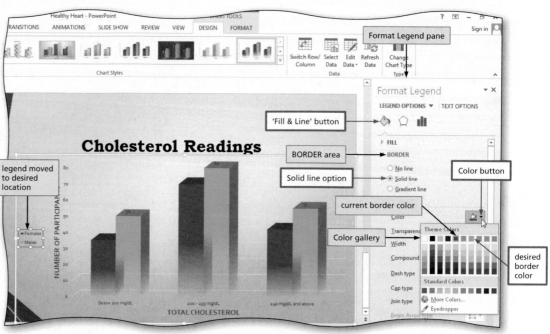

Figure 10–62

3
- Tap or click Gold, Accent 3 (seventh color in the first Theme Colors row) to change the legend border line color.
- Increase the line width to 1.5 pt (Figure 10–63).

Q&A Is a live preview available?
No, this feature is not offered.

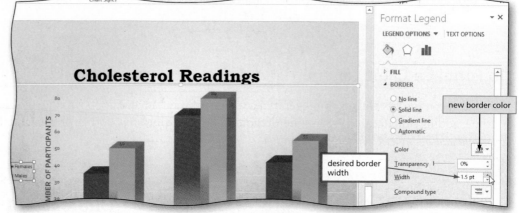

Figure 10–63

4
- Tap or click the Effects button (Format Legend pane) and then, if necessary, display the GLOW area. Tap or click the Presets button to display the Glow gallery (Figure 10–64).

Figure 10–64

- If you are using a mouse, point to Gold, 8 pt glow, Accent color 3 (third variation in the second row) (Figure 10–65).

- Tap or click the Gold, 8 pt glow, Accent color 3 variation to apply this Glow preset to the legend.

- Tap or click the Close button (Format Legend pane).

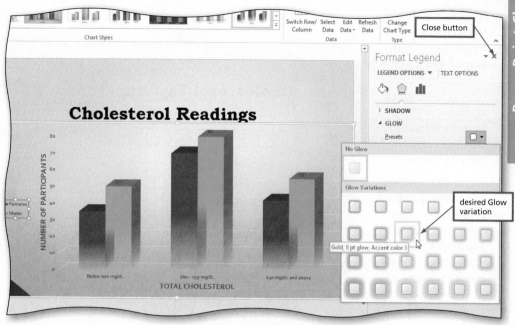

Figure 10–65

Other Ways

1. Press and hold or right-click legend, tap or click Format Legend on shortcut menu

To Format a Chart Background

1 INSERT & EDIT WORD FILE | 2 DRAW TABLE ROWS & COLUMNS | 3 FORMAT TABLE
4 INSERT & EDIT LINKED WORKSHEET | **5 COPY, FORMAT & EDIT CHART**

The background area behind and to the left of the chart bars is called the **chart wall**. You can format this portion of the chart by adding a fill, an outline, and effects such as a shadow. The following steps add a gradient fill to the background chart wall. **Why?** *The gradient adds a visual element and helps call attention to the white gridlines.*

- Press and hold or right-click an area of the chart wall to select this chart element and to display a mini toolbar and shortcut menu. If necessary, tap or click the Chart Elements arrow and then tap or click Walls in the list (Figure 10–66).

Q&A How will I know if this piece of the chart is selected? You will see six small blue circles, each one located at the upper or lower gridline corner.

Figure 10–66

- If necessary, display the shortcut menu again. Tap or click Format Walls in the shortcut menu to display the Format Walls pane. If necessary, tap or click FILL to expand the FILL section.

- Tap or click Gradient fill to display options related to gradient colors in the pane. Tap or click the Preset gradients button to display a palette of built-in gradient fill colors (Figure 10–67).

Figure 10–67

- Tap or click Light Gradient – Accent 2 (second gradient in the first row) to apply this gradient to the chart walls (Figure 10–68).

- Tap or click the Close button (Format Walls pane).

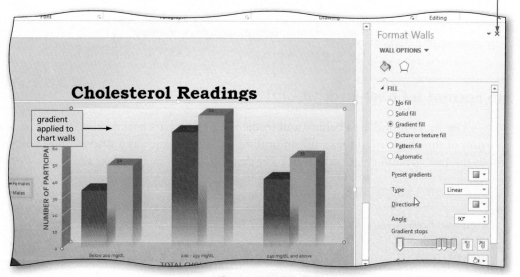

Figure 10–68

Other Ways

1. Tap or click the Chart Elements arrow (CHART TOOLS FORMAT tab | Current Selection group), tap or click Walls, tap or click Format Selection (CHART TOOLS FORMAT tab | Current Selection group), if necessary tap or click Fill & Line button, if necessary tap or click FILL, tap or click Gradient fill (Format Walls pane)

To Edit Data in a Chart

1 INSERT & EDIT WORD FILE | 2 DRAW TABLE ROWS & COLUMNS | 3 FORMAT TABLE
4 INSERT & EDIT LINKED WORKSHEET | 5 COPY, FORMAT & EDIT CHART

The data in Sheet2 of the worksheet is used to create the chart on Slide 4. If you edit this data, the corresponding bars in the chart change height to reflect new numbers. The chart is a linked object, so when you modify the data and close the worksheet, the chart will reflect the changes and the original file stored on your Data Files for Students also will change. The following steps edit three cells in the worksheet. *Why? You have obtained test results from additional fitness center members and want to update your chart and the Excel worksheet with this information.*

- Display the CHART TOOLS DESIGN tab and then tap or click the Edit Data button (CHART TOOLS DESIGN tab | Data group) to display Sheet2 of the worksheet.

Q&A

Why might I want to tap or click the Edit Data arrow instead of the Edit Data button?

You would be given the option to run Microsoft Excel and then edit the worksheet using that app. More options would be available using Excel. If you simply need to edit data, you can perform that task easily using PowerPoint.

- Tap or click cell B2 (Below 200 mg/dL for Females) to make cell B2 the active cell (Figure 10–69).

Figure 10–69

- Type 40 as the replacement number and then tap cell B3 or press the DOWN ARROW key to make cell B3 (200 – 239 mg / dL for Females) the active cell.

- Type 65 as the replacement number and then tap cell C3 or press the RIGHT ARROW key to make cell C3 (200 – 239 mg / dL for Males) the active cell.

- Type 85 as the replacement number and then press the ENTER key (Figure 10–70).

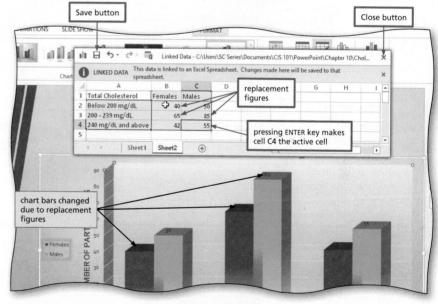

Figure 10–70

3

- Tap or click the Save button on the spreadsheet toolbar to save the data to the Excel spreadsheet.

- Tap or click the Close button on the spreadsheet to close the window.

- Tap or click the slide in a location outside the chart area (Figure 10–71).

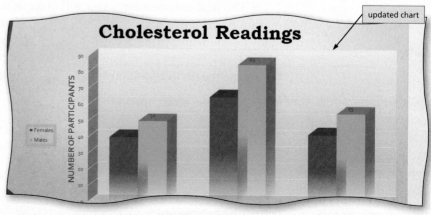

Figure 10–71

To Add a Hyperlink to a Table

A hyperlink connects one element on a slide to another slide, presentation, picture, file, webpage, or email address. Presenters use hyperlinks to display these elements to an audience. In this Healthy Heart presentation, you will create a hyperlink from a cell in the table on Slide 2 to an Adobe PDF file. *Why? You want to show your audience a simple form they can use to monitor their food intake each day.* When you tap or click this particular table cell during a slide show, Adobe Acrobat starts and then opens this PDF file. The following steps hyperlink a table cell to a PDF file.

- Display Slide 2 and then place the pointer in the word, Frequently, in the rightmost cell.

- Display the INSERT tab and then tap or click the Hyperlink button (INSERT tab | Links group) to display the Insert Hyperlink dialog box.

- If necessary, tap or click the 'Existing File or Web Page' button in the Link to area.

- If necessary, tap or click the Current Folder button in the Look in area and then navigate to the location where your Data Files for Students are stored (in this case, the PowerPoint folder in the CIS 101 folder [or your class folder] on your computer or SkyDrive).

- Tap or click Daily Food Diary to select this file as the hyperlink (Figure 10–72).

Figure 10–72

- Tap or click the OK button (Insert Hyperlink dialog box) to insert the hyperlink.

To Add a Transition between Slides

The final enhancements you will make in this presentation are to apply a transition, change the transition effect option, and change the transition speed. The following steps apply these transition effects to the presentation.

1 Apply the Doors transition in the Exciting category to all slides.

2 Change the effect option to Horizontal.

3 Change the transition speed from 1.40 to 3.00 seconds.

BTW

Conserving Ink and Toner

If you want to conserve ink or toner, you can instruct PowerPoint to print draft quality documents by tapping or clicking FILE on the ribbon to open the Backstage view, tapping or clicking Options in the Backstage view to display the PowerPoint Options dialog box, tapping or clicking Advanced in the left pane (PowerPoint Options dialog box), sliding or scrolling to the Print area in the right pane, placing a check mark in the 'Use draft quality' check box, and then tapping or clicking the OK button. Then, use the Backstage view to print the document as usual.

To Run, Print, Save, and Exit PowerPoint

The presentation now is complete. You should run the presentation, view the hyperlinked file, print the slides, save the presentation, and then exit PowerPoint.

1 Run the Healthy Heart presentation. When Slide 2 is displayed, tap or click 'FREQUENTLY FOUND IN…' in the table to display the Daily Food Diary document as the hyperlinked file. If the Microsoft Office dialog box is displayed, tap or click the OK button to open the PDF file.

2 Review the contents of the Daily Food Diary document. Swipe in from the left edge of the screen, and then back to the left, or point to the upper-left corner of the screen to display a live preview thumbnail of Slide 2. If the Slide 2 thumbnail is not displayed, point to the PowerPoint app button on the taskbar to see a live preview of Slide 2.

3 Tap or click the thumbnail of Slide 2 to display that slide and then display Slide 3 and Slide 4. End the slide show.

4 Print the Healthy Heart presentation as a handout with two slides per page (Figure 10–73).

5 Save the Healthy Heart presentation again with the same file name.

6 Exit PowerPoint, closing all open documents.

BTW
Printing Document Properties
To print document properties, tap or click FILE on the ribbon to open the Backstage view, tap or click the Print tab in the Backstage view to display the Print gallery, tap or click the first button in the Settings area to display a list of options specifying what you can print, tap or click Document Info in the list to specify you want to print the document properties instead of the actual document, and then tap or click the Print button in the Print gallery to print the document properties on the currently selected printer.

(a) Page 1

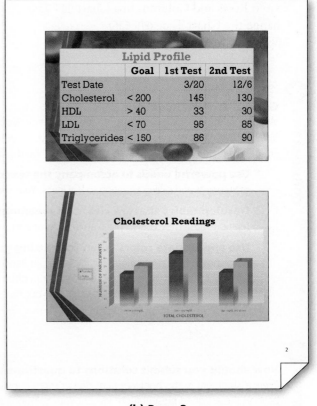

(b) Page 2

Figure 10–73

Chapter Summary

In this chapter you have learned how to develop a presentation using information you inserted from a Microsoft Word flyer and Microsoft Excel chart. These documents were either embedded or linked, and you edited each of them to update words or numbers. You also drew a table and enhanced it, and linked an Adobe PDF file to the table. You altered the Microsoft Excel object by changing the chart type, background, gridlines, and legend. The items listed below include all the new PowerPoint skills you have learned in this chapter.

Align Objects
Center a Table (PPT 625)
Align a Worksheet (PPT 628)
Align a Chart (PPT 633)

Create a Table
Draw a Table (PPT 610)
Draw Table Rows (PPT 611)
Draw Table Columns (PPT 613)
Erase a Table Line (PPT 615)
Split a Table Column and Row (PPT 617)

Edit Objects
Edit an Embedded File (PPT 608)
Edit a Linked Worksheet (PPT 629)
Edit Data in a Chart (PPT 642)

Format a Chart
Switch Rows and Columns in a Chart (PPT 634)
Change the Chart Type (PPT 635)
Apply a Style to a Chart (PPT 636)

Exclude Data in a Chart (PPT 636)
Change Chart Colors (PPT 637)
Display and Format Axis Titles (PPT 638)
Move a Chart Legend (PPT 639)
Format a Chart Legend (PPT 639)
Format a Chart Background (PPT 641)

Format a Table
Add Shading to a Table (PPT 620)
Add a Gradient Fill to a Table (PPT 621)
Add a Cell Bevel (PPT 621)
Distribute Table Rows (PPT 622)
Resize Table Columns and Rows (PPT 623)

Insert Objects
Insert a File with Graphics and Text (PPT 606)
Insert a Linked Excel Worksheet (PPT 626)
Copy an Excel Chart (PPT 631)
Add a Hyperlink to a Table (PPT 644)

CONSIDER THIS

General Project Guidelines

When creating a PowerPoint presentation, the actions you perform and the decisions you make will affect the appearance and characteristics of the finished document. As you create a presentation with illustrations, such as the project shown in Figure 10–1 on pages PPT 603 to PPT 604, you should follow these general guidelines:

1. **Use powerful words to accompany the text on your slides.** The slides are meant to enhance your talk by clarifying main points and calling attention to key ideas. Your speech should use words that explain and substantiate your visuals.

2. **Develop tables that are clear and meaningful.** Tables are extremely useful vehicles for presenting complex relationships. Their design plays an important part in successfully conveying the information to the audience.

3. **Use appropriate colors when formatting graphics you want people to remember.** Numerous studies have shown that appropriate graphics help audiences comprehend and remember the information presented during a speech. Color has been shown to increase retention by as much as 80 percent. When choosing colors for your graphics, use hues that fit the tone and objective of your message.

CONSIDER THIS

How should you submit solutions to questions in the assignments identified with a ✳ symbol?

Every assignment in this book contains one or more questions identified with a ✳ symbol. These questions require you to think beyond the assigned presentation. Present your solutions to the questions in the format required by your instructor. Possible formats may include one or more of these options: write the answer; create a document that contains the answer; present your answer to the class; discuss your answer in a group; record the answer as audio or video using a webcam, smartphone, or portable media player; or post answers on a blog, wiki, or website.

Apply Your Knowledge

Reinforce the skills and apply the concepts you learned in this chapter.

___

Changing a Chart, Formatting Chart Legends, and Editing a Table

Note: To complete this assignment, you will be required to use the Data Files for Students. Visit www.cengage.com/ct/studentdownload for detailed instructions or contact your instructor for information about accessing the required files.

Instructions: Run PowerPoint. Open the presentation, Apply 10-1 Teen's Survey, from the Data Files for Students.

You conducted a survey of your freshman class to find out how much time they spend on certain activities each day. You also asked if they had ever experienced bullying now or in the past. The document you open is a partially formatted presentation. You will change a chart type, format a chart legend, and add data to a table. Your presentation should look like Figure 10–74.

Perform the following tasks:

1. On Slide 1, apply the Blue, 18 pt glow, Accent color 5 text effect to the title text, and then enlarge the photo to approximately 6.07" × 13.33", move it to the bottom of the slide, and then apply the Soft Edge Rectangle picture style (the sixth style in the first row) as shown in Figure 10–74a.

2. On Slide 2, change the chart type from a bar chart to a 3-D Pie chart, and change the size to approximately 6.5" × 12.23". Increase the chart title font size to 40 point, change the chart colors to Color 4 (the fourth row in the Colorful area), and then change the chart style to Style 7.

3. On Slide 2, change the data labels fill to White, Background 1 (the first color in the first Theme Colors row), change the font size to 14 point, change the font color to Black, Text 1 (the second color in the first Theme Colors row), and then bold this text. Change the legend font size to 18 point, and then bold this text. Distribute the chart vertically and horizontally on the slide, as shown in Figure 10–74b on the next page.

4. Create a background on Slide 3 by inserting the photo called Bullying, which is available on the Data Files for Students, as shown in Figure 10–74c.

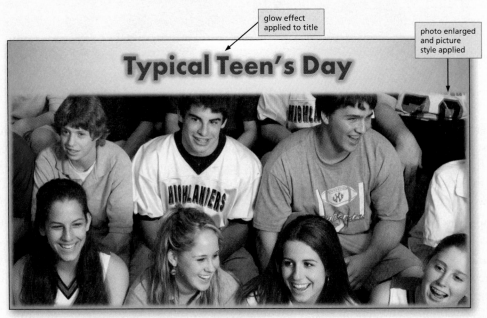

glow effect applied to title

photo enlarged and picture style applied

(a) Slide 1

Figure 10–74

Continued >

Apply Your Knowledge *continued*

(b) Slide 2

(c) Slide 3

Figure 10–74 (Continued)

5. Merge the three cells in the first row of the chart on Slide 3. Increase the size of the font in the first row to 24 point, bold the text, and then center the text both horizontally and vertically in the cell. Change the height of the first and second rows to 0.8", and then change the height of the third row to 0.6". Delete the bottom row of the table. Insert the numbers in the third row, and then center the numbers. Move the table to the location shown in Figure 10–74c.

6. Apply the Dark Style 2 – Accent 5/Accent 6 table style to the table (the fourth style in the second Dark row). Add all borders to the table, change the border weight to 3 pt, change the pen color to Dark Blue (the ninth color in the Standard Colors row), and then add two vertical lines and one horizontal line. Add the Offset Bottom shadow effect (the second effect in the first Outer row), as shown in the figure.

7. If requested by your instructor, add your birth year after the title of the table on Slide 3.

8. Apply the Peel Off transition (Exciting category) and change the duration to 4.00 for all slides.

9. Save the presentation using the file name, Apply 10-1 Typical Teen's Day.

10. Submit the revised document in the format specified by your instructor.

11. ☀ In this presentation, you changed the chart type on Slide 2 from a bar chart to a pie chart. Why? Did adding a table style to the table on Slide 3 improve the table?

Extend Your Knowledge

Extend the skills you learned in this chapter and experiment with new skills. You may need to use Help to complete the assignment.

Drawing and Formatting Tables

Note: To complete this assignment, you will be required to use the Data Files for Students. Visit www.cengage.com/ct/studentdownload for detailed instructions or contact your instructor for information about accessing the required files. You will need to use a mouse or other pointing device to draw tables.

Instructions: Run PowerPoint. Open the presentation, Extend 10-1 Sodium, from the Data Files for Students. You will format one table and then draw and format a second table, as shown in Figure 10–75 on the next page.

Perform the following tasks:

1. On Slide 1 (Figure 10–75a), delete the first row of the table, which contains the table title, Daily Sodium Levels. To delete this row, place the pointer in that row, tap or click the TABLE TOOLS LAYOUT tab, tap or click the Delete button (TABLE TOOLS LAYOUT tab | Rows & Columns group), and tap or click Delete Rows in the Delete menu.

2. With the table selected, display the TABLE TOOLS DESIGN tab and then click the Pen Weight arrow (TABLE TOOLS DESIGN tab | Draw Borders group). Tap or click 3 pt to change the border weight.

3. Change the pen color by tapping or clicking the Pen Color button (TABLE TOOLS DESIGN tab | Draw Borders group) and then selecting Green (the sixth color in the Standard Colors row).

4. Tap or click the Borders arrow (TABLE TOOLS DESIGN tab | Table Styles group) and then select All Borders in the Borders gallery to apply the new border settings to the entire table.

5. Change the table shading color to Blue-Gray, Accent 3 (the seventh color in the first Theme Colors row), and then apply the From Center Variation gradient (the second gradient in the second variations row in the Light Variations area). Change the table text font to Arial, bold this text, and then center the table horizontally on the lower area of the slide.

6. Display Slide 2 (Figure 10–75b) and then draw a table with five rows and five columns. Distribute the rows and the columns. (*HINT:* To distribute the columns, display the TABLE TOOLS LAYOUT tab and then tap or click the Distribute Columns button [TABLE TOOLS LAYOUT tab | Cell Size group].) Change the line weight to 3 pt and the pen color to Dark Blue (the ninth color in the Standard Colors row). Click the Draw Table button and then click the four main borders of the table to apply the new border settings.

7. Click the first cell in the first row, click the Table Eraser button, and then erase the vertical line between the first and second cells in the first row.

8. Erase the horizontal lines in the first, third, and fourth columns of the second row.

9. Erase the horizontal lines in the first, third, and fourth columns of the fourth row.

10. Enter the data in the table using Figure 10–75b as a guide. Select all text in the table and then change the font to Arial and the font size to 20 point. Center the text both horizontally and vertically in each cell. Select the first row of the table and then bold this text.

Continued >

Extend Your Knowledge *continued*

(a) Slide 1

(b) Slide 2

Figure 10–75

11. Select the table on Slide 2, adjust the size of the table to approximately 3.94" × 9.79". Change the shading color to Teal, Accent 2, Lighter 40% (the sixth color in the fourth Theme Colors row), and then apply the Linear Down Gradient (the second gradient in the first Variations row) to the table.

12. If requested by your instructor, replace the word, Our, in the title text of Slide 1 with your grandfather's first name.

13. Apply the Split transition in the Subtle category to all slides and then change the duration to 3.50 seconds.

14. Save the presentation using the file name, Extend 10-1 Sodium in Our Diet.

15. Submit the revised document in the format specified by your instructor.

16. ✳ In this presentation, you added borders to the table on Slide 1. Did these borders help separate the cells and make the data easier to read? On Slide 2, you formatted the table. How did these colors enhance this slide element?

Analyze, Correct, Improve

Analyze a presentation, correct all errors, and improve it.

Editing a Table, Linking a Chart from a File, Changing a Chart, Switching Rows and Columns in a Chart, and Adding a Hyperlink to a Table

Note: To complete this assignment, you will be required to use the Data Files for Students. Visit www.cengage.com/ct/studentdownload for detailed instructions or contact your instructor for information about accessing the required files.

Instructions: Run PowerPoint. Open the presentation, Analyze 10-1 College Courses, from the Data Files for Students. Based on recent enrollment, there is an increase in demand for certain courses, such as psychology and forensic science, and a decrease in enrollment in chemistry classes. You work part time in your school's registration office, and your supervisor has asked you to gather information based on enrollment and to create a PowerPoint presentation. There have been several inquiries about the upcoming Spring semester registration, so your supervisor asked you to add a hyperlink to the Spring Semester PDF file, Spring 2015. Modify the slides by making the indicated corrections and improvements.

1. Correct

a. Select the table on Slide 1 (Figure 10–76a) and delete the first row. Select the remaining text in the table and center it, and then align it in the middle of each cell. Change the width of the first column to 1.5", and then change the width of the fourth column to 1.7". Change the height of the second row to 1". Change the border line weight to 1 pt and the color to Black, Text 1 (the second color in the first Theme Colors row). Move the table to the lower-left corner of the slide.

b. Add a hyperlink from the word, Spring, in the second column to the Spring 2015 Adobe PDF file located in the Data Files for Students (Figure 10–76b on the next page).

c. Display Slide 2 (Figure 10–76c). Copy the chart on Sheet1 in the North Suburban Courses Microsoft Excel file located on the Data Files for Students and then paste it using the 'Use Destination Theme & Link Data' option. Size the chart so that it is 5" × 8.5", align it in the center of the slide, and then move it below the title text placeholder.

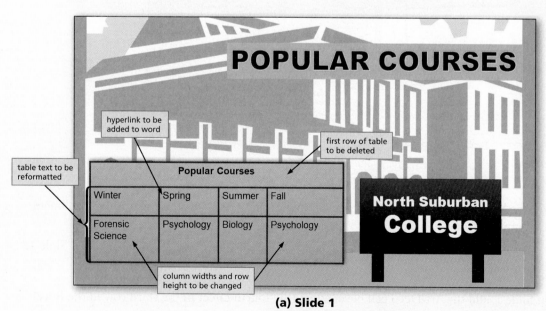

(a) Slide 1

Figure 10–76

Continued >

Analyze, Correct, Improve *continued*

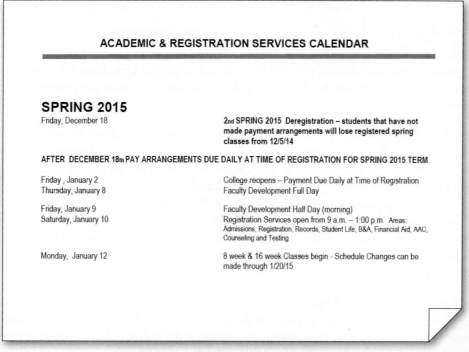

(b) Hyperlinked Adobe PDF File

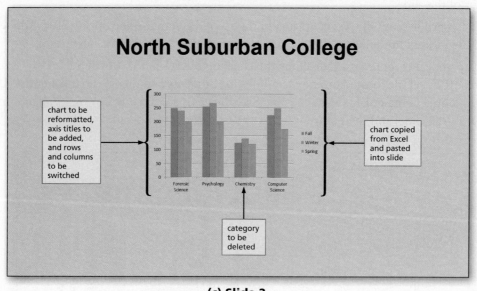

(c) Slide 2

Figure 10–76 (Continued)

d. Edit the Winter enrollment data for Psychology from 268 to 260 and the Spring enrollment for Computer Science from 175 to 300 (Figure 10–76d).

e. If requested by your instructor, add your birth year after the word, Fall, in the table on Slide 1.

2. Improve

a. On Slide 1, add the Art Deco cell bevel effect (the fourth effect in the third row in the Bevel area) to all cells in the table.

b. On Slide 2, switch the rows and columns. Delete the Chemistry category so that data for only Forensic Science, Psychology, and Computer Science is displayed.

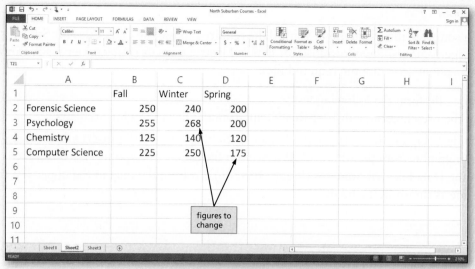

(d) Original Excel Worksheet
Figure 10–76 (Continued)

c. Change the Legend Position to the top of the chart and increase the font size to 16 point.

d. Change the style to Style 4 and the color to Color 4 (the fourth row in the Colorful area).

e. Display the Axis Titles. Select the Horizontal (Category) Axis Title and type **Popular College Courses** as the replacement text. Select the Vertical (Value) Axis Title and type **Enrollment** as the replacement text. Increase the font size to 20 point for both titles.

f. Apply the Top Spotlight – Accent 4 gradient (the fourth gradient in the second row of the Preset gradients) to the Chart Area.

g. Change the transition to the Window transition and then change the duration to 3.25 seconds for all slides.

h. Save the presentation using the file name, Analyze 10-1 North Suburban College.

i. Submit the revised document in the format specified by your instructor.

3. ✹ How did changing the table style on Slide 1 help? How did changing the chart style on Slide 2 improve the look of the slide? Why is linking the Excel file important in this presentation?

In the Labs

Design and/or create a presentation using the guidelines, concepts, and skills presented in this chapter. Labs 1 and 2, which increase in difficulty, require you to create solutions based on what you learned in the chapter; Lab 3 requires you to create a solution, which uses cloud and web technologies, by learning and investigating on your own from general guidance.

Lab 1: Inserting a Graphic from a File, Inserting a Linked Excel Worksheet, Inserting a Linked Word Document, and Entering Data in a Table

Problem: You and your family took a trip to Wisconsin Dells last summer. You also visited Kettle Moraine State Forest. Your travel club asked if you would share the experience of your trip and what your expenses were.

Continued >

In the Labs *continued*

Note: To complete this assignment, you will be required to use the Data Files for Students. Visit www.cengage.com/ct/studentdownload for detailed instructions or contact your instructor for information about accessing the required files.

Instructions: Perform the following tasks:

1. Open the presentation, Lab 10-1 Road Trip, from the Data Files for Students.

2. On Slide 1 (Figure 10–77a), use the Create from file option of the Insert Object dialog box to insert a graphic from the Microsoft PowerPoint file called Chicago to Wisconsin Dells Map from the Data Files for Students (Figure 10–77b). Position the map in the upper-left corner of the slide as shown in the figure.

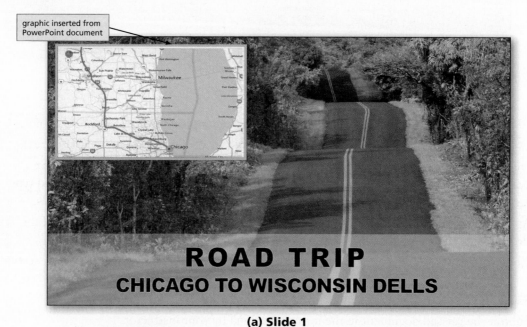

graphic inserted from PowerPoint document

(a) Slide 1

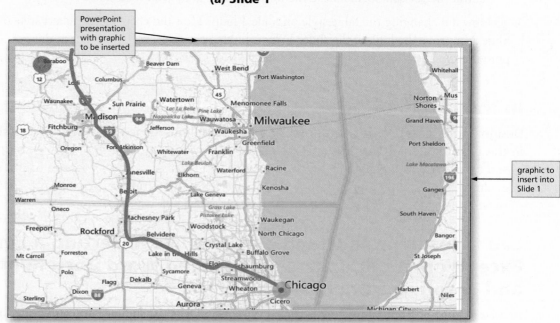

PowerPoint presentation with graphic to be inserted

graphic to insert into Slide 1

(b) PowerPoint Graphic

Figure 10–77

(c) Slide 2

(d) Original Word Document

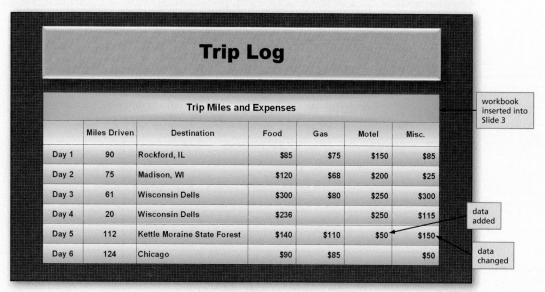

(e) Slide 3

Figure 10–77 (Continued)

Continued >

In the Labs *continued*

(f) Original Excel Worksheet

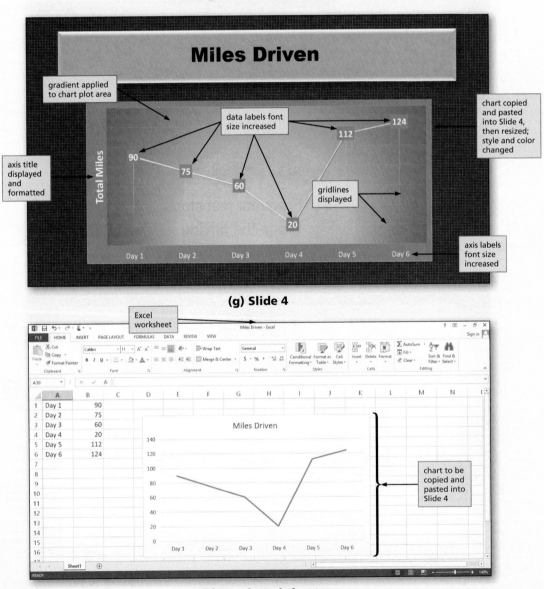

(g) Slide 4

(h) Excel Worksheet

Figure 10–77 (Continued)

3. On Slide 2 (Figure 10–77c on page PPT 655), use the Create from file option of the Insert Object dialog box to insert a table from the Microsoft Word file called Trip Planning (Figure 10–77d), from the Data Files for Students and link it. Change the size of the table to approximately 5.53" × 9.7", move it to the lower area of the slide, and center it as shown in the figure. Double-tap or double-click the table and enter data by typing `Get vehicle ready` in the third row, right column below Stop newspaper and mail, as shown in the figure.

4. On Slide 3 (Figure 10–77e), use the Create from file option of the Insert Object dialog box to insert a table from the Microsoft Excel file, Trip Miles and Expenses (Figure 10–77f), from the Data Files for Students and link it. Change the size of the table to approximately 4.8" × 11.47", center it on the slide, and then move it to the location shown in the figure. For the Kettle Moraine visit, type `$50` for camping fees in the motel column. Highlight the $85 in the seventh row, last column and type `$150` as the replacement text.

5. On Slide 4 (Figure 10–77g), copy and paste the chart in Sheet1 of the Microsoft Excel file, Miles Driven, from the Data Files for Students (Figure 10–77h). Use Destination Theme and Embed Workbook. Increase the size of the chart to approximately 4.5" × 10", position it in the area shown in the figure, and center it on the slide. Change the chart style to Style 12 and the color to Color 10.

6. Display the Primary Vertical Axis Title, highlight it, and then type `Total Miles` as the replacement text. Increase the font size to 24 point. Select the Gridlines check box in the CHART ELEMENTS pane so that the Primary Major Horizontal gridlines are added to the chart. Clear the Chart Title check box in the CHART ELEMENTS pane so that the title is not displayed.

7. Apply the Bottom Spotlight – Accent 4 gradient (the fourth gradient in the fourth row) to the chart Plot Area. Increase the size of the data labels to 20 point, as shown in Figure 10–77g.

8. Increase the size of the Horizontal (Category) Axis labels (Day 1 through Day 6) along the bottom of the chart to 16 point, as shown in the figure.

9. If requested by your instructor, add your home address in the last row, first column of the table on Slide 2.

10. Apply the Doors transition in the Exciting category and then change the duration to 3.75 seconds for all slides.

11. Submit the document in the format specified by your instructor. Save the presentation using the file name, Lab 10-1 Road Trip to Wisconsin Dells.

12. ✳ On Slide 1, you inserted a graphic from another PowerPoint presentation. How did this improve this slide? You increased the size of the labels on Slide 4. What other changes could make the slide more readable?

Lab 2: Inserting a Table from a Word Document, Inserting an Illustration from a Word Document, and Editing an Embedded File

Problem: In your earth science class, you are studying rainfall on earth. There are certain areas that receive a lot of rain and some that hardly get any. In your research you've discovered there is actually a desert in South America that has never had any recorded rainfall. It's known as the driest place on earth. To help you understand how rainfall is recorded, you decide to build your own rainfall gauge and track the rainfall for six months. You create a presentation with four slides, as shown in Figures 10–78a through 10–78d on the next page.

Continued >

In the Labs *continued*

Note: To complete this assignment, you will be required to use the Data Files for Students. Visit www.cengage.com/ct/studentdownload for detailed instructions or contact your instructor for information about accessing the required files.

Instructions: Perform the following tasks:

1. Open the presentation, Lab 10-2 Rainfall, from the Data Files for Students.

2. Display Slide 1 (Figure 10–78a) and then draw a table with five rows and two columns. Change the height of the first row to 0.7", the height of rows two through five to 0.6", and then change the width of both columns to 5".

3. Enter the data in the table using Figure 10–78a as a guide. Select all text in the table and then change the font to Arial and the font size to 24 point. Align all the text in the middle of each cell. Center the text in the first row and bold this text, as shown in Figure 10–78a.

4. Change the color of the table background to Gold, Accent 4 (the eighth color in the first Theme Colors row), and then apply the Linear Down gradient (the second gradient in the first Variations row) to the table. Apply the Convex bevel (the third bevel in the second Bevel row) to the table, as shown in Figure 10–78a.

(a) Slide 1

(b) Slide 2

Figure 10–78

(c) Original Word Document

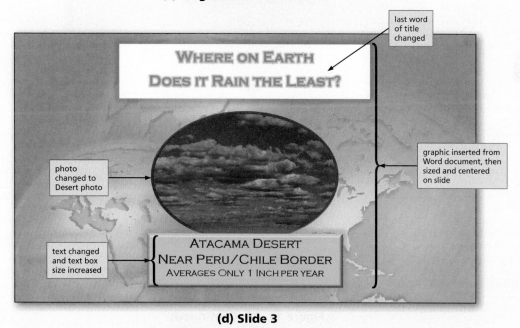

(d) Slide 3

Figure 10–78 (Continued)

5. On Slide 2 (Figure 10–78b), insert and embed the object Microsoft Word file, Most Rainfall Flyer (Figure 10–78c), from the Data Files for Students. Adjust the size of the graphic to approximately 7.82" × 8.08", align the graphic to the center and middle of the slide, as shown in Figure 10–78b.

Continued >

In the Labs *continued*

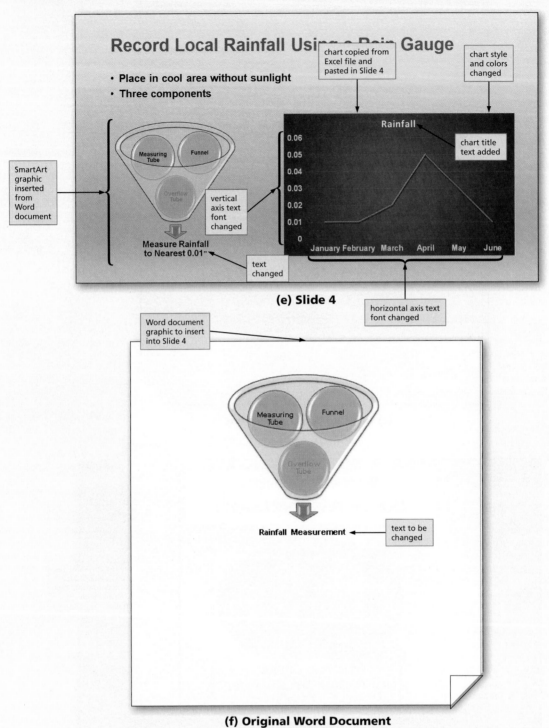

(e) Slide 4

(f) Original Word Document

Figure 10–78 (Continued)

6. On Slide 3 (Figure 10–78d on the previous page), repeat the steps for Slide 2. Select the flyer and replace the last word of the title, Most, with the word, Least. Change the photo in the flyer to the photo called Desert, from the Data Files for Students. Select the text in the text box on the bottom of the flyer, and then type `Atacama Desert, Near Peru/Chile Border,` `Averages only 1 inch per year` as the new text. Increase the size of the text box so that the text fits on three lines as shown in Figure 10–78d. *Note:* To keep this Word document in its original format, do not save this file.

7. On Slide 4 (Figure 10–78e), use the Create from file option of the Insert Object dialog box to insert the rain gauge SmartArt graphic from the Microsoft Word file, Rainfall Gauge

(g) Excel Worksheet

Figure 10–78 (Continued)

(Figure 10–78f), from the Data Files for Students. Highlight the text below the graphic, Rainfall Measurement, type `Measure Rainfall to Nearest 0.01"`, as the replacement text, and then change the font size to 18 point, as shown in Figure 10–78e.

8. On Slide 4, copy the chart on Sheet1 in the Measure Rain Microsoft Excel file (Figure 10–78g), located on the Data Files for Students, and then paste it using the 'Use Destination Theme & Link Data' option. Move the chart to the right side of the slide, as shown in Figure 10–78e.

9. Change the chart style to Style 7, and then change the colors to Color 9 (the fifth row in the Monochromatic area). Highlight the chart title text and type `Rainfall` as the replacement title. Change the Vertical (Value) Axis and the Horizontal (Category) Axis font to Arial, and then change the size to 16 point.

10. If requested by your instructor, type the name of your current pet after the word, components, in the second bulleted paragraph on Slide 4.

11. Apply the Ripple transition in the Exciting category and then change the duration to 2.00 seconds for all slides.

12. Save the presentation using the file name, Lab 10-2 Rainfall Worldwide.

13. Submit the document in the format specified by your instructor.

14. ✸ On Slides 2 and 3, you inserted a graphic from a Microsoft Word flyer and made changes to the graphic, including changing the photo on Slide 3. Was this an effective way to show the countries where there is the most and least amount of rainfall? Could you have used a different chart type to show recorded rainfall on Slide 4?

Lab 3: Expand Your World: Cloud and Web Technologies
Using the PowerPoint Web App to Create and Format SmartArt

Problem: You are using a mobile device or computer at your fitness center that does not have Power-Point but has Internet access. To make use of time between your personal training session and your nutrition class, you use the PowerPoint Web App and the data in Slide 2 of the Healthy Heart presentation in this chapter to create a SmartArt graphic (Figure 10–79 on the next page). This graphic can be used as a replacement for Slide 2 if you decide to present the same information in an alternate manner.

Continued >

In the Labs *continued*

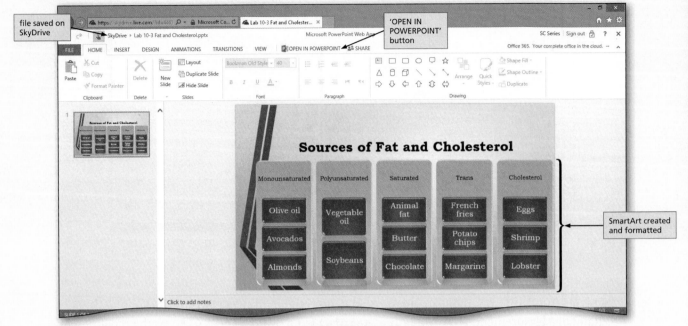

Figure 10–79

Instructions: Perform the following tasks:

1. Run a browser. Navigate to the Office Web Apps website. You will need to sign in to your SkyDrive account.

2. Tap or click the Create button to begin creating a PowerPoint presentation using the PowerPoint Web App. Name the document Lab 10-3 Fat and Cholesterol.

3. Use the Title and Content layout, apply the Parallax theme and then change the variant to Variant 4 (the rightmost variant with the gray and red stripes).

4. To create the SmartArt graphic, tap or click the SmartArt icon in the content placeholder, select the Grouped List design (the eighth design in the third row), and then enter the data from Slide 2 of the Healthy Heart presentation, which is shown in Figure 10–1(c) on page PPT 603.

5. Apply the Polished SmartArt style (the first style in the second row) and change the colors to Colored Fill – Accent 1 (the second color in the Accent 1 row). Change the font of all text to Bookman Old Style and then bold the title text. Use the SmartArt corner sizing handles to increase the graphic's size, as shown in Figure 10–79.

6. Tap or click the 'OPEN IN POWERPOINT' button and then tap or click the Yes button (Microsoft Office dialog box) to open the document in the PowerPoint desktop app. If necessary, sign in to your Microsoft account when prompted.

7. In the PowerPoint desktop app, apply the Cartoon SmartArt style (the third design in the first 3-D row) to the graphic and bold the five column headings (Monounsaturated, Polyunsaturated, Saturated, Trans, and Cholesterol). Save the table on your SkyDrive account with the file name, Lab 10-3 Fat and Cholesterol Modified.

8. Redisplay your SkyDrive account and open the file Lab 10-3 Fat and Cholesterol Modified in the PowerPoint Web App. Select the option to edit the modified document in the PowerPoint Web App.

9. Using either the PowerPoint Web App or the PowerPoint desktop app, submit the Lab 10-3 Fat and Cholesterol document in the format requested by your instructor. Sign out of your SkyDrive account. Sign out of the Microsoft account in PowerPoint.

10. ✳ Which SmartArt features that are available in the PowerPoint desktop app are not available in the PowerPoint Web App? Did the file retain the SmartArt style you applied? Is the information presented more clearly in the Healthy Heart chart or in the SmartArt graphic? Why?

✳ Consider This: Your Turn

Apply your creative thinking and problem-solving skills to design and implement a solution.

1. Design and Create a Presentation about Caffeine Content of Beverages

Personal

Part 1:   Your doctor recently told you to reduce caffeine consumption for health reasons. You have researched the beverages you consume, and you found that the highest amount of caffeine is in brewed coffee that you drink several times a day (8-ounce serving) - 95–200 mg. Other beverages that you consume have high amounts of caffeine as well. They are: hot chocolate (5-ounce serving) - 2–10 mg; cola (12-ounce serving) - 30–50 mg; green tea (8-ounce serving) - 30–50 mg; other teas (5-ounce serving) - 40–100 mg; and energy drinks (8-ounce serving) - 80 mg. You also learned that a 5-ounce serving of decaffeinated coffee has between 2 and 5 mg of caffeine. You decide to create a PowerPoint presentation for your family and friends to share your findings. Use the concepts and techniques presented in this chapter to prepare a presentation. Select a suitable theme, create a table showing caffeine levels, insert a chart, and use WordArt or SmartArt graphics where appropriate. You can use photos and illustrations from Office.com if they are appropriate for this topic. Submit your assignment in the format specified by your instructor.

Part 2:   ✳ You made several decisions while creating the presentation in this assignment: where to place text and how to format the table and chart. What was the rationale behind each of these decisions? When you reviewed the document, what further revisions did you make and why? Where would you recommend showing this slide show?

2. Design and Create a Presentation about Your Shoe Business

Professional

Part 1:   You are the owner of Terry's Tennis Shoes, a small athletic shoe store in your town. Business has been so good that you decided to open another store in a nearby town. You rented a building and hired a manager for the new location. The new manager has hired employees, and you suggested having a meeting with employees from both stores. You decide to put together a PowerPoint presentation for this meeting. Your top-selling shoes for the last six months were: Pink High Top (950 pairs sold), Patterned High Top (1,200 pairs sold), Black High Top (1,750 pairs sold), and Checkered (850 pairs sold). Use the PowerPoint file called Tennis Shoes Top Sellers, which is available on the Data Files for Students, to show these four styles and some of your other top sellers. Insert the file called Terry's Sport Shoes Flyer, located on the Data Files for Students, to show an example of an ad for the store. Select a suitable theme. The presentation could contain other photos and illustrations from Office.com if they are appropriate for this topic. Customize your presentation by creating a table and chart. Submit your assignment in the format specified by your instructor.

Continued >

Consider This: Your Turn *continued*

Part 2: ✺ You made several decisions while creating the presentation in this assignment: where to place text, how to format the text (such as font, font size, and colors), which image(s) to use, and what type of table and chart you used to make the presentation look professional and consistent. What was the rationale behind each of these decisions? When you reviewed the document, what further revisions did you make and why? Where would you recommend showing this slide show?

3. Design and Create a Presentation about World Energy
Research and Collaboration

Part 1: In your science class you are studying world energy. Energy is required for many essential functions in our everyday living, such as driving vehicles and using electricity. For many years, our energy came from fossil fuels: coal, oil, and gas. Now, other forms are prevalent, including renewables such as hydroelectric, geothermal, solar, wind, and biodiesel. Hydroelectric plants use dams to harness running water to generate energy. Geothermal power comes from ground water heated by molten rock. Solar panels capture and store energy from the sun. Biodiesel fuel can be made from both used and unused sources of vegetable oil and animal fats. Currently, our energy comes from these sources worldwide: Coal/Peat - 27 percent; Oil - 33.2 percent; Gas - 21.1 percent; Renewables - 12.9 percent; Nuclear - 5.8 percent. Your class has divided into three groups. One group will study fossil fuels and another group will study renewables. The third group will pull all the information together and create a PowerPoint presentation. Create a chart using the data furnished above. For just the renewables, you can change the chart type to 'Pie of Pie' or you can create a separate pie chart with approximate percentages of the renewable sources. Use at least three objectives found at the beginning of this chapter to develop the presentation. You can use your own pictures or those available from Office.com if they are appropriate for this topic.

Part 2: ✺ You made several decisions while creating the presentation in this assignment, including where to place text and how to create and format the energy sources data. What was the rationale behind each of these decisions? When you reviewed the document, what further revisions did you make and why? Where would you recommend showing this slide show?

Learn Online

Reinforce what you learned in this chapter with games, exercises, training, and many other online activities and resources.

Student Companion Site Reinforcement activities and resources are available at no additional cost on www.cengagebrain.com. Visit www.cengage.com/ct/studentdownload for detailed instructions about accessing the resources available at the Student Companion Site.

SAM Put your skills into practice with SAM! If you have a SAM account, go to www.cengage .com/sam2013 to access SAM assignments for this chapter.

11 | Organizing Slides and Creating a Photo Album

Objectives

You will have mastered the material in this chapter when you can:

- Create a section break
- Rename a section
- Reorder a section
- Create a custom slide show
- Create a photo album
- Reorder pictures in a photo album
- Adjust the quality of pictures in a photo album

- Add captions to pictures in a photo album
- Use the Research task pane to look up information
- Change slide orientation
- Set up a custom size slide
- Copy and compress a video file
- Email a presentation
- Create a video from a presentation

11 | Organizing Slides and Creating a Photo Album

Introduction

BTW
Using Photographs
A carefully selected image can convey an engaging message that your audience will remember long after the presentation has ended. One picture can evoke emotions and create a connection between the speaker and the listeners. The adage, "A picture is worth a thousand words," is relevant when audience members view PowerPoint slides.

Sharing photographs and videos has become a part of our everyday lives. We often use digital cameras and visit online social media websites to share our adventures, special occasions, and business activities. The presentations can be organized into sections so that particular slides are shown to specific audiences. For example, one large presentation created for freshmen orientation can be divided into one section for registration, another for financial aid, and a third for campus activities; each section could be shown to different audiences.

In addition, PowerPoint's ability to create a photo album allows you to organize and distribute your pictures by adding interesting layouts, vibrant backgrounds, and meaningful captions. These photo albums can be emailed, published to a website, or turned into a video to distribute to friends and business associates, who do not need PowerPoint installed on their computers to view your file.

Project — Presentation with Sections and a Photo Album

BTW
Designing Postcards
A postcard is an effective means of sending information to a specific audience, according to marketing experts. The size is large enough to support eye-catching images yet small enough to get the message into the readers' hands. Designers recommend using two-thirds of the postcard for a graphic and one-third for text.

Alaska is a travel destination unlike any place in the world. The state's 570,000 square miles are home to moose, bears, bald eagles, blue and humpbacked whales, and hundreds of other species. Visitors enjoy whale watching, fishing, hiking, and relaxing in the state's natural beauty. Float plane trips and rail excursions take travelers deep within the mountains to view wildlife and the trails prospectors traveled more than 100 years ago in search of treasures during the gold rush. Many travel groups plan vacations to Alaska, and they welcome experts and vacationers who share insights and photos of their travels. Members of the Travel Club in your community have asked you to present highlights of your Alaskan vacation that you enjoyed recently.

The presentation you create in this chapter (Figure 11–1) contains photos you took during this trip, which began in Seattle and included stops in Juneau, Skagway, and Ketchikan. You divide the slide show into sections for Lakes (Figure 11–1a), Train Excursion, Glaciers, and Float Plane trip. You then create a photo album, add pictures, make adjustments to brightness and contrast, and add captions (Figures 11–1b and 11–1c). You also create a second photo album with black-and-white images (Figure 11–1d). In addition, you create two slides with a custom size to use as a marketing tool to promote the annual Travel Expo and insert a video file on one of the slides (Figure 11–1e). You then email the meeting announcement file to a member and also convert another file to a video so that Travel Club members who do not have PowerPoint installed on their computers can view a glacier you visited during your vacation.

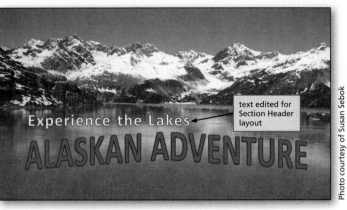

text edited for
Section Header
layout

Photo courtesy of Susan Sebok

(a) Alaskan Adventure Section Slide

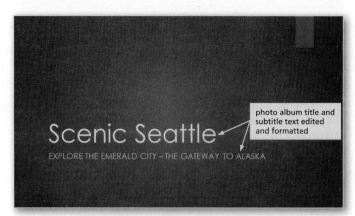

photo album title and
subtitle text edited
and formatted

(b) Photo Album Title Slide

photo
enhanced

Photo courtesy of Susan Sebok

(c) Photo Album Slide

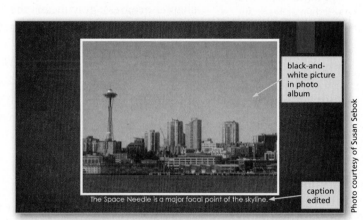

black-and-
white picture
in photo
album

caption
edited

Photo courtesy of Susan Sebok

(d) Black-and-White Photo Album Slide

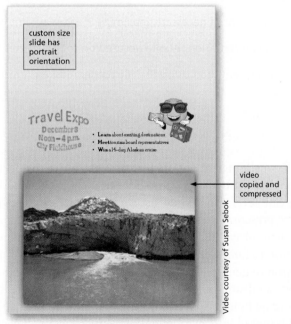

custom size
slide has
portrait
orientation

video
copied and
compressed

Video courtesy of Susan Sebok

(e) Custom Size Slide

Figure 11–1

Roadmap

In this chapter, you will learn how to create the slides shown in Figure 11–1 on the previous page. The following roadmap identifies general activities you will perform as you progress through this chapter:

1. CREATE and ORGANIZE SECTIONS in a presentation.
2. Select specific slides to CREATE a CUSTOM SLIDE SHOW.
3. CREATE a PHOTO ALBUM and ENHANCE photo album ELEMENTS.
4. SPECIFY a CUSTOM SLIDE SIZE and ADD a VIDEO CLIP.
5. SHARE and DISTRIBUTE a PRESENTATION by emailing and creating a video.

At the beginning of step instructions throughout the chapter, you will see an abbreviated form of this roadmap. The abbreviated roadmap uses colors to indicate chapter progress: gray means the chapter is beyond that activity; blue means the task being shown is covered in that activity, and black means that activity is yet to be covered. For example, the following abbreviated roadmap indicates the chapter would be showing a task in the 2 CREATE CUSTOM SLIDE SHOW activity.

1 CREATE & ORGANIZE SECTIONS | 2 CREATE CUSTOM SLIDE SHOW | 3 CREATE PHOTO ALBUM & ENHANCE ELEMENTS

4 SPECIFY CUSTOM SLIDE SIZE & ADD VIDEO CLIP | 5 SHARE & DISTRIBUTE PRESENTATION

Use the abbreviated roadmap as a progress guide while you read or step through the instructions in this chapter.

To Run PowerPoint and Save a File

If you are using a computer to step through the project in this chapter and you want your screens to match the figures in this book, you should change your computer's resolution to 1366 × 768. The following steps run PowerPoint and then save a file.

1 Run PowerPoint. If necessary, maximize the PowerPoint window.

2 Open the presentation, Alaska, located on the Data Files for Students.

3 Save the presentation using the file name, Alaskan Adventure.

Creating Sections and a Custom Slide Show

Quality PowerPoint presentations are tailored toward specific audiences, and experienced presenters adapt the slides to meet the listeners' needs and expectations. Speakers can develop one slide show and then modify the content each time they deliver the presentation. In the Alaskan Adventure slide show, for example, a speaker may decide to place the slides that showcase spectacular glaciers at the end of the presentation to build suspense. Or, these slides can appear at the beginning of the presentation to generate interest.

You can divide the slides into **sections** to help organize the slides. These sections serve the same function as dividers in a notebook or tabs in a manual: They help the user find required information and move material in a new sequence. In PowerPoint,

One of the few differences between Windows 7 and Windows 8 occurs in the steps to run PowerPoint. If you are using Windows 7, tap or click the Start button, type **PowerPoint** in the 'Search programs and files' box, tap or click PowerPoint 2013, and then, if necessary, maximize the PowerPoint window. For a summary of the steps to run PowerPoint in Windows 7, refer to the Quick Reference located at the back of this book.

BTW
The Ribbon and Screen Resolution
PowerPoint may change how the groups and buttons within the groups appear on the ribbon, depending on the computer's screen resolution. Thus, your ribbon may look different from the ones in this book if you are using a screen resolution other than 1366 × 768.

you can create sections, give them unique names, and then move slides into each section. You then can move one entire section to another part of the slide show or delete the section if it no longer is needed. Each section can be displayed or printed individually.

A **custom show** is an independent set of slides to show to a specific audience. These slides can be in a different order than in the original presentation. For example, you may desire to show a title slide, the last nine slides, and then Slides 2, 5, and 8, in that order. One PowerPoint file can have several custom shows to adapt to specific audiences.

To Insert Slides with a Section Layout

1 CREATE & ORGANIZE SECTIONS | 2 CREATE CUSTOM SLIDE SHOW | 3 CREATE PHOTO ALBUM & ENHANCE ELEMENTS
4 SPECIFY CUSTOM SLIDE SIZE & ADD VIDEO CLIP | 5 SHARE & DISTRIBUTE PRESENTATION

Your presentation will have four sections: Lakes, Train Excursion, Glaciers, and Float Plane. One of PowerPoint's layouts is named Section Header, and it is similar to the Title Slide layout because it has a title and a subtitle placeholder. To ensure consistency and save time, you can create one slide with a Section Header layout and then duplicate and modify it for each section. *Why? You can help your audience understand the organization of your slide show if you have one slide announcing the content of each section.* The following steps insert the four section slides.

- With Slide 1 selected and the HOME tab displaying, tap or click the New Slide arrow (HOME tab | Slides group) to display the Office Theme gallery (Figure 11–2).

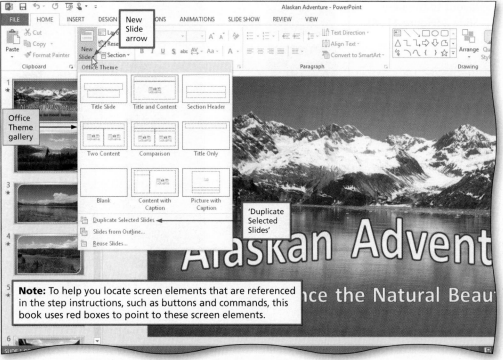

Figure 11–2

Photo courtesy of Susan Sebok

● Tap or click 'Duplicate Selected Slides' in the Office Theme gallery to create a new Slide 2 that is a duplicate of Slide 1.

● Tap or click the Slide Layout button (HOME tab | Slides group) to display the Office Theme layout gallery (Figure 11–3).

Figure 11–3

● Tap or click the Section Header layout to apply that layout to the new Slide 2 (Figure 11–4).

Figure 11–4

Other Ways

1. Press and hold or right-click Slide 1, tap or click Duplicate Slide on shortcut menu; then press and hold or right-click Slide 2, tap or click Layout on shortcut menu

BTW
Touch Screen Differences
The Office and Windows interfaces may vary if you are using a touch screen. For this reason, you might notice that the function or appearance of your touch screen differs slightly from this chapter's presentation.

To Edit the Subtitle

The slide with the Section Header layout should have characteristics similar to the title slide to give the presentation continuity. One method of slightly altering the title slide is to change the text to reflect the next set of slides in the presentation. The following steps edit the subtitle text.

1 With Slide 2 displaying, select the words, Natural Beauty, in the subtitle text placeholder and then type **Lakes** as the replacement text.

2 Select all the subtitle text, tap or click the Character Spacing button (HOME tab | Font group), and then change the character spacing to Loose.

3 Change the title text font color to Blue (eighth color in the Standard Colors row) (Figure 11–5).

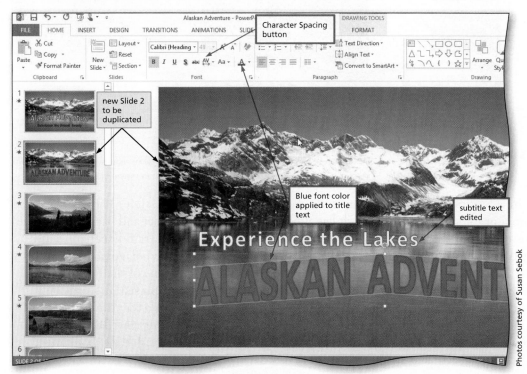

Figure 11–5

To Duplicate and Edit the Section Slides

Slide 2 is formatted appropriately to display at the beginning of the Lakes section of the slide show. A similar slide should display at the beginning of the Train Excursion, Glaciers, and Float Plane sections. The following steps duplicate Slide 2 and edit the title text.

1 With Slide 2 selected and the HOME tab displaying, tap or click the New Slide arrow and then tap or click 'Duplicate Selected Slides'.

2 Repeat Step 1 twice to insert two additional duplicate slides.

3 Display Slide 3, select the words, the Lakes, and then type **a Train Excursion** in the subtitle text placeholder.

4 Display Slide 4, select the word, Lakes, and then type **Glaciers** in the subtitle text placeholder.

5 Display Slide 5, select the words, the Lakes, and then type **a Float Plane** in the subtitle text placeholder (Figure 11–6 on the next page).

BTW

Q&As
For a complete list of the Q&As found in many of the step-by-step sequences in this book, visit the Q&A resource on the Student Companion Site located on www.cengagebrain.com. For detailed instructions about accessing available resources, visit www.cengage.com/ct/studentdownload or see the inside back cover of this book.

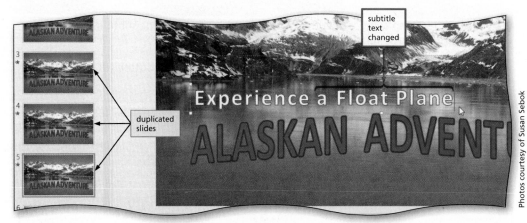

Photos courtesy of Susan Sebok

Figure 11–6

To Arrange Slides in Slide Sorter View

1 CREATE & ORGANIZE SECTIONS | 2 CREATE CUSTOM SLIDE SHOW | 3 CREATE PHOTO ALBUM & ENHANCE ELEMENTS
4 SPECIFY CUSTOM SLIDE SIZE & ADD VIDEO CLIP | 5 SHARE & DISTRIBUTE PRESENTATION

The four slides with a Section Header layout currently are displayed after the title slide. They are followed by 16 slides grouped into four categories, each of which has a distinct photo style or effect and background. The Lakes slides have photos with a rounded diagonal white border and a blue background, Train Excursion slides have photos with a gray border and a mountain background, Glacier photos have snipped diagonal corners and a water background, and Float Plane photos have soft edges and a cloud background. One of the four section slides you formatted should be positioned at the beginning of each category. When the presentation has only a few slides, you easily can drag and drop the slide thumbnails in the Slides pane. Your Alaskan Adventure presentation, however, has 21 slides. The following steps arrange the slides in Slide Sorter view. *Why? To easily arrange the slides, you can change to Slide Sorter view and drag and drop the thumbnails into their desired locations.*

1
• Tap or click the Slide Sorter view button to display the slides in Slide Sorter view and then tap or click the Slide 3 thumbnail (Experience a Train Excursion) to select it.

• Drag the Zoom slider to the left to change the zoom percentage to 50% so that all the slides are displayed (Figure 11–7).

Photos courtesy of Susan Sebok

Figure 11–7

- Drag the Slide 3 thumbnail between the Slide 9 and Slide 10 thumbnails so that it is positioned in the desired location between these two slides (Figure 11–8).

Photos courtesy of Susan Sebok

Figure 11–8

3

- Release your finger or the mouse button to display the Slide 3 thumbnail in a new location as Slide 9.
- Select the new Slide 3 (Experience Glaciers) and drag it between Slide 13 and Slide 14.
- Select the new Slide 3 (Experience a Float Plane) and drag it between Slide 17 and Slide 18 (Figure 11–9).

Photos courtesy of Susan Sebok

Figure 11–9

To Create a Section Break

1 CREATE & ORGANIZE SECTIONS | 2 CREATE CUSTOM SLIDE SHOW | 3 CREATE PHOTO ALBUM & ENHANCE ELEMENTS
4 SPECIFY CUSTOM SLIDE SIZE & ADD VIDEO CLIP | 5 SHARE & DISTRIBUTE PRESENTATION

The slides in the presentation are divided into four categories: Lakes, Train Excursion, Glaciers, and Float Plane. You can create a section break to organize slides into a particular group. *Why? At times, you may want to display slides from one particular category or move a section of slides to another part of the presentation.* The steps on the next page create five sections in the presentation.

1

- In Slide Sorter view, position the pointer between Slide 1 and Slide 2 and then tap or click once to display the vertical bar (Figure 11–10).

Q&A | I am using a touch screen. When I tap between the slides to display the vertical bar, a shortcut menu also displays with an Add Section button. Can I just tap that button instead of using the HOME tab Section button?
Yes.

Figure 11–10

2

- With the HOME tab displaying, tap or click the Section button (HOME tab | Slides group) to display the Section menu (Figure 11–11).

Figure 11–11

3

- Tap or click Add Section in the menu to create a section.
- Position the pointer between Slide 6 and Slide 7, which is the start of the slides with the Train Excursion, and then tap or click once to display the vertical bar (Figure 11–12).

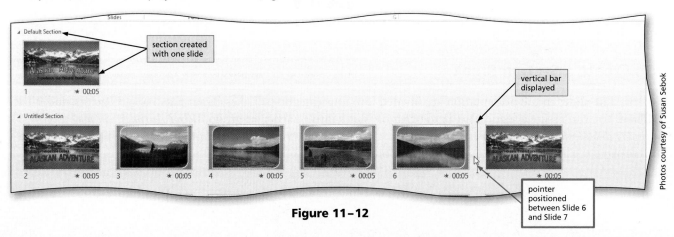

Figure 11–12

Photos courtesy of Susan Sebok

4

- Tap or click the Section button (HOME tab | Slides group) to display the Section menu and then tap or click Add Section in the menu to create a section with the name, Untitled Section.

- Position the pointer between Slide 11 and Slide 12, which is the start of the slides with glacier photos (Figure 11–13).

Figure 11–13

5

- Tap or click the Section button and then tap or click Add Section in the menu to create a section with the name, Untitled Section.

- Scroll down to display the final slides in the presentation, position the pointer between Slide 16 and Slide 17, and then create a section (Figure 11–14).

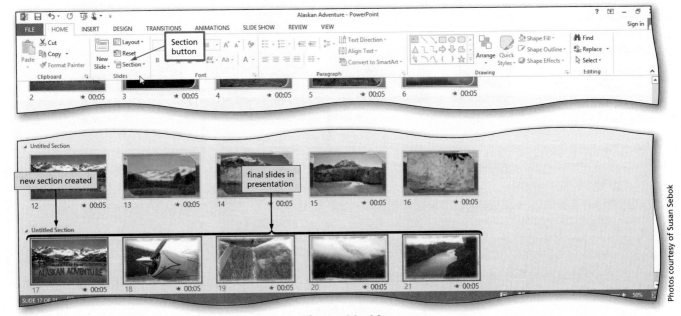

Figure 11–14

To Rename a Section

The default section names, Untitled and Default, do not identify the content of the slides in the group. The following steps rename each of the five sections in the presentation. *Why? Giving each section a unique name helps to categorize the slides easily.*

1

• With the last section featuring the float plane photos selected and the HOME tab displaying, tap or click the Section button (HOME tab | Slides group) to display the Section menu (Figure 11–15).

 If the Float Plane section is not highlighted, how can I select it?
Tap or click the divider between the sections. You will know the section is selected when the thumbnails have a red border and the text and slide numbers have a red font color.

Figure 11–15

Photos courtesy of Susan Sebok

2

• Tap or click Rename Section in the menu to display the Rename Section dialog box.

• Type **Float Plane** in the Section name box (Figure 11–16).

Figure 11–16

Photos courtesy of Susan Sebok

3

- Tap or click the Rename button (Rename Section dialog box) to change the section name.

- Tap or click the Untitled Section divider for the Glaciers section (Slide 12 through Slide 16) to select it and then tap or click the Section button (HOME tab | Slides group) to display the Section menu (Figure 11–17).

Figure 11–17

Photos courtesy of Susan Sebok

4

- Tap or click Rename Section to display the Rename Section dialog box, type `Glaciers` in the Section name box, and then tap or click the Rename button to change the section name.

- Select the divider for the Train Excursion section (Slide 7 through Slide 11), display the Rename Section dialog box, type `Train Excursion` as the new section name, and then tap or click the Rename button (Figure 11–18).

Figure 11–18

Photos courtesy of Susan Sebok

- Scroll up to display the first two sections, select the divider for the Lakes slides (Slide 2 through Slide 6), display the Rename Section dialog box, type **Lakes** as the new section name, and then tap or click the Rename button.

- Select the Default Section divider for Slide 1, display the Rename Section dialog box, type **Alaskan Adventure Title** as the new section name, and then tap or click the Rename button (Figure 11–19).

Figure 11–19

Photos courtesy of Susan Sebok

Other Ways

1. Press and hold or right-click section divider, tap or click Rename Section on shortcut menu

To Collapse and Reorder Sections

1 CREATE & ORGANIZE SECTIONS | 2 CREATE CUSTOM SLIDE SHOW | 3 CREATE PHOTO ALBUM & ENHANCE ELEMENTS
4 SPECIFY CUSTOM SLIDE SIZE & ADD VIDEO CLIP | 5 SHARE & DISTRIBUTE PRESENTATION

Why? *Travel Club members have expressed much more interest this year in glaciers than the train excursion, so you want to change the order of these two sets of slides in your presentation.* When slides are organized into sections, it is easy to change the order in which the sections display. Because your presentation consists of multiple sections, you can collapse the sections so that only the section titles are displayed. You then can reorder the sections and expand the sections. The following steps collapse the sections, reorder the Glaciers and Train Excursion sections, and expand the sections.

- With the first section, Alaskan Adventure Title, selected and the HOME tab displaying, tap or click the Section button (HOME tab | Slides group) to display the Section menu (Figure 11–20).

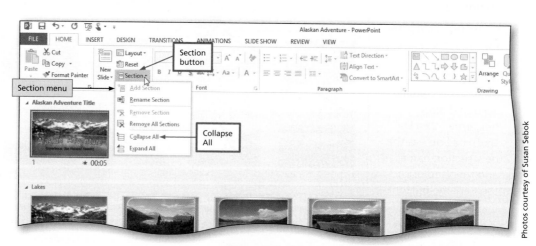

Figure 11–20

Photos courtesy of Susan Sebok

Q&A Can I remove a section?
Yes. To delete one section, select the title and then tap or click Remove Section in the Section menu. To remove all sections, display the Section menu and then tap or click 'Remove All Sections'.

2

- Tap or click Collapse All in the Section menu to display only the section names.

- Tap or click the Glaciers section name to select it and then drag the section upward between the Lakes and Train Excursion sections (Figure 11–21).

Figure 11–21

3

- Release your finger or the mouse button to move the Glaciers section between the Lakes and Train Excursion sections.

- Tap or click the Section button (HOME tab | Slides group) to display the Section menu (Figure 11–22).

Figure 11–22

 4

- Tap or click Expand All in the Section menu to display all the slides in their corresponding sections (Figure 11–23).

 5

- Run the presentation to display all the slides in the desired order.

Photos courtesy of Susan Sebok

Figure 11–23

Other Ways

1. Press and hold or right-click section name, tap or click Move Section Up, Move Section Down, Collapse All, or Expand All on shortcut menu

TO SHOW A PRESENTATION WITH MANUAL TIMING

The Alaskan Adventure slides are set to display for specified times. If you desire to override the automatic timings and advance the slides manually, you would perform the following steps.

1. Display the SLIDE SHOW tab and then tap or click the 'Set Up Slide Show' button (SLIDE SHOW tab | Set Up group) to display the Set Up Show dialog box.

2. Tap or click Manually in the Advance slides area (Set Up Show dialog box) and then tap or click the OK button.

Break Point: If you wish to take a break, this is a good place to do so. Be sure to save the Alaskan Adventure file again and then you can exit PowerPoint. To resume at a later time, run PowerPoint, open the file called Alaskan Adventure, and continue following the steps from this location forward.

To Create a Custom Slide Show

1 CREATE & ORGANIZE SECTIONS | 2 CREATE CUSTOM SLIDE SHOW | 3 CREATE PHOTO ALBUM & ENHANCE ELEMENTS
4 SPECIFY CUSTOM SLIDE SIZE & ADD VIDEO CLIP | 5 SHARE & DISTRIBUTE PRESENTATION

Many presenters deliver their speeches in front of targeted audiences. For example, the director of human resources may present one set of slides for new employees, another set for potential retirees, and a third for managers concerned with new regulations and legislation. Slides for all these files may be contained in one file, and the presenter can elect to show particular slides to accompany specific speeches. PowerPoint allows you to create a **custom show** that displays only selected slides. The following steps create a custom show. *Why? You want to create a smaller file in case your speech time at the meeting is less than planned and you need to shorten your talk.*

1
- Tap or click the Normal view button to display the slides in Normal view and then display the SLIDE SHOW tab.

- Tap or click the 'Custom Slide Show' button (SLIDE SHOW tab | Start Slide Show group) to display the Custom Slide Show menu (Figure 11–24).

Photos courtesy of Susan Sebok

Figure 11–24

• Tap or click
Custom Shows to
open the Custom
Shows dialog box
(Figure 11–25).

Figure 11–25

• Tap or click the New
button (Custom
Shows dialog box)
to display the
Define Custom
Show dialog box.

• Tap or click
the '1. Alaskan
Adventure' check
box in the Slides in
presentation area
to select this slide
(Figure 11–26).

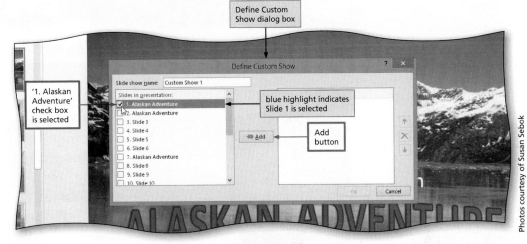

Figure 11–26

4

• Tap or click the
Add button (Define
Custom Show dialog
box) to add this
slide to the Slides in
custom show area.

• Scroll down and then
tap or click the check
boxes for Slide 3,
Slide 6, Slide 9,
Slide 11, Slide 13,
Slide 14, Slide 19,
and Slide 21 in the
Slides in presentation
area.

• Tap or click the
Add button (Define
Custom Show dialog
box) to add these
slides to the Slides in
custom show area (Figure 11–27).

Figure 11–27

- Select the text in the 'Slide show name' text box (Define Custom Show dialog box) and then type **Travel Club Favorites** as the new name (Figure 11–28).

Figure 11–28

- Tap or click the OK button (Define Custom Show dialog box) to create the new Travel Club Favorites custom show and display the Custom Shows dialog box (Figure 11–29).

- Tap or click the Close button (Custom Shows dialog box) to close the dialog box.

Figure 11–29

BTW
Hyperlinking Custom Shows
You can hyperlink to a custom show with slides relating to a specific topic in your presentation. Click the Hyperlink button (INSERT tab | Links group), click the 'Place in This Document' button, and then select the custom show in the Select a place in this document list.

To Open and Edit a Custom Slide Show

1 CREATE & ORGANIZE SECTIONS | 2 CREATE CUSTOM SLIDE SHOW | 3 CREATE PHOTO ALBUM & ENHANCE ELEMENTS
4 SPECIFY CUSTOM SLIDE SIZE & ADD VIDEO CLIP | 5 SHARE & DISTRIBUTE PRESENTATION

A PowerPoint file may have several custom slide shows. You can elect to display one of them at anytime depending upon the particular needs of your audience. If you need to reorder the slides, you can change the sequence easily. The following steps open a custom show and edit the slide sequence.

1

- With the SLIDE SHOW tab displaying, tap or click the 'Custom Slide Show' button (SLIDE SHOW tab | Start Slide Show group) to display the Custom Slide Show menu (Figure 11–30).

Q&A Why does 'Travel Club Favorites' display in the Custom Slide Show menu?
The names of any custom shows will be displayed in the menu. If desired, you could click this custom show name to run the slide show and display the selected slides.

Figure 11–30

Photos courtesy of Susan Sebok

2

- Tap or click Custom Shows to display the Custom Shows dialog box (Figure 11–31).

Figure 11–31

Photos courtesy of Susan Sebok

3

- With the Travel Club Favorites custom show selected in the Custom shows area, tap or click the Edit button (Custom Shows dialog box) to display the Define Custom Show dialog box.

- Tap or click Slide 19 in the Slides in custom show area to select it (Figure 11–32).

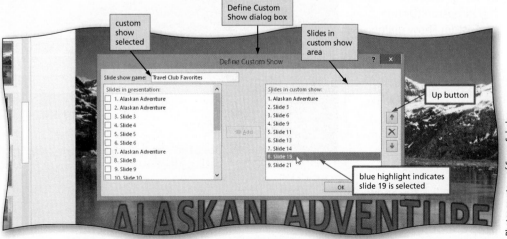

Figure 11–32

Photos courtesy of Susan Sebok

• Tap or click the Up button six times to move Slide 19 below Slide 1 as the second slide in the custom show (Figure 11–33).

Figure 11–33

• Tap or click Slide 21 in the Slides in custom show area to select it and then tap or click the Up button six times to move Slide 21 below Slide 19 as the third slide in the custom show.

• Tap or click Slide 9 in the Slides in custom show area to select it and then tap or click the Down button once to move Slide 9 below Slide 11 as the seventh slide in the custom show (Figure 11–34).

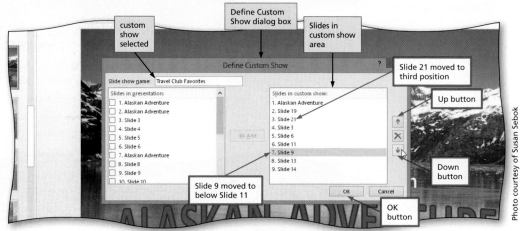

Figure 11–34

Q&A Can I move the slides so they display later in the custom show?
Yes. Select the slide you want to reorder and then tap or click the Down button.

• Tap or click the OK button (Define Custom Show dialog box) to create the revised Travel Club Favorites custom show and display the Custom Shows dialog box (Figure 11–35).

• Tap or click the Show button (Custom Shows dialog box) to run the Travel Club Favorites custom show.

• When all the slides have displayed, exit the custom show.

• Save the Alaskan Adventure file. Do not close this file because you are going to use it later in this project.

Figure 11–35

Break Point: If you wish to take a break, this is a good place to do so. You can exit PowerPoint now. To resume at a later time, run PowerPoint, open the file called Alaskan Adventure, and continue following the steps from this location forward.

Use photographs with sharp focus and contrast.

Clear, sharp pictures provide details that draw an audience into your presentation. High-quality photographs impress your audience and state that you have an eye for detail and take pride in your work. When your slides are projected on a large screen, any imperfection is magnified, so you must take care to select photographs that are in focus and have high contrast.

Creating a Photo Album

A PowerPoint **photo album** is a presentation that contains pictures to share with friends and business colleagues. It can contain a theme, a vibrant background, custom captions, a specific layout, frames around pictures, and boxes. You can enhance the quality of the pictures by increasing or decreasing brightness and contrast, and you can rotate the pictures in 90-degree increments. You also can change color pictures to display in black and white.

You can share your photo album in a variety of ways. You can, for example, email the file, publish it to the web, or print the pictures as handouts.

BTW
Printing in Grayscale
In this project you will convert your photos from color to black and white. If you desire to keep your images in color but want to print in black and white, PowerPoint provides that option. Display the FILE tab, tap or click the Print tab, tap or click the Color button, and then tap or click Grayscale. If you then want to print in color, tap or click the Grayscale button and then tap or click Color.

To Start a Photo Album and Add Pictures

1 CREATE & ORGANIZE SECTIONS | 2 CREATE CUSTOM SLIDE SHOW | **3 CREATE PHOTO ALBUM & ENHANCE ELEMENTS**
4 SPECIFY CUSTOM SLIDE SIZE & ADD VIDEO CLIP | 5 SHARE & DISTRIBUTE PRESENTATION

Why? Once you have gathered files of digital pictures, you can begin building a photo album. You initially create the album and then later enhance its appearance. The following steps start a photo album and add pictures.

1
- Display the INSERT tab and then tap or click the 'New Photo Album' button (INSERT tab | Images group) to display the Photo Album dialog box (Figure 11–36).

 Why am I viewing a menu with the 'New Photo Album' and 'Edit Photo Album' commands instead of the Photo Album dialog box?
You mistakenly clicked the 'New Photo Album' arrow instead of the 'New Photo Album' button.

Figure 11–36

- Tap or click the File/Disk button to display the Insert New Pictures dialog box.

- If necessary, navigate to the location where your Data Files for Students are stored (in this case, the PowerPoint Chapter 11 folder in the CIS 101 folder [or your class folder] on your computer or SkyDrive) (Figure 11–37).

Figure 11–37

- If necessary, tap or click the Views arrow on the toolbar (Insert New Pictures dialog box) to display the view settings (Figure 11–38).

Figure 11–38

- Tap or click List in the view settings to change the view setting and display only the picture file names.

- Tap or click Mount Rainier in Background to select the file name, and then select the file names Pike Place Market, Safeco Field View from Water, Safeco Field, Salmon Bake, Seattle Great Wheel, Seattle Map, and Seattle Skyline as additional files to insert (Figure 11–39).

Figure 11–39

Photo courtesy of Susan Sebok

Q&A

If I mistakenly select a file name, how can I remove the selection?
Tap or click the file name again.

I'm having trouble selecting multiple files on the touch screen. What can I do?
You may need to use a mouse in combination with the onscreen keyboard CTRL key, or you can select and insert each file individually.

- Tap or click the Insert button (Insert New Pictures dialog box) to add the pictures to the album.

BTW

Selecting Slides or Other Items
To select sequential or adjacent files or items, select the first item, press and hold down the SHIFT key, and then select the last item. All items between the first and last item will be highlighted. To select nonadjacent files or items, select the first item and then press and hold down the CTRL key. While holding down the CTRL key, select additional items.

To Reorder Pictures in a Photo Album

1 CREATE & ORGANIZE SECTIONS | 2 CREATE CUSTOM SLIDE SHOW | 3 CREATE PHOTO ALBUM & ENHANCE ELEMENTS
4 SPECIFY CUSTOM SLIDE SIZE & ADD VIDEO CLIP | 5 SHARE & DISTRIBUTE PRESENTATION

PowerPoint inserted the pictures in alphabetical order, which may not be the desired sequence for your album. You easily can change the order of the pictures in the same manner that you change the slide order in a custom show. The following steps reorder the photo album pictures. *Why? Showing the map of Seattle at the beginning of the presentation orientates your audience members to the geography of the region.*

- Tap or click the check box for the seventh picture, Seattle Map, to select it (Figure 11–40).

Photo courtesy of Susan Sebok

Figure 11–40

- Tap or click the Move Up button six times to move the Seattle Map photo upward so that it now is the first picture (picture 1) in the album.

- Tap or click the Seattle Map check box to remove the check mark.

- Select the eighth picture, Seattle Skyline, and then tap or click the Move Up button once to move this picture between the Salmon Bake and Seattle Great Wheel photos so that it now is the seventh picture.

- Tap or click the Seattle Skyline check box to remove the check mark.

To Adjust the Rotation of a Photo Album Image

1 CREATE & ORGANIZE SECTIONS | 2 CREATE CUSTOM SLIDE SHOW | 3 CREATE PHOTO ALBUM & ENHANCE ELEMENTS
4 SPECIFY CUSTOM SLIDE SIZE & ADD VIDEO CLIP | 5 SHARE & DISTRIBUTE PRESENTATION

Digital images have either a portrait (vertical) or landscape (horizontal) orientation. If a picture is displayed in your album with the wrong orientation, you can rotate the image in 90-degree increments to the left or the right. The following steps rotate a photo album picture. *Why? The map of Seattle is tilted toward the left, and audience members will be able to read the town names more easily if the picture is rotated.*

1

- Tap or click the check box for the first picture, Seattle Map, to select it and display a preview (Figure 11–41).

Figure 11–41

2

- Tap or click the 'Rotate Left 90°' button (Photo Album dialog box) to turn the picture to the left (Figure 11–42).

3

- Tap or click the Seattle Map check box to remove the check mark.

Figure 11–42

To Adjust the Contrast of a Photo Album Image

A picture you insert may need correcting to enhance its visual appeal. You can adjust the difference between the darkest and lightest areas of the picture by increasing or decreasing the contrast. The following steps adjust the contrast of a photo album picture. *Why? The Mount Rainier photo shows the mountain peak in the distance, and its prominence would be enhanced if the image had more dark and light areas.*

- Tap or click the check box for the second picture, Mount Rainier in Background, to select it and display a preview (Figure 11–43).

- Tap or click the Increase Contrast button (Photo Album dialog box) four times to change the contrast of this picture.

Figure 11–43

Photos courtesy of Susan Sebok

To Adjust the Brightness of a Photo Album Image

If a picture in the photo album is too light or too dark, you can adjust its brightness to enhance its appearance. The following step adjusts the brightness of a photo album picture. *Why? The Mount Rainier photo is somewhat dark, so increasing the brightness would help the colors stand out on the slide and give more depth to the image.*

- With the Mount Rainier picture selected, tap or click the Increase Brightness button (Photo Album dialog box) two times to intensify the colors in the picture (Figure 11–44).

Figure 11–44

Photos courtesy of Susan Sebok

To Change a Photo Album Layout

PowerPoint inserts each photo album picture so that it fills, or fits, one entire slide. You can modify this layout to display two or four pictures on a slide, display a title, or add white space between the image and the slide edges. You also can add a white or black frame around the perimeter of each picture. The following steps change an album layout. ***Why?*** *The photos are spectacular, so you want to display only one on each slide. Adding a frame provides contrast between the photos and the background.*

- With the Photo Album dialog box displayed, tap or click the Picture layout arrow in the Album Layout area (Photo Album dialog box) to display the Picture layout list (Figure 11–45).

Figure 11–45

Photos courtesy of Susan Sebok

- Tap or click 1 picture in the Picture layout list to change the layout so that one picture is displayed on each slide and a rectangular frame is displayed around each picture.

- Tap or click the Frame shape arrow in the Album Layout area (Photo Album dialog box) to display the Frame shape list (Figure 11–46).

Figure 11–46

Photos courtesy of Susan Sebok

- Tap or click 'Compound Frame, Black' in the Frame shape list to add a double black frame around the picture.

To Add a Photo Album Theme

The themes that are used to design a presentation also are available to add to a photo album. These themes determine the colors and fonts that complement each other and increase the visual appeal of the slides. The following steps add a theme to the photo album. *Why? Seattle is known as the Emerald City, so you want to select a theme that has a green background and a simple layout and font that will complement the majestic photos.*

- Tap or click the Browse button in the Album Layout area (Photo Album dialog box) to display the Choose Theme dialog box.

- Tap or click Ion in the theme list to select this theme (Figure 11–47).

- Tap or click the Select button (Choose Theme dialog box) to apply this theme to the presentation.

Figure 11–47

To Add Captions below All Pictures

If you desire a caption below each picture, you can request PowerPoint add this feature to the slides. The file name is displayed as the caption text, but you can edit and add effects to this text. The following step selects the option to add a caption below all pictures in the photo album. *Why? The audience members will see the text on the slide and hear you describe the images. Because they are using these two senses, they should be able to recall the information you are presenting. In addition, absent Travel Club members could view the presentation during their free time and learn the names of the places and objects presented on the slides.*

1

- In the Picture Options area (Photo Album dialog box), tap or click the 'Captions below ALL pictures' check box to select the check box (Figure 11–48).

Figure 11–48

To Create a Photo Album

Once you have inserted the pictures, determined the picture sequence, layout, and frame shape, you are ready to make the photo album. *Why? You have specified all the information PowerPoint needs to create this album.* The following step creates the photo album.

1

- Tap or click the Create button (Photo Album dialog box) to close the dialog box and create a photo album with a title page and nine pictures (Figure 11–49).

Q&A Why does a particular name display below the Photo Album title? PowerPoint displays the user name that was entered when the program was installed. To see this name, display the Backstage view, tap or click Options to display the PowerPoint Options dialog box, and then view or change the name entered in the User name box in the Personalize your copy of Microsoft Office area.

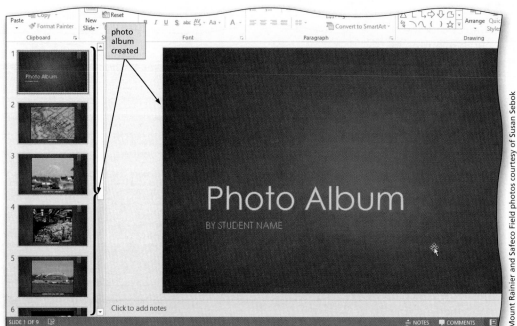

Figure 11–49

Mount Rainier and Safeco Field photos courtesy of Susan Sebok

To Edit a Photo Album

Once you review the photo album PowerPoint creates, you can modify the contents by adding and deleting pictures, changing the layout and frames, and adding transitions. The following steps edit the photo album. *Why? You want to change the frame style and color, add a text box on a new slide, and add a transition to add interest and to give additional information to your audience members.*

1

- Display the INSERT tab and then tap or click the 'New Photo Album' arrow (INSERT tab | Images group) to display the New Photo Album menu (Figure 11–50).

Figure 11–50

Mount Rainier and Safeco Field photos courtesy of Susan Sebok

2

- Tap or click 'Edit Photo Album' in the menu to display the Edit Photo Album dialog box.

- Tap or click the Frame shape arrow to display the Frame shape list and then tap or click 'Simple Frame, White' in the list to change the frame from a compound black border to a single white border.

- Tap or click the 'New Text Box' button (Edit Photo Album dialog box) to insert a new slide in the album with the name, Text Box.

- Select the Text Box picture check box and then tap or click the Move Up button once to move this picture upward as the first picture in the Pictures in album list (Figure 11–51).

Figure 11–51

Q&A Can I insert a box on one slide that already has a picture?
Yes. Tap or click the Text Box button (INSERT tab | Text group) and then tap or click the slide where you want to insert the box. You then can arrange the box and picture on the slide.

3

- Tap or click the Update button (Edit Photo Album dialog box) to make the changes to the photo album.

- Apply the Gallery transition and then change the duration to 5 seconds for all slides.

To Insert and Format Text in a Photo Album

PowerPoint inserts text into the slides, such as the file name for captions and the user name associated with the Microsoft Office installation as the subtitle text on the title slide. You can revise and format this text by changing the font, font size, color, and any other font styles and effects. The following steps edit text in the photo album.

1 With Slide 1 displaying, select the title text, Photo Album, and then type `Scenic Seattle` as the replacement text.

2 Select the subtitle text, By Student Name, and then type `Explore the Emerald City - The Gateway to Alaska` as the replacement text.

3 Increase the font size of the subtitle text to 24 point.

4 Display Slide 2, select the words, Text Box, and then type `Seattle is the Pacific Northwest's largest city and is a major port for commercial trade. The city is the birthplace of Starbucks, Pearl Jam, and Jimi Hendrix.` as the replacement text.

5 Press the ENTER key two times and then type `Precipitation falls an average of 150 days per year.` as the second paragraph.

6 Display Slide 3, select the caption text, and then type `Seattle is located on an isthmus between Puget Sound and Lake Washington.` as the new caption.

BTW
Resetting Placeholders
You can reset all customization changes to the preset options. Tap or click the Reset button (HOME tab | Slides group) or press and hold or right-click the slide or thumbnail and then tap or click Reset Slide on the shortcut menu. To retain custom formatting changes and move the placeholders to their original locations, tap or click the Layout button (HOME tab | Slides group) or press and hold or right-click the slide or thumbnail and then click Layout on the shortcut menu. Then, reapply the active layout from the Layout gallery.

7 Display Slide 9, select the caption text, and then type `The Space Needle is a major focal point of the skyline.` as the new caption.

8 Display Slide 1 and then run the slide show.

9 Save the presentation with the file name, Seattle Photo Album (Figure 11–52).

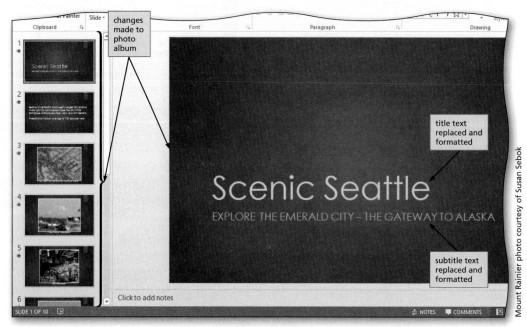

Figure 11–52

To Create Black-and-White Images in a Photo Album

1 CREATE & ORGANIZE SECTIONS | 2 CREATE CUSTOM SLIDE SHOW | 3 CREATE PHOTO ALBUM & ENHANCE ELEMENTS
4 SPECIFY CUSTOM SLIDE SIZE & ADD VIDEO CLIP | 5 SHARE & DISTRIBUTE PRESENTATION

Why? *Black-and-white pictures often generate interest and give a unique version of the color photographs. The series of shades ranging from black to white, or grayscale, provide a different perspective of our world.* The following steps edit a photo album to use black-and-white images.

1

• Display the INSERT tab, tap or click the 'New Photo Album' arrow, and then tap or click 'Edit Photo Album'.

• Tap or click the 'ALL pictures black and white' check box to select the check box (Figure 11–53).

Q&A Can I change the view to see my slides in grayscale or black and white?
Yes. Display the VIEW tab and then tap or click the Grayscale or the 'Black and White' button (Color/Grayscale group). The Grayscale option shows a variety of shades ranging from white to black whereas the Black and White option displays only black-and-white objects.

Figure 11–53

2

- Tap or click the Update button (Edit Photo Album dialog box) to change the photographs from color to black-and-white images on the slides.

- Run the slide show.

- Save the presentation with the file name, Seattle Photo Album Black and White.

- Print the presentation as a handout with three slides per page (Figure 11–54).

(a) Handout Page 1

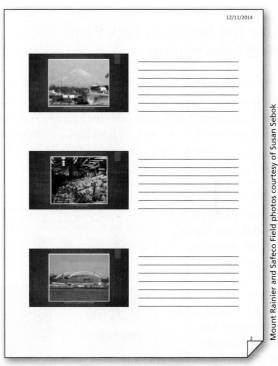

Mount Rainier and Safeco Field photos courtesy of Susan Sebok

(b) Handout Page 2

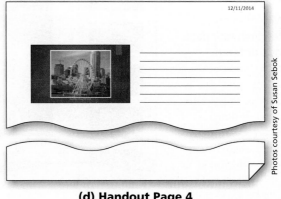

Photos courtesy of Susan Sebok

(d) Handout Page 4

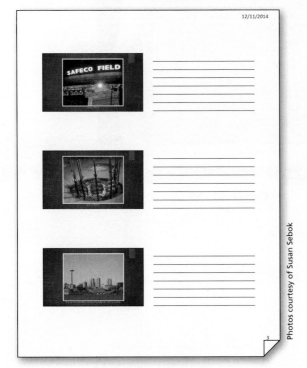

Photos courtesy of Susan Sebok

(c) Handout Page 3

BTW

Conserving Ink and Toner

If you want to conserve ink or toner, you can instruct PowerPoint to print draft quality documents by tapping or clicking FILE on the ribbon to open the Backstage view, tapping or clicking Options in the Backstage view to display the PowerPoint Options dialog box, tapping or clicking Advanced in the left pane (PowerPoint Options dialog box), sliding or scrolling to the Print area in the right pane, placing a check mark in the 'Use draft quality' check box, and then tapping or clicking the OK button. Then, use the Backstage view to print the document as usual.

Figure 11–54

BTW
Printing Document Properties
To print document properties, tap or click FILE on the ribbon to open the Backstage view, tap or click the Print tab in the Backstage view to display the Print gallery, tap or click the first button in the Settings area to display a list of options specifying what you can print, tap or click Document Info in the list to specify you want to print the document properties instead of the actual document, and then tap or click the Print button in the Print gallery to print the document properties on the currently selected printer.

To Use the Research Task Pane to Find Information

1 CREATE & ORGANIZE SECTIONS | 2 CREATE CUSTOM SLIDE SHOW | 3 CREATE PHOTO ALBUM & ENHANCE ELEMENTS
4 SPECIFY CUSTOM SLIDE SIZE & ADD VIDEO CLIP | 5 SHARE & DISTRIBUTE PRESENTATION

You can search for information regarding a wide variety of topics using PowerPoint's reference materials. A commonly used research tool is the thesaurus to find synonyms for words on your slides or in the Notes pane. The Research task pane also includes a dictionary, encyclopedia, and translation services. In addition, if you are connected to the web, it provides a search engine and other useful websites. The following steps use the Research task pane to look up a definition of a word. *Why? You want to know more about the word, isthmus, which you typed as part of the Slide 3 caption text.*

1

• Display the REVIEW tab and then tap or click the Research button (REVIEW tab | Proofing group) to display the Research task pane, and then, if necessary, tap or click the Research list arrow and select 'All Reference Books' (Figure 11–55).

Q&A
Why does my Research task pane look different?
Your computer's settings and Microsoft's website search settings determine the way your Research task pane is displayed.

Figure 11–55

- Type **isthmus** in the Search for box and then tap or click the Start searching button to perform a search for definitions of this word (Figure 11–56).

Q&A | What is Encarta?
It is the name of Microsoft's encyclopedia, which contains thousands of articles, illustrations, photos, and other reference materials.

What should I do if I see the message, No results were found, instead of a list of search results?
If a 'Get services on Office Marketplace' icon is displayed at the bottom of the Research pane, tap or click it, follow instructions to update your services, and then repeat your search.

Figure 11–56

- Tap or click the Search for arrow in the Research task pane to display a list of search locations (Figure 11–57).

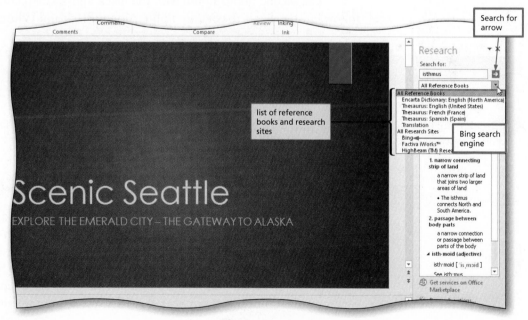

Figure 11–57

4

- Tap or click Bing in the list to perform an Internet search for websites with information about this search term (Figure 11–58).

Q&A

What is Bing?
It is the name of Microsoft's search engine, which is a program that locates websites, webpages, images, videos, news, maps, and other information related to a specific topic.

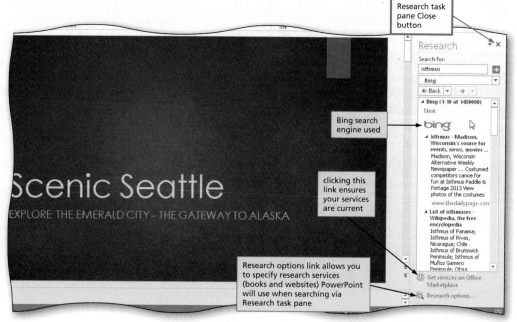

Figure 11–58

5

- Tap or click the Close button in the Research pane.

To Close a Presentation

The second photo album with the black-and-white pictures is complete. The following step closes the Seattle Photo Album Black and White file.

1 With the Backstage view open, tap or click Close to close the open Seattle Photo Album Black and White file without exiting PowerPoint.

Break Point: If you wish to take a break, this is a good place to do so. You can exit PowerPoint now. To resume at a later time, run PowerPoint and continue following the steps from this location forward.

Sharing and Distributing a Presentation

Many people design PowerPoint presentations to accompany a speech given in front of an audience, and they also develop slide shows to share with family, work associates, and friends in a variety of ways. For example, they can print a slide on thick paper and send the document through the mail. They also can email the file or create a video to upload to a website or view on a computer. Video files can become quite large in file size, so PowerPoint allows you to reduce the size by compressing the file.

CONSIDER THIS

Use hyperlinks to show slides with landscape and portrait orientations.
When you are creating your presentation, you have the option to display all your slides in either the default landscape orientation or in portrait orientation. You may, however, desire to have slides with both orientations during a single presentation. Using hyperlinks is one solution to mixing the orientations. Apply a hyperlink to an object on the last slide in one orientation and then hyperlink to another presentation with slides in the other orientation. If you desire to hyperlink to one particular slide in a second presentation, tap or click the Bookmark button in the Insert Hyperlink dialog box and then select the title of the slide you want to use as your link. Once you have displayed the desired slides in the second presentation, create another hyperlink from that presentation back to a slide in your original presentation.

To Change the Slide Orientation

By default, PowerPoint displays slides in landscape orientation, where the width dimension is greater than the height dimension. You can change this setting to specify that the slides display in portrait orientation. *Why? In portrait orientation, the height dimension is greater than the width dimension, so it is useful to display tall objects, people who are standing, or faces.* The following steps change the slide orientation.

1

- Open the presentation, Travel Expo, located on the Data Files for Students.

- Display the DESIGN tab and then tap or click the Slide Size button (DESIGN tab | Customize group) to display the Slide Size gallery (Figure 11–59).

Figure 11–59

2

- Tap or click 'Custom Slide Size' to display the Slide Size dialog box and then tap or click Portrait in the Slides area of the Orientation section to change the slide orientation from Landscape to Portrait (Figure 11–60).

Figure 11–60

To Set Up a Custom Size

Why? To announce the Travel Expo event and encourage community members to attend, you want to mail postcards to the residents' homes. To simplify the process, you can create a PowerPoint slide that is the precise measurement of a postcard, print the card on heavy paper stock, and mail the card to club members. You can specify that your PowerPoint slides are a precise dimension. The steps on the next page change the slide size to a custom size.

1

- With the Slide Size dialog box displaying, tap or click the 'Slides sized for' arrow to display the size list (Figure 11–61).

Figure 11–61

2

- Tap or click Custom in the size list.

- If necessary, change the slide width to 5 inches in the Width box.

- Change the slide height to 7 inches in the Height box (Figure 11–62).

 If I am using a mouse, can I type the width and height measurements in the boxes instead of clicking the down arrows repeatedly?
Yes. You also can click and hold down the mouse button instead of repeatedly clicking the arrows until the desired dimensions are displayed.

Figure 11–62

3

- Tap or click the OK button (Slide Size dialog box) to display the Microsoft PowerPoint dialog box (Figure 11–63).

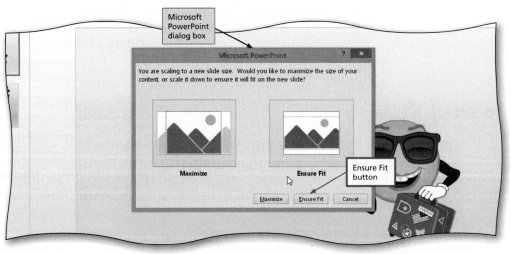

4

- Tap or click the Ensure Fit button (Microsoft PowerPoint dialog box) to apply the custom sizes and close the dialog box.

Figure 11–63

To Display Multiple Presentation Windows Simultaneously

Why? *When you are reviewing elements of several presentations, it often is efficient and convenient to open and display them simultaneously on the screen.* The following steps display three open presentations simultaneously.

1

- Open the presentation, Glacier Bay, located on the Data Files for Students and then display the VIEW tab (Figure 11–64).

- If necessary, open the Alaskan Adventure file if you closed it earlier in this project.

Figure 11–64

Photos and video courtesy of Susan Sebok

2

- Tap or click the Cascade button (VIEW tab | Window group) to display the three open presentations – Glacier Bay, Travel Expo, and Alaskan Adventure – from the upper-left to the lower-right corners of the screen.

Q&A What is the difference between the Cascade button and the Arrange All button?
When you tap or click the Cascade button, the open windows display overlapped, or stacked, on each other. Tapping or clicking the Arrange All button tiles all the open windows side by side on the screen. Each window may display narrower than in Normal view so that all the open windows are visible simultaneously.

Figure 11–65

Photos and video courtesy of Susan Sebok

- If necessary, tap or click the Glacier Bay presentation title bar to display that presentation in the front of the screen (Figure 11–65).

Q&A The Glacier Bay title bar is not visible on my screen. Can I move the presentation album windows so that it is visible?
Yes. You can drag the presentation title bars to arrange the windows.

To Copy a Video File

Why? Slide 2 in the Glacier Bay presentation contains a video clip of the glacier that you want to insert at the bottom of Slide 2 in the Travel Expo file. With multiple presentations open simultaneously on your screen, you can view all the slides quickly and decide which elements of one presentation you desire to copy to another. The following steps copy the video file from Slide 2 of the Glacier Bay presentation to Slide 2 of the Travel Expo presentation.

1

- Tap or click the Slide 2 thumbnail of the Glacier Bay presentation to display that slide.

- Press and hold or right-click the video image in the center of the slide to select it and to display the shortcut menu (Figure 11–66).

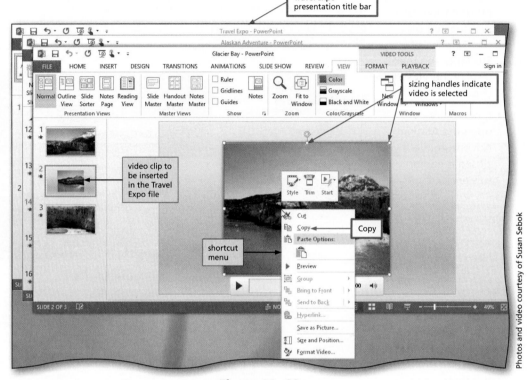

Photos and video courtesy of Susan Sebok

Figure 11–66

2

- Tap or click Copy on the shortcut menu.

- Tap or click the Travel Expo presentation title bar to display that presentation in the front of the screen.

- Tap or click the Slide 2 thumbnail of the Travel Expo presentation to display that slide.

- Press and hold or right-click the slide to display the shortcut menu and then point to the 'Use Destination Theme' button under Paste Options to display a preview of the video clip on that slide (Figure 11–67).

Video courtesy of Susan Sebok

Figure 11–67

3

- Tap or click the 'Use Destination Theme' button in the Paste gallery to insert the video into the slide.

- If necessary, drag the Travel Expo presentation title bar downward so the Glacier Bay title bar is visible (Figure 11–68).

Figure 11–68

Video courtesy of Susan Sebok

4

- Tap or click the 'Glacier Bay Close' button to close that presentation.

- Tap or click the 'Travel Expo Maximize' button to maximize the PowerPoint window.

- Select the video, display the VIDEO TOOLS FORMAT tab, size the video to 3" × 4", and move the clip to the location shown in Figure 11–69.

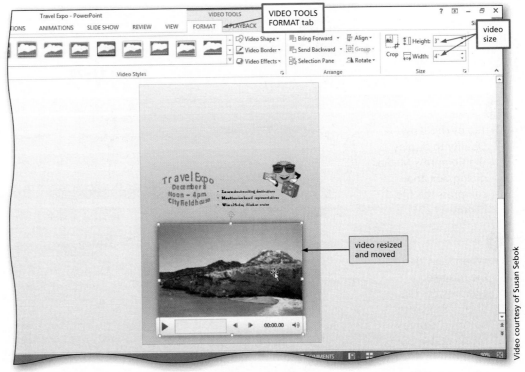

Figure 11–69

Video courtesy of Susan Sebok

To Compress a Video File

Why? The file size of videos can be quite large. This size can pose a problem if you desire to email a presentation or if the space on a storage device is small. PowerPoint includes a feature that will compress your file to reduce its size. You can specify one of three compression qualities: Presentation, Internet, or Low. In this project, you are going to email the Travel Expo file, so you desire to keep the file size as small as possible without sacrificing too much resolution quality. The following steps compress the video file.

1

- With the video clip selected on Slide 2, display the Backstage view and then tap or click the Compress Media button (Info tab | Media Size and Performance section) to display the Compress Media menu (Figure 11–70).

Figure 11–70

2

- Tap or click Low Quality to display the Compress Media dialog box and compress the file (Figure 11–71).

3

- When the video file has been compressed, tap or click the Close button (Compress Media dialog box) to return to the Backstage view.

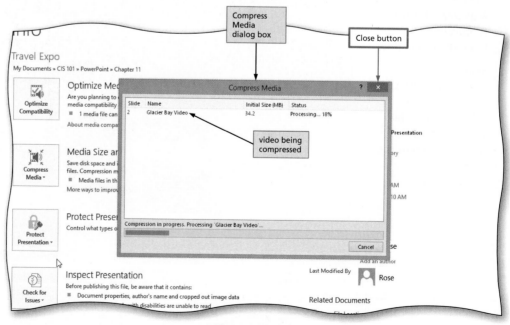

Figure 11–71

To Record Narration

In some situations, you may want your viewers to hear recorded narration that accompanies slides. You can record narration separately and then add this file to the slide. You also can record narration while the slide show is running. To record this narration, you would perform the following steps.

1. Display the SLIDE SHOW tab and then tap or click the 'Record Slide Show' arrow (SLIDE SHOW tab | Set Up group).

2. Tap or click 'Start Recording from Beginning' if you want to begin with the first slide or click 'Start Recording from Current Slide' if you want to begin with the slide that is displaying on your screen.

3. Tap or click the 'Narrations and laser pointer' check box (Record Slide Show dialog box) and, if appropriate, tap or click the 'Slide and animation timings' check box ('Record Slide Show' dialog box) to select or remove the check mark.

4. Tap or click the Start Recording button (Record Slide Show dialog box).

5. When you have finished speaking, press and hold or right-click the slide and then tap or click End Show on the shortcut menu.

To Preview Narration

Once you have recorded narration, you can play the audio to review the sound. To preview this narration, you would perform the following steps.

1. In Normal view, tap or click the sound icon on the slide.

2. Display the AUDIO TOOLS PLAYBACK tab and then tap or click the Play button (AUDIO TOOLS PLAYBACK tab | Preview group).

To Show a Presentation with or without Narration

If you have recorded narration to accompany your slides, you can choose whether to include this narration when you run your slide show. You would perform the following steps to run the slide show either with or without narration.

1. Display the SLIDE SHOW tab and then tap or click the Play Narrations check box (SLIDE SHOW tab | Set Up group) to remove the check from the box.

2. If you have chosen to show the presentation without narration and then desire to allow audience members to hear this recording, tap or click the Play Narrations check box (SLIDE SHOW tab | Set Up group) to check this option.

BTW

Turn Off Slide Timings
If you recorded narration with slide timings, you might decide to play the comments for your audience but want to advance the slides manually. PowerPoint gives you the option to turn slide timings off and then turn them back on without having to recreate them. Tap or click the 'Set Up Slide Show' button (SLIDE SHOW tab | Set Up group) and then tap or click Manually in the Advance slides area (Set Up Show dialog box). To turn the slide timings back on, tap or click 'Using timings, if present' in the Advance slides area (Set Up Show dialog box).

BTW

Certification
The Microsoft Office Specialist (MOS) program provides an opportunity for you to obtain a valuable industry credential — proof that you have the PowerPoint 2013 skills required by employers. For more information, visit the Certification resource on the Student Companion Site located on www.cengagebrain.com. For detailed instructions about accessing available resources, visit www.cengage.com/ct/studentdownload or see the inside back cover of this book.

To Email a Slide Show from within PowerPoint

1 CREATE & ORGANIZE SECTIONS | 2 CREATE CUSTOM SLIDE SHOW | 3 CREATE PHOTO ALBUM & ENHANCE ELEMENTS
4 SPECIFY CUSTOM SLIDE SIZE & ADD VIDEO CLIP | 5 SHARE & DISTRIBUTE PRESENTATION

Why? *Presenters often email their presentations to friends and colleagues to solicit feedback and share their work.* PowerPoint offers a convenient method of emailing a presentation directly within PowerPoint. The steps on the next page create a message, attach a presentation, and send a slide show to Mary Halen.

1

- With the Backstage view displaying, display the Share gallery.

- Tap or click the Email button to display the Email options (Figure 11–72).

Figure 11–72

2

- Tap or click the 'Send as Attachment' button in the Email area to open the Travel Expo.pptx – Message (HTML) window in Microsoft Outlook (Figure 11–73).

Q&A | Must I use Microsoft Outlook to send this email message?
No, you do not have to have Outlook installed; however, you need to have an email program installed in Windows to send the email. If you don't use Outlook, you could install Windows Live Mail or another email program.

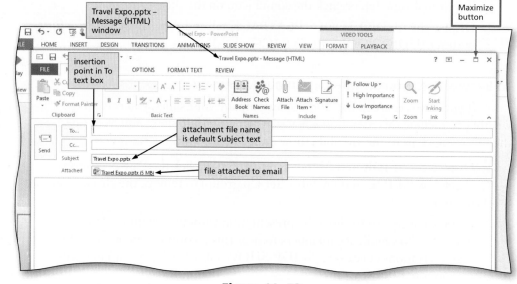

Figure 11–73

3

- If necessary, tap or click the Maximize button in the Travel Expo.pptx – Message (HTML) window to maximize the window.

- With the insertion point in the To box, type **mary_halen@hotmail.com** to enter the email address of the recipient.

- Tap or click to position the insertion point in the Subject box, select the file name that is displaying, and then type **Upcoming Travel Expo** as the subject.

- Tap in the message area or press the TAB key two times to move the insertion point into the message area.

- Type **Miss Halen,** as the greeting line.

- Press the ENTER key to move the insertion point to the beginning of the next line.

- Type **The announcement for our upcoming Travel Expo is attached. I hope you will be able to attend.** to enter the message text.

- Press the ENTER key twice to insert a blank line and move the insertion point to the beginning of the next line. Type **George Alexander** as the signature line (Figure 11–74).

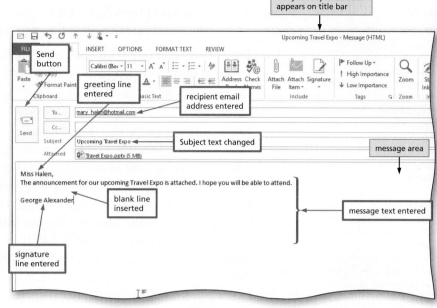

Figure 11–74

Q&A May I type my own name instead of George's name?

Yes. You may desire to have your name on the title slide, or your instructor may request that you substitute your name or provide other identifying information.

5

- Tap or click the Send button in the message header to send the email message and to close the message window.

To Run and Save the Presentation

When you run the Travel Expo presentation, the video will play automatically because the file had that setting in the Glacier Bay presentation. The following steps run the slide show and then save and close the document.

1 Display Slide 1 and then run the presentation.

2 Save the presentation with the file name, Travel Expo Mail.

3 Display the Backstage view and then tap or click Close to close the Travel Expo Mail file without exiting PowerPoint.

BTW

Restricting Permissions
You can allow PowerPoint users to see your presentation but not allow them to change the slide content, copy the slides, or print the presentation. To protect your presentation, display the FILE tab, display the Info tab in the Backstage view, tap or click the Protect Presentation button, tap or click the Restrict Access button, and then tap or click 'Connect to Rights Management Servers and get templates'.

Rehearse, rehearse, rehearse.
Speakers should spend as much time practicing their presentations as they do preparing their PowerPoint slides. Frequently, however, they use the majority of their preparation time designing and tweaking the slides. Audience members expect to see a presenter who is prepared, confident, and enthusiastic. Practicing the presentation helps convey this image. As you rehearse, focus on a strong introduction that grasps the audience's attention and previews the main points of your talk. You have only one chance to make a good first impression, so begin the speech by establishing eye contact with audience members in various parts of the room. Resist the urge to stare at the slides projected on the screen. Your audience came to your presentation to hear you speak, and rehearsing will help you deliver a high-quality talk that exceeds their expectations.

CONSIDER THIS

TO PRESENT A SLIDE SHOW ONLINE

Microsoft's Office Presentation Service feature allows you to share your presentation remotely with anyone having an Internet connection. As you display your slides, they see a synchronized view of your slide show in their web browser, even if they do not have PowerPoint installed on their computers. To present your presentation, you would perform the following steps.

1. Tap or click the Present Online arrow (SLIDE SHOW tab | Start Slide Show group) to display the Present Online menu.

2. Tap or click 'Office Presentation Service' to display the Present Online dialog box.

3. Tap or click the CONNECT button to agree to the service terms, if necessary, enter your Windows Live ID email address, tap or click the Next button (Sign in dialog box), enter your Windows Live ID email address and password, and then tap or click the Sign in button (Sign in dialog box).

4. After PowerPoint has connected to the service and completed preparing the presentation, share the presentation link with up to 50 remote viewers and then tap or click the START PRESENTATION button (Present Online dialog box). People visiting the website can view your presentation with any annotations you make.

5. When you have displayed the last slide, tap or click the 'End Online Presentation' button (PRESENT ONLINE tab | Present Online group) and then tap or click the 'End Online Presentation' button (Microsoft PowerPoint dialog box).

To Create a Video

1 CREATE & ORGANIZE SECTIONS | 2 CREATE CUSTOM SLIDE SHOW | 3 CREATE PHOTO ALBUM & ENHANCE ELEMENTS
4 SPECIFY CUSTOM SLIDE SIZE & ADD VIDEO CLIP | 5 SHARE & DISTRIBUTE PRESENTATION

Why? Watching video files is a common activity with the advent of easy-to-use recording devices and websites that host these files. You can convert your PowerPoint presentation to a video file and upload it to a website or share the file with people who do not have PowerPoint installed on their computers. The following steps create a video of the Alaskan Adventure presentation.

- Display the Alaskan Adventure file and, if necessary, tap or click the Maximize button in the title bar to maximize the window.

- Display the Backstage view and then display the Export gallery.

- Tap or click the 'Create a Video' button to display the Create a Video section.

- If 'Internet & DVD' is not selected as the screen resolution in the Create a Video section, tap or click the 'Computer & HD Displays' button to display a list of screen resolutions (Figure 11–75).

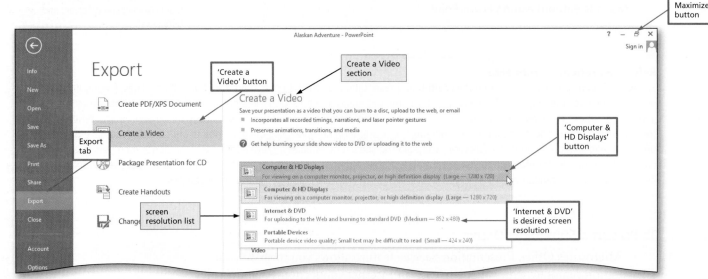

Figure 11–75

2

- If 'Internet & DVD' is not selected as the screen resolution, tap or click the 'Internet & DVD' button to select the Medium (852 × 480) resolution.

- If 'Don't Use Recorded Timings and Narrations' is not selected as the default duration, tap or click the 'Use Recorded Timings and Narrations' button in the Create a Video section to display a list of recording options (Figure 11–76).

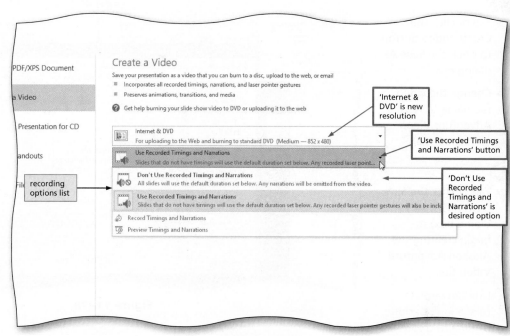

Figure 11–76

3

- Tap or click 'Don't Use Recorded Timings and Narrations' to select that option.

- Change the 'Seconds spent on each slide' time to 10 seconds (Figure 11–77).

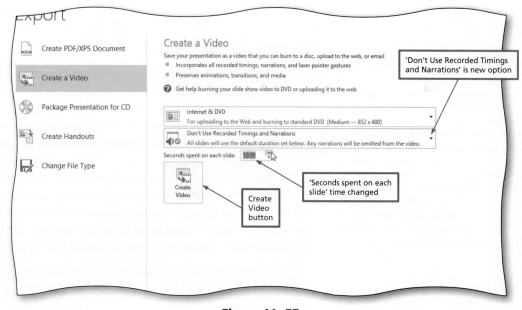

Figure 11–77

BTW
Quick Reference
For a table that lists how to complete the tasks covered in this book using touch gestures, the mouse, ribbon, shortcut menu, and keyboard, see the Quick Reference Summary at the back of this book, or visit the Quick Reference resource on the Student Companion Site located on www.cengagebrain.com. For detailed instructions about accessing available resources, visit www.cengage.com/ct/studentdownload or see the inside back cover of this book.

- Tap or click the Create Video button to open the Save As dialog box.

- Change the video file name to Alaskan Adventure Video (Figure 11–78).

- Tap or click the Save button (Save As dialog box) to begin creating the Alaskan Adventure Video file.

Q&A

Does PowerPoint take a long period of time to create the video?

Yes. It may take several minutes to export the presentation to a video. Windows Media Player will display an error message stating that the file is in use if you attempt to open the video file while it is being created.

Figure 11–78

Video courtesy of Susan Sebok

6

- When the video has been created, save the presentation again.

BTW

Practice Using Presenter View
One of the new features in PowerPoint 2013 is Presenter view, which allows a speaker to use dual monitors: one that displays what the audience is seeing, and another with controls to aid the presenter. You can rehearse using Presenter view with one monitor so that you are comfortable using the features. Be certain that 'Use Presenter View' is selected (SLIDE SHOW tab | Monitors group) and then press ALT+F5. You will not be able to edit the slides while using Presenter view.

BTW

Printing Selections
When you are developing slides or creating handouts for a particular audience, you may not want to print every slide in your presentation. To print specific slides, select the desired slides in the Thumbnail pane. Then, display the FILE tab, tap or click the Print tab in the Backstage view, tap or click the first button in the Settings area, tap or click Print Selection in the list to specify you want to print the slides you have selected, and then tap or click the Print button in the Print gallery to print these slides.

To Set Up Presenter View

Experienced speakers often deliver a presentation using two monitors: one to display their speaker notes privately, and a second to display the slides and project them on a large screen for the audience to view. PowerPoint's Presenter view supports the use of two monitors connected to one computer so presenters can view the slide currently being projected while viewing the slide thumbnails, seeing a preview of the next slide or animation, reading their speaker notes, viewing the elapsed time, lightening or darkening the audience's screen, or customizing the presentation by skipping the next slide or reviewing a slide previously displayed. A computer must support the use of multiple monitors and must be configured to use this feature. To use Presenter view, you would perform the following step.

1. Display the SLIDE SHOW tab and then tap or click the 'Use Presenter View' check box (SLIDE SHOW tab | Monitors group).

To Run and Print the Presentation

The presentation now is complete. You should run the slide show, print handouts, and then exit PowerPoint.

1 Run the slide show.

2 Print the presentation as a handout with six horizontal slides per page (Figure 11–79).

3 Exit PowerPoint, closing all open documents.

(a) Handout Page 1

(b) Handout Page 2

(c) Handout Page 3

(d) Handout Page 4

Figure 11–79

Chapter Summary

In this chapter you have learned how to organize a presentation into sections and then rename and move entire sections in the file. You then created a photo album, added and organized pictures, selected a theme and layout, adjusted a photo's contrast and brightness, and edited captions. You also changed the images to black and white in a separate photo album. Then, you specified a custom size and modified two slides by changing the slide orientation to portrait and inserting and compressing a video file. You then emailed the file and converted another file to video. The items listed below include all the new PowerPoint skills you have learned in this chapter.

Add and Compress a Video Clip
Display Multiple Presentation Windows Simultaneously (PPT 701)
Copy a Video File (PPT 702)
Compress a Video File (PPT 704)

Create and Organize Sections
Insert Slides with a Section Layout (PPT 669)
Arrange Slides in Slide Sorter View (PPT 672)
Create a Section Break (PPT 673)
Rename a Section (PPT 676)
Collapse and Reorder Sections (PPT 678)

Develop a Photo Album
Start a Photo Album and Add Pictures (PPT 685)
Reorder Pictures in a Photo Album (PPT 687)
Create a Photo Album (PPT 692)
Edit a Photo Album (PPT 692)

Develop and Edit a Custom Slide Show
Create a Custom Slide Show (PPT 680)
Open and Edit a Custom Slide Show (PPT 682)

Enhance Photo Album Elements
Adjust the Rotation of a Photo Album Image (PPT 688)
Adjust the Contrast of a Photo Album Image (PPT 689)

Adjust the Brightness of a Photo Album Image (PPT 689)
Change a Photo Album Layout (PPT 690)
Add a Photo Album Theme (PPT 691)
Add Captions below All Pictures (PPT 691)
Create Black-and-White Images in a Photo Album (PPT 694)
Use the Research Task Pane to Find Information (PPT 696)

Share and Distribute a Presentation
Show a Presentation with Manual Timing (PPT 680)
Record Narration (PPT 705)
Preview Narration (PPT 705)
Show a Presentation with or without Narration (PPT 705)
Email a Slide Show from within PowerPoint (PPT 705)
Present a Slide Show Online (PPT 707)
Create a Video (PPT 708)
Set Up Presenter View (PPT 710)

Specify a Custom Slide Size
Change the Slide Orientation (PPT 699)
Set Up a Custom Size (PPT 699)

CONSIDER THIS

General Project Guidelines
When creating a PowerPoint presentation, the actions you perform and the decisions you make will affect the appearance and characteristics of the finished document. As you create a presentation with illustrations, such as the project shown in Figure 11–1 on page PPT 667, you should follow these general guidelines:

1. **Use photographs with sharp focus and contrast.** The adage, "A picture is worth a thousand words," is relevant in a PowerPoint presentation. When your audience can see a visual representation of the concept you are describing during your talk, they are apt to understand and comprehend your message. Be certain your pictures are sharp and clear.

2. **Use hyperlinks to show slides with landscape and portrait orientations.** All slides in one presentation must be displayed in either landscape or portrait orientation. If you want to have variety in your slide show or have pictures or graphics that display best in one orientation, consider using hyperlinks to mix the two orientations during your presentation.

3. **Rehearse, rehearse, rehearse.** Outstanding slides lose their value when the presenter is unprepared to speak. Always keep in mind that the visual aspects are meant to supplement a speaker's verbal message. Practice your presentation before different types of audiences to solicit feedback, and use their comments to improve your speaking style.

How should you submit solutions to questions in the assignments identified with a symbol?
Every assignment in this book contains one or more questions identified with a ❋ symbol. These questions require you to think beyond the assigned presentation. Present your solutions to the questions in the format required by your instructor. Possible formats may include one or more of these options: write the answer; create a document that contains the answer; present your answer to the class; discuss your answer in a group; record the answer as audio or video using a webcam, smartphone, or portable media player; or post answers on a blog, wiki, or website.

Apply Your Knowledge

Reinforce the skills and apply the concepts you learned in this chapter.

Creating and Reordering Sections and Creating Custom Slide Shows

Note: To complete this assignment, you will be required to use the Data Files for Students. Visit www.cengage.com/ct/studentdownload for detailed instructions or contact your instructor for information about accessing the required files.

Instructions: Run PowerPoint. Open the presentation, Apply 11-1 Tennis, from the Data Files for Students.
    The slides in this presentation provide information about tennis lessons at the CHF Racquet Center. The document you open is a partially formatted presentation. You will insert slides, insert section breaks, reorder and rename sections, and create two custom slide shows so that the presentation matches the one shown in Figure 11–80 on the next page.

Perform the following tasks:
1. Select Slide 1 (Figure 11–80c on page PPT 715), create a new Slide 2 that is a duplicate of Slide 1, change the layout to Section Header, and then change the transparency of the background to 35%. Create a new Slide 3 that is a duplicate of Slide 2.

2. On Slide 2, select the title text and then type `Women's Tennis Lessons` as the new title text. On Slide 3, select the title text and then type `Men's Tennis Lessons` as the new title text. Decrease the title text font size to 54 point on Slides 2 and 3.

3. Change the view to Slide Sorter view (Figures 11–80a and 11–80b), select Slide 4, and then add a section break. Rename the section divider, Women's Tennis.

4. Select the Default Section divider (before Slide 1) and rename it, CHF Racquet Center - Tennis.

5. Select Slide 5, add a section break, and then rename it, Men's Tennis. Move the Women's Tennis section header slide to the beginning of the Women's Tennis section, and move the Men's Tennis section header slider to the beginning of the Men's Tennis section.

6. Select Slide 6, add a section break, and then rename it, Mixed Doubles.

7. Select Slide 7, add a section break, and then rename it, Scoring.

8. Reorder the sections by moving the Men's Tennis section before the Women's Tennis section. The slides should now appear in the order shown in Figures 11–80c through 11–80i on pages PPT 715–717.

9. Create a custom slide show called Men's and Women's Tennis Lessons. Include only Slides 2, 3, 4, and 5 in this custom slide show.

10. Create a second custom slide show called Tennis Schedule. Include only Slides 3, 5, and 6 in this custom slide show.

11. If requested by your instructor, add the city where you were born as the second line of the subtitle on Slide 1.

12. Apply the Window transition (Dynamic category) and change the duration to 2.50 for all slides.

13. Save the presentation using the file name, Apply 11-1 Tennis Lessons.

Continued >

Apply Your Knowledge *continued*

14. Submit the revised document in the format specified by your instructor.

15. ❂ In this presentation, you created two new slides (duplicates of the title slide) and used them as section headers. How did this help when creating sections in the presentation? Did changing the background photo transparency for the section header slides make a difference? Why?

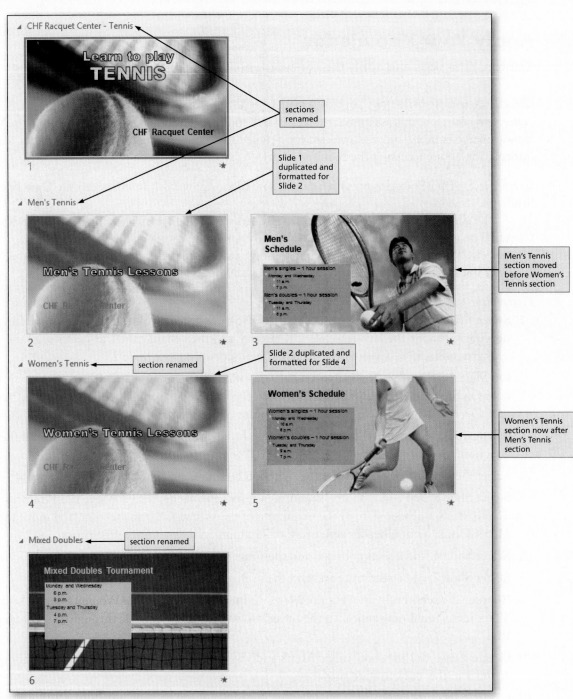

(a) First Six Slides of Presentation in Slide Sorter View

Figure 11–80

(b) Last Slide of Presentation in Slide Sorter View

(c) Slide 1

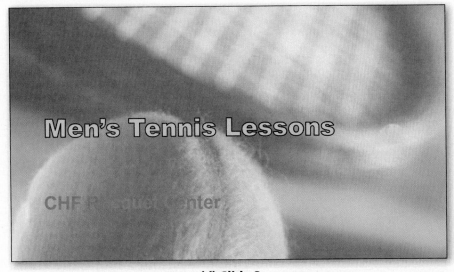

(d) Slide 2

Figure 11–80 (Continued)

Continued >

Apply Your Knowledge *continued*

(e) Slide 3

(f) Slide 4

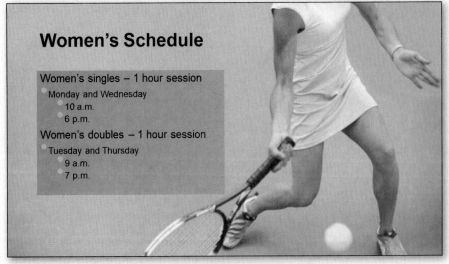

(g) Slide 5

Figure 11–80

(h) Slide 6

(i) Slide 7

Figure 11–80 (Continued)

Extend Your Knowledge

Extend the skills you learned in this chapter and experiment with new skills. You may need to use Help to complete the assignment.

Formatting Sections and Proofing a Presentation

Note: To complete this assignment, you will be required to use the Data Files for Students. Visit www.cengage.com/ct/studentdownload for detailed instructions or contact your instructor for information about accessing the required files.

Instructions: Run PowerPoint. Open the presentation, Extend 11-1 Bears, from the Data Files for Students. A koala is sometimes mistaken for a bear, but it is actually a marsupial. You will remove the section with the two koala slides (Slides 7 and 8) and proof the presentation shown in Figure 11–81 beginning on the next page through page PPT 720.

Continued >

Extend Your Knowledge *continued*

Perform the following tasks:

1. On Slide 1 (Figure 11–81a), there are only six of the eight living species of bears in the world in the numbered list. Add the names of the last two types of bears by using the Research proofing tool. (*Hint:* Type **8 types of bears** in the Search for box.)

2. Select Slide Sorter View (see Figures 11–81b and 11–81c). Remove the section named Koala and the two slides. (*Hint:* You may need to use Help to learn how to remove a section.)

3. Rename the Untitled Section divider after Slide 1 to Black Bear.

4. Rename the Untitled Section divider after Slide 2 to Grizzly Bear.

5. Rename the Untitled Section divider after Slides 3 and 4 to Giant Panda.

6. Rename the Untitled Section divider after Slides 5 and 6 to Polar Bear.

7. Present the slide show online to your instructor and to two classmates.

8. If requested by your instructor, add the number of bones you have broken after the word pounds on Slide 8.

9. Apply the Peel Off transition in the Exciting category, change the duration to 2.25 seconds, and then apply to all slides.

10. Save the presentation using the file name, Extend 11-1 Bears of the World.

11. Submit the revised document in the format specified by your instructor.

12. ✳ In this presentation, you removed the section with the koalas. Why? Which website did you use to find the names of the two missing bear species for Slide 1? Was it easy to find this information?

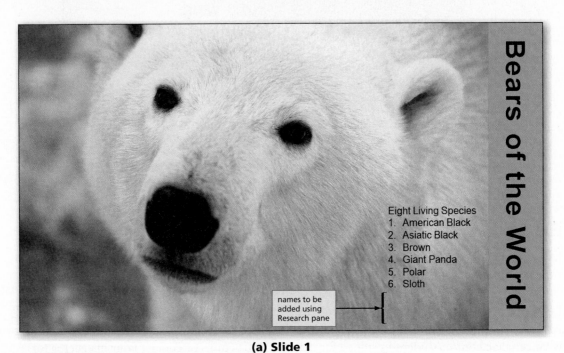

(a) Slide 1

Figure 11–81

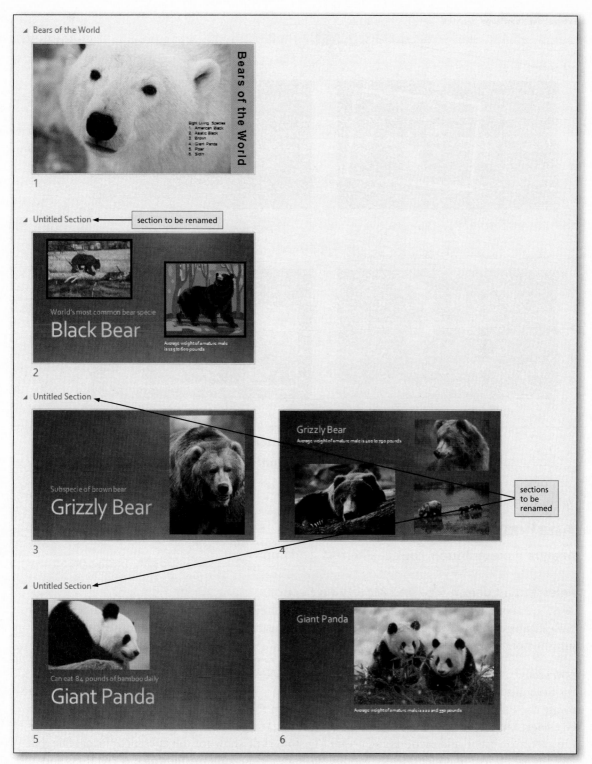

(b) First Six Slides of Presentation in Slide Sorter View
Figure 11–81 (Continued)

Continued >

Extend Your Knowledge *continued*

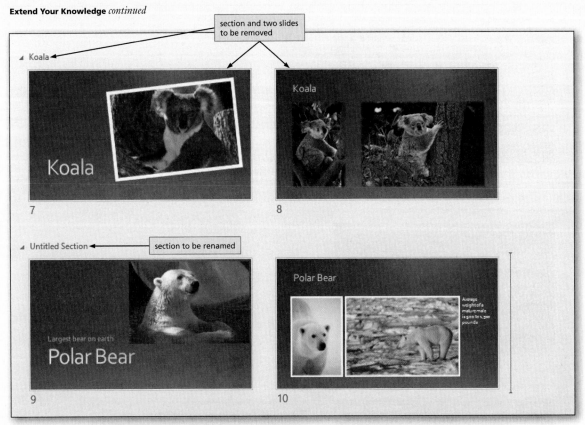

(c) Last Four Slides of Presentation in Slide Sorter View

Figure 11–81 (Continued)

Analyze, Correct, Improve

Analyze a presentation, correct all errors, and improve it.

Selecting a Custom Size and Modifying Sections

Note: To complete this assignment, you will be required to use the Data Files for Students. Visit www.cengage.com/ct/studentdownload for detailed instructions or contact your instructor for information about accessing the required files.

Instructions: Run PowerPoint. Open the presentation, Analyze 11-1 Flowers, from the Data Files for Students. You work for a florist and their specialty is wedding flowers. Your manager asked you to use the PowerPoint presentation that is running on the kiosk in the store and revise it for the city's next business expo. She will be making a presentation and handing out 14" × 8.5" flyers at the expo. You are to add sections and create a custom slide show for the upcoming bridal fair that just features bridal bouquet flowers. Modify the slides by making the indicated corrections and improvements.

1. Correct

    a. On Slide 1, insert a Double Wave shape (the last shape in the Stars and Banners shapes), size it to approximately 1.44" × 2.9", and then apply the Subtle Effect – Green, Accent 6 shape style (the seventh style in the fourth row). Type **Izabella's Flowers** on the first line, change the font to Lucida Calligraphy, and then change the point size to 20 point. Type **100 Main Street** on the second line, type **Open 7 days** on the third line, and type **10 a.m. to 6 p.m.** on the fourth line. Select the second, third, and fourth lines of text, change the font to Arial, and then change the font size to 14 point. Rotate the shape to the left and then move it to the upper-left corner of the slide, as shown in Figure 11–82a on the next page.

b. Select Slide 2 and create a new Slide 3 that is a duplicate of Slide 2. On Slide 2, delete the three small photos and leave the large center photo. Reduce the size of the heart shape to approximately 2.65" × 2.86", rotate it to the right (rotation should be 370 degrees), and then move it to the upper-right corner of the slide. Copy and paste the Double Wave shape from Slide 1 to the upper-left corner of Slide 2.

c. With Slide 2 still selected, use the Research proofing tool to look up **popular bridal flowers** and add at least three or four more flower names to the purple square shape in the lower-right corner of the slide. Change the font for all the text in the purple shape to Arial.

d. Select Slide 3 and reduce the size of the heart shape to approximately 2.65" × 2.86", and if necessary, move the heart shape so that it is not hanging off the edge of the slide. Delete the purple square shape in the lower-right corner of the slide.

e. Display the slides in Slide Sorter view (see Figure 11–82a). Select Slide 2 and add a section break. Select the section divider and rename the section **Bride's Flowers** as the new section divider. Select Slide 4 and add a section break. Select the section divider and rename the section **Other Wedding Flowers**, as shown in Figure 11–82a.

f. With the Slide Sorter view still displayed, move the Other Wedding Flowers section before the Bride's Flowers section. (Not shown in the figure.)

g. Create a custom slide show called Bride's Flowers. Include only Slides 1, 6, and 7 in this custom slide show.

h. If requested by your instructor, add your mother's middle name in place of the word, Izabella, in the shape on Slide 6.

2. Improve

a. Rename the Default section divider, Izabella's Flowers.

b. On Slide 2, reduce the size of the heart shape to approximately 2.52" × 2.97" and move the shape to the upper-left corner of the slide (not shown in the figure).

c. On Slide 6, select the purple shape in the lower-right corner of the slide, and increase the font size to 28 point. If necessary, increase the size of the shape and move the shape up and slightly to the left on the slide (not shown in figure). Apply the Metal Frame picture style to the photo on the slide (the third style in the first row).

d. Change the size of the slides to a custom width of 14" and a height of 8.5". (*Hint:* Click the Maximize button [Microsoft PowerPoint dialog box] to adjust the slide content.)

e. Change the transition from Curtains to Glitter (Exciting category), change the duration to 3.25 seconds, and then apply to all slides.

f. Save the presentation using the file name, Analyze 11-1 Wedding Flowers.

g. Submit the revised document in the format specified by your instructor.

3. ✸ Which errors existed in the starting file? When you created the custom slide show for Bride's Flowers, do you think the correct slides were included? Would you have selected different slides? Why or why not?

Continued >

Analyze, Correct, Improve *continued*

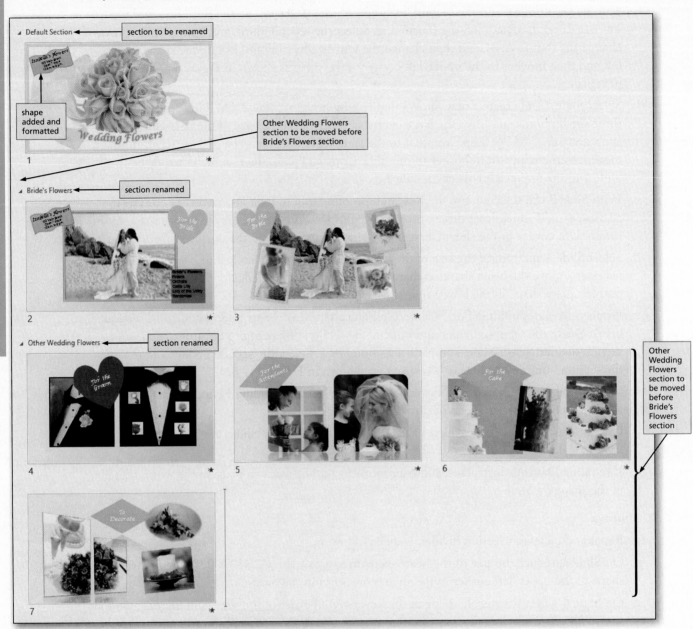

(a) Presentation in Slide Sorter View

Figure 11–82

(b) Slide 2

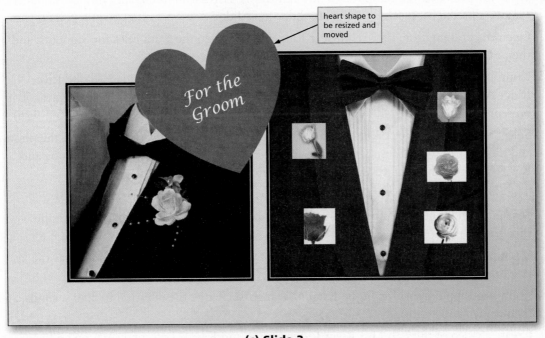

(c) Slide 3

Figure 11–82 (Continued)

In the Labs

Design and/or create a presentation using the guidelines, concepts, and skills presented in this chapter. Labs 1 and 2, which increase in difficulty, require you to create solutions based on what you learned in the chapter; Lab 3 requires you to create a solution, which uses cloud and web technologies, by learning and investigating on your own from general guidance.

Lab 1: Working with Multiple Presentation Windows Simultaneously, Setting Manual Timing, and Creating a Video

Problem: While attending school, you work for River Ridge, a canoe and kayak outfitter located on the beautiful Watson River near your college campus. You are preparing a presentation for the outdoor adventure club on campus. River Ridge won a special award for the Best Guided Kayak Adventure. You will be working with two PowerPoint presentations. One has all the information about canoe and kayak trips and the other one shows the award that River Ridge won. You will create a video of your final combined presentation.

Note: To complete this assignment, you will be required to use the Data Files for Students. Visit www.cengage.com/ct/studentdownload for detailed instructions or contact your instructor for information about accessing the required files.

Instructions: Perform the following tasks:

1. Open the presentation, Lab 11-1 Canoe and Kayak Trips, from the Data Files for Students, and remove all sections. Insert a new blank slide after Slide 5.

2. Open the presentation, Lab 11-1 River Ridge Award, from the Data Files for Students, and then cascade the two open document windows on the screen.

3. Copy and paste the explosion shape from the upper-right corner of Slide 1 on the River Ridge Award presentation to the upper-right corner of Slide 1 on the Canoe and Kayak Trip presentation. Select the new Slide 6 of this presentation (Figure 11–83f on page PPT 726).

4. Select Slide 2 of the River Ridge Award presentation. Select the award illustration, the photo, and the text box, copy these three items, and then paste them on Slide 6 of the Canoe and Kayak Trip presentation. Close the award presentation without saving changes.

5. The slides now should appear in the order shown in Figures 11-83a through 11-83f.

6. Set up the slide show to advance slides manually. Use Presenter View when you run the slide show.

7. If requested by your instructor, add the name of your grade school or high school as the last line in the text box on Slide 5.

8. Apply the Ripple transition in the Exciting category, change the duration to 2.50 seconds, and then apply to all slides.

9. Create a video of the Lab 11-1 River Ridge Canoe and Kayak Trips presentation and name it Lab 11-1 River Ridge Canoe and Kayak Trips Video.

10. Save the presentation using the file name, Lab 11-1 River Ridge Canoe and Kayak Trips. Submit the document and the video in the format specified by your instructor.

11. ✳ On Slide 6, you copied the illustration, photo, and a text box from another presentation. What did this add to your presentation?

shape copied
and pasted
from other
presentation

(a) Slide 1

(b) Slide 2

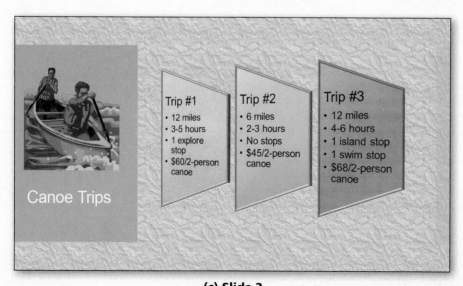

(c) Slide 3

Figure 11–83 (Continued)

Continued >

In the Labs *continued*

(d) Slide 4

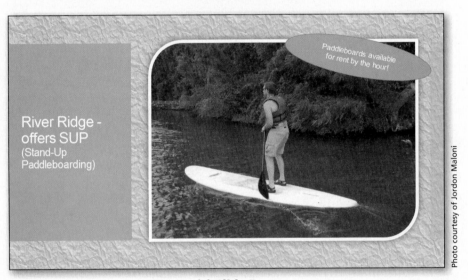

Photo courtesy of Jordon Maloni

(e) Slide 5

(f) Slide 6

Figure 11–83 (Continued)

Lab 2: Creating Photo Albums in Color and Black-and-White, Adding Captions, Reordering Photos, Adjusting Rotation of an Image, Adjusting Brightness and Contrast of an Image, Copying and Compressing a Video File, and Recording a Narration

Problem: Your geology class took a trip to Arizona to see the Grand Canyon. You decide to create a photo album to share your experiences. To add interest to the color photo album, your instructor gave you a short video he took of the Grand Canyon. You will copy the video into your color photo album. You create a presentation shown in Figures 11–84a on page PPT 729 through 11–84d on page PPT 732.

Note: To complete this assignment, you will be required to use the Data Files for Students. Visit www.cengage.com/ct/studentdownload for detailed instructions or contact your instructor for information about accessing the required files.

Instructions, Part 1:   Perform the following tasks:

1. Insert a new photo album.

2. Insert the Grand Canyon1, Grand Canyon2, Grand Canyon3, Grand Canyon4, Grand Canyon5, Grand Canyon6, Grand Canyon7, and Grand Canyon8 photos from the Data Files for Students.

3. Do not create the album (tap or click the Create button in the Photo Album dialog box) until you are asked to do so.

4. Select the Grand Canyon3 photo in the album and move it above the Grand Canyon2 photo.

5. Select the GrandCanyon7 photo in the album and move it below the Grand Canyon8 photo.

6. Change the GrandCanyon1 layout to '2 pictures', select the 'Captions below ALL pictures' option, and then select the 'Simple Frame, White' frame shape.

7. Select the Facet theme for the photo album. Create the photo album. Save the presentation using the file name, Lab 11-2 Grand Canyon Color Album.

8. Change the theme to Berlin for the color photo album, and keep the orange variant (the first variant).

9. On Slide 1, change the title to `Grand Canyon` and then, if necessary, enter your name in the subtitle placeholder. The slide should appear as shown in Figure 11–84a.

10. On Slide 2, type the caption of the left photo as `Established in 1919` and then type `You have to see it to believe it!` as the caption of the right photo. The slide should appear as shown in Figure 11–84b.

11. On Slide 3, type the caption of the left photo as `One South Rim view` and then type `Another great view` as the caption of the right photo. The slide should appear as shown in Figure 11–84c.

12. On Slide 4, type the caption of the left photo as `Colorado River runs through it` and then type `Colorado River traces a course` as the caption of the right photo. The slide should appear as shown in Figure 11–84d.

13. Edit the photo album using the Photo Album arrow (INSERT tab | Images group). Remove the two photos Grand Canyon8 and Grand Canyon7. Insert the Grand Canyon Bird, Grand Canyon Lizard, Grand Canyon Sign, and Grand Canyon Squirrel photos. Rotate the Grand Canyon Sign photo clockwise. Tap or click the Update button. Slides 5 and 6 should appear as shown in Figures 11–84e and 11–84f.

14. Insert a new slide after Slide 6 and select the Title Only layout. Type `Grand Canyon Live` as the title text placeholder text.

Continued >

In the Labs *continued*

15. Open the Grand Canyon Video presentation located on the Data Files for Students and then cascade the two open document windows on the screen. Copy the video and paste it into Slide 7 of the Lab 11-2 Grand Canyon Color Album as shown in Figure 11–84g on page PPT 731. Change the video to Start Automatically, and apply the Reflected Bevel, White video style to the video (the fourth style in the first Intense row). Close the Grand Canyon Video presentation. Maximize the Lab 11-2 Grand Canyon Color Album presentation.

16. Apply the Gallery transition, change the duration to 2.50 seconds, and then apply to all slides.

17. Set up the presentation to run in Presenter view. The slides should appear as shown in Figures 11–84a through 11–84g.

18. Compress the media file in the presentation to Presentation Quality and then email this presentation to your instructor.

Instructions Part 2: Perform the following tasks:

1. Start a new photo album.

2. Insert the Grand Canyon9, Grand Canyon10, Grand Canyon11, Grand Canyon12, Grand Canyon13, and Grand Canyon14 photos from the Data Files for Students.

3. Do not create the album until you are asked to do so.

4. Select the 'ALL pictures black-and-white' picture option, the 2 pictures option layout, the Compound Frame Black Frame shape, and the Slice Theme.

5. Select the Grand Canyon9 picture in the album and increase the contrast of the picture two times.

6. Select the Grand Canyon11 picture in the album and decrease the brightness of the picture two times.

7. Create the photo album. The slides should appear as shown in Figures 11-84h through 11-84k on page PPT 732 when this lab is complete.

8. Select Slide 1. Type **Grand Canyon** as the title text. If necessary, add your name in place of the subtitle text.

9. Select Slide 2. Record the slide show from the current slide. Note: The following steps contain narration that you will read while progressing through the slides. Read the following narration: **"Join us as we explore the Grand Canyon."** for this slide.

10. Advance to Slide 3 and then read the following narration: **"Breathtaking views and the Colorado river runs through it."** for this slide.

11. Advance to Slide 4 and then read the following narration: **"It's hard to look at the Grand Canyon and not be curious about geology."** for this slide.

12. Stop the presentation so that the recording session ends.

13. Display Slide 1 and then run the slide show to view the presentation and to hear the narration you just recorded.

14. Apply the Fade transition, change the duration to 3.00 seconds, and then apply to all slides.

15. Save the presentation using the file name, Lab 11-2 Grand Canyon Narration.

16. Submit the revised document in the format specified by your instructor.

17. If requested by your instructor, type the year you started college after your name on Slide 1.

18. ✳ When you created the color and black-and-white photo albums of Grand Canyon photos, you set up the album with two photos per slide. Do you think it would have been better to do one photo per slide? Why? Do you think adding captions to the color album was effective? In the black-and-white photo album, you used the Slice design with the blue variant. Was this a good choice? Why?

(a) Slide 1

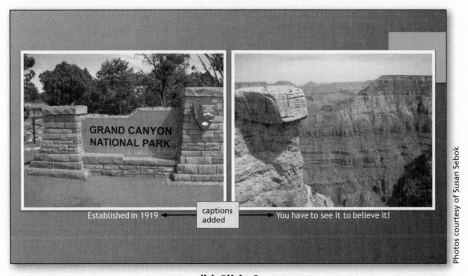

Photos courtesy of Susan Sebok

(b) Slide 2

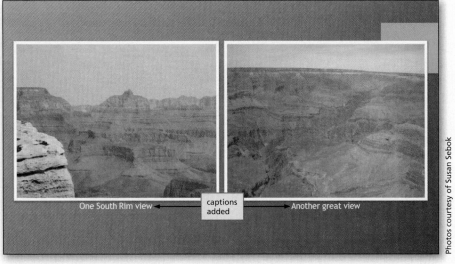

Photos courtesy of Susan Sebok

(c) Slide 3

Figure 11–84 (Continued)

Continued >

In the Labs *continued*

(d) Slide 4

(e) Slide 5

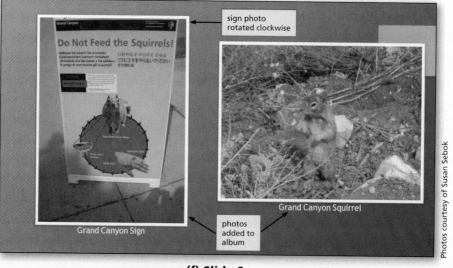

(f) Slide 6

Figure 11–84 (Continued)

(g) Slide 7

(h) Slide 1 (Narrated Presentation)

(i) Slide 2 (Narrated Presentation)

Figure 11–84 (Continued)

Continued >

In the Labs *continued*

photo brightness decreased

Photos courtesy of Susan Sebok

(j) Slide 3 (Narrated Presentation)

Photos courtesy of Susan Sebok

(k) Slide 4 (Narrated Presentation)

Figure 11–84 (Continued)

Lab 3: Expand Your World: Cloud and Web Technologies
Exploring Apps for Office

Problem: You use apps on your phone and tablet regularly to look up a variety of information. You see that you can use apps not only in PowerPoint, but in other Office apps. You would like to investigate some of the apps available for PowerPoint to determine which ones would be helpful for you to use.

Note: You will be required to use your Microsoft Account to complete this assignment. If you do not have a Microsoft account and do not want to create one, read this assignment without performing the instructions.

Instructions: Perform the following tasks:

1. Use Help to learn about Apps for Office. If necessary, sign in to your Windows account.

2. If you are not signed in already, sign in to your Microsoft Account in PowerPoint.

Figure 11–85

3. Display the INSERT tab and then tap or click the 'Insert an App' button (INSERT tab | Apps group) to display the Apps for Office dialog box. (If a menu is displayed, tap or click the See All link to display the Apps for Office dialog box.) On the FEATURED APPS tab, view the Editor's Picks apps (Figure 11–85). Your list of Editor's Picks featured apps may differ.

4. Tap or click the More apps link to visit the online Office Store. View the apps that will work with PowerPoint 2013. Locate a free app that you feel would be helpful to you while you use PowerPoint, tap or click the Add button, and then follow the instructions to add the app to PowerPoint.

5. In PowerPoint, tap or click the 'Insert an App' button (INSERT tab | Apps group) to display the Apps for Office dialog box. Tap or click the app you added and then tap or click the Insert button to add the app. Tap or click the 'Insert an App' arrow (INSERT tab | Apps group) to see the added app in the list.

6. Practice using the app.

7. ✹ Which apps are available for PowerPoint in the online Office Store? What were their costs to download? Which app did you download and why? Does the app work as you intended? Would you recommend the app to others?

Consider This: Your Turn

Apply your creative thinking and problem-solving skills to design and implement a solution.

1. Design and Create a Presentation about Stand-Up Paddleboarding (SUP)

Personal

Part 1: Your part-time job at River Ridge has been a fulfilling experience. The company received special recognition when it was awarded the Best Kayak Adventure of 2014. You have been a guide on many canoe and kayak trips. You also have become skilled at paddleboarding and have

Continued >

Consider This: Your Turn *continued*

taught this fun activity to people of all ages. River Ridge is planning to develop a schedule for paddleboarding lessons. Use the concepts and techniques presented in this chapter to prepare a presentation for promoting the business. You can shoot a short video to include in the presentation, search online for photos and videos, or use photos and illustrations from Office.com if they are appropriate for this presentation. Select a suitable theme, create section breaks, record narration, and create a video from the presentation. Change the slide orientation to portrait for a handout. Submit your assignment in the format specified by your instructor.

Part 2: ☀ You made several decisions while creating the presentation in this assignment: where to place text, photos and illustrations, how to divide the presentation into sections, which words to include in your narration, and whether to create a photo album. What was the rationale behind each of these decisions? When you reviewed the document, what further revisions did you make and why? Where would you recommend showing this slide show?

2. Design and Create a Presentation about Your Ice Cream Parlor Business
Professional

Part 1: You are the owner of your town's only ice cream parlor called Ice Cream Creations. It is a small family-owned business that has been serving delicious ice cream desserts for more than 30 years. The business recently has expanded to include homemade candy and added a plant where you make your own ice cream and create new flavors. You decide to put together a PowerPoint presentation for the next Chamber of Commerce meeting. Select a suitable theme, create section breaks, record narration, and create a video from the presentation. Change the slide size to a size suitable for posters to hang in your shop. The presentation could contain photos from a PowerPoint file called Ice Cream Creations available on the Data Files for Students or you can use photos and illustrations from Office.com if they are appropriate for this topic. You can create a photo album with narration showing some of your special ice cream dishes. Submit your assignment in the format specified by your instructor.

Part 2: ☀ You made several decisions while creating the presentation in this assignment: where to place text, photos and illustrations, where to use WordArt, how to divide the presentation into sections, and whether to create a video. What was the rationale behind each of these decisions? When you reviewed the document, what further revisions did you make and why? Where would you recommend showing this slide show?

3. Design and Create a Presentation about Traveling by Steamboat on the Mississippi River
Research and Collaboration

Part 1: You are studying rivers in your geography class and your group has been assigned the topic of traveling by steamboat on the Mississippi River, also called the Mighty Mississippi. Your group has divided into three small groups. One group will gather facts about the history of the river when people could travel by boat on the river in the early 1800s. Another group will look into the history of steamboats, including the different types and when they were first used to travel on the river. The third group will gather photos, illustrations, and videos about steamboat travel on the Mississippi River and develop several itineraries and places to visit along the routes. Your group will put together a PowerPoint presentation using at least three objectives found at the beginning of this chapter. Select a suitable theme, create section breaks, create a custom slide show, record narration, and create a video from the presentation. Three illustrations are available on the Data Files for Students: Steamboat, St. Louis, and Mississippi River Map. You can use your own photos or those available from Office.com if they are appropriate for this topic. Change the slide orientation to portrait for a handout to the class during your group's presentation. You also should create a black-and-white photo album for this topic.

Part 2:   ✹ You made several decisions while creating the presentation in this assignment: where to place text, photos and illustrations, where to use WordArt, how to divide the presentation into sections, whether to create a photo album in color or black and white, and the words to use in the script for narration. What was the rationale behind each of these decisions? When you reviewed the document, what further revisions did you make and why? Where would you recommend showing this slide show?

Learn Online

Reinforce what you learned in this chapter with games, exercises, training, and many other online activities and resources.

Student Companion Site   Reinforcement activities and resources are available at no additional cost on www.cengagebrain.com. Visit www.cengage.com/ct/studentdownload for detailed instructions about accessing the resources available at the Student Companion Site.

SAM   Put your skills into practice with SAM! If you have a SAM account, go to www.cengage .com/sam2013 to access SAM assignments for this chapter.

Appendix A

SAM Projects

Introduction

With SAM Projects—SAM's hands-on, live-in-the-application projects—students master Microsoft Office skills that are essential to academic and career success. SAM Projects engage students in applying the latest Microsoft Office 2013 skills to real-world scenarios. Immediate grading and feedback allow students to fix errors and understand where they may need more practice.

This appendix provides the printed instructions for one SAM Project that corresponds to this text. This project was created by an instructor currently teaching an Introduction to Computing course:

- PowerPoint Project: created by Barbara M. Waxer, Instructor & Trainer, Santa Fe Community College

To complete the project in this appendix, you must log into your SAM account. Go to sam.cengage.com for more information or contact your instructor.

PowerPoint 2013: Student Engagement Project 1a

SAM Gamitopia EdTech

Enhanced Skills

PROJECT DESCRIPTION
Created by Barbara M. Waxer, Instructor & Trainer, Santa Fe Community College

Your company, Gamitopia EdTech, has received a federal grant to create classroom-based gaming systems that help students identify their interests and develop 21st century learning skills—a trend called "gamification." Because gamification is new and not well understood, you will first educate parents and the community about how it works and the benefits it offers to students.

You will introduce the first game, which is aimed at high school freshmen, at a state school board meeting, where your team will demonstrate the game for board members and other attendees. While your team finishes the game, you will complete an informative presentation on gamification using tables, charts, animation, and graphics in PowerPoint.

GETTING STARTED

- Download the following file from the SAM website:
  - ○ **SAM_PPT2013_SE_P1a_*FirstLastName*_1.pptx**
- Open the file you just downloaded and save it with the name:
  - ○ **SAM_PPT2013_SE_P1a_*FirstLastName*_2.pptx**
  - ○ *Hint*: If you do not see the **.pptx** file extension in the Save file dialog box, do not type it. PowerPoint will add the file extension for you automatically.
- To complete this Project, you will also need to download and save the following support file from the SAM website:
  - ○ **support_SAM_P13_SE_P1a_brain.jpg**
  - ○ *Hint*: Opening an image may alter its file size. If you open an image support file, delete the file and download a new copy from the SAM website.
- With the file **SAM_PPT2013_SE_P1a_*FirstLastName*_2.pptx** still open, ensure that your first and last name is displayed in the presenter notes on Slide 1. If the presenter notes do not display your name, delete the file and download a new copy from the SAM website.

PROJECT STEPS

1. Apply the **fourth** variant of the **Slice** theme to the presentation.
2. On Slide 1 ("Gamification and Education"), select the text "Gamification and Education: Top Things to Know" and apply the WordArt style **Fill - White, Text 1, Shadow** (1st column, 1st row in the WordArt Style gallery).
3. On Slide 2 ("What is Gamification?"), select the text "What is Gamification?" Change the font to **Georgia**, and then **bold** the text.
4. With Slide 2 still displaying, move the round trophy picture down and to the left so that it is vertically centered across from the middle of the badge picture and positioned to the immediate right of the progress bar picture.
5. With Slide 2 still displaying, select all three pictures, and then group them.
6. On Slide 3 ("Hours Spent Playing Video, Mobile, & Computer Games"), select the text box "3 Billion" (in the blue sphere) and complete the following:
   a. Apply the animation **Grow & Turn** (10th option in the Entrance section of the Animation gallery).
   b. Apply the animation timing **Start After Previous**.
   c. Set the animation delay to **01.00** seconds.
7. With Slide 3 still displaying, insert a new text box and complete the following:
   a. Type **Globally per week** in the new text box.
   b. **Bold** the text.
   c. Resize the text box to a width of **2.5"**.
   d. Position the text box so that it is centered immediately above the blue sphere.
8. On Slide 4 ("What Leads to Learning?"), convert the bulleted list to a numbered list.
9. On Slide 5 ("Results"), change the chart data in cell B3 to **28**, and change the chart data in cell B5 to **32**.
10. On Slide 6 ("Learning Impacts"), use the content placeholder to insert a table with **2 columns** and **5 rows**, and then enter the data shown in Table 1.

Table 1 Data for Slide 6	
Activity	**Retention**
Read	10%
Listen with visuals	30%
Observe action	50%
Perform action	90%

© 2014 Cengage Learning.

11. On Slide 7 ("Brain Food"), in the content placeholder, type the following bulleted list items:

   Confidence

   Motivation

   Deeper learning

   a. Change the font size of the list items to **32 pt.**

   b. Apply the animation **Wipe** (6th option in Entrance section of the Animation gallery) using the animation timing **Start After Previous**.

12. On Slide 8 ("Brain Science"), complete the following:

   a. Convert the bulleted list to the SmartArt graphic **Vertical Box List** (2nd column, 2nd row in the List section of the Choose a SmartArt Graphic gallery).

   b. Apply the SmartArt style **Moderate Effect** (4th column, 1st row in the SmartArt Styles gallery).

13. With Slide 8 still displaying, insert the picture **support_SAM_P13_SE_P1a_brain.jpg** available for download from the SAM website. Move the picture so that its right edge touches the right side of the slide, and then apply the **Send to Back** option.

14. Move Slide 8 to become the new Slide 7.

15. Apply the transition **Reveal** (7th option in the Subtle section of the Transition to This Slide gallery) to all slides in the presentation. Set the duration to **02.00** seconds.

16. On the new Slide 8 ("Brain Food"), apply the transition **Peel Off** (8th option in the Exciting section of the Transition to This Slide gallery) only to this slide.

17. Add a footer to all slides except the title slide.

   a. Type the footer text:

   Gamitopia EdTech

   b. Include the **slide number**.

Save your changes, close the presentation, and exit PowerPoint. Follow the directions on the SAM website to submit your completed project.

Appendix B

Capstone Projects

Capstone Project 1

Problem: You have been working on a class assignment to research the issues of global e-waste and will then share your findings with your classmates. To prepare for your oral presentation, you have created some slides to emphasize the key points in the information that you gathered. To enhance the slides and make them more appealing and effective, you will add some additional photos, a video, and some special effects—including animations and transitions.

    Note: To complete this assignment, you will be required to use the Data Files for Students. Visit www.cengage.com/ct/studentdownload for detailed instructions or contact your instructor for information about accessing the required files.

    Instructions: Run PowerPoint. Open the presentation SC_PPT2013_Capstone_1-1. pptx and save it with the name SC_PPT2013_Capstone_1-2.pptx. You will also need the following support files from the student data files:

SC_PPT2013_Capstone_devices.jpg
SC_PPT2013_Capstone_waste_basket.jpg
SC_PPT2013_Capstone_throw_away.mp4

Hint: Opening an image may alter its file size. If you open an image support file, delete the file and download a new copy from the student data files.

Perform the following tasks:

1. Apply the Facet theme to the presentation. Apply the Recycled Paper texture background to all the slides.

2. On Slide 1 ("E-Waste Today"), left-align the title text. Next, change the font color of the subtitle text to Green, Accent 1, Darker 25% (5th column, 5th row in the Theme Colors palette), change the font size to 40 pt., and add the font attribute Text Shadow.

3. On Slide 2 ("Increased Use of Electronic Devices"), use the content placeholder to insert the picture SC_PPT2013_Capstone_devices.jpg, available from the student data files. Resize the picture so that it is 3.5" high, and then reposition the picture so it is centered horizontally under the title.

4. On Slide 2, apply the Beveled Matte, White picture style to the picture.

5. On Slide 3 ("Devices Become Unwanted or Outdated"), change the slide layout to Title and Content. In the title placeholder, apply bold and italics to the word "Outdated".

6. On Slide 3, use the content placeholder to insert the video SC_PPT2013_Capstone_throw_away.mp4, available for download from the student data files. Use the default On Click setting to start the playback.

7. On Slide 3, apply the transition Wind to that slide only.

8. On Slide 4 ("The Impact of Improper Disposal"), change the color of the picture on the right to Grayscale (2nd column, 1st row in the Recolor category in the Color gallery). Next, change the picture brightness and contrast to Brightness: 0% (Normal) Contrast: +20% (3rd column, 4th row in the Brightness/Contrast area of the Corrections gallery).

9. On Slide 4, insert the shape Multiply (in the Equation Shapes area in the Shapes menu). When complete, the shape should be 4" high and 4" wide. Position the shape so it is centered over the two pictures.

10. On Slide 4, apply the shape style Intense Effect – Red, Accent 5 (6th column, 6th row in the Shape Styles gallery) to the Multiply shape just inserted. With the shape still selected, enter the text **Hazardous**. Then select the shape text and apply the font Arial Rounded MT Bold.

11. On Slide 4, apply the Entrance animation Appear to the Multiply shape. Use the default start On Click. Then change the order of animations so that the Multiply shape animation appears first, before the bulleted list animation.

12. With Slide 4 still displaying, insert a new Slide 5 using the Title and Content layout. In the title placeholder, enter **Waste Reduction**. In the content placeholder, type the multilevel bulleted list as shown in Figure 1–1.

- Reuse
  - Donate or update
  - Sell
  - Trade
- Refurbish
  - Recover or repair
  - Trade in
- Recycle

Figure 1–1

13. On the new Slide 5 ("Waste Reduction"), select the bulleted list and apply the Entrance animation Appear, using default start On Click.

14. On Slide 5, insert the picture file SC_PPT2013_Capstone_waste_basket.jpg, available for download from the student data files. Resize the picture proportionally so that it is 3.5" high, and then reposition the picture in the area on the right, aligning the top of the picture with the top of the first bulleted item. Next, apply the Simple Frame, Black picture style.

15. On Slide 5, enter the following speaker note: **In municipal solid waste, e-waste is the largest source of lead.**

16. Move Slide 7 ("Purchase Green Devices") so that it becomes Slide 6. Add a border to the Energy Star picture using the border color Black, Text 1 (2nd column, 1st row in the Theme Colors palette) and the border weight 6 pt. Then move the content placeholder with the bulleted list so that the top of the first bulleted item aligns with the top of the picture.

17. On the new Slide 7 (no title), delete the title placeholder. Insert a WordArt image using the WordArt style Fill – Green, Accent 1, Shadow (2nd column, 1st row). In the WordArt text box, enter **Recycle Responsibly**. Then reposition the WordArt text box so it is centered horizontally at the top of the slide, above the bulleted list and picture.

18. On Slide 8 ("E-Waste Challenges"), in the subtitle placeholder, enter **Apply the Solutions**. Go to Slide 1 and use the Format Painter to copy the formats for the subtitle text, and then use the Format Painter to apply those formats to the subtitle on Slide 8.

19. Insert a footer with the text **E-Waste Challenges** and the slide number.

20. In the Header and Footer dialog box, use the Don't show on title slide check box to apply the footer to all the slides except the title slide. (Note: The footer will not appear on the last slide of the presentation because it uses a title slide layout.)

21. Check the Spelling in the presentation to identify and correct any spelling errors. (Hint: You should find and correct at least one spelling error.)

22. Update the document properties by entering the keywords **e-waste challenges** in the Tags box.

23. Save your changes, close the presentation, and exit PowerPoint. Submit the assignment as specified by your instructor.

Capstone Project 2

Problem: You are working to roll out a new line of high-end picnic baskets for Open Air Dining. Open Air is known as the top supplier for luxury woven products and imports from artisans in Europe and Southeast Asia. The marketing department wants to reveal the new line at the International Basket Goods for Fancy Foods Festival in Paris.

Your manager is finalizing a PowerPoint presentation for the sales team. He has asked you to complete the final review of the presentation by addressing comments and editing the various animations, bulleted lists, SmartArt graphics, tables, and charts. You will also add hyperlinks and action buttons to help the team access information easily and stay focused on the message.

Note: To complete this assignment, you will be required to use the Data Files for Students. Visit www.cengage.com/ct/studentdownload for detailed instructions or contact your instructor for information about accessing the required files.

Instructions: Run PowerPoint. Open the presentation SC_PPT2013 _Capstone_2-1.pptx and save it with the name SC_PPT2013_Capstone_2-2.pptx. You will also need the following support files from the student data files:

SC_PPT2013_Capstone_history.docx
SC_PPT2013_Capstone_fun.jpg
SC_PPT2013_Capstone_gingham.jpg
SC_PPT2013_Capstone_romance.jpg
SC_PPT2013_Capstone_work.jpg
SC_PPT2013_Capstone_app.pptx

Hint: Opening an image may alter its file size. If you open an image support file, delete the file and download a new copy from the student data files.

Perform the following tasks:

1. On Slide 1 ("Open Air Dining"), view the comment, and then insert a reply with the text: **Thanks! We love the new look**. On Slide 2 ("We love all things picnic and it shows"), change the bullets to pictures using the file SC_PPT2013 _Capstone_gingham.jpg, available from the student data files.

2. Next, change the size of the bullets to 115%.

3. On Slide 2, edit the action button by adding a hyperlink to the file SC_PPT2013 _Capstone_history.docx, available from the student data files.

4. On Slide 2, format the table: Apply the Medium Style 1 - Accent 6 table style (7th column, 1st row in the Medium section of the Table Styles gallery).

5. On Slide 3 ("Why picnic?"), convert the bulleted list to the Vertical Picture List SmartArt graphic (2nd column, 6th row in the List section of the SmartArt gallery).

6. Insert the picture file SC_PPT2013_Capstone_work.jpg, available from the student data files, in the first box.

7. Insert the picture file SC_PPT2013_Capstone_romance.jpg, available from the student data files, in the second box.

8. Insert the picture file SC_PPT2013_Capstone_fun.jpg, available from the student data files, in the last box.

9. Apply the Moderate Effect SmartArt style (4th column, 1st row in the SmartArt Styles gallery) to the SmartArt graphic.

10. Change the colors to Colorful Range - Accent Colors 5 to 6 (5th column, 1st row in the Colorful section of the SmartArt Colors palette).

11. On Slide 4 ("And the most popular side dishes are…"), follow the instructions in the comment, and then delete the comment.

12. On Slide 4, create a pie chart using the data shown in Table 2–1.

Table 2–1 Data for Pie Chart on Slide 4	
	Salad
Fruit	35%
Pasta	27%
Potato	25%
Coleslaw	13%

13. On Slide 5 ("The secret to our success"), apply the Color Pulse animation (2nd option in the Emphasis section of the Animations gallery) to the bulleted list. (Hint: Select the entire bulleted list object before adding the animation; do not highlight the text and then apply the animation.) Set the animation to start After Previous.

14. On Slide 6 ("Find Your Perfect Picnic Basket"), animate the SmartArt diagram with the Turns motion path (3rd option in the Motion Paths section of the Animations gallery), and then make the following changes: Change the effect option to Down Right.

15. If necessary, open the Animation Pane to reorder the items by moving the SmartArt diagram up to the top of the list.

16. Change the sequence to One by One.

17. Change the duration to 00.75 seconds.

18. Expand the Diagram animation in the Animation pane, make sure each animation is selected, and then set the Start setting to After Previous.

19. On Slide 7 ("Highland Collection"), change the Line Spacing of the text box to the left of the first picture to 1.5.

20. On Slide 7, format the action button as follows: Change the size to 0.5" high and 0.7" wide.

21. Change the shape style to Intense Effect - Green, Accent 6 (7th column, 6th row in the Shape Styles gallery).

22. Edit the action button so it advances the presentation to the next slide. (Hint: Change the default Hyperlink to setting in the Action Settings dialog box.)

23. Copy the modified action button from Slide 7. On Slide 8 ("Concord Collection"), paste the action button.

24. On Slide 9 ("If you can pack it, we can keep it fresh"), paste the action button, and then make the following change: Edit the action button so it advances the presentation to Slide 7 ("Highland Collection"). (Hint: Change the default Hyperlink to setting in the Action Settings dialog box.)

25. On Slide 10 ("Feeling creative?…"), insert a comment with the text: This slide will change once we get the food container photos.

26. On Slide 11 ("Need to protect something fragile?"), remove the picture background. (Hint: Adjust the handles on the marquee lines to only remove the white background and none of the imagery.)

27. With Slide 11 displayed, reuse the presentation called SC_PPT2013_Capstone _app.pptx, available from the student data files. Then, insert the slide "Picnic mobile app launching next month!" (Hint: Do not use source formatting.)

28. Close the Reuse Slides, Animations, and Comments panes, if necessary.

29. On Slide 12 ("Picnic mobile app launching next month!"), animate the title text box with the Color Pulse animation (2nd option in the Emphasis section of the Animations gallery).

30. Set the animation to start After Previous.

31. On Slide 12, add the Chime sound to the animation applied in Step 29.

32. On Slide 12 only, apply the Drape transition (2nd option under the Exciting section of the Transitions gallery).

33. Insert the slide number and the footer text **Baskets and more** on every slide in the presentation except the title slide.

34. Save your changes, close the presentation, and exit PowerPoint. Submit the assignment as specified by your instructor.

Capstone Project 3

Creating a Photo Album with Sections and Narration

The Camden Coastal Marine Museum (CCMM) is a small facility on the coast of Maine. The museum attracts school groups, tourists, history buffs, and amateur oceanographers to its exhibits featuring sea life and underwater exploration. Simon MacAllan is the outreach director of CCMM and has asked for your help in creating a presentation.

Instructions, Part 1: Simon wants a photo album that he can share with museum board members and visitors. The photo album should highlight the museum's one-of-a-kind collection of underwater photography. The presentation that you will create should consist of a title slide, section slides, and multiple photo slides. You will also add a narration recording.

Create a new presentation and save the presentation as Camden Album. Delete the placeholders. Change the theme to Ion and apply the Blue II color variant. Change the theme fonts, using the TrebuchetMS fonts. Name the new theme, Camden. Format the background using the Watercolor Sponge artistic effect with a transparency of 20%, as shown in Figure 3–1. Apply the Title Slide layout to Slide 1 and add the title shown in Figure 3–1. Move the lower placeholder down and to the left, add the subtitle text for the slide, and change the subtitle font to Teal, Accent 6, Lighter 40%. Change the font size to 28 pt.

To add visual interest and customize the presentation to match the museum's corporate identity, you will add a figure. Open the Sea star file from the Data Files for Students and place it on Slide 1. Remove the figure background and resize and reposition the sea star as shown in Figure 3–1.

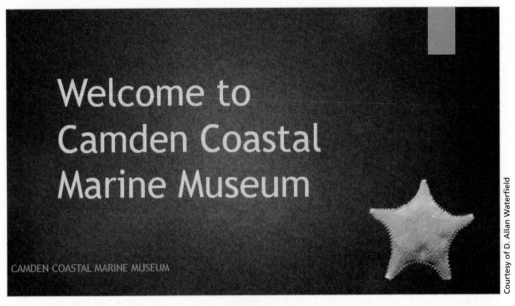

Figure 3–1

Instructions, Part 2: The photo album will consist of two sections, the Underwater Exploration section and the Sea Life section. Add a section between Slides 1 and 2. Change the Section name to Exploration. Ensure that Slide 2 has a blank layout. Insert the Exploration 1.jpg figure as the artwork for the first Section Header. Insert a text box below the figure, as shown in Figure 3–2. Change the font color of the text to Orange and change the font size to 40. Center the title in the text box. Apply a solid fill to the text box using White, Text 1, a 70% transparency level. Using Shape Effects, change the text box outline to 5 point soft edges, no outline.

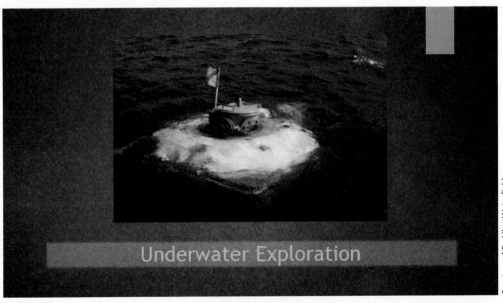

Figure 3–2

Slide 3 will be the beginning of the Exploration section of photo album. Create the first album slide with a Title and Content layout style. Copy the sea star image from the title slide, and then paste it into Slide 3. Duplicate Slide 3 eight times, for a total of nine slides in the Exploration section. Using the information from Table 3–1, insert titles and photos into the nine slides. Resize the images as needed.

Table 3–1		
Slide Number	**Image**	**Title**
3	Exploration 2	Deepstar 2000 two-person sub
4	Exploration 3	Beaver Mark IV mini sub
5	Exploration 4	Jim Suit self-contained exploration suit
6	Exploration 5	Jim Suit arm
7	Exploration 6	Helgoland undersea habitat
8	Exploration 7	Helgoland undersea habitat
9	Exploration 8	Helgoland interior
10	Exploration 9	Helgoland submerged
11	Exploration 10	Ice diving practice unit

Instructions, Part 3: Duplicate Slide 2 and move it to the end of the presentation. Change the image to the sea star image, Sea star. Add a section between Slides 11 and 12 and rename the section, Sea Life. Because Simon has so many sea life images that he wants in the photo album, you will create a separate presentation containing the photo album, and then copy and paste the photo album into the Camden Album presentation.

Open a new presentation and insert a photo album. Select File/Disk as the image source, and then navigate to the Data Files for Students. Select all the figures in the Data Files for Project 3\Exploration\Sea life folder. The layout of the album should have a 1 Slide picture layout with Soft Edge Rectangle frame. Select the Ion theme, and display captions below all images. Create the photo album, and then change the Theme color to the Blue II variant, to match the Camden album. On the first slide, change the album title to Sea Life Photo Album. Your name should appear as the creator of the photo album. If it does not, change the placeholder content to your first name and last name. Copy all the photo album slides, change to the Camden Album presentation, and then paste the photo album below Slide 12.

Instructions, Part 4: Record a brief audio welcome that will play while the opening slide is visible. You will need a microphone or other recording device that is compatible with your computer. Select Slide 1, and then click Record Slide Show and record the following narration: "Thank you for visiting the Camden Coastal Marine Museum, where the oceans reveal their secrets. We encourage you to view our slide show and tour the museum at your own pace. Our collection of photos and historical information is unparalleled on the East Coast. We welcome your questions." When you are finished speaking, stop the narration. Play the slide show from the start, and then manually proceed through the slides after the narration finishes.

Save the presentation as Camden Album and submit it in the format specified by your instructor.

Appendix C

Microsoft Office 2013 Specialist and Expert Certifications

What Are Microsoft Office Specialist and Expert Certifications?

Microsoft Corporation has developed a set of standardized, performance-based examinations that you can take to demonstrate your overall expertise with Microsoft Office 2013 programs, including Microsoft Word 2013, Microsoft PowerPoint 2013, Microsoft Excel 2013, Microsoft Access 2013, and Microsoft Outlook 2013. When you successfully complete an examination for one of these Office programs, you will have earned the designation as a specialist or as an expert in that particular Office program. These examinations collectively are called the Microsoft Office 2013 Specialist and Microsoft Office 2013 Expert certification exams.

Why Should You Be Certified?

Microsoft Office 2013 certification provides a number of benefits for both you and your potential employer. The benefits for you include the following:

- You can differentiate yourself in the employment marketplace from those who are not Microsoft Office Specialist or Expert certified.
- You have proved your skills and expertise when using Microsoft Office 2013.
- You will be able to perform at a higher skill level in your job.
- You will be working at a higher professional level than those who are not certified.
- You will broaden your employment opportunities and advance your career more rapidly.

For employers, Microsoft Office 2013 certification offers the following advantages:

- When hiring or promoting employees, employers have immediate verification of employees' skills.
- Companies can maximize their productivity and efficiency by employing Microsoft Office 2013 certified individuals.

Skills Mapping

The following mapping information shows where each skill in the PowerPoint 2013 certification exam is covered in this text.

Table C–1 Specialist-Level Skill Sets and Locations in Book for Microsoft PowerPoint 2013	
Skill Set	**Page Number**
1.0 Create and Manage Presentations	
1.1 Create a Presentation	
creating blank presentations	OFF 11
creating presentations using templates	Chapter 2
importing text files into presentations	PPT 607
importing Word document outlines into presentations	PPT 343
1.2 Format a Presentation Using Slide Masters	
applying a slide master	Chapter 8
adding new layouts	Chapter 8
modifying existing layouts	Chapter 8
adding background images	PPT 488
controlling page numbers	PPT 504
inserting headers and footers	PPT 300, PPT 485
modifying presentation themes	Chapter 8
1.3 Customize Presentation Options and Views	
changing page setup options	PPT 699
changing to view in color/grayscale	PPT 694
using views to navigate through presentations	PPT 49, PPT 157
modifying presentation properties	PPT 48, PPT 312
1.4 Configure Presentations to Print or Save	
setting handout print options	PPT 52, PPT 188
printing selections from presentations	PPT 710
packaging presentations for CD	PPT 308
saving presentations as web pages	PPT 68, PPT 142
printing presentations in grayscale	PPT 52, PPT 685
printing speaker notes	PPT 121
maintaining backward compatibility	PPT 310
1.5 Configure and Present Slideshows	
creating custom slideshows	PPT 680
configuring slideshow options	PPT 317
rehearsing timing	PPT 450
configuring slideshow resolution	PPT 304, PPT 708
using Presenter View	PPT 710
navigating within slideshows	PPT 317
annotating slideshows	PPT 317
2.0 Insert and Format Shapes and Slides	
2.1 Insert and Format Slides	
adding slides layouts	PPT 23
duplicating existing slides	PPT 41
hiding slides	PPT 370

Table C–1 Specialist-Level Skill Sets and Locations in Book for Microsoft PowerPoint 2013 *(continued)*

Skill Set	Page Number
deleting slides	PPT 79
modifying slide backgrounds	PPT 108–112
applying styles to slides	PPT 26–27
2.2 Insert and Format Shapes	
modifying shape backgrounds	PPT 568
applying borders to shapes	PPT 576
resizing shapes	PPT 93
inserting shapes	PPT 92, PPT 94
creating custom shapes	PPT 570–574
applying styles to shapes	PPT 95
2.3 Order and Group Shapes and Slides	
inserting section headers	PPT 673
modifying slide order	PPT 42
aligning and grouping shapes	PPT 567, PPT 570, PPT 571
displaying gridlines	PPT 636
3.0 Create Slide Content	
3.1 Insert and Format Text	
changing text to WordArt	PPT 103
creating multiple columns in a single shape	PPT 376
inserting hyperlinks	PPT 347–350, PPT 358–362
applying formatting and styles to text	PPT 11–13, PPT 21
creating bulleted and numbered lists	PPT 380–389
3.2 Insert and Format Tables	
creating new tables	PPT 239, PPT 610
modifying number of rows and columns	PPT 248, PPT 617
applying table styles	PPT 244
importing tables from external sources	PPT 626
3.3 Insert and Format Charts	
creating and modifying chart styles	PPT 235
inserting charts	PPT 228
modifying chart type	PPT 635
adding legends to charts	PPT 233
modifying chart parameters	PPT 235–237
importing charts from external sources	PPT 631
3.4 Insert and Format SmartArt	
adding shapes to SmartArt	PPT 558
changing color of SmartArt	PPT 224
moving text within SmartArt shapes	PPT 555–556
reversing direction	PPT 554
converting lists to SmartArt	PPT 222
3.5 Insert and Format Images	
resizing images	PPT 35–39
cropping images	PPT 415
applying effects	PPT 90, PPT 150–152
applying styles	PPT 87

Table C–1 Specialist-Level Skill Sets and Locations in Book for Microsoft PowerPoint 2013 *(continued)*	
Skill Set	**Page Number**
3.6 Insert and Format Media	
adjusting media window size	PPT 175
trimming timing on media clips	PPT 169
setting start/stop times	PPT 170
setting media options	PPT 170, PPT 172
linking to external media	PPT 534
4.0 Apply Transitions and Animations	
4.1 Apply Transitioning between Slides	
inserting transitions between slides	PPT 45
managing multiple transitions	PPT 447
modifying transition effect options	PPT 446
4.2 Animate Slide Content	
applying animations to shapes	PPT 437
applying animations to text strings	PPT 183, PPT 440
adding paths to animations	PPT 430–431
modifying animation options	PPT 177, PPT 445
4.3 Set Timing for Transitions and Animations	
modifying duration of effects	PPT 180–182, PPT 443
configuring start and finish options	PPT 176–178
reordering animations	PPT 423
using the Animation Pane	PPT 423–425, PPT 441
5.0 Manage Multiple Presentations	
5.1 Merge Content from Multiple Presentations	
merging multiple presentations	PPT 277
reusing slides from other presentations	PPT 296
viewing multiple presentations	PPT 701
5.2 Track Changes and Resolve Differences	
setting track changes	*Functionality not found in PowerPoint 2013
modifying options for track changes	*Functionality not found in PowerPoint 2013
discarding changes from specific users	PPT 282–287
managing comments	PPT 279–292
5.3 Protect and Share Presentations	
encrypting presentations with a password	PPT 314
proofing presentations	PPT 116
marking as final	PPT 316
compressing media	PPT 417, PPT 704
embedding fonts	PPT 630
restricting permissions	PPT 707
removing presentation metadata	PPT 312
checking for accessibility issues	PPT 614
checking for compatibility issues	PPT 311

Index

Note: **Boldface** page numbers indicate key terms.

A

Access, **OFF 63**
See also databases
introduction to, OFF 63–64
starting, OFF 63
unique elements of, OFF 64
Access work area, **OFF 64**
accessibility, checking for issues, PPT 614
accounts
signing in to Microsoft, OFF 37–38
signing out of Microsoft, PPT 55, PPT 125, PPT 191, PPT 255–256, PPT 523
Acrobat Reader, PPT 121
action buttons, **PPT 350**
built-in (table), PPT 351
changing fill colors, PPT 354–355
copying, PPT 355–356
editing action settings, PPT 356–357
running slide show with, PPT 389–391
sizing, PPT 354
active cell, **OFF 59**, OFF 60, **PPT 227**
Active Directory Synchronization, **CLD 8**
adding
See also inserting
artistic effects to photos, PPT 152
borders to tables, PPT 245–246
charts to slides, PPT 226–229
effects to tables, PPT 246–247
footers to slides, PPT 300–301
footers with fixed information, PPT 300–301
and formatting placeholders, PPT 489–493
gradient fills to tables, PPT 621
guides, PPT 366
hyperlinks to paragraphs, PPT 349–350
hyperlinks to slides, PPT 347
hyperlinks to tables, PPT 644
images to tables, PPT 251–252
picture borders, PPT 88–90
shading to tables, PPT 620
shapes to slides, PPT 92–93, PPT 94–95
slide transitions, PPT 45–47, PPT 119–120, PPT 517, PPT 644
SmartArt bullets, PPT 557
SmartArt shapes, PPT 558
text boxes to documents, PPT 156
video styles, PPT 173–174
address bar, folder windows, OFF 27
Adobe Reader, PPT 52
align, **PPT 363**
aligning
centering. *See* centering
charts, PPT 633–634

data in table cells, PPT 624
illustrations, PPT 368–369
objects, PPT 363–366
paragraph text, PPT 154–155
placeholder text, PPT 374
text in table cells, PPT 253–254
worksheets, PPT 628–629
alignment options (table), PPT 364
All Caps effect, PPT 9
animating
charts, PPT 438–439
content placeholder paragraphs, PPT 183–184
illustrations using Animation Painter, PPT 435–436
illustrations using emphasis effect, PPT 177–178
illustrations using entrance effect, PPT 176
illustrations using exit effect, PPT 178–179
lists, PPT 440
photos using emphasis effects, PPT 419–420
photos using entrance effects, PPT 418
photos using exit effects, PPT 420
slide content, PPT 175–184, PPT 417–418
SmartArt graphics, PPT 436–437
text boxes by applying motion path, PPT 430
text boxes using entrance effects, PPT 428–429
title text placeholder paragraphs, PPT 422–423
animation effect icon colors, PPT 175
animation effects
icon colors for, PPT 410
transition, PPT 46
triggering, PPT 445–446
using, PPT 418
Animation gallery, PPT 184
animation order, changing, PPT 423–424
Animation Painter
animating illustration using, PPT 435–436
copying animations using, PPT 442–443
Animation Pane, PPT 424
animations
associating sounds with, PPT 432
changing direction, PPT 176, PPT 179, PPT 419
custom, PPT 175–184
developing, PPT 422
modifying emphasis, exit timings, PPT 182–183
modifying timing, PPT 180–181
numbered animation events, PPT 420
previewing, PPT 421

removing, PPT 429
selecting individual, PPT 421
text options, PPT 444
types of, PPT 410
annotate, **PPT 274**
app, **OFF 3**
App bar, **OFF 8**
Apple iPads, access to Office 365, CLD 8
Apple iPhones, access to Office 365, CLD 8
applications. *See* apps
Apply, Apply to All buttons, PPT 119
apps
exiting Office, with one document open, OFF 42–43
Microsoft Office 2013, OFF 9
pinning, unpinning, OFF 8
running, OFF 63
running from File Explorer, OFF 57–59
running from Start screen, OFF 11–12
running using Search box, OFF 46–48
running using Start menu using Windows 7, OFF 12
switching between Start screen and, OFF 13
switching from one to another, OFF 30–31
arranging slides, PPT 42
arrows, inserting, PPT 565–566
artistic effects, adding to photos, PPT 152
assignments, OFF 83
audience, considering their interests, PPT 389
audio files, inserting into presentations, PPT 172–173
automatically updated properties, **PPT 48**, **PPT 518**
axis titles, displaying and formatting, PPT 638

B

background graphics, hiding or unhiding, PPT 499–500
backgrounds
Format Background dialog box, PPT 516
formatting chart, PPT 641–642
formatting slide, PPT 108–112
graphics, inserting into slide masters, PPT 488
printing, PPT 122
removing, PPT 411–415
slide masters, PPT 484–485
Backstage view, **OFF 31**
closing Office files using, OFF 53–54
creating new Office documents from, OFF 51–52

Quick Reference Summary

Microsoft PowerPoint 2013 Quick Reference Summary

Task	Page Number	Mouse	Ribbon	Other On-Screen Areas	Shortcut Menu	Keyboard Shortcut
Accessibility, Check for Issues	PPT 614		'Check for Issues' button (FILE tab | Info tab), Check Accessibility			
Action Button, Change Fill Color	PPT 354		Shape Fill arrow (DRAWING TOOLS FORMAT tab | Shape Styles gallery)		Fill	
Action Button, Copy	PPT 355		Copy button (HOME tab | Clipboard group)		Copy	CTRL+C
Action Button, Edit Setting	PPT 356		With button selected, Action button (INSERT tab | Links group), edit desired setting			
Action Button, Insert	PPT 351		Shapes button (INSERT tab | Illustrations group), Action Buttons area			
Action Button, Size	PPT 354		Set size in vertical and horizontal size boxes (DRAWING TOOLS FORMAT tab | Size group)	Drag sizing handles of action button		
Animation, Add	PPT 176		ANIMATIONS tab | Animation group			
Animation, Add to Existing	PPT 177		Add Animation button (ANIMATIONS tab | Advanced Animation group)			
Animation, Adjust a Motion Path	PPT 431			Drag red stopping point or green starting point on motion path		
Animation, Associate Sound with	PPT 432		Add sound to slide, tap or click sound icon, then tap or click Play button (ANIMATIONS tab | Animation group), set start timing to With Previous			
Animation, Change Direction	PPT 177		Effect Options button (ANIMATIONS tab | Animation group)			
Animation, Change Order	PPT 423		Display Animation pane, select animation, Move Earlier or Move Later buttons (ANIMATIONS tab | Timing group)	Select animation in Animation pane, up or down arrow buttons in Animation pane		

Microsoft PowerPoint 2013 Quick Reference Summary *(continued)*

Task	Page Number	Mouse	Ribbon	Other On-Screen Areas	Shortcut Menu	Keyboard Shortcut
Animation, Delete	PPT 179					Tap or click number associated with animation, DELETE
Animation, Dim Text After	PPT 441		Animation Pane button (ANIMATIONS tab | Advanced Animation group), Animation Order list arrow, Effect Options, After animation arrow, tap or click color for dim effect			
Animation, Draw Custom Motion Path	PPT 433		Add Animation button (ANIMATIONS tab | Advanced Animation group), Custom Path (Motion Paths section)			
Animation, Modify Timing	PPT 180		ANIMATIONS tab | Timing group			
Animation, Preview Sequence	PPT 180		Preview button (ANIMATIONS tab | Preview group)		Play Selected button (Animation task pane)	
Animation, Trigger Effect	PPT 445		Animation Pane button, (ANIMATIONS tab | Advanced Animation group), select trigger object in Animation pane, Trigger button (ANIMATIONS tab | Advanced Animation group)			
Animation Painter, Use to Copy Animations	PPT 435 PPT 442		Select object with animation effects, Animation Painter button (ANIMATIONS tab | Advanced Animation group), then tap or click object to which you want to copy animation			
Audio File, Insert	PPT 170		Audio button (INSERT tab | Media group)			
Audio Options, Add	PPT 172		Start arrow (AUDIO TOOLS PLAYBACK tab | Audio Options group)			
Bullet, Change Size	PPT 384		Bullets arrow (HOME tab | Paragraph group), Size box		Bullets, Bullets and Numbering, Size	
Bullet, Format Color	PPT 385		Bullets arrow (HOME tab | Paragraph group), Color button		Bullets, Bullets and Numbering, Color	
Bullet Character, Change to Number	PPT 386		Numbering arrow (HOME tab | Paragraph group), choose desired numbering option		Numbering	
Bullet Character, Change to Picture	PPT 380		Bullets arrow (HOME tab | Paragraph group), Bullets and Numbering, Picture button (Bullets and Numbering dialog box)		Bullets, Bullets and Numbering	

Microsoft PowerPoint 2013 Quick Reference Summary (continued)

Task	Page Number	Mouse	Ribbon	Other On-Screen Areas	Shortcut Menu	Keyboard Shortcut
Bullet Character, Change to Symbol	PPT 382		Bullets arrow (HOME tab | Paragraph group), Bullets and Numbering, Customize button (Bullets and Numbering dialog box)		Bullets, Bullets and Numbering, Customize	
Bullet Characters, Remove	PPT 388		Bullets arrow (HOME tab | Paragraph group), None	Select bulleted text, Bullets button		
Character Spacing, Change	PPT 495		Character Spacing button (HOME tab | Font group); Font dialog box launcher (HOME tab |Font Group), Character Spacing tab (Font dialog box)		Font, Character Spacing tab	
Chart, Align	PPT 633		Align button (DRAWING TOOLS FORMAT tab | Arrange group)			
Chart, Animate	PPT 438		More button (ANIMATIONS tab | Animation group), select effect from Animation gallery			
Chart, Apply Style	PPT 235 PPT 636		More button (CHART TOOLS DESIGN tab | Chart Styles group)	Chart Style button (paintbrush icon) on right side of chart area		
Chart, Change Colors	PPT 637		'Change Colors' button (CHART TOOLS DESIGN tab | Chart Styles group)	Chart Style button (paintbrush icon on right side of chart area), COLOR tab		
Chart, Change Layout	PPT 233		Quick Layout button (CHART TOOLS DESIGN tab | Chart Layouts group)			
Chart, Change Type	PPT 635		'Change Chart Type' button (CHART TOOLS DESIGN tab | Type group)			
Chart, Copy from Excel	PPT 631		(In Excel) Copy button (HOME tab | Clipboard group), switch to PowerPoint, Paste arrow (HOME tab | Clipboard group), 'Use Destination Theme & Link Data'		Copy (in Excel), Paste (in PowerPoint)	
Chart, Display Gridlines	PPT 636		'Add Chart Element' button (CHART TOOLS DESIGN tab | Chart Layouts group), Gridlines			
Chart, Display and Format Axis Titles	PPT 638		'Add Chart Element' button (CHART TOOLS DESIGN tab | Chart Layouts group), Axis Titles	Chart Elements button (plus icon on right side of chart area), Axis Titles check box		
Chart, Edit Data	PPT 642		Edit Data button (CHART TOOLS DESIGN tab | Data group)			
Chart, Exclude Data	PPT 636			Chart Filters button (funnel icon on right side of chart area)		

Microsoft PowerPoint 2013 Quick Reference Summary *(continued)*

Task	Page Number	Mouse	Ribbon	Other On-Screen Areas	Shortcut Menu	Keyboard Shortcut
Chart, Format Background	PPT 641		Current Selection arrow, Walls (CHART TOOLS FORMAT tab | Current Selection group), Format Selection button		Format Walls	
Chart, Format Legend	PPT 639		Current Selection arrow, Legend (CHART TOOLS FORMAT tab | Current Selection group), Format Selection button	Chart Elements button (plus icon on right side of chart area), Legend arrow	Format Legend	
Chart, Insert	PPT 228		Chart button (INSERT tab | Illustrations group)	Insert Chart icon in content placeholder		
Chart, Move Legend	PPT 639		Add Chart Element button (CHART TOOLS DESIGN tab | Chart Layouts group), Legend arrow	Chart Elements button (plus icon on right side of chart area), Legend arrow	Format Legend, Legend Position	
Chart, Resize	PPT 233			Drag sizing handles	Format Chart Area, Size & Properties icon	
Chart, Rotate	PPT 235		Format Selection button (CHART TOOLS FORMAT tab | Current Selection group), set desired degrees of rotation		Format Data Point	
Chart, Separate a Pie Slice	PPT 236			Select slice and drag	Format Data Point, set Point Explosion percentage	
Chart Shape, Change Outline Color	PPT 232		Shape Outline arrow (CHART TOOLS FORMAT tab | Shape Styles group), click desired color		Chart Area in Chart Elements box, Outline button, choose color	
Chart Shape, Change Outline Weight	PPT 231		Shape Outline arrow (CHART TOOLS FORMAT tab | Shape Styles group), Weight		Chart Area in Chart Elements box, Outline button, Weight	
Chart, Switch Rows and Columns	PPT 634		Switch Row/Column button (CHART TOOLS DESIGN tab | Data group)			
Clip Object, Change Color	PPT 161		Shape Fill arrow (DRAWING TOOLS FORMAT tab | Shape Styles group)		Fill button; or Format Shape, Fill & Line icon, FILL, Solid fill, Color button (Format Shape task pane)	
Clip Object, Delete	PPT 163		Cut button (HOME tab | Clipboard group)		Cut	
Columns, Adjust Spacing	PPT 377		Columns button (HOME tab | Paragraph group), More Columns, Spacing box			
Columns, Create in a Placeholder	PPT 376		Columns button (HOME tab | Paragraph group)			
Comment, Delete	PPT 290		Delete Comment button (REVIEW tab | Comments group)	Delete button (Comments pane)		

Microsoft PowerPoint 2013 Quick Reference Summary *(continued)*

Task	Page Number	Mouse	Ribbon	Other On-Screen Areas	Shortcut Menu	Keyboard Shortcut
Comment, Insert	PPT 289		New Comment button (REVIEW tab | Comments group)	New Comment button (Comments pane)		
Comment, Reply to	PPT 288			Reply box (Comments pane)		
Comments, End Review	PPT 293		End Review button (REVIEW tab | Compare group)			
Comments, Print	PPT 279		Print button (FILE tab, Print tab, check 'Print Comments and Ink Markup' box)			CTRL+P
Comments, Review	PPT 287		Next Comment and Previous Comment buttons (REVIEW tab | Comments group)	Next Comment and Previous Comment buttons (Comments pane)		
Comments, Show or Hide	PPT 278		Show Comments button (REVIEW tab | Comments group)	Comments button on status bar		
Copy	PPT 101, PPT 166		Copy button (HOME tab | Clipboard group)		Copy	CTRL+C
Credits, Create	PPT 443		More button (ANIMATIONS tab | Animation group), More Entrance Effects, Credits			
Custom Slide Show, Create	PPT 680		In Normal view, 'Custom Slide Show' button (SLIDE SHOW tab | Start Slide Show group), Custom Shows, New			
Custom Slide Show, Edit	PPT 682		Normal view, 'Custom Slide Show' button (SLIDE SHOW tab | Start Slide Show group), Custom Shows, select show, Edit			
Digital Signature, Create and Add	PPT 309		Protect Presentation button, Add a Digital Signature (FILE tab, Info tab)			
Document Inspector, Start	PPT 312		'Check for Issues' button (FILE tab, Info tab), Inspect Document, Inspect button			
Document Properties, Change	PPT 48		Properties button (FILE tab, Info tab)			
Document Properties, Print	PPT 122		'Print All Slides' button (FILE tab, Print tab), Document Info, Print button			
Document Theme, Change Color Variant	PPT 5		Choose color variant (DESIGN tab | Variants group)			
Document Theme, Choose	PPT 5		FILE tab, New tab; More button (DESIGN tab | Themes group)			
Embedded File, Edit	PPT 608	Double-click embedded object to open source program		Double-tap embedded object to open source program	Document Object, Edit	

Microsoft PowerPoint 2013 Quick Reference Summary *(continued)*

Task	Page Number	Mouse	Ribbon	Other On-Screen Areas	Shortcut Menu	Keyboard Shortcut
Excel Worksheet, Edit Linked	PPT 629	Double-click linked worksheet to edit		Double-tap linked worksheet to edit		
Excel Worksheet, Insert Linked	PPT 626			Object button (INSERT tab | Text group), 'Create from file', browse to Excel file		
Exit PowerPoint	OFF 42, PPT 55		Exit (FILE tab)	Close button on title bar	Right-click PowerPoint app button on taskbar, click Close window	ALT+F4 or CTRL+Q
Eyedropper, Use to Format Text	PPT 444		Font Color arrow (HOME tab | Font group), Eyedropper, place pointer over desired color, tap or click to apply color to selected text			
File with Graphics and Text, Insert	PPT 606		Insert Object button (INSERT tab | Text group), 'Create from file', browse to file			
Fill Color, Apply to Slide	PPT 515		Format Background button (DESIGN tab | Customize group), FILL section (Format Background pane)		Format Background, FILL section (Format Background pane)	
Fill Color, Set Transparency	PPT 515		Format Background (DESIGN tab | Customize group), FILL section (Format Background pane), Transparency slider		Format Background, FILL area (Format Background pane), Transparency slider	
Font, Embed in Presentation	PPT 630		Tools button (FILE tab | Save As tab, Save As dialog box), Save Options, 'Embed fonts in the file'			
Font Size, Decrease	PPT 100		Decrease Font Size button or Font Size arrow (HOME tab | Font group)	Decrease Font Size button or Font Size arrow on mini toolbar	Font, Size arrows (Font dialog box)	CTRL+SHIFT +LEFT CARET (<)
Font Size, Increase	PPT 12		Increase Font Size button or Font Size arrow (HOME tab | Font group)	Increase Font Size button or Font Size arrow on mini toolbar	Font, Size arrows (Font dialog box)	CTRL+SHIFT +RIGHT CARET (>)
Font, Change	PPT 98		Font arrow or Font dialog box launcher (HOME tab | Font group)	Font arrow on mini toolbar	Font	CTRL+SHIFT+F
Font, Change Color	PPT 13		Font Color button or Font Color arrow or Font dialog box launcher (HOME tab | Font group)	Font Color button or Font Color arrow on mini toolbar	Font, Font Color button on Font tab (Font dialog box)	CTRL+SHIFT+F
Footer, Add	PPT 300		'Header & Footer' button (INSERT tab | Text group)			
Format Painter, Use	PPT 101		Double-click Format Painter button (HOME tab | Clipboard group), select text with format you want to copy, select text to apply previously selected format; press ESC to turn off Format Painter	Format Painter button on mini toolbar		

Microsoft PowerPoint 2013 Quick Reference Summary *(continued)*

Task	Page Number	Mouse	Ribbon	Other On-Screen Areas	Shortcut Menu	Keyboard Shortcut
Grayscale, Print in	PPT 685		Color button (FILE tab, Print tab), Grayscale			
Gridlines, Display	PPT 636		Gridlines check box (VIEW tab | Show group)			
Guides, Display/Hide	PPT 365 PPT 367		Guides check box (VIEW tab | Show group)		Grid and Guides, Guides	ALT+F9
Handout Master, Use	PPT 504 PPT 520		Handout Master button (VIEW tab | Master Views group)			
Handout, Create by Exporting File to Microsoft Word	PPT 582		'Create Handouts in Microsoft Word' button (HOME tab | Handouts group); or Create Handouts button (FILE tab | Export tab)			
Handout, Print	PPT 188		Full Page Slides button (FILE tab | Print tab), select layout in Handouts section, tap or click Print button			CTRL+P
Header, Add	PPT 301		Header & Footer button (INSERT tab | Text group)			
Hyperlink, Add	PPT 347 PPT 349		Hyperlink button (INSERT tab | Links group)		Hyperlink	CTRL+K
Hyperlink to a Word File	PPT 361		Action button (INSERT tab | Links group), Hyperlink to, Other File, select file			
Hyperlink to Another PowerPoint File	PPT 358		Action button (INSERT tab | Links group), Hyperlink (Action on click area), Hyperlink to, Other PowerPoint Presentation; Hyperlink button (INSERT menu | Links group), Existing File or Web Page			
Illustration, Placeholder, or Shape, Move	PPT 39, PPT 155			Drag		ARROW KEYS move selected image in small increments
Illustration, Regroup	PPT 165		Group button, Regroup command (DRAWING TOOLS FORMAT tab | Arrange group)		Group, Regroup	
Illustration, Ungroup	PPT 160		Group button, Ungroup command (PICTURE TOOLS FORMAT tab | Arrange group), click Yes to convert to Microsoft Office drawing, click DRAWING TOOLS FORMAT tab, Group button, Ungroup		Group, Ungroup	CTRL+SHIFT+G
Illustrations, Align	PPT 368		Align button (PICTURE TOOLS FORMAT tab | Arrange group), select desired alignment			

Microsoft PowerPoint 2013 Quick Reference Summary *(continued)*

Task	Page Number	Mouse	Ribbon	Other On-Screen Areas	Shortcut Menu	Keyboard Shortcut
Illustrations, Distribute	PPT 369		Align button (PICTURE TOOLS FORMAT tab | Arrange group), Distribute Horizontally or Distribute Vertically			
Line Break, Insert	PPT 303 PPT 378					SHIFT+ENTER
Line, Change Weight or Color	PPT 573		Shape Outline arrow (DRAWING TOOLS FORMAT tab | Shape Styles group), Weight or choose color			
Line, Draw	PPT 572		Shapes arrow (DRAWING TOOLS FORMAT tab | Insert Shapes group)			
Line, Set Formatting as Default	PPT 574				Set as Default Line	
Line Spacing, Change	PPT 367		Line Spacing button (HOME tab | Paragraph group); Paragraph Dialog Box Launcher (HOME tab | Paragraph group), Line Spacing arrow		Paragraph, Line Spacing	
List, Animate	PPT 440		More button (ANIMATIONS tab | Animation group), select effect from Animation gallery			
List Level, Decrease	PPT 19		Decrease List Level button (HOME tab | Paragraph group)	Decrease List Level button on mini toolbar		SHIFT+TAB
List Level, Increase	PPT 19		Increase List Level button (HOME tab | Paragraph group)	Increase List Level button on mini toolbar		TAB
Markup, Hide/Show	PPT 293		Show Comments arrow (REVIEW tab | Comments group), uncheck Show Markup to hide, check Show Markup to show			
Master View	PPT 480		Slide Master button (VIEW tab | Master Views group)			
Master View, Close	PPT 510		'Close Master View' button (NOTES MASTER tab | Close group)			
Merge a Presentation	PPT 277		Compare button (REVIEW tab | Compare group)			
Move to Another Slide in Normal View	PPT 29			Next Slide or Previous Slide buttons on vertical scroll bar; drag scroll box on vertical scroll bar; click slide thumbnail in Thumbnail pane

Touch Mode: Tap desired slide in Thumbnail pane | | PAGE DOWN (next slide); PAGE UP (previous slide) |

Task	Page Number	Mouse	Ribbon	Other On-Screen Areas	Shortcut Menu	Keyboard Shortcut
Move to Another Slide in Slide Show View	PPT 50			Click to display next slide; click Next Slide or Previous Slide icons on Slide Show toolbar Touch Mode: Swipe forward or backward on slide		PAGE DOWN (next slide); PAGE UP (previous slide); RIGHT ARROW or DOWN ARROW (next slide); LEFT ARROW or UP ARROW (previous slide)
Narration, Preview	PPT 705		In Normal view, select sound icon on slide, Play button (AUDIO TOOLS PLAYBACK tab | Preview group)			
Narration, Record	PPT 705		'Record Slide Show' arrow (SLIDE SHOW tab | Set Up group), 'Start Recording from Beginning' or 'Start Recording from Current Slide', 'Narrations and laser pointer' check box (Record Slide Show dialog box), Start Recording button (Record Slide Show dialog box), End Show			
Notes, Add	PPT 115			Notes button on status bar; type notes in Notes pane		
Notes, Print	PPT 121		FILE tab, Print tab, tap or click Notes Pages (Print Layout area), tap or click Print button			CTRL+P
Notes Master, Use	PPT 507 PPT 521		'View Notes Master' button (VIEW tab | Master Views group)			
Notes Pane, Hide/Show	PPT 278			Notes button on status bar		
Numbered List, Format	PPT 388		Numbering arrow (HOME tab | Paragraph group), Bullets and Numbering		Numbering, Bullets and Numbering	
Open Presentation	OFF 54		Open (FILE tab)			CTRL+O
Outline, Open as Presentation	PPT 343		Open (FILE tab, File Type arrow, All Outlines, select Word file, Open); New Slide arrow (HOME tab | Slides group), 'Slides from Outline', File Type arrow, All Outlines, select Word file, Insert			
Password, Remove or Change	PPT 316		Open file with current password, Save As button (FILE tab, Save As tab), Tools button (Save As dialog box), General Options, 'Password to open' or 'Password to modify'			

Microsoft PowerPoint 2013 Quick Reference Summary *(continued)*

Task	Page Number	Mouse	Ribbon	Other On-Screen Areas	Shortcut Menu	Keyboard Shortcut
Password, Set	PPT 314		Protect Presentation button (FILE tab, Info tab), 'Encrypt with Password'			
Paste	PPT 101, PPT 166		Paste button (HOME tab | Clipboard group)		Paste	CTRL+V
Pattern Fill, Apply to Slide	PPT 516		Format Background button (DESIGN tab | Customize group), FILL section (Format Background pane) Pattern fill		Format Background, FILL section (Format Background pane), Pattern fill	
Permissions, Restrict	PPT 707		Protect Presentation button (FILE tab, Info tab), Restrict Access			
Photo Album, Add Captions Below All Pictures	PPT 691		Photo Album dialog box, 'Captions below ALL pictures' check box			
Photo Album, Add Theme	PPT 691		Photo Album dialog box, Browse button in Album Layout area			
Photo Album, Change Layout	PPT 690		Photo Album dialog box, Picture Layout arrow			
Photo Album, Create	PPT 692		Create button (Photo Album dialog box)			
Photo Album, Create Black and White Images	PPT 694		'New Photo Album' arrow (INSERT tab | Images group), 'ALL pictures black and white' check box (Edit Photo Album dialog box), Update			
Photo Album, Edit	PPT 692		'New Photo Album' arrow (INSERT tab | Images group), 'Edit Photo Album'			
Photo Album, Reorder Pictures	PPT 687		Photo Album dialog box, select photo, Move Up or Move Down button			
Photo Album, Start and Add Pictures	PPT 685		'New Photo Album' button (INSERT tab | Images group)			
Photo Album Image, Adjust Brightness	PPT 689		Photo Album dialog box, Increase Brightness or Decrease Brightness button			
Photo Album Image, Adjust Contrast	PPT 689		Photo Album dialog box, Increase Contrast or Decrease Contrast button			
Photo Album Image, Adjust Rotation	PPT 688		Photo Album dialog box, 'Rotate Left 90°' or 'Rotate Right 90°' button			
Picture, Add an Artistic Effect	PPT 152		Artistic Effects button (PICTURE TOOLS FORMAT tab | Adjust group)		Format Picture, Effects icon, ARTISTIC EFFECTS (Format Picture pane)	

Microsoft PowerPoint 2013 Quick Reference Summary *(continued)*

Task	Page Number	Mouse	Ribbon	Other On-Screen Areas	Shortcut Menu	Keyboard Shortcut
Picture, Add Border	PPT 88		Picture Border arrow (PICTURE TOOLS FORMAT tab | Picture Styles group)			
Picture, Change	PPT 85 PPT 551		Change Picture button (PICTURE TOOLS FORMAT tab | Adjust group)		Change Picture	
Picture, Clear Formatting	PPT 302		Reset Picture button (PICTURE TOOLS FORMAT tab | Adjust group)		Format Picture, Picture icon (Format Picture pane), PICTURE CORRECTIONS, Reset	
Picture, Color or Recolor	PPT 150		Color button (PICTURE TOOLS FORMAT tab | Adjust group)		Format Picture, Picture icon, PICTURE COLOR (Format Picture pane)	
Picture, Compress	PPT 417		Compress Pictures button (PICTURE TOOLS FORMAT tab | Adjust group)			
Picture, Correct	PPT 87		Corrections button (PICTURE TOOLS FORMAT tab | Adjust group)	Picture Corrections Options (Corrections gallery)	Format Picture, Picture Corrections (Format Picture dialog box)	
Picture, Crop	PPT 415		Crop button (PICTURE TOOLS FORMAT tab | Size group), drag cropping handles		Crop	
Picture, Insert	PPT 31		Pictures button or Online Pictures button (INSERT tab | Images group)	Pictures icon or Online Pictures icon in slide		
Picture, Move	PPT 39			Drag		ARROW keys to move in small increments
Picture, Remove Background	PPT 413 PPT 414		Remove Background button (PICTURE TOOLS FORMAT tab | Adjust group)			
Picture, Rotate	PPT 498	Drag rotation handle	Rotate button (PICTURE TOOLS FORMAT tab | Arrange group)		Format Object, 3-D ROTATION	
Picture Border, Change Color or Weight	PPT 88–89		Picture Border arrow (PICTURE TOOLS FORMAT tab | Picture Styles group)		Format Picture, Fill & Line, Line (Format Picture pane)	
Picture Effects, Apply	PPT 90		Picture Effects button (PICTURE TOOLS FORMAT tab | Picture Styles group)		Format Picture, Effects (Format Picture pane)	
Picture Presentation, Save as	PPT 584		'Change File Type' (FILE tab | Export tab), 'PowerPoint Picture Presentation'			
Picture Style, Apply	PPT 87		More button (PICTURE TOOLS FORMAT tab | Picture Styles group)			

Microsoft PowerPoint 2013 Quick Reference Summary *(continued)*

Task	Page Number	Mouse	Ribbon	Other On-Screen Areas	Shortcut Menu	Keyboard Shortcut
Placeholder, Delete	PPT 156				Cut	select placeholder, DELETE or BACKSPACE
Placeholder, Move	PPT 155			Drag		
Placeholder, Resize	PPT 154			Drag sizing handles		
Placeholder Text, Align	PPT 372 PPT 374		Align Text button (HOME tab | Paragraph group)		Paragraph, Alignment arrow	CTRL+E (center) CTRL+R (right) CTRL+L (left)
Placeholder Text, Change Line Spacing	PPT 375		Line Spacing button (HOME tab | Paragraph group)		Paragraph, Line Spacing arrow	
Presentation, Check for Compatibility	PPT 311		'Check for Issues' button (FILE tab, Info tab), Check Compatibility			
Presentation, Create Self-Running	PPT 453		'Set Up Show' button (SLIDE SHOW tab | Set Up group), 'Browsed at a kiosk (full screen)'			
Presentation, Display Multiple Windows Simultaneously	PPT 701		With multiple presentations open, Cascade button or Arrange All button (VIEW tab | Window group)			
Presentation, Email from within PowerPoint	PPT 705		Email button (FILE tab | Share tab), 'Send as Attachment'			
Presentation, Mark as Final	PPT 316		Protect Presentation button (FILE tab, Info tab), 'Mark as Final'			
Presentation, Package for CD or DVD	PPT 308		'Package Presentation for CD' (FILE tab, Export tab), 'Package for CD' button			
Presentation, Set Resolution	PPT 304		'Set Up Slide Show' button (SLIDE SHOW tab | Set Up group), Resolution arrow in Multiple Monitors section (Set Up Show dialog box)			
Presentation, Show with Manual Timing	PPT 680		'Set Up Slide Show' button (SLIDE SHOW tab | Set Up group), Manually (Advance slides area)			
Presentation Change, Accept	PPT 282		Accept Change button (REVIEW tab | Compare group)	Check boxes on DETAILS or SLIDES tabs (Revisions pane), Presentation Changes section		
Presentation Change, Reject	PPT 282		Reject Change button (REVIEW tab | Compare group)	Uncheck boxes on DETAILS or SLIDES tabs (Revisions pane), Presentation changes section		

PowerPoint Quick Reference

Microsoft PowerPoint 2013 Quick Reference Summary *(continued)*

Task	Page Number	Mouse	Ribbon	Other On-Screen Areas	Shortcut Menu	Keyboard Shortcut
Presentation Changes, End Review	PPT 293		End Review button (REVIEW tab | Compare group)			
Presentation Changes, Preview	PPT 281		Reviewing Pane button (REVIEW tab | Compare group)			
Presenter View, Use	PPT 710		'Use Presenter View' check box (SLIDE SHOW tab | Monitors group)			
Print a Presentation	PPT 52		Print button (FILE tab, Print tab)			CTRL+P
Reading View, Run Presentation in	PPT 292		Reading View button (VIEW tab | Presentation Views group)	Reading View button on status bar		
Research Pane, Use to Find Information	PPT 696		Research button (REVIEW tab | Proofing group)			
Resize	PPT 36, PPT 93, PPT 175		Enter height and width values (PICTURE TOOLS FORMAT tab | Size group or DRAWING TOOLS FORMAT tab | Size group or VIDEO TOOLS FORMAT tab | Size group)	Drag sizing handles	Format Picture or Format Shape or Format Video, Size & Properties icon	
Resolution, Set for Slideshow	PPT 708		'Set Up Slide Show' button (SLIDE SHOW tab | Set Up group), Resolution arrow (Set Up Show dialog box)			
Ribbon, Customize	PPT 579		Customize Ribbon (FILE tab, Options tab)			
Ribbon, Reset	PPT 585		Reset button (FILE tab, Options tab), Customize Ribbon, Reset			
Rulers, Display/Hide	PPT 367		Ruler check box (VIEW tab | Show group)		Ruler	
Run PowerPoint	PPT 46, PPT 4			PowerPoint 2013 tile on Start menu; search for PowerPoint 2013 using Search charm on Charms bar		
Save a Presentation	PPT 82		Save (FILE tab)	Save button on Quick Access toolbar		CTRL+S or SHIFT+F12
Save a Presentation with a New Name	PPT 15		Save As (FILE tab)			
Save a Slide as an Image	PPT 307		'Change File Type' button (FILE tab, Export tab), 'JPEG File Interchange Format'; Browse button (FILE tab, Save As tab), 'Save As Type' arrow, 'JPEG File Interchange Format'			

Microsoft PowerPoint 2013 Quick Reference Summary *(continued)*

Task	Page Number	Mouse	Ribbon	Other On-Screen Areas	Shortcut Menu	Keyboard Shortcut
Save as a PowerPoint Show	PPT 306		'Change File Type' button (FILE tab, Export tab), PowerPoint Show in Presentation File Types section; Browse button (FILE tab, Save As tab), 'Save As Type' arrow, PowerPoint Show			
Save in a Previous Format	PPT 310		'Change File Type' button (FILE tab, Export tab), 'PowerPoint 97-2003 Presentation'; Browse button, (FILE tab, Save & Send tab), 'Save As Type' arrow, 'PowerPoint 97-2003 Presentation')			
Screen Clipping, Use	PPT 299		Screenshot button (INSERT tab | Images group), Screen Clipping command			
Section, Create Break	PPT 673		In Slide Sorter view, Section button (HOME tab | Slides group), Add Section		In Slide Sorter view, tap where break desired, tap Add Section	
Section, Rename	PPT 676		Section button (HOME tab | Slides group), Rename Section		Rename Section	
Sections, Collapse or Expand	PPT 678		Section button (HOME tab | Slides group), Collapse All or Expand All		Collapse All or Expand All	
Sections, Reorder	PPT 678	Drag section name			Move Section Up or Move Section Down	
Selection, Print	PPT 710		'Print All Slides' button, Print Selection (FILE tab, Print tab)			
Shape, Add	PPT 92, PPT 94		Shapes button (Insert tab | Illustrations group); Shapes More button (HOME tab | Drawing group or DRAWING TOOLS FORMAT tab | Insert Shapes group)			
Shape, Apply Fill	PPT 568		Shape Fill arrow (DRAWING TOOLS FORMAT tab | Shape Styles group)		Format Shape, Fill icon (Format Shape pane)	
Shape, Apply Style	PPT 95		Quick Styles button (HOME tab | Drawing group); 'Shape Styles More' button or Format Shape dialog box launcher (DRAWING TOOLS FORMAT tab | Shape Styles group)		Format Shape	
Shape, Change Fill Color	PPT 354		Shape Fill arrow (DRAWING TOOLS FORMAT tab | Shape Styles gallery)		Fill	
Shape, Set Formatting as Default	PPT 577				Set as Default Shape	

Microsoft PowerPoint 2013 Quick Reference Summary *(continued)*

Task	Page Number	Mouse	Ribbon	Other On-Screen Areas	Shortcut Menu	Keyboard Shortcut
Shape, Subtract	PPT 570		Merge Shapes button (DRAWING TOOLS FORMAT tab | Insert Shapes group), Subtract			
Shape Fill, Increase Transparency	PPT 487		Drawing Dialog Box Launcher (HOME tab | Drawing group), Format Shape dialog box, Transparency slider			
Shapes, Merge	PPT 571		Merge Shapes button (DRAWING TOOLS FORMAT tab | Insert Shapes group), Union			
Slide, Add	PPT 15		New Slide button (HOME tab | Slides group)		New Slide	CTRL+M
Slide, Arrange	PPT 42		Slide Sorter button (VIEW tab | Presentation Views group), drag thumbnail to new position	Drag slide in Thumbnail pane to new position, click Slide Sorter icon on status bar, drag thumbnail to new position		
Slide, Delete	PPT 79				Delete (touch screen) or Delete Slide	DELETE
Slide, Duplicate	PPT 41		New Slide arrow (HOME tab | Slides group), Duplicate Selected Slides		Duplicate Slide	
Slide, Format Background	PPT 109–111		Format Background button (DESIGN tab | Customize group)		Format Background (Format Background pane)	
Slide, Hide	PPT 370		Hide Slide button (SLIDE SHOW tab | Set Up group) (must be in Slide Sorter view)		Hide Slide (Slide Sorter view or thumbnail on Slides tab)	
Slide, Insert Picture as Background	PPT 108		Format Background button (DESIGN tab | Customize group)		Format Background, Picture or Texture Fill, Insert from File (Format Background pane)	
Slide, Reuse from an Existing Presentation	PPT 296		New Slide arrow (HOME tab | Slides group), Reuse Slides command			
Slide, Select Layout	PPT 23		Layout button or New Slide arrow (HOME tab | Slides group)			
Slide, Set Size	PPT 303		Slide Size button (DESIGN tab | Customize group)			
Slide, Set Up Custom Size	PPT 699		Slide Size button (DESIGN tab | Customize group), 'Slides sized for' arrow, Custom			
Slide Change, Accept	PPT 286		Accept Change button (REVIEW tab | Compare group)	Check boxes on DETAILS or SLIDES tabs (Revisions pane), Slide Changes section		

Microsoft PowerPoint 2013 Quick Reference Summary *(continued)*

Task	Page Number	Mouse	Ribbon	Other On-Screen Areas	Shortcut Menu	Keyboard Shortcut
Slide Change, Reject	PPT 286		Reject Change button (REVIEW tab | Compare group)	Uncheck boxes on DETAILS or SLIDES tabs (Revisions pane), Slide changes section		
Slide Layout, Delete	PPT 502		Delete button (HOME tab | Slides group)		Delete Layout	DELETE
Slide Master, Delete Slide Layout	PPT 502		Delete button (SLIDE MASTER tab | Edit Master group)		Delete Layout	DELETE
Slide Master, Insert Placeholder	PPT 489		Insert Placeholder arrow (SLIDE MASTER tab | Master Layout group)			
Slide Master, Apply Slide and Font Themes	PPT 481		Themes button (SLIDE MASTER tab | Edit Theme group)			
Slide Master, Delete, Move, and Add Text to Footer	PPT 485		Slide Master button (VIEW tab | Master Views group), 'Header & Footer' button (INSERT tab | Text group)			
Slide Master, Display	PPT 480		Slide Master button (VIEW tab | Master Views group)			
Slide Master, Format Background and Apply a Quick Style	PPT 484		Background Styles button (SLIDE MASTER tab | Background group)			
Slide Master, Hide and Unhide Background Graphics	PPT 499		'Hide/Unhide Background Graphics' check box (SLIDE MASTER tab | Background group)			
Slide Master, Insert a Background Graphic	PPT 488		Insert Picture button (INSERT tab | Images group)			
Slide Master, Save as a Template	PPT 510		Save as type arrow (FILE tab, Save As tab), PowerPoint Template			
Slide Master and Slide Layout, Rename	PPT 500		Rename button (SLIDE MASTER tab | Edit Master group)			
Slide Number, Insert	PPT 118		'Insert Slide Number' button (INSERT tab | Text group) or 'Header & Footer' button (INSERT tab | Text group), click Slide number check box			
Slide Objects, Rename	PPT 425		Rename objects in Selection pane (Select button, HOME tab | Editing group, Selection Pane)			
Slide Orientation, Change	PPT 699		Slide Size button (DESIGN tab | Customize group), 'Custom Slide Size'			

Microsoft PowerPoint 2013 Quick Reference Summary *(continued)*

Task	Page Number	Mouse	Ribbon	Other On-Screen Areas	Shortcut Menu	Keyboard Shortcut
Slide Show, Adjust Timings Manually	PPT 452		In Slide Sorter view, select slide and set timing (TRANSITIONS tab | Timing group)			
Slide Show, Change Highlighter or Pen Color	PPT 319		'Pen and laser pointer tools' button (Slide Show control bar), tap or click desired color			
Slide Show, Draw on Slides During Show	PPT 319		'Pen and laser pointer tools' button (Slide Show control), Pen			
Slide Show, End	PPT 51			Tap or click black ending slide	End Show	ESC or HYPHEN
Slide Show, Highlight Items During Show	PPT 318		'Pen and laser pointer tools' button (Slide Show control bar), Highlighter			
Slide Show, Keyboard Shortcuts	PPT 317					Table 5-1
Slide Show, Present Online	PPT 707		Present Online arrow (SLIDE SHOW tab | Start Slide Show group), 'Office Presentation Service'			
Slide Show, Rehearse Timings	PPT 450		Rehearse Timings button (SLIDE SHOW tab | Set Up group)			
Slide Show, Show/Hide Pointer and Control Bar	PPT 320 PPT 321			Options button on control bar, Arrow Options		
Slide Show, Start	PPT 49		Slide Show button (SLIDE SHOW tab | Start Slide Show group)	Slide Show button on status bar; 'Start from Beginning' button in Quick Access toolbar		F5
Slide Show Control Bar, Use	PPT 318					Table 5-2
Slide Sorter View	PPT 672		Slide Sorter button (VIEW tab | Presentation Views group)	Slide Sorter view button in taskbar		
Slides, Insert with a Section Layout	PPT 669		Slide Layout button (HOME tab | Slides group), Section Header layout		Layout, Section Header	
SmartArt, Add Shape	PPT 558		Add Shape arrow (SMARTART TOOLS DESIGN tab | Create Graphic group)			
SmartArt, Change Layout	PPT 557		More button (SMARTART TOOLS DESIGN tab | Layouts group)			

Microsoft PowerPoint 2013 Quick Reference Summary *(continued)*

Task	Page Number	Mouse	Ribbon	Other On-Screen Areas	Shortcut Menu	Keyboard Shortcut
SmartArt, Convert to Text or Shapes	PPT 563 PPT 565		Convert button (SMARTART TOOLS DESIGN tab | Reset group)			
SmartArt, Remove Shape	PPT 558				Delete	select shape, DELETE
SmartArt, Resize Graphic	PPT 559 PPT 560		Smaller or Larger button (SMARTART TOOLS FORMAT tab | Shapes group); or enter desired settings in Height and Width boxes (SMARTART TOOLS FORMAT tab | Size group)		Size and Position, SIZE area (Format Shape pane)	
SmartArt Bullet, Add	PPT 557		Add Bullet button (SMARTART TOOLS DESIGN tab	Create Graphic group			
SmartArt Bullet Level, Promote or Demote	PPT 555 PPT 556		Promote or Demote button (SMARTART TOOLS DESIGN tab | Create Graphic group)			
SmartArt Graphic, Animate	PPT 437		More button (ANIMATIONS tab | Animation group), select effect from Animation gallery			
SmartArt Graphic, Apply Style	PPT 218		More button (SMARTART TOOLS DESIGN tab | SmartArt Styles group)		Style button	
SmartArt Graphic, Change Color	PPT 219		Change Colors button (SMARTART TOOLS DESIGN tab | SmartArt Styles group)		Color button	
SmartArt Graphic, Enter Text	PPT 215		Text Pane button (SMARTART TOOLS DESIGN tab | Create Graphic group)	Text Pane arrow icon in center-left edge of graphic	Show Text Pane	Table 4-2
SmartArt Graphic, Format Text	PPT 216		Text formatting buttons (HOME tab | Font group)	Select text in Text Pane, apply formatting		
SmartArt Graphic, Insert	PPT 214		SmartArt button (INSERT tab | Illustrations group)			
SmartArt Graphic, Insert Picture	PPT 217		Shape Fill button (SMARTART TOOLS FORMAT tab | Shape Styles group), Picture	Insert Picture from File icon in picture placeholder	Fill button, Picture	
SmartArt Graphic, Resize	PPT 221			Drag sizing handles	Size and Position	
SmartArt Shapes, Reorder	PPT 554		Move Up or Move Down button (SMARTART TOOLS DESIGN tab | Create Graphic group)			
Spelling, Check	PPT 117		Spelling button (REVIEW tab | Proofing group)	Spell Check icon on status bar	Spelling (or click correct word on shortcut menu)	F7

Microsoft PowerPoint 2013 Quick Reference Summary *(continued)*

Task	Page Number	Mouse	Ribbon	Other On-Screen Areas	Shortcut Menu	Keyboard Shortcut
Stacking Order, Change	PPT 153		Bring Forward or Send Backward button (PICTURE TOOLS FORMAT tab | Arrange group)		Send to Back or Bring to Front	
Symbol, Insert	PPT 241		Symbol button (INSERT tab | Symbols group)			
Synonym, Find and Insert	PPT 114		Thesaurus button (REVIEW tab | Proofing group)		Synonyms	SHIFT+F7
Table, Add Borders	PPT 245		Borders arrow (TABLE TOOLS DESIGN tab | Table Styles group)			
Table, Add Cell Effects	PPT 621		Effects button (TABLE TOOLS DESIGN tab | Table Styles group)			
Table, Add Gradient Fill	PPT 621		Shading arrow (TABLE TOOLS DESIGN tab | Table Styles group), Gradient			
Table, Add Effect	PPT 246		Effects button (TABLE TOOLS DESIGN tab | Table Styles group)			
Table, Add Hyperlink	PPT 644		Hyperlink button (INSERT tab | Links group)		Hyperlink	
Table, Add Shading	PPT 620		Shading arrow (TABLE TOOLS DESIGN tab | Table Styles group)			
Table, Align	PPT 625		Align button (TABLE TOOLS LAYOUT tab | Arrange group)			
Table, Align Text in Cells	PPT 253		Choose desired alignment (TABLE TOOLS LAYOUT tab | Alignment group)			
Table, Apply Style	PPT 244		More button (TABLE TOOLS DESIGN tab | Table Styles group)			
Table, Clear Formatting	PPT 239		Clear Table command in Table Styles gallery (TABLE TOOLS DESIGN tab | Table Styles group)			
Table, Distribute Rows	PPT 622		Distribute Rows button (TABLE TOOLS LAYOUT tab | Cell Size group)			
Table, Draw	PPT 610		Table button (INSERT tab | Tables group), Draw Table, drag pencil pointer			
Table, Insert	PPT 239		Table button (INSERT tab | Tables group)	Insert table icon in content placeholder		
Table, Merge Cells	PPT 248		Merge Cells button (TABLE TOOLS LAYOUT tab | Merge group)		Merge Cells	
Table, Resize	PPT 247			Drag table sizing handles		
Table, Resize Columns and Rows	PPT 623	Drag column or row borders	Table Row Height or Table Column Width boxes (TABLE TOOLS LAYOUT tab | Cell Size group)			

Microsoft PowerPoint 2013 Quick Reference Summary *(continued)*

Task	Page Number	Mouse	Ribbon	Other On-Screen Areas	Shortcut Menu	Keyboard Shortcut
Table, Split Columns or Rows	PPT 617		Split Cells button (TABLE TOOLS LAYOUT tab | Merge group)		Split Cells	
Table Cell, Add Image	PPT 251			Shape Fill arrow on mini toolbar, Picture	Format Shape, FILL tab, 'Picture or texture fill'	
Table Cell, Center Text Vertically	PPT 253		Center Vertically button (TABLE TOOLS LAYOUT tab | Alignment group)		Format Shape, TEXT OPTIONS tab, Textbox, Vertical alignment arrow	
Table Cell, Change Text Direction	PPT 250		Text Direction button (TABLE TOOLS LAYOUT tab | Alignment group)		Format Shape, TEXT OPTIONS tab, Textbox, Text direction arrow	
Table Line, Erase	PPT 615		Table Eraser button (TABLE TOOLS DESIGN tab | Draw Borders group), click line to erase			
Table Rows and Columns, Draw	PPT 611 PPT 613		Draw Table button (TABLE TOOLS DESIGN tab | Draw Borders group), drag pencil pointer			
Template, Open and Save as Presentation	PPT 512		Computer button (FILE tab | Open tab), Custom Office Templates, then Save As tab (FILE tab), 'Save as type', PowerPoint Presentation			
Text, Add Animation	PPT 183		More button (ANIMATIONS tab | Animation group)			
Text, Add Shadow	PPT 100		Text Shadow button (HOME tab | Font group)			
Text, Align Horizontally	PPT 154		Align Text buttons (HOME tab | Paragraph group)	Align Text buttons on mini toolbar; Paragraph dialog box launcher (HOME tab | Paragraph group), Indents and Spacing tab (Paragraph dialog box), Alignment arrow	Paragraph, Indents and Spacing tab (Paragraph dialog box), Alignment arrow	CTRL+R (right), CTRL+L (left), CTRL+E (center)
Text, Align Vertically	PPT 366		Align Text button (HOME tab | Paragraph group), Top, Middle, or Bottom			
Text, Bold	PPT 21		Bold button (HOME tab | Font group)	Bold button on mini toolbar	Font, Font tab (Font dialog box), Font style arrow, Bold	CTRL+B
Text, Change Color	PPT 13		Font Color button or Font Color arrow or Font dialog box launcher (HOME tab | Font group)	Font Color button or Font Color arrow on mini toolbar	Font, Font Color button (Font dialog box)	CTRL+SHIFT+F
Text, Change Direction	PPT 492		Text Direction button (HOME tab | Paragraph group)			
Text, Convert to SmartArt Graphic	PPT 222		'Convert to SmartArt' button (HOME tab | Paragraph group)		Convert to SmartArt	

Microsoft PowerPoint 2013 Quick Reference Summary (continued)

Task	Page Number	Mouse	Ribbon	Other On-Screen Areas	Shortcut Menu	Keyboard Shortcut
Text, Delete	PPT 43		Cut button (HOME tab | Clipboard group)		Cut	DELETE or CTRL+X or BACKSPACE
Text, Find and Replace	PPT 113		Replace button (HOME tab | Editing group)			CTRL+H
Text, Italicize	PPT 11		Italic button (HOME tab | Font group)	Italic button on mini toolbar	Font, Font style arrow (Font dialog box), Italic	CTRL+I
Text, Select	PPT 11			Drag to select; double-click to select word; triple-click to select paragraph Touch Mode: Tap to position insertion point and drag selection handles		CTRL+SHIFT+RIGHT ARROW (select word); CTRL+SHIFT+DOWN ARROW (select paragraph)
Text Box, Add	PPT 156		Text Box button (INSERT tab | Text group)			
Text Box, Align	PPT 550		Align button (DRAWING TOOLS FORMAT tab | Arrange group)			
Text Box, Animate	PPT 428 PPT 430		More button (ANIMATIONS tab | Animation group); select effect from Animation gallery			
Text Box, Apply a Gradient Fill	PPT 549		Shape Fill arrow (DRAWING TOOLS FORMAT tab | Shape Styles group), Gradient fill (Format Shape pane)		Format Shape, FILL section (Format Shape pane), Gradient fill	
Text Box, Apply a Pattern Fill	PPT 547		Shape Fill arrow (DRAWING TOOLS FORMAT tab | Shape group), Gradient, More Gradients, Pattern fill (Format Shape pane)		Format Shape, FILL section (Format Shape pane), Pattern fill	
Text Box, Apply an Effect	PPT 544		Shape Effects button (DRAWING TOOLS FORMAT tab | Shape Styles group)			
Text Box, Apply Fill	PPT 496		Shape Fill arrow (HOME tab | Drawing group)		Format Shape, FILL pane	
Text Box, Apply Picture	PPT 561		Shape Fill arrow (DRAWING TOOLS FORMAT tab | Shape Styles group), Picture		Format Shape, FILL section (Format Shape pane), Picture or texture fill	
Text Box, Change Internal Margin	PPT 497		Shape Styles dialog box launcher (DRAWING TOOLS FORMAT tab | Shape Styles group), Format Shape pane, TEXT BOX options		Format Shape, TEXT OPTIONS	
Text Box, Change Outline Weight, Color, or Style	PPT 542 PPT 543 PPT 544		Shape Outline button arrow (DRAWING TOOLS FORMAT tab | Shape Styles group), choose Weight, color, or Dashes			
Text Box, Insert	PPT 237 PPT 426		Text Box button (INSERT tab | Text group)			
Text Box, Move	PPT 221			Drag text box to desired location		

Microsoft PowerPoint 2013 Quick Reference Summary *(continued)*

Task	Page Number	Mouse	Ribbon	Other On-Screen Areas	Shortcut Menu	Keyboard Shortcut
Text Box, Rotate	PPT 498	Drag rotation handle	Rotate button (DRAWING TOOLS FORMAT tab | Arrange group)		Format Shape, Effects icon, 3-D ROTATION	
Text Box, Set Formatting as the Default	PPT 545				Set as Default Text Box	
Text File, Import	PPT 607		Object button (INSERT tab | Text group), 'Create from file', browse to .txt file			
Theme, Change	PPT 26, PPT 185		More button (DESIGN tab | Themes group)			
Theme, Download	PPT 77		Choose category from Suggested searches (FILE tab, New tab), choose theme, tap or click Create button			
Theme Colors, Change	PPT 187		More button (DESIGN tab | Variants group), Colors			
Theme Font, Customize	PPT 482		Theme Fonts button (SLIDE MASTER tab | Background group)			
Transition, Add	PPT 45		More button (TRANSITIONS tab | Transition to This Slide group)			ALT+A, T
Transition, Apply to a Single Slide	PPT 447		Select transition from Transitions gallery (TRANSITIONS tab | Transition to This Slide group) (do not click 'Apply to All')			
Transition, Change Duration	PPT 46		Duration box or arrows (TRANSITIONS tab | Timing group)			
Transition Effect, Modify	PPT 446		Effect Options button (TRANSITIONS tab | Transition to This Slide group)			
Transparency, Change	PPT 109		Background Styles button (DESIGN tab | Background group), Format Background, move Transparency slider		Format Background, Transparency slider	
Undo Changes	PPT 8			Undo button (Quick Access toolbar)		CTRL+Z
Video, Create from Presentation	PPT 708		'Create a Video' button (FILE tab, Export tab)			
Video File, Compress	PPT 704		Compress Media button (FILE tab, Info tab), Media Size and Performance area, select quality			
Video File, Insert	PPT 167		Video button (INSERT tab | Media group)	Insert Video icon in slide		

Microsoft PowerPoint 2013 Quick Reference Summary *(continued)*

Task	Page Number	Mouse	Ribbon	Other On-Screen Areas	Shortcut Menu	Keyboard Shortcut
Video File, Trim	PPT 169		Trim Video button (VIDEO TOOLS PLAYBACK tab | Editing group), drag video start/end points or edit Start Time and End Time boxes		Trim	
Video Options, Add	PPT 170		VIDEO TOOLS PLAYBACK tab | Video Options group		Format Video, Video icon (Format Video task pane), VIDEO, Presets button	
Video Style, Add	PPT 173		More button (VIDEO TOOLS FORMAT tab | Video Styles group)			
View, Change	PPT 157		View buttons (VIEW tab | Presentation Views group)	View buttons on status bar (Normal, Slide Sorter, Reading View, Slide Show)		
View, Change to Color/ Grayscale	PPT 694		Color or Grayscale button (VIEW tab | Color/Grayscale group)			
WordArt, Add Text Effects	PPT 104		Text Effects button (DRAWING TOOLS FORMAT tab | WordArt Styles group)			
WordArt, Apply Text Fill	PPT 106		Text Fill arrow (DRAWING TOOLS FORMAT tab | WordArt Styles group)			
WordArt, Change Outline Color or Weight	PPT 106–107		Text Outline arrow (DRAWING TOOLS FORMAT tab | WordArt Styles group)			
WordArt, Convert to SmartArt	PPT 553				Convert to SmartArt	
WordArt, Insert	PPT 103		WordArt button (INSERT tab | Text group)			
Worksheet, Align	PPT 628		Align button (DRAWING TOOLS FORMAT tab | Arrange group)			
Zoom for Viewing Slides	PPT 10		Zoom button (VIEW tab | Zoom group)	Zoom slider on status bar; Zoom In or Zoom Out buttons on Zoom slider; change percentage in Zoom level box on left side of slider		
				Touch Mode: Pinch two fingers to zoom out; stretch two fingers apart to zoom in		